T0133712

CISO Compass

CISO Compass
Navigating Cybersecurity Leadership
Challenges with Insights from Pioneers

Todd Fitzgerald

CRC Press
Taylor & Francis Group
Boca Raton   London   New York

CRC Press is an imprint of the
Taylor & Francis Group, an **informa** business
AN AUERBACH BOOK

For my two children—favorite son Grant and favorite daughter Erica. Because you grew into amazingly intelligent, thoughtful, caring, and productive adults, I could take the time to write this book for those unlocking their own potential and pursuing their dreams to keep all of us safe. Go unlock yours and help others along the way in your own passionate journey.

Contents

SECTION 2   STRATEGY

SECTION 5   SHARED VALUES

SECTION 7 SKILLS

SECTION 8 STYLE

CISO Insights from Industry Leaders

THE CISO ROAD MAP 1

STRATEGY 51

STRUCTURE 129

SYSTEMS 183

SHARED VALUES 311

STAFF 417

SKILLS 461

STYLE 489

INDEX 513

Foreword

Today's information technology (IT) security leaders are often working in unchartered waters to keep their enterprises secure and competitive in the face of increasingly sophisticated and stealthy cyberattacks. These security leaders are keenly aware, and feeling the pressure, that recent well-publicized mega breaches are creating a sense of urgency among Chief Executive Officers and boards of directors to have highly qualified IT security professionals at the helm.

CISO Compass: Navigating Cybersecurity Leadership Challenges with Insights from Pioneers, authored by IT security luminary Todd Fitzgerald, is the most thorough road map to being a successful IT security leader and should be in the library of every current and future Chief Information Security Officer (CISO). CISO Compass is unique, not only in the breadth and depth of the topics covered but also in the practical guidance and wisdom provided by more than 75 prominent CISOs, security leaders, professional association leaders, and cybersecurity standards setters. For example, Steve Katz, the first CISO and Executive Advisor Security and Privacy, Deloitte, is interviewed on the topic: the Role of CISO: Evolution or Revolution? This thoroughly researched book also features at the end of each chapter a section on suggested readings on the topic.

Our research has often examined the evolving role of the CISO and the importance of having skilled staff to manage cybersecurity risks and, when the inevitable data breach strikes, to have an effective cybersecurity incident response plan in place. We conclude from our research that the CISO role will become more critical, especially in managing enterprise risk, deploying security analytics, and ensuring the security of Internet of Things (IoT) devices. However, to play a bigger role in their organizations, it is essential that CISOs not only have the necessary technical expertise and leadership skills but also understand their companies' operations and will be able to articulate IT security priorities from a business perspective.

A 2018 Ponemon Institute Study on "What Worries CISOs Most" illustrates just how challenging their roles can be and why Mr. Fitzgerald's book is especially timely. Specifically, the human factor is the top security threat, with 70% of CISOs calling "lack of competent in-house staff" their number one concern and 65% stating "inadequate in-house expertise" as the top reason they are likely to have a data breach. Other problems include the inability to protect sensitive and confidential data from unauthorized access (59%), inability to keep up with the stealth of the attackers (56%), and the failure to control the third party's use of our sensitive data.

On the positive side, 65% of respondents expect cyber intelligence to be improved, 61% believe that the ability to staff the IT security function will improve, and 60% say that technologies will improve.

As noted above, CISOs need to be able to demonstrate to senior management that the cybersecurity program they have built is supportive of their companies' business goals and mission. To help overcome this hurdle, Mr. Fitzgerald draws upon The McKinsey 7-S Framework, developed in the 1980s by Tom Peters and Robert Waterman, as a way to measure the organizational effectiveness of a cybersecurity program. Chapters on Strategy, Structure, Systems, Shared Values, Skills, and Style present the cybersecurity program objectives that should be met. Specifically, the chapter on Strategy details a six-step process from creating the vision to building an action plan. In addition to the McKinsey Framework, more than a dozen cybersecurity control frameworks and standards are presented and explained.

CISO Compass also covers in detail emerging technologies and trends, the cybersecurity organization structure, functions CISOs should be responsible for, and the various CISO reporting models. Not often covered in other books and presentations, CISO Compass highlights the importance of understanding generational differences in the workplace and their possible effect on insider risk as well as the value of having soft communications skills so CISOs can more effectively negotiate, present, listen, and, in the end, achieve their goals.

Given the mounting need for security expertise, CISO Compass can be key to strengthening CISOs' capabilities, improving their effectiveness, and expanding their numbers. To that end, it is a welcome addition to the IT security body of knowledge.

Dr. Larry Ponemon
Chairman & Founder
Ponemon Institute
Traverse City, Michigan

Acknowledgments

When I was in college, I knew *exactly* what I wanted to be "when I grew up," albeit some would argue I am still working on the growing up part. I was a mathematics major, took calculus, and then switched to an accounting major, took tax accounting, and then switched to a business administration major with an emphasis in human resources—leading to my first job as a computer programmer. I was not so excited sitting in a cubicle all day coding stuff (or very good), so after 2 years, I became a database administrator (DBA), then figured I would be better leading DBAs and data modelers... did that for a decade, and then fell into a security job when a company needed a leader for DBAs, business intelligence, and information security. Along the way, I was outsourced, changed companies, moved, was outsourced again, outsourced some more, moved, moved again—in other words, could not hold a job I guess. Good way to see the country's Midwest, south, and east coast and travel a bunch to the west coast.

I should feel lucky, I was employed by two companies for exactly 10 years 7 months each. That must be my expiration date written on a label somewhere. I honestly thought I would be like my Dad and be at the same company for 37 years and get the gold watch. Was not happening. Times changed.

When we start out our careers, we have very little idea about where the journey will take us. Will we have to move? Will we get the promotion? Will our job be outsourced? Will we be competent enough in our jobs to be able to make a living? And most of all...

Will we be happy doing what we are doing?

And I am. Gratefully so. Grateful to all the experiences I have been given. Grateful to those leaders who took their time to teach me another way. Grateful to my colleagues that challenged me. Grateful for all those who showed up at my presentations. Grateful to those that gave presentations. Grateful to those companies that outsourced their IT functions. Grateful to those who randomly came up to me at a conference and said they read something I wrote or asked how the next book was coming along—it inspired me to write more. Grateful to those whom I shared work and personal lives with, it would be impossible to name all of you, but you know you are—I hope, or I still have more work to do.

In recent years, I have had the memorable leadership of Kevin Novak, Rob McGillen, Linda Pelej, and Kin Lee. Prior career development would never have happened without the leadership and support of Robert Krebs, Bud Loveless, Hugh Brownstone, Michael Cautin, Walter Koenig, Alex Weigel, Sandy Coston, Cheryl Leissring, Liz Bartlett, and Sally Wood. The list would not be complete without the friendship and opportunity to work with talented leaders Kevin Potter, Tim Waggoner, and Chris Moir as we secured Medicare systems.

I was influenced heavily by the opportunities they provided and interactions with these leaders.

Networking is an important part of learning, and I am grateful to those that have dedicated their time and energy to bringing communities of CISOs together, so we can have the discussion. I first met Marci McCarthy (T.E.N.) 15 years ago, have emceed her North America awards events multiple times, and have seen first-hand the good work she has done in awarding CISOs and bringing us together. Bill Sieglein holds CISO breakfast meetings as Founder of the CISO Executive Network, Tom Ward organizes Evanta CISO Summits, David Lynas have passionately led COSAC for 25 years, Britta Glade passionately builds speaker sessions for the best attendee experience for the RSA Conferences, and Wayne Johnson diligently organizes the local CISO Community in Chicago with monthly dinner groups—all models of CISO collaboration success. John Johnson's and Dimitra Kane's support and passion for bringing the local Chicago security community together is also rather commendable.

This book could not be written without the more than 75 key CISOs, security leaders, professional association leaders, and cybersecurity standards setters that contributed. I tapped into some of the busiest people on the planet, and they made time to write—for you. These leaders were not chosen at random—they all have one trait in common—they were chosen for their passion and success in building security programs, as well as their commitment to help others advance themselves and their programs. They share. I like sharing. That is why they are in the book. To share their knowledge with you. And hats off to Dr. Larry Ponemon for graciously writing the forward and opening our eyes to so much cybersecurity industry research with integrity. Rich O'hanley suggested I write my first article, explaining the Health Insurance Portability and Accountability Act of 1996 (HIPAA) Security Rule 3 weeks after it was finalized, over 15 years ago, and has been a joy to work with ever since.

This book was written half in Dublin, Ireland, and half in the Chicago, Illinois, area. Many thanks to Patrick Walsh and Jake Phillips of Dogpatch labs (www.dogpatchlabs.com), Dublin, Ireland, and the great entrepreneurs, each working there chasing their own dreams, for creating a friendly, productive co-sharing work environment. And finally, this field has lead me to meet many intelligent, thoughtful, supportive, and authentic people that eventually became big parts of my life—thanks much to Valerie Lyons for support and encouragement beyond the imaginable in so many ways.

Contributors

Phil Agcaoili has been an influential leader in the security industry for 30 years and has established world-class organizations from startups-to-the-Fortune 1. He has been the CISO at Elavon, Cox Communications, VeriSign, and SecureIT and led successful, global teams at General Electric, Alcatel, Scientific-Atlanta, and Dell. He has also served on industry committees for National Institute of Standards and Technology (NIST), FS-ISAC, PPISC, Communications Sector Coordinating Council, Communications Information Sharing and Analysis Center (ISAC), Cloud Security Alliance (CSA), and the Ponemon Institute. He is also a technology entrepreneur and has been involved in three consecutive and successful startups—co-founded SecureIT (sold to VeriSign), an early foundation member of Internet Devices (acquired by Alcatel), and Chief Security Architect for Scientific Atlanta (acquired by Cisco Systems). He sits on the boards of several startups, advises several venture funds, and is an investor.

Candy Alexander, CISSP CISM, is an industry leader with 30 years of experience in information security working for various high-technology companies. She serves on the Information Systems Security Association (ISSA) International Board of Directors, has held several positions as CISO, and is now working as a virtual CISO assisting companies to improve their security initiatives. She has received numerous awards and recognitions, including that of Distinguished Fellow of the ISSA, ranking her as one of the top 1% in the association, and she was inducted into the ISSA Hall of Fame in 2014. She is a frequent speaker, blogger, and author of professional development articles.

Dr. Edward G. Amoroso is a Chief Executive Officer of TAG Cyber LLC, a global cybersecurity advisory, training, consulting, and media services company supporting hundreds of organizations across the world. He recently retired from AT&T after 31 years, culminating as Senior Vice President and Chief Security Officer. He was elected an AT&T Fellow in 2010. He has been an Adjunct Professor of Computer Science at the Stevens Institute of Technology for the past 29 years. He is also a Research Professor in the Computer Science Department at the NYU Tandon School of Engineering and a Senior Advisor at the Applied Physics Laboratory.

Chris Apgar, CISSP, CEO, and President of Apgar Associates, LLC, is a nationally recognized information security, privacy, and electronic health information exchange expert. He has over 19 years of experience assisting health-care organizations to comply with HIPAA, Health Information Technology for Economic and Clinical Health (HITECH), and other privacy and security laws. He has assisted health-care, utilities, and financial organizations implement privacy and security safeguards to protect against organizational harm and harm to consumers.

Bret Arsenault is the Corporate Vice President and CISO for Microsoft. He is widely recognized as a luminary and thought leader in the cybersecurity industry. In addition to his responsibilities as CISO, he serves as a Chairman of Microsoft's Information Risk Management Council and as an outside Cyber-risk Advisor to executives and boards at numerous Fortune 100 companies. He is also a founding member of Security 50 and the Executive Security Action Forum.

Michael Boucher has over 20 years of information security experience working in the financial services, retail, manufacturing, and pharmaceutical industries. He joined FTD in 2013 as the Senior Director of Information Risk Management and is responsible for all information security and compliance activities across the company. Prior to FTD, he worked in information security leadership roles at PwC and Xerox where he was responsible for delivering information security solutions and advising clients. He is an active member of the Chicago InfraGard Chapter and other professional information security organizations. He received a BA in Economics from Lewis University and an MBA from the University of Notre Dame, and he maintains the CISSP certification.

Bob Bragdon is the Senior VP and Founding Publisher of Chief Security Officer (CSO)—a media brand of IDG Communications, Inc. He works closely with industry vendors, enterprise security leaders, government officials, and law enforcement agencies in identifying and addressing the challenges of today's complex security and risk management environments. A frequent speaker and panel moderator on enterprise and national security issues, he has presented and keynoted at numerous industry events. Prior to launching CSO in 2002, he held various management positions in marketing, sales, and product development at SOFTBANK, Ziff-Davis, and Cahners (now Reed Elsevier) Publishing.

Joyce Brocaglia In 1986, Joyce Brocaglia founded Alta Associates, the leading executive search firm specializing in information security, cybersecurity, and IT risk management. Named as one of the top 50 executive search firms in the United States, Alta has filled many of the most high profile Chief Information Security Officer roles and built world-class information security, cybersecurity and IT risk organizations. Joyce founded the Executive Women's Forum (EWF) on Information Security, Risk Management and Privacy in 2002. Today, the EWF is the largest member organization serving emerging leaders as well as the most prominent and influential female executives in their field.

Devon Bryan oversees cybersecurity policy, compliance, strategy, and incident response for the Federal Reserve System (FRS). Devon came to the FRS from Fortune 500 payroll and human resources provider Automatic Data Processing (ADP), where he has served as Global CISO. Devon led ADP's information security strategy, collaborating across the company's geographically dispersed business operations to ensure coordination, consensus, and effective execution across global operations. Prior to joining ADP, he has served as the Deputy CISO for the Internal Revenue Service (IRS). Prior to the IRS, he has served 11 years in the USAF (United States Air Force).

Mark Burnette has 21 years of experience in information security and risk management. During his decorated career, he has served as the Global Practice Leader for a national information security consulting company, has built and led information security functions for two major publicly traded corporations, and has worked for several years in key leadership roles with two of the Big 4 accounting firms. He was named the 2005 Information Security Executive of the Year and in 2008 was named one of Information Security Magazine's "Security 7" top seven security leaders. He has also been named a Fellow by the ISSA.

Dawn Cappelli, VP Global Security and CISO at Rockwell Automation since 2016, is responsible for protecting Rockwell Automation and its Connected Enterprise ecosystem from the global threat landscape. In 2013, she started at Rockwell Automation as Director, Insider Risk to build their Insider Risk Program. She was Founder and Director of Carnegie Mellon's Computer Emergency Response Teams (CERT) Insider Threat Center and has worked on the insider threat problem since 2001 with federal agencies, the intelligence community, private industry, and academia. She co-authored the book "The CERT Guide to Insider Threats: How to Prevent, Detect, and Respond to Information Technology Crimes (Theft, Sabotage, Fraud)."

Shaun Cavanaugh is the CISO for the National Park Service. Prior to this, he worked for the U.S. Nuclear Command and Control System Support Staff in Virginia, the U.S. European Command in Germany, and the U.S. Army TACOM in Michigan. He studied at the University of Detroit Mercy College of Business where he received a bachelor's and master's degree in Computer and Information Systems, the National Defense University where he completed their CISO Certificate Program and is a CISSP. For the past four years, he has lived in Springfield, Virginia, with his wife Katie, daughter Charlotte, and dog Eggs.

Ann Cavoukian, Ph.D., is recognized as one of the world's leading privacy experts. She is presently the Distinguished Expert-in-Residence, leading the Privacy by

Design Centre of Excellence at Ryerson University, and is also a Senior Fellow of the Ted Rogers Leadership Centre at Ryerson University. She has served an unprecedented three terms as the Information and Privacy Commissioner of Ontario, Canada. There, she created Privacy by Design (PbD), a framework that seeks to proactively embed privacy into the design specifications of information technologies, networked infrastructure, and business practices, thereby achieving the strongest protection possible. In 2010, International Privacy Regulators unanimously passed a Resolution recognizing PbD as an international standard. Since then, PbD has been translated into 40 languages.

John Ceraolo is an internationally recognized author and speaker with more than 25 years of experience in the information security industry. He has served in security leadership roles in the health-care, mobile technology, automotive, and software industries. He has led these organizations' enterprise risk management (ERM), business continuity, and information security initiatives. As an expert in audit and compliance assessments, he has also led several organizations in SOX compliance, Payment Card Industry Data Security Standards (PCI DSS) certification, SAS70 auditing, and HIPAA compliance. He holds his CISM, CISSP, and CISA as well as his master's in Information Assurance from Norwich University.

James Christiansen is a Global CISO for Teradata. He brings extensive expertise as a leader in information security. Prior to joining Teradata, he is the CISO at Experian, General Motors, and Visa International. He has been featured at the Business Round Table, Research Board, American Bar Association, American Banker, RSA, BankInfoSecurity, ISSA, ISACA, and HIMSS, and quoted in USA Today, New York Times, Wall Street Journal, Reuters, and Bloomberg. He is a patent inventor and has received three innovation awards in cybersecurity. He is the author of the Internet Survival Series and contributing author of CISO Essentials and numerous industry papers.

Jason Clark is the Chief Strategy Officer at Netskope and has decades of experience in building and executing successful strategic security programs. He has previously served as the Chief Security and Strategy Officer for Optiv, the CISO, and Vice President of infrastructure for Emerson Electric, CISO for the New York Times, and has held security leadership and technical roles at Everbank, BB&T, and the U.S. Army.

Richard A. Clarke is the Founder and CEO of Good Harbor Cyber Security Risk Management and is an advisor to leaders in the public and private sectors on all issues of cybersecurity and crisis management. He has served in the White House for an unprecedented 10 years as Special Advisor to the President on Cyber Security, serving under President George H.W. Bush, President Bill Clinton, and President George W. Bush. In this role, he also advised on counter-terrorism and other national security issues and served on the National Security Council for 10 years. In his role as the nation's "Cyber-Czar," he developed the country's first National Strategy to Defend Cyberspace.

Roland Cloutier As Staff VP and Global Chief Security Officer of Automatic Data Processing, Inc. (ADP), Roland Cloutier brings an unprecedented understanding and knowledge of global business operations protection and security leadership to one of the world's largest providers of human capital management solutions. With over 25 years of experience in the military, law enforcement, and commercial sector, he has functional and operational responsibility for ADP's cyber, information protection, risk, workforce protection, crisis management, and investigative operations worldwide. He is the author of his book, "Becoming a Global Chief Security Executive Officer," and has been honored with numerous industry recognitions and awards.

Michael J. Daugherty is CEO of LabMD, a cancer testing laboratory. He has spent the last decade defending LabMD against charges that it had deficient cybersecurity practices. The early years of his fighting Washington, DC, are recorded in his book, "The Devil Inside the Beltway." He has become the only litigant to challenge the basic authority underlying more than 200 enforcement actions relating to cybersecurity and online privacy that the Federal Trade Commission (FTC) has brought over the past 15 years. In so doing, he may topple key pillars of the FTC's cybersecurity and online privacy edifice, successfully exposing and challenging The Administrative State.

Erik Decker is a seasoned Information Security Executive with a career-specific focus within Healthcare and Academic Medicine. He currently serves as the Chief Security and Privacy Officer for the University of Chicago Medicine. In this role, he is the Chief Executive responsible for cybersecurity and HIPAA. He also serves as the Chairman of the Board for the Association for Executives in Healthcare Information Security (AEHIS), which is an association of over 800 CISOs in health care. In addition, he leads a Department of Health and Human Services cybersecurity task group chartered with developing consensus-based guidelines, best practices, and methodologies to strengthen health care's cybersecurity posture, as mandated by the Cybersecurity Information Sharing Act of 2015.

Steve Durbin is Managing Director of the Information Security Forum (ISF). His main areas of focus include strategy, IT, cybersecurity, and the emerging threat landscape. He has served as a Digital 50 Advisory Committee Member in the United States, a body established to improve the talent pool for Fortune 500 boards around cybersecurity and information governance, and has been ranked as one of the top 10 individuals shaping the way that organizations and leaders approach information security careers. Previously Senior Vice President at Gartner, Steve is a Chartered Marketer and Fellow of the Chartered Institute of Marketing.

Melanie Ensign is a Security Communications Advisor with expertise in reputation management, media relations, employee education, incident response, disclosure incentives, consumer engagement, and public policy. She currently leads security and privacy communications at Uber and previously was a Security Communications Manager at Facebook. She also leads the press team for DEFCON, the world's largest hacker con, and serves on the board of Women in Security and Privacy (WISP), a nonprofit advancing woman to lead these converging fields.

Summer Craze Fowler is the Technical Director of Cybersecurity Risk and Resilience at Carnegie Mellon University's Software Engineering Institute CERT Division. She leads an amazing team of experts who are anticipating and solving the nation's toughest cybersecurity challenges in critical infrastructure protection, insider threat mitigation, and risk management. Summer is very active in the community as a member of the faculty at CMU's Heinz college, a member of several Boards, and an advisor to Board members in the healthcare and fintech sectors. She is often asked to speak at events around the world with favorite topics being cybersecurity measurement, organizational resilience, and why Pittsburgh is the birthplace of cybersecurity!

Stephen Fried is an accomplished Information Security Leader with over 25 years of experience in information risk management, security, and technology for both large and small organizations. He has provided leadership in the development, implementation, and operation of effective information risk management programs and led the creation of the security programs for two Fortune 500 companies. His expertise covers a wide range of security areas, including risk management, regulatory compliance, policy development, security architecture, cloud security, Identity and Access Management (IAM), incident response, outsource relationship management, business continuity, and IT auditing.

Renee Guttmann-Stark is an accomplished Global Information Security and Privacy Executive. She has extensive Information Security and Privacy expertise spanning a 25-year career. She was the first CISO at Royal Caribbean, Coca-Cola, and Time Warner Inc. At Royal Caribbean, she established the company's first Maritime Cybersecurity Program. She is a frequent speaker at industry events including addressing the U.S. Travel Association at the inaugural Secure Tourism Summit in NYC 2017. She is an avid early adopter of new information security technologies and participated as a judge at RSA's Innovation Station.

Ron Hale, Ph.D. CISM, is the VP of Cyber Training, Development, and Policy at DarkMatter, a cybersecurity solution provider and consultancy in the United Arab Emirates. Prior to this, he was the Chief Knowledge Officer at ISACA and served a term as the acting CEO. He brings wide professional experience gained from serving as a forensic investigator, information security manager, security consultant, and researcher. Ron has a master's degree in criminal justice from the University of Illinois and a doctorate in Public Policy from Walden University.

Lance Hayden Ph.D.'s information security career spans 30 years and includes roles in the private sector, government, and academia. He is currently the Chief Privacy and Security Officer for a health-care startup in Austin, TX. Lance is the author of the books "IT Security Metrics" and "People-Centric Security" and a regular contributor to security publications and events. He is also an Assistant Professor in the University of Texas School of Information.

Emily Heath is United's VP and CISO. In this role, she oversees the airline's global information security program as well as the IT regulatory, governance, and risk management functions. Prior to joining United Airlines, she was the Global CISO at AECOM, a Fortune 500 architecture, engineering, and construction company. Originally from Manchester, England, she is a former police detective from the U.K. Financial Crimes Unit where she led investigations into international investment fraud, money laundering, and large-scale identity theft. She also ran joint investigations with the Federal Bureau of Investigation, U.S. Securities and Exchange Commission, and London's Serious Fraud Office.

Rebecca Herold is the CEO and Founder (2004), the Privacy Professor (consultancy) and President and Co-founder (2014), and SIMBUS, LLC (cloud services). Rebecca has authored 19 books and contributed to dozens of other books and hundreds of articles. Rebecca led the U.S. NIST Smart Grid Privacy Subgroup for 7 years, was Adjunct Professor for the Norwich MSISA program for 9 years, received numerous awards, and keynoted on five continents. Rebecca hosts the Voice America radio show "Data Security & Privacy with the Privacy Professor." Rebecca has degrees in Mathematics, Computer Science, and Education and the following certifications: CISM, CISA, IAPP-FIP, CIPT, CIPM, CIPP/US, CISSP, and FLMI. Rebecca is based in Des Moines, Iowa. privacyprofessor.org, privacyguidance.com, SIMBUS360.com, www.voiceamerica.com/show/2733.

Dawn-Marie Hutchinson is a well-known thought leader and published author and speaker. She is an expert on the subjects of ERM, crisis management, privacy, cybersecurity strategy, and leadership. She is credited with establishing standards and controls for the anonymization of identifiable data and authored the white paper for defining those levels, as well as use cases for the secondary uses of medical data. In addition to being recognized by CSO Magazine as one of the 12 most influential women in cybersecurity, she was also honored as SC Magazine's "8 Women to Watch," and the CRN Women's Power 50 list honoring outstanding female executives prominently involved in the IT channel ecosystem for their successes and the far-reaching impact they are having on the technology industry.

Paul Hypki has a varied IT background, primarily with banking and brokerage companies, with a few years of retail and engineering. His information security journey began in the early 2000s as the Risk Officer to "Keep us off the front page of the Wall Street Journal." Moving from finance, with generous budgets, to nonprofit health care, relying on older technology and smaller budgets, was a culture shock at first. After years in health care, Paul understands that information security risk must be measured, evaluated, and prioritized across the entire enterprise, and monies allocated where the greatest risk reduction can be achieved.

John Iatonna is the CISO at Spencer Stuart, an international executive search and leadership consulting firm, where he is responsible for all aspects of the organization's global security program. Prior to joining Spencer Stuart, he held a leadership role as Senior VP of Information Security, Governance, and Risk at Edelman, Inc. a public relations, marketing, and digital firm. He holds a master's degree in IT management from Northwestern University and a bachelor's degree in Business Administration from DePaul University.

Todd Inskeep consults on Commercial Cybersecurity at Booz Allen Hamilton and has over 30 years of security leadership and innovation experience including:

Being interim CISO for two Booz Allen clients
Leading cybersecurity assessments for global and regional companies (Oil and Gas, high tech and global manufacturing, pharmaceuticals, and financial service)
Worked on online banking and cybersecurity at Bank of America
Multiple patents, and time at the MIT Media Lab
Information assurance and security at the National Security Agency (NSA)
a BSEE and an MS in Strategic Intelligence.

Jack Jones has worked in technology, information security, and risk management for over 30 years, with 10 years as a CISO for three different companies, including 5 years at a Fortune 100 company. In 2006, he received the ISSA Excellence in the Field of Security Practices Award at that year's RSA conference, and in 2012, he received the CSO Compass Award for leadership in risk management. He is also the creator of the "Factor Analysis of Information Risk" (FAIR) Framework, an international standard. Currently, he is the Executive VP Research and Development of RiskLens, Inc., and Chairman of the FAIR Institute.

Glenn Kapetansky has a passion for building systems, organizations and teams that endure, and a knack for ensuring regulatory compliance in the process. For over 20 years, he has advised senior executives and built teams throughout the delivery cycle: financial and project management, strategy, architecture, development, quality assurance, deployment, and operational support. He has general expertise in data insights, data privacy, data warehouse, eBusiness, and Internet technologies. His current focus areas—as Senior Principal and Chief Security Officer at Trexin Group—are agile management, data protection, and audit/regulatory compliance.

He speaks and publishes on occasion.

Steve Katz For over 30 years, Steve Katz has been directly involved in establishing, building, and directing Information Security and Privacy functions. He is the Founder and President of Security Risk Solutions, providing consulting and advisory services to major, mid-size, startup companies. He is also an Executive Advisor to Deloitte. Steve has served as a member of the (ISC)² Americas Advisory Board for Information Systems Security.

Steve organized and managed the Information Security Program at JP Morgan for 10 years. In 1995, he joined Citicorp/Citigroup, where he was the industry's first CISO.

Steve has testified before Congress on numerous information security issues and was appointed as the first Financial Services Sector Coordinator for Critical Infrastructure Protection by the Secretary of the Treasury. He was also the first Chairman of the Financial Services Information Sharing and Analysis Center (FS/ISAC) and is an Advisor to the NH-ISAC Board of Directors.

Mischel Kwon is the Founder and CEO of MKACyber. She has more than 35 years of broad IT and security experience, ranging from application design and development, to network architecture and deployment, to building and implementing security operations centers. Prior to starting MKACyber, she has served as a VP of Public Sector Security for RSA Security, the Director for the U.S. Computer Emergency Readiness Team (US-CERT), and she built the first Justice Security Operations Center (JSOC) to monitor and defend the Department of Justice network against cyber threats while serving as the Deputy Director for IT Security Staff there.

Ricardo Lafosse is the CISO for Morningstar. He is responsible for IT risk governance, software and product security, incident management, and determining enterprise-wide security policies. He regularly presents on security topics at global conferences, including MirCon and ISACA Computer, Audit, Control and Security (CACS). He has more than 14 years of experience in information security for the government, banking, legal, health-care, and education sectors. He began his career in information security consulting in finance and manufacturing. He holds a master's in Information Assurance from the Iowa State University. He also holds the CISSP and CISM designations.

Steven Lentz is the dynamic IT security management professional best known for Integrity, Innovation, Initiative, strategic planning and management, development of key performance metrics, negotiation tactics, customer service excellence in support, team development and mentorship, risk mitigation and compliance. Steven Lentz has over 19 years' experience in IT security and network security management. Steven Lentz bridges the gaps between business and IT, strengthening cross-functional communication. Steven Lentz translates complex technical information to audiences on all levels, generating support and consensus on common mission and goals. Steven Lentz involves in team and relationship building and motivation and leads high-performance teams, completing simultaneous projects within strict time and budget constraints.

Dan Lohrmann is an internationally recognized cybersecurity leader, technologist, keynote speaker, and author. During his distinguished career, he has served global organizations in the public and private sectors in a variety of executive leadership capacities, receiving numerous national awards including CSO of the Year, Public Official of the Year and Computerworld Premier 100 IT Leader. In 2017, he was awarded the cybersecurity breakthrough CISO of the year for global security products and services companies. Lohrmann led Michigan government's cybersecurity and technology infrastructure teams from 2002 to 2014, including Chief Security Officer (CSO), Chief Technology Officer (CTO), and CISO roles.

Valerie Lyons is the Chief Operations Officer of BH Consulting and a Senior Advisor in all things General Data Protection Regulation (GDPR). She was previously the Head of Information Security Risk Management in KBC Bank for almost 15 years and is currently undertaking a Ph.D. in Information Privacy from Dublin City University. Her Ph.D. research is in privacy risk management beyond legislation and its relationship with consumer trust. Between day job, Ph.D. and looking after two children, she also does some lecturing in information risk management.

Joe Manning is an Information Security/Privacy Professional with leadership and hands-on experience. Joe Manning's career focuses on establishing Information Security Office, defining and publishing policy and procedure, and auditing in the multichannel retail environment. Joe Manning has former experience in managing development and implementing information systems for manufacturers, distributors, financial institutions, and multichannel merchants.

Edward Marchewka is the Director of Information and Technology Services for Gift of Hope Organ & Tissue Donor Network. Before joining Gift of Hope, he was the Enterprise Information Security and Server Operations Manager (CISO) for Chicago Public Schools, the third largest school district in the country. He has completed, from Northern Illinois University, an MBA and an MS in Mathematics. He has also earned Certificates in Nonprofit Management and Leadership from the Kellogg School of Management at Northwestern University. He holds multiple active industry certifications from (ISC)^2, ITIL, PCI, Microsoft, and CompTIA.

Marci McCarthy is the CEO and President of Tech Exec Networks (T.E.N.), an information security executive networking and relationship marketing firm. She has more than 20 years of business management and entrepreneurial experience, including founding T.E.N.'s flagship program, the Information Security Executive® of the Year (ISE°) Program Series, which is lauded by the IT industry as the premier recognition and networking program for security professionals in the United States and Canada. In 2015, McCarthy launched ISE° Talent, which specializes in executive-level searches as well as high-demand security industry skill sets and specializations across all industry verticals. She has been a Guest Lecturer at George Washington University; speaker and moderator at national conferences such as the ISE° Executive Forum and Award Program Series, ISSA International Conference, Local ISSA Chapter Conferences to include the ISSA Middle Tennessee's InfoSec Nashville, ISACA, TiECON, and more; and is a nationally sought-after speaker on cybersecurity, women in technology/security/business, science, technology, engineering, and mathematics (STEM), entrepreneurism, and leadership topics.

Caitlin McGaw is the President of Candor McGaw Inc., an executive search firm specializing in the placement of IT Audit, Information Security, and IT governance, risk, and compliance (GRC) professionals. She has been in executive search since 1997. Prior to founding Candor McGaw, she was responsible for managing Lander International's IT Audit search practice for the Midwest. After earning an MBA from the U.C. Berkeley Haas School of Business, she worked for Apple and then worked in Malaysia for 9 years. She is passionate about the critical role that Information Security, IT Audit, and IT GRC professionals play in successful companies and the global economy.

Adel Melek is Deloitte's Global Vice Chair for Risk Advisory (2015–present), the former Global Managing Partner for Enterprise Risk Services (2011–2015), and the former Global Cyber-Risk Services leader (2007–2011). Adel specializes in advising boards and executives on broad strategic risk matters and more specifically on cyber-risks.

William Miaoulis, CISA, CISM, has more than 25 years of Information Security experience and is currently employed as the CISO for Auburn University, his Alma Mater. Previously, he was the first Data (Information) Security Officer, at the University of Alabama Birmingham (UAB) Medical Center, and was also in consulting for 15 years. He contributes to the industry by speaking at conferences and has been quoted by numerous publications including SC Magazine, Health Data Management, Briefings on Healthcare Security, Computerworld, and Health Information Compliance Insider. He authored the book "Preparing for a HIPAA Security Compliance Assessment" and assisted with updating the American Management Health Information Management Association (AHIMA) Security Practice Briefs.

Stacy Mill As CISO and VP, Global Compliance, of Spirit AeroSystems, Stacy Mill leads global compliance and cybersecurity strategy. She has a passion for protecting the company's digital assets bridges, security architecture, vulnerability management, information governance, and compliance initiatives. Her proven E4 strategy, Evolution via Education, Enablement, and Enforcement, has helped several organizations understand and address cybersecurity business needs. After receiving her BS in Computer Science and Mathematics, her 30+ year experience includes compliance, contracts, engineering, operations, implementation as well as business strategy. She has held positions on numerous CISO and nonprofit board of directors in addition to her speaking engagements across the country.

Sam Monasteri is the VP, CISO, at ACCO Brands. His primary responsibilities are the creation and execution of the cybersecurity strategy and program, including developing road maps and driving them to success. Other responsibilities include incident response, security awareness, data protection, and regulatory readiness. Through more than 20 years of information security experience, he has built long-standing relationships with information security professionals and has a reputation for success. His expertise combines consulting and corporate experience that creates a bridge between business processes, information security strategy, and regulatory compliance solutions. Colleagues praise Sam for his unwavering commitment to quality and result-driven approach.

Kevin Morrison, MBA, CISM, is the CISO for Pulte Group, a Fortune 500 company in Atlanta, GA, and was previously the Head of Information Security at Jones Day, one of the oldest and largest global law firms. His background spans nearly 20 years in IT, with 15 in Security, including building and leading teams engaged in holistic information/cybersecurity programs and business continuity across highly regulated environments in public and private industries. He holds a BS in IT, an MBA (Technology & Innovation Management emphasis), and maintains CISSP, CISM, and CISA certifications.

Suzan Nascimento is an innovative, avant-garde leader. She has lead mature, optimized application security programs for large organizations in industries such as information services and financial services. From clear governance to robust secure Systems Development Life Cycle controls to "sticky" application development enablement. Ultimately, she brings the organization results through innovation (like Lady Gaga), data-driven decisions (like Amazon), and high standards (like Elon Musk). Nascimento also believes that high employee engagement is a leading indicator of financial results. Therefore, she implements intentional team building and various leadership styles to increase employee engagement.

Richard Nealon has worked for more than 30 years in Information Security and many of its related disciplines within the financial sector. He has been involved with (ISC)² for many years and has a long-time involvement with the Irish Information Security Forum (IISF). He sits on the Irish TC428 mirror committee for e-competency. He currently sits on the (ISC)² Ethics Committee and is a past chair of that committee. He is honored to have received the COSAC award in 2003 and the James R. Wade (ISC)² Service Award in 2010.

Naiden Nedelchev Ph.D. maintains CISM, CGEIT, and ITIL Manager, Certified Ethical Hacker (CEH), Computer Hacking Forensic Investigator (CHFI), and Certified EC-Council Instructor (CEI) credentials; Naiden Nedelchev is a technically proficient business savvy security executive with experience in corporate and cross-industry settings. Naiden Nedelchev has over 20 years of hands-on domestic, international, and multicultural experience in setting service quality and security management systems. As an active ISACA and EuroCIO member, Naiden Nedelchev participated in professional workgroups involved with key associations projects like the development of COBIT 5 for Information Security and C-SIG support on cloud security and vendor management. Naiden Nedelchev is fully committed to rapidly advancing cybersecurity best practices. Naiden Nedelchev is the cybersecurity evangelist, mentor, author, speaker, and COBIT fanboy.

Jonathan Nguyen-Duy leads Strategy and Analytics Programs at Fortinet where he is responsible for innovative edge-to-edge solutions for digital transformation. Prior to joining Fortinet, he served as the Security CTO at Verizon Enterprise Solutions where he was responsible for strategic technology partnerships, the Verizon Cyber Intelligence Center, and the Verizon Data Breach Investigations Report. He also led the global public-sector security practice with a focus on the Department of Defense and national security agencies.

Jonathan has more than 20 years of cybersecurity and BCDR experience—including armed conflict, labor strikes, natural disasters, and a wide range of cyberattacks.

David Nolan As the Director of Information Security at Aaron's, Inc., David Nolan is accountable for information security leadership, strategy, budget, and operational excellence. He is a servant leader to teams of information security professionals and managers covering application security, incident response, GRC, and endpoint and information protection.

David Nolan has more than 15 years in the IT industry. He has previously served as a Manager of the Threat, Attack, and Penetration testing services team, Application Security Architect, Deployment Manager, and various Lead Developer roles for Caterpillar Inc. He has additionally held positions at companies including State Farm Insurance and the Central Intelligence Agency.

Kevin Novak is the CISO and Technology Risk Officer at a Large Global Financial Services firm. He is responsible for the security of Company and Client information and for the management of IT risks across the firm's global business. Prior to assuming this role, he worked for Discover Financial managing their information security, records management, and enterprise risk programs. Before joining corporate America, he spent 8 years as Chief Operating Officer and Director of Consulting Services for Neohapsis, a Chicago-based information security consultancy, and 5 years in senior technology roles at Ciber Network Services, a global IT consulting services provider.

Steve Orrin is the Federal CTO for Intel Corporation. He has held architectural and leadership positions at Intel driving strategy and projects on Identity, Anti-malware, HTML5 Security, Cloud, and Virtualization Security. He was previously CSO for Sarvega, CTO of Sanctum, CTO and co-founder of LockStar, and CTO at SynData Technologies. He is a recognized expert and frequent lecturer on enterprise security and was named one of InfoWorld's Top 25 CTOs of 2004 and, in 2016, received Executive Mosaic's Top CTO Executives Award. He is a fellow at the Center for Advanced Defense Studies and a Guest Researcher at NIST's National Cybersecurity Center of Excellence.

Michael Palmer is the VP and CISO for The National Football League. A business leader with deep technical expertise, he determines the NFL's security strategy, policies, and programs to meet the league's corporate objectives while protecting its brand, intellectual property, and assets. A proven leader change agent and subject matter expert in risk management, he is a key member of the executive team. He established and chairs the NFL's Information Risk Management Committee that identifies threats and vulnerabilities and the associated business risks and determines how to address them. With more than 20 years of professional experience across multiple industries including finance, insurance, technology, and retail, he builds and oversees teams and budgets. He is passionate about cybersecurity, and he works closely with his peers, providing guidance and sharing information.

Lee Parrish is the VP, CISO for Blucora, responsible for the strategic vision, execution, and ongoing operations of the cybersecurity program for the company. He has been published in information security trade journals and is a frequent speaker at multiple international security conferences. He has served as an Adjunct Professor of Information Security and Guest Lecturer at large universities. In addition to being CISSP certified, he holds two graduate degrees: an MBA from the University of Arkansas and a Master of Science from Norwich University. He is a combat veteran of the U.S. Marine Corps.

Mark Rasch is the owner and principal of the Law Office of Mark Rasch in Bethesda Maryland, providing legal and other support in the areas of computer crime, breach response, regulatory compliance, privacy law, and GDPR assessment. He was the former head of the U.S. Department of Justice computer crime unit, and prosecuted several high-profile computer and high-technology crimes, and was the Chief Privacy Officer (CPO) for Science Applications International Corporation (SAIC) and the Chief Security Evangelist for Verizon Enterprise Solutions. He is a prolific author and appears frequently on TV and radio as an expert on Internet and privacy law.

Jim Reavis For many years, Jim Reavis has worked in the information security industry as an entrepreneur, writer, speaker, technologist, and business strategist. Jim's innovative thinking about emerging security trends has been published and presented widely throughout the industry and has influenced many. Jim is helping shape the future of information security and related technology industries as co-founder, CEO, and driving force of the Cloud Security Alliance (CSA).

Kevin Richards is Marsh Risk Consulting's (MRC) Global Head of Cyber Risk Consulting. Based out of Chicago, Kevin Richards leads MRC's worldwide cyber-risk consulting team and its regional and local centers of excellence. He is an information risk management professional with over 28 years of experience in information security and ERM. Working with large multinational corporations, as well as the U.S. Department of Defense and other U.S. Federal agencies, Kevin Richards provides an array of technical and pragmatic perspectives on building and protecting an organization's critical information assets. Kevin Richards is a prior International President for and a Distinguished Fellow of the Information System Security Association (www.issa.org) and is a CISSP.

Jim Routh is the Chief Security Officer and leads the Global Security function for Aetna. He is the Chair of the NH-ISAC Board. He serves on the Board of the National Cyber Security Alliance and is a member of the Advisory Board of the ClearSky Security Fund. He was formerly the Global Head of Application and Mobile Security for JP Morgan Chase. Prior to that, he was the CISO for KPMG, Depository Trust & Clearing Corporation, and American Express.

Tony Sager is a Senior VP and Chief Evangelist for the Center for Internet Security. He leads the development of the CIS Controls, a community consensus project to identify and support best practices in cybersecurity. His "volunteer army" identifies practices that will stop the vast majority of attacks seen today, and he leads projects that will share, scale, and sustain these practices for worldwide adoption. He retired from the NSA in 2012 after 34 years as a Mathematician, Software Vulnerability Analyst, and Executive Manager. Tony oversaw all NSA Red and Blue Teams, as well as all security product evaluation teams.

Dane Sandersen is a Global Leader that brings over 20 years of experience in leading high-performance teams and implementing, supporting, and securing technology-based solutions. Most recently, he has been developing information security strategies and is building another Global Information Security Program. He truly enjoys working with business partners to collaboratively align InfoSec controls to business risks and rewards. Additionally, he is a Lieutenant Colonel in the U.S. Army Reserve and currently serves as a Cyber Battalion Commander.

Gene Scriven is an Information Security Veteran with over four decades of experience in many sectors and industries, including military, government, retail, hospitality, and finance. Prior to joining ACI worldwide less than 3 years ago, he was the CISO at a leading hospitality solutions provider, and the CISO at the world's largest home improvement retailer.

Gene Scriven holds a bachelor's degree from Hawaii Pacific University and a master's from Troy State University and is a frequent speaker at many industry conferences and events. Gene Scriven and his wife, Tammie, currently live in sunny, Southwest Florida.

Grant Sewell, CISSP, manages the Global Information Security Program at The Scotts Miracle-Gro Company, the world's largest marketer of branded consumer products for lawn and garden care. He serves on the board of directors for the R-CISC, the Retail ISAC, and has held information security leadership roles with several Fortune 500 companies and U.S. Government agencies. He has more than a decade of experience in security, holds numerous industry certifications, and is a frequent speaker at regional and national conferences.

Bill Sieglein is the Founder of the CISO Executive Network. He established and improved security programs, directed them for numerous companies, and oversaw the professional services organizations for security consulting firms.

His career started in the U.S. Intelligence Community where he pioneered the certification and accreditation process for the CIA and improved information security awareness training at the NSA. Bill is an accomplished author with numerous credits, including a book entitled "Security Planning and Disaster Recovery" by McGraw-Hill. He is frequently sought by news outlets for input to national-level information security stories.

Matthew Smith is a Senior Security Engineer at G2, Inc. He has been working on the Cybersecurity Framework team since its beginnings in 2013. He has moderated panels and presented at many local and regional conferences as well as RSA on cybersecurity-related topics. He is also the author of NIST Special Publication 800-184 Guide for Cybersecurity Event Recovery. He currently leads the contractor team which develops the framework, creates implementation guidance, and promotes ecosystem surrounding the framework.

Tony Spinelli has spent his entire 25+ year career devoted to advancing and developing cybersecurity and risk management capabilities through roles as CISO for some of the world's most critical companies and as a board member for both government and public traded corporations. He has been a major contributor to developing next-generation digital cybersecurity capabilities throughout his career and is the recognized leader in methods to secure Public Cloud technology. His most recent focus is pioneering methods to drive deeper insights into human and artificial intelligence teaming, machine learning, and time series graph analytics in cybersecurity. He currently serves as a Board Member at Peapack Gladstone Bank. Prior to those roles, he was Senior Vice President/CISO for Capital One Financial Corporation.

Jason Taule A 30-year industry veteran, Jason Taule has held executive positions in public and private sectors serving as CSO/CPO within government and at large integrators like General Dynamics Information Technology and Computer Sciences Corporation. His thought leadership contributions have advanced the science and practice of cybersecurity, privacy, and risk management. With passion and integrity as calling cards, his communication or interpersonal skills and numerous accomplishments as a Security Specialist have earned him recognition as Industry Luminary. Ever mindful to balance risk with business need, he has successfully adapted security controls in countless real-world implementations, a pragmatism that leads many to consider him the voice of reason.

Samantha Thomas For 25+ years, Samantha Thomas has worked in the information and people protection profession, mostly in the United States, for finance, health care, technology, government, and postsecondary education. She has been a key-note/speaker/panel member on five continents, in 14 countries, and most major U.S. cities. Her writings, interviews, and quotes have been published in books, newspapers, and magazines.

Mark Weatherford is the Chief Cybersecurity Strategist at vArmour. He has more than 20 years of information security experience, and his former roles include Principal, The Chertoff Group; Deputy Under Secretary for Cybersecurity, DHS; CSO, North American Electric Reliability Corporation; CISO State of California; CISO State of Colorado; and U.S. Navy Cryptologist. He holds a BS from the University of Arizona and an MS from the Naval Postgraduate School and is a CISSP. He was awarded SC Magazine's "2010 CSO of the Year" and named one of the "ten Most Influential People in Government Information Security" in both 2012 and 2013.

Michael J. Wilcox has more than 20 years of experience in providing IT Security Leadership across a comprehensive portfolio of security services during his IT career. He has developed programs and centers of excellence for IT security services including forensics, incident response, education and awareness programs, vulnerability assessments, penetration testing, data loss prevention, enterprise information security architecture, compliance, encryption, IAM, and disaster recovery. He joined Cisco from Newell Brands, a global manufacturer and marketer of consumer and commercial products. In his role, Michael advises business partners on business-driven cybersecurity initiatives including strategy, risk management, transformation, and security operations.

Greg Witte supports the U.S. National Institute of Standards and Technology in developing and updating information security guidance and reference materials. He works with organizations around the world to strategically apply that guidance for improving and monitoring the effectiveness of cybersecurity governance and risk management programs.

Jason Witty is the EVP, CISO at U.S. Bancorp, providing singular accountability for information security controls in the company. He has 24 years of information security and risk management experience gained at former employers including Bank of America, Options Clearing Corporation, Aon, Allstate, and NASA Langley. An award-winning CISO, he was the inaugural Chicago CISO of the Year in 2013 and was recently named the 2017 SecureWorld Ambassador of the Year in addition to a "CISO Superhero" at I.S.E. North America in 2015. Providing industry leadership, he simultaneously serves as the Chairman of the Board of Directors at the Financial Services Information Sharing and Analysis Center (FS/ISAC), as well as being FBI's Chicago InfraGard Sector Chief for Financial Services.

Caroline Wong's close and practical information security knowledge stems from broad experience as a Cigital Consultant, a Symantec Product Manager, and day-to-day leadership roles at eBay and Zynga. She is a well-known thought leader on the topic of security metrics and has been featured at industry conferences including RSA (USA and Europe), OWASP AppSec, and BSides.

Caroline Wong authored the popular textbook Security Metrics: A Beginner's Guide, published by McGraw-Hill in 2011. She graduated from UC Berkeley with a BS in electrical engineering and computer sciences and holds a certificate in finance and accounting from Stanford University Graduate School of Business.

Charles Cresson Wood, JD, MBA, MSE, CISA, CISSP, CISM, CGEIT, is an independent Information Security and Privacy Consultant based in Mendocino, California. He has been in the field for approximately 40 years, has done this work with over 125 organizations, and is the author of the well-known book entitled "Information Security Policies Made Easy." He specializes in the development/documentation of infrastructure components in support of information security and privacy, including policies, standards, guidelines, contingency plans, corporate governance systems, incentive systems, outsourcing agreements, as well as training and awareness materials.

Introduction

You are most likely reading this introduction because you picked this book off the shelf in the bookstore at a conference or local bookstore, and wondering will this book help me? Is it for me? Or you are a professor looking for a comprehensive semester course on cybersecurity leadership. Will I learn something new? Will it reaffirm what I already know? Or, maybe you bought the book from Amazon and are a collector of cybersecurity leadership books. Whatever the reason, thank you.

I am going to make a rather bold promise here—*you will learn something new*.

How do I know this? Because this is a different Chief Information Security Officer (CISO), Information Security Leadership, Cybersecurity Leadership, or Cybersecurity book than you have read before for one simple reason—I did not write it. You did. You wrote it from what you taught me while I prepared to speak at conferences, what you shared with me at workshops, and working with some of you who built security programs for Fortune 500/large companies over two decades with me. You wrote it when you asked me a question I did not know the answer to. You wrote it when you showed me a different way.

This is a soup-to-nuts book to provide a comprehensive roadmap, enhanced by *insights from experience* to help build, lead, and sustain a cybersecurity program (or information security program if you prefer—the debate on terminology would take up a whole book—this book will use the terms "cybersecurity" and "information security" interchangeably)—we do not have time to be stuck in old terminology, do we? We have systems and data to secure!

I also admit I cheated and solicited help from *over 75 award-winning CISOs, security leaders, professional association leaders, cybersecurity standards setters* you have seen speak at conferences and some CISOs leading security programs that you have not met yet—but I am confident someday you will. Some of the CISOs are still in the role at their companies, some have joined others, some have gone into consulting, some have joined vendors—check out their bios and past experiences highlighted in the *Contributors* section, and you will see they have done some amazing things, leading some of the most successful security programs in leading companies and creating today's standards. Many of them heavily influenced the developing role of the CISO and security practices we have today.

Each of them has taken the time to share their expertise with you. Is this cheating? Maybe not—it is what we all should be doing in our careers—*leveraging the expertise others have in different aspects of leading cybersecurity.* This book is based upon the principle of collaboration, the principle that says we are more than the sum of our parts.

We begin with an interview with the "First CISO," Steve Katz in Chapter 1 (*CISO Role: Evolution or Revolution?*). The book continues with cybersecurity leaders short, personal stories of the challenges, successes, lessons learned, and sharing of their insights.

Chapter 2, *Cybersecurity Leadership and the McKinsey 7-S Framework*, explains the framework developed in the 1980s by Tom Peters and Robert Waterman, to structure our thinking around reviewing cybersecurity organizational effectiveness. To my knowledge, no cybersecurity leadership book has leveraged this model to ensure an effective cybersecurity program to date. This framework does not replace any of the cybersecurity control frameworks (which are also reviewed in this text), but rather enhances the way we 'lead cybersecurity' by leveraging an existing management framework that has stood the test of time. Do we not want the CISO organization to run effectively? How do we ensure we have adequately supported our cybersecurity strategy with the other important organizational factors (structure, systems, staff, skills, style, and shared values)? I chose to apply cybersecurity practices to this model because we should be thinking about maturing our cybersecurity programs to incorporate the elements of the 7-S model to move to a higher level of effectiveness. For simplicity, this will be referred to as the *7-S Framework Applied to Cybersecurity Leadership.* To achieve this goal, the chapters in this book have been related to and organized around the 7 "Ss" of the McKinsey Framework—Strategy (Chapters 3–4), Structure (Chapters 5–6), Systems (Chapters 7–9), Shared Values (Chapters 10–12), Staff (Chapter 13), Skills (Chapter 14), and Style (Chapter 15). Ineffectiveness in anyone of these areas has the potential to impact the entire security program and negate investments made in other areas.

(STRATEGY) Using the framework defined in Chapter 2 as our *CISO ROADMAP* for the rest of the book, the *strategy* section begins with Chapter 3 *Developing Strategy*, whereby a six-step strategy process from creating the vision through to building an action plan is explained, as well as an introduction to other techniques. The section continues with a discussion of Chapter 4 *Emerging Technologies and Trends*, providing a discussion of how technologies are adopted plus discussion of some of the current technologies such as blockchain, IoT, artificial intelligence, machine learning, digital transformation, automation/orchestration, threat intelligence, others, and even Drones! Trends the CISO needs to consider are also presented.

(STRUCTURE) Chapter 5 *Cybersecurity Organization Structure* examines the structure and functions the cybersecurity program should include based on the model for leading organizations and related to traditional functions such as security awareness training, IAM, risk analysis, and newer functions such as security analytics, data science, threat intelligence, and managing vendor relationships. Chapter 6 *CISO Reporting Models* examines different reporting models and the pros and cons of each.

(SYSTEMS) Chapter 7 *Leveraging the Incidents of Others* starts off by highlighting some of the impactful recent security incidents and the lessons we can learn from them, Chapter 8 *The Security Control Framework Maze* explores the maze over a dozen cybersecurity control frameworks and standards and ending with an 11-Factor Cybersecurity Risk Assurance Manifesto to manage compliance with the frameworks. Chapter 9 *Risk Management Practices* closes out this section discussing qualitative and quantitative risk management approaches.

(SHARED VALUES) Chapter 10 *It's the Law* explores multiple laws and regulations such as HIPAA, GLBA, HITECH, FISMA, SOX that laid the ground-work, plus today's more recent laws such as CISA, New York Cybersecurity Requirements, and International emerging cybersecurity laws. Chapter 11 *Data Protection and Privacy Every CISO Must Know* provides the relevant privacy laws including the more recent GDPR, privacy nomenclature, eight privacy principles, privacy approaches such as PbD, and discussions of privacy and social media. Chapter 12 *Meaningful Policies and Procedures* provides guidance for policy, procedure, standards, and guidelines development and ways to make these effective.

(STAFF) Chapter 13 *Multigenerational Workforce Team Dynamics* provides insight into understanding, communicating, and leveraging the capabilities of the different generations, from traditional, boomers, Generation X, Millennials, to Generation Z, why we are the way we are, and the implications for the workforce. The chapter wraps up with using the MBTI Personality Type Indicator to understand teams and the organization.

(SKILLS) Chapter 14 *CISO Soft Skills* explores necessary skills for the CISO and team to relate to the organization to communicate, negotiate, influence, maintain an executive presence, present, listen, and achieve their goals.

(STYLE) Chapter 15 *The CISO and the Board of Directors* provides useful guidance for working with the board of directors in presentation and interaction.

I was pleased to learn that my second book, *Information Security Governance Simplified: From the Boardroom to the Keyboard* (Auerbach, 2012), was being used by several universities in their bachelor's and master's of Cybersecurity programs. The book was written in 15 chapters with that in mind, so I decided to structure this book with 15 chapters also, to enable ease of use as a core leadership course in a University CISO, cybersecurity leadership, or security governance semester course providing real-world experiences.

I have enjoyed collaborating with many experienced, intelligent, caring people to put this book together, and I hope you enjoy reading it and refer to it from time to time as needed. There may also be an issue in the future to look up again to provide a real, truthful, non-salesy, straightforward perspective as the leaders in this book have provided. I have brought some of the best minds in my network to you, so please thank them next time for volunteering their insights when you see them speaking at a conference or in your networking travels.

The opportunities to lead in this field are endless.

Enjoy the journey ahead and make a difference. Our families are counting on us to make them safe and secure. Go for it.

Todd Fitzgerald

Author

Todd Fitzgerald, CISSP, CISA, CISM, CIPM, CIPP/US, CIPP/E, CIPP/C, CGEIT, CRISC, PMP, ISO27000, and ITILv3 certified, is Managing Director/CISO of CISO Spotlight, LLC., has built and led multiple Fortune 500/large company information security programs for 20 years across multiple industries, was named 2016–2017 Chicago CISO of the Year by AITP, ISSA, ISACA, InfraGard, and SIM, ranked Top 50 Information Security Executive, T.E.N. Information Security Executive (ISE) Award Finalist, and was named Ponemon Institute Fellow (2013-present).

Fitzgerald coauthored with Micki Krause the first professional organization Chief Information Security Officer Book, *CISO Leadership: Essential Principles for Success* (ISC2 Press, 2008). Todd also authored *Information Security Governance Simplified: From the Boardroom to the Keyboard* (Auerbach, 2012), co-authored *Certified Chief Information Security Officer Body of Knowledge* (E-C Council, 2014), and has contributed to over a dozen others. Fitzgerald has participated in the development of materials for the *ISC2 Official CISSP Exam Study Guide*, *Information Security Handbook Series*, ISACA *COBIT 5 for Information Security*, and *ISACA CSX Cybersecurity Fundamentals*.

Fitzgerald is a top-rated RSA Conference Speaker and is frequently called upon to present at international, national, and local conferences for Information Systems Audit and Control Association (ISACA), Information Systems Security Association (ISSA), Management Information Systems Training Institute (MISTI), COSAC, Centers for Medicare and Medicaid Services, T.E.N., and others. Fitzgerald serves on the HIPAA Collaborative of Wisconsin Board of Directors (2002–present), Milwaukee Area Technical College Security Advisory Board, and University of Wisconsin-La Crosse College of Business Administration Board of Advisors (2007–present).

Prior senior leadership includes SVP, CAO Information Security and Technology Risk Northern Trust, Global CISO Grant Thornton International,

Ltd, Global CISO ManpowerGroup, Medicare Security Officer/External Audit Oversight WellPoint (now Anthem) Blue Cross Blue Shield-National Government Services, Manager Information Security North and Latin America Zeneca/Syngenta, and prior senior IT leadership positions in data management with IMS Health, American Airlines, and Blue Cross Blue Shield United of Wisconsin. Todd earned a BS in Business Administration from the University of Wisconsin-La Crosse and Master Business Administration with highest honors from Oklahoma State University.

THE CISO ROAD MAP

1

Chapter 1

CISO Role: Evolution or Revolution?

> One must not always think so much about what one should do, but rather what one should be. Our works do not ennoble us; but we must ennoble our works.
>
> **Meister Eckhart, 1260–1327**

The information security discipline has grown substantially over the past 20 years, evolving into a "profession" previously reserved for technical staff buried deep in the computer operations area. While security controls have been managed since there have been computers, dating back half a century, information security was not a focus area beyond establishing controls for who should have access to the system. The profession has grown substantially in recent years due to the cyber threats, increased connectivity, increased laws and regulations, and a desire to manage security holistically to mitigate the risk of financial loss due to the destruction, loss, or alteration of information.

The need to manage the security of information has given rise to a new role of the CISO, or Chief Information Security Officer. The role is "new" in relation to other industries and roles that have been around much longer. The first named "CISO" was Steve Katz, designated CISO in 1995 for Citibank. While there were individuals named as security managers prior to this time, organizations did not place the value of this role at the executive level. This was the beginning of the environment we know today where it is taken for granted that every organization of any size would have a CISO and even those smaller organizations would have an individual they could name as being accountable for information security.

Other industries such as accounting, construction, and manufacturing processes have been around for many years. For example, the accounting industry dates to Luca Pacioli, who first described the double-entry bookkeeping system used by Venetian merchants. Now those in the information security field may argue that the first information security thinking came from Julius Caesar (100–44 BC), where he created the "Caesar Cipher" substituting each letter of the alphabet with another letter further along. This was used to communicate with his generals and would not be viewed as very strong encryption today, as there were only 25 possible combinations of letters using the displacement. This is where the comparison to early thinking in information security and the accounting profession would stop. While there were advances in information security through such developments as the Enigma machine, first patented in 1919 and used by the German Navy in 1926 used to encipher and decipher messages through a much more complex mechanism than the Julius Cipher, using 17,756 ring settings for each of 60-wheel orders (compared to Julius's 2-wheel approach), there was still not the concept in organizations of a central person to manage the information security program. Contrast this to the accounting industry, where the industrial revolution necessitated the need for more advanced cost accounting systems and corporations were being formed with bond and stockholders, to the point where the American Association of Public Accountants was formed in 1887 and the first licensed Certified Public Accountants (CPAs) were licensed in 1896. Contrast this with the first broad industry-recognized information security credentialing organization, the International Information System Security Certification Consortium (known as ISC2) formed over 100 years later in 1989. The first credentialed Certified Information Systems Security Professional (CISSP) was issued in 1994, again almost 100 years after the CPA. Today, there are approximately 700,000 CPAs and over 110,000 CISSPs, almost a sevenfold multiple. This short history is essential to understand, as consistency between organizations, public or private sector, does not generally exist as this profession is in an evolution of "best practices" that has had to catch up to the other industries, such as the accounting industry, to standardize practices and generally accepted approaches. This makes the CISO job that much more challenging, as there is the need to review and select the appropriate methods, security frameworks, controls, and policies that will be valuable to the organization they are initiating and leading information security programs.

Clearly, this is a young, maturing industry that has made significant steps in a short period of time. For those that have been in the industry for many years, some days it may feel like the tasks are like those of 20 years ago. This may be true when considering the technical underpinnings are similar—such as the threat environment needs to be evaluated, an organization needs to determine their risk, and controls need to be put in place to mitigate the threats, just as in today's organizations. The difference between the CISO role today and in the early beginnings has to do with the transformation and maturity of the profession over this period as the attack surface changed, the threat model changed, and the regulatory environment has significantly changed.

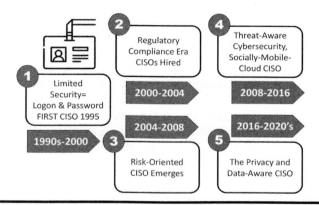

Figure 1.1 Five phases of CISO role evolution 1995–2020. (Adapted from Fitzgerald, Privacy Essentials for Security Professionals, 2018, San Francisco, RSA Conference.)

Understanding how the profession has evolved is instructive to the next-generation CISO to avoid repeating history. The CISO may be the first CISO in an organization or may be the fourth or fifth one in the role. More likely than not, the role of CISO will be something that was created within the last 5–10 years, and the organization may not have much history with the role.

Figure 1.1 illustrates the evolution of the CISO role from 1995 to 2020, depicting the role of the information security profession and the focus of the CISO as continually adapting and expanding. Over the past few decades, I would suggest there have been five distinct phases of information security program maturity, each phase requiring a different focus for the CISO as well as potentially a different type of security leader within the role. Security has been a concern since the beginning of time to keep those away from valuables that were not authorized to have them. The focus changes, and just as we no longer must roll rocks in front of our caves to protect ourselves, we now have other threats to deal with. Knowing the history and how this profession has evolved can be instructive to avoid repeating our previous mistakes or leverage the good ideas from the past. As we work with new technologies, some of the challenges may require new approaches; however, some of the fundamentals of what needs to be in place can leverage some activities of the past.

These stages should be regarded as cumulative or additive in nature. In other words, we expand our breadth as CISOs and the world that needs to be focused on becomes larger in scope.

CISO Phase I: The Limited Security Phase (Pre-2000)

The period prior to 2000 could be considered as the "Limited Security" phase. This is not to imply that organizations did not secure their information assets, but rather that as a formalized discipline that had the board attention of senior management, for most organizations, this was very limited, and in some organizations, nonexistent, compared to today. Financial institutions were clearly ahead of the curve, as there was a real threat to monetary loss if access was gained to the systems. In the 1990s, there was still the perception by many organizations that the information contained within their systems would not be interesting to external parties. Granted, there were firms concerned with intellectual property protection; however, the concern was typically around managing access to ensure that users were properly authenticated and authorized to the systems they needed access to, no more and no less. The focus was on internal logon ID and password provisioning, and physical access. Much of information security was security by obscurity, which today might be referred to as security by absurdity!

So why was the focus so internal for many companies? Much of this had to do with the connectivity of the computer equipment. The 1980s–1990s saw the changeover from "glass house data centers" where all the data was contained within the data center and accessed by terminals, to the introduction of the IBM PC in 1981 connected through local area networks to information. Security controls were necessary to ensure the isolation of human resource and financial systems, as well as to protect the stability of the production environment by implementing processes and controls for change management. Information was also starting to experience data sprawl and proliferation, as desktop computers now contained data previously stored in the data center. Still, the information concern was the flow of information within the organization, along with email to parties outside the organization.

The focus changed from internal protection of access between users to external threats (except for physical threats that were predominantly externally focused) in the mid-1990s as the World Wide Web (www), or the Internet we all take for granted today, was emerging and companies were trying to figure out the appropriate use cases for it. Companies sent questionnaires to employees asking for justification as to why they needed Internet access. This would seem silly today; however, that was the state of the technology in the mid-1990s. It was not until this connection to the Internet that organizations had to start to examine security threats more broadly than the information flow with their business partners (through direct communication links) and external email communications with customers. The Internet presence spawned an entire industry ensuring that firewalls and antivirus (AV) programs were blocking unwanted malicious traffic. On November 2, 1988, Robert Morris, a graduate student in Computer Science at Cornell University, wrote an experimental self-replicating and propagating program called a worm taking advantage of a bug in the Unix sendmail program and let it loose on the Internet. He released the worm from Massachusetts Institute of Technology, so it would not look like it came from Cornell. The worm continued to spread and wreaked havoc before researchers at Harvard, Berkley and

Purdue University developed solutions to kill the worm. He was convicted of violating the Computer Fraud and Abuse Act (1986), created to aid law enforcement agencies with the lack of criminal laws to fight the emerging computer crimes. He was sentenced to 3 years' probation, 400 hours of community service, fined $10,050 (over twice as much in today's dollars), and the costs of supervision. He appealed, and it was later rejected. This is a small fine in comparison to the estimated damage to the organizations suffering crashes due to the worm, costing universities, military sites, and medical research facilities between $200 and more than $53,000 each to fix. The numbers pale in comparison to the cost of breaches today; however, the impact was large to the organizations connected to the Internet.

As the World Wide Web initiated support for multimedia display in the mid-1990s using HyperText Markup Language along with the common Uniform Record Locaters to simplify address lookup, the Internet became a key technology for organizations to be able to promote their capabilities directly to the end consumer. Along with this new connectivity to the Internet came a new threat vector to organizations outside of the university/research domain—external access beyond email. Firewalls and AV were the panacea to protect the organization from external threats. As CISOs of today like to joke about the good old days, then "as long as you had a firewall and AV," you were good. Many executives would have that view when it came to security, infrastructure spending for security would end up with limited funding.

The type of leader hired to run the organizations during this period came primarily from a technical background and typically ended up somewhere in the Information Technology (IT) department. In many cases, those running the information security programs were reporting through the computer operations area. Progressive organizations viewed the security of the internal information important and combined the discipline with the database administrators , Data Modelers, software development life cycle practitioners, and systems quality assurance (SQA) testing, placing the security function within information resource management or data management organizations. While this was an important function in larger organizations, the visibility was rarely beyond the IT department. The function was also typically part of someone's job function, usually as part of a systems administration function or networking function within the IT area. The first CISO role was not named until 1995 (and highlighted by an interview with Steve Katz in this chapter), and the role was not given the high-level visibility except in the largest organizations. The norm was for this role to exist at a manager or director level or at a technical systems administrator level. Rarely would an organization see the need to place this function at a C-level. The Chief Information Officer (CIO) was just emerging in the 1990s as needed with IT becoming a larger impact to organizations; however, the CISO role was just emerging and was not a household word during this period.

STEVE KATZ: INTERVIEW WITH THE FIRST CISO

Executive Advisor Security and Privacy, Deloitte

TODD: Steve we are honored to have you join us today. How did you get into the security field?

STEVE: Thank you Todd. I fell into the information security field accidentally in the 1970s and serendipity is just fantastic! After getting out of school and starting at First National Citibank, I was working in an internal consulting group and was asked to help figure out and be part of the establishment of an SQA function and Systems Development Life Cycle (SDLC) function. We mandated the use of an ID and password module in Cobol and Fortran programs. Although stored in a primitive clear text table, it was the start of protecting the code. I then gained experience when Access Control Facility (ACF2), Resource Access Control Facility (RACF), and Top Secret came on the scene and we converted the programs to use the new security software.

TODD: How popular was the information security group?

STEVE: The security group at that time was as popular as poison ivy, and developers would say, "You want me to do what?" and would blame the security software when application changes would fail. We generally asked them to retest, because it rarely was a problem with the security software.

TODD: What was your experience with auditing security controls in those days?

STEVE: I recall a time when a new examiner, fresh out of school, was sent to audit us. He wrote up a "major issue" in the report sent for my review that there was no "RACF in the DEC VAX" (computing) environment. I let the report go through without comment, and the lead federal examiner from Washington, DC, called and said, "What are you doing over there?" I said, "You are absolutely right—we don't have RACF in the DEC VAX environment." He said, "Well, RACF doesn't run in the DEC VAX environment." I said, "You are right, next time please send competent examiner!"

TODD: How much information was shared during that period between institutions?

STEVE: In the mid-1980s, the Data/Information Security Officers for the New York banks started getting together on an ad hoc basis every 2–3 months. Every meeting was different, with only two consistent agenda items—when will the next meeting would be held and who was bringing the donuts. This was the forerunner of the

Information Sharing and Analysis Centers (ISACs). {Note: Steve was appointed to be the sector coordinator for financial services, following a task force commissioned by President Clinton to examine U.S. critical infrastructure security, holding formation meetings for FS-ISAC in 1997–1999}. We realized if one of us gets hit with a breach, we all eventually will. It was also effective for resolving vendor issues—one vendor once told me that I was the only bank in New York City complaining about an issue with their product and I should rethink it. At the next security officer meeting, I put him on the Polycom with the heads of security for ten other banks—needless to say, the issue was fixed!

TODD: How receptive was the board to information security issues?

STEVE: At Morgan Guaranty Trust (now J.P. Morgan), Dr. Peter Tippett demonstrated a new AV program, which eventually was acquired by Norton. The board was unfamiliar with information security issues, and I needed $400,000 to implement Peter's program. The CIO told me to come to the board meeting the next day, so I showed up and 5 minutes later I had to make my pitch. After taking a deep breath facing the hallowed hall of business-focused Chief Executive Officers, I said, "You may have seen something in the paper about computer viruses. Picture this, you are in the trading room and 3's become 6's and 5's become 8's and 9's become 0's—what does that do to your positions?" They asked if this could happen and I said, "You bet!" They asked if I could fix it, and I responded that I could not eliminate it, but could greatly reduce the problem. They funded the AV program. Why? Because this was put in business terms they could easily understand.

TODD: Great story. Would this method work with the technologies today?

STEVE: Absolutely. My focus has consistently been a business risk focus. I see companies over and over that have great technologies that solve great technical problems and my consistent question back has been, "So what, what is the business problem you are trying to solve?" If there is not an answer to "so what" for a solution, I did not need the solution.

TODD: What advice would you give to CISOs to engage business leadership?

STEVE: When you go to present to business leadership, every business executive knows they are there because they are smart. That may or may not be the case, it does not matter, and they know they are smart. When you present, and they do not get it, it is not because they were not smart enough—it is because you were too incompetent to explain it.

TODD: Very insightful, that certainly puts the onus on the CISO to prepare.

STEVE: There are times you are being paid to make a decision, times to make a recommendation or times to inform, and the CISO needs to let them know what they are being asked to do. More often than not, you are being asked to make a recommendation. You cannot take it personally if the recommendation is not followed. Your job is to get the message across (a meaningful "so what"), make recommendations, make sure they understand why, and the risks of doing something or not doing something, and then you step back.

TODD: Where did the term "CISO" come from?

STEVE: After Citibank was hacked in 1994, losing $400,000 in transfers that was noticed by an accounting clerk who said, "My clients don't do this type of transfer" and preventing a subsequent $10M in losses. The board decided they wanted an executive that could move freely among the executives in the bank, and this is where the CISO term was born.

TODD: Who did you report to?

STEVE: I reported to the CTO who reported to the CEO and to the corporate risk committee, which gave me leverage.

TODD: What changes did you make as the CISO in this role?

STEVE: My administrative assistant came to me with a stack of variance requests 12 inches high to the security policy in place. I decided to change the policy—as of now, I will not sign these. New policy—(1) there will be a risk acceptance, not a variance process, (2) approved by the business head or one permanent designee, (3) specification as to why the exception was necessary, (4) my recommendation, and (5) business signature. I also had one line at the bottom which said, "This is against the recommendation (not decision) of the CISO." I also indicated that two metrics would be reported to the risk committee—(1) the number of risks accepted by the business and (2) the number of risks accepted against my recommendation. In the 10 years, there were none accepted against my recommendation! We would have a conversation with the business executive as to why we were recommending against it and followed the recommendation. Visibility was very important.

TODD: How has the threat environment changed in the last 25 years since you first became CISO?

STEVE: My biggest concern was script kiddies wanting to make a name for themselves and a criminal element that wanted to make some money, and they were not particularly good at it. The attack surface has changed dramatically, borders have disappeared, and now there are state-sponsored and state-sanctioned security attacks, as well as organized crime making tons of money developing and selling products they can rent out to help break into systems. They are far more sophisticated, far more focused, far more knowledge-able, and as diligent as ever. The skills have improved remarkably, and they go after specific targets—they know what they are after.

TODD: What implications does this have for today's CISO?

STEVE: We continue to play catchup. The bad guys have somewhat unlimited budgets and we do not. We need to get a little better at prevent-ing attacks and significantly better at detecting and responding to them. We are developing much better cybersecurity profession-als through ungraduated and graduate training programs. We are also getting people in the CISO role that understand business leadership support is critical and explaining the impact when new security technologies are implemented.

TODD: Do we have too many cybersecurity regulations today?

STEVE: Many are confusing and, in some cases, conflicting. Some states are tougher than other states; by satisfying one country's regula-tion, you may be violating another country's regulation. Difficult to understand where the overlap and where the conflict are. We need (1) simplification, (2) fewer regulations, and (3) consistency.

TODD: How does a CISO sort through all the security products?

STEVE: Have vendor focus on the business problem—too often they do not understand that (the so what) that eliminate many of them. Leverage fellow CISOs and ISACs. Be confident enough to ask others for help.

TODD: What are a few traits for the successful CISO?

STEVE: Must maintain the technical knowledge; translate that into the business issues being addressed; incredible negotiation skill abil-ity to develop operational, managerial, and executive metrics (risk acceptances, audit findings, key examiner findings, risks applica-ble for us and our response, maturity models 3-4 categories, and swim lanes); and report the right metrics for the right audience. Have a good reason for the metric or get rid of it. The good CISO also understands how his company makes money.

TODD: How should the role of the CISO change in the future?

STEVE: I have been advocating the role of the CISO as a bifurcation whereby a Chief Information Risk Officer (CIRO) would focus on the what's, the why's, and the verification; a Chief Information Security Technology Officer will come up the most effective "how." The CIRO would verify the "how" met the needs. These are two different skill sets, and there are some people that can do both, but very few can do this. Too many CISOs are confident when talking about technology and less confident when talking with business leadership to help them understand why something is needed. Too many of us get into the details of the technology, and the business leader needs to know why it is important to them and how the risks are being dealt with. Security is just another risk. The CISO must make certain the cure is not worse than the disease. There are times the solution it may cost more to offset the risk than to accept it.

TODD: If you were to speak to your younger self, what would you have told yourself knowing what you know now?

STEVE: There are very few changes I would have made. In 1994, we focused on business risk issues and continued to do so. There are no silver bullets, and the best you can do is reduce risk and be confident to deliver that message to the steering committee or board, and then extensively market it. My first 2 years at Citibank I put in about 200,000 miles just going from region to region, business head to business head to build credibility and told them to call me if something did not sit right. You must become the Chief Information Security Evangelist in addition to the CIRO and CISO.

TODD: Any parting thoughts for those considering this career path?

STEVE: For those senior technical staff wanting to be a CISO, they should ask themselves if they are willing to give up their "technical safety net," as the more time is spent as a CISO, the less this safety net will exist.

This is probably the best profession you can ever get involved in, you will never get bored, and you will meet some of the best people in the world.

TODD: Well said, thanks for being so helpful and sharing your insights.

STEVE: Thank you, it was my pleasure.

While it was recognized that security controls were important through the passing of regulations such as the Computer Security Act of 1987, aimed at ensuring U.S. Federal Government systems were appropriately secured; the passage of several privacy laws such as the Privacy Act of 1974 requiring designated record sets be identified and secured and the EU Data Protection Directive (1995/1998); European developments including the BS7799 Code of Practice (CoP) (BSI, 1995); and for information assurance developed by the U.K. Department of Trade and Industry CoP for information security (1993), much of the regulations impacting the establishment of the "Information Security Officer" position came later after the turn of the millennium. One plausible reason for this is there was much focus on avoiding catastrophe from computers having to process transactions after the year 2000, known as Y2K in the IT industry, whereby programmers had coded systems for years using two digits for the year to save space, erroneously counting on the fact that the applications would be replaced prior to Y2K. Organizations are still running some applications on mainframes created before 2000 due to the complexity and cost of change. Organizations were focused on retiring old systems and upgrading infrastructure, and while attending to information security, were less concerned with establishing high-level positions focused on data protection and information assurance. The external threat was also viewed to be under control with the existing structure, as organizations were beginning to make the foray into e-commerce applications. For most companies, the "Internet" presence was still more informational and serving up static web pages vs. integrating with transactional data or was used for research purposes within their organization. Internal intranets were beginning to be developed, again with static information for most companies. The biggest threat at the time to these sites were script kiddies, or individuals intending to cause harm and earn their "badge of courage" by replacing the web page with their own "I was here" type page.

CISO Phase II: Regulatory Compliance (2000–2004)

The early 2000s witnessed the passage of several laws focused on protecting the privacy and security of information. There was beginning to be more concern than usual due to the computerization of not only back-office-type functions to support accounting, but rather the collection and storage of personal information and how this was stored. Industry vertical laws were passed in the United States, such as the Health Insurance Portability and Accountability Act of 1996 (HIPAA), which required the Secretary of the Department of Health and Human Services to publish standards for the exchange, privacy, and security of health information. Proposals were made in late 1999; however, the rules were not finalized and publicized until after public comment until December 28, 2000. The rule was subsequently modified in early 2002, while the Final Security Rule was also under discussion and the final rule was published February 20, 2003, and covered entities had 2–3 years, depending upon size, to become compliant. Other compliance laws such as the Gramm–Leach–Bliley Act (enacted November 1999) for the financial industry, and the Sarbanes–Oxley Act of 2002 (SOX) targeting internal controls to ensure financial statements were correct after the Enron scandal, each served to give rise to the establishment of the "Information Security Officer," or someone named and accountable for the security of the organization.

These changes were significant in the evolution of the present-day CISO as requirements were established, for the first time, across a broad set of industries, that someone in charge of information security was required. This may be regarded as the one-throat-to-choke type of establishment and accountability missing in organizations until these requirements arrived. The nomenclature in these laws did not refer to this role as the "Chief" Information Security Officer at this time, but merely the jargon Security Officer, Information Security Officer, or Systems Security Officer was used. "Cybersecurity" was not a common term used when referring to the individual in charge of protecting the organization's assets. Some organizations also had difficulty adding the word "officer" to the official title, as an officer of an organization typically implies those in charge of specific duties such as the Secretary, Treasurer, or President and named in corporation legal documents. The information security position during this period held the titles of Vice President (VP), Director, or Manager in primarily the largest organizations. This period represents the early stages of the CISO that we know today, specifying broad responsibilities for ensuring the protection of the organization's information from loss, destruction, or disclosure. It also became clear that the position needed to work with the (newly) appointed Privacy Officers in the organization to secure the appropriate information and paying special attention to information with a higher level of sensitivity, such as health-care or financial information.

Breach notification laws were also starting to be adopted state by state after California passed the breach notification law S.B. 1386 that became operative in July 2003. Subsequently, the state-by-state passage of the bill occurred where most of the states now have a breach notification law. Heretofore, there was no requirement to report the breaches. CISOs needed to work with compliance departments to define what constituted a breach vs. an event vs. an incident, a debate that still goes on whenever a new law has a breach reporting requirement.

This period also ushered in sets of requirements contained within the regulations for protecting information. One complaint frequently heard was that the regulations were not prescriptive enough and left much to interpretation! The laws needed to be created this way, or there would be a risk that by the time the regulation was passed, the technology referred to would be obsolete. The laws also needed to be written in such a way that small organizations, large organizations, and the public sector could each adhere to the regulations—no small feat. Frequently at conferences, security professionals would complain about the regulations and compliance requirements; however, this point in history was significant as it started the security conversation in many organizations that may not have begun otherwise. Each of the regulations had some combination of monetary penalties as well as the potential for directors in the companies to become personally and criminally liable for failing to ensure their organizations were complying with the laws.

With respect to the Internet, more organizations were also venturing into transactional-based websites, taking orders, and processing information. While Amazon opened its online doors in 1996 as a radical idea (why by a book online when you can go to the bookstore and see it), we all know today the success that was brewing in the early days of Amazon as a bookseller. The idea of online commerce was no longer a novelty during this period, and the CISO of this era needed to be concerned with compliance that the regulations mandated as well as a more sophisticated Internet presence.

Much energy was expended by organizations during this period to determine compliance through initiating gap analysis, remediating the gaps, and reporting compliance to company committees. This evolution of the CISO was also marked with limited enforcement of the security controls by some regulators such as HIPAA, and increased scrutiny by others, such as the Sarbanes–Oxley section 404 audits by the company external auditors. External enforcement may have been a mixed bag, as organizations tried to get to "100% compliant with X regulation." The valuable Information Security Officer at this time was one that comprehended the regulations and could offer administrative, technical, or operational safeguards to protect the organization. Organizational skills and working across the organization became more important than the deep technical skills. This era represented a shift in the expectations of a CISO as we know it today, as now the CISO needed to be able to interpret legal regulations, and work with the General Counsel and other executives to formulate the strategies required. This period is also responsible for the beginning of senior management to become engaged with the information security controls and privacy processes protecting the organization.

LEE PARRISH: THE COLONOSCOPY OF CYBERSECURITY

VP, CISO, Blucora

The companies I have worked for as CISO offer a generous life insurance policy that provides a standard amount, with an option to increase coverage at my own expense. I chose a higher level of coverage which required that I go through several administrative processes. I first completed a questionnaire asking me basic questions about age, current medical conditions, smoker/nonsmoker, and other standard questions. The results came back and said that I passed the first milestone, the next one being a medical examination. I scheduled the screening, and a representative from the medical firm came to my office and performed the examination. He efficiently and professionally took my blood pressure, resting pulse rate, height, weight, and a urinalysis screening. He asked a few more questions and then put the results into a report that was submitted to his firm. The results came back in 2 weeks and said that for the level of insurance I was requesting, I was in good health and insurable to the level. Separate but related to this, I visit my primary care physician each year. She takes my blood pressure and resting pulse rate, asks me multiple questions, performs several tests of my blood, conducts Electrocardiogram tests, and gives me a prostate examination, a urinalysis screening, and several other tests. Additionally, she puts me through other testing protocols such as stress tests for heart health and a colonoscopy procedure. At the end of all these tests, the physician makes the determination that I am in good health. Both scenarios seek to accomplish the same thing: determining the condition of my health. But both seek this condition for very different reasons. The life insurance policy examination is compliance; the full physician examination is security. I cannot use the results of my basic life insurance examination to conclusively determine that I am in good health. However, I can use the physician's examination to conclude that I am in good health AND insurable. Similarly, compliance cannot be used to show good security, but good security can be used to show compliance.

CISO Phase III: Risk-Oriented CISO (2004–2008)

The compliance era was beneficial in ushering in new regulations and focusing organizations on information security. One could also evaluate this phase as being necessary, but not sufficient. The problem was that information security became a check-in-the-box-done approach. After the implementations of the regulations were considered complete, organizations disbanded the working committees for the project and went back to their normal activities. Security spending may have become elevated; however, the institutional focus was no longer on information protection. After all, the security project was done and just needed an annual review, right?

In addition to complying with the regulation, it became clear that implementing the same controls across the entire organization was inefficient and maybe not the best investment. For example, does the internal employee newsletter need to have the same protections as an externally facing health information inquiry system? In recognition that different risks may require different levels of investment and protection, the focus shifted from compliance with all the regulations to taking a risk-based approach to the information being protected. For example, as more and more information was stored on laptops, the sensitivity of the information needed to be evaluated. A watershed moment for laptop encryption came in 2006 when the Veterans Administration lost a laptop containing personal information of 26.5 million veterans. Many organizations at that time were not encrypting laptops. I recall asking at conferences during those years how many had encrypted their laptops and only half of the hands would go up—today, it would be rare to see anyone (admit) in a publicly traded or government entity not encrypting their laptops as a fundamental control. A compliance approach, at the time, would have mandated all computers be encrypted. A risk-based approach would have evaluated the desktops or servers as being internal to the locked building, and a much less probability of being lost or stolen (today, most organizations move to encrypt all devices as the threat has increased and the cost of the software has decreased).

The shift to a risk-based CISO required that the CISO acquire new skills to evaluate the probability and impact of an adverse event occurring. This is not as simple as pulling out the checklist of requirements and determining which ones comply. Risk assessments involved either a qualitative (rating of low, medium, and high with greater subjectivity, but simpler to conduct) or quantitative (how much money would an adverse event cost) risk assessment.

This period also witnessed a greater formalization of the role and the view that the CISO needed to possess more than technical skills to be effective. The first CISO leadership book targeting the "soft skill" dimension published by a professional security organization (ISC2) was developed during this period (Fitzgerald and Krause, 2008) because of technical security individuals being thrust into the spotlight and assuming CISO leadership roles. It was during this period from 2004 to 2008 that the CISO role and title began to emerge in more companies. So as a profession, the role is still relatively young, with the real emergence for most medium to smaller organizations a decade or so at most. Given this short timeframe, organizations may have only had experience with one to two CISOs, with the first CISO building the awareness of the need and the second one obtaining the budget after the organization absorbs the message from the first CISO!

During this period, the CISO was predominantly still in IT, reporting to the CIO. These were where the projects needing security were primarily infrastructure projects requiring cooperation with the IT area. The legal departments were also a reporting place for the CISOs as companies were dealing with the regulations that were initiated in the early 2000s that needed to still be implemented. The financial services industry recognized that information contributed to the risk profile and a trend was to move pieces of information security, particularly the governance, to report within the risk management group that also managed operational, financial, credit, reputation, and strategic risks. The emergence of governance, risk, and compliance (GRC) tools appeared during this period to manage the risks across the enterprise, including information security now started to be recognized as an organizational risk.

This period also saw the emergence of a detailed set of government regulations aimed at U.S. government agencies and the contractors that served them, specifically the 800–53 controls. These controls operated at a very prescriptive detailed level and provided useful guidance for "how" to implement various security controls to satisfy the regulations.

Breaches were on the rise with most of the attention paid to large organizations having larger breaches. The groundwork for reporting these breaches was laid in the California Senate Bill in the preceding era, and now companies were figuring out when and when not to report breaches. As a result, tighter integration or cooperation with the privacy teams resulted. The CISO role was becoming elevated in the larger organizations due to the focus on risk that organizations were now facing.

MARK BURNETTE: THE BENEFITS OF FOCUSING ON RISK VS. COMPLIANCE

Shareholder, LBMC Information Security

Security compliance obligations represent a true irony for many security leaders. On the one hand, compliance obligations may provide the impetus that compels an organization to support and fund certain cybersecurity initiatives, providing some validation to the efforts of the security leader. However, on the other hand, in many cases, the business leaders at an organization are so focused on the entity's compliance obligations that they assume that once compliance is achieved, security is sufficient. Good security leaders know that true security is about proper cybersecurity risk management, and a well-designed program that enables company leaders to make well-informed decisions about security risks is the ideal state. Security leaders also agree that being compliant with an applicable security regulation does not necessarily equate to proper cybersecurity risk management (or sufficient security posture!). The challenge, then, is for security leaders to shift the mindset of their organization away from tracking compliance against regulations and towards the practice of security risk management. This shift is not easy, because company executives and board members are constantly bombarded by reminders of applicable rules and legislation, so they will continue to ask about the entity's compliance posture. When discussing and presenting your organization's compliance with the relevant regulations, be sure to continually bring the conversation back to how effectively cybersecurity risks are being identified, managed, and reported. Avoid building your dashboards and reports based on compliance posture if possible. While you will likely have to address the topic, an effective response can be something like "We expect to be fully compliant with XYZ law by the end of this year. While that is encouraging progress that we should acknowledge, XYZ law only applies to certain types of data, and we have at least three other types of sensitive data in our organization that must also be protected. Our most recent risk assessment highlighted the following areas of high risk. The company's security program and our security budget have been allocated to address those items by XXX date." Continually reinforce the concept of cybersecurity risk management with company leaders. Use data from your risk assessments to educate your executive team and inform their decision-making. If you can help them learn to make risk-based decisions rather than compliance-based reactions, your job satisfaction will be much higher, and your security program will be much more effective.

CISO Phase IV: The Socially Mobile Cloud-Enable Threat Aware CISO (2008–2016)

This period witnessed Facebook growing to from a school-based social media platform of 1 million users in 2004 to almost a billion users in 2009 (over 2.2 billion active monthly in 2018) and a constant in most people's lives that own a smartphone or a computer today. Speaking of smartphones, since the introduction of the iPhone in 2007, we have evolved to today where almost everyone has at least one smartphone in their pocket. The new-generation Z (born after 1995) has had a smartphone most of their lives. The technological changes that matured during this time had major societal impacts as to how people received their news, communicated with friends, researched and applied for jobs, and interacted with others. Texting replaced phone calls and voicemail, and meeting at the "yellow pole outside the concert" was no longer the way of finding someone.

It is easy to forget that dramatic changes are taking place when we are amid them. For the CISO, these new ways of communicating once again stretched the boundaries of what should be allowed or denied within organizations. Should Facebook be blocked or supported? Will this impact our millennial (born 1980–1995) recruiting efforts? If we block Facebook, should we block LinkedIn (used for business job-related connections) as well because the senior management needs visibility into these relationships for business? What about bringing their own smartphones into the workplace, should we allow access to email, calendaring, contacts, and storing documents? How do we ensure security with these new avenues of malicious software and links into our organizations?

This period created many questions that now had to be dealt with in addition to the existing regulations introduced in the early 2000s. New tools were available now to assess the risk, and with this lens, the CISO could look at these new platforms in terms of the risk management practices developed in the prior era. There was still a tendency of many CISOs to say no to the technology by blocking the social media sites and not allowing users to bring your own device (BYOD). Some Information Security Officers were so hesitant to allow BYOD, as are some today, they sometimes jokingly refer to BYOD as "bring your own disaster," highlighting the difficulty in controlling multiple devices across multiple platforms and versions of software. The CISO had to be part technologist, part marketing, and part politician to navigate these waters. Marketing departments were encouraging the use of social media to promote the brand and product, network departments did not want to punch holes in the firewall, Human Resources departments wanted to attract new candidates with the progressive technology and positive social experiences, and the CISO did not want to create new vulnerabilities in the environment. As with all technologies, eventually the desired human experience will win out and the Information Security Officer will either need to find a method to secure the new approach or find an organization that is not progressive and upgrades slowly.

Saying "no" has never been an option, and saying no during this period had a greater career-limiting effect on the CISOs than saying no would have been during the compliance era of 2000–2004. This is since the focus was primarily on meeting the regulations at that time, and there were clearer guideposts (i.e., penalties for not achieving the requirement). New technologies initiated during this period did not have these guideposts as the regulations had not caught up with providing guidance around them yet as they were just moving too fast. This period is a great example as to why security laws, regulations, and policies are written at a high level and not prescriptive, as they would become quickly outdated. For example, just when Facebook had become a household word, by August 2014, 40% of all U.S. 18-year olds were using Snapchat daily to take disappearing pictures. In the United Kingdom, the Snapchat penetration rate among teenage Internet users (3d Quarter, 2016) was an astounding 84%, with even higher rates in Ireland (89%), Singapore (89%), and Sweden (87%).

We also changed the mode of Internet surfing during this period from the laptop to the tablet with Apple Computer's introduction of the tablet (iPad), at the same time expanding the people who bought computers to those individuals that would never own a laptop or desktop. The thought of being able to access the Internet from the living room was a sleek idea that caught on quickly. For the workplace, this was a desired device by executives that traveled to be able to access email, calendar, and contacts while on the road without the need to carry a bulky device or must use their Blackberries (soon to be replaced by companies during this era as well with iPhones and Android devices). CISOs needed to be able to ensure that executives could have this support. Board of directors were also trading in their three-ring printed binders with documents loaded on tablets. This is arguably the most confidential strategic information a company may have, and this required special attention to secure.

Large breaches were making headlines during this period, and regulatory organizations were becoming more serious about enforcement (see Chapter 10 regarding the regulatory environment). The CISO role was being thrust into the spotlight like no period prior. The perfect storm was occurring between the regulatory environment, breaches, and technological change creating higher demand for this role. A new type of CISO was needed, one that could not only understand the technology but could also navigate the boardroom questions and promote the right level of investment for the company. The demand for talented CISOs started to outstrip the supply, causing salaries to rise and also encouraging more to seek the position.

The breaches gave rise to an increase in the need for more information on external threats and the establishment of threat intelligence sharing organizations. Laws were passed to make sharing among companies to share information. The recognition that companies are being hit by the same criminal actors and there was a need to cooperate was moving beyond the financial services organizations. This sharing has a long way to go; however, sharing in earnest started for more sectors during this period.

GENE SCRIVEN: THE PATH FROM TECHIE TO SUCCESSFUL CISO

CISO, ACI Worldwide

I grew up in the era of pay phones and eight-track tapes, both of which are now virtually extinct. When I started my professional career in technology, it was on mainframes that filled entire supercooled buildings, only understood assembly language, and stored programs on refrigerator-sized 20M storage devices.

The transition from 20th-century technologist to modern-day security executive has not been a simple one. It is more than just learning new network models, understanding the idiosyncrasies of security devices, and knowing the impacts of malicious traffic or activities. Table stakes require successfully juggling the latest cyber knowledge and skills, along with the leadership skills to manage diverse and geographically separated teams. But there is so much more. It is also about becoming a trusted partner to the business, which means being able to see the world through business goggles, while remaining true to your pledge to protect data and resources throughout the enterprise.

We are all experts on risk, but for the "*R* word" to mean anything, the business-oriented focus must be a top priority and is a mandatory prerequisite in the transition from techie to CISO. I can quote Common Vulnerabilities and Exposures (CVE) numbers and threat ratings all day long, and they will fall on deaf ears. But when the risks and impacts are put into business terms, which mean something to business people, a CISO will be so much more effective. For example, telling a retail store manager that you need a slice of his precious processing time to upgrade an AV engine means nothing. However, telling him that a virus or malware infection from an out-of-date solution can result in his store not being able to ring up sales for several hours or days…well, which has a much more meaningful impact.

Probably the most significant takeaway from this discussion is that I have learned over the years; to be a successful CISO today, you absolutely must be a business person first and a technician second. Those who can adapt this philosophy will thrive, whereas others are likely to become extinct—just like the pay phone and eight-track.

CISO Phase V: The Privacy and Data-Aware CISO (2016–2020s)

Predicting the future is a risky business; however, since a meteorologist can be right 50% of the time and keep his or her job, let us take a whack at it here. Just as with other eras where the seeds of an era are sown in the couple of years before the era where the change takes root, there has been an emerging concern around privacy in the past few years. As more and more information is aggregated about personal lives, shared, and processed through data analytics to understand behaviors, an ever-increasing concern about the protection of this information is surfacing. The first question to ask is, where is it? Structured (present in systems, data files, databases) and unstructured data (extracts, spreadsheets, documents) has sprawled across our organizations and across the cloud environments coming to maturity in the prior era. Increased regulations, such as the General Data Protection Regulation replacing the EU Data Protection Directive of 1995/1998 which mandated compliance expectations in mid-2018, necessitate review of the business and where data is stored and processed. Countries are establishing their own cybersecurity and privacy laws. The CISO needs to understand the new regulatory environment and compliance with these regulations, while at the same time not introducing excessive burdens on business operations.

This period is also experiencing a continued movement of offshoring IT resources, and the location and processing of the information must be evaluated for security when moving beyond the organizational confines. Increased attention is being paid to vendor management relationships and their security, in large part due to some of the breaches in the prior era that involved breaches at vendor/partners of the company experiencing the breach.

The CISO is now expected to be able to work with senior management as a partner, represent risk in the boardroom, leading critical initiatives, and respond to attacks from nation states, politically motivated attackers, organized crime, ensure compliance with privacy and security laws and regulations, evaluate external cloud operations, and support an agile business utilizing the latest technology.

CISO Role Today and Tomorrow— Increased Complexity

The CISO role has certainly become more complex over the past several years due to many external and internal company forces. As a result, the individual must be able to lead through changes that are much different from the five phases illustrated. The modern CISO has a broad range of focus, and failure to pay attention to any one of these areas can result in the one "career limiting gotcha" that makes it difficult for the CISO to recover from within his organization and may have to prepare for other external opportunities.

It is challenging to keep these items in focus and not become distracted from the day-to-day questions; however, the CISO should always have the following "list" of items and integrate the Steve Covey's landmark book, *The Seven Habits of Effective People*, method of using the Eisenhower Urgent/Important Principle and use the prescribed four quadrants to prioritize tasks. The system distinguishes between "important" and "urgency" by referring to "important" tasks as those

	URGENT	NOT URGENT
IMPORTANT	*Quadrant I:* Urgent & Important	*Quadrant II:* Not Urgent & Important
NOT IMPORTANT	*Quadrant III:* Urgent & Not Important	*Quadrant IV:* Not Urgent & Not Important

Figure 1.2   Four-quadrant prioritization matrix. (Adapted from Steven Covey, *The Seven Habits of Highly Effective People.***)**

responsibilities contributing to the achievement of the function's goals and "urgent" tasks as those responsibilities needing immediate attention. Urgent tasks are typically tied to the achievement of someone else's goal, and there will be consequences if these tasks are not dealt with. The quadrants for prioritizing tasks are shown in Figure 1.2.

Items in the first quadrant contain items of high importance and require high urgency—tasks and responsibilities needing immediate attention. The second quadrant requires items that are important, but do not require immediate attention. This quadrant is where the long-term strategizing would come into play, as if this is not done today, an immediate effect will not be felt. The third quadrant contains urgent tasks that are urgent, but not that important. These are the day-to-day distractions that do not contribute to your output—these may be an option to reduce, eliminate, or delegate to someone else. The fourth and final quadrant contains items that are unimportant and not urgent and therefore hold little value. These are time wasters that should be eliminated. Most of the activities that we perform are in Quadrants I and III, those urgent tasks that are either important or unimportant. The urgency of the moment grabs our attention. Many people spend too little time in the second quadrant, the long-term strategizing quadrant, as this quadrant is not urgent. When this happens, this means that we are most likely very operationally focused and not spending enough time on our business long-term development as well as our own personal long-term development.

CISO Forces at Play

Before discussing the application of the prioritization quadrant to the forces impacting the CISO's program, let us discuss the various forces impacting the CISO role, as shown in Figure 1.3. External and internal activities and trends influence the direction of the CISO, and subsequently, the prioritization of the CISO workload. Notice these forces occur at a higher level than the administrative, technical, and operational controls required to ensure the confidentiality, integrity, and availability of the systems and information.

Figure 1.3   Forces impacting CISO role.

Increased International Government Regulations and Scrutiny

There are increased regulations and the emergence of proposals to place more control over cybersecurity around the world such as China's Cybersecurity Law (2017), Singapore's Cybersecurity Bill (2018), and increased scrutiny by regulators such as the Office of Civil Rights for HIPAA, and the Federal Trade Commission. These laws can have a larger effect on the ability of small and medium businesses to comply with the regulations not utilizing third parties (i.e., Managed Systems Security Providers) to ensure the computing environment is consistent with the regulation. The CISO should be aware of the emerging laws and how it may impact both current business operations and strategic initiatives. These laws can influence where the company chooses to perform business and the controls that the company chooses within that country. For example, after China's Cybersecurity Law was issued, Apple Corporation decided to remove all virtual private network (VPN) mobile applications from their platform to comply with China's Cybersecurity Law. Whether or not enforcement of some of the foreign laws would take place, sometimes it is good business for companies desiring to expand into foreign countries to show they are following the local laws and will become good partners for the nation and respect their sovereignty. Apple indicated through a statement, "We have been required to remove some VPN apps in China that do not meet the new regulations." Each organization needs to evaluate local, national, and international regulations to determine if they are applicable to their business and to which business units would be impacted. The CISO also needs to know the penalties of noncompliance with the laws to enable proper education of the executive management team and the board of directors, as there may be personal liability attached to the regulations, both criminal and civil.

Privacy Compliance

Over the past several years, there has been an increased focus on privacy due to the amount of information collected and aggregated based on activity and location for targeted marketing. The CISO needs to pay attention to the privacy laws and how he or she is being compliant with the clauses within the privacy laws requiring safeguarding of the information. A regulation can become law in a country and have impacts beyond the borders of the country. Privacy concerns are having an ever-increasing impact on security programs and moving these programs to discover where the information resides so that the appropriate controls can be placed on the information. The largest impact today is the location of the information and assurance the personal highly sensitive information is being protected from those without a need-to-know.

Technical Advances

As technology continues to advance rapidly, the CISO must consider the impact these new technologies have on security—both the technology being used internally for the existing applications and the new technology that could be leveraged to reduce costs, add functionality, or provide a strategic benefit. For example, a few years ago, password controls with a logon ID and password were deemed sufficient for most operations (questionable if that really was sufficient; however, the expectation was adequate). Today, with the prevalence of two-factor or multifactor authentication, whereby something you know is also supported with something you have or are, this is becoming the emerging standard for authentications. Yahoo and Google both announced the availability of two-factor authentication in 2011; however, the usage is still optional. Many online banking sites provide the ability of two-factor authentication with the option to register the device (i.e., laptop, desktop, mobile phone, tablet) upon the first entry. Requiring two-factor authentication for remote access VPNs is a de facto standard today. This capability has been around for some time, with the issuance of RSA SecureID hard tokens available for several decades, prior to the smartphone. These hard tokens have been increasingly replaced by solutions that use Short Message Service text messaging and smartphones, email, or phone calls to provide the access code. Therefore, a CISO today recommending users carry a hard token with them would most likely be viewed as being out of touch with the current state of technology, as there are other software-based methods to provide the same functionality with less friction.

BRET ARSENAULT: ELIMINATING PASSWORDS: A JOURNEY

Corporate Vice President, CISO, Microsoft

Every modern CISO is aware of the weaknesses of passwords as a means of protecting identity. Years ago, when we started seeing the growing sophistication of hackers and their unfortunate success, we knew that multifactor authentication was a smarter approach. Initially, we used physical smart cards because this kind of authentication is much more secure, but it did not give people a smooth user experience. Additionally, the smart cards require infrastructure that can be challenging to implement. Further, while smart cards are more secure, they are still prone to being lost or forgotten. To sidestep the usability challenges of smart cards, we have now started a journey focusing on a nearly friction-free experience, from using nature's most unique characteristics: biometrics. These technologies are easier to use, more accessible for the needs and preferences of the person, and significantly harder for criminals to exploit. Right now, about two-thirds of the people at Microsoft perform their daily work without having to type in a password. There is a process for incorporating this technology across our organization and that requires some time to implement, which is why we are not totally password-free yet. It is worth noting that this approach only works when there is a deep integration between the hardware and the software. I genuinely believe that the effort involved is worth the work because the result delivers strong, tangible benefits: (1) a great user experience, (2) it drives operational costs down because there are fewer calls to the help desk for resetting passwords, and (3) better security! We are collaborating with our peers within the technology industry via the Fast IDentity Online (FIDO) Alliance to help propel the adoption of this approach more broadly. We have built a blueprint for the technology and shared it with hundreds of companies, some of whom are rolling out the technology now. Companies who are interested in adopting this approach should work with FIDO to learn more. We are optimistic that this innovation will become more widely adopted, and as it is deployed more, people will be safer.

New Products/Services

Paying attention to the strategic direction of the organization and the products and services on the horizon are essential to long-range planning. Failure to understand these developments will result in the CISO being out of the loop and ending up later supporting products not having the benefit of input by the CISO organization. The CISO must function as a business partner enabling the business through actions, and this means being directly involved in ensuring their team is helping to provide secure solutions for the product or service under consideration. Bolting on security after the fact is both expensive in the real dollar impact, and politically expensive through the perception that the CISO was not engaged with the business to help. By designing sufficient controls from the start, the CISO may be able to improve the user experience through suggesting items such as biometric authentication (i.e., smartphone integration with Touch ID, operating system integration with facial recognition, or usage of mobile devices as proximity badges).

Engaging with the applications management team is a must to ensure that security is baked into the systems through a Secure Systems Development Life Cycle (s-SDLC) process supporting newer methods of development, such as Agile Development where Scrum masters serve as shepherds to ensure development is cohesive. Agile-developed applications are developed in Sprints—small pieces of the project are developed in iterations, and later iterations continue to "bite off" a little more of the project until completed. Or using a Dev-Ops approach whereby the communication between the traditional development and operations teams is increased, thought to be a by-product of Agile Development. Use of these concepts, combined with the leveraging of cloud technology, has increased the automation developer's use within their jobs. Understanding these approaches will help the CISO understand how to be engaged in the development of new products and services within the IT organization.

GLENN KAPETANSKY: INTEGRATING SECURITY WITH SDLC/AGILE DEVELOPMENT

Chief Security Officer, Trexin Group

For a long time, I resisted working directly in the information security field. While at Bell Labs, we did not have a distinct security function—UNIX, the Internet, and Web were developed as open ecosystems with some trust assumed. But we did believe passionately in privacy, and that culture shaped my thinking.

I remained happy in IT operations for years. Later, on Mergers and Acquisition teams at banks and health-care insurers, I was able to shorten my due diligence time dramatically, often to 2–3 days. My trick was to focus on the Systems Development Life Cycle (SDLC) at the target company, very specifically on the protection of data as it moved from development, to test, into production. I invariably found this to be the weakest security in the company. This also shaped my thinking.

So, when challenged at ThoughtWorks to develop a framework for Secure Agile Development, my experience led me to split my advice into two parts: one for producing secure code, and the other for the preproduction environments that support the SDLC. I will spare you the details but share with you my conclusions:

For the first part, I went to the Web and searched on "top application security risks 201*" (where "*" was the last 5 years). You can try it too, and find that (for instance) for Web applications, there are vulnerabilities that persist: injection, cross-site attacks, breaking authentication and session management, etc. I turned to my colleagues and proclaimed the profound truth: "Don't ask me about Secure Agile Development. Go produce good code. Good code is secure code."

For the second part, I will summarize my advice from every single assessment I have performed. Pay attention to three things:

1. Identity and access management
2. Protecting your data and your endpoints
3. Comprehensive event logging.

The rest is left as an exercise for the reader.

Third-Party Outsourcing

As companies shift more processing overseas for the IT processing, many times the security administration/operations are also moved. This requires increased coordination with the offshore providers and an understanding of the functions remaining onshore and how they integrate with the offshore functions. For example, the testing of business continuity functions requires local business involvement, while the daily maintenance of the backups may be remotely covered offshore or be managed through a combination of internal and external data centers. Individuals may be dealing with service desks located in foreign countries and security administration functions supported by a combination of portals and staff. The countries supporting outsourcing may also be a patchwork of skills in multiple countries, leveraging the unique skills and cost advantages a country may offer. For example, technical resources may be more plentiful and cost-effective in India on a per-hour basis, and other countries such as the Philippines with an abundance of lower-cost, college-educated fluent English-speaking technical resources provide a large pool of resources to staff the call centers, where a projected revenue of $40 billion in call-center handling is expected by 2022 in the Philippines alone.

External/Internal Audits

Publicly traded companies are subject to SOX assessments made by external audit firms to ensure financial statements accurately represent the company's operations and correct results. The audits provide insight as to whether the operations are adequately supported by the security controls, attesting to the adequacy of design and effectiveness of the controls. The CISO needs to be aware of the timing of these reviews and the expectations for the correction of inadequate controls. Sometimes these audits in and of themselves can drive a significant work for the security program and need to be appropriately prioritized among the other initiatives. Many times, these initiatives will be viewed as more urgent and more important by the organization as the individuals involved want the audit issue noted by the auditors in their summary report to "disappear," so business can continue without the cloud of a deficiency hanging overhead. However, while the audits are very important to provide an independent review ensuring the security practices are sufficient, these are secondary to the operation of the security program and should have less importance than building and operating the security program for the organization. In practice, this is unfortunately not the case in many companies, whereby the audit process ends up driving the security program vs. the other way around. Audit findings are also reported to the audit committee and have visibility over time until closed. To maintain favorability with the audit committee, it is important to show consistent progress towards the audit items.

Internal audits are performed as the third line of defense (after the first-line security operations and second-line information security oversight) and should be taken just as seriously as the external audits. These audits are generally targeted at specific areas of risk to assist in helping the organization resolve outstanding issues impacting financial and operational activities.

Social and Cultural Trends

As the world becomes more connected and the availability of shared information continues to grow daily, information can "go viral" and be shared by millions of people in a short period of time. As news of company activity, whether it be unpopular with a hacktivist group or the changing demographics of the customer base, the CISO should be aware of how these changes may impact the way individuals access and use technology. Different policies may need to be constructed to manage the security in response. For example, with more and more workers wanting flexibility in their working arrangements across all demographics, desiring flexible work-at-home arrangements or work-in-coffee-shop capabilities, the CISO must be responsive to implementing policies with a balance between security and the ability to work remotely. We have progressed from the desktop to laptop to Personal Digital Assistant to smartphone to tablet era for the chosen device for our work. Offices have become smaller and no longer have large file cabinets for paper files, and in some modern offices, the concept of hoteling, or "borrowing a hot desk," for the day has become the norm. These social trends are moving more towards a paperless, portable society. The security policies need to be able to support these changes. This book, e.g., was writing entirely in a home office near Chicago, Illinois (34-inch monitor made life easy!), in coffee shops, on airplanes, on the road at conferences, and in a rented co-sharing office space in Dublin, Ireland. There was no storage of paper files in a big filing cabinet, and only a high-powered 2lb laptop and a 2lb second 16-inch portable monitor made the trip! Contrast this to several years ago, when moving offices, I had five large double-wide file cabinets full of papers and decided it was time to go digital. While the experience is different by environment depending upon the equipment, space, privacy, and noise level (hence earbuds everywhere), this truly represents a significant departure from the way of working in the past where everyone was in one office. Many of the offices today are moving to open floor plans with no or very little personal permanent space. The CISO today needs to make sure they support this mode of working from anywhere—securely.

Social networks such as Facebook, Snapchat, WhatsApp, Instagram, LinkedIn, and Google+ have grown in popularity in just a little over a decade, changing the way we communicate with distant friends and acquaintances, even changing how we think of a "friend." This has given rise to changes to acceptable use policies to ensure that appropriate content is posted externally and that when the individual posts information, they recognize they are still, in some manner, reflecting upon the organization where they work.

Organizational Culture

As management guru Peter Drucker is often credited with saying "Strategy eats culture for lunch" (however, this has been a topic of discussion as to who first said it), this is especially true for the plans of the CISO. Does everyone nod their heads in agreement in the meeting, however fail to provide the necessary funding or carry out their departmental security responsibilities? This is one of the priorities that is often not given much "thought" in the CISO's long-term strategic thinking—assuming that others are onboard. Have you ever left a meeting thinking everyone agreed, only to find out later that "silence" or "absence of verbal objection" does not mean agreement and commitment? Several issues may reveal themselves as conflicts requiring immediate attention or may not be visible until longer in the future when commitments of support were made, but not delivered.

MISCHEL KWON: COMMUNICATING SECURITY PROGRESS AND NEEDS WITH BUSINESS-FOCUSED LEADERSHIP

CEO, MKACyber

The average CISO's tenure at an organization is a fast 18 months of learning, educating, begging, and defending—the business of an organization, the executive process of an organization, and the security of the organization.

The CISO's entry and exit from an organization is either an inability to master these processes and move the ball forward, or an incident where the

CISO is made the sacrificial lamb and offered up to the board, the press, and the organization. The CISO's role is a relatively new executive role, which is just now being more clearly defined. In the early CISO days, it was viewed as more of a technical role than an executive role. In more recent years as the stakes in risk, loss, and cost have gone up—it is clear this is an executive role where it is imperative that the CISO bring extensive knowledge of the business, cybersecurity, use of IT to support the business, finance, and leadership to the table. No different than other executive roles, the CISO's role has grown into a truly accountable executive role.

Looking at resolving budget, programmatic, communication, and high-value events such as incidents are issues faced by all executives—whether business, finance, IT, or now security. All executives are required to educate the leadership about the problems, justifying the budget, presenting a plan, and executing on this plan. Cybersecurity and the job of the CISO are no different. The challenge the CISO faces is articulating technical issues into the executive and business-focused language and educating the executive leadership in the right level of technical information to allow them to make sound decisions.

Prioritizing the Forces Using the Four Quadrants

So how do we apply the matrix to the CISO's world? It would be prudent to examine each of the forces contributing to the complexity of the role and examine how we are prioritizing the activities of each of these forces by quadrant. We may not be explicitly assigning quadrants to the activities we perform today; however, we are always implicitly assigning a priority to each of these forces and the resources we assign to them, whether we are conscientious of the prioritization or not.

External and internal activities and trends influence the direction of the CISO, and subsequently, the prioritization of the CISO workload. Combining these forces with the four-quadrant prioritization matrix results in placement along important/unimportant and urgent/not urgent lines and serves to focus the CISO as to where he or she should be spending most of their valuable time. Just because an item falls into the "not important" category, does not necessarily mean it is not important, although it may be, but rather that it is less important for the CISO to deal with the issue than other more strategic issues, and could be eliminated or delegated depending upon the nature of the issue. A sample CISO four-quadrant prioritization matrix of where particular issues could be placed is shown in Figure 1.4.

The CISO Future Is Cumulative

Each of the eras has contributed to the CISO role today in a profound way. The concepts of regulation compliance, risk management, technology adaptability,

	URGENT	NOT URGENT
IMPORTANT	**Quadrant I:** Urgent & Important Increased International Government Regulations & Scrutiny Privacy Compliance	**Quadrant II:** Not Urgent & Important Technical Advances New Products & Services 3rd Party Outsourcing Social & Cultural Trends Organizational Culture
NOT IMPORTANT	**Quadrant III:** Urgent & Not Important Internal/External Audits Day-to-day tactical fire-fighting	**Quadrant IV:** Not Urgent & Not Important Unnecessary reporting

Figure 1.4 CISO four-quadrant prioritization matrix.

privacy, executive management interaction, and the expanding CISO scope did not happen overnight. The CISO role is still advancing and maturing; however, the "need for a CISO" is no longer a question for many of our organizations (and for those that do not think they need one, they will rethink that assumption after they have been breached). We still secure systems using logon IDs and passwords; even though the form of authentication has increased, the requirement remains. The perimeter has been moving away from companies for years, and the data has moved with it. Privacy concerns that were barely on the early CISO's radar are now a common topic of discussion. Boardroom presentations were something only a few would get to present in the past and IT security concerns (of which security was normally a part of), were covered off by the CIO. Presentations were usually requested in a crisis and are now considered a necessary core competency for today's CISO with scheduled updates to inform the board. CISOs still manage regulation compliance, risk, control selection, cloud, mobile, social media, privacy protection, emerging technology security, maturity mapping with control frameworks; obtain threat intelligence; detect intrusions; and ensure business resilience through response programs. And all this will be done with multiple service providers and employees working remotely.

In short, each of the challenges and methods to combat the threats in an ever-increasing threat environment is cumulative—we continue to add and expand, and the old stuff does not go away. More platforms and more places to put data increase susceptibility to a breach. Therefore, the organizations are concerned. The discussion for an organization to then recruit a CISO is not a "should we hire one," but rather, "let's get the right one for us."

Change is a funny concept really. When we are in the middle of change, sometimes we are so busy tending to our lives inside and outside of work that we do not realize that all along, our lives were changing. Our children who once needed our full attention reached the ripe old age of 4–5, and suddenly, we would hear "you are not the boss of me," until they tried to lock their bedroom door and we had to remove their doors. Then, we watched them progress through the teenage years, watching their dance recitals, baseball, soccer, and hockey games. Sometimes they thought we were great; sometimes, they thought we were reincarnated from the devil. Then, they grow up, get an education, enter adulthood, get married, and figure out their own career path. They evolved—but in a different way than we evolved, in a different world. The world did not start with them (except when they were teenagers, it revolved around them!), nor will it end with them. The changes did not happen all at once, but how many a parent looks back just 5–10 years on their child's life and says, "Wow, they grew up so fast?" The CISO world has been gradually evolving through these phases over the past 25 years, adapting, adding new skills, and just as a 30-year-old-something has different expectations on them than a 5-year-old-something does, the CISO of today and the future is expected to be the sum of all the parts of development (the five phases) which preceded them. To skip and under develop and not absorb the lessons learned from any of these parts will decrease the effectiveness of the CISO.

Never has the profession had a career path to those who want to seek it as there is today. The opportunities in this field will only increase in the future. The CISO is here to stay. The CISO has evolved among disruptive technology and services that have gradually revolutionized our world.

JOYCE BROCAGLIA: AN INSIDER'S VIEW OF THE CISO SEARCH

CEO, Alta Associates and Founder, Executive Women's Forum on Information Security, Risk Management, and Privacy

When conducting CISO searches, we advise our clients on the most important things to consider before and during the search process. The following information will give you an insider's view of many of our conversations and as such better prepare you for hiring a CISO or interviewing for the role itself.

As corporations' race to create competitive solutions through digitization and transformation, the role of the CISO has become more crucial and the selection of a uniquely qualified leader essential to the success of building a resilient corporation. Here are five things we advise our clients to consider when hiring that are important for you to know:

WHAT COMPELLING EVENT, IF ANY, PROMPTED YOU TO SEEK NEW LEADERSHIP?

The compelling event for hiring a new executive is directly tied to the characteristics, qualities, and experiences of the candidate that will be most likely to succeed. If the search for a CISO was prompted following the public exposure of a major breach, the newly hired executive will need to be immediately credible and able to quickly assess the current state, to safeguard the company, and to regain trust in the marketplace. Other companies recognize that the talent that got them to where they are today is not going to be the talent that takes them forward. They require an executive that can elevate the role with their strategic vision, leadership capabilities, and presentation skills.

HOW WILL THE CISO COMPLEMENT YOUR ORGANIZATION'S TRANSFORMATIONAL EFFORTS?

CISOs and IT risk executives must have the capability of engaging with business and technology leaders to proactively evaluate new technologies, enhance their capabilities, and mitigate their risks.

A transformative CISO is one that has the skills to reduce risk while still allowing adaptability in a volatile threat landscape. Keeping your organization safe goes far beyond purchasing technology solutions. CISOs are often able to accomplish a great deal in the way of improvements through collaboration and influence. Finding an executive with these complementary skills requires access to a deep network of security professionals and specialized recruiters with the knowledge to conduct in-depth interviews.

REPORTING STRUCTURE IN YOUR COMPANY

To be effective in an organization, CISOs need to be positioned strategically. Cybersecurity executives have moved from a role solely relegated to IT organizations to one of protecting brand, reputation, and profitability. The new breed of CISO is responsible for deploying a holistic approach to understanding and mitigating business and technology risks.

Since cybersecurity is an enterprise-wide risk management issue, not just an IT issue, the CISO will not be effective if buried deeply within an IT team. Recognize that this role requires the exertion of influence and the development of trusted relationships. If internal leaders or external regulators do not believe the CISO has the proper influence within the organization, it will negatively impact their ability to be effective. Make sure you engage a search firm that can help you think through these issues and determine the right reporting structure, level of responsibility, and scope required to ensure the CISO and their team are best positioned for success.

DEFINING THE SCOPE OF THE ROLE

To identify the right candidate, you first must define the scope of responsibilities and organizations they will be managing. The size, scope, and influence of the role will largely determine who you will be able to attract.

Potential functions that could report to the security leader include the following:

- Cybersecurity
- IT risk
- GRC
- Physical security
- Privacy.

Typically to attract the most senior security leaders, the role should contain the proper reporting structure and scope, and be combined with opportunities to interact with the board, participate as a thought leader in industry groups, and speak at industry events. Ensure that you partner with an executive search firm that is immersed in this industry, understands the nuances of the role and can quickly identify who will be successful.

A CISO'S EFFECTIVENESS IS HIGHLY DEPENDENT UPON THE TEAM THAT SUPPORTS AND SURROUNDS HIM OR HER

In order to be proactive in defending the company, a CISO must have a security team in place that they can rely on. Most CISOs struggle with limited resources, especially given the expanding nature and changing definition of the role they play. A skilled and dedicated team frees a CISO from repeatable tasks and allows them to delegate and drive projects more effectively. Without a robust support structure, your CISO is unable to focus proactively on long term and strategic protection efforts. Candidates consider the size and quality of their team as an important factor in enabling their success.

Suggested Reading

1. Secret Code Breaker. Caesar Cipher History. www.secretcodebreaker.com/history2.html.
2. Fitzgerald, T. and Krause, M. 2008. *CISO Leadership Essential Principles for Success*, The ISC2® Press Series. New York. Auerbach Publications.
3. Stripp, A. 2009. How the Enigma Works. NOVA (November 9). www.pbs.org/wgbh/nova/military/how-enigma-works.html.
4. Kehoe, B.P. 1992. *Zen and the Art of the Internet*. 2nd edn. Englewood Cliffs, NJ. P T R Prentice Hall, Inc.

5. Massachusetts Institute of Technology. The Robert Morris Worm. http://groups.csail.mit.edu/mac/classes/6.805/articles/morris-worm.html.
6. U.S. Department of Justice. 2015. Computer Fraud and Abuse Act Prosecuting Computer Crimes. www.justice.gov/sites/default/files/criminal-ccips/legacy/2015/01/14/ccmanual.pdf.
7. Strickand, J. 10 Worst Computer Viruses of All Time. How Stuff Works. http://computer.howstuffworks.com/worst-computer-viruses10.htm.
8. U.S. Department of Health and Human Services. Summary of the HIPAA Privacy Rule. Health Information Privacy. www.hhs.gov/hipaa/for-professionals/privacy/laws-regulations/index.html.
9. U.S. Department of Health and Human Services. The Security Rule. Health Information Privacy. www.hhs.gov/hipaa/for-professionals/security/index.html.
10. Webley, K. 2010. Online Shopping. Time (July 16). http://content.time.com/time/business/article/0,8599,2004089,00.html.
11. Bosworth, M. 2006. VA Loses Data on 26 Million Veterans: Employee Claims Laptop with Sensitive Data Was Stolen. Consumer Affairs (May 22). www.consumeraffairs.com/news04/2006/05/va_laptop.html.
12. California Legislative Information. Senate Bill No. 1386. www.leginfo.ca.gov/pub/01-02/bill/sen/sb_1351-1400/sb_1386_bill_20020926_chaptered.pdf.
13. Apple-History. iPhone 3G. http://apple-history.com/iphone_3g.
14. Phillips, S. 2007. A brief history of Facebook. The Guardian (July 2007). www.theguardian.com/technology/2007/jul/25/media.newmedia.
15. Zeevi, D. 2013. The Ultimate History of Facebook {INFOGRAPHIC}. SocialMediaToday (February 21). www.socialmediatoday.com/content/ultimate-history-facebook-infographic.
16. Vaynerchuk, G. 2016. The Snap Generation: A guide to Snapchat's History. www.garyvaynerchuk.com/the-snap-generation-a-guide-to-snapchats-history/.
17. Yan, S. 2017. China's New Cybersecurity Law Takes Effect Today, and Many are Confused. CNBC (May 31). www.cnbc.com/2017/05/31/chinas-new-cybersecurity-law-takes-effect-today.html.
18. Mueller, S. 2017. Steven Covey's Time Management Matrix Explained. Planet of Success (April 1). www.planetofsuccess.com/blog/2015/stephen-coveys-time-management-matrix-explained/.
19. Yu, E. 2017. Singapore Unveils First Look at New Cybersecurity Laws. ZDnet (July 10). www.zdnet.com/article/singapore-unveils-first-look-at-new-cybersecurity-laws/.
20. Danchev, D. 2011. Yahoo! Mail introduces two factor authentication. ZDNet (December 19). www.zdnet.com/article/yahoo-mail-introduces-two-factor-authentication/.
21. Philippines at a glance. https://ccap.ph/philippines-at-a-glance/#.
22. Zephoria Digital Marketing. 2018. The Top 20 Valuable Facebook Statistics. (April 25). https://zephoria.com/top-15-valuable-facebook-statistics/.
23. The Statistics Portal. 2016. Snapchat Usage Penetration Among Teenage Internet Users in Selected Countries as of 3rd Quarter 2016. www.statista.com/statistics/321076/leading-snapchat-market-teens/.

Chapter 2

Cybersecurity Leadership and the McKinsey 7-S Framework

> Only when we realize that there is no eternal, unchanging truth or absolute truth can we arouse in ourselves a sense of intellectual responsibility.
>
> **Hu Shih, 1891–1962**

Organizational Effectiveness

The 7-S Framework (known as the McKinsey 7-S Framework named for the two creators who were consultants for McKinsey & Co. at the time) has been around since the first publication of the idea several decades ago (Waterman & Peters, 1980) as a method to examine organizational effectiveness. At the time, it was believed that when organizations had difficulty in executing their strategy, they could hire external consultants skilled in organizational design and resolve the issues by changing the organizational structure. In the 1980 Waterman and Peters paper, *Structure Is Not Organization*, they asserted that there were more factors involved in executing a successful strategy than just reorganizing the workforce around a new structure. The structure of the organization follows the strategy, but the strategy, they believed, rarely dictated specific structural solutions. The main problem they observed for failing to execute the strategy was not in the structure of the organization, albeit that was one piece, rather the real issue was "getting it done." The visionary Larry the Cable Guy simplifies it for us in today's world by simply stating, "Git R Done!" Larry apparently never worked in our organizations and never had the challenges of getting the organization to move forward on a strategy, or he would know it was not that easy!

Organizations are slow to adapt to change and the reason is explainable by more than two variables (strategy and structure) that are usually attributed to (1) systems that have outdated assumptions, (2) management styles at odds with the strategy, (3) absence of a stated goal (i.e., vision) that binds the organization together to achieve a common purpose, and (4) not dealing with people problems and opportunities.

The 7-S Framework was used as the basis for this book to examine the Chief Information Security Officer (CISO) organizational effectiveness. The chapters are organized into sections relating to each of the components of the 7-S Framework. As the last chapter regarding the CISO evolution illustrated, we have been maturing the role of the CISO, and while building this role, we have not taken a pause to evaluate how well we are addressing all of the dimensions holistically to answer the questions—are we addressing each area and are we effective with our organizations? Therefore, the following chapters have been organized and examine cybersecurity leadership through the 7-S Framework lens, a powerful way to examine the organizational effectiveness, so we as an industry can have richer conversations about effectiveness. After all, as CISOs, our "raison d'être" is to run effective organizations with respect to cybersecurity. Before delving into the application with cybersecurity, let us briefly examine the 7-S Framework or Model.

The 7-S Framework Defined

Often in the cybersecurity community, we lament the creation of a new framework, control standard, law, or regulation and scream, "We already know what we are to do to protect the information!!!!" However, except for some laws that are redundant and require extra time to map, each of the control standards or frameworks tends to look at the cybersecurity issue with a slightly different intent or view. These control frameworks and standards are covered extensively in Chapter 8 and the benefits of using each one. So, what we are really advocating for is the *reuse of models that have stood the test of time.* Therefore, I chose the 7-S Framework as a model for structuring the content of this book to ensure we were addressing critical areas to build an effective cybersecurity organization to protect the information assets. To keep things simple, this model will be referred to herein as the *7-S Framework Applied to Cybersecurity Leadership.*

The model asserts that effective organizational change depends on the relationship between each of the 7 "S"s depicted in Figure 2.1. The 7 "S"s stand for *structure, strategy, systems, style, skills, staff, and shared values (originally called superordinate goals).* The premise is that organizational effectiveness is the result of the

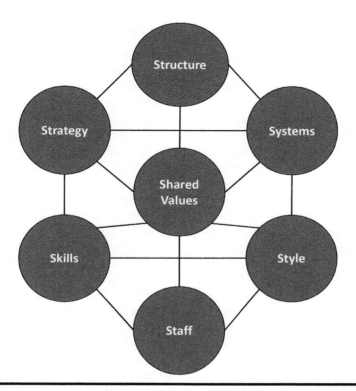

Figure 2.1 McKinsey 7-S Framework. (Adapted from Waterman, Jr., R. and Peters, T., Structure Is Not Organization, June 1980, *Business Horizons*.)

interaction between these factors, and some are not obvious and thus are often under-analyzed. The figure demonstrates several ideas: (1) there are multiple factors for organizational effectiveness, but many organizations only seem to spend time on structure and strategy; (2) the factors are all interconnected, and thus a change in one of the areas has an impact on another; and (3) the shape of the diagram is important—there is no starting point or hierarchy, and each is an important factor to achieve organizational effectiveness. At different times, different factors may be the driving force for change in the organization at the time.

The "S"s in the top half of the figure are known as the "hard" factors, including strategy, structure, and systems. These are called hard factors due to their feasibility and being easier to identify. Strategy documents, corporate plans, organizational charts, and other documentation make it easier to identify. The four soft factors are skills, staff, style, and shared values as these are continuously changing and highly dependent upon the people working in the organization at a time. It becomes much harder to plan on these factors, even though they have a great influence on the ability to be successful with the other three elements of strategy, structure, and systems.

7-S Framework Applied to Cybersecurity Leadership

While the McKinsey 7-S Model was geared towards examining an overall organization and creating changes that would succeed in delivering upon the strategy, this model can be leveraged by the CISO to build and lead an effective cybersecurity program, referred to as the *7-S Framework Applied to Cybersecurity Leadership*. If we think about it carefully, each CISO is running a business with stakeholders, customers, management, and staff to produce products and services (protection of business-critical information, reducing risk, and providing business resiliency). We can therefore leverage the model to organize the activities of the CISO and ensure we are proving ample coverage and attention to the areas of most concern. The CISO at times will focus more on structure, and at other times, focusing on the skills gap will be more essential. Imagine that we have just spent 3 days offsite with our teams to map out an elegant 3-year cybersecurity strategy, and then, we realize we do not have the staff to execute the strategy, the skill sets we need are difficult to hire, and the consultants with this expertise are either unavailable for our time frame or too expensive, then what? How successful will our strategy be? Would we want to present this strategy to the board knowing that we have gaps in other areas of the 7-S Framework? These interdependencies and using the model help us ensure that we are clearly understanding our current capabilities and what needs to change to be effective in the future.

Let us examine each of the seven factors of the framework (structure, strategy, systems, style, skills, staff, and shared values) applied to cybersecurity and how they are presented within the content of the rest of this book. The 7-S Framework applied to the cybersecurity topics in this book is shown in Table 2.1.

Cybersecurity Strategy

Strategy embodies those actions an organization plans to execute in response to or from anticipated changes in the external environment (i.e., cybersecurity threats, increased regulation), customers (i.e., new applications, methods of service, products), and competitors. The company must also be looking to improve their competitive position through adding more value, lowering the cost, increasing sales—or the competition will. The CISO must also build a vision and strategy to protect the most critical assets at the lowest cost, assisted by tools and methods to develop and maintain the strategy. The emerging technologies need to be understood so the proper investments can be made to either (1) leverage these technologies to provide increased cybersecurity and the appropriate protection and detection to match the new threat level or (2) help the organization to create new products and services by using emerging technologies, therefore needing protection.

Cybersecurity Structure

Organizations are structured to divide the tasks and provide coordination of activities. Over the years, companies have had centralized functions, decentralized

Table 2.1 McKinsey 7-S Framework Applied to Cybersecurity Leadership

7-S Factor	Cybersecurity Topic	Chapter	Coverage
Overall roadmap	The CISO road map	1	CISO role: evolution or revolution? (historical perspective)
			CISO forces at play (internal and external)
	Cybersecurity leadership and the McKinsey 7-S Framework	2	7-S Framework defined
			7-S Framework applied to cybersecurity leadership
Strategy How do we intend to meet our objectives?	Developing strategy	3	Cybersecurity development techniques
Deal with competitive pressures? Changes in customer demand?	Emerging technologies and trends	4	Five stages of technology adoption
			Emerging technologies to consider
Structure How is the team divided? What is the organizational hierarchy? How do team members align themselves? Is decision-making centralized? What are the lines of communication? Informal and formal?	Organization structure	5	Learning from leading organizations
			CISO functions
	CISO reporting models	6	Different reporting relationships
			Determining the best fit

(Continued)

Table 2.1 (Continued) McKinsey 7-S Framework Applied to Cybersecurity Leadership

7-S Factor	Cybersecurity Topic	Chapter	Coverage
Systems What systems does the CISO use to run the cybersecurity organization? What controls are in place to ensure they are being managed (maturity)? What is the impact of external incidents influencing the control development?	Leveraging incidents	7	Breach demographics
			Selected breaches lessons learned
	Security control framework maze	8	Control frameworks explained
			11-factor risk assurance manifesto
	Risk management practices	9	Risk management acceptance
			Qualitative vs. quantitative risk assessments
Shared values What are the core cybersecurity values shared across the organization (policies, procedures, standards, laws, and data protection)? How strong are these values? Does the culture support the mission of the CISO?	It is the law	10	Working with lawyers
			Cybersecurity laws and regulations
	Data protection and privacy every CISO must know	11	Data protection key components
			Privacy by Design
			Privacy laws and common principles
			Privacy and social media
	Meaningful policies and procedures	12	Policy development

(Continued)

Table 2.1 (*Continued*) McKinsey *7-S* Framework Applied to Cybersecurity Leadership

7-S Factor	Cybersecurity Topic	Chapter	Coverage
Staff What are the differences between the generations and how does this impact managing the team?	Multigenerational workforce team dynamics	13	Changes impacting work
			Different generations defined
			Leadership implications
			Understanding individual motivations (MBTI)
Skills What skills does the CISO need? What are the innate preferences of the CISO team and what are the implications for leadership?	CISO soft skills	14	Talking vs. listening
			Soft skills (influencing, negotiating, writing, presenting, networking, etc.)
			Technical excellence vs. organizational enablement
			Value of certifications
Style How effective is the CISO with the board? What is the role of the board with respect to cybersecurity?	The CISO and the board of directors	15	Board of directors cybersecurity reporting
			Driving effectiveness and efficiency

functions, specialized activities (such as cybersecurity), and varying degrees of organization by product line or functional area, each with varying spans of control. Matrixed organizations came about to be able to react to different formations of areas quickly. Cybersecurity has typically been organized in a central area due to the need to concentrate on coordination and skill development. This model is rapidly changing with the use of Managed Security Service Providers (MSSPs), offshore talent, engagement of external firms, global presence, and remote users.

The CISO organization structure cannot be fully discussed without paying attention to the reporting structure of the CISO. This has fueled much discussion over the years, with individuals in those roles wanting to report to the highest level in the organization possible. Smaller companies may have a higher reporting relationship (i.e., Chief Executive Officer or Chief Operations Officer), whereas in larger organizations, this role may still be at an executive level, with another intermediate reporting role such as the Chief Risk Officer, Chief Information Officer, and Chief Legal Officer. Each of these options has pros and cons that must be evaluated and may vary by company size, industry, and maturity state.

Cybersecurity Systems

Systems are the formal and informal procedures by which work gets done. This factor can dominate all the others, and if the systems are not aligned with the strategy and provide the necessary information, they can have a detrimental impact on achieving the strategy. Take for example, the organization that fails to select a cybersecurity control framework, a "system for the CISO," to measure maturity over time, or worse yet, the organization that picks 2–3, and changes the approach every other year. In either case, the firm will find it difficult to achieve an effective strategy as the "product du jour" is implemented without a sense of what currently exists (as would be mapped to a control framework), or what the current level and expected levels of maturity are there. In other words, without following a consistent system or approach, attaining the strategic goals related to effectiveness may be a struggle. Cybersecurity processes can also be informed by leveraging the security incidents of others to improve the ongoing processes. Finally, the risk management processes are key in any security program to determine the appropriate level of risk and mitigation strategies.

Cybersecurity Shared Values

Shared values, originally named superordinate goals, refer to the higher-order goals of the organization, or a set of aspirations and guiding concepts which are sometimes unwritten and may not be in the formal statements of objectives, but which represent ideas around which a business is built. For example, Steve Jobs discussed a marketing campaign called "Think Different" at Apple; however, the core value of the organization was to make the best products in the market and focus on selected products, so they can develop and innovate. After the iPod "killed" the Sony Walkman, they did not rest and developed the iPhone, iPad, iWatch, etc. The shared value was to make the best products. A shared value binds the company together and is a way of thinking. Tim Cook, who looks over the CEO role, echoed the need for value, stating "My belief is that companies should have values, like people do" in response to being challenged at an investor meeting to only make moves that would be profitable for the company.

Slogans are a way of expressing the shared values and are not just fancy slogans if used properly, used to drive the way people work within the organization. Consider BMW's "The Ultimate Driving Machine" sets a very high standard to claim that "experience" in the customer. Having a low-quality rating or having news stories surface like the 2018 report of the ability to hack BMW's 14 ways, this would clearly take away from this imagery. Or imagine being a grumpy employee serving a customer at Disneyland's "The Happiest Place on Earth"! Imagine being the cybersecurity department for Nike and saying "In cybersecurity, just don't do it, just say no" could be a career-limiting move. Or standing in line for 20 minutes to check out at a Staples office supply store where "That was Easy" is the slogan may cause you to start pressing Easy Buttons.

To infuse cybersecurity values into the organization, we first need to define what the values are. Here, we are not talking about the systems to achieve the results, such as those noted in the *Cybersecurity Systems* section(leveraging the incidents of others, the security control framework maze, and risk management practices), as these explain how we accomplish advancing the security posture of the organization through evaluating risk, applying control frameworks, and avoiding insecure systems and reducing the likelihood of a breach. The cybersecurity shared values, on the other hand, represent the higher-level values of the organization and are related to (1) laws and regulations our organizations are subject to, (2) our concern for and approach to data protection and privacy, and (3) meaningful policies and procedures stating the expectations of the organization. These shared values should drive our thinking about security for the company. Granted, the risk appetite plays a big role. Beyond the risk appetite, we need to consider that our risk appetite is directly related to the laws and regulations we are subject to. For example, the Federal Trade Commission has levied substantial fines in recent years and imposed 20 years of auditing on some organizations. This could greatly influence the direction of the shared values within the company to ensure that processes were built with privacy and security from the start for systems involving sensitive customer information.

Just as shown in Figure 2.1 for the 7-S Framework, the cybersecurity shared values are in the center, connecting the strategy, structure, staff, skills, and style factors, as they impact the delivery of each of those factors. For example, if privacy is not taken seriously within the organization as a core shared value, it is doubtful resources will be hired (staff), with appropriated privacy knowledge (skills), or there will be a function focused on privacy or data protection (structure). Introduce a law, regulation, and policies to the contrary, and the shared values of the organization may shift, embracing stronger protection of information, as the focus is placed on these regulations to become compliant.

Cybersecurity Staff

The 7-S Framework-posited organizations maintain two different views of staff: (1) people are treated in "hard" terms of salaries, performance measurement systems, and formal training programs and (2) a focus on the "soft" terms of morale, attitude motivation, and behaviors. The model asserts that top executives dislike either approach, as the first one leads the company to put the human resources department in charge of ensuring people are treated appropriately while the latter gives visions of psychologists analyzing the moves of the employees. The model indicates that top organizations focus on their talent from the time they are hired and throughout their career, many times allocating new hires to key departments where they can grow and make a difference, as well as promoting to higher-level positions early in their career (early to mid-30s). Top companies try and understand their talent and provide training to become effective managers and spend time continuing to develop their top managers.

There are many books on leadership development for developing employees and managers. One of the areas that has gained considerable conversation over the past decade has been the generational change of the workforce due to the large population of millennials (born 1980–1995), boomers (1946–1964) retiring at the rate of 10,000 per day for the next decade, Gen Xers sandwiched in the middle, and Generation Z (1996–) now entering the workforce. These are significant shifts in the workforce, each generation with different value systems and methods of working. The CISO needs to understand this shift in demographics as well as changes in women in executive leadership positions, diversity, and interaction with multiple global cultures. For this reason, the section *Multigenerational Workforce Team Dynamics* focuses on these differences to achieve a clearer understanding and appreciation of these differences.

The CISO that also takes time to understand the personability preferences indicated by the Myers-Briggs Type Indicator® (MBTI), DISC profiles, Enneagrams, Caliper assessments, etc. and begins to leverage these differences across team members and the organization, will also begin to understand, respect, and appreciate the differences, making for a more productive team environment.

Cybersecurity Skills

We characterize companies not by their strategies or structures, but rather by what they do best. Fortune Magazine annually publishes the top 100 companies to work for, and it is an insightful exercise to read the list and think of what comes to mind when reviewing the list? What are they good at? Salesforce was recently the number one company to work for, by richly rewarding their employees in both monetary rewards including pay bounties for referrals and helping employees going 18 months without a promotion to find new challenges, and nonmonetary rewards such as paying employees 56 hours per year to volunteer and dedicating floors to "mindfulness." This is a much different company than Wegman's Food Markets, holding the number 2 spot on the list for spending $50 million on employee development with employees feeling they have a sense of purpose.

Skills are clearly important as the strategy of the organization shifts into new markets and services or faces increased competition to fend off new disruptive startups aiming to cut into the business. Take for example, how taxicab companies dispatched vehicles before Uber and Lyft came on the scene—to arrange a cab pickup, the most common method was to make a call to the dispatcher or make a reservation on a website. After the disruptive ride-sharing services could be accessed immediately from a smartphone application, indicating the location and minutes away of the driver, the taxicab companies needed to invest in mobile applications, text messaging, and provide similar access to become responsive. Acquiring mobile application developers and securing the transactions was a shift in skill sets needed.

New skill needs are often accompanied with increased costs, and it is helpful to explicitly label these skill needs and replace old skills and their supporting systems and structures, so the focus can shift to the new skills. For example, in the past, the CISO may have supported security awareness training by maintaining staff to create newsletters, annual face-to-face awareness training sessions, and PowerPoint presentations. In recognizing this type of training is no longer scalable and not as effective for today's threats, the CISO may recruit videographers, phishing simulation expertise, mobile training specialists, and learning management systems expertise. The skills could be additive; however, a more cost-effective approach may be to eliminate some of the skills required, such as eliminating construction of the monthly newsletter and retraining or acquiring staff to create short interactive videos to be more effective with generations that have grown up on YouTube, Instagram, Snapchat, Twitter, etc.

The skills focus in the *CISO Soft Skills* chapter is on the fuzzier, softer skills the CISO needs to be effective in the role, such as influencing, negotiating, presenting, executive presence, communications, listening, as well as understanding the team personalities and individual motivations (MBTI) and generational differences noted in the staff dimension. Naturally, the CISO must also examine each of the staff functions outlined in the *Cybersecurity Structure* section and recruit talent possessing the appropriate technical, analysis, and soft skills to perform the jobs for each of those functions. Because the CISO maintains such a pivotal role in cybersecurity for the organization, the focus here is on the soft skills of the CISO. As the CISO demonstrates these skills through action vs. what they say they do, senior cybersecurity staff, and cybersecurity professionals will also grow through the example set by the CISO.

Cybersecurity Style

Different leaders have different styles and can still be effective. Each leader chooses to spend their time in different ways and must understand the organizational culture to know what is important. Some leaders manage by "walking around" to know their staff, peers, and other department staff, which others are holding meeting after meeting. One style of critical importance for the CISO is how senior leadership and board of director interactions are handled. Until recently, many CISOs, by and large, were not having frequent communications with the board; however, due to the risk of a cybersecurity incident and the penalties for being noncompliant with the various regulations, this has now changed. A CISO could be doing a great job managing the controls; however, if the board does not have confidence, the CISO has the appropriate skills to protect the company against increasing future threats (as indicated in the strategy), and the effectiveness of the organization will be diminished. Top-performing organizations have shared values supporting communication and alignment across the organization. If an employee does not understand or is unaware of the company values, soon you have a department out of alignment, a division, and the company gets off course and does not meet the forecasted goals.

A Holistic Tool for the CISO

The McKinsey 7-S Framework applied to cybersecurity becomes a holistic tool for the CISO to evaluate what is missing within the organization. When the strategy is not working, it may not be due to having an incorrect strategy, but rather the right skills are not present to carry it out, or the organizational shared values may be showing that the same level concern is not owned by the organization and there is more work to do. The *7-S Framework Applied to Cybersecurity Leadership* can be very powerful when building and sustaining the cybersecurity program.

Suggested Reading

1. Waterman Jr., R., Peters, T., and Phillips, J. 1980. Structure Is Not Organization. http://tompeters.com/docs/Structure_Is_Not_Organization.pdf.
2. Think Marketing. 2016. Have You Ever Read about Apple's Core Values? (January 11). https://thinkmarketingmagazine.com/apple-core-values/.
3. Fortune. 2018. 100 Best Companies to Work For. http://fortune.com/best-companies/list.

4. Lu, V. 2015. Taxi Companies Fight Uber with Own Updated Apps. The Star (May 20). www.thestar.com/business/2015/05/20/taxi-companies-fight-uber-with-own-updated-apps.html.
5. Leswing, K. 2016. Apple CEO Tim Cook: 'Companies should have values, like people do'. Business Insider, U.K. (August 9). http://uk.businessinsider.com/apple-ceo-tim-cook-companies-should-have-values-like-people-2016-8?r=US&IR=T
6. Peters, T. 1982. In Search of Excellence: Lessons from America's Best-Run Companies.
7. Zorz, Z. 2018. Researchers Hack BMW Cars, Discover 14 Vulnerabilities. HelpNet Security (May 23). www.helpnetsecurity.com/2018/05/23/hack-bmw-cars/.

STRATEGY

2

Chapter 3

Developing Strategy

The only thing new in the world is the history you don't know.

Harry S. Truman, 1884–1972

Imagine that you have been parachuted onto a piece of barren land near a town with a population of 12,000 people. The climate is very cold in the winter, and the people are friendly and community-minded as many small towns are (they say there may not be much to do in a small town, but what you hear makes up for it). Most people are working, and the jobs do not pay too much; however, the income is enough to enjoy a safe, reasonable life. Let us also assume that a large economic opportunity has just arrived in the area, and the population increases to over 30,000 people in just 3 years, live births at the local hospital increase by 50%, and airport passengers at the local airport increase by 400%. Incomes increase substantially, with many people making more than $100,000/year for jobs where the training was provided. Apartments cannot be built fast enough, a "man camp" is built for $40 million to house 1,200 people in a dormitory-type building because the demand for jobs is so great—the unemployment is less than 1%. People move here without an education and land high-paying jobs. The hotels able to accommodate 2,300 people are full almost every night. Life is good.

Now imagine you are the Mayor or the Chief of Police. The rapid influx of people requires the building of new apartments, businesses, eating establishments, and services—fast. Crime starts to increase as organized crime sees opportunity to expand the drug sales into the region. Traffic is very heavy, as the roads were built for 12,000 people, not 30,000. Milk costs $4/gallon, and McDonald's has a hard time finding workers, even paying $15/hour (50% more than minimum wage) plus a $300 signing bonus. Rent for a two-bedroom apartment increases from $350 to over $2,000 a month. A new $57 million high school is built due to the increasing population. As the Mayor, you are responsible for city planning; as the Chief of Police, you are responsible for keeping the community safe.

The situation described above is not hypothetical. This is what Williston, North Dakota, residents faced during the oil boom from 2010 to 2014, where the city grew by 67%, causing North Dakota to have the fasted growing economy in the United States in 2014. A process known as fracking was used to extract oil from the Bakken oil patch, centered there. And within a few short years after the boom years, as oil prices plummeted from $120 a barrel to $30 a barrel, the $40 million "man camp" became vacant, many of those who flocked to North Dakota left as jobs dried up, campers were left abandoned in fields, and apartment rents dropped significantly with many empty apartments available. Less than one-third of the hotel rooms were now full on any night for $99/night. Many of the oil rigs remain silent, hence resulting in the boom and bust cycle of oil.

This is where strategy comes in, having the vision to be able to adapt to a rapidly changing environment and build a better future. Strategy never is as clean as being able to start from scratch—we are parachuted in and must understand the current situation to create a better future, all the while changes are occurring rapidly. The Mayor is faced with the challenge of city planning to ensure the infrastructure and services are adequate to support the community. The new Mayor in town does not have the luxury of leveling the town and starting over, investments have been made, and he is dealt the hand and budget that he has. His job is to identify those areas needing improvement and solicit the appropriate funds, either through taxes, special assessments, or reallocating funds of other less productive or necessary projects. The Mayor does not know for certain what will happen in the future and must make the best decisions he can, leveraging the best available facts and advice at the time to support the community. The Chief of Police must maintain order and ensure new threats which the community did not experience before are handled. In Williston, North Dakota, the Williams County Jail planned a $49 million expansion to increase the inmate capacity from 132 to 240 prisoners. Federal and state officials launched "Project Safe Bakken" to pursue criminal networks to pursue drug and weapons dealers.

The Chief Information Security Officer (CISO) in many respects is like the Mayor and the Chief of Police. Just as the Mayor must adapt to the infrastructure, listen to his staff, and ensure the community needs are met to survive the next re-election, the CISO must ensure the right things are done at the right time adapting to the changes in the environment. The CISO is responsible for laying the groundwork and road map to enable growth so the community can prosper. Organizations rely on the CISO to provide the appropriate guidance, living within the constraints of the investment available. If new roads need to be built, the Mayor is responsible to ensure the right people are engaged to propose a reasonable level of spending based upon the projections of population growth and traffic patterns. This requires an analysis of the existing traffic data, as well as incorporating plans for growth of apartments, houses, businesses, and the like to meet the demands.

Tough decisions must be made as to which roads need to be torn up and rebuilt or moved all together. In the end, the Mayor is expected to show results, not through "the activity of road building," but rather the results derived from traffic moving at the stated speed limits. People expect results, not activity. The Chief of Police must ensure order is maintained and violators of the law are punished and removed from the public. The Chief has new threats of drugs, prostitution, theft, altercations, etc. that accompany the increase in population. Individuals in Williston, North Dakota, had more money, increasing the target environment and opportunity, and increasing the criminal element and scam artists. The CISO must pay attention to new emerging threats based upon emerging changes in the external environment as well as within the organization itself. As the organization opens new offices, expands into new markets, merges with and acquires other organizations, introduces new technologies, upgrades systems, and launches new products, the threat environment needs to be re-evaluated to ensure "order" is being maintained.

The Chief of Police cannot prevent every crime; however, this does not excuse him from working with the Mayor to promote sufficient deterrents such as educating the public, maintaining a visible police presence, installation of security cameras, maintaining well-lit areas, suggesting residents stop mail and newspapers while on vacation, and hiring security guards for local businesses. The Chief must also ensure he has the necessary trained resources to respond in the event of an emergency and can handle the calls made to the department. In Williston, North Dakota, the calls to the police department increased 100-fold during the boom years. In the boom years, the Chief of Police requested to hire an additional police officer early due to an officer leaving the force, and the Mayor asked whether he would like to hire two more positions early as well, which was unanimously by the City Council, illuminating the necessary partnership between the Mayor, Chief of Police, and the City Council. The CISO must also ensure the properly trained resources are available to minimize the threat, recognize when a critical security event has occurred, and respond in a timely manner. Just as the Mayor, Chief, and City Council must collaborate and work together to accomplish a safer city, the CISO must also ensure appropriate partnerships are established with the Chief Executive Officer, executive team, organization, and the board.

Making the Case for Developing a Security Strategy

The strategy for the City of Williston had to dramatically change over the past 20 years. In 2000, the median household income was $29,942, and in 2016, it was $93,245, while the U.S. median income grew less than 1% ($59,039 in 2016) over the same period. The population grew 96.3% from 2000 to 2014 (24,562). As the preceding artifacts indicate, many changes to the infrastructure were necessary, to enable the city to keep operating the oil wells and keep up with the oil business demand. This is not unlike many of our organizations as we grow revenues, merge with other companies, and introduce new products and services to market. *Without a strategy, our ability to ensure the protection of information assets and more importantly, become a partner with the business, enabling the development of these new products, services, and new business opportunities, is significantly curtailed.* Business changes, our teams change, and the strategy acts as the necessary road map to ensure the right things are developed. According to a 2018 Global Information Security Study by Price Waterhouse Coopers, only 56% of respondents had an overall information security strategy in place, and only 44% of company directors are very confident that their company has a comprehensive program to address data security and privacy. Just 10 years earlier, the same study indicated similar results, with 59% of companies having an overall information security strategy. In 2018, companies worth at least $25 billion fared better, with 70% having an overall information security strategy.

John Kotter best summarized the process of strategy by stating, "Leaders establish the vision for the future and set the strategy for getting there." This very succinctly sums up two key components of strategy: setting a vision and creating a mechanism to attain the vision. Both are necessary, or the target will not resonate with the team charged with implementing the strategy and the methods for getting there will be left to chance. Strategies must adapt over time, as seen in the oil example when the "bust" occurred as oil prices fell; however, thoughtful planning of contingencies for when the (inevitable) drop in oil prices was to occur can minimize the impact of the change in strategy.

Four Ways Organizations Develop Cybersecurity Strategy

What happens often is that a need for information security "appears one day" as the result of an incident, public disclosure of information, a new law or regulation which must be complied with, or an inquiry from a member of senior management that was reading about a security incident that was experienced by one of their competitors in the news. This scenario is depicted in Figure 3.1. What follows is that someone is assigned to resolve the incident or come up with what needs to be done for cybersecurity. The individual assigned is usually within the Information Technology (IT) department, as security is usually seen as an IT problem to be solved. The person then takes this assignment on, in addition to his or her other responsibilities and starts fixing the problem at hand. After a series of small successes and a further understanding of the broader scope of cybersecurity, the person charged with addressing information security/cybersecurity requests more resources, initially met with resistance. A few more projects are taken on, and problems tackled, increasing the visibility of the security function. In this scenario, the strategy is the result of looking in the rearview mirror and articulating the accomplishments of what has been completed to gain more funds to further

Figure 3.1   Incident-driven cybersecurity strategy approach.

initiatives. The focus becomes that of (1) attempting to prevent the next incident and (2) responding to the next incident in a more organized, timely manner. Since limited security expertise was most likely available within the organization, the focus of this strategy development is titled towards fixing the pieces related to the initial incident and working through an incident response plan.

A second approach is to make an assessment of the information security practices that are in place, usually by partnering with an external firm to conduct an objective review, creating a vision and mission, and then creating the short- and long-term multiyear plans for addressing the problem areas, concentrating on the areas of the highest risk first as illustrated in Figure 3.2. This top-down approach is beneficial in that it provides broad coverage for all the domains and can be

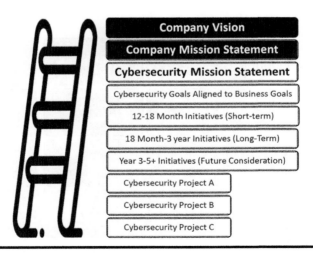

Figure 3.2   Top-down cybersecurity strategy approach.

established without focusing on an immediate trigger, as in the incident-driven cybersecurity strategy approach. The top-down approach also takes into consideration the risks of the security areas evaluated and future business projects and opportunities vs. focusing on the issue that is getting the most visibility at the time.

One could argue that using an immediate security incident to spur the organization into action is not developing a strategy at all and is more akin to "running by the seat of your pants" or managing by chaos. The reality is that organizations do not always have the foresight or the knowledge within the organization to recognize the role that cybersecurity should play within the business. They may not have an advocate for cybersecurity that can articulate how implementing or expanding this function can be good for the business by reducing costs, increasing market share, creating a competitive advantage, etc. Imagine also that a security incident is occurring, and the person assigned says, "We should create a strategy to develop and implement an information security program to deal with this." Using the nomenclature put so well within the book, *Good to Great*, there may not be a seat on the next bus for that individual! When there are urgent business problems to solve, the first order of action is to put out the fire, and then work on the fire suppression equipment and safety procedures, install additional smoke/carbon monoxide detectors, buy fire extinguishers, and so forth. The same principle applies to security incidents; while they may spur us into action and get the ball rolling, we must address the immediate issue at hand first.

The third approach, as shown in Figure 3.3, is the bottom-up cybersecurity strategy approach, whereby the CISO examines the infrastructure, various regulations, and control frameworks and begins to fill in the gaps based on those presenting the highest risk to the organization. Initially, the CISO may perform this activity without much involvement or buy-in from senior management, thus the characterization of a bottom-up approach. This approach usually entails an analysis

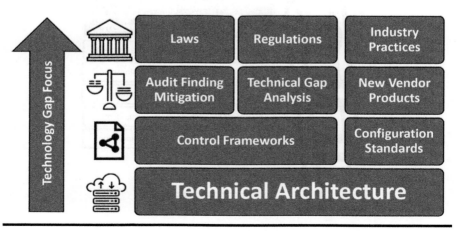

Figure 3.3 Bottom-up cybersecurity strategy approach.

of the current environment and focuses on "what is missing today" vs. expending energy on "where are we going tomorrow." The value in this approach is that it can inform the future direction and movement to a greater level of maturity driven by a subsequent top-down approach. Many organizations start the analysis using a bottom-up approach to understand the current state before engaging senior management to explore the expectations of how cybersecurity practices can protect and enable the business. The focus typically begins with the gaps in the technical infrastructure and becomes the de facto strategy as projects are added to fill in the gaps.

The fourth type of strategy development—the toss-a-softball-in-the-bushel-basket unconscious cybersecurity approach—is performed by not consciously creating a strategy at all, as shown in Figure 3.4. When the carnival came to town each year as a kid, we would try and toss a softball in a bushel basket to win the prize, only to see it continuously bounce out. We went back to our parents for more money, as we were sure that next time, the ball we tossed into the basket would stay there. We were sure we could fix the problem by doing the same thing over and over and just adjusting our technique a little. Frustrated, we would try something else—such as the basketball shoot with crooked backboards and smaller rims. When that failed, even for us tall kids, we just knew we could embrace a different technology and win, so we went over to the squirt gun carnival stand, shot our steady stream of water into the clown (all the while laughing at us and taking our parents money), as we tried to make our horse cross the finish line first. At least in this race, one of ten of us lined up with the squirt guns would win, finally!—a 10% chance of winning.

Organizations that could be classified as security unaware fall into this category. They are the organizations that have individuals performing security functions, however not in a premediated manner. Security "just happens" within these organizations as different individuals are assigned the various functions of cybersecurity,

Figure 3.4 Toss-a-softball-in-the-bushel-basket unconscious cybersecurity strategy approach.

whether it is called that or not. For example, the systems administrator may receive requests for access via email and grants the access requested. An individual is responsible for moving source code to production status within the version control software. The help desk administers' password resets upon request. Security functions are distributed across different individuals within the organization without a master plan of what should be performed. Human Resources provides guidance on confidentiality in new hire training. Risk assessments and reviews of the latest threats are usually nonexistent in this type of organization. Plans for upcoming initiatives are sparse and new initiatives are generated by the next large incident, as in the incident-driven approach, which impacts availability or results in an unintended public disclosure. Security solutions are implemented ad hoc to fix the issue of the day; other technologies are acquired when the problem is (perceived) to be from the former technologies without much attention to processes or the people performing the processes. The security vendors in the carnival tent are happy to take the money, as more money is spent moving from product to product, finally arriving at the best solution—a 10% chance of success.

So whatever method has been used to initiate the development of a cybersecurity strategy, whether leveraging the security incident in the incident-driven approach, the pre-planned systematic top-down vision-driven approach, the structured bottom-up cybersecurity approach, or the toss-a-softball-in-the-bushel-basket unconscious approach, it should be recognized that all organizations have a cybersecurity strategy, deliberate or not. The more planned the strategy is, the more likely that the strategy will be one that meets the needs of the business and is properly aligned with the business strategy. The incident-driven and unconscious strategy approaches have a relatively slim chance of meeting the needs of the business, as security events, problems of the day, or security vendors tend to drive what the security response will be vs. a thought-out plan. The bottom-up approach is where companies usually begin the formal process before senior management has embraced the program.

Few companies can afford to take risks without knowing the risk they are assuming by doing nothing. The chance that a strategy other than a top-down or bottom-up approach effort will address each of the information security domains prior to when they are needed in a proactive manner is like spinning the roulette wheel to determine what the next business strategy would be.

Cybersecurity Strategy Development Framework

The oft-asked questions by CISOs are where do I begin to develop the strategy? Is there a guide I can use? What is the preferred strategy? Because businesses have different challenges, operate in different vertical industries, are subject to different regulations, are facing some similar and some different threats, are in different geographical regions, are protecting different types of information assets, and have differing levels of resources available to commit to cybersecurity, the strategies are inherently different. Each consulting firm will have their own proprietary methodology to assist in building the information security strategy. While one security firm may be more efficient and have a thought-out structured process for developing the strategy, there is no proprietary "secret sauce" in these strategies and the results really come down to the extent the firm is able to quickly digest the business initiatives of the company, and match security policies, processes, and technology to the protection and detection of critical information asset compromise and envision the future. Surely, competent staff that understand the options are required, but equally important is the engagement of business staff internally to articulate the concerns, products, and services on the horizon and significant business changes. For several years, I facilitated a workshop at the RSA security conference whereby the participants, primarily CISOs, created a 2-year cybersecurity strategy in 2 hours. Granted, this was a training exercise limited by time; however, this exercise and the positive feedback from the participants clearly indicated that this process was effective in developing an initial starting point by which discussions could be held within the organization to flesh out a fuller information security strategy. This is not to suggest that a strategy should be created solely by the CISO, just as the Mayor and Chief of Police rely on many others to create their city strategies. The overall process for developing a cybersecurity strategy is shown in Figure 3.5.

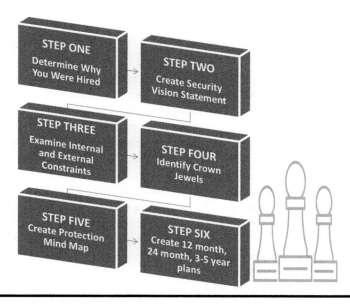

Figure 3.5 Cybersecurity strategy development framework.

Step 1—Determine Why Were You Hired

Before developing the cybersecurity strategy, it is useful to step back and ask, "Why was I hired for this position?" Was I the first CISO? Second? Third? Was there an issue that needed to be solved and I had a specific skill set they needed? Or why did I decide to take this job? More than a fleeting moment should be taken with this question. While we would like to think that we were hired because of our education, knowledge, and ability to run a security program for the hiring company, these factors are most likely, in truth, merely table stakes. To put it another way, it is expected that we know the right cybersecurity practices, or they would not have invited us to the party to be interviewed. The question of, "why were you hired?", goes deeper than the list of requirements on the job description. There was most likely some trigger event at the organization that prompted the hiring. The CISO position may be the first position being filled after a regulation has caught management's attention. There may have been a breach, and the last CISO was offered up as a sacrifice for the issue (aka "Chief Information Scapegoat Officer"). They may have had two or three CISOs previously that did not fit well with the culture. The prior CISOs may have left the organization due to a lack of additional security investment, the firm or the organization recruited them to satisfy a "CISO onboard checkbox," and they feel they have done their due diligence. Or the prior CISO may have left for a new opportunity.

Why is this important? This is important because understanding the conditions by which the CISO is hired helps understand what may be possible in executing a new strategy. For example, if the prior CISO was fired due to a very public breach, the new CISO may have much more latitude to change the existing program and secure greater investments. If this role is the first CISO hired, the time to implement the strategy may be longer as the executive culture adjusts to the requests to invest additional money to protect information assets in an environment where a breach has not previously occurred (that they are aware of). If a longtime incumbent running a bare-bones security program has left the company, the new CISO may be challenged with a "not broken, don't fix it" mentality and limited to the predecessor's budget, even though the focus may have been solely on security login ID/ password administration and not much on the other aspects of information security.

By listening to the stakeholders and understanding their needs during this period, a strategy can reflect the values of the organization and truly be in alignment with the business objectives. As in the case of Williston, North Dakota, we cannot always start from scratch and must deal with the infrastructure we are given as a starting point. If after reviewing the interview questions and talking with people, it is still unclear as to the "real" reason you were hired, just ask! The real answer may or may not be provided in response, and may vary by whom is asked, and that can be telling as to the motivations for the position as well.

Before developing the security strategy, the person responsible for developing the strategy needs to understand the organizational past experiences with cybersecurity.

Organizations tend to have long memories with projects that failed and relatively short-term memories with projects that were successes and had little visibility. If the preceding two CISOs implemented a strategy that failed, possibly evidenced by their short tenure or abrupt departure, then it would behoove the new CISO to obtain informally what some of the issues were and the approaches attempted to solve them. This does not mean that the same approach would not work by a new person with additional management support and investment, or attempted under a different set of new circumstances, but the reasons should be uncovered as quickly as possible. Failure may have been due to not enough resources applied, lack of available technical expertise, failure to communicate project vision, lack of management support, etc. Alternatively, it may have had more to do with clashes of personality of the individual responsible for the implementation utilizing an autocratic approach vs. a collaborative approach.

The CISO Chicken Little

One reason that the predecessor's information security strategy may not have been well received by the organization was that the security officer utilized the fear, uncertainty, and doubt (FUD) cycle. It works like this: Step 1: a security incident occurs that gets (unwanted) management attention. Step 2: the security officer indicates what a large problem this is and requests a large amount of funding to implement new controls, hire more resources, and so forth, to fix the problem. This is usually the response to a senior executive's question of, "How can we prevent this and ensure it does not happen again?" Step 3: the security officer implements the solution, and all is well… until the next time the same event happens. Step 4: repeat Steps 1–3. The security officer indicates that there is new technology that will reduce our risk even further. Step 5: a new incident occurs, and the same process is followed all over again.

What is wrong with this model? Many CISOs will echo the sentiment, "There is nothing like a good incident." While it is true that the first incident raises the level of awareness and importance that adequate controls be in place and many times does provide the necessary funding, the problem is that the second, third, and fourth time that the "sky is falling" message is given, Chicken Little tends to get little additional funding. The response from senior management is likely to be finding a way to prevent the issue from reoccurring with the resources that have already been provided. The reality is that the FUD message tends to dissipate over time and is not effective. It is much more effective to have a security strategy road map of a plan laid out which provides concrete enhancements to the business to deal with the threats facing the organization. This is not to assert that incidents in the news of others should not be leveraged, as this is a good approach. The difference from Chicken Little is to use the incident to articulate in clear terms what happened in the incident, articulating the risk of this event happening to the organization given the current control environment, and if susceptible, what the mitigation would be and the cost. This is a much different approach than asking for money after each incident in the news. The CISO needs to be strategic and judicious in the use of these incidents.

Step 2—Create a Security Vision Statement

Most organizations today have a vision statement to direct the company employees to conduct business in a way that meets the overall goals of the organization. Vision statements are generally very short so that employees can easily grasp the essence of the strategy and behave in a manner that is consistent with the strategy. This is helpful to determine the right course of action in the absence of a documented policy. Just as the overall business needs to have a vision, mission statement, goals, and action plans, so does the cybersecurity program if it is to sustain the long-term viability and be effective in meeting the needs of the business.

The security vision statement reflects the organization's core values and supports the mission of the organization. A vision should get people excited or inspired to move in the direction necessary. Why does the cybersecurity department exist? If the CISO could wave a wand, what would the perfect future look like? Paint that vision. Help people understand why the cybersecurity team is there and the value added to the organization, as well as what are the roles and responsibilities of everyone in the company to achieve this vision. These should be succinct statements that inspire action. When we plan a vacation, we can list out all the activities that need to be done: (1) determine the destination, (2) book a hotel, (3) schedule airline flights, (4) arrange for a fun activity, (5) pack our bags, (6) make a reservation at a restaurant, and so forth. As you read this, how inspiring is listing a set of tasks or activities that need to be accomplished? Not very. We should not fall into this trap of explaining what we do in a vision statement, these are left to individuals' goals, objectives, and plans to accomplish the vision. For our vacation, "renting a house in southern France, basking in the sun on the warm sandy beach, overlooking the crystal blue ocean and sipping Champagne as the sunsets…" congers up an entirely different image than our first attempt at describing "the vacation." Security visions should be treated the same way, even though they will not sound as glamorous as a vacation in southern France!

In a recent workshop, participants created vision statements embodying what they wanted to accomplish with the security program. These are clearly a first pass, as they had only 15 minutes to complete; however, they all express some general ideas about protecting information assets and enabling the business in some fashion:

■ To enable the business to operate securely and empower our people. To provide assurance to our customers.
■ To enable the business to deliver its mission efficiently by establishing a safe and secure platform and ensure trust.

- To enable business success through secure infrastructure and trusted transactions.
- Driving business objectives securely.
- To enable successful business outcomes, profitably and growth through balanced risk management, risk-aware culture, and the enablement of innovation.
- Deliver a program and strategy to protect our assets, values, and clients and reduce risk.
- Proactively provide: secure environment, deliver solutions to the business on time, securely, culture, enable security solutions to build confidence in the operations of the business and with customers, trusted companion of the business.
- Protect and enable the business to securely deliver the corporate mission in a digital transformation context.

Imagine if the CISO brought together members of the organization from different departments to construct the vision and spent more than 15 minutes on the exercise how rich and succinct the vision statement could become. The vision statements in the example above had common themes of business success, trust, and a sense of partnership. Security is never the end goal, and conducting business is the only reason security exists.

JASON CLARK: BUILDING A SECURITY VISION AND STRATEGY

Chief Strategy Officer, Netskope

An information security vision is the end result of an overall information security strategy, and in order to successfully establish a vision, you need to marry the vision to your strategy. That means that from day one, you need to be looking anywhere from 5 to 10 years ahead. Start asking yourself questions like "Where is the strategy of my company?" "Where does my organization want to go?" "What is its end goal?" "What are the forces giving me pressure (positive and negative), and how strong are they?" and "Given all of these forces, what are the steps I need to take to get to my desired outcome?"

Many strategies (and the vision associated with them) often fail because they have not been effectively communicated. In security, this is both an art and a science. There is science involved with understanding risk and threat models, but figuring out how to apply those models to the broader business and communicate it widely is an art. By clearly communicating your strategy in a digestible, visual format, your stakeholders will better understand the strategy. This puts you in a better position to equip your leader [CIO (Chief Information Officer), CEO, or the board] who will get the relevant stakeholders aligned and inspire the whole organization (whether the security team, the IT team, or the wider business) to execute against that strategy and realize your vision.

Finally, CISOs are almost always a change agent in an organization. You are either the first CISO, or you have been brought in to replace a CISO. Ask yourself questions like "What can I do differently and make an impact to build something sustainable?" and "How can I market myself to the organization?" Speak in the language of the business and demonstrate to the wider organization that you are helping solve business problems. This will show them that your job is tied to the wider organization, critical to making their jobs more productive, and most importantly never finished.

Step 3—Examine Internal and External Environment Constraints

Companies work within the context of a much larger environment and are subject to external circumstances beyond what is created by them. These include the regulatory environment, strategies of the competitors, being aware of the emerging threats, knowing the cost structures, and leveraging the external independent research that is available.

Regulatory

Each organization should understand the regulatory environment within which they participate. Is the organization a publicly traded company subject to the Sarbanes–Oxley rules? Are they transacting business involving European citizens and subject to the General Data Protection Regulation (GDPR)? Do they maintain Protected Health Information and subject to the Health Insurance Portability and Accountability Act (HIPAA)? Are they complying with each state's security incident notification laws and aware of the New York State's Cybersecurity Requirements for Financial Services Companies effective March 1, 2017? Are they processing credit cards and subject to the Payment Card Industry Data Security Standards? The regulatory environment will drive security rules that have been mandated for the specific public or private sector.

Competition

Most board of directors want to know how the security strategy and investment compares with the strategy of their competitors. The objective of many companies is to spend no more and no less than that of their competitors, unless security is seen to provide a competitive advantage that is worth the additional investment.

It can be very difficult in practice to ascertain what the competitors are spending on information security, as this information is not generally shared. Companies may discretely obtain information from social media websites (i.e., job profiles on LinkedIn articulating current function and activities for individuals in security roles), or from attendees at conferences. They may also have information from other employees that were hired away from competitors. Intelligence, whether formal or informal, is obtained at some level by an organization, hopefully through ethical means, to enable the organization to differentiate their products and services to obtain a competitive advantage.

The reason organizations prefer to spend the same amount on cybersecurity as their competitor is that an organization must allocate funds across the different business units in a way that maximizes profitability. Spending more on a function such as cybersecurity, which is traditionally viewed as an overhead cost (i.e., does not increase revenue), would normally be viewed as money that is not available to grow the business. This assumption makes security investment a hard sell in most organizations; however, being able to articulate competitor investments in developing the strategy is one way to garner support for the strategy. This is especially true if the competitor will be using this knowledge to bid on or obtain new business that the company is also pursuing. Spending the same amount in this context provides the board of directors the comfort that they are not overspending, while at the same time, providing the comfort that they are exercising due diligence in funding the security efforts. If a security breach occurs in the future and they are subject to external governmental review or a lawsuit, they can provide justification that they spent an appropriate amount on information security given the business climate in which they operated.

Emerging Threats

Many information security threats are common across industries in that they represent vulnerabilities to generally available software. Vulnerabilities in Microsoft Office or the latest vulnerability found within Adobe Reader represent opportunities for the hacker to exploit the code, irrespective of the industry that the company resides in. The ability to exploit the opportunity has more to do with how widespread the technology is used within the organization and how defense-in-depth strategies have been deployed to protect the information assets.

The strategy needs to consider the emerging threats in building the security strategy. As discussed further in the *Risk Management* chapter, certain types of information will need more protection focus than others and will need further protection strategies. For example, an organization that processes credit card information or handles social security numbers will want to know where that information is located via the data classification activities. This information is more likely to be the subject of a targeted attack than other, nonproprietary or nonsensitive information within the company and will need to be protected appropriately.

Technology Cost Changes

When developing an information security strategy, it may appear that the costs for a solution may be cost prohibitive when the strategy is initially developed. Since technology costs are continually dropping due to competition, increasing technology advances, the impact of mergers and acquisitions, and by companies trying to increase market share, once a security strategy is put in place, the initial cost assumptions should be revisited. For example, it was not uncommon for database administrators to be reluctant to implement logging of the database servers due to the perceived impacts to performance and the requirement that large amounts of disk space be used. In the mid-1990s, the cost for this disk space could easily run into the millions of dollars for a few terabytes of storage. Today, we know that the local electronics or office supply store can provide several terabytes storage capacity for laptop devices for less than $50. Thus, the cost of implementing a logging and monitoring solution today involving terabytes of information would not be nearly as expensive and should be part of the strategy for an organization with the appropriate resources. Today, the same debate goes on whether database server performance can handle the additional overhead of encryption for large data stores, or whether the current generation of firewalls with increased functionality and inspection capabilities can handle the throughput of the organization using increased volumes of digital media.

External Independent Research

Organizations such as Gartner, Forrester, industry associations, major consulting firms, and others are valuable sources for product evaluations, emerging strategies, and emerging trends. These organizations provide predictions, typically 2–3 years out, of what vendors and products are leaders in their field. They also provide a vast amount of information on the products themselves and how they may fit into the security solution. Organizations do not have the funds to research all these products themselves, even using a Request for Proposal (RFP) process. RFPs can yield a great deal of information for a given security business need, but at the same time require significant resource time to adequately send out the requests, evaluate the responses, score the responses, hold vendor presentations, and make a final selection. RFPs are good vehicles if the organization has the time and resources or is narrowing down the selection of an expensive long-term solution. The external independent reports can serve as input into jump-starting the RFP process, or in less expensive solutions, quickly provide a cost-effective path towards product selection.

The Internal Company Culture

The company external environment is clearly important to information security strategies, as they represent how the world is interacting with our organizations.

KEVIN MORRISON, MBA, CISM: MANAGING THE SECURITY PRODUCT SALESPERSON

CISO, Pulte Group

"Hi Kevin, we've never met, but my name is {fill in the blank} and I wanted to see if I could get just 10 minutes of your time to…". I returned from a short vacation in 2017 to nearly 40 identical voicemails from security vendors wanting to explain how their product was the best thing since sliced bread. And most voicemails lasted 1–2 seconds before I deleted them, as I (nor most of you) honestly do not have "just 10 minutes" to give to everyone who asks. As a result of that experience, I penned a LinkedIn article called "A CISO's Advice on Selling to CISOs." The challenge in the industry is real. CISOs need innovative and trustworthy solutions to address our organizations' risks, and security product salespeople need CISOs to succeed. To help reduce the friction that clearly exists between us, I have seen that we CISOs can also take a few actions to help smooth that friction. This includes the following: (1) taking up offers to meet for a coffee or lunch, even if you pay for your own; (2) when you meet with them or decide to take a call, be upfront about your budget cycle and when they should reach back out, or inform them that you do not see an opportunity for a current business relationship; (3) prior to a demo, provide salespeople with clear objectives or business challenges that the product must address; (4) get any offer or capability written within a contract if those have been verbally expressed; and (5) recognize that business partnerships that can form from these relationships are of benefit to us all, so treat them with the same respect that you expect in return.

Finally, as security companies seek to differentiate themselves in the market (admittedly a tough job), CISOs should expect no less than a salesperson who is well prepared with honest business cases that can help streamline the budget-building process. With the right solution, a good salesperson can and should make the process easy and even enjoyable.

The internal company culture has a great impact on how successfully our security programs will be received. While it would be nice to be able to copy another organization's security strategy, implement the strategy as ours, and call it a day, unfortunately no two organizations have the same "norm of operation" and a security strategy that may work for one company may not work for another. The following are areas to give some thought to. It may not even be clear how the organization is operating and may need the perspective of several individuals at different management/end-user levels to achieve an accurate assessment.

Risk Appetite

A community banking organization may have a low risk appetite and will tend to make very risk-averse decisions. A small credit union, e.g., may wait until the technology is well developed or many other companies have embraced the technology before committing to its use. Establishing an Internet banking presence, e.g., in the early days was only embraced by the large banks with sufficient resources to commit to the technology, thus minimizing the risk. Today, even small organizations have embraced the online banking technology as a business imperative. Smartphone deposits were initially rolled out by the large, well-funded banks, and now even the small credit unions have mobile applications supporting the smartphone deposits. The risk is perceived to be less when the application has been installed by several hundred banks and supported by a software vendor with the ability to spread the security development costs over multiple customers vs. building the application with the limited resources of a single small credit union.

Risk-averse organizations will tend to have more rigid rules for information security and less likelihood to grant exceptions. On the other hand, innovative organizations promoting creativity or research will tend to allow more creativity. Users may be allowed to purchase and download designer or specialized software on their machines, whereas a more structured environment would not. For example, a company such as Apple that is very innovative would be more permissive internally in design functions to promote creative expression than a pharmaceutical manufacturer would be with those engaged in tracking product shipments. This is not to say that one organization cares about security and the other does not, as both are concerned about the protection surrounding intellectual property within their companies. What differs is the internal approach to information security and securing the information in a way that provides security that is consistent with the culture, business operations, and management direction, and at the same time provides an adequate level of protection from unauthorized users.

Some organizations view new technologies similar to prescription drug research and are willing to invest the money in multiple initiatives knowing that several will fail, understanding there will be one that is successful and will make up for the others. Pharmaceutical companies, for instance, spend hundreds of millions on research and clinical trials for new drugs, knowing that most of these drugs will fail in the testing process. The prices for the drugs that are viable and effective then carry the costs of the research for the failed drugs. Likewise, large organizations can invest larger amounts in security because they can spread their costs across many more users, systems, or products and services. If the solution does not turn out to be effective within a few years, the same organization will invest funds to replace it with a better solution. The smaller organization is more likely to select a product that will last for a longer period and live with or incrementally enhance the usage of the product.

Speed

Organizations move at different speeds, some acquiring one business and then acquiring another before the first acquisition is fully implemented. A major airline published their new innovative sales promotions in the newspaper about 3 weeks prior to when the IT department needed to have the systems available for processing the new promotion. Several programmers made sure they read the ads in the newspaper each day, so they could be aware of what the marketing department was selling! This strategy was done to ensure that the promotion was kept under wraps until necessary so that the competition did not find out. This is an example of an organization working with lightning speed. How long do projects typically take? Weeks? Months? Years? An 18-month implementation will not be very well received in an organization that typically implements projects in a 3-month time frame. The security strategy needs to mirror the speed culture of the organization. With DevSecOps and Agile Development becoming more commonplace to refine products and deliver smaller sets of functionalities quickly, cybersecurity approaches must match the development culture, or the vision will not reflect "enabling the business."

Leadership Style: Collaborative vs. Authoritative

Organizations structured in a command-control-type organization where the subordinates are expected to follow the directives of their immediate supervisors tend to operate in an authoritative manner. Individuals may be encouraged within the organizations to suggest improvements to the existing practices or suggest new processes; however, the decision-making authority in this case typically resides within the superior manager and is pushed down through the organization. Security policies and procedures are introduced via directives and established at higher levels within the company. Alternatively, collaborative organizations tend to request input and more discussion prior to the decisions made. Decisions are made collectively by a team or steering committee to achieve consensus on a direction. Security Risk Councils/Committees are very well received within this type of organization, and security policies are less likely to emerge solely as directives from one department.

Knowing who are the individuals in an authoritative structure whose opinions shape most of the company actions and plans would be beneficial to know. Time would be well spent with these individuals early in the strategy planning process to get them behind the strategy. In the collaborative organization, the senior executive may be looking for clues that opinions were solicited from others within their organization before they will agree to the strategy.

Trust Level

An organization with low trust levels is a very difficult organization to work within, as it is unclear as to whom the message needs to be communicated to for it to be effective and who is ultimately in control. In this type of organization, it may be necessary to increase the number of stakeholders that need to accept the security strategy. By garnering broader support, it will be harder for a single individual acting on their own to undermine the security strategy. Trust level can be evaluated by matching up the statements made and the actions observed. Two-way trust is obviously preferred to exist at the beginning of strategy development; the CISO may have to take the first step by implementing projects within the committed timelines and functionality promised to build the trust over time.

Individuals may also have hidden agendas related to their own advancement that the CISO should be conscious of. If a security strategy is viewed as adding time to a project that the individual is responsible for implementing, or it is perceived that the project may not meet the deadline because of a new security policy, the individual may not fully support the implementation. The worst case may come when the manager appears to support the security initiative publicly, meanwhile does little to advance the effort. The manager could also not like the constraints that security places on their operations, not like structure, or may have been dissatisfied with the length of time it takes the security department to onboard a new employee. Whatever the reason, it is important to understand which individuals are advocates for the security program and which individuals will serve as detractors.

RICHARD NEALON: TRUST—A VERY DIFFERENT CONCEPT WHEN APPLIED TO PERSONAL INTEGRITY

Information Security Professional

On one occasion, I was tasked with leading an internal security investigation into suspicious activity carried out by a number of individuals, which brought one of my own team within scope. I had been a friend and mentor to that team member and had advised and encouraged them in their education and helped them to enhance their work prospects. They would often consult me for work and career advice.

I was asked if I wished to recuse myself from leading the task because of potential conflict, and I refused. I rationalized that I was just a professional doing a job and that my team member would fully understand. I told myself that if I was ever considered within the scope of an investigation, then I would be fully objective and would not personalize any actions being taken or outcome.

I was very happy with the process followed during the investigation, and it was successful in identifying a serious breach of policy. The investigation subsequently cleared the good name of my colleague, so I considered it a good outcome all around. I naturally assumed that our professional relationship would continue as was. However, as a result of being brought into the scope of the investigation, and the fact that I was leading the investigation, that person had lost their trust in me. They did not see it objectively (as I thought I would). They saw it as a challenge to their integrity. Within 6 months, they had left our organization and we lost a very valuable staff member.

Would that person have left anyway—possibly? Did I run the investigation as well as I could—yes? However, given the option again of leading the investigation, I perhaps would have handed that task to an independent third party.

Despite many of the decisions that we make every day in our professional life being colored in many differing shades of gray (risk management), the very best security professionals that I have worked with over the years have a very black and white view when it comes to their personal integrity and ethics (and rightly so).

Growth Seeker or Cost-Cutter

Stocks can be classified in many ways, such as large capitalization stocks (greater than $10 billion revenue), mid-cap stocks ($2–$10 billion), small capitalization stocks (less than $2 billion), domestic, international, or by the sector or industry they operate in. Stocks are also classified as to whether they are considered a growth stock or a value stock. A growth stock is one in which there appear to be significant opportunities for the stock to grow in the future. These stocks typically represent either new start-ups or innovative established companies with product ideas that have not reached their full potential. Value stocks are those stocks where companies are perceived to be worth more than their book asset value, but for some reason, have been beaten down by the market and are now out-of-favor. These stocks are purchased in the hopes that someday the negative events pushing down the stock price are changed, and the stock will rise in value.

All companies want to increase revenues and cut costs. The distinction that is important here is that growth companies tend to invest more money than value companies in future product development and are more likely to embrace a growth security strategy that projects initiatives into the future that may not have immediate payback. Value companies, on the other hand, may be out of favor and are looking for significant cost reductions to increase the stock value. Projects may be cut, and layoffs may be the norm to regain financial viability. If an organization is in cost-cutting mode, and the CISO suggests a project with a large financial commitment with a payoff several years into the future, this may be embraced by a growth-oriented company that is willing to take the risk and has the investment projects for growth, but not by the value-oriented company that is searching for new ways to cut costs. There needs to be an immediate or short-term payback to gain the support of leadership with the cost-cutting company.

Company Size

Large companies tend to be more willing to invest in more initiatives as noted earlier, in large part because the total impact to the budget of the organization will be less when initiatives do not work out as anticipated. In other words, the larger organization can hedge their bets. On the flip side, larger organizations are sometimes more bureaucratic, with more buy-in and management approval necessary before the initiative can move forward. Security strategies need to take this into account when establishing time frames for implementation. Whereas a smaller organization may accept a contract more readily from a vendor without challenging it due to the lack of legal support or leverage with the large vendor, a large organization may require a couple of months to move the contract through the legal negotiation process. Similarly, a small organization may not need the level of documentation that a large organization may need to conduct business. For example, a small doctor's office with an office staff of two people may not need as formal of a termination process ensuring that the keys to the office are changed vs. a large organization of 100,000 employees that would need card access systems and documented proximity badge collection policies, recertification policies, and new badge issuance policies. The small organization still needs to address each of the security domains within the security strategy albeit the degree of definition, documentation, and approach to satisfying the domain will be vastly different.

Outsourcing Posture

The security strategy should consider the company's inclination to outsource functions or processing. What has the history of the company been? Is someone else currently providing the IT services for the organization? Is processing occurring outside of the United States? The outsourcing posture has implications not only for how the security organization should be managed as a function (employees, contractors, or outsourcing of pieces of the security function), but also for the controls that must be put in place for information assets being processed by another company or beyond company's borders. If the cost savings are significant or if the quality of work is viewed to be superior to the work that could be done internally, the security strategy must be written to incorporate controls that make the processing feasible. Quite often, the outsourcing decisions are made at a very high company level with a limited detailed input of costs at the time of agreement, as they tend to be kept very confidential. Few individuals are in the loop at this juncture. As the security program matures and the CISO becomes the trusted partner, involvement in the mergers and acquisitions discussion should increase. However, since leakage of these mergers can have significant consequences, involvement and information flow is typically limited to a select few. In either case, the CISO needs to be prepared to provide high-level estimates and process, either during or shortly after the business partner engagement.

The security strategy needs to ensure that contractual obligations are established, and it is clear how the external functions will be managed. Take the case of outsourcing the internal email systems to a cloud-based provider. The questions that should be addressed by the security strategy are as follows: "Who is responsible for the disaster recovery of the information if it is lost?" "Is the outsourcer responsible for maintaining and testing backups on a regular basis?" "Is there a hot site in the strategy or is there redundant hardware supported by the outsourcer?" "Is the email archived for e-discovery purposes?" "What antivirus and spam filtering are performed?" "What has been the history of availability?" Nothing is inherently wrong with outsourcing functions, where it typically goes wrong is when expectations are not clear. Finding out that the outsourcer only retains backups for 1 month when the security strategy indicates that the organizations' servers are recoverable for a period up to 1 year could cause an unwanted issue for the organization. Without the proper strategy and agreements in place, such as Service Level Agreements, the lack of backups beyond 1 month may not be discovered until there is a need for recovery of critical information, a point that would be too late and could have been prevented by creating the appropriate security outsourcing strategy.

Prior Security Incidents, Audits

Evaluation of the prior security incidents can be of great value in developing an information security strategy. Did an end user leave a box of confidential information in his car with the engine running, only to have it stolen? Did an executive share her password with her administrative assistant so she could access his email? Was the business strategy sent unencrypted across the Internet? Was a mis-configured firewall responsible for an external party using the mail server to send spam? Did a review of external background checks by the contracting company reveal that only 5 out of 25 background checks occurred? Incidents provide a wealth of information as to what actions are not being performed within the company. Security incidents are like mice—where you see one, there must be many more that are not seen. The question to ask when building the security strategy is, "Do I have a stated control in place, as evidenced by the existence of a policy, procedure, and implemented activity which serves to mitigate or reduce the likelihood or impact of this event occurring?" If the answer is no, then this item needs to be included in the security strategy. The tendency to evaluate how important an incident is by the number of occurrences should be avoided, as there may only be one incident, but the potential impact may be large.

Internal and external audits also provide a significant knowledge as to the process breakdowns within an organization. For instance, companies may do a very good job in documenting the policies and procedures but may do a very poor job of executing them. Is the problem one of communication (awareness)? Is the problem due to shortcuts taken to implement a new system or change a system by the weekend? Is the problem one of misinterpretation? Or is there a personal disagreement with the standard or lack of supporting technical controls to support the policy? Audits should be reviewed, and unresolved findings should be used to enhance the security strategy. Previously resolved findings can also provide input, as an issue may have been resolved by a quick fix to remove the finding, but a better long-term solution may be warranted and should be reflected within the security strategy.

External audits may or may not provide recommendations to mitigate the audit issue depending upon the nature of the audit (some firms will not provide recommendations in the post-Enron era as this may be viewed as a conflict of interest as it could possibly be viewed as providing consulting services). If they are providing an attestation of the controls, they are not supposed to provide advice. However, many auditors will informally be willing to provide their opinions outside of the formal written report as to what types of actions would have made the situation be a nonissue and not result in a finding. This information can be very valuable in constructing the strategy, as the auditors are exposed to many different solutions across industries and companies.

If the organization is in the business of contracting work to other organizations, the government or a parent company, other formal reviews of past performance should be reviewed. Reviews of past performance may include metrics such as quality, timeliness, and meeting project deadlines. These reviews can highlight areas where information security may be able to help. For instance, if there are delays in the early morning call center availability due to virus scans starting off at undesirable times, the information security strategy could examine the methods to shift the running of the scans, reduce the time of the scans by allocating more hardware or faster desktops, or examine alternative products for deployment.

Step 4—What Are the Crown Jewels?

Without knowing what to protect, we end up trying to protect everything at the same investment level. None of our companies have the resources to achieve this. Therefore, we need to identify exactly what we are protecting. Different industries will have different assets needing protection. This is a great exercise to engage the business areas, as any one organization may have hundreds or thousands of asset types needing protection; however, only a few will be considered "the crown jewels" of the organization. The CISO should have a good handle on what the crown jewels are and where they are. In the end, the definition of what is or is not a crown jewel is up to the business with guidance for determining the crown jewel from the CISO. Crown jewels will be those information systems and assets which if lost, compromised, or disclosed would have the largest financial impact or damage to the brand (reputation). Figure 3.6 shows some examples of "crown jewels" an organization may need to protect.

People	Customer Data	Board Minutes	Trade Secrets
Compensation Data	Intellectual Property	Physical Infrastructure	Strategic Plans
Financial Data	Client Information	Customer Lists Contracts	Core System Processes
Existing Vulnerabilities	New Product Development	Security Processes & System Designs	Credit Card Information
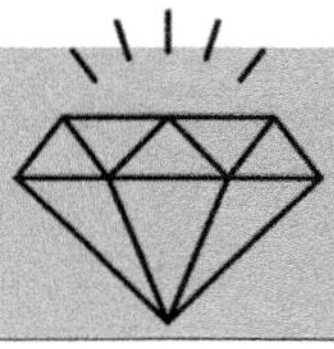	Sales Data & Profitability	Protected Health Information	Mergers and Acquisitions

Figure 3.6   Identify the crown jewels to protect.

STEVE DURBIN: PROTECTING THE "CROWN JEWELS"

Managing Director, Information Security Forum, Ltd.

Data breaches are happening with greater frequency and are compromising larger volumes of data, than at any time in our history. As breaches continue, and the number of compromised records grows, organizations are being subjected to stronger financial penalties, greater legislative and regulatory scrutiny, and tangible reputational damage. But business leaders often fail to recognize the extent to which critical information assets are exposed to threats and the potential business impact should they be compromised. The extensive footprint of these assets provides more opportunities for attackers to gain access or their inadvertent loss to occur. Few organizations continue to give the consistent, highly focused attention to defining and protecting these assets across the enterprise at all stages of the information life cycle. As a result, they are frequently incorrectly classified and poorly managed. While the need to provide mission-critical information assets with specialized protection can appear obvious, organizations can experience difficulties in identifying these assets, evaluating the extent of their exposure to adversarial threats, and understanding the true level of risk to the organization. The work required to get in shape for the European GDPR at my own organization is a case in point. Identifying the assets, in this case personal information, was just the start of the journey—enabling the business transformation, the people awareness, and the tracking and monitoring of the assets at each stage to ensure they remain protected, often while being processed by a third party, has been a major business and strategic undertaking and one that has impacted every corner of the organization. Not protecting these assets is not an option. The lesson moving forward, and what exercises such as the GDPR compliance have shown, is that information risk must be a board-level issue and given the same attention afforded to other risk management practices. Organizations face a daunting array of challenges interconnected with cybersecurity: the insatiable appetite for speed and agility, the dependence on complex supply chains, and the rapid emergence of new technologies. To be effective, cybersecurity chiefs must drive collaboration across the entire enterprise, transforming the security conversation so it resonates with decision makers while also supporting the organization's business objectives.

Step 5—Create a Cybersecurity Mind Map® of Protection

Mind Mapping is a very powerful technique to extract thoughts out of different individuals and subsequently organize those thoughts. Mind Mapping encourages the free flow of thoughts and concepts together. The greatly simplified process works according to the following steps:

1. The topic is drawn in a circle in the center of a flip chart for a group or on a piece of paper if done individually.
2. Lines are drawn outward from the circle in a spiderlike fashion to represent the main thoughts. These lines are labeled with the thought.
3. Thoughts come to people's mind from the main spokes drawn in #2 and are added as smaller perpendicular lines from the main spokes and labeled.
4. This process is repeating, drawing more perpendicular lines, or branches from the prior lines, until most of the thoughts around the subject noted in the circle are expressed.

For example, if the circle in the middle was labeled "Develop an Information Security Program," some of the thoughts that may come to mind are policies, procedures, staffing, vulnerability testing, access control, business continuity planning, strategy development, etc. These could form the spokes coming from the circle, and then as the brainstorming continued, more and more thoughts could be added. The word "staffing" may cause expression of the word's experience, certifications, education, years in the industry, security tool knowledge, budgets, number of staff, training, and so forth. Then, the training spoke could be explored, and

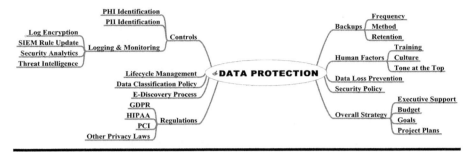

Figure 3.7   Cybersecurity Mind Map® example.

the concepts of cost, training organization, type, prerequisites, tracking, etc. could be added to the training branch. A sample cybersecurity Mind Map® for Data Protection is shown in Figure 3.7.

The power comes from obtaining multiple thoughts from different people with different perspectives or seeing other vantage points of the issue being discussed. Many ideas can be captured in quick succession. As an experiment at a workshop of 64 CISOs and security leaders, each person was given 1 minute to draw a Mind Map® with at least 10 thoughts coming from the word "happiness." As one can imagine, happiness means many different things to many different people. Each person was asked to recite one different meaning from their Mind Map®, and amazingly, out of all people in the room, they were each able to come up with something different! The key takeaway is that even as experienced as the CISO may be, he or she should recognize that the organizational knowledge, experience, and ideas contained in others need to be understood. The Mind Mapping tool is an excellent method of capturing the components that should be addressed in a cybersecurity strategy. As a side note, each chapter of this book started with the creation of a Mind Map® to capture the content to be covered for the chapter, applying cybersecurity topics to the McKinsey 7-S Framework.

The facilitator of the Mind Map® process must ensure that all thoughts are captured, no matter how ridiculous they seem or how they may be viewed as "we tried that before." The objective is to spur thought and then build upon those thoughts. The best thought may not come from the loudest, most talkative person in the room and may come from the contribution of the quietest one at the table. The beauty of the tool is the free flow of ideas without the limited flow by adding too much structure in the idea generation.

Step 6—Planning the Next 12 Months, 24 Months, 3–5 Years

The action planning is where the "rubber meets the road." While determining the internal and external environment in Step 3, crown jewels in Step 4, and Mind Mapping the protections in Step 5 are critical to protecting the right assets in the

MICHAEL J. WILCOX: MIND MAPS®—EFFECTIVE METHOD FOR ORGANIZING CYBERSECURITY INFORMATION

Commercial Central CISO, Cisco

Do you feel overwhelmed by numerous headlines about breaches, new vulnerabilities, the Internet of Things, and other security concerns? Do you have difficulty tracking the numerous meetings you attend, tasks to be completed, and prioritizing your projects and schedule? Legacy security challenges have not disappeared, and new threats are stacked on top of the old, daily. Keeping abreast of all this information and sorting through all the noise can be a daunting challenge, so I have made it a priority to use various learning techniques and organization systems to help me acquire, retain, and quickly recall important information, particularly the use of Mind Mapping.

A Mind Map® is a visual way to organize information; it is a hierarchical method of outlining ideas to establish relationships between events, concepts, images, or essentially anything you are trying to organize. A sample of a typical Mind Map® is shown in Figure 3.8.

Mind Mapping can be performed with pen and paper, but software is much more flexible and powerful, since it provides the ability to hyperlink between different Mind Maps®, files, white papers, and sites. Over the years, I have created hundreds of Mind Maps® for team projects, each person I regularly interact with, outlining the narrative for presentations, to brainstorm and to map various cybersecurity frameworks to compliance requirements and most importantly as a tool for follow-up and tracking progress and accountability. Rather than relying on contact management software, poorly organized browser bookmarks and numerous spreadsheets, Mind Mapping is used as the centralized organizing tool to provide an easy and efficient access to information.

Mind Mapping can be as simple or detailed as you want it to be. The benefits of Mind Mapping go beyond the organization. Scientific research shows that Mind Mapping boosts memory, fosters creativity, facilitates learning, and is an effective tool for improving presentations and collaborating with others. If you would like to become more organized and effective at managing your cybersecurity priorities, contacts, and meetings, try Mind Mapping. With a little bit of practice, you will find it easy to use. Although there are many applications available, I have been using FreeMind, which is open source software, and iThoughts, a licensed app for mobile devices.

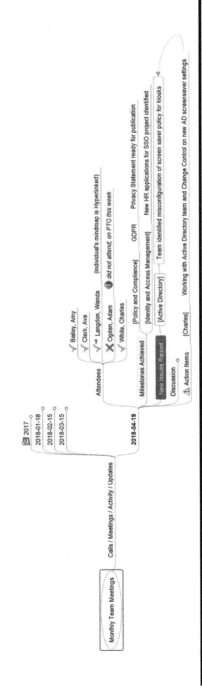

Figure 3.8 Sample Mind Map®.

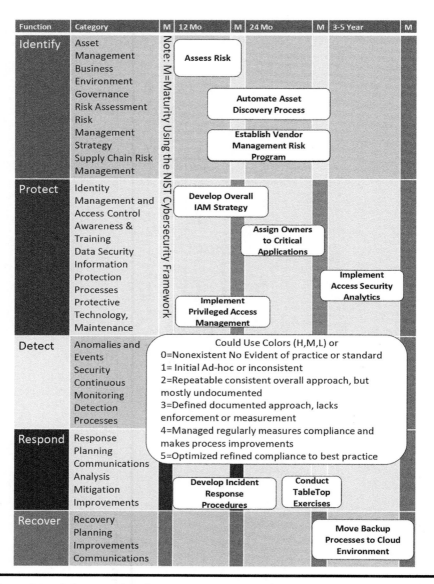

Figure 3.9 Cybersecurity plan 2020–2025 example.

best way, without a plan the protection becomes a vision without substance. Real progress to the vision needs to be achieved within 12–24 months to gain confidence of the organization. Budget cycles are determined on an annual basis in most organizations and typically consume 3–5 months of the year to determine. By having a 12- to 24-month cycle, progress can be shown and changes in the environment can be reacted to in a sufficient time frame. As shown in Figure 3.9, the initiatives to advance security are mapped to a control framework, in this case the NIST Cybersecurity Framework, and progress to new states of maturity is shown in 12-month, 24-month, and 3- to 5-year horizons. This permits communication within the organization to see the short-term goals (12–24 months) as well as the long-term goals taking 3–5 years. If additional funding becomes available, or a threat is deemed to have a higher risk level (such as was the case of ransomware protection after the 2017 Petya/NotPetya infections), the strategy can be adjusted. While this charge shows the maturity related to a framework, the same mapping can be done by replacing the NIST categories with the business processes, products, or services which will be rolled out and the initiatives used to protect those business imperatives.

Once there is consensus on what needs to be protected and the approaches for protection, alternatives can be produced with cost estimates for management approval. Business cases may need to be developed according to organizational templates and processes for approval. Approval for these initiatives may be very time-consuming in larger organizations and can take months to go through the socialization and acceptance process. The CISO needs to ensure the time for approval is built into any multi-year projections, as well as understanding the timing of the budget cycle. These business cases sometimes may request return on investment (ROI) calculations, as the business must decide on security investments in conjunction with other company investments. These calculations are very often difficult to project, as the security function does not in itself generally produce revenue and is viewed as a cost. However, costs can be associated with products and

PAUL HYPKI: WHERE IS THE ROI?

CISO, Children's Minnesota

When I heard that one of our hospital's buildings was being renovated because the façade was failing, I realized I had a phenomenal information security opportunity!

The face of the building was failing, threatening everyone who entered or left the building with falling debris. Since a similar building failure had recently killed someone in our city, our executives quickly approved the remodeling, to the tune of over $10 million.

So why was this an information security opportunity? Let me tell you the story. I was asking for an increase in spending for much-needed information security tools but had been asked what the ROI was on the investment. I explained again that most information security investments have little or no ROI. They are investments that reduce risk. I had defensible costs for initial investment and ongoing support cost. However, putting a value on risk reduction is still incredibly hard.

Our next meeting to discuss investing in information security tools with our executives finally came. I started out by asking how much we had spent replacing the façade of this one building. It was a bit over budget, coming in at about $13 million. Then, I asked what the ROI was on replacing the façade. And let that settle a minute.

Upgrading the building so it would not fall on people was expensive, had $0 return on investment, yet our executive team quickly approved the work and even accepted the cost overrun. I explained that information security might not directly put lives in danger, but it, too, is a risk reduction effort. The investment in information security tools does not immediately translate to increased income. However, it does protect your reputation and avoid the costs of managing an incident. It may even save the life of a patient, due to the inherent risk of our medical devices. But there will be no ROI.

I would love to say they approved everything I asked for, but that did not happen. However, the conversation got us over a hurdle, so our executive team better understood how information security reduces organizational risk and opened the door to start getting projects approved.

services being brought to market, the protection of the revenue streams from those products, and the reduction of risk.

7-S Framework Applied to Cybersecurity Leadership Strategy

The premise of the 7-S Model as articulated in Chapter 2 is that an organization is not just structure, and the organization effectiveness consists of seven elements—the three "hard elements," strategy, structure, and systems, and the four "soft elements," style (culture), staff, skills, and shared values developed and expanded upon by Peters and Waterman in the early 1980s. The six-step strategy process satisfies the "Strategy S" portion of the *7-S Framework Applied to Cybersecurity Leadership*, and the other 6"S"s need to be evaluated as well to support the strategy. For example, identification of the crown jewels and protections for the crown jewels will lead to identification of certain systems, or processes necessary to protect them, such as utilizing data security analytics to determine who has been accessing the information over the past month and the business areas they represent. Upon reviewing the skills as part of the framework, a gap in available Data Scientists may be identified to enable this job to be performed well. So, while the protections may be in place, without the right skill set to set up the right rules and understand the information being reviewed, a change would need to be made to the strategy to recruit (or outsource) the Data Science capability, amplifying the importance of the interrelationships between the other 6 "S"s in constructing a viable cybersecurity strategy.

Alternative Strategy Development Techniques

The cybersecurity development process utilized the Mind Mapping® process to determine the potential methods of protection for the crown jewels. There are other approaches for developing the "Strategy S" of the cybersecurity program as well. These techniques can be used as the basis for increasing the maturity of the program or can be used as tools to analyze different aspects of the program. For example, strengths, weaknesses, opportunities, and threats (SWOT) analysis could be leveraged to determine the state of the overall program or could be leveraged to analyze the ability to provide business resiliency in the core systems and where improvements could be made in the future.

SWOT Analysis

When businesses are embarking on a new business venture, a SWOT analysis is typically used to determine the organization's current ability to compete in that marketplace. The process involves a facilitated brainstorming discussion whereby a box is drawn divided into four quadrants (each representing one of four dimensions of the SWOT acronym) and each of the quadrants is then evaluated by the team. An example of SWOT analysis for a security program is shown in Figure 3.10. In practice, much time is usually spent on defining the strengths and weaknesses as these appear to be easier to grasp as they tend to be based upon past observations

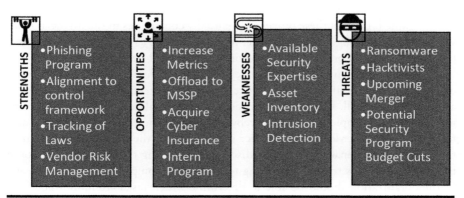

Figure 3.10   SWOT analysis.

of performance within the organization. Opportunities require an understanding of items that are more abstract, such as possibilities of the future without necessarily being currently equipped to develop the product or service. Threats are those actions that may serve to derail our future or disrupt our existing environment.

Applied to information security strategy development, the SWOT process can illuminate areas where security could make a positive, proactive impact on the organization (opportunity), but to date has not acted. For example, creating and deploying an Identity Access Management system that would ease the manual burden of submitting paper forms while providing faster access to the needed systems would benefit the business process by making it more efficient. Other benefits could be added into the security strategy such as the integration with the corporate help desk ticketing system, enabling password resets, and reducing the number of profiles by implementing role-based access. Each of these would represent an opportunity for the business.

In the example, through the SWOT analysis, it may be determined that the skills are not available in-house to implement a complex Identity Access Management product and resources from outside need to be obtained. It may also be identified that it is not well understood what access should be granted to what job function, making the construction of accurate profiles difficult, or that a role-discovery tool is needed to jump-start the effort. Strengths may include project management expertise in-house, knowledge of the existing processes, or the ability to receive excellent pricing on the security software.

Balanced Scorecard

The Balanced Scorecard was developed by Kaplan and Norton and gained popularity after the idea was published in the Harvard Business Review. Essentially, the Balanced Scorecard approach encourages organizations to not only examine the financial measures of profitability, but rather also continuously examine the measurements of how well the customer, process (quality), and learning perspectives are being attained. Each of these processes eventually contributes to the financial measures, and by focusing upon these other measures as well as the financial measures, the overall financial profitability of the organization will be improved.

Some organizations identify a few key measures such as growth in the number of customers, nonconformance to processes, or the percentage of staff that have acquired a new skill. Other organizations drive the Balanced Scorecard concept to an individual employee level, whereby goals are created for each employee and rolled up into higher-level goals (or vice versa). Driving the Balanced Scorecard to the employee level enables a valuable discussion regarding the tasks each employee performs and if it is truly contributing to the overall company strategy. Everyone in the organization should be able to determine which tasks are more important in attaining the company objectives. The downside of this approach is it is very labor-intensive and can become an exercise in compliance if the intent is not valued.

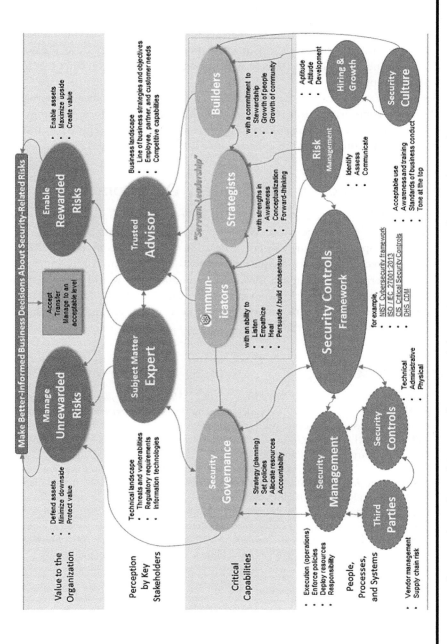

Figure 3.11 Cybersecurity Balanced Scorecard. (From Brink, D., A Strategy Map for Security Leaders, 2018.)

Organizations that structure tasks at the higher levels track the metrics and often base the annual bonus on these numbers, thus making them meaningful at the company and department level. Some employees may not feel connected to the overall strategy. In either case, the Balanced Scorecard provides an excellent mechanism to review the progress of the organization in meeting their goals. As the quality guru Deming is frequently credited with saying by many, "if you can't measure it, you can't improve it."

Security strategies can be developed using the Balanced Scorecard approach and building appropriate measures to track if the customer, quality, learning, or financial perspectives are being enhanced by the cybersecurity strategy. An example of the Balanced Scorecard tied to cybersecurity is shown in Figure 3.11.

Business Interaction with Strategy Development

Key to each of these techniques is designed to determine the cybersecurity strategy with the input of the business leaders and appropriate technical staff. What may appear as an important security concern heard at a security conference may not be the largest security concern facing the business. The CEO may have some real concerns concerning brand image now, and an opportunity would be missed by not connecting the cybersecurity strategy to the needs of the CEO. Demonstrating how applying the proper security controls can protect the brand, e.g., would enable maturity of the security program.

Suggested Reading

1. Kaplan, J., Sharma, S., and Weinberg, A. 2011. *Meeting the Cybersecurity Challenge.* McKinsey & Co (June 2011). www.mckinsey.com/business-functions/digital-mckinsey/our-insights/meeting-the-cybersecurity-challenge.
2. Collins, J. 2001. *Good to Great: Why Some Companies Make the Leap and Others Don't.* New York. HarperCollins Publishers Inc.
3. Fitzgerald, T., Goins, B., and Herold, R. 2007. Information Security and Risk Management. *In Official ISC2® Guide to the CISSP CBK*, eds. Tipton, H. A. and Henry, K., 9–17. Boca Raton Auerbach Publications.
4. Kaplan, R. S. and Norton, D. P. 1996. *The Balanced Scorecard, Translating Strategy Info Action.* Boston, MA. Harvard Business School Press.
5. Buzan, T. and Buzan, B. 1996. *The Mind Map® Book: How to Use Radiant Thinking to Maximize Your Brain's Untapped Potential.* Plume. The Penguin Group publishers.

Chapter 4

Emerging Technologies and Trends

> New opinions are always suspected, and usually opposed, without any other reason but because they are not already common.

John Locke, 1632–1704

Ask anyone that has been in the information security field more than 10 years about how they view managing security today vs. earlier in their career, and they are bound to say something like, "ahhh, those were the good old' days" or "security was so much easier and less complex then." The reality is the "good old days" when life was rainbows and butterflies really never existed, our minds just tend to forget the bad things of the past and focus on the good things, or we think about the lack of complex technology and not having the threat environment of today. The past was just "different," and there were different challenges as noted in the *discussion of the CISO evolution* in Chapter 1. We may have been more focused on deciding the best antivirus (AV) vendor or firewall product in those days and spent a significant amount of time doing so—today, we regard many of these products as commodities with similar features, issue a Request for Proposal, decide on a product, and move on. We tend to spend more time trying to understand what threats we are subject to, where the data is, and what other methods we should be employing to protect and detect the intrusions in addition to the firewalls and AV products. These products are still important, as the feature sets within both these technologies have expanded through the addition of threat intelligence, user behavioral analytics (UBA), cloud-based firewall products, and so forth; however, other technical concerns and solutions and different approaches have emerged to address other endpoints such as mobile devices, Internet of Things (IoT), and the massive amount of information collected by our organizations.

Attend any security conference, and it becomes clear very quickly the sheer number of sessions dedicated to "the next-generation technology," combined with the number of vendors with solutions involving the "next technology" and the conference can feel like you are in the middle of a live game called security buzzword bingo. The "next-generation, military-grade, bank-grade, single-pane-of-glass products with threat intelligence built into their artificial intelligence (AI) machine-learning security analytic engines" are the only products needed, to solve the issues across the environment. While these products are admirable in their attempts to be the end-all solution, it is not of a surprise that Chief Information Security Officers (CISOs) and senior security technical staff are confused with the bombarding of choices to be "the solution" or the "solution to fill a major hole" within the organization. An old joke was of the major security conferences, 50% of the vendor names changed each year—either through acquisition, merger, went out of business, or the two guys that borrowed from their credit cards could not afford another booth this year. This creates a very difficult situation for CISOs. The 2018 USA RSA Conference alone drew 42,000 attendees and 600 companies competing for their attention on the exposition floor and afterward. Since we know each of these vendors has multiple products to sell to solve different problems, the scenario is mind-boggling. Add in *700 speakers talking* about the security issues, products, and solutions, and the view of complexity is even greater… all in less than a week. How is a CISO supposed to keep all this straight? And this is just one of many security conferences with companies promoting their solutions.

With that said, we need vendors to keep innovating with new products and services to reduce the time spent and increase the effectiveness of managing the security programs. With many security departments still run by rather small budgets today, and by small I am referring to several large organizations with a staff under ten people and outsourcing some of the functions, there is a need to be as productive as possible. With the threat environment increasing, there is a need to be as effective in detecting and managing the threats. The Gartner hype cycle, as shown in Figure 4.1, shows the path by which a product moves from the initial idea through general acceptance, using the stages of innovation, peak of inflated expectations, trough of disillusionment, slope of enlightenment, and the plateau of productivity. Some products and ideas may show great promise in the beginning and have high expectations; however, as they are developed, tested, and adopted by industry, the product or service may fall still short of the promise of the innovation and early-stage adoption. This generates a tough of disillusionment, whereby the product has not lived up to expectations; however, further maturing and understanding where and how the product may be best used results in the maturing and enhancing of a product. The product may reach production-level capability and usefulness. Not all products reach the plateau of productivity; however, those that do typically become mainstream commodities and accepted practices within the

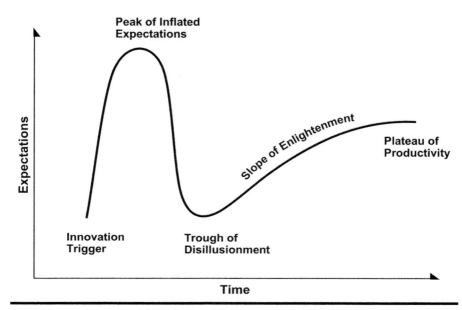

Figure 4.1   Gartner hype cycle. (From Reprinted with permission Gartner, *Hype Cycle*.)

security arsenal. Gartner creates several hype cycles related to security such as the threat-facing technologies hype cycle, application security hype cycle, data security hype cycle, and mobile security hype cycle.

Figure 4.2 highlights the threat-facing technologies related to different stages of the hype cycle. Relating this table to the stages in Figure 4.1, we can see that products on the right-hand side of the chart such as unified threat management, network intrusion prevention systems, vulnerability assessments, and Security Information Event Management (SIEM) systems have reached their plateau (2019). These are also products implemented as staples in organizations to the degree that not having these products in place would be viewed by many regulators as having "inadequate or unreasonable" security practices. The processes around using these products have also matured within the products and services as well as how they are integrated and reported on within the organization. For example, implementing a vulnerability management system to discover the potential exploits before the attackers are run on a scheduled basis, either internally or by a cloud service in most organizations and those which are not, most likely does not have a security program in place or are in planning stages to acquire and implement a product. The metrics from the vulnerability scans may be reported to the operational teams to fix the exploits by installing patches or upgrading the software and hardware. The metrics may be further reported to management and ultimately the board to demonstrate the timeliness in resolving new vulnerabilities and working off the

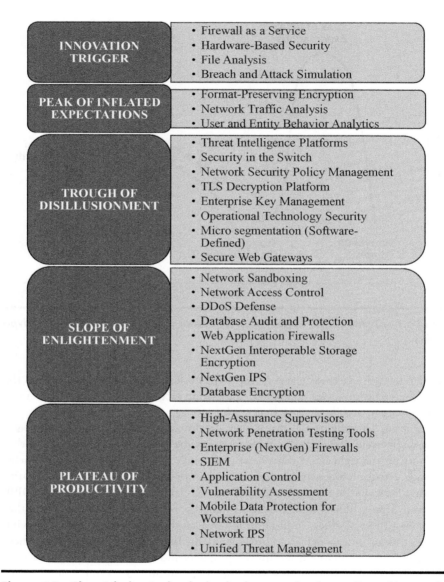

Figure 4.2 Threat-facing technologies by hype cycle phase. (From Young, G., *Hype Cycle for Threat-Facing Technologies*, 2017, Gartner.)

backlog of old vulnerabilities. In short, the products on the right-hand side are typically "staples" in our organizations, and if they are not in your environment, this would be a good opportunity to evaluate why they are not. Products on the far left-hand side are newer ideas not having the benefit of broad-scale adoption or the test of time to mature; however, they may be exciting ideas showing promise. Over the past several years, user entity behavior analytics has been at the peak of inflated expectations; however, it has not been put through the paces in many organizations yet to show this will be here in the current form to stay. Threat intelligence has been emerging the past few years, and with the number of information sharing organizations emerging along with the integration of threat intelligence into cloud services and security products, this may end up as a long-term staple for organizations, large and small. Note that these technologies can take upward of 5–10 years before reaching the plateau period, further indicating that the time for market penetration follows a long cycle and during this time new technology ideas will enter the market. The CISO should be aware of these trends to keep up with the protections and their industry practices. As the board will often be concerned with, "what are our competitor's doing", so should we in the application of technologies so that thoughtful decisions can be made as to whether the technologies apply to us.

Each of these emerging technologies could easily justify a chapter or book on their own to explain the technology, the maturity of the industry, and success stories of the technology. The following technologies and trends are a few to pay attention to in the 2020s and beyond, as solutions will continue to be refined to address these areas. Thousands of startups will be focusing their resources to solve targeted problems, much like the early days of Facebook, where according to CEO Mark Zuckerberg said, "Punch above your weight class. If your product is better than anything out there, the users will let you know it," as he aimed at major universities such as Stanford, Columbia, and Yale first with the expectation that his product had to be better than the college social media networks at large universities to succeed. Security spending was estimated to be $96 billion in 2018 by Gartner Group; with growth through 2023 driven by a shift towards detection and response, Gartner stated, "This increased focus on detection and response to security incidents has enabled technologies such as endpoint detection and response, and user entity and behavior analytics to disrupt traditional markets such as endpoint protection platforms and SIEM." The breakdown of the spending is shown in Figure 4.3.

Five Stages of Technology Adoption

The technologies and/or trends listed in the upcoming section are by no means an exhaustive list; however, these are receiving attention among security professional discussions in networking groups, conferences, and social media discussions and worth exploring further. Organizations will approach these technologies at different stages, depending upon the resources available and the type of organization the CISO is working within, as well as the risk appetite of the organization. Everett Rogers in 1962 published a research called "Diffusion of Innovations" and developed a theory of adoption of innovations by individuals and organizations. He posited there are five stages as shown in Figure 4.4. "Diffusion" is the term used to express how an innovation will spread.

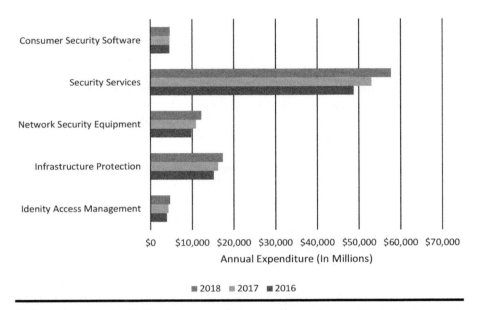

Annual Expenditure (In Millions)

■ 2018 ■ 2017 ■ 2016

Figure 4.3 2016–2018 Cybersecurity spending. (From *Gartner Forecasts Worldwide Security Spending Will Reach $96 Billion in 2018, Up 8 Percent from 2017,* **December 7, 2017, Gartner.)**

Stage 1 Knowledge

Here, the individual has been exposed to the innovation but does not have enough information about the innovation and is not yet inspired to learn more about the innovation. The home user may hear that Amazon has a new product for the home called Alexa but does not know what it does or thinks maybe it is a stereo speaker and is uninterested.

Stage 2 Persuasion

In this stage, the individual is intrigued by the innovation and actively seeks out more information. The user may hear that Alexa has the capability to receive voice commands and is connected to a smartphone device, such as having Siri functionality, and wants to learn more to hear how it could be used and if the device would be of personal use.

Stage 3 Decision

Now that the individual has acquired some facts about the product, the user examines the pros and cons of acquiring the product. Is the product from a

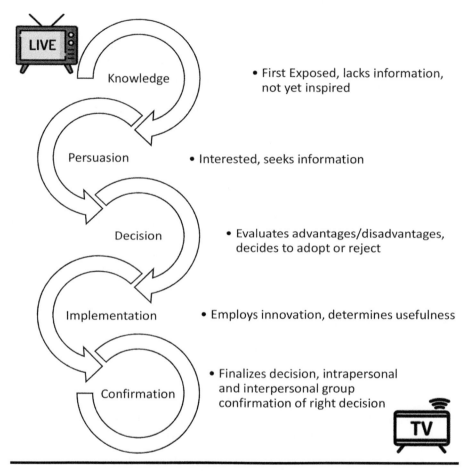

Figure 4.4   Five stages of the decision innovation process.

reliable company? Do I need this innovation? Would I use it? Is it priced right? Are there other alternatives to using this product, or is it truly something new that does not exist? The iPad went through a similar cycle—how is this different from a laptop computer and why would I need such a device that lacks a keyboard and a mouse? How would this be used differently? (As we know today, the iPad/iPad Pro product line is a huge success for its portability and ability to quickly access the Internet thru built-in Wi-Fi or cellular options, and lags in functionality as a full laptop would add-on options such as a keyboard, mouse, enhanced processors, etc.) The decision to adopt in this stage is largely an individual preference based on the individual's perceived value of the innovation across many evaluated factors, which would vary from person to person based upon their experience.

Stage 4 Implementation

The individual selects the innovation and begins to use it. Evaluation may still be occurring in this stage, as the product or service may or may not live up to the expectations. As noted earlier, the Gartner "peak of inflated expectations stage" may set up high hopes for the product and the actual implementation may lead to the "trough of disillusionment" or the "slope of enlightenment" depending upon the testing and the perception of the individual. More information about the innovation may be sought after in this stage to confirm the understanding of the innovation. When hooking Alexa up to the home, the individual may be concerned with privacy issues of having a device that could be activated accidentally or the user may be uncomfortable with the amount of information captured by Alexa and the analytics processing of the data to send more marketing materials. Alternatively, the user could really see the benefits of this innovation and the time-saving ability to ask Alexa questions, obtain the weather at a moment's notice, or add products to a shopping list while the item is on their mind. Others may decide further products, such as Google Home, deserve to be included in the analysis to determine if there is more functionality or better operability with other devices used by the family.

Stage 5 Confirmation

The decision is finalized to either go forward with the innovation or decide that the innovation is not a good fit.

DAN LOHRMANN: CISOs NEED TO BE ENABLERS OF BUSINESS INNOVATION—HERE IS HOW.

Chief Security Officer, Security Mentor, Inc.

Back in 2004, I was firmly against Wi-Fi. Why? It was not secure, in my view. I had plenty of wardriving stories, scary magazine breach headlines, and an abundance of Washington DC three-letter agency white papers to back up my "Wi-Fi is a bad idea" arguments. Until one day, I almost got fired when I insisted that we could not put Wi-Fi in our government conference rooms. I said, "We just can't do it. Not secure. Bad idea. I'm vetoing the project!" My boss, and Michigan Chief Information Officer (CIO) at the time, was Teri Takai. Teri later went on to become the CIO in California Government and at the Department of Defense. Teri said, "Dan, if that's your answer, you can't be the CISO in Michigan." Teri went on, "I've been to Dow, Ford, Chrysler and GM, and they all have Wi-Fi in their conference rooms. So, you need to figure out what they know that you don't know and then come back and tell me how we're going to implement Wi-Fi securely. And I'm giving you one week." That meeting started a transformation in my security career. I began to rethink my role, my team's mission, and how we were being perceived. I refocused my tactical and strategic initiatives to become an enabler of innovation—with the "right" level of security. We went on to win awards for secure Wi-Fi deployments in government a few years later. And there was a larger lesson for me from this experience. I now constantly ask myself: I am bringing the organization problems or workable solutions? As I look back at my early years as a CISO, I see so many blind spots. Yes, I cared passionately about information security. I had the necessary technical skills. But I was putting up unnecessary roadblocks. I was a hindrance to management and not offering the business a range of technology solutions with different risk levels. I never truly learned up to that point, the real reason for the security team's existence. The security leader (and team) must be trusted advisors offering the business secure technology solutions. Security does not exist if the business fails. I believe that history repeats itself regarding technology and security. No doubt, the specific hardware, software, operating systems, frameworks, issues, vulnerability, and threats change daily. But whether we are talking about Wi-Fi, cloud computing, bring your own device (BYOD), or IoT, are you bringing problems or solutions?

Types of Adopters

Adopters also fall into several types and tend to mirror the risk appetite of the organization. The adopters follow a distribution as shown in Figure 4.5, including Diffusion of Innovations, innovators, early adopters, early majority, late majority, and laggards, indicating how innovation is adopted over time. For an innovation to be sustainable, it must have the penetration of sufficient market share through wide acceptance of the idea, or the innovation will parish. Innovations need a social system such as government regulations and media communications as well as time for the idea to take root, ways for the innovation to be communicated, and the introduction of a new idea. Note that sometimes the ideas themselves may not seem new, such as the introduction of the Apple iPod, whereby the product was essentially a portable way to play music and could be argued this already existed through the Sony Walkman or other Mpg players on the market. The new feature was the ability to store many songs on the device without an external media (i.e., Compact Discs, tapes), and the design was compact and simple. Apple marketed a new experience surpassing the other technologies at the time, even though the primary functionality of playing a song was not different.

The first adopter type (2.5% of the adopters) is willing to take risks to try new products, has the financial resources to absorb failures, and is socially networked with other innovators. Information security startups partner with private equity

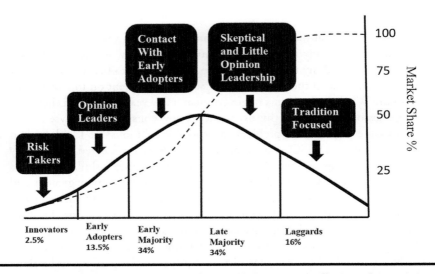

Figure 4.5 Adopter-type distribution. (From Rogers, E., *Diffusion of Innovations*, 2003, Free Press.)

firms based upon an idea showing promise. Private equity firms invest in multiple products knowing that they will not all succeed, but those that do will pay for those that do not. When working for a subsidiary of an $18 billion annual revenue pharmaceutical/life sciences company, I learned we had many products in the pipeline in research and development; however, many of these ideas fail. One drug created accounted for $6 billion of the annual revenue, or 33% of the company's $18 billion total. The product was priced beyond the cost for just the development of that product, as the other innovations resulting in failure had to be paid for. Similarly, startups developing new ideas partner with private equity firms and other individuals with the financial wherewithal to take calculated risks. Additionally, individuals at companies with larger budgets, typically in the financial and technology sectors, may take risks with new ideas if it solves problems other products have not been able to adequately resolve.

The early adopters (13.5%) are many times regarded as the "thought leaders" and work to influence the opinion of others to help spread the technology ideas. Just as with the innovators, early adopters take a leading role with the technology and will typically try the technology out on a section of the environment, i.e., implementing a new method of detecting malware using a mathematical model vs. AV signatures on a small segment of the workstations to test the efficacy. These individuals are risk-takers and have a desire to become in-the-know early on with the technology. They are also willing to know they may need to swap out and reinvest in the technology down the road as a new standard appears; however, the experience of understanding the technology is viewed as being valuable by this group. Some drivers could not wait to get their hands on the new Tesla; even though there were concerns about driving an electric car—where would you recharge? How far would it go? Was it too expensive compared to a gas car? These parameters were not as important—they wanted to be the first on their block to have the new technology and experience it—as well as become the opinion leaders for those curious about this new concept. These early adopters would be the ones sought after for their opinions on the experiences and liked being in this role. Some individuals take this tact, and some organizations are viewed as early adopters. According to Pew Research (2014), 28% of Americans consider themselves to be strong early adopters of technology, and those households earning $150,000 or more have a stronger preference for early adoption (39%). The study also indicated these individuals are more likely to be Internet users and own cellphones, tablets, and laptop or desktop computers. They are also most likely to score higher in the "openness to new experiences" and "extroversion" dimensions. Organizations are really representations of the industry and the people recruited within them. Organizations also attract the talent based upon the values of the company. For example, it is no surprise that Tesla, Google, Apple, Netflix, and Microsoft are some of the most sought-after companies for internship programs due to the technical innovation these companies represent. Likewise, the organizations desiring to deploy the technologies created by these companies early in the life cycle will also most likely be filled with early adopter individuals. Check to see if they are driving a Telsa or have the latest iPad/laptop with the latest applications—this will provide a clue as to their adoption strategy. Entrepreneurs need to be careful when surrounding themselves with other early adopters, as they may add in more bells and whistles than the average consumer needs, more than individuals in the early and late majority adopters that make up 68% of the market. The early adopters will sign up as beta testers for the products and will provide feedback on product quality; however, they are not as apt to give opinions on the usability and ease of operation as the larger market of regular customers will.

Early majority adopters (34%) adopt the innovations after the early adopters but are not seen as the opinion leaders as the early adopters are. This stage is when products are becoming mainstream and the average consumer is adopting the product. The Tesla Model 3, e.g., created such a buzz that over 325,000 orders were placed for the car in the first week. This was for a car that would not be delivered for 2 more years in mid-2018! Contrast this to the more expensive Model S which only had orders for 10,000 cars as it entered 2015 (truly early adopters of the electric technology). These innovation buyers have received more information about the product due to the media, view the viability of the product as acceptable, and are willing to pay a higher price for the product to become an early adopter, or in some cases are drawn in by attractive discounts. When behavioral analytics were integrated into AV programs or firewalls started ingesting threat intelligence feeds, firms saw the potential of this technology and it made sense to pursue based upon "the idea" and produce some anecdotal early case studies. Others would wait until a later stage of adoption until "evidence" suggests 0-day exploits could be detected by behavioral analysis in the AV engines. The early majority tend to follow the market leader and will exercise more caution than the early adopters. In the Tesla case, many people signed up as they did not want to "miss out," while at the same time, a guarantee was made they could get a refund if they decided not to pursue the purchase.

Late majority adopters (34%) are skeptical about innovation and will not adopt the innovation until most of society has adopted the innovation. The proposal to eliminate signature-based AV software in favor of a behavioral, analytics-based product will not be adopted by this group until the major companies have implemented this scenario with enhanced success, the AV vendor market share has been seen to substantially decrease, or this class of products occupies the Gartner Leader Quadrant or is reflected in the Forrester Wave Report. These individuals will be buying Tesla's after the 500,000+ cars are on the road, great reviews have been written, gas prices are high, batteries can now support the same distance as a tankful of gas, and charging stations are as commonplace as gas stations.

The laggards are the last group to adopt a technology, have the lowest social status of all the adoption types and lowest financial ability, and may not be as networked socially as the other adopter types. As in the other types, individuals and organizations can share this characteristic. We all know of the doctor who was practicing for 35 years when the introduction of electronic medical records (EMR) came available and the health-care system was met with resistance, "I have been treating patients for my entire career without needing a computer and a paper chart works just fine. Besides, now I must take patient time to fill out these records vs. helping my patient! I think I will just retire." These are the laggards averse to change and focused on the "way things have always been done," or the traditions of the past. These individuals will eventually adopt the technology, as the organization will force it by system changes, policy, or the need to meet an external mandate [such as the 2009 Health Information Technology for Economic and Clinical Health (HITECH) Act requiring the meaningful use of interoperable electronic health records (EHRs)]. The laggards may also refer to those organizations not investing in security technology, or still of the mindset that "we have nothing they need."

Each adopter type has their place, and our organizations and people will fit into one or more of these types of adoption. Some departments may be more risk-averse than others and have different styles with respect to technology. A Chief Marketing Officer may be willing to be an early adopter, using new technologies to gain a competitive advantage, knowing that they will not be perfect and some of the technologies will fail. He or she may be investing in social media data analytics with graphical analysis based on an individual's current location and proximity to one of the company's retail outlets to send a message or coupon when they are near the store. This may involve cloud storage, mobile applications, and multiple social media platforms. Alternatively, the same company's finance department may be much more comfortable with using their contained on-premise, database-centric financial application to manage the general ledger and company transactions and not see a need to upgrade to a new technology.

Why is all this important to understand? The technology may be the coolest, newest, awesome, most innovative technology ever—to you or me—but if management and users needing to support this new way forward are primarily a different kind of adopter, there will be much groundwork to sell the idea. A small community bank may not be too keen performing beta testing new wire transfer software, whereas a larger bank may have the ability, infrastructure, and may want to participate to show technology leadership as one of the key values. Mobile Check deposits were introduced by USAA Federal Savings Bank in 2009, and 72% of the institutions at that time indicated they had no plans to roll out mobile remote deposit capture. As the innovation was embraced by consumers, by 2012, only 18% indicated they had no plans. Sometimes these innovations and the desire for adoption can come quickly, and organizations need to be able to respond—with a secure implementation. Sometimes a security technology will become widely known, as promoted by the opinion leaders (early adopters), and others will follow suit. There was a time not long ago when cloud adoption was viewed as highly insecure and should be avoided—Gartner projected in 2016 that by 2020 a corporate "No-Cloud" policy would be as rare as a "No-Internet" policy, with most organizations having at least some part of their technology innovation cloud-centric, with most organizations embracing some form of a hybrid cloud.

Emerging Technologies to Consider

The following technologies are the technologies that may or may not apply to the industry vertical in which the CISO operates. These technologies should be reviewed for applicability, and if not applicable, review them in a year and see if this is still the case.

Blockchain/Cryptocurrencies

Cryptocurrencies have received much press in recent years due to the rapid increase in value experienced in 2017, where the primary cryptocurrency Bitcoin surged from a starting price of $995 on 1/1/2017 per digital Bitcoin to a peak of $19,065 in less than 1 year on 12/10/2017. Early entrants gained much more, as $100 invested in Bitcoin 6 years earlier on 1/1/2011 at the rate of 30 cents—yes cents—per Bitcoin would be worth over $6 million at the peak. The value has moved up and down since this time, as the price hovered around $6,200 USD in the fall of 2018, with many people speculating on the currency. Some view each Bitcoin as being worth hundreds of thousands of dollars due to the limited supply (system is designed for a maximum of 21 million coins), and promise of the cryptocurrency, while others view the currency has no intrinsic value, meaning it has no underlying assets or earnings as a stock in a company would and the value is only derived by supply and demand. While there are hundreds of cryptocurrencies emerging and vying for this space, Bitcoin is the most well-known and has been the payment of choice, due to its anonymous owner identity characteristics being untraceable. The currency has faced halted trading on some of the exchanges, such as the Japan's largest digital currency exchange, Coincheck in January 2018 as Coincheck indicated that over 500 NEM tokens worth $533 million were stolen from the digital wallets. This was not the first time an exchange suffered an attack by hackers, as Japan's Mt. Gox exchange suffered several breaches between 2011 and 2014 and the breaches forced the company into bankruptcy. In June 2018, South Korean cryptocurrency exchange Coinrail reported that 30% of the coins in storage, or $37.2 million USD, were stolen. Just as banks and financial services companies are the targets of hackers due to the financial assets under custody, these cryptocurrencies represent large opportunities for skilled hackers. The cryptography itself has not been the aspect broken, but rather the processes surrounding the use of the cryptography.

The debate among investors will continue well into the future as to the long-term viability of the currency—one thing is for certain, the idea of a cryptocurrency for transactions has legs and is one of those technologies CISOs need to become more familiar with—if for no other reason, the primary form of payment for ransomware is in a cryptocurrency (Bitcoin)! How many organizations have purchased a few Bitcoins as part of their security budget for that case where they may decide the best alternative is to pay for the ransom (i.e., no backups were in place, backups corrupted, time to restore beyond critical time frame information needed, or no other choice)? Some cybersecurity consulting firms have a stockpile of Bitcoins in the event a client needs to pay, as many clients have not thought in advance that this might be necessary. This is not surprising that clients have not planned to purchase a cryptocurrency if they have not ensured their backups were maintained and adequately protected in the event of a breach. The organization also needs to ensure these Bitcoin wallets are adequately secured as well including backing up the wallet, encrypting any backup exposed to a network, storing in multiple secure locations, encrypting the primary wallet, using strong complex passwords at least 16 characters long, and maintaining offline wallets not exposed to the network. Essentially, the same foundational controls apply to cryptocurrency wallets as securing the infrastructure for any asset of value.

While the cryptocurrencies have generated considerable debate between neighbors and friends, gathering conversations among all generations, the real story here may be the underlying technology supporting the cryptocurrencies—blockchain. Blockchains are distributed, decentralized ledgers not managed by a central, single entity and instead are managed by a group of people that "mine transactions" called "miners." The blockchain is a series of blocks appended to each other, each with a digital timestamp of the date it is created. Once information is recorded inside the block, it becomes very difficult to back-date or change the integrity of the block. It works simply like this: a block is added to the chain containing some data, a hash of the block, and the hash of the previous block in the chain. If someone was to tamper with the block, the hash value for the block would change and not be correct. Hackers could get around this by recomputing the hashes for all the blocks; however, the feature known as the "proof of work" slows down the process by implementing a 10-minute process to add a new block to the chain. Since tampering would require the recomputing of all the other blocks in the chain (as the hash values would all change) to tamper with a block, this wait time is a security feature to mitigate this risk. The blocks are also distributed through a peer-to-peer network, and everyone receives a full copy of the blockchain. The added block is sent to everyone, and the blocks are added to each person's previous block in the chain. If the block has been tampered with, it will be rejected. The truth is derived by the consensus of everyone on the network, with a majority achieving the consensus.

The technology provides a way for the truth of a transaction to be known without the need of one person, company, or government entity to be able to vouch for the truth. For example, consider the case of holding a deposit savings account with a bank—the user initiates a transaction to deposit or withdraw funds from the bank and initiates a transaction. The bank, or holder of the "real truth," credits or debits the funds from the account and maintains the account balance. The bank is the central, single entity maintaining the truth of the transaction, just as the register of deeds maintains the truth of who owns which house in a location. With blockchain, the knowledge of the transaction is shared between all the members of the blockchain, as they have a copy. They have the truth because of the hashing of the block, inclusion of the hash in the next block, the distributed copies shared by many people, and the time for the process to create a block on the chain. The perceived value is that a bank would not be paid for the process of holding the information, as any costs would be for the exchange and paying miners to mine the truth.

Other applications are emerging using the technology concepts to solve other problems and create efficiencies beyond managing the financial currency. Anywhere information is shared among multiple people provides an opportunity for blockchain. Other uses may include storing medical records, contracts, voting, background checks, logistics transparency, origins of products in a supply chain, transactions between parties, serving as a notarizing function, and others. Other applications are sure to evolve where the reliance on records that cannot be updated is important. Trade could be decentralized by reducing the need for intermediaries. Most likely, someone in the organization is already experimenting with this technology to improve business processes, and it would behoove the CISO and security team to understand what is being considered and ensure the surrounding processes of managing wallets, keys, backups, configurations, and so forth are appropriately managed securely.

Blockchain could become a disruptor as the concept of trade, move to decentralization of buyers and sellers, and will require an understanding of the users as to the safety of the technology and standards evolve. In the 2020s, expect to see a growing number of proof of concepts for applications where the users do not need the ability to trust each other (think of PayPal as a mechanism to pass payments from one untrusted person to another). Trust is established rather by trusting the underlying mechanism (PayPal comes with guarantees; the other party does not have access to the bank account). Many new applications by startups are sure to emerge. Blockchains within the business environment are likely to emerge through a set of defined parties where there is an inherent trust relationship established, reducing the risk, unlike the cryptocurrency environment where no one is trusted.

Internet of Things

IoT, whereby almost any device imaginable is being connected to the Internet, clearly presents security challenges for the environment. Does the organization have policies and standards related to these devices? Are these devices being detected by the organization? Is the connectivity being segmented or do these represent a new entry point into the network or data on a device? This frontier is like the questions asked when organizations were trying to figure out who should have access to the Internet in the mid- to late 1990s and the BYOD mobile device discussions that followed the penetration and price reductions of the smartphones, tablets, and personal computers. Individuals want to interact with their smartphones, watches, and with products bridging their home and work life such as thermostats, home security cameras, doorbells, bathroom scales, and wearable technology. Even the toothbrush is being connected to the Internet and providing feedback information. Some organizations have started to use their smartphones to serve as access devices reducing the need for passwords, proximity card badges, and access to applications. The devices can provide identity intelligence by using telemetry such as global positioning system with tracking ability, and Bluetooth communications for short-range communications.

The usage of IoT has the potential to impact any business. The energy sector could benefit from increased accuracy in drilling oil wells, improving the safety of workers by monitoring devices and reducing costs through monitoring parts when they may be at the end of life. Smart meters are used in homes to increase energy efficiency by better forecasting of energy demands and by the consumer being able to monitor their usage. IoT provides the capability for monitoring more detailed information—such as which device is consuming more energy? Is it the vending machine in the mall? Which machine on the shop floor is using the most energy and should be upgraded? Water sensors can track the water consumption, pressure, temperature, and so forth and communicate with the company to monitor water consumption.

Health care should benefit from IoT, as a number of installed IoT devices, not counting wearables such as fitness trackers, experience projected growth from 95 million in 2015 to 646 million in 2020, a significant growth curve. Health care was traditionally an under-invested space, with paper medical charts being the norm for many organizations prior to the HITECH Act of 2009, where only 16% of hospitals were using an EHR or EMR, increasing to 80% in just a few short years (2013). Today, having an EHR is considered vital in the hospital environment. By providing the ability to have access to medical information securely directly by the consumer through a smartphone, website, tablet, or laptop/desktop, the implementation and expectations of technology became commonplace. The next logical step for a health-care organization is to utilize IoT to assist in the monitoring and care of patients remotely. Devices such as ultrasounds, thermometers, glucose monitors, electrocardiograms, smart beds, heart monitors, medication dispensers, and other emerging connected devices can improve the quality of health care. As much as an average consumer may not want an IoT Toilet in the home, there may be some applications where monitoring the activity and frequency can help improve the treatment of a patient. Wearable fitness technologies may also be used to collect information on exercise and lower insurance premiums. Products such as Bluetooth-enabled smart socks record a runner's speed, pace, and cadence and use analytics to provide a real-time training plan and feedback to help improve performance and reduce injury.

The CISO and their team need to be able to secure the IoT, as Gartner indicated that by 2020 more than half of new business processes and systems will incorporate some elements of the IoT. Physical items previously disconnected will be connected. The introduction of IoT in an organization will increase the need for more spending in the security group to address the security concerns, adding in network segmentation, device-to-device authentication, data encryption, and establishing the appropriate privacy policies. The IoT devices have the capability to collect much information about the environment, such as using the temperature to determine who is and who is not at home, or working as indicated, or using the information to send commands to machines or make medical decisions. Much security in the past with sensitive information has been concerned mostly with confidentiality; however, the integrity of the information will become an even greater concern, as modification or substitution of this information could cause a risk. The technology holds great promise, and the technology estimates of the number of devices diverge greatly, with 2020 estimates between 18 and 50 billion, depending upon the forecaster. The actual number is not as important to the cybersecurity professional as the recognition that this is a freight train that has either just left the company station and is well down the tracks, or it is the small light approaching from the near distance and we need to be ready to board. How will we secure this technology? How may it be used? Could this be an access point open to compromise? Are the products in this space mature and do we know how we would isolate and secure them according to the asset risk if the base product does not have that capability?

ERIK DECKER: HEALTH-CARE CYBERSECURITY

Chief Security and Privacy Officer, University of Chicago Medicine

As you may be aware, the health-care sector is undergoing a cybersecurity paradigm shift. You have probably read the articles in the news about hospitals being shut down by ransomware, or patient data being stolen during a sophisticated cyberattack. What you may not know are the unique challenges the health-care industry presents when it comes to securing its assets and operations, and protecting its patients.

Health-care cybersecurity comes with a unique challenge. Long ago are the days of a single clinician or doctor providing the care for a patient. In some of the more sophisticated systems, for every patient being treated, there might be upward of 100 employees providing support for that patient's health. It ranges from the direct care team that interfaces with the patient, such as doctors, nurses, and residents. To provide support for the patient's long-term health, there are patient care service teams, social workers, nutritionists, and other specialty care professionals. There are also teams that support the infrastructure, facilities, bill for services, and so much more. As you can easily see, the patient's information must travel and traverse through all corners of a typical health-care system to properly care for any given patient.

CISOs within this space have the unique challenge of securing all this data that wants to move. They also must secure the ecosystem itself to protect against real attacks that try to monetize its digital operations, such as ransomware. How can they possibly be successful?

There are many answers to this question, and this book will most certainly address many of them. For the CISO in health care, it is imperative to be part of the executive business leadership, a risk manager, and explain risks without technical jargon. Establishing cybersecurity governance processes is the first step. Convene your C-suite, preferably with your highest executive. Charter them with risk ownership, setting risk tolerance and approving policy. In my experience, this is most effective by ensuring the chair of these committees is anyone but the CISO. It starts by sitting down with your CEO or President and explaining the role of the CISO—we are risk advisors, not risk owners. More specifically, to tackle the challenge of data movement or digital ecosystem challenges, and the ensuing clinical workflow practices that will inevitably need to be adjusted, it will become quickly apparent that it is not appropriate for information technology (IT) or cybersecurity departments to make such policy changes. Only the business can make these adjustments; these governance groups are your pathway to influence those changes.

Drones

Drones are sophisticated devices pushing into global mainstream use, no longer the "toy" of hobbyists. As the battery-life improves and drones can fly for longer periods, these could become delivery mechanisms of the future. Amazon was awarded the patent by the U.S. Patent and Trademark Office for a drone that can respond to human gestures such as thumbs up, shouting, or frantic arm waving and adjust its behavior in the delivery of packages. This capability may permit the drone to release the package, alter the flight path to avoid crashing, ask questions, or abort the delivery. This is accomplished by infrared and ultraviolet light sensors interacting with the humans. These drones are larger in size, and running into a person could injure them. The Federal Aviation Administration regulates drones from 0.55 to <55 lbs. As seen by the drone statistics in Figure 4.6, the number of nondefense drones is expected to increase at an accelerated rate as the technology matures.

Commercial use cases may include areas such as aerial photo/videography, surveillance monitoring, payload delivery, first aid and disaster response, agriculture, engineering, communications, and security services. Drones should be

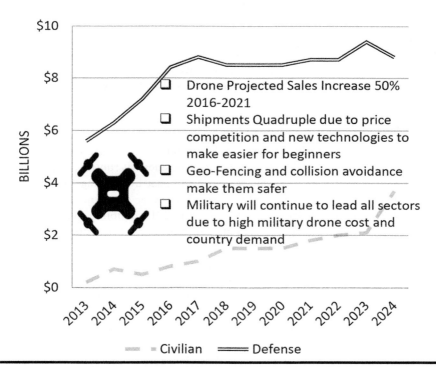

Figure 4.6 **The growth of drones. (From *The Drones Report: Market forecasts, regulatory barriers, top vendors, and leading commercial applications*, 2016, BI Intelligence (June 10).)**

accompanied with an incident response plan in the event there is an issue. Drones can only be flown in areas where the airspace is not restricted, which includes areas beyond airports and major cities and includes areas such as national parks, the White House, Camp David, stadiums, and Walt Disney World. The airspaces could also include areas around wildfires and whether there is an emergency, so individuals are not interfering with emergency and rescue operations. The organization needs policies and procedures to manage these conditions.

We care about drones as they may be used within our organizations and the products come with varying degrees of encryption, run on 3G/4G or Wi-Fi networks, and above all, may create privacy issues. At issue is the potential for a drone filming, and in full high-definition quality video of activities on your property from a position several hundred feet up. What rights does the homeowner have? These could be viewed as a nuisance, harassment, or an invasion of privacy, yet there are few specific laws to date clearly protecting individuals from drones. As noted in the *Privacy and Data Protection* chapter, the 1890 Harvard Law Paper by Warren and Brandeis advocating "the right to be left alone" was of a very similar concern—providing photographic evidence of something going on in a person's home. At least 38 states considered legislation to regulate unmanned aircraft (drones) in 2017. Many countries have started drone laws, including countries such as the United Kingdom requiring that there is no breach of any privacy laws with the images obtained from the drone, the drone must be in visual sight, and the drone cannot be flown further than 500 m from the location and no higher than 122 m. There has been concern over drones and engines of airplanes being susceptible to a disaster, like a bird strike causing engine failure.

Ransomware

Recent ransomware attacks indicate the significant damage these attacks can have including destruction of files, system outages, business disruption, and unanticipated financial costs, let alone the reputation impact by creating the perception the security program is not properly managed, fairly or not. One estimate of the ransomware paid out by victims was $2 billion in 2017, doubling the amount paid out in 2016. Total damage inflicted by the ransomware was estimated to exceed $5 billion, including NotPetya costs of $310 million to Merck Pharmaceuticals, $310 million to FedEx, and $200 million for shipping firm Maersk. A U.S. Government Agency Report indicated there have been more than 4,000 ransomware attacks daily since 2016 and this number is rising. The full extent of the ransomware payouts may be even higher, as businesses may privately pay the ransoms to recover files. The amounts are increasing, up from an estimated $24 million paid to hackers in 2015, representing a very accelerated glide path. Ransomware hackers are upping their game and increasing ways to avoid detection, such as providing malware that can morph (polymorphism) to avoid detection. Some of these are packaged as malware botnets that can be rented on the black market, i.e., ransomware-as-a-service, requiring less skill by those creating the techniques. The cloud is being leveraged, as well as using graphics processing units instead of central processing units to increase the speed of the encryption.

According to Europol's 2017 Internet Organized Crime Threat Assessment, "ransomware has eclipsed most other cyber threats with global campaigns indiscriminately affecting victims across multiple industries in both the public and private sectors. Some attacks have targeted and affected critical national infrastructures at levels that could endanger lives. These attacks have highlighted how connectivity, poor digital hygiene standards, and security practices can allow such a threat to quickly spread and expand the attack vector." Their recommendations for combating this problem involved recommendations for law enforcement, policy makers and regulators, and advice for organizations. Specifically, CISOs and security leaders need to ensure company employees are educated to recognize and respond accordingly to the changing criminal tactics such as social engineering, spam botnets, and support the prevention and awareness programs. They also advocated public and private partnerships between law enforcement and Computer Emergency Response Teams to enable fast response during a global cyberattack.

CISOs and their teams should be performing tabletop exercises to prepare in the event of a ransomware attack. By pre-thinking under what circumstances the organization would or would not pay the ransom would enhance the incident response process vs. making this decision in the heat of the moment. Working through this exercise with management, once the potential impact of ransomware is assessed, this may also lead to an increase in funding and the strengthening of the critical vulnerability management processing and user awareness training, as well as investing in more robust backup and recovery solutions. There are no guarantees when paying the ransom ensuring that the keys will be provided by the attacker (even though it is to the attackers' advantage to do so, so that future victims will also pay) and the files may not be recovered. There are also no guarantees the same company will not end up paying the ransom again in the future, possibly at a higher amount, as the attacker now knows the systems are weak and more importantly, the company will pay up. The bottom line is to prepare upfront in the event of an attack, perform foundational cybersecurity vulnerability management to limit risk, educate the users, ensure backup/recovery mechanisms are in place and tested, and have the capability to pay the ransom if necessary as the last line of defense to restore the environment to the state prior to the attack. Ransomware is considered a breach under the Health Insurance Portability and Accountability Act (HIPAA) unless the covered entity or business associate can demonstrate there is a "low probability that the PHI has been compromised," based on the Breach Notification Rule. In other words, a breach of PHI is assumed since a breach is defined as "the acquisition, access, use, or disclosure of PHI in a manner not permitted under the HIPAA Privacy Rule which compromises the security or privacy of the PHI." This example infers that since the PHI was "accessed" during the ransomware process, it may be considered a breach, and the CISO would be wise to use this example when reviewing other regulations to interpret whether a ransomware attack would be considered a breach of sensitive information, even if the information was not exfiltrated from the system.

AI/Machine Learning

Go to any vendor floor at a security conference, and security products indicating usage of AI seem to be everywhere. The nomenclature of AI is attractive because the security problems faced are so large and complex, and there is something intriguing about having a machine capable of replacing or augmenting human thought to solve a problem, able to take in vast amounts of information, and process it quickly. Computers have been performing rote sequential tasks for many years now, and the difficulty is in implementing programs requiring generalization, or applying experience to analogous new situations. For example, the word "detect" if coded by rote learning would need to have "detected" coded as the past tense if the word was to be discovered, as opposed to generalization where the "add ed rule" would be applied from knowledge of how other past tenses were formed, to form the past tense of "detect" resulting in "detected." Reasoning draws inferences relevant to the task or solution. AI can integrate perception through sensors to identify individuals, help self-driving vehicles drive at appropriate speeds, and enable robots to work in factories. One of the early robots was named *Freddy*, able to recognize objects such as a toy car in a heap of random objects. Freddy was created at the University of Edinburgh in Scotland from 1966 to 1973.

AI is used today on our smartphones for speech understanding, and Natural Language Programming was used to develop an IBM supercomputer dubbed Watson used on the TV show Jeopardy to defeat the champion, enabling fast processing of web searches. The IBM supercomputer named Watson shows promise in applications for medical diagnosis, genetic testing result interpretation, drug research, call centers, and other complex analysis such as computer threat detection. There is promise in the technology to provide AI to automatically investigate indicators of compromise, produce insights faster, and accelerate the time to respond cycle. The capabilities may also reduce the error rate from missing threats due to overburdened staffs.

We do need to be cautioned, as any new buzzword or solution enters the security solution space of what is AI and what is merely a repackaging of a prior product. AI has the potential to change the way individuals interact with machines. A large population has become comfortable with touching and talking to smartphones (i.e., ask Siri, selecting applications for most aspects of our lives), and home devices such as Alexa and Google Home. Sanford University created a panel and subsequent study published in 2015 entitled "The One Hundred Year Study on Artificial Intelligence" to examine the long-term effects of AI on the community, people, and society. The study indicated that AI has been patchy and unpredictable in the results over the past 60 years, as each application of AI involves years of specialized research and construction to achieve the results desired. In industries struggling to attract younger workers, AI and robotics will be deployed increasingly in areas such as agriculture, food processing, fulfillment centers, and factories. They will guide the delivery of items through drones, self-driving cars and trucks, and robots capable of walking upstairs. The report indicates there are several challenges with moving forward, such as the difficulty of creating safe and reliable hardware, difficulty of smoothly interacting with human experts in such fields as education and health care, gaining public trust, overcoming fears of marginalizing humans in employment and the workplace, and the social risk of diminishing interpersonal interactions. The panel suggested that even with these challenges, AI is likely to have a profound impact on our society by 2030. There will be missteps and legal and ethical issues along the way, such as the self-driving cars injuring or killing passengers. As these events happen in testing, companies are expected to have bugs as they are rolled out; however when the impact involves human life, the societal and government reaction is typically swift. A study by AAA indicated 63% of people would not feel safe in a self-driving car today. This is one example where AI has promise, evaluating millions of data inputs to make the right decisions, and just as the automobile has evolved since Henry Ford's 1896 Model T, so will the self-driving car. The self-driving car is just one example of AI's promise. Complex applications where decisions need to be made quickly, as in the security threat detection space, hold promise for the future.

Digital Transformation

Cloud adoption by companies has rendered the network almost borderless with data and processing in many different places, using faster networks and adding to the complexity of the network design. Digital technology is being integrated into many areas of business leading to changes in the way businesses must operate and how value creation for the customer is achieved. The various technologies all combine to create a digital experience and capability for the customer, combining mobile devices, wearables, virtual reality, IoT platforms, sensors, cloud computing, big data analytics, and understanding the customer and their needs through AI. The movement of firms to integrate these different platforms with a goal of a seamless experience increases the attack surface, as the devices are now connected to cloud applications and physical objects through IoT.

TONY SPINELLI: INFORMATION SECURITY APPROACH TO DIGITAL TRANSFORMATION

Former CISO, Capital One

In the current environment, companies are seeking to become more agile and competitive regarding using technology and becoming more digital. In the digital sense, businesses seeking to thrive and, in many cases, survive have to meet the technology demands of their consumers and stay relevant vs. their competitors. But, what does becoming digital actually mean as it seems to be part of the hype cycle and a buzzword that slides into marketing materials and discussions with ease?

Clearly, I can recall leading a keynote discussion for the global conference of Chief Risk Officers (CROs) where they asked me to deliver a discussion on the future of digital disruption and how this relates to the cybersecurity imperative. As I began the keynote, I asked the audience of CROs to raise their hand if their company was embarking on becoming digital? This means you are doing one of a few constructs, and this list is not exhaustive:

1. *Mobility and presence*—branding is no longer where you are, but it's where your customer is
2. *Analytics and AI*—learning drives deeper contextual experiences with your customers
3. *Social media*—drives your interaction model with customers
4. *IoT*—everything is on its way to being connected with everything
5. The software is the new hardware
6. Cloud is the new data center
7. *Maker culture*—leveraging open source for innovations sourced by a crowd of experts.

As you might imagine, every hand went up from the CRO audience. I then quickly asked, keep your hands up if your cybersecurity program is digital? Sadly, every hand went down amid mild discussion breaking out in the crowd, but this was not unexpected in my experience. And this is why digital adoption in enterprises is challenged, failure rates are high, and digital leaders feel as if they are pushing against two walls closing in on them.

Cybersecurity keeps moving farther away from becoming digital. For much too long in cybersecurity, we have bought vendor products that do one thing and all the while knowing few of them have any possibility of integrating or working together. We typically watch Security Operations Center (SOC) analysts "alt-tabbing" between the 60–70 products that the typical cybersecurity program of a Fortune 500 has deployed, and we expect to correlate this data together from the millions of inbound attacks while piecing together whether the attack is real or is a false positive. All the while, our other cybersecurity products continue to send our analysts more binary decisions they have made from alerts and guess what—send them to humans. Think about this. The very definition of human and machine teaming in AI is that the machines do the complex and the humans make decisions. How did we get this so backward?

We ask humans in cybersecurity to continually work off of lists of alerts, lists of vulnerabilities, and lists of threat advisories all the while attackers are attacking us with digital concepts. Alt-tab will never win against graph thinking which hackers employ to understand how to laterally move and escalate privileges to successfully acquire our crown jewel assets. If we are to win in cybersecurity, we must become digital in cybersecurity as well.

In my experience, if your business wants to become digital, your cyber-security program has to be the first mover by deploying digital cyberse-curity capabilities around graph analytics, cloud capabilities, time series databases, micro-services architectures, container-based services, deep insights from real analytics, and the deep use of open source technologies. As noted, these are not in vendor cybersecurity products as of this writing, and many of the digital cybersecurity approaches you can deploy require a new mindset. I often ask CISOs that are embarking on the digital journey what is their number one tool of choice for cybersecurity as they make this shift, and I hear a multitude of responses around this vendor product or that one. In reality, it is simply harnessing the power of unlimited com-pute that cloud technologies can offer you and your enterprise and sourc-ing the vast array of open source technologies and data science around graph analytics and times series data. A CISO that understands how to leverage these digital concepts for cybersecurity can offer their business new opportunities, new business agility, and a stronger capability for their business to achieve the digital destination with a risk-managed competi-tive advantage.

Multifactor Authentication and Privilege Restriction

With the number of breaches escalating each year providing account and password information to potential attackers, organizations should be moving towards multifactor authentication. Organizations have been traditionally cautious about implementing this technology beyond the network administrators and remote access users. Multifactor solutions today employ the use of SMS text messages or applications leveraging the smartphone and authenticator applications to provide the secondary authentication. Implementing a scheme with something you have (phone, token) and something you know (pin, password, random generated num-ber), or something you are (fingerprints, iris scans, biometrics), adds one more step of complexity for the attacker. The consumer attitude appears to be shifting due to the public nature of all the data breaches and the likelihood they were involved in one or more data breaches themselves and desires to be protected if the "friction" of the transaction is not excessive. Some implementations of multifactor authentica-tion are rolled out at the same time as single sign-on to show another benefit to the consumer beyond their protection. Some products also provide context and behavioral information, such as the location of the device and the actions of the end user to determine if the end user is the same end user. The future of "the password" lies with the implementation of multifactor techniques leveraging devices for identity verification such as smartphones, tablets, and watches. Individuals have become accustomed to using the fingerprint biometric reader on smartphones due to the benefit to the user—it is easy to use.

Automation/Orchestration

Combine the different platforms and technologies used with the number of security products within the organization, and this becomes a challenge to manage. Is it better to have one vendor with a "single pane of glass," or the best of breed with multiple vendors? To gain efficiencies with the information security staff and leverage the technical expertise for high-value items, the focus should always be on automating the repetitive, manual tasks to provide information for the analyst requiring action vs. spending time to determine the items needing action. Orchestration holds the promise of integrating the disparate tools in the security analyst's toolbox to provide focus on the alerts and issue areas requiring the most attention. Orchestration should not be attempted until the processes are well understood and documented internally, as this will waste time and most likely result in rework. Orchestration can take the analysts out of fire-fighting mode trying to respond to too many alerts from different systems, causing fatigue and burnout of the analysts. Another benefit is that the orchestration can address the cybersecurity skills gap by automating the analyses of common attacks. As SOCs leverage more external providers for part of the function, combined with the operations in different geographies with varying skill sets, the need for coordination for fast response could not be greater. Without automation, incidents could be missed, and duplication of efforts with individuals working on the same incident and difficulties in capturing metrics and reporting for management are likely to occur. Many organizations have a limited number of skilled analysts working on these issues. However, orchestration is not without cost—integration of disparate security products is not a once-and-done process—as the products themselves are upgraded, this can change the integration of the products into the process. Integration of Identity and Access Management systems or SIEM systems followed a similar challenge as the connectors to feed information from one system to the other were either an additional cost or worst case needed to be customized for the specific application. The CISO needs to evaluate the products understanding the full life cycle cost and whether this would outweigh the benefit of making investments in standardizing incident response playbooks, training additional staff, leveraging the existing product capabilities, and strengthening current metrics.

Automation and orchestration will continue to evolve as the current workload and lack of talent will drive more organizations to a combination of automation, outsourcing, and investing in talent. Companies will be more attractive to those that have reduced the mundane work. The question remains, "Will the automation/orchestration live up to the vendor promise?" The SIEM toolset, e.g., has been criticized as having too many alerts, not providing the right amount of data for an investigation, lack of prioritizing alerts for incident response, time involved to manage the SIEM, vendor support, and lack of skilled individuals to operate the SIEM. The SIEM tool was held out as the promise to determine the alerts. Some vendors have added AI to the SIEM products. The questions the CISO must ask is, "Why was AI needed, was the SIEM not sufficient to perform the job?" Orchestration does hold promise to integrate case management, forensic tools, SIEM, threat feeds, sandboxing, endpoint detection, response tools, and other security tools into the mix. The costs of this integration may make the effort reserved for the medium and large institutions or developed by an outsourcer for the small environments. According to one security orchestration company's research, while 54% of respondents believed automating incident response would provide immediate benefits, only 10.9% had automated this facet. Whether or not the number of those believing the orchestration would provide benefits was as high as 54%, the low number should cause some pause—this indicates there is much room for upside automation of the security processes and something leading CISOs should investigate once the foundational security technologies are in place.

Threat Intelligence

Several information sharing organizations were formed over the last several years with varying levels of maturity in providing threat intelligence. The most well-known and oldest threat intelligence sharing organization was formed more than 20 years ago in 1999, established by the financial services community in response to 1998 Presidential Directive 63, recognizing national and economic security was "increasingly reliant on certain critical infrastructures and upon cyber-based information systems." The directive was subsequently updated by Homeland Security Presidential Directive 7 in 2003, stating the government agencies "shall collaborate with the private sector and continue to support sector-coordinating mechanisms: a) to identify, prioritize, and coordinate the protection of critical infrastructure and key resources; and b) to facilitate sharing of information about physical and cyber threats, vulnerabilities, incidents, potential protective measures, and best practices." While the term "threat intelligence" was never mentioned in the text, this term has become the commonly accepted term used to represent sharing of cybersecurity threats across the various sectors. The sharing organizations provide anonymous indicators of compromise and procedures and best practices for safeguarding against emerging and known security threats.

GRANT SEWELL: EXPERIENCE WITH AN INFORMATION SHARING AND ANALYSIS CENTER

Head of Global Information Security, The Scotts Miracle-Gro Company

Information Sharing and Analysis Centers (ISACs, for short) were established to promote centralized gathering and sharing of threat information within an industry sector. Since the first centers were established in the late 1990s, the footprint has grown to support more than 20 sectors and become an indispensable tool in the modern security program.

As a consumer products manufacturing company, our customer relationships are our top priority. Our job is to make consumer goods, and those operations are dependent on sensible risk management.

We joined an ISAC to be a better partner to our customers. As a supplier to other member companies, we are cognizant of the strengths and potential risks inherent to the nature of our partnerships. We are committed to running a strong security program, and sharing our common threats demonstrates that to our customers. By sharing information within the retail ISAC, we deepen those relationships and enhance the confidence our customers have in us.

Upon becoming members, my team quickly realized that the threats we thought belonged exclusively to us were actually shared problems. The visibility we gained helped deepen our understanding of the threats we saw day-to-day and opened our eyes to the sheer volume of threats we were facing as an industry. Through the ISAC, we gained an understanding of the full scope of the threats in the retail supply chain—from supplier, to manufacturer, to retailer.

Sharing information among competitors is one of the biggest roadblocks perceived in an ISAC relationship. It comes down to one simple fact: security threats are a shared problem. We are all members of the same ecosystem. If we can work together to formulate solutions that provide better protection for customers and stop security threats, that is a win for the industry. It is not about competition; it is about building a unified approach to protecting our customers. We are stronger together.

The challenge of the ISACs is to provide timely, relevant, and actionable information to the members of the ISAC. Threat intelligence feeds are available from vendors to be ingested into security tools and can be matched with an organization's own telemetry gleaned from analyzing external connections to the company network. The challenge of these feeds is that they can lack context and not be applicable to the user's environment, taking analyst time to sort out. The feeds can include domains, hashes, and IP addresses known to relate to malicious botnet activity and could be used to blacklist the connection requests coming from those potentially malicious sources. Because these IP addresses move around, the information needs to be near real-time or the stale information may have a limited value. The information can also be compared with firewall and Domain Name System logs to determine if an attack has occurred, and then, the attack can be subsequently triaged. Feeds - free, purchased, or obtained as the result of a membership with an ISAC and may include information originating from open source, honeypots/deception technology, Dark web, scanning engines, malware processing and human intelligence of planned actions. Some vendors aggregate these feeds into platforms and perform additional research examining different criminal forums, blogs, and code repositories. Threat hunting uses manual and automated procedures to discover security incidents through leveraging various forms of threat intelligence information, data analysis tools, and technical ability.

As the ISACs emerge in the retail, health-care, legal, and other sectors, these groups are primarily focused within their sectors and there is limited sharing and coordination across the ISACs. As more ISACs emerge and companies are more willing to share their information with others and between ISACs, the capture of threat intelligence will become more useful across industries. Companies are structured to compete with product, service, and revenue; however, the cybersecurity problem is too large, and the enemy is too large to not coordinate together and share for the public good. The international messaging service for the financial institution Society for Worldwide Interbank Financial Telecommunication (SWIFT), headquartered in Belgium formed to communicate regarding cross-border payments between financial institutions, instructed banks to share information about hacks using SWIFT messages following the $81 million theft from the Bangladesh central bank in 2016. SWIFT released a Customer Security Controls Framework (CSCF) in April 2017 as part of the Customer Security Program (CSP), requiring members to attest compliance by the end of 2017 (subsequently updated with clarifying guidance, adding mandatory and advisory controls with mandatory compliance attestation by the end of 2019). The framework not only required the standard prevention and detection requirements, but also focused on "share and prepare" as being part of the community, as well as introducing a SWIFT ISAC global information sharing portal to "share detailed and technical intelligence to allow the community to protect itself, to take mitigating actions, and to defend against further attacks." This example of information sharing with a sector or technology is likely to see more activity and formation of more threat intelligence centers, threat feeds, and adoption of threat intelligence platforms in the future. In March 2018, Swift issued a release stating, "The industry has a shared interest in cyber fraud and cybersecurity, so it (will be) important to be able to share information about the risks. For example, the FS-ISAC weekly communications have got people talking. This type of sharing is the next frontier—every organization should not have to figure this out on their own." Well said. CISOs and their threat analysts need to become engaged in a threat intelligence sharing activity as a participant contributor.

DevSecOps

Agile development has required changing the mindsets of developers from the waterfall techniques of the past where the system implementation would be mostly designed and delivered a few years out. Agile development has changed this by iterating the delivery of the functionality and making development and operations activities more seamless. Information security has still been an afterthought in many of these environments where the pressure is to develop and make available new functionality quickly. Security must be integrated within the processes in a way that does not significantly slow the processes down, or time-to-market will win out. When there is a security concern that develops after the code is released, this increased cost and rework results. The CISO and the security team need to work with the developers to integrate security within the ecosystem, or they will be left behind the development. To be successful, Gartner recommends ten tips for integrating with the development process to form an effective DevSecOps:

1. Adapt security testing tools and processes to the developers, not the other way around.
2. Do not try and eliminate all vulnerabilities during the development phase.
3. Focus first on identifying and removing known vulnerabilities.
4. Do not expect to use traditional dynamic application security testing and static application security testing methodologies without making changes.
5. Train all developers on the basics of secure coding, but do not expect them to become security experts.
6. Adopt a security champion model and implement a simple security requirement gathering tool.
7. Eliminate the use of known vulnerable components at the source.
8. Secure and apply operational discipline to automation scripts.
9. Implement strong version control on all code and components.
10. Adopt an immutable infrastructure mindset.

Development is still the Wild West in many organizations, and security needs to become part of the process to become successful. The International Organization of Standards (ISO) has released a secure development life cycle standard (ISO/IEC 27034-1), which could be a good starting point for organizations to place some structure on the development life cycle to include security. The battle is not new; however, including security in the automation processes and implementing the steps above can serve to limit the resulting security vulnerabilities. The earlier security can be put into the life cycle with incentives for adoption the better. The application teams need to be communicating with the security teams and vice versa. There is benefit to both teams by increasing their capabilities, with security teams understanding more about the development process and the developers understanding more about creating secure code. Tossing code over the wall between development, operations, and security teams also leads to inefficiencies and sets up unnecessary barriers impacting time to market and product quality. If the security team does not get involved with DevOps and create DevSecOps, the risk is faster code being generated without adequate security, increasing the rate of vulnerabilities. Integration into the life cycle reduces the need for infrastructure experts and expert security staff to resolve the issues, again reducing the cost and increasing system availability.

REBECCA HEROLD: CHANGE CONTROLS ARE MORE NECESSARY THAN EVER

Co-Founder and President, Privacy Professor and SIBMUS, LLC

In recent years, I have helped many clients whose programming teams caused business disruptions, some severe and quite costly, because of the changes they made in the program code of their online service, or in their operating systems. The IT folks who made these changes, and many of my other clients, have expressed the opinion that they can just code something and plop it out into production, without testing and then try to tell me that is "agile programming." No, it is not. It is unsecure and, quite frankly, lazy programming. And most of my clients that are startups, mobile apps developers and cloud service providers did not have any change control processes in place. Too many of them started their business with basic programming knowledge, but absolutely none of the very important knowledge necessary for secure programs that will not fail, cause disruptions, or even leak personal information and cause privacy breaches. I have often covered the importance of program change control management over the years, and I want to emphasize it again here because as important as it is, it typically does not get the attention it deserves. The many continuing exploits of online applications show there is still work to be done around application program change controls. Every organization must implement change control procedures to consistently make the following:

■ Changes involving new program code implementations
■ Installations of new code into your existing environment
■ Changes within the existing codes to change, improve, etc., a feature or process
■ A fix to a discovered error or bug
■ Technical changes and enhancements
■ Emergency changes
■ Configuration and parameter code changes.

Some Tips

■ Be sure to look beyond just the documentation and the system's capabilities within any change control system; also, observe how well individuals are following those procedures.

■ Technology tools are necessary and good to support information security and privacy, but they cannot, by themselves, provide effective safeguards for business information. Well-written and correct code is necessary for ensuring incidents and breaches do not occur.

■ Personnel must receive effective training and ongoing awareness communications to know not only what they must do to build program code to safeguard information, but also why.

■ Noncompliance with change control policies and procedures must be consistently enforced, or the policies and procedures will not be effective.

Privacy/Data Protection

The privacy/data protection issues covered extensively the *Data Protection and Privacy* chapter notwithstanding, the emphasis on the information captured and analyzed by companies will undergo increasing scrutiny in the future. The Facebook and Cambridge Analytica issue made public in 2018 regarding the access to private Facebook information on millions of Facebook users, allegedly used to identify the personalities of American voters to influence their voting behavior, highlights the concern over who should have access to our information. Because of these efforts, the CEO of Facebook was faced with hours of congressional hearings, outrage by consumers, and many questioning the practice. Transparency and appropriate use will be the key question for companies, and for individuals, the key question will be the amount of information an individual is willing to give up and their awareness of the extent of the information they are giving up obtaining the service. Regulations and enforcement will need to evolve, as today much is left up to the companies and their privacy practices as stated in the privacy notice and internal privacy policies. Expect to see more regulations and fines in the future, as organizations are made examples to discourage overreaching practices. As more and more information becomes monetized through data analytics, more applications are moved to the cloud, and the issue will become more challenging to determine where the information is and who is performing what analysis on it.

Increased Cloud Migration—Including Security Services

A 2017 annual study on cloud adoption by McAfee indicated that hybrid cloud adoption grew by 3X over the prior year, from 19% to 57% of organizations surveyed; in 15 months, 80% of all IT budgets would be committed to cloud solutions;

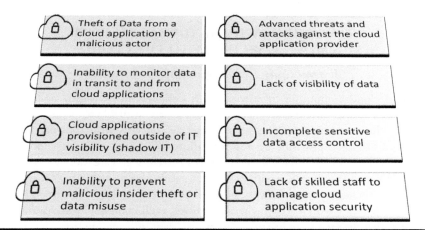

Figure 4.7 Cloud cybersecurity concerns to mitigate. (From *Navigating a Cloudy Sky*, 2018, McAfee.)

73% of companies would move to a software-defined data center within 2 years; and 49% of businesses are delaying cloud deployment due to a cybersecurity skills gap. The relevant takeaway from this study is not the actual numbers as much as the "cloud trajectory"—in other words, the increase in the cloud adoption, while at the same time being slowed by the lack of cybersecurity expertise. Customer experience is driving a cloud first strategy at many organizations.

There is still a lack of trust with the public cloud, albeit the chart shows those numbers are dropping. This does not mean that there are not issues with the cloud, as shown in Figure 4.7.

As the infrastructure matures and organizations can control the authentication, encryption, and application control within the cloud, organizations will become more comfortable with placing the data in the cloud. The herd mentality is also at play here, whereby the rest of the herd is moving to the cloud due to the speed to market, ability to scale, difficulty finding and retaining local resources, reduction in capital investment, and increased security capabilities than a small to midsize organization can deliver. The promise of economies of scale is clearly available, and the key impediment being able to trust the service provider is delivering the services contracted for. Service providers are building this trust, and the migrations to the cloud can be expected to increase.

Organizational Focus on Vendor Risk Management and Supply Chain

Organizations are accustomed to managing themselves from the inside-out; in other words, investments are normally directed at "getting our own house in order."

STEVE ORRIN: WHY HARDWARE MATTERS IN MOVING SECURELY TO THE CLOUD

Federal Chief Technologist, Intel Corporation

Shared cloud computing infrastructure is designed to be highly agile and flexible, transparently using whatever resources are available to process workloads. However, there are security and privacy concerns with allowing unrestricted workload provisioning and migration. Whenever multiple workloads are present on a single cloud server, there is a need to segregate those workloads so that they do not interfere with each other, gain access to each other's sensitive data, or otherwise compromise the other's security or privacy. Imagine two rival companies with workloads on the same server; each company would want to ensure that the server can be trusted to protect their information from the other company. Similarly, a single organization might have multiple workloads that need to be kept separate because of differing security or regulatory requirements for each workload and/or its data. Another concern is that workloads could move from cloud servers located in one country to servers located in another country. Each country has its own laws and regulations for data security, privacy, and other aspects of data handling (e.g., data retention). Geolocation can be accomplished in many ways, with varying degrees of accuracy. Often, the traditional geolocation methods are not secured and are enforced through management and operational controls that cannot be automated and scaled.

These challenges around workload policy/separation and geolocation were the motivation behind the industry collaboration to develop a solution for implementing trusted cloud architectures and enabling geolocation controls and attestation in collaboration with the National Institute of Standards and Technology (NIST). NIST published the IR7904 "Trusted Geolocation in the Cloud" in 2015, which documents a reference architecture and guidance for improving the cloud security by establishing an automated hardware root of trust method for enforcing and monitoring geolocation restrictions for cloud servers. A hardware root of trust is an inherently trusted combination of hardware and firmware that maintains the integrity of the platform security measurements and the geolocation information. This information is accessed by management and security tools using secure protocols to assert the integrity of the platform and confirm the location of the host and is then used for policy controls, enforcement, compliance, and audit.

When a company selects a security control framework such as COBIT 5 for information security, ISO 27001/2, NIST Cybersecurity Framework, CIS Controls, or a combination proprietary framework from an external consultant, the primary focus in the past has been on the internal systems and the security controls within these systems. With the increased migration to the cloud and the use of Software as a Service applications where the security controls are primarily provided by an external vendor, the focus has shifted. The rise in breaches, particularly those involving third-party vendors, has created an increased concern and focus with those vendors hosting systems and information or connected to the systems. Companies are often surprised when an analysis of the number of vendors and products used by the various departments is more than retained in the application inventory. This is often the result of Shadow IT with departments purchasing software outside of the IT governance practices. Procurement is not always engaged in the purchasing and contract process, also leading to application products and services with weak or nonexistent contracts. The 2017 Verizon Data Breach Report indicated 27% of the security breaches were discovered by third parties. The 2013 Target Breach where a third party was breached (HVAC vendor) caused many programs to examine third-party security more seriously and issue questionnaires. Third-party services such as BitSight and Security Scorecard examine the Internet-facing and known company vulnerabilities obtained through their sources to provide a relative rating of the security of the organization from an external viewpoint. Banks have been issuing questionnaires containing hundreds of questions modeling security requirements based on the regulations for several years, with large financial institutions dedicating resources solely to vendor risk management.

Unfortunately, even with the external products to provide vendor risk management emerging, consensus on "the framework" or "the question set" to be used is several years away. Organizations are struggling with the selection of one of the frameworks, let alone specifying what framework or set of controls other organizations should adopt. The problem becomes very large very quickly. For example, consider an organization has 1,000 suppliers they do business with, from hosting cloud applications, development, exchange information with, or procure products and services from. They send out 1,000 questionnaires to the vendors, as at this stage, they are unsure what information is being retained and need to more accurately determine the risk level. Subsequently, the questionnaire responses reveal that 200 of the vendors are at higher risk, and more detailed questionnaires and follow-up need to be performed. Let us also assume that these 200 suppliers also each have 200 high-risk suppliers they need to send questions to. Now, we have 40,000 questionnaires to provide assurance. Clearly, it is easy to see why this current environment is unmanageable and unsustainable. Digital solutions in the next several years are likely to emerge to address the issue, whereby a central "trusted" source, or repository of information, can be accessed to provide the assurance. An analogy may be found with single sign-on, where a token is passed indicating the user is valid, possibly such a product could minimize the time spent by organizations to provide assurance for the suppliers. If supplier Y is used by X companies, this creates XY questionnaires when only one comprehensive is needed! Of course, aggregating this information has the downside of being a treasure trove of desirable information for hackers as well.

In the meantime, many organizations will continue the manual processes, with leading innovators exploring ways to cut down on this workload where a majority of the questions are the same between issuing organizations, as they are based on similar control frameworks and risk management processes.

JOE MANNING: VENDOR RISK MANAGEMENT— MASTER SERVICE AGREEMENT TERMS

Former Diirector Information Security and Privacy, Crate and Barrel

With the surge of cloud and other service providers handling confidential information, it has become increasingly important to establish InfoSec and Privacy expectations in writing. We established a tracking system to ensure IT, InfoSec and Privacy, Risk, Finance, Legal, and other departments as appropriate approved "ALL" new and renewal agreements. Upon initial discussions with a vendor or service provider, a nondisclosure agreement must be signed by all parties prior to any exchange of confidential or proprietary information. Once an agreement is reached to acquire goods or services, the NDA is generally replaced by a Master Service Agreement, which further protects each party. It has been helpful to establish a "repository" of MSA language for each of the points below, then used that to compare with the draft of the MSA during negotiations, requesting modifications where desired.

- Vendor (aka company) may only use customer information for the purpose of fulfilling the contract. All exceptions must be approved in writing, including using the information anonymously or in aggregate.
- Vendor may retain information only as long as required to fulfill contract unless other retention agreed upon in writing.
- Customer (aka client) owns the information, and the vendor must provide a method to return customer information within 30 days of contract expiration.
- Vendor must disclose additional third parties that may be utilized in fulfillment of transmitting, storing, and processing customer information.
- Vendor must provide attestation of compliance upon request (for PCI or for other attestations for confidential data types).
- Vendor must provide documentation describing information security posture upon customer request, including compliance to industry standards (SAS70, NIST, SANS, ISO, or another acceptable standard).
- Customer reserves right to audit vendor annually or after significant modifications.

- Vendor must maintain an incident response program and notify customer of suspected or actual breach within 24 hours. Breach is defined as unauthorized access, unauthorized disclosure, or corruption of customer information.
- Indemnification clauses define the limits of legal liability.
- Vendor must maintain a cyber-liability insurance policy with acceptable coverage limits.

Vendors may not agree to all MSA requests, but it is better to ask than ignore.

Breaches Will Continue due to a Lack of Fundamentals

Even as the focus has shifted from prevention to detection (i.e., not a matter of if you will get hacked, but when) may be misinterpreted that prevention is no longer as critical. This perspective could not be more wrong, as organizations can avoid a substantial amount of pain by having fundamental controls in place. Do all the users have local administrative rights or are these limited to those needing them and controlled by software to whitelist, blacklist, or graylist applications? Are the users trained to detect phishing emails and has the organization invested in secure email gateways to reduce the likelihood of occurrence? Has the organization identified and segmented critical assets? Are these networks scanned for vulnerabilities frequently? Has a control framework been selected and investment allocated to manage the program? Performing these functions and the others may not prevent a breach; however, they will significantly reduce the attack surface. While public relations will posit breaches as advanced and persistent, I suspect the likelihood for many organizations is that there was some gap in security exploited that was not all that sophisticated.

Suggested Reading

1. Isaac, M. 2012. Mark Zuckerberg on Facebook's Early Days: Go Hard or Go Home All Things D (October 20). http://allthingsd.com/20121020/mark-zuckerberg-on-facebooks-early-days-go-hard-or-go-home/.
2. Gartner News Room. 2017. Gartner Forecasts Worldwide Security Spending Will Reach $96 Billion in 2018, Up 8 Percent (December 17). www.gartner.com/newsroom/id/3836563.
3. Kennedy, B. and Funk, C. 2016. 28% of Americans are 'Strong' Early Adopters of Technology. Pew Research Center (July 12). www.pewresearch.org/fact-tank/2016/07/12/28-of-americans-are-strong-early-adopters-of-technology/.
4. Zwilling, M. 2014. Early Adopters Are Great, But They Aren't Most Customers. Entrepreneur Europe (November 14). www.entrepreneur.com/article/239606.

5. Warren, T. 2016. Tesla has received almost 400,000 preorders for the Model 3. The Verge (April 21). www.theverge.com/2016/4/21/11477034/tesla-model-3-preorders-400000-elon-musk.

6. Nelson, G. 2015. Tesla Meets Model S Production Goal, But Losses Widen Automotive News (February 11). www.autonews.com/article/20150211/OEM/150219951/tesla-meets-model-s-production-goal-but-losses-widen.

7. Wisniewski, M. 2013. Mobile Check Deposit Boom Brings Risks. American Banker (July 11). www.americanbanker.com/news/mobile-check-deposit-boom-brings-risks.

8. Gartner News Room. 2016. Gartner Says By 2020, a Corporate "No-Cloud" Policy Will Be as Rare as a "No-Internet" Policy Is Today (June 22). www.gartner.com/newsroom/id/3354117.

9. Mitchell, J. 2018. How Machine Learning and Other Tech Trends Will Disrupt Cyber Security In 2018. *Forbes* (January 31). www.forbes.com/sites/julianmitchell/2018/01/31/how-machine-learning-and-other-tech-trends-will-disrupt-cyber-security-in-2018/#36c281948009.

10. Five New Year's Resolutions to Help CISOs Improve Enterprise Security in 2018. Security Intelligence (January 2). https://securityintelligence.com/five-new-years-resolutions-to-help-cisos-improve-enterprise-security-in–2018/.

11. Bitcoin USD. https://finance.yahoo.com/chart/BTC-USD.

12. Cao, S. 2018. $500M of Digital Coins Stolen on Japan's Largest Crypto Exchange. *Observer* (January 26). http://observer.com/2018/01/500m-digital-coins-stolen-japans-largest-crypto-exchange/.

13. Bitcoin. Securing Your Wallet. https://bitcoin.org/en/secure-your-wallet.

14. Carmody, B. 2018. 7 Ways Blockchain Will Enable Entrepreneurs in 2018. Inc. www.inc.com/bill-carmody/7-ways-blockchain-will-enable-entrepreneurs-in-2018.html.

15. Meola, A. 2016. Internet of Things in healthcare: Information Technology in Health. Business Insider. www.businessinsider.com/internet-of-things-in-healthcare-2016-8.

16. Gartner, Inc. 2016. Gartner Says By 2020, More Than Half of Major New Business Processes and Systems Will Incorporate Some Element of the Internet of Things. Gartner Newsroom (January 14). www.gartner.com/newsroom/id/3185623.

17. Shaban, H. 2018. Amazon is Issued Patent for Delivery Drones That can React to Screaming Voices, Flailing Arms. The Washington Post (March 22). www.washingtonpost.com/news/the-switch/wp/2018/03/22/amazon-issued-patent-for-delivery-drones-that-can-react-to-screaming-flailing-arms/?utm_term=.dea0a56797b5.

18. Frank, M. 2016. Drone Privacy: Is Anyone in Charge? Consumer Reports (February 10). www.consumerreports.org/electronics/drone-privacy-is-anyone-in-charge/.

19. National Conference of State Legislatures. 2018. Current Unmanned Aircraft State Law Landscape. Blog (February 1). www.ncsl.org/research/transportation/current-unmanned-aircraft-state-law-landscape.aspx.

20. Howell O'Neill, P. 2017. Ransomware is Now a $2 Billion-Per-Year Criminal Industry. Cyberscoop (November 21). www.cyberscoop.com/ransomware-2-billion-bitdefender-gpu-encryption/.

21. Europol. 2017. 2017, The Year When Cybercrime Hit Close to Home. (November 27). www.europol.europa.eu/newsroom/news/2017-year-when-cybercrime-hit-close-to-home.

22. Department Health and Human Services. Fact Sheet: Ransomware and HIPAA. www.hhs.gov/sites/default/files/RansomwareFactSheet.pdf.

23. Los Angeles Times. 2011. Watson Wins 'Jeopardy!' Finale; Ken Jennings Welcomes 'Our New Computer Overlords'. (February 16). http://latimesblogs.latimes.com/showtracker/2011/02/watson-jeopardy-finale-man-vs-machine-showdown.html.
24. Government Publishing Office. 1998. 63 FR 41804- Presidential Decision Directive 63 on Critical Infrastructure Protection: Sector Coordinators. Federal Register Volume 63, Issue 150. (August 5). www.gpo.gov/fdsys/granule/FR-1998-08-05/98-20865.
25. U.S. Department of Homeland Security. 2015. Homeland Security Presidential Directive 7: Critical Infrastructure Identification, Prioritization, and Protection. 1st Ed Dec 17, 2003, last published September 22, 2015. www.dhs.gov/homeland-security-presidential-directive-7.
26. Reuters. 2016. SWIFT Tells Banks to Share Information on Hacks. (May 20). www.cnbc.com/2016/05/20/swift-tells-banks-to-share-information-on-hacks.html.
27. Swift. Customer Security Programme. www.swift.com/myswift/customer-security-programme-csp/programme-description.
28. Swift. 2018. Fraud and Cyber High Alert. (March 19). www.swift.com/news-events/news/fraud-and-cyber-high-alert.
29. The ThreatHunting Project. www.threathunting.net/.
30. MacDonald, N. 2017. 10 Things to Get Right for Successful DevSecOps. Gartner. October 3. www.gartner.com/doc/3811369/-things-right-successful-devsecops.
31. Granville, K. Facebook and Cambridge Analytica: What You Need to Know as Fallout Widens. New York Times (March 19). www.nytimes.com/2018/03/19/technology/facebook-cambridge-analytica-explained.html.
32. Columbus, L. 2017. 2017 State of Cloud Adoption and Security. Forbes (April 23). www.forbes.com/sites/louiscolumbus/2017/04/23/2017-state-of-cloud-adoption-and-security/#7c032bd21848.
33. Goodman, M. 2015. *Future Crimes*. New York. Doubleday/Random House.

STRUCTURE

3

Chapter 5

Cybersecurity Organization Structure

> Order and simplification are the first steps toward the mastery of a subject—the actual enemy is the unknown.
>
> **Thomas Mann, 1875–1955**

The cybersecurity structure within an organization will evolve over time. In recent years, with some organizations newly appointing the Chief Information Security Officer (CISO) role, the CISO may find themselves with a blank slate to be able to build the team necessary to perform the function. This does not mean cybersecurity was not performed in the past at the organization—it just means that the function may not have been provided the level of visibility necessary to develop a program. Each organization will need to structure themselves for what works for that organization, we just do not need to start from scratch. There are functions the CISO needs to ensure that are performed somewhere within the organization, and while they may not initially report to the CISO, the CISO can build the team with a vision to grow the team to add these functions.

The McKinsey 7-S Framework article *Structure Is Not Organization* operated on the premise that structure follows strategy, but was not entirely responsible for the successful execution of the strategy (as the other factors of *shared values, systems, skills, staff,* and *style* were also critical). This does not mean the structure of the organization is not important, as the appropriate functions need to be defined to deliver the strategy. The same is true in the *7-S Framework Applied to Cybersecurity Leadership*, where the functions necessary to drive the cybersecurity strategy must be thoughtfully designed. Otherwise, the strategy may be missing necessary components for the program. This chapter and the following chapter discussing reporting models provide the thought processes for developing the structure to support the strategy.

Learning from Leading Organizations

To understand what leading organizations were doing to meet the information security challenges, the General Accounting Office (GAO) studied several leading organizations in 1998 to determine what activities were performed by organizations that were leaders in information security at the time. As far back as over two decades ago, there was a growing concern over how information was being protected (to ensure privacy) by organizations aggregating information and storing this information electronically. The effort was led by U.S. Senators John Glenn and Fred Thompson, two leaders outside of politics as an astronaut and television actor (Law and Order), and the findings of this study still hold true today for successful security programs. The concepts from this study are worth "updating" and bringing forward as to the implications for today's information security leadership for the 2020s. I like to think of this framework as the foundation for how a house should be built, and if a strong foundation is built to begin with, the house can be updated periodically to be attractive to buyers through the years. Just as building a house needs architects, engineers, electricians, carpenters, plumbers, and so forth—our organizations need certain functions delivered by people dedicated to those roles with those skill sets. Let us examine the five critical functions that the study found

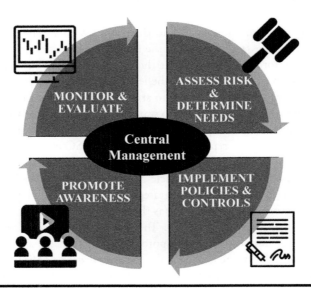

Figure 5.1 Security leadership—learning from leading organizations. (From General Accounting Office Report "Learning from Leading Organizations", 1998.)

were consistently applied, as shown in Figure 5.1, and then update the framework for today's security functions.

Assess Risk and Determine Needs

To many security practitioners, this would appear as a logical, if not obvious first step. However, how many times have we seen a knee-jerk reaction to implement a new policy and procedure or buy a technical product without first understanding what the real business risk is to the organization? Assessing risk, which is provided in more detail in the *Risk Management* chapter, weighs out the cost of implementing the control against the losses that would be experienced by the organization if the risk is not mitigated. The analysis may bear out the fact that it is costlier to implement sufficient security controls than to accept the risk. For example, a commuter train could erect cement barricade barriers at the edges of the train platform, between the rider and the train to protect someone from accidentally falling onto the train tracks before an approaching train. This would be an expensive endeavor to place these barricades along the length of the train. Most of us would find either of these controls as silly or unwarranted, as most people would take personal responsibility to stand behind a yellow line and "mind the gap" while boarding the train. The yellow line would be sufficient and not present a substantial risk. Implementation of a control of this type would be unnecessary and would be viewed by many as an overreaction. People appear to understand they are traveling around a potentially dangerous hazard. Additional controls of signage indicating to "mind the gap," announcements of oncoming trains, and conductors helping with safety add to this control environment. The purpose of the risk assessment is to determine what the adequate level of controls needs to be. Organizations that "best manage security" view the risk assessment as a critical first step in the process.

Implement Policies and Controls

Once the risk is determined, the appropriate policies and controls to support the policies are implemented. Policies are specific to the organization and consider the needs of the organization and support the business operations. Controls that match the risk profile of the organization and reduce the likelihood and impact of a security breach are selected. Policies need to be written so that individuals know what is expected of them. In the case above, there are policies for ensuring there are yellow lines on the platform by the train, policies for announcements proclaiming "mind the gap," and policies for the conductor to ensure safety. Before the National Institute of Standards and Technology (NIST) created the Cybersecurity Framework, the organization produced many useful information security documents free of charge (paid for by U.S. tax dollars), including the excellent special publication (800–53) for Federal information systems for control selection entitled, "Recommended Controls for Federal Information Systems and Organizations."

This reference contains controls for low-, medium-, and high-risk systems and can be applied to nongovernment environments as well. The publication has detailed controls and can be used to formulate policy statements. The publication ISO27002:2013 Security Techniques—Code of Practice for Information Security Management is also an excellent resource for the types of control that should be implemented, albeit this framework does not go to the level of detail that the NIST publication 800–53 does. ISO27002:2013 is designed to be used by organizations intending to select controls in support of implementing an Information Security Management System based on ISO/IEC 27001, implements common security controls, and provides flexibility for the organization to develop their own security management guidelines. COBIT 5 for information security is another framework that could be leveraged to build controls to satisfy this activity. These are just a few of the more widely used control frameworks available.

Traditionally, laws have not been very prescriptive in defining the information security controls needed, as this must be governed by the risk of the system, the technology that is available, scalability, and the resources that are available to the organization. Hence, the assessment of adequate controls is somewhat subjective and depends upon the exposure of the individual making the assessment of different alternatives that have been successfully implemented in organizations with similar sizes and similar issues. Guidance is starting to emerge from the experiences within vertical industries to create "best practices," "good practices," "essential practices," etc. to deal with some of the issues. One organization may determine that they are willing to accept the risk of smartphone protection by requiring a password be implemented on the phone. Other organizations may view this control as insufficient and require that the password also be made a "strong password" by company policy, requiring that the password by eight characters includes at least one uppercase and one lowercase character, along with at least one special character (@, &, $, %, etc.). Another organization may require even stronger controls and require that the password be technically enforced and that the device is remotely "wiped" after three invalid attempts, and the user attests to a smartphone security training if a reset is required. Another organization may require the use of biometrics, such as using a fingerprint touch-id to authenticate before the phone may be accessed, as well as requiring touch-id on each application itself. Another organization may decide that the technology of the Android or iPhone is not appropriate for business usage and is not allowed, while another may yet encourage the use of a non-company-owned device and provide a complete support with the addition of a third-party security product. These perspectives change over time: about 97% of Fortune 500 companies use an iPhone and 98% use an iPad somewhere in their business today, whereas that would have been unheard of when the iPhone was introduced. The perception of the Apple product at the time of introduction was the smartphone, a consumer device without the robust security of Blackberry, at the time the market leader with 63% market share. This example shows how the policies and controls must be re-evaluated periodically to determine whether they still make sense, driven by the risk assessment.

The choices may seem endless for each decision that must be made, further illustrating the importance of performing an adequate risk analysis and then implementing the appropriate controls to mitigate or reduce the risk to an acceptable level. Just as new risks are continually emerging, so are the methods with which to mitigate the risk.

Promote Awareness

Most people want to do the right thing in life; they just need to be aware of what "the right thing" is! If policies and controls are not properly communicated, this step becomes very difficult. Security departments often will draft voluminous policy documents and then wonder why they are not being followed. Individuals cannot be held responsible for policies that they have not seen or understand. Much effort that went into determining the risk and deciding what controls were appropriate similar effort should be made in ensuring that the individuals responsible for executing the policies and procedures understand and are able to implement the controls. Otherwise, nice documents exist, but the security controls are not protecting the information assets as desired.

Monitor and Evaluate

If everything worked well the first time around, monitoring would be unnecessary. Unfortunately, security controls are not implemented once and address the security risk for years without re-evaluation. Threat levels may increase, technology changes, procedures are found to be implemented differently than designed, the business requirements change, etc. Organizations may change, and the person that once was very diligent in performing the control has now left and the new person has not been executing the control as frequently or worse yet, not at all. Controls once performed internally by a relatively constant department of long-term employees with less formal partially documented processes may now be performed by an external third party, or Managed Systems Security Provider (MSSP) with higher turnover and reliance on documented processes. Without proper monitoring to ensure the policy and control are being executed, it may never be discovered that employees were not made aware of the policy change and it was not being practiced consistently.

JONATHAN NGUYEN-DUY: MANAGING THE MSSP

Vice President (VP), Strategy and Analytics, Fortinet

Given the complexities of cybersecurity—from common, opportunistic attacks to advanced campaigns, as well as compliance and staffing challenges—it is easy to understand why so many organizations are using

MSSPs. Here are just a few practical considerations for managing your service provider:

- *Risk management*—MSSP users do not transfer responsibility. The customer is always ultimately responsible for security. Controls and technologies are perishable. Regularly review and ensure your controls are relevant and MSSP services are aligned with controls and compliance requirements.
- *Expectations*—Trade-offs are required with MSSPs as it is a one to many model where standardized technologies and processes are the rule, and custom is the exception, and often expensive. Painstakingly, review services and respective roles and responsibilities. It is critical to understand the volume of alerts and quality of analysis to be provided with clear demarcation of responsibilities. MSS users often encounter unexpected complexity when outsourcing part or all security requirements.
- *Integration*—Relying on MSSPs requires integration with their security monitoring and device management methods and procedures. Using an MSSP does not mean "set and forget it"—it requires a hands-on approach from planning and onboarding to daily operations and finally, separation. Pay special attention to process bottlenecks around detection and incident response. There, both parties must be in sync as the speed and complexity of threats grow. Conduct drills and tabletop exercises with your MSSP, and establish working relationships. The MSSP will appreciate your efforts to work with them, and it will pay dividends when problems occur, and you need fast escalation and attention. I am always surprised by how many customers do not work with their MSSP before an incident.
- *Outcome-based Service Level Agreements (SLAs)*—Align your business outcomes such as application availability, revenue, and productivity, to SLAs. Enhanced risk management and security is what you want when using an MSSP, not a 1/30th monthly recurring charge credit. Demand more than simple availability SLAs. Seek proactive SLAs along with portal-based, automated reporting that can show security and compliance improvements as well as risk reduction for each incremental MSSP spend. While this consideration is just emerging, it will soon become a standard.

Central Management

Leading organizations also recognized that someone needed to be focused on ensuring that these four activities were occurring. Organizations are busy, dynamic institutions that have many competing demands for expenditures and resources. Just as other parts of the organization need management to set direction and ensure that resources are being appropriately used to meet the mission of the business, management is also needed to be focused on managing information security. While there will be components that may be decentralized, typically due to business unit differences, or geographic differences, the overall security program should be unified to provide the sharing of practices across the multiple business units and locations.

This model while appearing simple can be a very powerful way to address cybersecurity management by guiding the program to perform the right activities. Every organization is constrained by the resources available to it—whether time, cost, materials, or labor—and by starting with the risk assessment to determine the real needs, implementing the appropriate controls, communicating those controls, and following up to ensure that the controls are still adequate and properly implemented, the organizations will continually enhance the security of the environment they operate within.

Functions the CISO Should Be Responsible For

If we accept the proposition that leading organizations address each of the five security critical functions in the model previously described and depicted in Figure 5.1, then a useful approach would be to identify the related security activities that must be performed to achieve the due diligence suggested by the model. Organizations may have all these functions reporting to the CISO or may decide to segregate the functions between multiple departments, such as a CISO maintaining responsibility for overall governance-type oversight functions, such as assessing risk, while an information technology (IT) security manager retains responsibility for security violation monitoring. Before delving into the discussion as to what functions should report to whom within the organization, let us describe the core security functions that must be addressed somewhere, as shown in Figure 5.2.

Assessing Risk and Determining Needs Functions

The six security functions that support the assessing risk and determining needs activity in the model are risk assessment and analysis, systems security plan development, internal and external penetration testing, privacy, cyber insurance, and third-party vendor risk management. In other words, performing these six activities well will satisfy this activity within the model. These should be considered functions that need to be performed somewhere within the company. Larger organizations may have whole departments performing risk assessments, where smaller organizations may assign one person to complete the risk assessment and systems

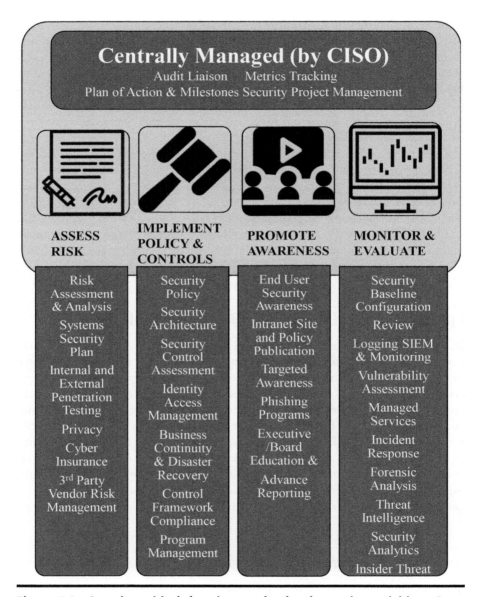

Figure 5.2 Security critical functions and related security activities. (From Author, title in italics, year, city, publisher.)

security plan (SSP) development and may outsource external penetration testing. What is important is that each of these functions is performed by someone, or an important component of information security will be missed, and the controls chosen may not be sufficient to protect the information assets.

Risk Assessment and Analysis

Risk assessment, or also known as risk analysis, is the formal process of reviewing the threats facing the organization; reviewing the likelihood or probability that vulnerability could be exploited; and the impact of the event should it occur. This is a key function of the information security department, and making the risk assessment as accurately as possible is the key to ensuring that money is spent in a productive manner to reduce the security risk. This is also one of the most difficult functions to perform for the information security department, as it can be very challenging to obtain information on what the real risk may be. Risk assessments have the appearance of being objective; however, they are at the core more subjective in nature. For example, what is the risk that a newly drafted first-round National Football League Quarterback will face a career-ending injury during the first 5 years after the draft? Or the likelihood that the quarterback will take the team to the Super Bowl within 5 years? Past statistics may be used, such as their college win and post-championship record; however as noted in many investment recommendations, "past performance does not guarantee future results." How many times have we seen a top prospect having a short career due to an injury or suboptimal performance? A full 47% (24/51) of the Super Bowls have been won by quarterbacks not drafted in the first round, such as Brett Favre of the Green Bay Packers in the second round and Tom Brady of the New England Patriots in the sixth round. These teams made the best risk decision they could. Likewise, sometimes it is very difficult to determine the risk by not having a specific security control in place. Organizations many times do not have the broad perspective to determine what the risk would be and will hire an external consultant to provide an assessment, or gap analysis of the security controls. External consulting organizations, whether they are large Big Four Accounting firms or smaller boutique security firms, can bring the experience gained from multiple assessments at multiple clients into the organization. This is not to suggest that adequate risk analysis cannot be done solely from staff within the organization; however, to leverage the external experience from other organizations, this is one area where external firms are typically engaged as a first step. Once the organization has more experience in performing risk assessments and has a clearer understanding of the threats, vulnerabilities, and controls in place, they may decide to make the risk assessment solely in-house.

CHRIS APGAR, CISSP: SECURITY AND SENIOR MANAGEMENT—BUY-IN IS CRITICAL TO SUCCESS

Adjunct Professor, Apgar & Associates, LLC

I have seen a fair number of health-care industry vendors that have not figured out that finding the same risks year after year is not good when it comes to risk avoidance and keeping their customers. Usually, I run into these situations because there is no solid commitment from the top to incentivize (and fund) enhancements in an entity's information security program. As an example, a software development client I have worked with since 2010 for years promised customers that my client would implement appropriate security measures— even something as basic as policies. I was challenged along the way to keep the attention of senior management. I also found myself attempt to mollify unhappy customers. It took a combination of events to turn the tide and build solid information security initiatives. Now my client is in pretty good shape. In late 2016, the board replaced the CEO. I saw an opportunity to pitch my plan to the new CEO and emphasize that compliance and sound security were more than risk avoidance measures. In the health-care industry, if you are a vendor, you will likely get pressure from your customers to demonstrate sound security measures have been implemented, and if you cannot, your customers may well find yet another vendor. Over the last few years, security has become differentiators in the market—if I have sensitive data and I have a reputation on the line, you, my vendor, will better be able to demonstrate that you are paying attention to security and you are doing it better than the next guy. With that in mind, the new CEO listened. Over the past year and a half, my client has gone through a number of changes including implementing a more robust security. At this point, I have had the opportunity to assist my client to successfully survive a Security Operations Center (SOC) 2 Type 1 audit, and now we are in the middle of a SOC 2 Type 2 audit. The key is explain to senior management that this is more than risk avoidance and a cost to the bottom line. It amounts to vendors out there need to differentiate themselves from their competitors and demonstrate they have what it takes to adequately secure their customers' valuable data.

SSP Development

The name "Systems Security Plan" is somewhat misleading, as an SSP is not really a plan at all, but rather a document that provides a snapshot of the security controls at a point in time. The SSP contains the contact information for the system, documents the level of criticality/sensitivity level of the system, describes the business use of the system, defines the system boundaries and system interconnections, and describes the managerial, operational, and technical controls that are in place to protect the information assets contained within the system. Systems may be general support systems, whereby they represent interconnected sets of information resources under the same direct management control that shares common functionality," or they may be major applications that are defined because they require special attention due to risk and magnitude of harm resulting from loss, misuse, or unauthorized access or modification of information in the application."

Developing an SSP is much more than just a documentation exercise, as the process of creating the plan brings clarity to the information system, the boundaries, and how it is protected. In medium to large organizations, a common answer when asking people about specifics of the computing environment or security controls is, "I don't know." The larger the organization, the more specialized the knowledge is across knowledge workers (i.e., information security, mid-range infrastructure, network, application development, mobile platforms, cloud processing, etc.), and the more this type of response should be expected. Individuals in different areas know their piece of the puzzle and are not necessarily expected to know what is going on in the rest of the organization. For example, the firewall administrator on the network team may know what firewalls are in place, what ports are open, and what baselines are applied, but may or may not know how often the firewall logs are reviewed by the security network monitoring team reporting to the IT security operations manager, or what types of events are being monitored. So, whether the organization views the development of the SSP document as purely a documentation exercise, or whether it is viewed as an opportunity to obtain clarity around the security controls, will determine the ultimate value to the risk assessment process.

Internal/External Penetration Testing

Ethical penetration testing provides some comfort, or discomfort, that the security controls intended to block external entry into the systems are functional and working as designed. These are typically performed minimally on an annual basis, usually in conjunction with an overall risk assessment. Penetration testing is also typically done by an external organization, as most organizations do not have the resources available to keep up with the latest tools and attacks that may be used to gain unauthorized access from an external source. However, larger institutions are standing up Red Teams these days to perform more frequent internal ethical hacking to discover holes in the network and to provide insight into whether the controls have been implemented as planned. The value of external penetration tests is subject for debate, as it shows at one point in time the controls that a skilled attacker may be able to circumvent. Since organizations do not have the resources to spend to be 100% secure, it is likely with the budgets of more security departments that the attacker will find some way to infiltrate the organization. Technical means using a step-by-step procedure to locate weaknesses through the running of foot printing and reconnaissance tools, and the use of social engineering (i.e., pretending to be someone from the help desk to obtain information or entering the building and plugging into an open LAN jack in a conference room) are both used to attempt entry. Odds are the penetration test that will reveal one or more vulnerabilities within the environment. Security managers are often required to have penetration testing performed at least once a year to meet a compliance regulation or may use penetration testing as a method to raise visibility to security vulnerabilities to obtain more resources or funding to reduce the risk.

Staffing a Red Team function and keeping up with the required training within an organization may be cost prohibitive; however, this is a growing trend, driven by increased regulation beyond the financial sector for in-house testing. Red Teams typically partner with an external specialized firm adept at ethical hacking. Where this was once viewed as primarily a solely external activity performed by consultants, more companies are building these teams internally, leveraging the skills of ethical hackers to perform simulated advanced persistent threat–type attacks against components of the applications or infrastructure.

Cyber Insurance

In recent years, cyber insurance has been added to organizations as a method to mitigate some of the financial impacts in the event of a breach. Cyber insurance is not a substitute for good security practices, just as buying car insurance does not mean that one can drive recklessly because some of the costs will be covered in the event of an accident. The global market is expected to grow 28% between 2016 and 2022 to $14 billion globally, with 70% of the current products purchased by large companies (coverage of $1 billion or more) where brand damage could be significant. North America accounts for 87% of the policies written today; however, with increased regulation in the European Union and significant increases in ransomware attacks in the Asia-Pacific, these areas could experience high growth rates. Cyber insurance also has provisions that may deny the claim, such as the requirement that laptops be encrypted, or the policy will not cover the damages. There is normally a minimum threshold by which the company will be responsible for damages (i.e., analogous to the auto insurance deductible) and limits set on the coverage.

The cyber insurance function is noted here within the CISO functional area because the CISO most likely will be the one initiating the conversation around cyber insurance within the organization, possibly prompted from the board of directors' inquiries as an option to mitigate risk. More than likely, the contracting and execution of cyber insurance will be carried out by the department responsible for company general liability insurance, legal counsel, or a risk-oriented area. However, the CISO needs to recognize that there will be involvement to demonstrate the security controls to reduce the premium, such as being able to demonstrate compliance with a security framework or regulation. Within the cybersecurity team, there should be an individual responsible for liaising with the other departments to determine the right level of coverage for the organization.

Vendor Risk Management

The *Emerging Technologies and Trends* chapter highlighted this growing area of concern for cybersecurity departments. Not only must the organization ensure the internal controls are sufficient and operating effectively, with the amount of information being outsourced, system interconnections with external business partners, and the prevalence of cloud-based software, it is imperative that the CISO dedicates resources to ensure vendor management risks are adequately understood and risks mitigated according to the organizational appetite. There will be contracting, purchasing, and legal department responsibilities outside of the cybersecurity team; however, the team needs to have a designated person or team responsible for managing the external risk.

SUMMER CRAZE FOWLER: MANAGING THIRD PARTY RELATIONSHIPS (EXTERNAL DEPENDENCIES)

Technical Director, Cybersecurity Risk and Resilience, Carnegie Mellon University Software Engineering Institute CERT Division

The CISO role of today looks very different than the role of yesterday, and we can guarantee that it will continue to evolve as technology and innovation advance. There are many articles written about the skills required for a successful CISO, and almost all of them correctly note technical competence is still an obvious requirement. However, strategic thinking, communication skills, and a mind for metrics are shown as at least or even more essential skills for the CISO. Another skill that is often overlooked is the ability to manage third party relationships. The CISO role is no longer solely about protecting company data that is housed in an on-prem, company-managed data center. The CISO of today and the future must treat third party relationships as another asset that requires identification, prioritization, and assignment of cybersecurity requirements for confidentiality, integrity, and availability (CIA). These relationships are called external dependencies and are defined at Carnegie Mellon University as entities that have access to, control of, ownership in, possession of, responsibility for, or other obligations to assets internal to the organization. These include vendors that are part of the supply chain (e.g., sources of hardware or software components), those that provide a service (e.g., cloud service providers), and those that provide a capability or resource (e.g., internet service provider). External dependencies are formalized through service level agreements (SLAs), which ITIL defines as a "formal, negotiated document that defines the service being offered to a customer." Three essential ways that a CISO can effectively manage the risks associated with external dependencies are 1) to establish and maintain CIA requirements for external dependencies, 2) to include CIA requirements in the SLA, and 3) to monitor performance of the external dependency against the SLA. The CISO must understand contents and limitations of the SLA with all external dependencies—this is a critical aspect of managing the cybersecurity risks of the organization! SLA development, monitoring, and management is an increasingly important responsibility for every CISO.

Implement Policies and Controls Functions

Security Policy Development

Security policy development is covered extensively in another chapter. Suffice it to say that without a formal, documented information security policy, the organization has no assurance that there is a common set of rules or practices that can be depended upon. The information security policy is the most visible document that the information security department creates. The document is necessary to guide the actions of everyone with respect to information security and needs to be easily available and read by everyone.

Security Architecture

Security architecture provides the security research and technical review of information security products to ensure that the appropriate security tools are purchased to solve the right problems. There are different methods to protect the environment, such as deciding between one vulnerability scanner over another. One may have more robust reporting features, while the other may be more accurate, delivering fewer false positives and representing more value to the organization. Likewise, security architecture needs to be considered when purchasing products to ensure that they are compatible with the existing products that are already in use. The purchase of an Identity Management system running on a Unix platform may not have interfaces with the Windows-based help desk ticketing system and require custom coding to make the system operational. Alternatively, the product may come bundled with an internal ticketing system that may not be robust. The goal of security architecture is to define a set of compatible products and processes to support the security controls that are necessary to mitigate the risks discovered in the risk assessment.

Security Control Assessment

If the risk assessment is the brain of the security program, the security controls are the heart. Keeping the security controls flowing through the organizational veins on a continuous basis provides the protection needed. Security controls can be divided into three primary classifications: managerial, operational, and technical. Controls should be assessed on an annual basis at a minimum and, in practice, are examined much more often by internal and external auditors. A good practice is to review all controls annually and further test one-third of the controls each year. Processes and technologies rarely stay static year over year and should be tested when changed. Regulations may have their own time frame for control review, which should be minimally adhered to.

Identity and Access Management

This function is typically a department on its own due to the size of the staff required to administer the function and the focus being primarily operational in nature. This area ensures that logon IDs are created, and access is appropriately authorized by management and provisioned to the end user. Organizations that are more mature have embraced automation of the ID creation, whereby access is then requested based upon a profile (set of predefined accesses for a job function or role vs. an individual need) and is automatically provisioned. The benefit of this approach is the speed at which requests can be filled, as once the electronic approvals are received from the manager; the system is performing the provisioning work. These products have been around since the early 2000s, and while they are maturing, applications typically require custom coding to provide the automation, which can be very expensive. These implementations can cost well into the millions with customization, placing them out of reach for small- to medium-sized companies. Short of purchasing a product, simplified solutions using electronic forms and email can be created at a relatively low cost to reduce the workflow time to manage the access administration. This function is the function which most people think of when they think of information security. Increasingly, this function is being challenged with finding ways to lower costs and perform the same work with fewer resources, as this area represents an operational, nonstrategic overhead cost to the business.

Even with the challenges of having the proper Identity and Access Management (IAM) tool set within a company, the real challenge is maintaining accountability with the end user's managers to ensure they only have access to applications needed to perform their jobs and identifying a business application owner or data owner to ensure the application accesses granted are well documented and understood by those managers assigning the access rights. Since a typical organization has 1000's of applications in use, this can be a daunting task and assigning owners can be a challenge. Furthermore, discovery of cloud-based Software as a Service applications requires additional tools to discover the external applications obtained by individual users outside of the IT department (Shadow IT). IAM is further complicated by systems with many different roles and permutations or combinations of access that are not clearly understood by the business manager taking responsibility for the system. Monitoring of these activities beyond update access may also be required with increased privacy regulations of sensitive data, leading to even further investment in security analytics to determine who has accessed the information. Each of these ventures adds to the cost of managing the infrastructure. Firms should consider the costs of onboarding new applications and users and strive to move towards a standard model for managing the applications vs. utilizing the individual onboarding mechanisms of each individual application to minimize the cost.

NAIDEN NEDELCHEV: IAM NIGHTMARE

Experienced CISO

It was in the early days of a promising new technology that came with the assurance to deliver the key to cybersecurity heaven, to provide the means of governance for everything access control related, reduce IT workload, facilitate business processes, and so on where I learned a valuable lesson. At the end of 2003 and early 2004, I launched an enterprise-wide project aiming to deploy a full-scale IAM solution in support of an employee onboarding program and a logical access management process. Many first-rate professionals combined their efforts, fully supported by management in a forecasted 1-year project that later turned into 3+ years of painful effort to achieve a minimal level of acceptable results. It was not for lack of understanding the difference between identities and accounts, nor was it the endless coding and development efforts that became additional action items to the day-to-day operational plans. Neither was it the constant changes in the company's organization nor the introduction of new technologies, although many of these and other factors had a significant impact on the project work. What was not considered was the fact that IAM was nothing else but a concept at that time, not a science, which all vendors were reading in their own way. Instead of automating a business logic that was fit to the business according to the opinion of all process stakeholders, the team was forced to revise and continuously adjust to the evolving understanding of the vendor as to what IAM is and how it should be implemented. And the lesson out of this to me was as follows: Do not over-trust a vendor no matter how famous it is, and no matter how flexible a solution claims to be, it will never be 100% compatible with your environment so be prepared to change if you want to take 100% out of it. To be completely correct, I must say that before selecting the solution, the decision-making process had gone through all the phases and good practices, including a comparison of several products, documentation of a base set of functional and nonfunctional requirements, full formal description of the activities at all levels, as well as an assessment of short- and long-term direct and hidden costs. None of this helped in avoiding the nightmares of development, implementation, and support of a product and technology that was not mature enough to be developed favorably to support the business. Fortunately, these times have passed, and the IAM products that are now available on the market offer significantly more business-oriented rather than technologically dictated functionality.

Business Continuity and Disaster Recovery

Business continuity provides the analysis as to whether the business can sustain operations in the event of a disaster, whereas disaster recovery is largely thought of as bringing the IT resources back online in the event of a disaster. The level of maturity of these two areas supports the business resilience, or the ability to be up and running quickly after an incident. The world has no shortage of disasters, whether it is an East Coast power grid blackout, flooding in North Dakota, earthquakes in Japan, oil spills in the Gulf of Mexico, the closing of European airports due to volcanic ash, or the collapse of major bridge in Minnesota. Recent years have added massive forest fires and mudslides in California and hurricanes damaging Florida, Texas, and the Caribbean. A malfunction at two hospitals in 2018 devastated families as the storage tanks containing thousands of frozen embryos fell below the minimum acceptable temperature and human error or a technical malfunction may have been involved. Each disaster brings new attention to business continuity/disaster recovery practices. The business continuity and disaster recovery teams need to exercise tests each year to ensure that the computer systems can be brought up in a remote location. They also conduct mock tests with different departments to ensure their business continuity plans are still accurate and, with lead emergency crisis management teams, made up of senior management to ensure that the organization can react to a crisis or unexpected event. For example, if there are blizzard conditions near the call center, should the call center close? Will call center employees be able to work from home and provide the same level of service? Should the work shift to another, geographically different location to handle the calls? How will people get to work if the offices remain open? Who makes the decision and based upon what information? All these questions would be answered by the business continuity and disaster recovery function. This function would also create business impact assessments to determine the amount of time the company could afford to be without the information. They would also, with business participation, prioritize the systems in the order they needed to be brought back online.

Each of these functions contributes towards defining the requisite controls to protect the information system. Due to the different skills required in each of the control areas, as well as the diverse interest areas, it is also likely in medium- to large-sized organizations that different individuals are performing each of these functions. For example, security policy development requires the ability to translate technical jargon into communications that the nontechnical end user can understand. Likewise, the business continuity and disaster recovery areas require the ability to work with management and understand where their business needs may not be met in the event of a disaster, as well as manage the technical ability to bring up the system operating environment and coordinate end-user testing to ensure the functionality is present.

The ransomware exposure with events, such as WannaCry and Petya/Not Petya, has created a greater awareness around the importance of business continuity and disaster recovery planning. These events serve as a reminder that the threat to the information assets is not just the result of a natural threat such as a fire, flood, or hurricane. The necessity for a good backup and recovery program can also easily be justified by the need to recover digital assets quickly to bring up the systems. Without adequate tested plans in place, the only alternative may be to pay the attackers and hope the information can be "unlocked"—not a strategy that would pass the due diligence test.

Control Framework Compliance

The arguments are plenty for "compliance does not equal security." This should not be misinterpreted to say that we can ignore the compliance frameworks, to the contrary. A better way to view them is that they are "necessary but insufficient" to ensure appropriate security. They become the starting point by which holistic security programs are built and combined with appropriate risk analysis and proper implementation of controls to meet the threats to the organization's systems and assets—they can become necessary *and* sufficient. Therefore, it is only prudent that the CISOs ensure that the organization is tracking compliance to the chosen framework to (1) understand the current state of security, (2) implement plans to increase the maturity level, and (3) provide a communication tool for the organization. The tracking may take the form of using more expensive governance, risk, and compliance tools, or using tools as simple as a spreadsheet or database to track compliance.

ROLAND CLOUTIER: CRITICAL CYBER ASSET PROTECTION PLANNING—LEARNING CONCEPTS AND OPERATIONAL IMPERATIVES FOR PROTECTING WHAT NEEDS TO BE PROTECTED

Staff VP, Global CISO, Automatic Data Processing, Inc (ADP)

All things are not created equally. Since the beginning of our careers in protection, we have always heard the requirement to "protect the crown jewels" by our bosses, and our business. They were not wrong. But the practical side of determining "what" needs to be protected and "how" has been a convoluted maze of academics, taxonomies, frameworks, and inconsistencies. From risk ranking to risk assessments and from secure enclave to the digital moat, our education and on-the-job training have enabled us to learn to prioritize and protect but have left a gap in educating us on a better way to operationalize a mature and consistent capability. A Critical Asset Protection Program (CAPP) helps prioritize, evaluate, protect, and deliver a relevant and effective business operation protection program.

Five Critical Elements of Your CAPP Life Cycle are as follows:

1. A well-formulated integrated risk program that draws expertise, resources, and ideas from a variety of areas such as cyber-risk, IT risk, audit, compliance, and Enterprise Risk Management (ERM) is the first component necessary to deliver a CAPP. From critical asset identification, risk evaluation, and prioritization, straight through to risk tracking and reporting; if you cannot measure it, track it, or report it, it will never work.
2. Next is what "it" "is". What is an asset? Is it a computer, a network, a piece of data, or an integrated set of systems, networks, applications, and data that makes up your crown jewel? Whatever it is, you must have a documented mechanism that provides logical and physical identification of those assets, clear data mapping, and validation of critical configurations and management information. To be clear, you have to know what you are protecting. If you do not know what it is, where it is, or how it works, all of the technology resources spent on it will be woefully mismanaged.
3. Next, standards matter. By applying a standard of testing for whatever type of asset it is, you ensure a consistency of your approach. This demands a checklist approach to the potential of human failure. Whether it is pen testing and code testing, data loss prevention (DLP) scanning, red teaming, architecture evaluation, threat modeling, BCP/DR validation, client-side access reviews, or identity access verification assurance, just do it EVERYTIME! Create a list of required tests or processes by asset type, and make sure they are followed.
4. Next, remediation. You will find bad things, and yes, they will need to be fixed. Some of these things are as simple as filling in a business or IT change request, while others will require a full-on business case with funding and business buy-in. Make sure you take all of your findings, work with your integrated risk groups, and validate risk issues against the risk appetite of your organization. If warranted, drive remediation as a critical part of your risk program. Assign project managers, executive sponsors, and due dates, and make sure that CAPP remediation items are tracked "more special" than your everyday risk.
5. Your last focus area is monitoring. If you identify your CAPP, evaluate it, and fix every known issue, it will not make any difference if it is attacked and you fail to defend it. Make sure that CAPP assets are treated as truly critical and your monitoring platform, operations, and response protocols are aligned to it. CAPP alerts should sound bells and whistles that other issues do not and force the attention where

needed. Additionally, your analysts and responders should have special protocols for handling incidents associated with CAPP assets, and your monitoring capabilities and response procedures should be tested accordingly.

ROME WAS NOT BUILT IN A DAY

Once you deliver a CAPP service to your business, your next level of maturity should be automation. It is not only helpful in any normalized process for operational sustainability but also helpful in many other areas. The use of scripts, data aggregators, and automation platforms will enable speed, allow for you to accomplish more throughout a calendar year, and provide a baseline in quality and delivery assurance. Additionally, it will allow you to collect better data and create security business intelligence capabilities needed for better reporting, metrics, and decision making. Finally, automation will allow you to focus precious resources on more critical and analytical tasks rather than mundane manual efforts such as data collection and controls verification.

If done right, a CAPP can be one of the most impactful services you deliver to your business. Reporting, scoring, and asset status allow you to educate, inform, and involve your business in their own security issues. A well-executed and repeatable CAPP can make the difference between protecting the right thing, or not.

Promote Awareness Functions

The goal of promoting awareness is to ensure that the security policies and procedures are available to those beyond the information security department. Everyone in the organization should be able to locate them. A random test asking questions about the security policy across the organization would reveal how effective the communications are. Many organizations put much effort into the development of information security policies, only to see them not followed because of a lack of communication. Timely security incidents or currents news items can be leveraged in a subtle way to highlight the existence of internal security policies.

EDWARD AMOROSO: EDUCATING SENIOR MANAGEMENT IN CYBERSECURITY

CEO, Tag Cyber, LLC

In 1985, I got my first inkling of how sloppy security practices can make employees feel bad. Here is what happened: I was a young member of the technical staff in Bell Labs and was making money for the first time in my life. My salary was $27,000, and I felt like Rockefeller. To that end, I was proud of my checkbook, which finally had a nonzero balance in it—and I would keep that darn thing with me all the time, just so that I could glance at my newfound riches. One evening, I forgot to bring my checkbook home from work, leaving it instead in that thin top desk drawer where we stupidly try to hide our most important papers. Anyway, the next morning, I came into work only to find a stern note on my desk from a senior security manager in the company explaining that I was putting the firm at risk by storing my checkbook in my desk. I remember trying so hard to figure out what the actual security risk was with my action. And I was not happy that someone had been going through my desk. It made me feel almost violated, even though I fully understood that the desk was not mine. It was the company's. Now, I suspect I was wrong, but I can tell you that I was super angry, and it affected my work for many months, perhaps even years afterward. My advice: Keep this sort of thing in mind as you deploy security—especially intrusive methods. Always do the right thing from both a security and a people perspective.

End-User Security Awareness Training

In addition to understanding their role and actions to take to protect the information assets under their care, business users need to be able to do two basic actions, in addition to complying with security control practices, with respect to cybersecurity: (1) recognize when an incident occurs or what could cause an incident to occur and (2) where to report the incident when the incident does happen. The business users are the eyes and ears of cybersecurity and a crucial piece in ensuring that security is being administered. Security "awareness" is just that—not the in-depth technical understanding that a security analyst may need for their jobs, but rather an understanding of how they are to handle and protect information entrusted to them. This function ensures that this training is provided prior to any systems access, refreshed and administered at least annually, and supplemented with interim emails, newsletters, awareness campaigns, and so forth.

STEVEN LENTZ: SECURITY AWARENESS THAT WORKS

Director Security, Samsung Research America

The overriding question is: "How to get employees to pay attention to security awareness?" I have tried many ways to get the word across—email phishing tests, email spamming employees, etc. Do any of these actually work? Hardly.

No matter how much you test or email your employees, there will be many who ignore and do what they want. Most security practitioners create presentations that are just facts and bullet points. Most times, especially late in the day, this will bore or put the audience to sleep. So how do you get them to pay attention in order to prevent a serious incident or exposure? For me, I have found a way to grab employee attention right off the bat. I have used this method in presentations for cybersecurity summits in Las Vegas and here in Silicon Valley. So, you ask, "Steve what is it?" Simple. I am very enthusiastic concerning security, but my main three secret weapons are as follows: (1) I always wear a Hawaiian shirt in order to stick out. Everyone knows me, and it helps to remind or trigger employees when they see the shirt, "oh I need to ask Steve about this." Wearing the shirt is a visual aid and a trademark that aids in grabbing attention. (2) I use my dog as the presenter in my slides who also wears a Hawaiian shirt (usually same pattern). Using my boy Hulk grabs the audience's attention IMMEDIATELY. Throughout my presentations, I have Hulk in different poses relevant to the subject. For instance, if talking about keeping your employee badge visible, Hulk states this while wearing his badge. (3) I send out monthly security awareness email bulletins with Hulk having the opening remarks. Most are related to the ever-growing email phishing scams. I receive many kudos because of this from executives and employees. But the overall satisfaction is that weekly I get several emails from employees asking/saying this looks like a phishing email. The plus here is that the employees are actually reading and heeding the security awareness bulletins and they can share with family and friends.

Intranet Site and Policy Publication

The security policies need to be readily accessible by all associates and contractors within the organization. The policies can be posted on the intranet site or made available through policy management software that can track user acknowledgment that they have read, understand, and accept the security policies. Providing the end users with a Google-type search engine is also very useful in delivering security policy content to enable end users to quickly locate information. The shelf may be a good place for an Elf on the Shelf™, who makes sure the boys and girls are behaving before the holidays; however, this is a bad place for a security policy and is less effective than the Elf on the Shelf™.

Targeted Awareness

Delivering the information security message should not be limited to the training sessions and posting of the policies, as the message needs to be continually communicated at all levels. The security department should establish a formal communication plan, whereby different audiences are made aware of the information security requirements. Information can be distributed through participation by a standing agenda item in the manager's meetings, IT steering committees, or by monthly attending a different departmental staff meeting to communicate plans and listen to their issues. Specific technical training should also be provided to those areas in need, such as the server engineer that needs to understand the security settings in active directory, or the network administrator that learns about the audit capabilities for the network firewalls and routers, and messaging/infrastructure team to understand the capabilities of mobile device management software for controlling mobile phone inventory and management. While all users can benefit from the generalized end-user security awareness training, others will need training adapted to their specific needs. Targeted awareness may also take the form of hosting internal events for the IT areas, hosting mechanisms such as an internal DEFCON, providing education, guest speakers, and fun exercises on how hackers penetrate systems. Management and business users could also be engaged by retaining external speakers from international or U.S. government agencies such as the Federal Bureau of Investigation (FBI), Central Intelligence Agency (CIA), National Security Agency (NSA), U.S. Department of Homeland Security (DHS), or an industry group such as the Information Security Forum or Cloud Security Alliance to provide an external company view.

KEVIN NOVAK: INNOVATIVE, FISCALLY RESPONSIBLE WAYS TO TRAIN/BUILD COMMUNITY

Chief Information Security and Technology Risk Officer, Large Financial Services Firm

Not everyone has the time or budget to attend quality, highly technical training, so Kevin Novak, a long-time attendee of DEFCON (one of the original "hacker" conferences), thought to himself: "Many of the people at my firm are extremely technical; why not host our own, private version of DEFCON?" Kevin set the following goals: (1) provide an affordable educational opportunity for high staff, (2) provide a safe venue for team members to demonstrate and hone their skills through speaking/teaching, and (3) provide a venue for team members across varied technical disciplines to socialize and build community. The ground was set. In September 2015, a private version of DEFCON was born. The private event included internal and external speakers and an attacker vs. defender game, hosted by PWC, which pitted teams of attendees against one another in a simulated cyber war-game exercise. The event also included a set of security challenges, similar to DEFCON's "villages," such as lock picking, breaking cryptograms, wireless cracking, packet capture analysis, snap circuits, and "spot the phishing attack." The objective of the conference was not to turn team members into hackers, but rather to provide an enjoyable forum for people to learn fundamentals that they could carry into their day jobs. Following the success of the initial event, the team has hosted several more annual events, each adding a little more to the mix, including consecutively hosting the event across four disparate corporate locations on three separate continents (Northern America, Europe, and Asia). Over the years, the event has hosted talks on hacking Internet of Things devices, hacking mobile phones, container security, threat intelligence, micro-segmentation, blockchain, and digital transformation. In addition to the original list of challenges, the event has added Bluetooth low-energy (BLE) sniffing, breaking out of a kiosk, and the secret room challenge (similar to the now commercialized "room escape" adventures), where teams have to incorporate all the skills they had honed in the previous challenges in order to be successful. The annual event continues to adhere to and meet ALL of the originally stated goals.

Phishing Programs

Conducting phishing campaigns is one of the best additions to security programs in recent years, as these programs have grabbed the attention of users in a way that other programs in the past have failed. Why? Because it showed the users (1) they were vulnerable, (2) these attacks were becoming more sophisticated (i.e., no misspelled words, logos from other sites, more information about a company's style/language reflected in the phish), and most importantly, (3) the users could really benefit from increased education. The phishing programs go beyond "phishing emails" and set up a platform for other modules to be introduced covering more topics such as mobile device security, cloud application use, money transfers, protected personal information, and so forth. Entire security programs can be built using the software generated over the past several years. These programs require staffing to administer, set up the emails, manage the distribution lists, respond to the user questions, track compliance, issue campaigns, etc. Even when many of these functions are outsourced with a vendor, there will be involvement internally to manage the implementation of the software to provide whitelisting (for the company phish to bypass phishing controls), establishment of user lists, communication with the appropriate support teams, and management reporting.

Executive/Board Education and Advance Reporting

Board of directors and executives are increasingly becoming involved at a closer level to cybersecurity issues due to the risk to the organization. Their background and experience with cybersecurity issues may be limited. Tabletop exercises to simulate the actions with boards and executive management to prepare them for a breach should be planned and executed on a periodic (minimally annually) basis. Education concerning the current threats in the news and how our own organizations are prepared for the threat, or what the impact would be to the organization, would be appreciated. These communications can take place as part of a regular process when new threats are in the news and can save time in regularly scheduled management meetings as the executives will already be prepared with the information. This also demonstrates the proactive actions of the CISO and cybersecurity department.

Monitor and Evaluate Functions

The functions below are excellent candidates for the creation of a "Security Operations Center" or SOC team within the information security department. This group provides the oversight for the other areas outside of information security to ensure security is given the appropriate attention. Separating the function provides stronger control through the separation of duties.

Security Baseline Configuration Review

Each computing platform should have a defined security baseline to limit the exposure of exploits. For example, parameters such as password lockout attempts, revision history, or what services should be enabled are set. The security department should ensure that the security configurations are reviewed and monitored on a frequent basis, preferably quarterly at a minimum.

Maintenance of the security baselines typically resides in the operational, infrastructure areas that are responsible for those platforms. It is important that baselines be developed for each platform and are frequently reviewed when new releases of the standards are available. This can be a time-consuming task to ensure that (1) baselines are developed for each operational platform (i.e., Windows, Unix, Mainframe, Resource Access Control Facility (RACF), Oracle, Structured Query Language (SQL) databases, virtualization servers, network devices, desktops, mobile platforms), (2) the baselines are kept up-to-date, (3) they are properly documented, (4) exceptions to the baselines are approved by management and documented, (5) baselines are tested prior to rolling out to production, (6) all devices are monitored and compared to the baseline, (6) a corrective action plan process exists to upgrade to the current baseline if necessary, and (7) quarterly reviews of compliance are conducted. The cybersecurity department is in the best position to provide leadership to ensure that the baselines are updated and applied to the devices within the environment.

The security department can coordinate weekly meetings with the operational areas to review the compliance with the baselines and track the process that is being made. The additional oversight increases the likelihood that security baselines will receive the proper attention. The security department can also play a role in ensuring that changes to the standards the baselines are built upon are communicated to the operational areas in a timely manner.

Logging, Security Information and Event Management, and Monitoring

An organization cannot be sure what attempts are being made to exploit vulnerabilities to access information unless there is an active monitoring program in place. Some organizations do a great job of collecting logs; however, there is no formal log review process in place and the logs are merely saved in the event an investigation is initiated. This can cause undesired events to go undetected, as the reliance then becomes dependent upon some other external stimulus to kick off an investigation. Log monitoring should be a daily event to be effective, even if a subset of the information is reviewed (i.e., administrator privilege access and escalation).

Since log data can be voluminous, security departments will often use a Security Information and Event Management (SIEM) product to aggregate and correlate the log information, a reporting tool, or create scripts to reduce the amount of data that must be reviewed. Logs are reviewed for external infiltration events, administrator access attempts, as well as the review of internal users and excessive login attempts. A threshold of the number of violations should be established, after while follow-up is required. Training can then be provided to the habitual user that is not following information security access policy. Due to the time-consuming efforts in reviewing the log, automation has a large payoff in this area. Many times, the reports produced for the platforms are rudimentary and can be difficult to use unless some automation of the output is created to determine the exceptions.

JASON TAULE: KEEPING UP WITH THE JONES (WHEN YOUR NEIGHBORS ARE BAD ACTORS)

Chief Security Officer/Chief Privacy Officer, FEI Systems

What are others doing is a question many CISOs can expect from their boards. Although benchmarking your program against peers or competitors may have value (especially in highly regulated sectors), it is more important to keep your leadership apprised of new and emerging threats and how the organization is responding. By now, most CISOs are board conversant, and translating the arcane and technical is no longer the issue. The challenge is that despite our best efforts, most of us are still looking in the rearview mirror. Consider that an SIEM/SOC cannot tell us what is going to happen because alerts are based on near-real-time analysis of past activity at best. Even so-called predictive analytics tools still depend on data, which, by definition, is historical. As it happens, I was preparing a presentation for an upcoming conference and had an epiphany. Exploring several deep web marketplaces to research and understand how bad actors were operating, I encountered an individual seeking to purchase exploit code. Nothing new right? Well, this time the threat actor was shopping by Common Vulnerabilities and Exposures (CVE) number. The next morning I shared the CVEs in question with our network security team and learned that we had patched most but not all of our systems. We immediately remediated those outstanding, and good thing we did because several days later, a particularly large ransomware attack began targeting those very holes. I realized then that we do not always have to lock every door and window in the house if we know which one a burglar intends to use. Hopefully, by sharing this insight, others may be able to justify for themselves a trial deployment of a small threat hunting team augmented with a third-party threat intelligence feed (which I highly recommend as a way of addressing the associated language barrier and inevitable ethics questions). In the end, I am not saying we can ignore the basics, merely that with actionable forward-looking Intel we are better equipped to make carefully reasoned and defensible choices in allocating limited resources across our various risk exposures. And in the end, that is what it is all about.

Vulnerability Assessment

Vulnerability assessments are frequently confused with penetration testing, and they represent two different activities. Penetration testing is the practice of attempting to gain entry to the system and typically obtaining higher-level privileges to demonstrate that the information assumed to be protected by the organization could be disclosed, modified, corrupted, or deleted by an unauthorized user outside of the organization. Vulnerability assessments, on the other hand, test for flaws in the system, mainly software and hardware, to determine where the exposures are that could be potentially exploited. The vulnerabilities are usually determined by running software tools (i.e., Tenable's Nessus/Security Center, Tripwire's IP360, Rapid 7) against the computing platform. Individual identifiers are associated with each vulnerability for tracking and remediation purposes. The risk level is also reported by the tools so that those of the highest risk can be acted on immediately. Most tools also provide the links to the patch/release level that should be applied to fix the issue.

The vulnerability scans should be run on a frequent basis, at least quarterly, with many organizations moving to monthly or weekly or even daily scans (partial infrastructure) due to the increasing frequency of new exploits. A good process is for information security to administer or provide oversight for the reporting of the scans and feed the information into a tracking document for the high- and medium-risk items, such as an access database or excel spreadsheet, and establish owners and commitment dates for mitigation of the issues found in the scans. Most of the vendor products now offer a cloud-based scanning engine and analysis tool to aggregate the results across environments. This can be particularly useful in a large, global organization desiring to have a consolidated view of risks across multiple countries or entities. Weekly meetings to resolve the issues can be held, and the expectation to complete all issues within 60–90 days of the scan, or a senior executive [i.e., Chief Information Officer (CIO)] justification and approval is needed. There will always be some issues that the operational areas will not be able to complete within 60–90 days; however, these should be the exceptions due to a lengthy process to resolve or a major system implementation/upgrade that is preventing progress. For example, a vendor product may require a version of Java that is 5 versions back, which contains known exploits; however, the product is not scheduled for update/new release until 3 months from now. The organization may decide to temporarily accept the risk until the new release is available.

Vulnerability scans are necessary to ensure that holes have not been inadvertently created within the computing infrastructure. After all, the attackers have these same tools and can run them against the infrastructure. Products have emerged in the past several years (i.e., BitSight, Security Scorecard) to produce an analysis of an organization by using externally available information, including information obtained from the Dark Web, a hacker underground. If the threat of an attacker is not enough to motivate an organization to close their holes, the fact other organizations are running scans and making this information available to others should help jolt the organization into action. The external scoring will be refined over time, as the practice is relatively new for most organizations; however, over time, this may morph into an external scoring of companies, providing, aside from the obvious problem of having a vulnerability open for exploit, a greater push for CISOs to take the scanning and subsequent patching programs seriously.

CAROLINE WONG: SHARING THE METRICS GOAL BETWEEN DEPARTMENTS

VP, Security Strategy, Cobalt.io

Years ago, I led the metrics function on the Global Information Security (GIS) Team at eBay. We had a problem in application security—GIS was great at finding security vulnerabilities using methods such as manual pen testing, scanning, and responsible disclosure, but we struggled to get developers to prioritize and fix issues. Week after week, we would approach them with the numbers. Here is how many new issues have been found, we would say.

Time and time again, we were met with resistance. Sometimes we could not even get the development teams to respond to our emails or attend our meetings. When they did respond, they seemed annoyed and angry with us.

Our approach was not working, so we had to try something new. Our CISO and the VP of engineering met and agreed that AppSec should be a shared goal between GIS and engineering. After all, eBay is an online platform that allows strangers to transact with each other over the Internet. Trust and security are critical to the business.

With buy-in from decision makers, we decided to meet with the folks doing the work. We talked to developers and asked them about their (nonsecurity) priorities and goals. We found that they were evaluated based on new features implemented and that their bonuses were tied to completing this work. I began to realize why they had been responding to us with so much resistance. We were asking them to take valuable time away from the work they needed to do in order to get their jobs done and bonuses paid.

With this new context, we then asked the developers how much work effort could reasonably be put into fixing security issues.

Together, we came up with a measurable objective. We would work together to drive down the number of security vulnerabilities for the customer-facing applications by 20% in 1 year. We took a baseline number of known security vulnerabilities and divided it by millions of lines of code to get to a defect density number so that we could reasonably compare different applications.

It worked.

Managed Services

Companies that do not have the staff to provide 24×7 monitoring of the externally facing devices may consider the use of MSSP to provide the monitoring. These organizations can achieve economies of scale by monitoring multiple clients in different shifts. Outsourcing to an external company does not dismiss the need to internal staff to respond to the security incidents. It typically requires an on-call person on the company security team that will be able to respond if there is a critical threat. SLAs should be put in place as to the services that will be provided, and the time frames expected to respond to issues.

RICARDO LAFOSSE: SUCCESS IMPLEMENTING A SHARED SECURITY CENTER

CISO, Morningstar

The SOC is Dead…long live the SOC, at least an Open SOC (OSOC, yeah, another acronym!). Throughout my career, I have been exposed to various

SOCs, and until recently, they have been predominantly dedicated and iso-lated to information security. I would like to focus on a reoccurring theme: the lack of sharing. The SOC is at the frontline for data, analysis, alerting, and intelligence; however, many organizations tend to use the informa-tion gathered in a siloed way, and information tends to remain within the department who gathered it. I decided to embark on a quest to really open the SOC and have it act more of an information center across an organiza-tion. I created three goals to keep track of this quest. Putting a stake in the ground really made it easier to conquer this quest. My three goals were as follows: (1) solicit feedback from the organization, (2) share the knowledge with the organization, and (3) share knowledge with our community. With my tasks engraved on a cocktail napkin, I embarked on a marketing road trip to obtain legitimate feedback from our business stakeholders and IT. The business really solidified my gut feeling, they did not know we existed or the services we offer (Infosec marketing failure!). IT enjoyed working with our department but felt that we did not provide enough information and context (communication issue). Armed with real feedback, I regrouped with the team and started a brainstorming session. Keeping the goals in mind, I decided to push our department into the limelight by instituting an internal Information Sharing and Analysis Center (ISAC), instead of a formal SOC. The ISAC was represented by key stakeholders and security liaisons. Our team would meet monthly to disseminate security advisories (with actionable intelligence) and discuss projects in flight, business realignments, and policy comments/updates. This effort ensured that there were accountability and transparency across the organization and gave everyone a voice (inclusion is critical to the success of the ISAC). The model was so successful that we offered these services to local municipalities to give the greater community access to actionable threat information, deidentified of course.

Incident Response

The ability to respond quickly to incidents depends largely on how well the pro-cess is thought-out in advance. Valuable time can be lost during an incident if there is not a process in place, and the result may be following a very chaotic, unorganized process of determining what has happened, containing the security incident, and eradicating the damage that was caused. Mistakes can be made with-out a well-defined process. The security department's role should be to facilitate the resolution of the incident to ensure that all the right departments are engaged and the Computer Security Incident Response Team (CSIRT) process defined by the organization is generally followed. Not all incidents will require the enactment of the CSIRT, so it should be understood under what conditions the team will be invoked. Other departments such as the business owners, infrastructure teams (server, desktop), and network teams are also engaged, either as a responsible party or an informed party.

The response mechanisms go beyond the involvement of the IT department and need to plan for the business response after the incident involving legal, public relations/communications, executives, and business partners. If financial information was disclosed, it is normal to offer credit monitoring services and staff call centers for the influx of calls following a breach. Notifications to impacted business partners would need to be prepared in advance so the organization is not scrambling when the time is of the essence. Retainers with firms are often created in advance to ensure the support is there when the breach happens, and the organization can quickly move into execution mode. Some of these retainers are implemented in conjunction with cyber insurance companies, who may specify the vendor to be used in case of a breach.

SAM MONASTERI: SECURITY FROM SCRATCH: INCIDENT RESPONSE ON A SHOESTRING BUDGET

VP, CISO, ACCO Brands

Protecting the organization from a data breach is the primary goal of a CISO and one of their greatest challenges. Bad guys and threats get more sophisticated every day, so it is imperative that CISOs and their teams stay apprised of new attack methods, hacking strategies, and potential internal vulnerabilities. This challenge is compounded by budget limitations, which are common across the industry. Most CISOs report having a smaller than necessary operating budget, often well below the 3%–6% of the total IT budget that is recommended by information security experts.

Despite being at high risk, with often low budgets, CISOs are expected to deliver an appropriate level of security to the organization, meeting the expectations of various stakeholders outside of IT, including the board of directors, executive leadership, regulators, and shareholders.

There are several cost-free ways to improve your security posture and establish a strong Security Incident Response Program. I advise following these four steps:

■ *Get executive-level buy-in*—Gaining the support of executives across business units is important and can be accomplished by communicating the impact a security breach may have on their individual functions.
■ *Establish a multidisciplinary team of incident responders*—Your incident response team should include IT and information security

professionals, as well as representatives from key business units such as human resources, legal, supply chain, finance, and media relations.
■ Implement the three Ps.
 – Plot your incident response plan, and share it with stakeholders and the individuals making up your incident response team.
 – Plan for possible threat scenarios. Create incident playbooks that include step-by-step action plans for the top ten incidents that may affect your organization.
 – Practice your action plan via tabletop exercises to ensure incident responders are clear on their individual roles and responsibilities to quickly contain and recover from any incidents that arise.
■ Build relationships.

Establish strong relationships with outside organizations, such as the FBI and local law enforcement. These relationships can be beneficial in the event you need outside assistance if a major incident occurs.

Forensic Analysis

This area has not received much attention within information security departments and tends to receive little investment. If the number of investigations is low, outsourcing this function may be a viable alternative. The time required to build a level of forensic expertise can be very expensive. Performing this function in-house can also be risky if the evidence is to be presented in court, primarily because the opposing counsel will ask, "How many forensic investigations have you performed?", "What training have you had that ensures you have the sufficient level of knowledge?", or "demonstrate that the appropriate chain of custody was followed completely throughout the process." Still, this is valuable expertise to develop within the organization at a basic level, as the act of going through forensic investigations will highlight gaps in the current logging/monitoring/configuration processes, as well as creating further learning opportunities for the cybersecurity staff. At a minimum, an organization should have this capability on a retainer in the event the service is needed. The costs can be high, particularly if having to retrieve information in another country and there is not an existing relationship. I once had a situation where I had to obtain a forensic image of a desktop halfway around the world, and the costs of travel were added on to the costs of copying the drive with a major, reputable provider, as there was no one in the local market we could reliably identify and establish a contract quickly. This resulted in a charge of $10,000 USD to copy one drive. This cost did not include the subsequent analysis of the drive, only the procurement. The processes will run more efficiently and be less expensive if they are arranged in advance.

Threat Intelligence/Security Analytics/Machine Learning

Various sources of threat intelligence and indicators of compromise may come from subscription-based services, vendor products, news media, and Information Sharing and Analysis Centers (ISACs) and need to be shared with the appropriate parties within the organization to ensure the appropriate actions are taken (i.e., the infrastructure teams need to be aware of critical patches to be applied immediately, board reporting needs to include the latest threats, security awareness training may need knowledge of the latest phishing scams, and financial areas may require knowledge of fraudulent transaction attempts). The CISO and their team may not directly manage all the threat feeds, such as those being ingested into vendor products; however, they should be aware of the feeds being received and their use within the organization to evaluate the effectiveness and demonstrate the external knowledge that is being obtained.

The security analytics/machine learning product capabilities can be leveraged to assess the patterns and intrusions of the organization. The analytics can also be used to proactively examine unauthorized or excessive access to systems. Staffing these functions are labor-intensive and may require data scientist skills beyond the cybersecurity team (i.e., consultants or outsourcing the function completely to an MSSP) to keep up with the emerging threats. With security artificial intelligence approaches emerging, the ability to examine large amounts of information with significantly less human intervention holds promise. Organizations should be exploring these approaches with pilot effort initiatives and may decide to recruit data scientists, or have access to, to augment the security team to automate some of the routine workloads to enable security staff to focus on higher-value activities such as evaluating the exceptions from these tools and processes.

JIM ROUTH: MODEL-DRIVEN SECURITY IS MAKING FUNDAMENTAL CHANGES TO SECURITY POSTURE

CSO, Aetna

In the fall of 2016, I decided to bring a chief data scientist to Aetna, focused on developing models to help us improve our cyber hunting capabilities. In retrospect, the decision was a good one, but the rationale for the decision was flawed. We were fortunate to have hired an exceptional person with incredible talent. However, the notion of improving cyber hunting capability through model development was the misguided part. We discovered that improving cyber hunting using better analytics was far too narrow a focus for the organization.

We were able to create and implement models using unsupervised machine learning, allowing us to identify online fraud trends and patterns, effectively eliminating threat actor tactics for compromising health savings accounts. We were thrilled with the results of the more than 100 data and machine learning models developed by the team. However, at the same time that this work was underway, several small teams of engineers implemented machine learning models driving frontline security controls across eight distinct platforms. These smaller, interdependent work efforts using vendor-developed products and custom-developed models contributed to a fundamental wave of emerging technology supporting frontline security controls. These controls represent what we call "model-driven security." We believe this trend is revolutionizing security control design and implementation.

We teach all security professionals the fundamentals of data science to equip them with the tools required to design, develop, and implement new security controls. We hire data scientists and teach them security techniques. A growing number of open roles today require data science experience and aptitude. This wave of model-driven security has triggered a fundamental change to our talent management strategy.

We have several examples of models driving security controls in production today. The first is what many in the industry call an insider threat. We address by this threat by identifying when behaviors of employees that request privilege break normal patterns. This is triggered by a change in behavior or an external threat actor using a privileged credential of an insider. Every registered user of the network has a behavioral profile represented in a model based on the entitlements they use most often, the websites they use, the emails they send, and the buildings they access. Once they request and are granted a privilege, their actual online behavior is compared in real time to their profile represented in a model. Deviation from a pattern could trigger an email alert to their leader to confirm the recent activity is appropriate. A significant deviation from the normal pattern of behavior—measured by a risk tolerance score—will trigger an automatic revocation of privilege. A security incident response will also be orchestrated automatically and in real time, with no human interaction necessary.

The next example uses a machine learning-enhanced model developed based on discerning domain attributes from all sending email domains. With this approach, an email inbound filter drops email sent from known bad email domains based on the behavior exhibited by that respective domain. Aetna receives email messages sent from approximately 29,000 email servers daily. About 14,000 of them are known to send fraudulent email based on an analysis of the attributes of the sending domain, so we do not deliver email from them. This increases trust in all emails by employees while reducing the probability of a phishing email achieving its objective.

The next example is enabling an enterprise to eventually eliminate the use of passwords and evolve to continuous behavioral-based authentication. This approach is needed because the assumption that you are the only person that knows your password to any website or mobile application is no longer valid. Threat actors can harvest credentials (user IDs and password combinations) and use Sentry MBA to try these credentials on any website they wish. They will be successful in taking over an online account 2% of the time, because we all use the same password across different websites, given how difficult it is to remember unique passwords for all sites. This is called credential stuffing, and it is one reason that binary authentication controls can be defeated by threat actors. Continuous behavioral-based authentication does not require you to remember a password. It uses benign attributes of your behavior and turns them into a model or mathematical formula to compare with your actual behavior in real time. The deviation score alerts the application of how much access to provide. It is one of the first examples of improving security and the consumer experience at the same time, and it is not possible without models driving it.

Aetna has more than 300 models at work currently, and we expect to have close to 500 in 2019. We should be able to share models through an ISAC with other members for them to use derivatives of our models or plug them into a similar platform to drive security controls. Whether you hire a chief data scientist and build a team of data scientists or choose vendor solutions using models, the evolution to model-driven security is underway. Threat actors are using data science to attack our enterprises and consumers, so creating friction for them while making it easier for consumers requires model-driven security.

Insider Threat

Organizations need to account for the insider threat and plan for how these issues will be handled. The cybersecurity focus is directed externally in most organizations as there is limited resource availability to also spend much time with insider threats, other than those threats reported that really are the "tip of the iceberg," or in other words, are not the result of an ongoing program to proactively manage the insider risk, but rather are incidents that come to light in conjunction with other employee/contractor suspicious activity. Organizations have a propensity to want to trust their employees. Some of this may be changing with the introduction of DLP initiatives to monitor the flow of sensitive information leaving the organization. The insider threat is often thought of as related to the theft of intellectual property for personal gain; however, it is not just limited to malicious activity but includes those activities of carelessness as well.

Central Management Functions

Along with providing the general management of the cybersecurity program, the security department must also provide the following two functions to interface with the audit requirements and ensure that issues are formally tracked to closure.

Audit Liaison

The security controls may be audited frequently depending upon the type of industry that the company is participating in. The security area is well advised to have someone designated to coordinate these audits that understand information security controls. While the internal audit department may lead the overall audit with the audit firm, they may not have the technical expertise to understand what is being requested, or the potential alternative, compensating controls within the environment which can be provided. The audit team within the organization may also be operationally or financially focused and my co-source or outsource the IT audit function.

Plan of Action and Milestones

Security deficiencies need to be tracked, and corresponding Plan of Actions and Milestones (POA&Ms) are developed to establish interim steps and dates for completion. Care should be taken in setting realistic dates, or these POA&Ms are recorded as delayed. A formal approval process for the submission of evidence, to whom, and who will review and approve the items for closure should be established.

Security Metrics Tracking

Organizations measure performance by tracking metrics, and the CISO should regard this activity as essential to demonstrating value is being provided to the company and as a vehicle for increasing performance and maturity. Without measuring the activities, the evidence becomes anecdotal-based and, therefore, not as trustworthy in the eyes of those seeking an objective opinion. The metrics collection should start with a few key metrics and build out the program from there. Board-level metrics are typically derived by aggregating lower-level metrics collected at an activity-based level. For example, being able to report on metrics of how the organization is subject to an attack related to the latest outbreak would require a detailed understanding of what patches have been applied and to how many machines. Understanding the effectiveness of the vulnerability management process would require knowledge of mean time before critical/high vulnerabilities were closed, a number of new vulnerabilities introduced, and a number of vulnerabilities not patched where a security incident subsequently was successful. Tracking of the metrics can also demonstrate the effectiveness after the implementation of new controls. The individual(s) collecting the metrics will need to interface with many departments to define the metrics to be collected, collect the metrics on a periodic basis (monthly minimally for operational metrics), validate the metrics, and determine the "meaning" of the metrics. Selected metrics of interest can then be provided to the board.

EDWARD MARCHEWKA: SECURITY METRICS TO MEASURE PROGRAM EFFECTIVENESS

Director, Information and Technology Services, Gift of Hope

Metrics help to tell a story to the right audience in terms they will understand. We, CISOs, have different audience members that include the board, executives, auditors/regulators, and engineers. As we tell each of these audiences the story of information security, it must be appropriate for our audience's level of understanding and their background keeping in mind they ask of or from them.

- The board is strategic, and we are asking for resources. The board, usually, receives an aggregated total score and maturity score, with average risk rating. This tells them where we are and how tight the controls are. We can use this to build a road map too and show how the resources are helping to move the needle.
- Executives need actionable information, usually, by subject area, and we need to answer their ask, "What's in it for me?" Executives need to see how the security program is affecting them. We need to aggregate by topics they care about. For example, the CMO might care about integrity and reputation, to address concerns of report accuracy and potential reputation damage. I aggregate my tactical metrics around six key business indicators: confidentiality, integrity, availability, human resources, finance, and reputation.
- Auditors/regulators need to know we know about our environment and that we are doing something about it. This is the blend of the aggregated and tactical metrics. They may understand that a program exists with the tactical metrics but may also want to see the details.
- Engineers need the details, and we are going to ask them to fix something. With the engineers, we can show them detailed tactical metrics such as patch cycle times or incident mean time to resolution.

NIST and Center for Internet Security (CIS)have great listings of tactical metrics with parameters for different levels of risk. From there, you can tie the results to specific technologies. Your metrics are not a burden to the job but should be a tool to help you tell a better story.

Security Project Management

Project management is a specialized skill that should not be minimized in importance to creating a successful project. According to CIO Magazine (2016), more than half of IT projects were still failing. While not all of this can be attributed to the lack of a good project manager, this does illustrate the complexity involved in delivering a successful project. Security projects are the same way—someone needs to have the skills to ensure the proper planning, staffing, decisions, and direction are being followed. The CISO should ensure the project management skills are resident on the team or can be acquired from somewhere within the organization (i.e., project management office organization). The most widely recognized credential for project management is the Project Management Professional (PMP®), which, like the credentials for information security, demonstrates knowledge of the global language of project management.

Future Structure Considerations

The cybersecurity organization will continue to evolve in a manner like those staff functions that went before it, such as human resources, finance, legal, IT, and risk management—each managing their aspects of their own "assets," whether people, money, contracts, systems, or financial/operational loss. For a successful cybersecurity program, all the functions listed in this section contribute to reducing the cybersecurity risk for the information assets in some way, and each organization should explicitly consider the impact of not performing any of these functions. As the environments become more complex, more activities are likely to be added to the organization. The CISO will rarely have the budget/staffing for all these functions initially; however, using the laws, regulations, control frameworks, and risk assessments discussed in the following sections, the goal should be to incorporate these functions as necessary, build incremental success in a few areas to protect the systems and information assets, and grow the security program through increased investment.

Suggested Reading

1. Russell, K. 2014. How Apple became the Dominant Force in the Enterprise, Business Insider. (February 19). www.businessinsider.com/why-apple-is-dominating-enterprise-2014-2.
2. Vergara, A. 2017. The 15 Super Bowl-Winning Quarterbacks Who Weren't First-Round Draft Picks. Fox Sports (June 3). www.foxsports.com/nfl/gallery/nfl-draft-15-super-bowl-winning-quarterbacks-not-first-round-picks-tom-brady-joe-montana-kurt-warner-brett-favre-042817.
3. Friedberg, S. 2017. Stroz Friedberg's 2017 Cybersecurity Predictions Report. https://content.strozfriedberg.com/2017-stroz-friedberg-cybersecurity-predictions-report.

4. Schmidt, S. 2018. 2,000 Frozen Eggs and Embryos Possibly 'Compromised' After Fertility Clinic Temperature Malfunction. Washington Post (March 19). www.washingtonpost. com/news/morning-mix/wp/2018/03/09/2000-frozen-eggs-and-embryos-possibly-compromised-after-fertility-clinic-temperature-malfunction/?utm_term=.c6ed22bc2e36.
5. Collette, S. 2016. What's in a Security Score? CSO Online (August 4). www.csoonline. com/article/3103293/security/what-s-in-a-security-score.html.
6. General Accounting Office Report. 1998. "Learning from Leading Organizations".
7. Sanborn, M. 2006. *You Don't Need a Title to Be a Leader: How Anyone, Anywhere, Can Make a Positive Difference.* New York. Crown Business.
8. Drucker, P. F. 2004. *The Effective Executive.* New York. Collins publishers.
9. Johnson, S. 2003. *The Present: The Gift That Make You Happier and More Successful at Work and In Life.* New York. Today! Doubleday and Company.
10. Covey, S. 2004. *The 7 Habits of Highly Effective People.* New York. Free Press (Revised Edition, 2004).
11. Peters, T. 2005. *Tom Peters* Essentials Series *(Leadership).* New York. DK Publishing.
12. Collins, J. 2001. *Good to Great: Why Some Companies Make the Leap and Others Don't.* New York. HarperCollins Publishers Inc.
13. Morgenstern, J. 2004. *Never Check E-mail in the Morning.* New York. Simon and Schuster.
14. Kroeger, O. and Thuesen, J. M. 1992. *Type Talk at Work: How the 16 Personality Types* New York. *Determine Your Success on the Job.*
15. Fitzgerald, T. and Krause, M. 2008. *CISO Leadership: Essential Principles for Success,* The ISC2® Press Series. New York. Auerbach Publishers.
16. United States General Accounting Office. 1998. Executive Guide Information Security Management: Learning from Leading Organizations. www.gao.gov/archive/1998/ ai98068.pdf.
17. Sharma, Y. Cyber Insurance Market to Reach $14 Billion, Globally, by 2022. Allied Market Research. www.alliedmarketresearch.com/press-release/cyber-insurance-market. html.
18. Florentine, S. 2016. More Than Half of IT Projects Still Failing. CIO (May 11). www. cio.com/article/3068502/project-management/more-than-half-of-it-projects-still-failing. html.

Chapter 6

CISO Reporting Models

One of the things that distinguishes ours from all earlier generations is this, that we have seen our atoms.

Karl Kelchner Darrow, 1891–1982

The security officer and the information security organization should report as high in the organization as possible to (1) maintain visibility of the importance of information security and (2) limit the distortion or inaccurate translation of messages that can occur due to hierarchical, deep, and siloed organizations. The higher up in the organization, the greater the ability to gain other senior management's attention to security and the greater the capability to compete for the appropriate budget and resources. Where the information security officer reports in the organization has been the subject of debate for several years and depends upon the culture of the organization. There is no one best model that fits all organizations, but rather the pros and cons associated with each placement choice. Whatever the chosen reporting model, there should be an individual chosen with the responsibility for ensuring information security at the enterprise-wide level to establish accountability for resolving security issues. The discussion in the next few sections should provide the perspective for making the appropriate choice for the target organization.

Business Relationships

Wherever the information security officer reports, it is imperative that he or she establishes credible and good working relationships with executive management, middle management, and the end users who will be following the security policy. Information gathered and acted upon by executive management is obtained through their daily interactions with many individuals, not just executive management. Winning their support may be the result of influencing a respected individual within the organization, possibly several management layers below the executive. Similarly, the relationship between the senior executives and the Chief Information Security Officer (CISO) is important if the security strategies are to carry through to implementation. Establishing a track record of delivery and demonstrating the value of the protection to the business will build this relationship. If done properly, the security function becomes viewed as an enabler of the business vs. a control point slowing innovation, providing roadblocks to implementation, and represents an overhead cost function. Reporting to an executive that understands the need for cybersecurity and is willing to work to obtain funding is clearly preferable.

Reporting to the CEO

Reporting directly to the CEO greatly reduces the message filtering of reporting further down the hierarchy and improves the communication, as well as demonstrating to the organization the importance of information security. Firms that have high security needs, such as credit card companies, technology companies, and companies whose revenue stream depends highly upon Internet Web site purchases, such as eBay or Amazon, might utilize such a model. The downside to this model is that the CEO may be preoccupied with many other business issues and may not have the interest, time, or enough technical understanding to devote to information security issues.

Reporting to the Information Technology Department

In this model, the CISO reports directly to the Chief Information Officer (CIO), Director of Information technology (IT), the Vice President of systems, or whatever the title of the head of the IT department is. Most organizations are utilizing this relationship, as this was historically where the data security function was placed in many companies. According to Larry Ponemon's research (2013), 56% of CISOs were still reporting to the CIO. There appears to be evidence that this trend is changing, as Georgia Tech Information Security Center produced a study indicating 40% of the CISOs were reporting to the CIO (2015). The history of reporting to the CIO is due to security being viewed as only an IT problem, which it is not. The breaches starting with the 2013 Target Breach have helped to change the placement of the CISO. The advantage of this model is that the individual to which the security officer is reporting understands the technical issues and typically has the clout with senior management to make the desired changes. It is also beneficial because the information security officer and their department must spend a good deal of time interacting with the rest of the information systems department, building the appropriate awareness of project activities and issues, and building business relationships. The downside of the reporting structure is the conflict of interest. When the CIO must make decisions with respect to time to market, resource allocations, cost minimization, application usability, and project priorities, the ability exists to slight the information security function. The typical CIO's goals are more oriented towards the delivery of application products to support the business in a timely manner. If the perception is that implementation of the security controls may take more time or money to implement, the security considerations may not be provided equal weight. Reporting to a lower level within the CIO organization should be avoided, as noted earlier; the more levels between the CEO and the information security officer, the more challenges that must be overcome. Levels further down in the organization also have their own domains of expertise that they are focusing on, such as computer operations, applications programming, or computing infrastructure.

The CIO is also driven to appease the users and maintain uptime and ensure availability vs. protecting the information. The CIO wants to avoid taking down systems to implement new security technologies, delaying user access by requiring multifactor authentication, or having systems unavailable 24×7 due to patching cycles. IT also wants to support the business with new initiatives and not have them slowed down by the "Dr. No" view of the CISO and may override the CISO without having to have these decisions visible to others due to the direct reporting relationship. In these reporting relationships, it takes a stronger CISO with the ability to raise and confront security issues with the CIO. Some of the information security decisions may fall outside of the information security realm, such as physical security, contracts, personnel security, and privacy, and require the CISO to have access with other departments such as legal, human resources (HR), and risk management.

A conflict of interest may also occur, as insider threats sometimes involve members of the IT department due to the elevated access typical in IT staff required to perform their roles. The CISO's ability to carry out an investigation may be limited in this reporting scenario.

CISOs are typically hired for their ability to understand the adversary and lead threat modeling efforts to map out the actions a threat adversary may take. Effective CISOs also understand compliance and privacy constructs, a discipline not typically the focus of IT departments. In other words, the IT staff are predominantly focused on building and supporting systems to provide business functionality, not to think about how the system could be circumvented or compromised to use it in ways it was not intended.

Some regulations are starting to surface, which clearly indicates the CISO, if appointed, needs to have an independent reporting relationship. In the past, some organizations have implemented dotted-line reporting relationships for the CISOs to an audit committee or another senior executive management member, such as the CEO. The 2017 Israeli Privacy Protections Regulations (Data Security), with a compliance date of May 8, 2018, stated in Section 17B, if an organization does appoint a CISO, the regulations require the CISO to report directly to senior management, to be independent and free of conflicts, and to be sufficiently resourced. While auditors may have previously noted a separation of duties conflict for the CISO reporting to the CIO, laws may start to shape the future reporting relationships by making the CISO reporting relationship independence from the CIO more explicit.

STEPHEN FRIED: THE BEST REPORTING RELATIONSHIP FOR A CISO MAY NOT BE WHAT YOU THINK!

IT Security Director, American Family Insurance

I am often asked what seems like a very simple question, "Where should the security organization report?" Unfortunately, the answer is far from simple. With the increased recognition of information security as a risk management discipline (as opposed to its traditional view as a technical discipline), many organizations are now trying to understand security's proper placement and relationship with other enterprise functions. In my many years, creating and developing security programs I have reported to many different places in the organization: IT, risk, legal, HR, facilities, and as a direct report to the CEO. In all those cases, there were very good business, cultural, and political reasons for security's reporting relationship. Sometimes it worked, and sometimes it did not. When it did not, we would change to make it better. Many consultants (and many in the security field) will issue bold statements, such as "Security should NEVER report to the CIO, that's a conflict of interest!" I completely disagree. In the hands of the right leadership—one that can objectively balance risk, business, and operational needs—IT can be a great place for security to effect real change to the risk profile of an organization. Under the wrong IT leadership—one that consistently places operational needs above true risk considerations—there is a real conflict and the reporting relationship needs to be changed. There are no absolute rules here; it is all about organizational leadership and maturity. Asking "Where should the security organization report?" is asking the wrong question. The real question to ask is, "Where is the best place in my organization for Security to get the resources, coverage, and executive support it needs to be most effective?" It is different for every organization. The security function should not be placed somewhere because it looks good in an organization chart, or because a consultant recommends it, or because your peer companies are doing it that way, or even because it addresses some theoretical conflict of interest. It should be placed where it can be the most effective at its charter: reducing information risk to the organization, wherever that may be. Placing security in any other part of the organization for any other reason is a recipe for frustration and ineffectiveness.

Reporting to Corporate Security

Corporate security is focused on the physical security of the enterprise, and most often, the individuals in this environment have backgrounds as former police officers, military, or were associated in some other manner with the criminal justice system. This alternative may appear logical; however, the individuals from these organizations come from two different backgrounds. Physical security is focused on criminal justice, protection, and investigation services, while information security professionals usually have different training in business and IT. The language of these disciplines intersects in some areas such as a desire to protect assets from harm and handle incidents through a managed process but is vastly different in others. Another downside is that the association with the physical security group may evoke a police-type mentality, making it difficult to build business relationships with business users to enable business functions. Establishing relationships with the end users increases their willingness to listen and comply with the security controls, as well as to provide knowledge to the security department of potential violations. The late Howard Schmidt, former Cybersecurity Czar under Presidents George Bush and Barack Obama, was previously the CISO for eBay, and he had combined the physical and information security functions together while at eBay. He ended up separating them for an unanticipated reason—the members of the physical security team wanted to be paid the same as the members of the information security (technical) team since they were all members of the same team. Because these were two different fields competing for talent with different pay structures, he ended up separating the groups.

Reporting to Administrative Services (Chief Administrative Officer)

The information security officer may report to the Vice President (VP) of Administrative Services, or Chief Administrative Officer (CAO), which may also include the physical security, employee safety, and HR departments. As in reporting to the CIO, there is only one level between the CEO and the information security department. The model may also be viewed as an enterprise function due to the association with the HR department, also seen to have an organization-wide purview. This is attractive because of the focus on security for all forms of information (paper, oral, electronic) vs. residing in the technology department, where the focus may tend to be more on electronic information. The downside is that the leaders of this area may be limited in their knowledge of IT and the ability to communicate with the CEO on technical issues.

Reporting to the Risk Management Department

Information-intensive organizations such as banks, stock brokerages, and research companies may benefit from this model. The Chief Risk Officer (CRO) is already concerned with the risks to the organization and the methods to control those risks through mitigation, acceptance, insurance, etc. The downside is that the Risk Officer may not be conversant in the information systems technology, and the strategic focus of this function may give less attention to day-to-day operational security projects. Increasingly, organizations are recognizing that information security is a key risk to the organization and is reflected at the enterprise level. The 2014 guidance by the National Association of Corporate Directors (NACD) promoting the five principles for managing cybersecurity risk, as discussed, has helped to move the discussion into a risk-based vs. technology discussion. If cybersecurity is not one of the top five risks for an organization today, this is more likely to be an anomaly.

Large organizations have enterprise risk management (ERM) or governance, risk, and compliance departments where the security function could reside. The advantage is that these departments may already have tools and organizational processes for ERM whereby the cybersecurity risks could be integrated and reviewed alongside these other risks to help establish priority and investment. The ERM departments organize cross-functional assessments of risk and bring parties to discuss all risks, such as how much should be spent on branding, new mergers and acquisitions, risk of upcoming legislation, risk of key company business, and IT projects. Some companies do not have an extensive risk management department; however, financial institutions usually do, as they are managing credit risk, operational risk, investment risk, etc., as this is core to the business of investing. In these environments, reporting to the Chief Risk Officer may be an excellent choice.

Reporting to the Internal Audit Department

This reporting relationship can create a conflict of interest, as the internal audit department is responsible for evaluating the effectiveness and implementation of the organization's control structure, including those of the information security department. It would be difficult for the internal audit to provide an independent viewpoint if the attainment of meeting the security department's objectives is also viewed as part of its responsibility. The internal audit department may have adversarial relationships with other portions of the company due to the nature of its role (to uncover deficiencies in departmental processes), and through association, the security department may develop similar relationships. It is advisable that the security department establishes close working relationships with the internal audit department to facilitate the control environment. The internal audit manager most likely has a background in financial, operational, and general controls and may have difficulty understanding the technical activities of the cybersecurity department. The exception to this are the audit departments focused on IT auditing, normally a subset of a larger audit group responsible for all the company's audits.

On the positive side, both cybersecurity and internal audit are focused on improving the controls of the company. The internal audit department does have a preferable reporting relationship for audit issues through a dotted-line relationship with the company's audit committee on the board of directors. The cybersecurity function should have a path to report security issues to the board of directors as well, either in conjunction with the internal audit department or through its own.

Reporting to the Legal Department

Attorneys are concerned with compliance with regulations, laws, and ethical standards, performing due diligence, and establishing policies and procedures that are consistent with many of the information security objectives. The company's general counsel also typically has the respect or ear of the CEO. In regulated industries, this may be a very good fit. On the downside, due to the emphasis on compliance activities, the cybersecurity department may end up performing more compliance-checking activities (vs. security consulting and support), which are typically the domain of internal audit. An advantage is that the distance between the CEO and the information security officer is one level.

The Chief Privacy Officer (CPO), or Data Protection Officer (DPO), is typically located in a legal or compliance function, and alignment with this role is becoming of increasing importance and requires a close working relationship with the CPO/DPO. There may be some synergy working within the same department, as many security issues are discussed within the privacy realm. I have reported to the Chief Legal Officer (CLO) in the past and found this to be an excellent working relationship, as the organization viewed the cybersecurity issues as a business issue. The reporting relationship also placed the CISO position at the same level of influence as the CIO and improved the working relationships between the CIO and CISO to resolve the security gaps together.

The CLO reporting relationship also has the benefit of close access to interpretation of laws and expertise with contractual agreements. Today, there is an expectation that an organization is managing the vendor relationships and security control requirements "flow down" to subcontractors and cloud services.

Three Lines of Defense

A common framework advocated by many accounting firms after the dot.com failures and Enron scandal in the early 2000s is the three lines of defense model, whereby there is a separation between the operations management, oversight, and independent assurance of the organizational activities. As shown in Figure 6.1, the three lines of defense model is favorable as the variety and complexity of the risks are rising rapidly, roles can be clarified within the organization, and the board of directors and audit committee can be provided with assurance that people are

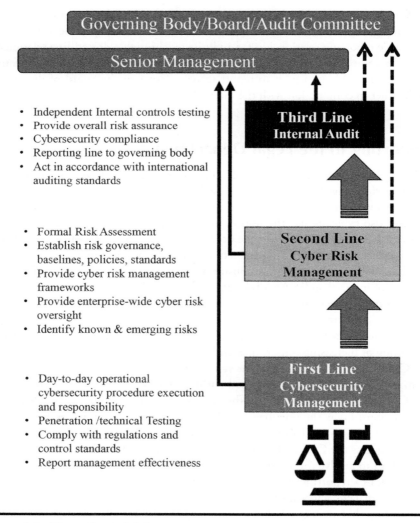

Figure 6.1 Three lines of defense.

working together to avoid gaps in risk management and duplication of efforts are being avoided. The first line of defense is the day-to-day operational area responsible for identifying, assessing, mitigating, and reporting on the risks. The second line provides risk oversight and designs and implements a risk program, developing a framework to be supported by the first line to manage risk. Overall governance is provided as this group evaluates the risks across operational areas. As such, this provides a top-down view of the risk profile relative to the strategy and acceptable risk appetite. Cybersecurity is just one of the organizational risk areas within the organization and may be providing input into an overall corporate ERM team. The third level of defense is an internal audit, which is to be fully independent and objective and conducts audits and reviews of a sample of the activities of the first and second lines to ensure controls are designed and operating effectively. This balance of controls provides multiple checks to ensure the controls are operating as planned.

In practice, the activities are not as clear-cut as in Figure 6.1, and the operational or business areas in the first line of defense may not have the ownership of the risk issues and look to the second line to provide those, taking away from second-line activities, which should be spending time providing deeper insights into the risk areas. New regulations have also increased the burden on the second-line oversight areas, spreading their time across more activities. The audit process conducted by the third line is also still predominantly a manual process, limiting the number of areas that may be audited. Even with these constraints, the organization should develop a responsible, accountable, informed, and consulted (RACI) model to define which area performs which activity in line with the three lines of defense model to identify areas of oversight weakness.

Determining the Best Fit

The primary reporting relationships for the CISO and cybersecurity team along with the pros and cons are summarized in Figure 6.2. Each organization must view each of these types of relationships and develop the appropriate relationship based upon the company culture, type of industry, and what will provide the greatest benefit to the company. Conflicts of interest should be minimized, visibility increased, funding appropriately allocated, and communication effective when the optimal reporting relationship is decided for the placement of the cybersecurity department.

The largest predictor of success will be the relationships the CISO has built across departments and with the various stakeholders up, down, and across the organization. I have led cybersecurity in organizations where the CISO reporting relationship was to the CIO, CLO, internal audit, and the CRO. I am a strong advocate for reporting into a risk management or legal function in larger firms or the CEO (most likely in a smaller firm). I do not advocate reporting to the

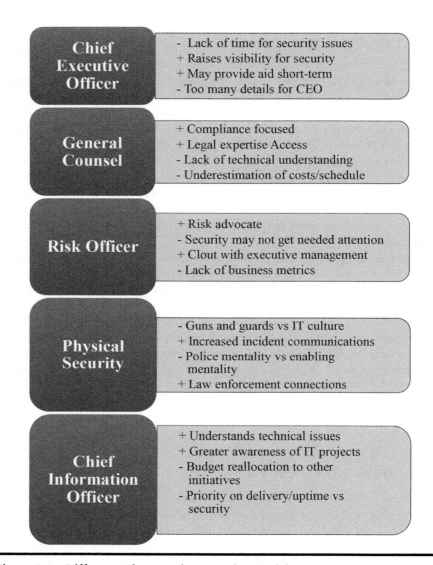

Figure 6.2 Different cybersecurity reporting models.

CIO except possibly for high-technology organizations. There is one exception to this—initially, the reporting relationship may be to the CIO while attention is placed on shoring up fundamental security issues; however, once this objective has been achieved, the organization needs to mature and move the function to an organization-wide function. Organizations have been moving the cybersecurity function around since the initial spike in the recruitment of the security officer at the turn of the millennium, and the move away from the CIO will continue to be slow for some organizations, particularly those with large technology investments.

MICHAEL PALMER: LEADERSHIP
CREATING A SEAT AT THE TABLE

VP—CISO, National Football League (NFL)

Those that know me know that I am a huge Game of Thrones fan. I think there are many lessons contained within the story that can help CISOs navigate through the corporate political arena. In regard to leadership and having a seat at the table, one cannot wait for a seat to be given to you. One must create opportunities for one self to receive a seat. I am reminded of the scene when Tyrion Lannister relocated a seat and positioned it so that he was at the head of the table. He did so by making as much noise as he possibly could by dragging the chair screeching across the floor. Then, he took control of the room by speaking first and setting the agenda. I am not saying that you should walk into your boardroom and drag a chair and sit next to the CEO. But you can work on creating relationships and become a trusted advisor to many that already have a seat so that you are invited in. You have to do some homework. Learn about who is in the room and what drives them. Find something that they need and give it to them. Here are a couple of things I have done over the years that drove engagement with "those that have seats at the table." One of the leaders was having issues where intellectual property (IP) in their control was being leaked out. I launched an investigation and determine the source of the leak. I then provided him with methods to protect his IP. Another person was having personal challenges with identity theft. I helped him through it and showed him how to protect his personally identifiable information. This allowed me to trade favors to get a couple of minutes on the agenda. I made sure to cover several items that peeked the curiosity of many of the stakeholders in the room. The next meeting, I was given more time and then I was a regular reoccurring topic in meetings moving forward. Never underestimate the "what's in it for me" factor.

Suggested Reading

1. Westby, J. 2015. *Governance of Cybersecurity: 2015 Report, How Boards and Senior Executives are Managing Cyber Risks.* Atlanta, GA. Georgia Tech Information Security Center. (October 2).
2. Pompon, R. 2017. CIO of C-Suite: To Whom Should the CISO Report? Darkreading.com (September 7). www.darkreading.com/partner-perspectives/f5/cio-or-c-suite-to-whom-should-the-ciso-report/a/d-id/1329807?piddl_msgorder=asc.
3. Teme, O. 2017. The New Israeli Data Security Regulations: A Tutorial, International Association of Privacy Professionals. https://iapp.org/news/a/the-new-israeli-data-security-regulations-a-tutorial/.

SYSTEMS 4

Chapter 7

Leveraging the Incidents of Others

> The social progress, order, security and peace of each country are necessarily connected with the social progress, order, security, and peace of all other countries.
>
> **Pope John XXIII, 1881–1963**

"We had an intrusion!" say the information security analyst as he walks away from his screen after studying the summarized information and reviewing the exfiltration of large files. The Chief Information Security Officer (CISO) responds with an inquisitive, "Are you sure?" and the journey begins... Soon other information technology (IT) people will be involved, along with the executives from various departments, and least of all—the media. In a best-case scenario, the organization has prepared for this day with the creation of playbooks for different types of scenarios from the detection of the intrusion, the handling of the evidence, and the subsequent managing of the incident through to recovery and communication with the media.

The *systems* factor of the *7-S Framework Applied to Cybersecurity* begins with a discussion of the incidents, as it is not only our own history which should be leveraged to build the proper controls, but we should also be leveraging the experiences of others. The follow-on chapters discuss the control frameworks (Chapter 8) and risk management practices (Chapter 9) as systems for the CISO to reduce the risk of a breach and protect the systems and information assets.

Breach Demographics Tracking

In recent years, there has been a greater focus in the security industry on detection and response over protection. This is not to suggest that prevention is not important, but rather that in the past, organizations did not place much emphasis on what to do in the event of a breach—assuming the organization had even detected it. According to the 2018 Verizon Data Breach Investigations Report, who has been tracking breaches for the past decade, the time for discovery has not changed much over the years, even with the focus on cybersecurity, and still takes months (68% of the time) to discover intrusions from point of sale, privilege misuse, cyberespionage, business email compromise, phishing, footprinting for future hacking, pretexting, the use of stolen credit cards, and other malware. Another report by the Ponemon Institute suggested that the average time to detect a data breach was 98 days for financial firms and retailers were taking up to 197 days.

While there has been debate within the security officer community over the past decade as to the source of the breaches, prior reports from earlier Computer Security Institute/Federal Bureau of Investigation (CSI/FBI) studies, a source of breach analysis for 15 years until ending in 2011, as a forerunner to the Verizon studies (started in 2009), indicated a high percentage of the attacks were due to the "insider threat." The studies showed a decline in the insider threat experienced by organizations in the later years from 2005 to 2011, from 48% in 2005, to a high of 59% in 2007, ending with 25% in 2011. These abuses included the abuse of Internet access, email, pornography, or pirated software. The major abuses in the final year of the 2011 CSI/FBI survey were related to malware infection (67%), phishing messages (39%), laptop/mobile phone theft (34%), and bots (29%). While the percentage of insider threats is still relatively substantial at 25%, this represents a significant reduction. Furthermore, most (59.1%) of the organizations did not feel that the actions were due to "malicious" insiders, but rather through the carelessness or inattention of end users (39.5%), thus providing some opportunity for security awareness and greater end-user controls.

As we wind forward to the 2018 Verizon Data Breach Investigations Report, the perceived attack surface, based upon the breaches currently experienced, has not changed substantially from the 2011 report, indicating 73% of attacks were perpetrated by outsiders and 28% involved internal actors. Not surprising, given the movement of hacking for website defacement activities and into criminal, profit-making motives, over 50% of the attacks involved organized crime and 12% were associated with state-sponsored actors. In 2017, not surprising is the highest percentage of breaches occurred where the money is—financial institutions (24%), followed with a tie between retail (15%), also where the money is in the form of credit card processing, and health-care organizations (15%), where medical information can be monetized for identity theft and medical fraud. The third largest breach victim was the public sector, containing confidential government and defense-related information (12%). Over 73% of the breaches had a financial motive. However, in

2018, the winner of the top spot for breaches was health-care organizations, rising to 24% of breaches, and 76% of the breaches were financially motivated. Also, the prevalence of malware being involved in the breaches has not changed much over the years either, with 67% of organizations experiencing malware in the 2011 CSI/FBI Study to 66% of the malware being installed by malicious emails in 2017 and 49% in 2018.

Hackers can be said to be opportunistic in the sense that they rattle door knobs (company firewalls, end user's email boxes, sniffing traffic) to find ways into the environment. Why rob a bank through the front door involving danger and possibly life, when one can hack into the computer systems to gain what is needed? Each organization has information they need to protect, and these controls will be different depending upon the organization. For example, a manufacturer or educational institution may need to be most concerned with protecting the intellectual property (IP) from cyberespionage, and a hospital may need to be concerned more with insider abuse accessing records or physical theft and secure disposal of information. Each of these threats may pose different solutions, such as segmenting, encrypting, and monitoring IP information for one manufacturing organization, vs. ensuring appropriate visibility into health-care access records, and sensitive information is appropriately shredded for another health-care organization.

DAWN CAPPELLI: MITIGATE THE RISK OF INSIDERS STEALING COMPANY CONFIDENTIAL INFORMATION

Vice President Global Security, CISO, Rockwell Automation

Insiders—employees and contractors—have stolen trade secrets and created competing products in other countries, exposed confidential information, and sabotaged source code, operations, or networks. We researched over 800 insider threat cases at the Computer Emergency Readiness Team (CERT) Insider Threat Center. At Rockwell Automation, we used that research to build an Insider Risk Program that won the Society of Women Engineers Global Team Leadership Award. Here is how we got started—focusing on theft of confidential information.

Get Human Resources (HR) on board. You cannot be successful without HR. Most insiders who steal confidential information take it within 90 days of resignation. Who knows when people are leaving? HR. You need HR to notify you when insiders with access to confidential information will be leaving the company.

Get Legal and IT on board. Get legal approval to audit activity for all insiders leaving the company who have access to critical information. You need ITs help to run reports of Universal Serial Bus (USB) flash drives, cloud, document management system, and email activity for those users for the past 90 days.

Prove it works. A global survey found 50% of people who changed jobs admitted they took confidential corporate information with them. Run reports for employees who left recently who had access to confidential information. You will find things, and your program will take off.

Automate. Once you prove the program's value, invest in a user behavioral analytics (UBA) tool to integrate diverse data sources and create models so you can proactively investigate users with the highest risk scores by drilling into the details on the UBA dashboard.

Most employees are honest, ethical people. While we typically think "it won't happen here," it is our responsibility to our customers and shareholders to make sure it does not. Some employees take confidential information unintentionally—they create their own backups or have information at home that they took to a customer and forgot to return to the office. The bottom line is that if you are not checking, you have no idea what information is walking out your door.

One final warning: after addressing insider theft, you are not finished … next is the more complex risk of insider cyber sabotage.

Breach Economics

At what point does the time and energy of a data breach payoff for the hacker? Depending upon the nature and sophistication of the data breach, and their motives and patience, it may or may not be profitable. The firm may have been targeted by another organization due to the size of the organization and the data they contain. A smaller entity may have less security and not have been attacked, as the profit motive would have been smaller and not worth as much time. Hackers make an investment of time and money to attack these organizations. An interesting study conducted by the Ponemon Institute (2016) researched the income made by an attacker vs. income made by information security professionals to protect their organizations. Dr. Larry Ponemon concluded that computer hackers made about $28, 744 per year, about one-fourth of the income they could earn as an information security practitioner! So, crime does not pay! However, the computer hacker works less, on average 705 hours per year compared with a computer security analyst logging 1,918 hours per year. As shown in Table 7.1, hackers spend an average of 70 hours hacking a typical IT infrastructure, 147 hours hacking an excellent IT infrastructure, and quit after 209 hours of trying. The lesson here? There is a cost benefit to the hacker, where it becomes time to move on. This suggests that it is clearly in our best interest to be at least better than the company next door and raise the bars on our controls. This also illustrates that there must be sufficient financial

Table 7.1   Economics of Hacking

Calculus	Overall*
Hours spent on the attack against typical IT security infrastructure	70
Hours spent on the attack against excellent IT security infrastructure	147
Hours before quitting	209
Value per successful attack	$14,711
Number of attacks per year	8.26
Percent of successful attacks	42.0%
Percent of successful attacks yielding nonzero return	59.0%
Cost of specialized tools	$1,367
Annual compensation	$28,744
Total hours spent per year	705
Labor rate per hour	$40.75
Rate per hour (benchmarks)	$60.36
Labor rate differential	$19.61
Percentage differential	38.8%

Source: Ponemon Research Report, *Flipping the Economics of Attacks*, 2016.

*Analysis conducted on the combined U.S., U.K., and German samples.

gain in what we have within our organization to justify the cost. While the large organization with many records and opportunity for financial gain may not be able to avoid being a target, the small to medium business would benefit greatly by knowing there is a threshold where the hacker will move on. The absolute best, most expensive security is not necessary for these environments, rather, just enough whereby the hacker will move on to another environment.

Customer Impact

In recent years, the breaches have appeared to go mainstream with high visibility. In other words, the types of breaches are impacting so many people going about their normal shopping, paying for health insurance, or subscribing to an email service. One must wonder what information has not been breached by someone yet! Let us review some recent breaches and the lessons learned from each breach.

The company that has the unawarded distinction of "biggest breach of the year award" seems to become the poster child at security conferences and is held up as the example of inadequate security practices. An organization could be diligent in administering security practices and still be breached because of a targeted, sustained, or advanced attack. However, in many of the breaches, while there may have been a nation-state or organized crime actor behind the attack, this does not necessarily translate into a "sophisticated attack" as some of the public relations material companies present after a breach would lead the public to believe. These statements post-breach are usually like:

"Cyberattackers conducted a very sophisticated attack to gain unauthorized access to our IT systems and have obtained personal information belonging to our customers. The information accessed includes names, birthdays, addresses, email addresses, social security numbers, and credit card information. As soon as we learned of the attack, we immediately made every effort to mitigate the security vulnerability, contacted the FBI, and cooperated fully in the investigation. We have also retained an expert-independent security company, a world leader in cybersecurity, to evaluate our systems and identify solutions based on the current threat environment. We are notifying all customers individually and will be offering free credit monitoring services. A website has been established for more information, along with the establishment of multiple toll-free phone numbers to report any concerns. We take our customer's privacy very seriously and work hard each day to make our systems and security processes more secure. We will continue to provide updates as new information becomes available."

The message conveys several key messages: (1) the attack was sophisticated and beyond our control, (2) we work hard every day to secure the systems, (3) we care about your privacy, (4) steps that are being taken to demonstrate action, (5) easy access to current and future information, and (6) an offering of caring. The intent is to satisfy the customer to make them feel whole, so they do not take their business elsewhere, referred to as "churn" from the result of a breach. In the 2017 Cost of a Data Breach Report, this "churn" of customers was 3.24%. These costs can be reduced by implementing practices to retain the customer, such as offering credit monitoring after the breach.

Whatever the reason for the breach, communication with the customers is vitally important, whether the breach was the result of a sophisticated breach or not. Organizations have become smarter, and some have individuals dedicated to ensuring the communication is truthful and prompt, and inspires confidence with the consumer that while the breach has happened, and may or may not have been prevented, the organization is acting in the best interest of the customer to mitigate any damage. Obviously, when information has been compromised, it is difficult for the consumer to be "made whole," as the information is now disclosed and the price on this disclosure is hard to calculate. The best the organization can do at this point is to execute a pre-planned response to minimize future damage.

MELANIE ENSIGN: IMPORTANCE OF COMMUNICATIONS BEFORE, DURING, AND AFTER THE BREACH

Security and Privacy Communications, Uber

A common misconception about security communications is that it is a post-incident function, akin to traditional crisis communications, brought in to navigate a negative press cycle. However, just as strong technical teams are constantly engaged in proactive and preventative efforts, so are the most effective communicators. Not only can a dedicated security communications specialist help you avoid potential pitfalls as advisors in your product development process, but they can also help build a resilient reputation and ensure the work of your internal teams is known and accurately reflected in public reports.

As a by-product of ongoing engagement with technical teams, security communicators force continuous stress testing of an organization's response process, forging important relationships with other resourceful teams, and helping to connect bodies of knowledge across the company. This institutional and procedural experience is critical for quick, accurate, and transparent communications during and after a security incident. It also equips your communications team with the ability to address both the current state of an incident and the characteristics of the environment in which it occurred. This level of detail is important for developing informative and actionable communications for external stakeholders and helping business leaders understand potential risks.

Every company has at least two things in common. First, you will experience a serious security incident at some point in time, and likely more than once. Second, you do not want your security team's first introduction to the world to be a breach. Your credibility and commitment must be established in advance. In fact, frequent and proactive external communications can be a security team's greatest asset in building trust for the brand, recruiting top talent, and contributing to the industry's knowledge base.

So, whether it is helping customers understand the backend systems in place to protect their information or guiding engineering teams towards a shared security goal, the most impactful work of security communications happens long before the breach—and quite possibly, could help prevent it.

Significant Breaches

According to the Privacy Rights Clearinghouse, an organization tracking breach statistics since 2005, there were 1.9 billion records breached in 2017 alone and 239 breaches comprising almost 500 million records in the first half of 2018. Since they started tracking breaches, there have been almost 10.5 billion records breached from over 8,000 breaches made public since 2005. An important consideration here is that this only includes *publicly reported breaches and* does not include breaches in organizations not required to or chose not to report the breach, as well as the organization that may have been breached but were unaware of the breach.

The following are a sampling of some of the most noteworthy breaches in the past few years and what we can learn from them for our security programs.

Under Armour 150M Records (2018)

In March 2018, Under Armour announced a breach involving the MyFitnessPal application, which tracks user's eating and nutrition habits by maintaining 5 million food items in their database and integrating with activity tracking devices such as FitBit, Garmin, Polar, and others. The breach involved usernames, email addresses, and hashed passwords (most using bcrypt to secure passwords) and were requiring users to change their passwords. They indicated they do not know the identity of the unauthorized party.

Given that between 31% and 55% of users reuse passwords across sites, this could be troublesome. Some companies have started employing services to check if a password used within the company is also used on another website or being sold on the Dark Web. Discover Financial Services has implemented tracking of social security numbers for sale on the Dark Web and is using this surveillance capability as a competitive service offering—a good example of leveraging a security practice not only to limit fraud but also to provide customer value and build trust by notification when the social security number is located on another site. Given the number of breaches in the past several years and exposed authentication credentials, adding proactive Dark Web monitoring for userID–password combinations may be an activity to consider. Shortly after the breach was announced, users were targeted with scam phishing emails to change the passwords, compounding the problem.

According to Under Armour, payment information and social security numbers were not disclosed, as they were protected by separate systems. Aside from the exposure of many user account password hashes being disclosed, the lesson here is that the separation of systems is still an effective mitigation control to reduce the impact of the breach. Since the financial information was not involved, there was no offering of credit monitoring services by Under Armour.

While the eating habits do not currently constitute protected health information, as these applications are developed and contain information about the eating habits, diet, and exercise goals, at what point does the aggregation of information start to resemble health information that should be protected? Could inferences be drawn from this data as to a health condition that may exist? Who should be able to access body mass information or the physical activity, or location of the individual? For example, the U.S. National Cancer Institute publishes a guide advising cancer patients of the best foods to eat and not eat—could a "cancer diagnosis" be inferred from the eating habits stored by the applications such as MyFitnessPal? The company has not indicated that the information was accessed at this juncture. As more and more fitness applications are produced, with as many as 58% of users downloading a fitness or health application, this information may become target-rich in the future.

Facebook/Cambridge Analytica (2018)

The Facebook/Cambridge Analytica incident involved as many as 87 million Facebook members account data accessed (according to Facebook), because of taking a personality quiz and passing the information off to Cambridge Analytica, a firm engaged in influencing political campaigns. The issue gained large media coverage after the story broke on March 4, 2018, by the New York Times, followed by warrants to search the political consultancy's U.K. office, hours of testimony by Chief Executive Officer Mark Zuckerberg before Congress in April 2018, with Cambridge Analytica closing its doors on May 2, 2018. The incident occurred after Facebook users were presented with an application created by Dr. Aleksandr Kogan that invited users to find out their personality type. The application was used by 305,000 users, which also recorded the public data of their friends, gathering data on as many as 87 million people, numbers that have been denied by Cambridge Analytica. It is alleged that the data was sold to Cambridge Analytica and was subsequently used to profile users for the 2016 U.S. election, also denied by Cambridge Analytica. Cambridge Analytica indicated they licensed 30 million records from the application's creator but did not use them in the U.S. election and have deleted all the information. Facebook has apologized and is reviewing their applications and access to the information by third parties.

John Rust, Director of the Psychometrics Center at the University of Cambridge, informed the head of the legal department at the University in 2014 warning that an issue may be developing with the application being developed by Aleksandr Kogan, a social psychologist and lecturer at the University of Cambridge, due to the extensive nature of the data collection of the "friends." He indicated that the university could be at risk of much (adverse) media attention. He was asserting at that time this information would be used in an election. John's own center discovered how Facebook "likes" could be used to deduce the personalities and political persuasions. His concern was one of privacy for the individual—particularly of the potential millions of users whose information would be available without their consent.

In addition to the subsequent investigations conducted by U.S. and U.K. authorities, the public relations fallout for Facebook, the incident has impacted thousands of third-party Facebook application developers that may have siphoned off data about users and their friends to provide understandings of people's preferences and relationships. Game makers such as Farmville and dating applications

Tinder had access to large amounts of Facebook information. Developers that designed applications to use the "log-in through Facebook" capability would have the ability to see profile, location, and behavior of that Facebook user and all that person's friends.

So, what does all this mean? Some would argue this is not a "breach" in the traditional sense, where someone stole information for unauthorized means. Cambridge Analytica may have accessed the information under false pretenses (data initially acquired via Facebook academic license), but that thought aside, developers of applications were provided with this Facebook access—unbeknownst to the Facebook users. This may have never surfaced as an issue had, (1) the use of the information was to be used to influence a major election, (2) information on other users who never consented to use that information—innocent bystanders of sorts—was not collected, and (3) users did not feel manipulated by using "personality-type information" and their "likes" to influence their views.

Whatever the outcome in this he-said-she-said case is less interesting than what this case represents—a compromise of trust. Online search engines, social media platforms, and companies collecting information have established privacy notices (which some incorrectly call privacy policies on their websites), whereby full consent to access any information about any related information to that which is provided, plus that of your connections. The privacy chapter goes into this in more detail; for the moment, let us just say this case highlights where we may have entered a world where posting a broad company privacy notice to "collect whatever we want to" may no longer be acceptable. Not that it ever was per the privacy laws and data collection/usage limitation privacy limitation principles that already existed—what has changed is the voice of public opinion, which was strong on this issue. People do not want to feel duped.

There are a few takeaways we can learn for our own organizations from this case, (1) just because users have signed a consent to the application sometimes a long time ago to collect a broad range of data, does not mean we *should* collect it, (2) manipulating users is likely to produce a public relations issue, (3) contracts with third parties need to be clear as to what they have access to and how they can use the information provided, (4) aggregated analytic data should be protected as one of the "crown jewels," and (5) failure to self-regulate will invite regulation.

RENEE GUTTMANN-STARK: SIX-MINUTE RULE

Board Member, Netshield

My first CISO role was at Time Inc. in 2000. I worked alongside some of the most talented people in the media industry. I had the opportunity to attend town hall meetings where journalists spoke about interviews with people like Nelson Mandela. I learned how they dealt with reporting while trying to avoid being kidnapped or killed. In addition to the magazines, Time Inc. published magazine content on their websites. That meant that every fact was checked at least three times! For context, the year 2000 predates Payment Card Industry Data Security Standard (PCIDSS) and the Sarbanes-Oxley Act (SOX) and just about every other regulation. Let us say compliance overhead was minimal.

About a year into my job, the job got a little more challenging. Parenting magazine had the vision to build a website that would allow expecting mothers to create an online pregnancy journal. Planned functionality would enable women to share their sonograms, create birthing instructions for the doctors, and much more! The option of telling creative folks: "NO WAY" was not an option. My role was to help identify the potential risks and define the "appropriate security controls." The bad news was that Parenting magazine was on the cutting edge in terms of their plans for personal information and the only other CISOs that I knew were in the financial arena. I was positive that Parenting would not appreciate it if I proposed financial system controls. I looked inside the company for help. The good news is that I had a solid relationship with the attorneys who reviewed the most controversial articles and were most skilled at evaluating risk. I asked for their help to review the project. The attorneys and I sat in meetings and watched the creative juices flow. We provided input to the project team about privacy and security controls, and we told them when we thought that certain functions seemed creepy. In the absence of relevant benchmarks and other compliance checklists, we developed the "Six-Month Rule". Basically, the "Six-Month Rule" was as follows: How will our work look after a breach and after Time Inc. journalists have spent 6 months reviewing all our emails and interviewing every member of the project team—multiple times? I still use the "Six-Month Rule" today. The difference is that it is now the "Six-Minute Rule." How will our decisions look in 6 minutes after someone posts an issue on the Internet, fact checked or not?

The bottom line is as follows: Do not be afraid when your business partners want to push the envelope. Companies must take the risk to survive and thrive. The risk/reward equation demands informed decision making by appropriate stakeholders. The Six-Minute Rule works for me. It enables me to sleep better at night and look myself in the mirror in the morning.

Equifax 143M Records (2017)

Equifax garnered much attention during the 2017 breach due to the number of individuals impacted and the information obtained, including names, social security numbers, birth dates, addresses, and in some instances driver's license numbers. Credit card information was also exposed for 209,000 customers.

There were several breach response missteps because of this breach that is worth noting, notwithstanding the investigation as to whether the $1.8 million stock sale by three executives of the company prior to public announcement of the breach will result in criminal or civil actions. The Chief Information Officer (CIO) of U.S. consumer reporting division charged in March 2018 with insider trading for selling almost $1 million in company stock after he learned of the breach and before it was announced publicly. One of the missteps was the creation of a site called "equifaxsecurity2017.com" directing consumers to enter the last six digits of their Social Security Number to determine if they have "potentially been impacted." Asking users to reenter the information that may have been stolen does not give the appearance of good security controls. Instead of directing users to www.equifax.com and posting information prominently on the landing page, they were directed to a different site. A researcher established a fake website, "securityequifax2017.com" to see if users would click on this link, and not only did they click on the simulated phishing link, but the site was linked in the company's official Twitter account, as shown in Figure 7.1. The link was blocked by some anti-malware programs as it appeared to be a phishing address.

Equifax also incurred other public relations issues when they encouraged those visiting the site to determine whether they have been impacted to enroll in the Equifax TrustedID Premier Service, as well as telling individuals to come back to the site in 4 days. There did not seem to be the urgency in protecting the consumer information. Probably the largest snafu was the inclusion of language in the fine print of accepting the service that rights were being given up being able to sue the company. A few days after the breach, Equifax pulled back the arbitration language stating, "In response to customer inquiries, we have made it clear that the arbitration clause and class action waiver included in the Equifax and TrustedID Premier terms of use does not apply to this cybersecurity incident." While it was good that the clause was redacted for this incident, individuals still wasted their time calling the company and expressing concern, as well as appearing that Equifax was being less than fully transparent and attempting to trick consumers into agreeing to

Figure 7.1 Equifax Twitter account communicates phishing site. (From Larson, S., Equifax tweets fake phishing site to concerned customers, CNN Tech, September 20, 2017.)

waive liability when this was still early days of the breach and the ultimate impact was unknown. Additionally, the ten-digit PIN number issued when enrolling in the protection was simply the time/date stamp of the enrollment time, reducing the number hackers would need to guess from 1 in a billion to 1 in 5,000 (since changed to be random). Due to this perceived lack of transparency, there was concern that once individuals enrolled in the free year of credit monitoring service, they would be automatically enrolled in a paid service, increasing profits to the company experiencing the breach.

Aside from the breach response, which had the appearance of being inadequate based upon the number of retractions and changes during the days following the breach, there is the issue of what caused the breach in the first place. The cause was a critical vulnerability that was known in March 2017, a flaw in Apache Struts software (CVE-2017-5638) used to provide web server access, and was not patched when the breach occurred in mid-May 2017 and discovered July 29, 2017. When Apache announced the vulnerability in March, they were advising organizations to immediately patch the 0-day vulnerability. Due to pending Equifax litigation, it is not immediately known why the systems were not patched in a timely matter. According to Gartner Analyst Avivah Litan, the information may be exploited by the hackers in the future in four different ways: (1) sold and resold on the underground; (2) used to update existing, already-stolen records about individual consumers that get bought and sold by cybercrime underground data brokers; (3) it will be used to take over existing accounts, e.g., bank accounts, brokerage accounts, phone service accounts (a common occurrence these days, e.g., with Bitcoin wallet holders), and retirement accounts. This compromised personally identifiable information (PII) data is used by call centers and online systems to verify identities when they are conducting high-risk transactions such as moving money or changing an account's phone number on record; (4) purchased by nation-states to build better dossiers on potential individuals they might try to recruit or blackmail, for intelligence-gathering purposes. The dataset may be worth as much as $27 million in the data underground according to Trend Micro. The true impact of this breach may not be known for years to come. The immediate impact to the consumers involved time-consuming requests of credit freezes on their accounts, as well as the inconvenience and reminder of the breach each time credit needed to be unfrozen each time a new credit card or line of credit was needed. This impact was also shared by individuals whose data was breached, not because consumers chose to provide this information to Equifax (other than by the fine print in our credit card applications), but because Equifax operated as the custodians of it.

There are several lessons from this breach that bear repeating and marking in bold letters. First, while there may be a policy within the organization to conduct vulnerability scans and patch on a regular basis, the timely execution of applying the patches, particularly to 0-day critical security vulnerabilities, is critical. These processes need to be monitored and the acceptance of "open critical vulnerabilities" must be measured and aged appropriately. If this is not done, with visibility to senior management, the processes can become accepted as "the new normal." On January 28, 1986, the space shuttle challenger exploded, killing seven astronauts due to the "O" rings failing while experiencing low temperatures, permitting the hot gas to blow by and destroy the spaceship. The engineers were in a heated discussion the day before with the leadership team, with the engineers arguing it was too cold to launch. In a book by Dr. Diane Vaughn entitled, "The Challenger Launch Decision," she created a phrase "the normalization of deviation"; in other words, where over time, organizations deviate from safe practices so regularly that they become the new normal. Whether or not this was the case in the Equifax breach has not been publicly communicated; however, what can be learned is that the patch was not applied in a timely manner and the issue could have been avoided with prompt patching. We can learn from our own organizations that we should not be accepting a "normalization of deviation," whereby we so regularly put off patches that it becomes the new norm.

Secondly, breach response is important. Failure to pre-think what will be said and have systems in place to adequately respond to the breach can result in a public relations nightmare. The media will jump on every misstep and highlight it. Consumers will be unhappy and may take their business elsewhere (whereas in the Equifax breach, consumers did not have a choice). Attorneys will circle the wagons with class action suits, tying up expensive internal and external resources. There will be government investigations into the matter. Individuals will be forced to retire, particularly where the "buck stops," including the CEO and members of the board of directors, and of course, the CISO (the CEO and CISO retired shortly following the breach). News stories will surface about the credentials of the CISO, fair or unfair assessments. It just gets ugly without an appropriate, planned-out response.

Third, transparency is critical to consumers. All the information may not be known at the time of the breach, and there still needs to be a review of "How would this appear to the consumer?" as the information is communicated. If customers do have a choice in the future, will they return to us? As the CEO of Equifax, Rick Smith indicated in his video after the breach, "Equifax will not be defined by this incident, but rather, by how we respond," indicates the importance of making the commitment to respond to the consumers. As highlighted previously, Equifax received much criticism for the execution of this promise; however, the promise was clearly on point.

Fourth, organizations must leverage learnings from prior breaches to strengthen the security practices, not so much with the specific vulnerability or patch, but by taking the opportunity to holistically review the processes to avoid a similar execution flaw in the future (Equifax experienced a breach in the TALX subsidiary, which provides online payroll, HR, and tax services by resetting a four-digit PIN and stealing W-2 data between April 17, 2016 and March 29, 2017). While this breach may not be related to the July 29, 2017, breach, the existence of the breach may prompt an internal review of processes to determine if there are other gaps needing to be addressed.

And finally, breaches involving sensitive information impacting many consumers will get more than their fair share of media attention due to the scope of the breach. Legislators will weigh in on the issue, such as Elizabeth Warren stating, "I've called for Equifax executives to be held legally accountable for their role in failing to stop this data breach and hiding it from the public for forty days." Notice the words were targeted towards the response of the breach and the failure to stop it. This is a tall order for many organizations to completely "stop a breach" and may have been more influenced by the company's response to the breach than the real efforts to stop it.

Spambot "Onliner" 711 Million Records (August 2017)

Spammers need many email addresses to each a wide audience as well as needing to produce targeted attacks to bypass spam filters. In August 2017, a Paris-based security researcher operating under the pseudonymous handle Benkow discovered that an open and accessible web server hosted in the Netherlands contained the email addresses, passwords, and email servers used to send spam of many individuals. The spammer apparently leveraged credentials obtained from the prior LinkedIn breach (a 2012 breach that fully came to light in 2016) and a suspected Badoo dating site breach (2016) and some other sources. The information also contained the Simple Mail Transfer Protocol (SMTP) server and port used to send the email. Using this information, the spammer would send targeted emails from the 80 million accounts to the remaining 630 million targets using fingerprinting emails, containing a pixel image that would send back to the sender the type of computer system, operating system, and other information. Once this information was collected, the attacker would know who to target to install malware, usually an invoice from a delivery service, hotel, or insurance company, with a JavaScript Ursnif malware attached. This technique allowed the spammer to send out millions of emails undetected by spam filters, as the emails were being sent from legitimate users in small quantities and harvest thousands of credentials including passwords, credit card numbers, and other personal information. Benkow estimated over 100,000 infections of the malware had occurred.

A database established by security researcher Troy Hunt helps users determine if their email address has been "pwned" or owned and made available as the result of a breach. By typing in the email address, the individual can see if the address was one of the addresses from a prior breach. Troy indicates that he does not store the credential information, as this would create a security risk (and a go-to place for hackers to target). The website haveibeenpwned.com aggregates the datasets from prior breaches as individuals tend to use the same password across sites.

There are several key lessons that can be learned from this breach. First, with the massive number of breaches occurring over the past several years and the accounts being sold via the Dark Web, much information is already known by the attackers. Armed with an email address and password, the attacker could access accounts and harvest even more information, potentially sensitive information contained in the emails. Password resets could be accomplished with this information, as resets are sent to the email address for verification. If these accounts are compromised, or "pwned," there is now a hole in the reset process. Second, users need to be educated about the reuse of passwords across personal, work, and the websites accessed. By using the same passwords, these passwords may have already been harvested, along with the email address. Training should stress the establishment of different passwords using different routines for business websites. Third, while much attention has been given to phishing programs over the past few years advising, "don't click on the link" or "don't open the attachment from someone you don't know," we need to recognize that the mere act of opening an email can trigger providing the attacker with information about our equipment, operating system, patch levels, etc.—information of great use to the attacker to limit the future targeted attack systems to make their campaigns "less noisy." Finally, while Troy has created a great service to check on whether an email address was involved in a breach, we should recognize that these files exist with attackers, but with richer information included as mentioned in this section. As the CISO, discussions should center around—what is the impact to our organization if this information was known? Would we change our password policies? Would we change our approach to training?

WannaCry, NotPetya, Petya Ransomware (2017)

Ransomware made a large splash in 2017 through the unleashing of several malware attacks, starting with the WannaCry attack in May 2017 that infected 300,000 computers in 150 countries. WannaCry, was alleged by the United States, British government, and several security researchers to have originated from North Korea's Lazarus Group working for the North Korean Government, the same group believed to be responsible for the 2014 attack on Sony Pictures in response to the pending release of a movie "The Interview." The movie depicted the leader of North Korea, Kim Jong-un, in an unflattering light. The malware created unprecedented damage by taking British hospitals offline, disrupting businesses globally. More than 80 England health organizations were impacted, resulting in over 20,000 canceled appointments and 600 surgeries having to rely on manual pen and paper methods. Five hospitals had to divert ambulances to other facilities. The ransomware page, as shown in Figure 7.2, demanded Bitcoin payment to recover the encrypted files.

Ransomware was not new, as CryptoLocker has been in the wild since 2013; however, this is the first case where the ransomware became widespread, as prior ransomware leveraged direct mail campaigns using phishing emails to entice a user to download malware. With WannaCry, the scale of the damage was much greater than an instance of CryptoLocker, as it spread like a "worm," self-replicating itself onto other vulnerable computers without user interaction. The last wide-scale worm was in 2009, when Conficker spread to over 20 million machines in 1 month. The most recent worm was the Mirai worm in October 2016 using poorly secured

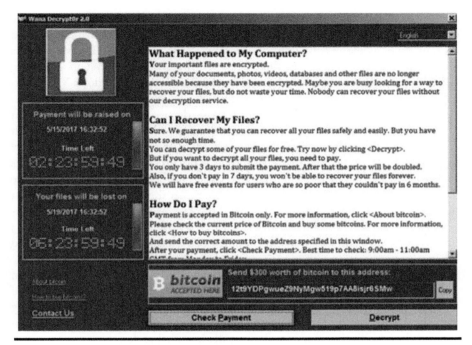

Figure 7.2   Ransomware WannaCry 2017.

Internet of Things (IoT) devices to create a botnet to attack websites through distributed denial-of-service (DDoS) attacks, including the servers of Dyn, and sites including Reddit, Amazon, New York Times, and Twitter websites. The Mirai Botnet attack also leveraged IoT devices with flawed security in September 2016 to take down the website of Brian Krebs, an investigative journalist who focuses on cybersecurity issues, sending 500–600 gigabits per second, much greater than the 3–4 gigabit DDoS attacks seen previously. The three creators of this worm plead guilty in the U.S. District Court for Alaska in November 2017 to the developing and operating the Mirai Botnet. WannaCry with the worm-like encrypting capabilities not only had the potential to produce massive damage for organizations that were unprepared for the malware but also was successful in wreaking havoc for several organizations.

The origins of WannaCry are thought to have come from a weakness in the Microsoft operating system released in April 2017 by a group known as the Shadow Brokers, which provided the ability to run on other systems within the same network. The weakness was code-named EternalBlue and was believed to have been stolen from the National Security Agency (NSA) hacking tool set from a group within NSA the Shadow Brokers referred to as the Equation Group. The weakness was fixed by Microsoft issuing a critical-level security patch (Microsoft Bulletin MS17-010) in March 2017 because of the NSA concerns over the potency of this attack, prior to the Shadow Brokers release. However, according to Kaspersky, 98% of the machines impacted by the virus were Windows 7 machines, which operated on four times as many computers as Windows 10 at the time. Windows XP was not much of a factor, except in the case of the British hospital system still using XP computers. Patches were also issued for the unsupported Windows XP operating system due to the criticality of the breach, for which security updates were no longer being made. The WannaCry worm stopped spreading due to the execution of a poorly constructed "kill switch" within the code, whereby if it could not reach a hard-coded Uniform Record Locator (URL) in the program, the WannaCry worm would shut down and stop encrypting. A British security researcher, Marcus Hutchins, made the discovery of the URL connection and was able to register the domain for $10.96, set up a website, and slow down the spread of the virus. As a side note, after receiving awards for his role in the WannaCry worm, Marcus was arrested in August 2017 after leaving the DEFCON conference in Las Vegas for his suspected role in a prior malware development, Kronos, in 2014 and he has denied his involvement.

Some security practitioners question as to why the kill switch was included in the malware—was it to enable the creators the ability to shut the software down if it went out of control? Was the malware meant to be released or was it in a testing phase and accidentally was deployed? Or was the ransomware really a distraction and not about collecting money and was really intended to destroy certain computers? The victims of WannaCry were asked to pay between $300 and $600 in Bitcoin to get their data back. However, given that only an estimated USD $100 K was paid to the attackers, in contrast to CryptoWall that earned $325 million for 406,000 attempted infections. The motives are unclear, as this was not profitable.

In March 2016, the Petya virus, named after a 1995 James Bond Film GoldenEye satellite, attached a file to an email claiming to be a job applicant's resume. Once the Portable Document Format (PDF) attachment was clicked, the user would agree to the Windows User Access Control warning indicating the executable would be making changes to the computer. The user's computer would subsequently reboot, install a boot loader, overwrite the system's master boot record, and encrypt the master file table, making the files inaccessible. This differs in other ransomware approaches, whereby the files are encrypted. This is possible because the user has granted high-level privileged administrative access.

In June 2017, a more potent form of the virus called NotPetya began circulating with the capability to spread without requiring spam emails or tricking the user to gain administrative access. NotPetya leveraged a backdoor in an accounting software package used by many companies in Ukraine to spread the malware. To spread to other computers, NotPetya enhanced the capabilities of Petya using EternalBlue (used in WannaCry) and EternalRomance, as well as a tool to locate the network administration credentials in memory of the infected machines and then use the remote access tools built into Windows to access other computers and infect them. In other words, this shifted the need for the end user to provide the admin privileges NotPetya also encrypted everything on the drive. Unlike Petya, which maintained the ability to reverse the encryption, the NotPetya appears to be intended to wipe drives without the intention of restoring them. NotPetya came just weeks after the WannaCry worm, exploiting the same Microsoft vulnerability that could be fixed by the patch released 3 months earlier. Security firm Cyberreason provided an analysis of the costs of NotPetya by reviewing the U.S. Securities and Exchange filings and investor statements and came up with an aggregated 2017 cost of $595 million and growing. They examined hard-hit companies including Nuance Communications, Beiersdorf, Mondelez International, Maersk, Merck, Reckitt Benckiser, and FedEx. Real dollar impact was experienced by these organizations, including FedEx's statement in the September 2017 earnings call, "the worldwide operations of TNT Express were significantly affected during the first quarter by the June 27 NotPetya cyberattack. Most TNT Express services resumed during the quarter, and substantially, all TNT Express critical operational systems have been restored. However, TNT Express volume, revenue, and profit still remain below previous levels." FedEx indicated the cost would be about $300 million following the attack. Danish shipper Maersk also indicated costs in the $300 million range.

We can glean several lessons from the various forms of ransomware that hit in 2017. First, the forms of ransomware are changing and able to replicate themselves without user intervention due to some of the exploit code that was made available. Second, these exploits are being packaged in the form of fully functional tool sets that can be executed by attackers that do not require the level of sophistication as the creator. Third, patching, patching, patching. While this is a general theme throughout these breaches, the destruction caused either through the encryption or through the wiping of information was extensive for some organizations. Fourth, governments may speculate as to the origin of the breaches, or the targets of the breaches—to the typical organization, this analysis almost becomes irrelevant when the objective is resiliency of business operations. While the discussion may be interesting, the real question is what would the impact to our organization be? Fifth, small businesses and individuals are often targeted by ransomware as many of these organizations do not have the rigor of regular backups and will find it necessary to pay the relatively small amount to get the key to unlock their files, whereas large organizations typically have the backups and will not pay. Sixth, even if the organization does pay the ransom, there is no assurance the file keys will be provided. In the case of Hancock Health, Greenfield, Indiana, in January 2018, they reported paying $55,000 in Bitcoin to attackers to release 1,400 files (renamed to "I'm Sorry" and encrypted). This was viewed as a business decision, as it would take them weeks to recover everything and substantially disrupt operations. In this case, the files were recovered; however, there are no guarantees the attackers will not also ask for more ransom money before handing over the keys, as they did in the case of the Kansas Heart Hospital, who changed strategies after the second ransom request. Seventh, backup recovery plans must be in place in the event the ransomware does hit. This includes not only ensuring that backups on key systems are current and will work (i.e., are readable and available) but also ensuring that impact to business operations has been assessed and plans are in place for handling the outage or system failover. Finally, these costs are sure to increase, as businesses assess the outage time with the cost of getting up quickly. As more businesses pay the ransom, the rates will go up, and a different protection strategy needs to be in place to manage the knowledge of the end user, technical endpoint solutions, appropriate monitoring, and rigorous recovery plans if all else fails.

TODD INSKEEP: DEALING WITH NOTPETYA

Principal Cybersecurity Consulting, Booz Allen Hamilton

June 27, 2017 started out as an ordinary day, acting as CISO for pharmaceutical laboratory company, when the IT Chief started sharing. Our team members at both a supplier and a customer were watching these partners' systems go down with a ransomware lock screen. With dedicated network connections to both partners, our first question is, "When do you cut the network connections you worked to establish for business?"

We checked Cable News Network (CNN), Twitter, and the National Health-Information Sharing and Analysis Center, and this early we did not learn much. There was malware, spreading, seemingly by rumor. Maybe it was spread through phishing with an attachment/ link or spread through the same exploit that fed WannaCry's spread nearly 2 months earlier.

We cut the network connections. We banned the machines at both partners from connecting to our network, and virtual private network connections. We formulated a plan to scan, patch, and verify the machines before letting them back on.

With NotPetya spreading at the end of the month, and end of a quarter, the business asked the IT team to restore the underlying services as accounting practices prevented counting revenue for stock not in transit—we had to find a way to process shipping.

On the fly, we were building the business continuity plan—we did not really have. The IT "heroes" fixed the IT systems, learning about the business processes broken by the external impact of NotPetya on suppliers and customers.

Key takeaways from NotPetya are as follows:

■ The next cyberattack may impact business without impacting IT systems; business continuity plans need to address business processes from end to end.

- NotPetya spread exponentially within affected companies, at rates over 10,000 computers per minute; an attack may be over before you identify it. Fast-spreading malware requires managing lateral movement:
  - Use multifactor authentication to limit hijacking of privileged accounts,
  - Segment networks to separate key systems and processes from others.
- Executing a business continuity plan requires access:
  - Printed or backup copies accessible without corporate technology,
  - Practice exercising the plan through different scenarios.
- Be clear on the decision-making roles and responsibilities before an event happens; 2 hours before, a payment deadline is not the time to buy Bitcoins and argue about paying a ransom to recover data.

Our pharmaceutical company was not fully prepared for NotPetya on June 27, but with a solid team, we were able to deal with the limited impact on our business. Other companies were not so lucky. CISOs today need to be prepared for all kinds of event scenarios—from those we see in the paper every week, to those we can only imagine today.

Apple vs. FBI (2016)

This case did not involve an incident or breach; however, this case has implications for the forensic handling of incidents and what happens when vulnerabilities become public, as noted in the Shadow Brokers case earlier. In December 2015, the FBI requested that Apple help the FBI unlock an iPhone belonging to the person responsible for the San Bernardino shooting that killed 14 people. Apple refused. In February 2016, the judge asked Apple to provide "reasonable technical assistance" to unlock the phone (which was set to eliminate all data after ten failed password attempts of a four-digit password). Apple argued this would result in creating a type of master key that in the wrong hands could provide hackers the ability to unlock millions of phones. A day before the March 2016 hearing, the request was withdrawn as the government said they found a third party to assist in unlocking the phone and announced a week later that the FBI had unlocked the phone.

The situation fueled a debate as to how much the courts could compel a technology company to weaken their encryption process by essentially creating a backdoor. Apple claimed they had no ability to bypass the security on their newer phones. According to a Poll conducted at the time of the 2016 rulings, 38% of those surveyed indicated Apple should not unlock the iPhone, 51% felt they should, and 11% did not know. Was this merely promoting a brand image for Apple or was it being altruistic in maintaining civil liberties and consumer privacy rights? Was this really about a one-time critical terrorism investigation attempt by the FBI, or was it meant to obtain the keys to the iPhone for other cases that would not have garnered the same public support for as needing the keys to fight "terrorism"? Clearly, the public is divided on the issue and across age groups.

Aside from personal opinions of whether they should or should not assist to unlock the smartphone, the question for us is, "What are the implications for our companies?" First, the security technology built into products today may or may not be at the same strength tomorrow due to a government action. Apple "won" this case by continually refusing to comply in the court system, and the FBI "won" by being able to find someone (or were able to internally—name of the company used has not been confirmed by the government) to bypass the security. A future court case aimed at a company to bypass security without the financial resources of Apple could compel a company to create a backdoor in the software or hand over the keys. What risk would this present to our own organization's applications? Knowledge of vendor products, asset inventories, and software versions within our organizations now becomes even more critical. The risk should be evaluated when these events occur. Second, as solutions make it into the wild, we could be in the same situation as the Shadow Brokers release of exploit code. If there was an external company that provided the FBI with a solution, how secure is the authentication process of the iPhone? Would that company be a good target for hacking from a foreign government (to obtain the technique)? Are their employees a risk for insider threat or external extortion/blackmailing to obtain information? Third, from the surveys, users expect a certain degree of privacy, even in the extreme case of giving up privacy to thwart terrorism—they are expecting the same from our organizations.

Anthem 80 Million Records (January 2015)

Anthem Blue Cross Blue Shield is the second largest health insurer in the United States and the largest licensee of the Blue Cross Blue Shield brand, operating in more than a dozen, covering over 40 million people. Anthem discovered a breach on January 29, 2015, and issued a memo to clients indicating, "On January 27, 2015, an Anthem associate, a database administrator, discovered suspicious activity—a database query running using the associate's login information. He had not initiated the query and immediately stopped the query and alerted Anthem's Information Security department. It was also discovered the login information for additional database administrators had been compromised."

Anthem indicated the attackers had access to names, member ID numbers, dates of birth, social security numbers, addresses, phone numbers, email addresses, and employment information including income data. They clarified further in the memo that no credit/debit card information and no medical health treatment information were compromised. Anthem soon made similar explanations of their website from the CEO following the breach.

The note indicated they determined on January 29 that they were a victim of a "sophisticated cyberattack" and executed an "advanced persistent threat." The memo further indicated that the attacker had a proficient understanding of the data platforms and successfully utilized valid database administrator login information. Anthem fed the information to the Health Information Trust Alliance (HITRUST) Cyber Threat Intelligence and Incident Coordination Center including the MD5 malware hashes, IP addresses, and email addresses used by its attackers. HITRUST then provided the information to its automated threat exchange, United States Computer Emergency Readiness Team (US-CERT), the Department of Homeland Security and the Department of Health and Human Services (DHHS). According to a HITRUSTAlert issued, "This crucial observable information was anonymously shared with the HITRUST C3 Community, through the automated threat exchange. It was quickly determined that the Indicators of Compromise (IOC)s were not found by other organizations across the industry and this attack was targeted at a specific organization." Several reports indicated the suspected breach involved the Deep Panda hacking group from China; however, this has not been publicly confirmed by Anthem, but was indicated in a June 5, 2015 FBI Report warning of a "group of cyber actors who have and stolen sensitive business information and Personally Identifiable Information (PII). Information obtained from victims indicates that PII was a priority target." This announcement followed on the heels of the Office of Personnel Management (OPM) breach (breach of 4.2 million former and government employees and security background clearance information on 21.5 million individuals), suspected to be originating from China via Deep Panda, although some security researchers are of the opinion the breaches came from different sources.

According to a multistate market conduct and financial examination conducted in response to a 2/26/15 Examination Warrant issued by the Indiana Department of Insurance, the breach started when a user in the Amerigroup subsidiary opened an email containing a malicious link, subsequently installing malware on the computer, and enabling remote access to the computer. The attacker then moved laterally across the Anthem systems and escalated privileges, leveraging 50 accounts and compromising 90 or more systems including the enterprise data warehouse, a system containing consumer PII. Subsequent queries to that system resulted in the exfiltration of 78.8 million records. The firm CrowdStrike confirmed with high confidence they knew the identity of the attacker. The review indicated that Anthem removed the attacker's ability to access the network within 3 days of identifying the breach.

Anthem agreed in June 2017 to pay $115 million to settle more than 100 lawsuits related to the matter to "protect settlement class consumers from future harm." The lawyers for Anthem indicated this was the largest settlement for a data breach and would be used, in part, to cover 2 years of credit monitoring for the consumers. For the 79 million records involved, this settlement amounts to $1.46 per record to protect from future harm and the consumer receives 2 years of credit monitoring or $50 cash if they choose. The attorneys in the case would receive up to $37.95 million of the $115 million fund, plus reimbursement expenses of up to $3 million. In addition, 29 Settlement Class Representatives would receive $597,000 each. The class action required those impacted (79 million "defendants") to respond by January

29, 2018 if they wanted to be excluded from the class action lawsuit. If individuals did nothing, as stated in the lawsuit settlement, they would "not be eligible to receive any Credit Monitoring Services or compensation from the Settlement, and if the Settlement becomes final, you will give up your rights to sue Defendants and every other person or entity (with certain limited exceptions) regarding the Data Breach, as described in detail above." In other words, unless action prior to January 29, 2018 was taken to specifically exclude oneself from the lawsuit, there was no future legal remedy, other than taking advantage of fraud resolution services provided through an arrangement made between Anthem and Experian.

When this breach occurred, it garnered widespread attention and was disturbing due to the possibility sensitive personal data, specifically health-care information, would be disclosed. In Anthem's operating capacity as a health insurer, they clearly had retained information on sensitive medical procedures, payments, diagnoses—the "holy grail" of information individuals want protected. From the beginning, Anthem maintained that no medical information was released. Why was this so important to confirm that? Aside from the obvious that this information could be used for medical identity theft, extortion, and other insidious criminal purposes, disclosure of the breach could be subject to the Health Insurance Portability and Protection Act of 1996 (HIPAA) and the subsequent HIPAA Privacy and Security Rules, resulting in fines up to $1.5 million for each violation. There appears to be a stronger appetite by the U.S. Human and Health Services Office for Civil Rights (OCR) to levy fines on organizations disclosing health-care records. For example, Advocate Healthcare of Illinois had reported three breaches between July and November 2013, the first breach occurring when four desktop computers containing records on 4 million patients were stolen from their offices. Advocate settled with OCR in 2016 for $5.55 million. Extrapolating this to the Anthem Breach would create a fine more than $100 million for HIPAA violations, not counting a class action suit. This number would go higher if the determination indicted there was willful neglect as well. There is also the added cost of further lawyer fees to negotiate with the OCR regarding HIPAA. In other words, it was crucial to Anthem, as it would be for all CISOs involved with health-care companies, to conduct the appropriate investigation to determine if health-care information was exposed. This does not minimize the fact that sensitive, personal information was accessed, as social security numbers, date of birth (DOB), medical IDs, and other individual information were disclosed; however, these items may be sensitive, but since they do not contain health information, would most likely not be deemed as "protected health information" under the HIPAA Law.

Armchair quarterbacking is always a sport among security professionals after a data breach. For lessons to be learned from this breach, it may be useful to examine the steps Anthem took after the breach. One could argue these steps should have been in place prior to the breach; however, organizations make choices based on their own implementation time frames, priorities, investment available at the time—without knowledge of "when" the attacker may strike. Some of these items may have been on a prior implementation road map, but not implemented. First, after the breach, they implemented two-factor authentication on all remote access tools, implemented a privileged account management (PAM) solution, added resources to their security event and incident management solutions, reset passwords of all privileged users, suspended remote access pending two-factor authentication implementation, replaced Network IDs with new Network Admin IDs and acquired more monitoring products for the databases.

Within 2 weeks of the breach, Anthem worked with a credit monitoring service to provide credit monitoring services to the impacted users. Anthem also notified each person potentially impacted by a letter and set up call centers. They also issued statements immediately, from the CEO. The announcement off the Anthem Breach, in stark contrast to other breaches that took weeks, months, or years to make public, the Anthem Breach was communicated to the clients of Anthem within 3 days of the initial discovery. External firms such as Mandiant and Crowdstrike were retained and immediately involved. Incident response teams were working the case internally. The database administrator had the foresight to notice the query, notice that "something was wrong," and knew who to alert and did so in a timely manner. These are all excellent post-breach practices executed by Anthem. So, what could be missing (emphasis on the word could)? For one, one may want to consider why a single query could access sensitive information on almost 79 unintended disclosure million records containing health-care information? The HIPAA Final Security Rule (2003) was enacted specifically for this reason—the concern over the aggregation of sensitive information falling into the wrong hands. As with any business venture, an investment in a product should only be made if the benefit of the product is at least marginally equal to the added cost. Was the benefit of aggregating this information in a data warehouse greater than the cost, in this case, the cost being the risk of unintended disclosure factored as a component of cost, of the data warehouse? In other words, did Anthem receive greater than the development, maintenance, security costs, and resulting fine ($115 M+ post-breach costs) from having this warehouse in place? If the answer is no, then this could drive investment, e.g., of the products acquired and implemented post-breach to reduce the cost of the loss. I state this as a thought process, not as a critic of Anthem decisions, but rather to highlight the thought process with respect to the impact of potential fines and post-breach costs when working to influence the company on a specific security product investment opportunity.

It appears Anthem acted swiftly in responding to the breach and appeared to be following textbook advice for post-breach execution through investigation, communication with stakeholders, cleaning up the breach, implementing additional technologies, etc. The question remains—now that the information is out there, including very sensitive information such as social security numbers, DOB, employment information, medical IDs for individuals that may not even be out of diapers yet, what will the long-range impact be? How do we factor this knowledge into building our systems that rely on social security numbers and DOB information? The settlement of $115 M by Anthem may not provide much comfort to the individuals involved ($1.46 per record), representing a value of at most 2 years of credit monitoring and fraud protection should there be evidence of identity theft. Will this breach and the liability be forgotten

10–15 years hence, while the information is still exposed? Time will tell what the ultimate impact is. Anthem settled with the DHHS in October 2018, admitting no liability, agreeing to pay a record $16 million fine to settle privacy violations for the largest healthcare attack in the U.S. history. The department cited Anthem for failure to deploy adequate measures to counter hackers, lack of an enterprise-wide risk analysis, insufficient monitoring procedures, failure to identify and respond to suspected or known security incidents, and did not implement minimum access controls dating back to February 2014. While the fine may seem large to some, this represents only 20 cents per record exposed for a company with almost $90 billion in Revenue in 2017. This is an interesting conclusion, since the statement issued at the onset of the breach indicated '...nor is there evidence at this time that medical information such as claims, test results or diagnostic codes were targeted or obtained' was disclosed. Anthem also agreed to a corrective action plan with government monitoring, implement appropriate safeguards and maintain ongoing surveillance. The privacy-related fine levied by DHHS is in stark contrast with the approach to privacy fines imposed by the EU General Data Protection Regulation, which could have started fine negotiations as high as $3.6 billion (4% of annual revenue). The current disparity in pricing the 'cost of privacy' indicates this is an area case law, which will help define realistic fines in the years to come.

As a CISO, it should be recognized that while there may have been gaps in security, Anthem clearly had processes in place to deal with the breach so promptly. This would be expected for a large organization; however, the CISO of a smaller organization needs to have the education of employees to report suspicious activity, react quickly, engage senior management, and being ready to promote proposed projects that may have been on the road map or new projects to mitigate the breach in the future.

Target 110 Million Records (December 2013)

In May 2017, Target Corporation settled lawsuits with 47 states and the District of Columbia for the Data Breach in Late 2013 that began over the holiday Black Friday period (breach experienced November 12, 2013–December 15, 2013), compromising 40 million credit and debit cards (including customer name, card expiration date, card verification value) and exposing information for an additional 70 million people including names, mailing addresses, phone numbers, and email address in their databases. The cyberattackers had accessed Target's gateway server through credentials stolen from a third-party heating and air conditioning vendor. The costs were estimated to be approaching $300 million, with $90 million covered by cyber insurance. The costs include $10 million paid to affected consumers (March 2015), $19 million paid to MasterCard (April 2015), $67 million paid to Visa (August 2015), $39.4 million to banks and credit unions for losses (December 2015), and the most recent $18.5 million settlement. Losses due to the breach also amounted to $17 million, $145 million, and $39 million in 2013–2015, respectively. This is substantial, however less than the $1 billion estimates that several media outlets were projecting soon after the breach was made public.

Why mention a breach that occurred in 2013 with all the other breaches occurring since? The main reason—the board. Target became a landmark breach for several reasons. One, only 5 months after the breach, the President and CEO Gregg Steinhafel resigned amid questions about how much Target had protected the customers. According to the board of directors, Steinhafel "held himself personally accountable and pledged the Target would emerge a better company." A week earlier, Target had appointed a new CIO, replacing the CIO in place at the time of the breach. Target did not have a CISO in place at the time of the breach and subsequently hired a CISO to guide the organization through the implementation of chip-and-PIN cards. This was a wake-up call to CEOs, senior management, and their board of directors across corporations. Even though the CEO was a 30+-year veteran of the company, this was the first CEO of a major corporation to lose their job in conjunction with a customer data breach. Prior to this point, the CISO seemed to be the "fall person" or the Chief Information ScapeGoat Officer (CISO). The Target Breach is significant by representing the beginning of a sea change where board of directors would become responsible—responsible not just in an accountable sense ensuring cybersecurity was being addressed, but also, as the chapter on *Boardroom presentations* articulates, they need to be proactive and involved in cybersecurity issues. The Target Breach represented a turning point for those companies not investing in security at the senior leadership level by employing a CISO and providing adequate funding, to turn the corner and get serious about information security.

The timing of the 2014 guidance by the National Associate of Corporate Directors (NACD) entitled "Cyber-Risk Oversight" follows closely behind the fallout from the Target Breach. Was this a coincidence? Maybe. However, boards now had the recommendation of the five principles to lead the organization strategically through the cybersecurity responsibly. The elevation of the cybersecurity responsibility beyond the CISO was now clear—we (senior management and the board) are all in this together.

The second positive development coming from the Target Breach was the attention of retailers on the security of the credit card transactions. European countries have had chip and PIN since the 1990s. The U.S. credit card companies maintained that they had stronger fraud systems and did not need the chip and PIN to provide security. This changed with the Target Breach, with the major credit card companies requiring retailers to accept chip cards by October 2015, or the liability of a breached card would shift to the merchant for counterfeit cards.

Since the Target Breach, presentations at security conferences started to appear for "how to talk to the board" that were rarely seen prior. CISOs and CIOs were getting first time exposure to the board on cybersecurity issues, and for those already established with their boards, they were getting deeper probing questions, requests for metrics, and more frequent (i.e., quarterly) updates and a permanent place on the agenda.

Finally, recall that Target did not have a CISO at the time responsible for the security function; rather, the security fell under different departments reporting to the CIO and the CIO was replaced because of the breach and there was no CISO in place. Organizations that were lacking in the CISO role now had new energy and justification to recruit and hire a CISO position to focus on cybersecurity. This is a positive change for the industry, as the CIO has a different focus to create new products to support the business and ensure the appropriate infrastructure is available, limiting time to devote to ensuring the systems and information are secure.

Breaches may come and go; however, this breach was so visible with (1) the impact to the boardroom and (2) the change in credit card processing; this breach will remain in the minds of security practitioners for some time, while others will fade away. The Target Breach could be considered a "Tipping Point," a concept articulated so well by Malcolm Gladwell, where a "magic moment occurs when an idea, trend, or social behavior crosses a threshold, tips, and spreads like wildfire." The Target Breach accelerated the discussions by the board of directors and cemented the appointing of the CISO role for firms that were on the fence in appointing an individual with the sole responsibility of leading cybersecurity.

Yahoo Breach 3 Billion Records (2013–2016)

Yahoo disclosed on December 14, 2016 over 1 billion accounts had been compromised in an August 2013 theft. Much criticism was levied at the time due to the long delay in reporting the data theft. This breach was disclosed after it was disclosed in September 2016 that 500 million records were compromised. Yahoo was subsequently purchased by Verizon (and the company was renamed Oath but retained Yahoo product branding), which announced on October 3, 2017, evidence indicating all of Yahoo's 3 billion accounts had been compromised. Verizon indicated they had acted to protect the accounts by contacting the additional users, requiring password changes, and invalidating unencrypted security questions and answers so they could not be used to access accounts in the future. Verizon also indicated they obtained new intelligence after their acquisition and during their integration that led them to believe all the accounts were compromised. When the story initially broke in December 2016 of the breach 3 years prior, Verizon reduced the price they paid for the company by $350 million to $4.48 billion in June 2017. The 3 billion accounts included email, Tumblr, Fantasy, and Flickr product lines including names, email addresses, and passwords, but not including any financial information. In March 2017, the U.S. Department of Justice issued indictments against four people, including two officers of the Russian Federal Security Service, successor to the Soviet Union KGB, indicating the information was used to "obtain unauthorized access to the contents of accounts at Yahoo, Google, and other Webmail providers, including accounts of Russian journalists, US and Russian government officials and private-sector employees of financial, transportation and other companies."

This breach highlighted several lessons that are experienced in other breaches, but were made very apparent because of the scale, billions of records, and garnered attention. First, there were delays in the reporting of the breach, angering customers and investor, when the executives knew about the breach. According to the New York Times, the security team was "marginalized" and known internally as the "Paranoids" in an organization focused on new application functionality development. The suggestion by Yahoo's CISO to implement an automatic reset of all user passwords after the breach was rejected by Yahoo senior management for fear that the change would drive users to other services. Does this represent your culture? Education of the senior executives may require an increase in the CISO's time to increase the investment and visibility of the security team. Second, individuals were put at risk not only within the Yahoo systems, but other systems as well—as unencrypted security questions and answers (used for password resets) were disclosed. How often does someone's mother's maiden name change? Never. How often does the "first girlfriend," "best friend," "high school mascot," or your "model of your first car" change? Problem is, they do not, and sites implementing these types of questions typically ask the same types of questions as they are memorable. Other sites have used different types of questions that are changeable such as "What is your favorite color?" However, these are harder to remember (did I answer blue? Red? Green?). So, this information was made available to the hackers to potentially use on other access compromises. Third, Yahoo had implemented the availability of two-factor authentication in 2011; however, this is an optional feature for end users that may not take advantage of the option. Yahoo indicated less than 10% of the users take advantage of two-factor authentication. Yahoo also introduced some mechanisms using an application on the mobile phone producing an "Account Key" to enter in the other platform to login, eliminating the need for a password. The lesson here is that security solutions to add more security need to be easy for the end user, even in the light of a breach, or the adoption will not occur. Fourth, the breach had a material impact, $350 million worth of material, or almost 8%, to the final price paid for the company. Clearly, there would be some damage control required to gain trust in the company, along with security investigations and investments. Fifth, when acquiring an organization, due diligence must be performed and there still may be areas where "new information post-acquisition" will appear via the investigations. Has the company allowed for this possibility? Financially? Customer impacts? These costs need to be considered for those companies previously communicating beaches and those stating they have "never had a breach." And finally, just because this is an "email system" does not mean that it would not be treated as containing personal information. U.S. District Court Judge Lucy Koh, of the Northern District of California, rejected a motion by Yahoo to throw out a consolidated class action lawsuit asserting damages due to potential identity theft and compromising PII. The reason? She was not persuaded by the arguments of a sophisticated attack and noted the argument of the plaintiffs who stated, "Users used their Yahoo for a variety of personal and financial transactions, and thus Yahoo email accounts contained, 'records involving credit cards, retail accounts, banking, account passwords, IRS documents, and social security numbers from transactions conducted by email, in addition to other confidential and sensitive information.'" The case could get very expensive considering the number of accounts and is most likely reflected in the $350 million reductions taken by Verizon in the acquisition. The information retrieved could and was used by attackers for credit card transactions, IRS filing scams, and theft of benefits.

DAWN-MARIE HUTCHINSON: SERVER ROOM TO WAR ROOM...ENTERPRISE INCIDENT RESPONSE

Executive Director, Optiv, Inc.

The C in many CISO titles is silent, meaning they may have the title on their business card but do not hold a seat at the big executive table often instead toiling away in proverbial "kitchens" with episodic visits to the big table but no seat. Frequently, this is a cultural nuance or demonstration of lack of "buy-in" at the executive and board level but it can also be symptomatic of a security leader grappling with communications and leadership challenges of managing up. The executive may report to one executive but ultimately achieving buy-in from multiple stakeholders is essential to any meaningful success—something that may be new and unfamiliar. Throw in an active security incident, especially one that is truly a crisis, and virtually, all the organization's competencies may be tested. Sadly, only the security leader is often held accountable directly. In our work with companies, we have sought to think about this dilemma recognizing that for those facing it is anything but existential—it is professional life and death or at least often the difference between termination and promotion. How did we get here and what can we learn and then do about it? We see several recurring patterns which, once observed, can help CISOs and the organizations they support improve effectiveness.

TEAM SELECTION

In many organizations, especially in a breach, the CISO will be looked to as the leading expert in incident response but often has very little involvement in the selection, planning, and training for the execution of the Enterprise Incident Management program. While many of the decisions around which third-party service providers are used are not within their control, as with any team activity, being familiar with others on the team can be essential to success. Insurance carriers, outside legal counsel, crisis communications, and forensic and security operations support all play a critical role, and only the largest organizations frequently have well-developed resources ready and prepared to work together internally. CISOs can and should leverage their expertise and professional networks to support the selection process and subsequently work with the selected partners in validating the effectiveness of the incident response program and subsequent forensic activities. Ultimately, the best lead teams are able to rely on "muscle memory"—something that comes with relentless practice (and experience) to respond effectively. Play Like You Practice.

Lastly, security breaches are and can be very, very stressful. In many instances, they may be among the most challenging personal experiences many executives may face. At the same time, few organizations meaning-fully test themselves. Many do so-called tabletops by simulating actual crisis conditions, and generating actual real-life, stressful situations for these teams will at least give the team a better chance for success during a real-life crisis. A CISO may be a fantastic peacetime soldier but, given that perfect defense cannot exist, cultivating adaptive skills may be far more important because failing to plan is often planning to fail.

Ultimately, hiring for soft skills, and creating situations to cultivate and develop them, is essential for CISO success. Whether it is picking the team, influencing the team, or visualizing what the team will do (and then doing it) when the game is on the line, forward-thinking organizations increasingly recognize that security leadership is much, much more than knowing which wire goes into which box.

Other Noteworthy Breaches

The breaches for 2018 alone could fill a whole book, but there are a few others worth mentioning here. The Spectre Meltdown news in January 2018 uncovered a sig-nificant hardware-based vulnerability that could allow attackers to bypass protec-tions on personal computers, servers, and smartphones to access information held in protective memory. Essentially, the hardware features of caching and computing instructions (branch prediction and speculative execution) to speed up execution created potential vulnerabilities on many of the modern processors. There were some initial problems with the patch rollouts as vendors were working on fixes. This may be an issue that takes some time to resolve and could impact performance as well.

Ashley Madison, a dating-cheating website, was hacked in 2015 and exposed at many as 37 million members when the database was hacked. The unverified information was posted online after the company refused to shut down the site. Ashley had promised to delete members' data for $19; however, it was not deleted and was exposed in the breach, prompting the Federal Trade Commission (FTC) to fine them $1.6 M ($17.5 million fine suspended for inability to pay) for deceptive practices, creating fake profiles, misleading consumers about security practices, and lax security. The parent company, Ruby Corporation, admitted to no wrongdoing in settling two dozen breach lawsuits in July 2017 and agreed to pay $11.2 million ($3.7 million to attorneys) to settle. This is another example of the FTC's ability to levy fines citing deceptive practices and promises made to consumers.

Several data leaks have been reported against India's Aadhaar database, a data-base managed by the government's Unique Identification Authority (UIDAI) containing 1.1 billion users. The government has been using Iris scanners and fin-gerprint scanners, and collecting demographic information on every Indian indi-vidual. The reports indicated that access to all the individuals in the database could be accessed for under $8 USD. The government has denied the breach. Even if biometric data was not breached, and if demographic information and other private information including services used and bank details were exposed, the information could be used in phishing and hacking attempts. The existence of the database is being challenged in India's Supreme Court on the grounds that it is unconstitutional, as well as citing privacy rights concerns (i.e., there is no concept of consent, and without the ID, Indian citizens could be denied benefits).

Reducing Data Breach Costs

Implementing practices to mitigate the specific situations above in the security program will strengthen the security program and reduce the likelihood these same methods will make the organization an easy target. The 2017 Cost of Data Breach Study: Global Overview identified 20 factors, as shown in Figure 7.3,

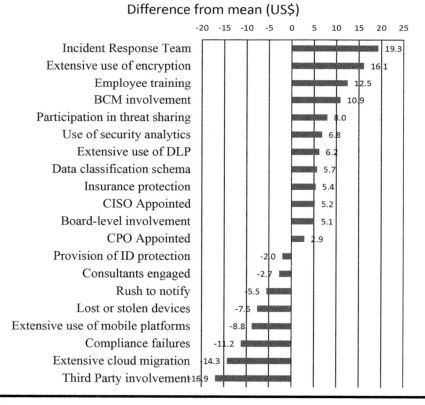

Figure 7.3   Twenty factors influencing the cost of data breach. (From Ponemon Institute, 2017 Cost of Data Breach Study: Global Overview, 2017.)

on the $141 per capita cost of a data breach per customer record, factors that either increased or decreased the cost of a breach. For example, implementing employee training reduced the cost of a data breach by $12.50, whereas having an extensive use of mobile platforms increased the average cost of a data breach by $8.80.

As new major breaches appear in the news, the CISO and cybersecurity team should evaluate the breach not in terms of the specific vulnerability or issue, but in the context of the broader process and would our organization suffer the same outcome. Are we patching vulnerabilities quickly when patches are available (or do we also have a 2 to 3-month time to patch delay)? Would we be ready with credit monitoring services and public communications immediately following the breach (or would we stumble with our messaging?) Would our cybersecurity teams be operating the breach evaluation in a planned and managed environment (or would we have distractions of constant management updates)? Would we have a high probability of responding to the alert immediately (or would we not have the right technology in place or have period gaps in our monitoring?) By taking the opportunity to review the breaches of others, we can learn and build stronger controls within our organization. We may not be able to prevent the breach, but we need to be able to reduce the impact of the breach by implementing security controls and processes throughout the information life cycle (beyond detection) to mitigate the risk.

Suggested Reading

1. Verizon Business. 2018. Verizon 2018 Data Breach Investigations Report. www.verizon-enterprise.com/verizon-insights-lab/dbir/.
2. Sullivan, B. 2016. So, You want to be a Hacker? The Economics of Computer Crime. Third Certainty (March 11). http://thirdcertainty.com/news-analysis/so-you-want-to-be-a-hacker-the-economics-of-computer-crime/.
3. Ponemon Institute. 2016. *Flipping the Economics of Attacks*. (February 16).
4. Safi, M. 2018. Personal Data of a Billion Indians Sold Online for £6, Report Claims. The Guardian (January 4). www.theguardian.com/world/2018/jan/04/india-national-id-database-data-leak-bought-online-aadhaar.
5. Khaira, R. 2018. Rs 500, 10 minutes, and You have Access to Billion Aadhaar Details. The Tribune (January 4). www.tribuneindia.com/news/nation/rs-500-10-minutes-and-you-have-access-to-billion-aadhaar-details/523361.html.
6. Perez, S. 2014. Target's Data Breach Gets Worse: 70 Million Customers had Info Stolen, Including Names, Emails and Phones. TechCrunch (January 10). https://techcrunch.com/2014/01/10/targets-data-breach-gets-worse-70-million-customers-had-info-stolen-including-names-emails-and-phones/?utm_source=feedburner&utm_medium=feed&utm_campaign=Feed%3A+Techcrunch+%28TechCrunch%29&utm_content=Netvibes.
7. KrebsonSecurity. https://krebsonsecurity.com/category/data-breaches/.

8. Bruck, L. 2018. Lessons Learned from Data Breaches in 2017. Business 2 Community (January 28). www.business2community.com/cybersecurity/lessons-learned-data-breaches-2017-01997512.

9. Burcham, J. 2017. Equifax Data Breach Exposes 143 Million. (September 8). www.fightingidentitycrimes.com/equifax-data-breach-exposes-143-million/.

10. Tynan, D. 2017. The Many Problems with Equifax's Response to The Privacy Breach Crisis. Forbes (September 26). www.forbes.com/sites/quora/2017/09/26/the-many-problems-with-equifaxs-response-to-the-privacy-breach-crisis/#41f6edb0725f.

11. Schwartz, M. 2017. Is Unpatched Apache Struts Flaw to Blame for Equifax Hack? Data Breach Today (September 12). www.databreachtoday.com/unpatched-apache-struts-flaw-to-blame-for-equifax-hack-a-10285?rf=2017-09-13_ENEWS_SUB_DBT_Slot1&mkt_tok=eyJpIjoiTmpkalpUUXdaRGt4T0RCaSIsInQiOiIzbGgwaFo1cm9wMGR1eVwvN0 5nQmpNdjV3MlR2cTVWclJ3QUZRRZjhMcEZwTjZlUTFwdEhVS1.

12. Litan, A. 2017. Our Country has been Hijacked and Equifax is Only the Latest Casualty. Gartner (September 10). https://blogs.gartner.com/avivah-litan/2017/09/10/our-country-has-been-hijacked-and-equifax-is-only-the-latest-casualty/.

13. Vaughan, D. 2016. *The Challenger Launch Decision*. Chicago, IL. University of Chicago Press.

14. KrebsonSecurity. 2017. Fraudsters Exploited Lax Security at Equifax's TALX Payroll Division. Krebsonsecurity blog (May 18). https://krebsonsecurity.com/2017/05/fraudsters-exploited-lax-security-at-equifaxs-talx-payroll-division/.

15. Office of Elizabeth Warren, US Senate. 2018. Bad Credit: Uncovering Equifax's Failure to Protect American's Personal Information. (February 7). www.warren.senate.gov/files/documents/2018_2_7_%20Equifax_Report.pdf.

16. Hopkins, N. 2017. Deloitte Hit by Cyber-Attack Revealing Clients' Secret Emails. The Guardian (September 25). www.theguardian.com/business/2017/sep/25/deloitte-hit-by-cyber-attack-revealing-clients-secret-emails.

17. Deloitte. 2017. Deloitte Statement on Cyber-Incident. (September 25 and October). www2.deloitte.com/global/en/pages/about-deloitte/articles/deloitte-statement-cyber-incident.html.

18. Breach Level Index. http://breachlevelindex.com/.

19. Ong, T. 2017. 711 Million Email Accounts Susceptible to New Spambot. The Verge (August 31). www.theverge.com/2017/8/31/16232144/onliner-largest-malware-spambot.

20. Hunt, T. 2013. Introducing "Have I been pwned?" - Aggregating Accounts Across Website Breaches. (December 4). www.troyhunt.com/introducing-have-i-been-pwned/.

21. Larson, S. 2017. Every Single Yahoo Account was Hacked -3 Billion in all. CnnTech (October 3). http://money.cnn.com/2017/10/03/technology/business/yahoo-breach-3-billion-accounts/index.html.

22. Oath. 2017. Yahoo Provides Notice to Additional Users Affected by Previously Disclosed 2013 Data Theft. (October 3). www.oath.com/press/yahoo-provides-notice-to-additional-users-affected-by-previously/.

23. The Conversation. 2016. Will the Hack of 500 Million Yahoo Accounts Get Everyone to Protect Their Passwords? (September 23). http://theconversation.com/will-the-hack-of-500-million-yahoo-accounts-get-everyone-to-protect-their-passwords-65987.

24. Perlroth, N. 2016. Defending Against Hackers Took a Back Seat at Yahoo, Insiders Say. New York Times (September 29). www.nytimes.com/2016/09/29/technology/yahoo-data-breach-hacking.html.

25. Waqas. 2017. Hackers Behind Mirai Botnet & DYN DDoS Attacks Plead Guilty. Hackread (December 13). www.hackread.com/mirai-botnet-hackers-2016-ddos-attacks-plead-guilty/.
26. KrebsOnSecurity. 2017. Who is Anna-Senpai, the Mirai Worm Author? (January 18). https://krebsonsecurity.com/2017/01/who-is-anna-senpai-the-mirai-worm-author/.
27. Volz, D. 2017. U.S. Blames North Korea for 'WannaCry' Cyber-Attack. Reuters (December 18). www.reuters.com/article/us-usa-cyber-northkorea/u-s-blames-north-korea-for-wannacry-cyber-attack-idUSKBN1ED00Q.
28. Nakashima, E. and Timberg, C. 2017. NSA Officials Worried about the Day its Potent Hacking Tool Would Get Loose. Then it Did. The Washington Post (May 16). www.washingtonpost.com/business/technology/nsa-officials-worried-about-the-day-its-potent-hacking-tool-would-get-loose-then-it-did/2017/05/16/50670b16-3978-11e7-a058-ddbb23c75d82_story.html?utm_term=.83279f4a0f43.
29. Fruhlinger, J. 2017. What is WannaCry Ransomware, How Does it Infect, and Who was Responsible? CSO Online (September 27). www.csoonline.com/article/3227906/ransomware/what-is-wannacry-ransomware-how-does-it-infect-and-who-was-responsible.html.
30. Hern, A. and Levin, S. Briton Who Stopped WannaCry Attack Arrested Over Separate Malware Claims. The Guardian (August 3). www.theguardian.com/technology/2017/aug/03/researcher-who-stopped-wannacry-ransomware-detained-in-us.
31. Trend Micro. 75% of UK Companies Targeted by Ransomware Believe They will Fall Prey to the Attack Again. (October 5). www.trendmicro.com/en_gb/about/newsroom/press-releases.html.
32. Suiche, M. 2017. Petya.2017 is a Wiper not a Ransomware. Camaelo (June 28). https://blog.comae.io/petya-2017-is-a-wiper-not-a-ransomware-9ea1d8961d3b.
33. Fruhlinger, J. 2017. Petya Ransomware and NotPetya Malware: What you Need to Know Now. CSO Online (October 17). www.csoonline.com/article/3233210/ransomware/petya-ransomware-and-notpetya-malware-what-you-need-to-know-now.html.
34. O'Connor, F. 2017. NotPetya's Fiscal Impact: $592.5 Million and Growing. Cybereason (September 6). www.cybereason.com/blog/blog-notpetyas-fiscal-impact-592-5-million-and-growing.
35. Quinn, S. 2018. Hospital Pays $55,000 Ransom; No Patient Data Stolen. Daily Reporter (January 15). www.greenfieldreporter.com/2018/01/16/01162018dr_hancock_health_pays_ransom/.
36. Dalton, A. 2016. Ransomware Hackers Get Their Money, then Ask for More. Engadget (May 24). www.engadget.com/2016/05/24/ransomware-hackers-get-paid-ask-for-more/.
37. Pierson, B. 2017. Anthem to Pay Record $115 million to Settle U.S. Lawsuits Over Data Breach. Reuters (June 23). www.reuters.com/article/us-anthem-cyber-settlement/anthem-to-pay-record-115-million-to-settle-u-s-lawsuits-over-data-breach-idUSKBN19E2ML.
38. Higgins, K. 2015. How Anthem Shared Key Markers of Its Cyberattack. Darkreading (February 12). www.darkreading.com/analytics/threat-intelligence/how-anthem-shared-key-markers-of-its-cyberattack/d/d-id/1319083.
39. Stone, J. 2015. Deep Panda Group Wasn't Behind Massive OPM Hack, But Other Chinese Hackers Were: FireEye. Ibtimes (June 19). www.ibtimes.com/deep-panda-group-wasnt-behind-massive-opm-hack-other-chinese-hackers-were-fireeye-1975658.
40. Oversight and Government Reform. 2016. The OPM Breach: How the Government Jeopardized Our National Security for More than a Generation. (September 7). https://oversight.house.gov/wp-content/uploads/2016/09/The-OPM-Data-Breach-How-the-Government-Jeopardized-Our-National-Security-for-More-than-a-Generation.pdf;

Mangan, D. 2016. Huge data breach at health system leads to biggest ever settlement. CNBC (August 4). www.cnbc.com/2016/08/04/huge-data-breach-at-health-system-leads-to-biggest-ever-settlement.html.

41. Walker, D. 2015. Exclusive: Mandiant Speaks on Anthem Attack, Custom Backdoors Used. SC Magazine (February 5). www.scmagazine.com/anthem-brings-in-mandiant-to-investigate-resolve-breach/article/536302/.
42. California Department of Insurance. 2016. Report of the Multistate Targeted Market Conduct and Financial Examination. (December 1). www.insurance.ca.gov/0400-news/0100-press-releases/2016/upload/Anthem-Examination-Report-AM-2016-12-01.pdf.
43. Fortune. 2017. Target Pays Millions to Settle State Data Breach Lawsuits. (May 23). http://fortune.com/2017/05/23/target-settlement-data-breach-lawsuits/.
44. McGrath, M. 2014. Target Data Breach Spilled Info on As Many As 70 Million Customers. Forbes (January 10). www.forbes.com/sites/maggiemcgrath/2014/01/10/target-data-breach-spilled-info-on-as-many-as-70-million-customers/#73cfccb2e795.
45. Huston, W. 2017. Report: Cost of Target's Data Breach Nearing $300 Million. (May 28). www.breitbart.com/tech/2017/05/28/cost-targets-data-breach-nearing-300-million/.
46. Elkins, K. 2015. Why it Took the US So Long to Adopt the Credit Card Technology Europe has used for Years. UK Business Insider (September 27). http://uk.businessinsider.com/why-it-took-the-us-so-long-to-adopt-emv-2015-9?r=US&IR=T.
47. Larson, S. 2017. Equifax Tweets Fake Phishing Site to Concerned Customers. CNN Tech (September 20). http://money.cnn.com/2017/09/20/technology/business/equifax-fake-site-twitter-phishing/index.html.
48. Data Breaches. www.privacyrights.org/data-breaches.
49. Pew Research Center. 2016. More Support for Justice Department than for Apple in Dispute Over Unlocking iPhone. U.S. Politics & Policy (February 22). www.people-press.org/2016/02/22/more-support-for-justice-department-than-for-apple-in-dispute-over-unlocking-iphone/.
50. CIS Center for Internet Security. Reusing Passwords on Multiple Sites. www.cisecurity.org/reusing-passwords-on-multiple-sites/.
51. National Cancer Institute. Eating Hints: Before, During, and After Cancer Treatment. www.cancer.gov/publications/patient-education/eatinghints.pdf.
52. Pai, A. 2015. Survey: 58 Percent of Smartphone Users have Downloaded a Fitness or Health App. Mobihealthnews (November 5). www.mobihealthnews.com/48273/survey-58-percent-of-smartphone-users-have-downloaded-a-fitness-or-health-app/.
53. Lapowsky, I. 2018. The Man Who Saw the Dangers of Cambridge Analytica Years Ago. Wired (June 19). www.wired.com/story/the-man-who-saw-the-dangers-of-cambridge-analytica/.
54. Neidig, H. 2018. Cambridge Analytica-linked researcher: Data wasn't helpful to Trump campaign. The Hill (June 19). http://thehill.com/policy/technology/393095-researcher-linked-to-cambridge-analytica-says-data-wasnt-useful-for-trump.
55. Attorney General Barbara D. Underwood. 2016. Press Release (December 14). https://ag.ny.gov/press-release/ag-schneiderman-announces-175-million-settlement-owner-ashleymadisoncom-joint-multi.
56. Whittaker, Z. 2018. A New Data Leak Hits Aadhaar, India's National ID Database. www.zdnet.com/article/another-data-leak-hits-india-aadhaar-biometric-database/.
57. Anthem. 2015. Statement regarding cyber attack against Anthem (February 5). https://www.anthem.com/press/wisconsin/statement-regarding-cyber-attack-against-anthem/.
58. Alonso-Zaldivar, R. 2018. Insurer Anthem will pay record $16M for massive data breach. AP News (October 15). https://www.apnews.com/591ed32303df48c0b3f86358fe8a58eb.

Chapter 8

The Security Control Framework Maze

> You have to take chances for peace, just as you must take chances in
> war.... The ability to get to the verge without getting into the war is the
> necessary art. If you try to run away from it, if you are scared to go to
> the brink, you are lost.

John Foster Dulles, 1888–1959

Imagine two guys walking down the street in the middle of a large city, looking
up at all the tall skyscrapers, admiring them, and they stumble across a parking lot
overlooking a river. The one guy says to the other, "Hey, this would be the perfect
place to put a tall building of condos, with a swimming pool on an elevated terrace
overlooking the river." Let us assume these two guys have all the money they need
to build their skyscraper, being billionaire trust-fund babies (we should all be so
lucky eh?). They are both into video games, because that is their true expertise and
decide to build a big media room on the dirt first. No pilings to bedrock, no concept
of how the building will stand... you get the picture. The other guy says, "Yeah, that
is a great idea, let's do it! But, where do we start?" We may have a vision of building
a skyscraper on ground where there is dirt, or worse, brownfields—whereby the
U.S. Environmental Protection Agency (EPA) defines this as "real property, the
expansion, redevelopment, or reuse of which may be complicated by the presence or
potential resource of a hazardous substance, pollutant, or contaminant." Now this
example may seem outlandish and the thinking of dreamers without a chance in
the world to achieve this—but, how many times do we approach security the same
way? With limited resources (staff, skills, knowledge due to funding constraints),
how do we make the best security decisions for our organizations? We may be

starting with a "cybersecurity brownfield" in our own organization resulting from years of cybersecurity neglect, previous systems—built years ago unable to withstand today's attacks, or a security culture accustomed to bypassing or ignoring the security policies to get the job done. Before our security skyscraper can be built, we need to understand our current situation and understand what policies, procedures, standards, and technologies need to be developed to get there.

Control frameworks provide us with a road map to measure our maturity and, more importantly, provide the "what" we need to accomplish to build our security skyscraper. Some of our security buildings will be taller than others, as more

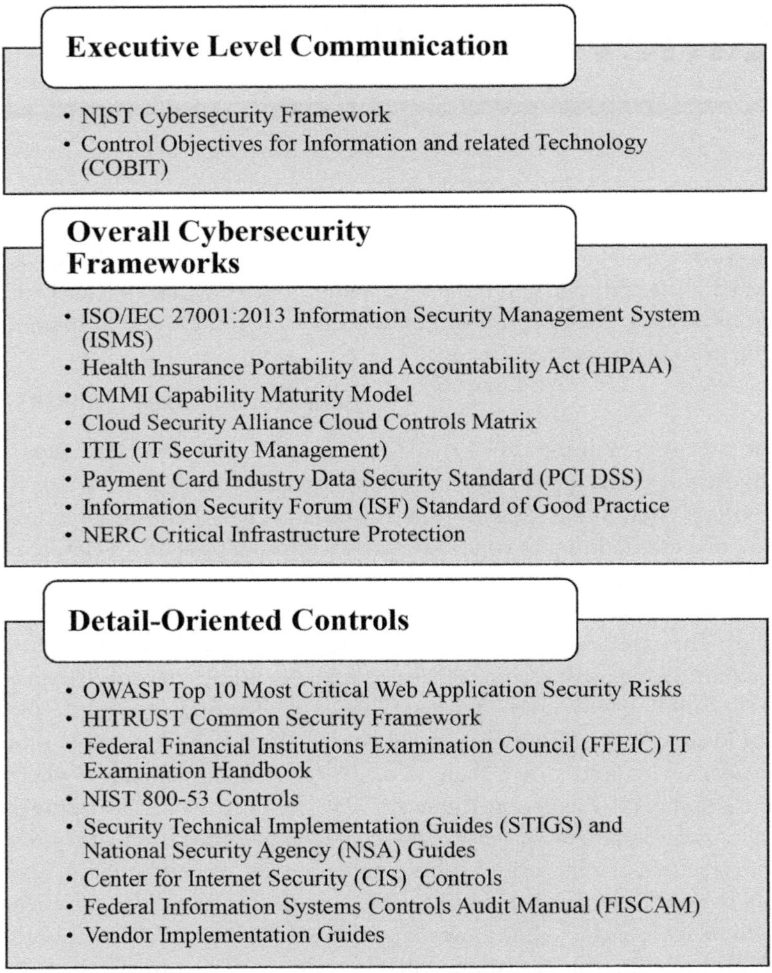

Executive Level Communication

- NIST Cybersecurity Framework
- Control Objectives for Information and related Technology (COBIT)

Overall Cybersecurity Frameworks

- ISO/IEC 27001:2013 Information Security Management System (ISMS)
- Health Insurance Portability and Accountability Act (HIPAA)
- CMMI Capability Maturity Model
- Cloud Security Alliance Cloud Controls Matrix
- ITIL (IT Security Management)
- Payment Card Industry Data Security Standard (PCI DSS)
- Information Security Forum (ISF) Standard of Good Practice
- NERC Critical Infrastructure Protection

Detail-Oriented Controls

- OWASP Top 10 Most Critical Web Application Security Risks
- HITRUST Common Security Framework
- Federal Financial Institutions Examination Council (FFEIC) IT Examination Handbook
- NIST 800-53 Controls
- Security Technical Implementation Guides (STIGS) and National Security Agency (NSA) Guides
- Center for Internet Security (CIS) Controls
- Federal Information Systems Controls Audit Manual (FISCAM)
- Vendor Implementation Guides

Figure 8.1 Security control frameworks and industry standards.

resources are available. Some will have better finishing by using more advanced technologies. But there are several commonalities among those engaged in creating skyscrapers—(1) the current situation is assessed, (2) the project is broken down into discrete elements with different skill sets required, (3) a plan is created, and (4) progress to completion is measured. Just as every skyscraper is different, so is every security program.

The fundamental building blocks are amazingly similar, thanks to the security control frameworks available. Every few years when a framework does not seem to be meeting the needs, another one is created vs. extending the existing framework. There are many reasons for this, such as different political forces, control framework ownership by different organizations invested in the framework, and a different focus, purpose, or level of granularity. Some Chief Information Security Officers (CISOs) would argue that the ones we have are incomplete, while the others would argue we have too many of them. Whatever your viewpoint, we may be able to share the view that we should be thankful we have this guidance so that we do not have to recreate the wheel for every organization—many volunteer hours have already gone into creating and enhancing the control frameworks. Control frameworks are sometimes called standards, and some would argue that standards are not control frameworks, but rather requirements. Avoiding a religious war over nomenclature, for discussion, all of these can be lumped into "security control frameworks and industry standards," or for brevity sake referred to as just security control frameworks. Figure 8.1 represents the most common security control frameworks and where these are most useful.

PHIL AGCAOLI: LEVERAGING CONTROL FRAMEWORKS

SVP, CISO, Evalon

The biggest reason that companies are getting hacked today is because they are not rigorously following the standards that articulate basic cyber hygiene. Early in my career, I witnessed a few other CISOs implementing security standards (also known as security controls frameworks) to secure their organizations and demonstrate their level of security maturity. At the time, I did not think that I had the resources to use/adopt/implement those standards [e.g., ISO 27001, Control Objectives for Information and related Technology (COBIT), National Institute of Standards and Technology (NIST) SP 800–53, Payment Card Industry Data Security Standard (PCI DSS), HIPAA, and Sysadmin, Audit, Network, Security (SANS) 20]. As I progressed in my career, I worked in a wide variety of industries (technology, Internet, critical manufacturing, communications, and financial services), so knew that several dozen security standards existed for the past 15–30 years for the various industries (e.g., BS7799, the forerunner to ISO 27001/27002, was first published in 1995). The goal for each of these standards was to answer the same basic question—"How can we become secure?" In many ways, each of these control frameworks was like using a paint by numbers system to consistently and systemically secure each company I was at. My eyes opened with respect to the use of the security standards while at Dell in 2008. At the time, "the cloud" was becoming very popular, and Dell purchased six cloud service providers for 7 billion dollars. Unfortunately, security was always one of the top issues why companies would not adopt "the cloud." Around the same time, I had helped co-found the Cloud Security Alliance (CSA). One of my first projects, CSA Cloud Controls Matrix (CCM), was to use my understanding of these seemingly disparate security frameworks to answer all the customer security, privacy, and data protection inquiries that we were being bombarded with by hundreds of our customers regarding the security practices for our cloud solutions. What became very apparent to me is that each of the different industry verticals had some different ideas of what it took to be secure based on the security standard they developed (paint by numbers), but generally the standards had similar concepts and requirements expectations among the various standards regardless of industry. Take password requirements; e.g., some said they needed 6–8 characters, and some 8–12, while some required the use of uppercase, lowercase, and special characters and some only required uppercase and lowercase characters, and then some said passwords needed to change every 45 days, while others said 90 days. Regardless, there were common truths in all the security requirements, and the trick (that unlocked me) was selecting the most stringent requirements in each of the standards to find the root of all the standards. Some people call this "harmonization" of the control standards or controls mapping or crosswalk, evolving the paint by numbers system with each standard to become blueprints on how to secure multiple environments at the same time. Today roughly 15 different industry security controls standards are cross-mapped in the CSA CCM to describe good security practices to support many industry verticals and cloud architectures (answering the question—Is your cloud secure?). Fast forward to 2013, the U.S. President issued Executive Order 13,636 giving NIST the responsibility to define what was basic cyber hygiene for critical infrastructure. Instead of developing a new security standard (reinventing the wheel), I recommended that we follow the same principles as we used to develop the Controls Matrix at the CSA. For me, developing the functions, categories, and subcategories seemed like developing version 2 of the CCM to harmonize the different security standards that defined good security practices to secure critical infrastructure in cyberspace.

An example of the controls mapping for the NIST Cybersecurity Framework v1.0 (2014) is as follows:

PR.AC-7: users, devices, and other assets are authenticated (e.g., single-factor, multifactor) commensurate with the risk of the transaction (e.g., individuals' security and privacy risks and other organizational risks).

Center for Internet Security Critical Security Controls (CIS CSC) 1, 12, 15, 16

COBIT 5 DSS05.04, DSS05.10, DSS06.10

ISO/IEC 27001:2013 A.9.2.1, A.9.2.4, A.9.3.1, A.9.4.2, A.9.4.3, A.18.1.4

NIST SP 800–53 Rev. 4 AC-7, AC-8, AC-9, AC-11, AC-12, AC-14, IA-1, IA-2, IA-3, IA-4, IA-5, IA-8, IA-9, IA-10, IA-11

An example of the controls mapping for the CSA CCM v1.0 controls mapping (2010) is as follows:

System and Services Acquisition (SA)-02: security architecture—user ID credentials.

Implement and enforce (through automation) user credential and password controls for applications, databases, and server and network infrastructure, requiring the following minimum standards:

- User identity verification prior to password resets.
- If the password reset initiated by personnel other than the user (i.e., administrator), then the password must be immediately changed by the user upon first use.
- Timely access revocation for terminated users.
- Remove/disable inactive user accounts at least every 90 days.
- Unique user IDs and disallow group, shared, or generic accounts and passwords.
- Password expiration at least every 90 days.
- Minimum password length of at least seven characters.
- Strong passwords containing both numeric and alphabetic characters.
- Allow password reuse after the last four passwords used.
- User ID lockout after not more than six attempts.
- User ID lockout duration to a minimum of 30 minutes or until the administrator enables the user ID.
- Reenter password to reactivate terminal after session idle time for more than 15 minutes.
- Maintain user activity logs for privileged access or access to sensitive data.

EQUALS

COBIT 4.1 DS5.3

COBIT 4.1 DS5.4

EQUALS
    HIPAA 164.308 (a)(5)(ii)(D)
    HIPAA 164.312(a)(2)(i)
    HIPAA 164.312 (a)(2)(iii)
    HIPAA 164.312(d)
EQUALS
    ISO/IEC 27002-2005 11.2.3
    ISO/IEC 27002-2005 11.5.5
EQUALS
    NIST SP800-53 R2 AC-1
    NIST SP800-53 R2 AC-11
    NIST SP800-53 R2 IA-1
    NIST SP800-53 R2 IA-2
    NIST SP800-53 R2 IA-5
    NIST SP800-53 R2 IA-6
    NIST SP800-53 R2 SC-10
EQUALS
    PCI DSS v1.2 8.1
    PCI DSS v1.2 8.2
    PCI DSS v1.2 8.3
    PCI DSS v1.2 8.4
    PCI DSS v1.2 8.5
    PCI DSS v1.2 8.5.4
    PCI DSS v1.2 8.5.5
    PCI DSS v1.2 8.5.10
    PCI DSS v1.2 8.5.11
    PCI DSS v1.2 8.5.12
    PCI DSS v1.2 8.5.13
    PCI DSS v1.2 8.5.14
    PCI DSS v1.2 8.5.2
    PCI DSS v1.2 8.5.3
    PCI DSS v1.2 8.5.9
    PCI DSS v1.2 8.5.15
    PCI DSS v1.2 10.1
    PCI DSS v1.2 12.3.8

Here are some tricks to using controls frameworks and standards. First, you need to know what your scope is. What assets to apply control requirements based on risk assessments? The next is to judge or use the rating systems such as the capability maturity model (CMM) to assess how you are doing and where you are failing. Applying a risk management methodology such as ISO 31000/27005 or NIST SP 800-39/800-37 allows you to prioritize areas of highest risk, connects them to your investment requests, provides a common language that can be used with senior management and your board of directors that they are already familiar with (audit and risk committee), and then provides you a way to give status and connect your activity to your implementation strategy. Ultimately communicating cyber-risk to your senior team and your board of directors is of the utmost importance. In the end, using controls standards frameworks is like painting by numbers. Over the past 30 years, thousands of other security practitioners have already defined what secure is through the development and ratification of these security standards. That is how buildings are built safely. These are the blueprints that plan whole cities. As CISOs, we must all use them and be diligent and rigorous on how we apply the controls. Select the use of one of the major security controls frameworks, apply it to your environment, and then use it to demonstrate your level of security maturity (when someone asks, "How secure are you?" or "Tell me about your security?").

Heath Insurance Portability and Accountability Act of 1996 Security Safeguards

The Health Insurance Portability and Accountability Act (HIPAA) final rule for adopting security standards was published February 20, 2003, with a compliance deadline of April 21, 2005, for large providers, 1 year later for smaller providers. The scope was modified by the Office for Civil Rights, Department of Health and Human Services, through publishing a final omnibus rule on January 25, 2013, in the Federal Register to include business associates handling Protected Health Information (PHI) (i.e., contractors and subcontractors). The rule clarified when breaches needed to be reported to U.S. Department Health and Human Services (HHS). HIPAA required a series of administrative, technical, and physical security procedures for entities to use to assure the confidentiality of PHI. The standard was intentionally non-technology-specific and intended to provide scalability to small providers and large providers alike. A key goal of the HIPAA Security Rule is to protect the privacy of PHI while enabling covered entities to adopt new technologies to improve the quality of health care. The security rule applies to e-PHI (electronic Protected Health Information), whereas the privacy rule applies to all forms of information.

A key requirement of the framework is the necessity to perform a risk analysis to determine if the security safeguards are reasonable and appropriate. The risk analysis evaluates the likelihood and impact of potential risks to e-PHI, identification of security measures to reduce the risk, documentation of the rationale for choosing these safeguards, and performing the risk analysis on a continuous basis.

Administrative safeguards included a security management process, designation of a security official, information access management, workforce training and management, and evaluation. Physical safeguards specified requirements for securing the facilities as well as the workstation and devices. Technical safeguards included access control, audit controls, integrity controls, and ensuring information transmitted was secure. The safeguards were presented as "required" or "addressable," meaning the addressable standards could be evaluated for the appropriateness for the organization. These measures need to be evaluated continuously, as what was deemed reasonable at one time may no longer be reasonable given an increased threat environment.

HITRUST Alliance Common Security Framework

One of the difficulties with implementing the HIPAA Security Rule for many organizations was determining the "reasonable and appropriate" controls necessary to satisfy the administrative, technical, and physical security safeguard requirements. Since the regulation was intended to be flexible and scalable to support large health-care covered entities as well as smaller ones, the regulation was not prescriptive. The Final HIPAA Security Rule represented policy, and to stand the test of time and allow for technical innovation, the regulation could not be prescriptive. I recall sitting next to Dr. Bill Braithwaite (a.k.a. Dr. HIPAA for authoring HIPAA) when the first National Coordinator of Health Information Technology (HIT) was announced in Washington, DC, at an event to launch HIT in 2004. The podium at the front of the room included senators and government officials enthusiastically showing their support as the Office of the National Coordinator for HIT, and the focus on health-care interoperability under George W. Bush was announced. Bill turned to me and said to me in a half-jokingly way, "I'll bet this policy-making stuff drives you guys that are trying to implement something nuts!" His words could not have been truer. It is good when there is bipartisan support on an issue or a direction for the future—determining how to make it happen is another complex issue that takes a long time. We are now almost two decades after that 2004 announcement, and while advances have been made, we have further to go to become securely interoperable across the health-care system, particularly in securing small–medium providers.

The lack of prescriptive security controls left some CISOs in a quandary—there was a desire to comply with the law, but they were not exactly sure what would pass the audit litmus test and what practices would ultimately be secure enough. In response to this dilemma, an organization was founded in 2007 named the Health Information Trust Alliance (HITRUST) made up of an executive council with leaders from some of the largest health-care organizations for guidance and run separately by a management team. The HITRUST Common Security Framework (CSF) was created to provide a framework of prescriptive and scalable controls. The framework is intended to harmonize the other frameworks, standards, regulations, and business requirements including ISO27000 series security requirements, NIST, Payment Card Industry (PCI), HIPAA, and state laws. The idea was that the framework would provide more targeted guidance to satisfy the requirements of the HIPAA Security Rule, organizations would be assessed, and then the organizations become "HITRUST-certified" by an independent assessor. The theory was that if an organization was "HITRUST-certified," then other health-care organizations could trust that their information would be protected when in the certified organization's care, without having to answer extensive questionnaires and make their own assessment. Some health-care organizations, such as Anthem, Health Care Services Corp. (HCSC), Highmark, Human, UnitedHealth Group, and others required partners to become HITRUST-certified if they are using e-PHI. Other organizations are making self-assessments and obtaining independent audits to show due diligence and ensure they are prepared for potential Office of Civil Rights (OCR) audits.

Since the HITRUST CSF draws on requirements of other regulations and standards, one would expect to see a similar set of categories as the other frameworks. The framework consists of 13 control categories, each identified with a control ID and a control objective. The controls within these control categories contain a control specification (policies, procedures, or organizational structures), risk factor (regulatory, organizational, and system factors driving requirements), implementation requirement (one of three levels to support the requirements based upon the relevant organizational or system scope), and control assessment guidance. The control categories are as follows:

■ Information security management program
■ Access control
■ Human resources (HR) security
■ Risk management
■ Security policy
■ Organization of information security
■ Compliance
■ Asset management
■ Physical and environmental security
■ Communications and operations management
■ Information systems acquisition, development, and maintenance
■ Information security incident management
■ Business continuity management
■ Privacy practices.

The tool used for the assessment scopes the assessment based upon the organization type and industry, number of customers, employees, users or transactions per day, Internet accessibility, mobile devices, use of third parties for access or transmission, interfaces to other systems, and regulatory factors affecting the organization.

The self-assessment contains 120–140 controls in the minimum level assessment, each of which requires the artifacts, or evidence of compliance, to be uploaded into the tool. The U.S. Government Accountability Office (GAO) released Critical Infrastructure Protection (CIP): Additional Actions Are Essential for Assessing Cybersecurity Framework Adoption Report in February 2018, which noted, according to sector officials, the health-care and public health sector "encourages the alignment of the NIST Cybersecurity Framework with existing cybersecurity guidelines currently in use within its respective sector. For example, the sector aligned the Health Information Trust Alliance Framework to the Cybersecurity Framework. This mapping fully incorporated the framework and provided for 135 individual security controls and 14 individual privacy controls that can be implemented by health-care providers. Department officials stated that the alignment of the framework to the Health Information Trust Alliance Framework allows organizations to demonstrate compliance with NIST through their implementation of the preexisting Health Information Trust Alliance Framework."

HITRUST has enhanced the ability to specify controls to be compliant with the HIPAA regulation. Critics of HITRUST assert that the framework has too many controls, requiring a significant amount of time and expense to prepare and review. This could result in not focusing on the right things that will contribute the most to securing the system, such as patch management, removal of administrative rights, encryption, two-factor authentication, and network segmentation. Larger organizations may have the resources to complete and can bear the expense, whereas smaller organizations with tighter budgets may not. In either case, the framework represents a significant body of work mapping the controls to the relevant laws that are kept current, as evidenced by consistently updating the framework as new laws and regulations appear. This activity to keep the controls mappings up-to-date by an organization without using HITRUST would be a massive undertaking for many organizations. For example, the September 2017 version reflected OCR Audit Protocol Phase II Clarification of HIPAA Security requirements, and the February 2018 version reflected the European Union General Data Protection Regulation (GDPR) and New York Department of Financial Services Cybersecurity Requirements for Financial Services Companies (23 NYCRR 500). HITRUST is a good example of a framework embodying other requirements and developing concrete security actions to take. Each organization would need to weigh the cost of adoption with the internal capabilities of the team.

Federal Financial Institutions Examination Council IT Examination Handbook

The Federal Financial Institutions Examination Council (FFIEC) is empowered to provide uniform principles, standards, and reporting forms for the examination of financial institutions by the Board of Governors of the Federal Reserve

System, the Federal Deposit Insurance Corporation, the National Credit Union Administration, the Office of the Comptroller of the Currency, and the Consumer Financial Protection Bureau. Several booklets have been issued by the council, including audit, business continuity planning, development and acquisition, electronic banking, management, operations, outsourcing technology services, retail payment systems, supervision of technology service providers, and wholesale payment systems. Information security was also added as a booklet in July 2006, which includes guidance for the security process, risk assessment, security strategy, security controls implementation, security monitoring as well as the examination procedures and related laws. The handbook issued by the FFIEC serves as a supplement to the member agencies expectations for meeting the Gramm-Leach-Bliley Act (GLBA) 501(b) requirements.

In 2014, the FFIEC piloted a Cybersecurity Assessment Tool (CAT) used to evaluate their cybersecurity preparedness and to help organizations identify their risks at more than 500 financial institutions (released generally June 30, 2015, as an optional tool), managing internal and external threats to the infrastructure and information assets. The tool was mapped to the baseline maturity statements in the FFIEC IT Examination Handbook and the NIST Cybersecurity Framework. The tool contained two parts: Part 1 is used to assess the inherent risk profile of the organization (least, minimal, moderate, significant, most) using five different categories (technologies and connection types, delivery channels, online/mobile products and technology services, organizational characteristics, external threats), and Part 2 is used to determine the level of cybersecurity maturity, or the preparedness represented by levels (baseline, evolving, intermediate, advanced, innovative) across five domains (Cyber-Risk Management and Oversight, Threat Intelligence and Collaboration, Cybersecurity Controls, External Dependency Management, Cyber Incident Management and Resilience), as shown in Figure 8.2.

The FFIEC provides guidance for assessing the inherent risk levels of the organization and institutions with limited use of technology that would score on the low end of the scale (i.e., least or minimal inherent risk), to organizations using complex, emerging technologies with multiple delivery channels.

The maturity of the cybersecurity capability is assessed by responding to declarative statements with yes, no, or yes with compensating controls (added in May 31, 2017 update). One of the challenges to move up the maturity level is that all the declarative statements (requirements) in each maturity level and the previous levels must be sustained (yes, or yes with compensating controls) to achieve the higher maturity level. For example, in the Cyber-Risk Management and Oversight domain, designated members of management may be held accountable by the board or an appropriate board committee for implementing and managing the information security and business continuity program (baseline maturity-level declarative statement). Cybersecurity tools and staff may be requested through the budget process (evolving maturity-level declarative statement), but if a written report on the overall status of the information security and business continuity program is not

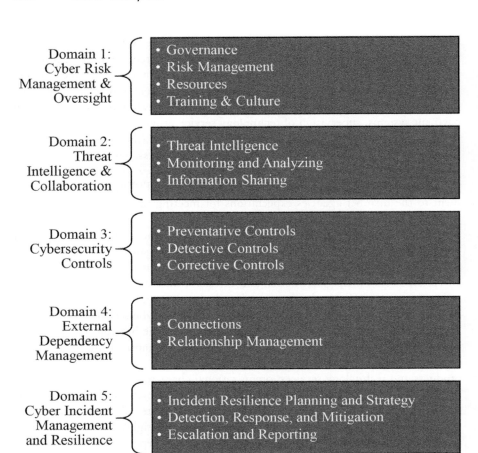

Figure 8.2 FFIEC CAT domains. (Adapted from FFIEC Cybersecurity Assessment Tool (CAT), 2017.)

provided to the board annually (baseline maturity-level statement), and even if the rest of the evolving maturity-level statements were satisfied, the maturity level would be assessed at the "baseline" maturity level. This really behooves the CISO to pay attention to the details of each level and to ensure completeness. It is also expected that as the inherent risk of the institution increases, so does the cybersecurity maturity level.

The FFIEC announced a frequently asked questions document in October 2016, answering 18 questions and to reaffirm that the CAT was voluntary and was not a regulatory requirement. While the FFIEC indicated they did not intend on releasing an automated version of the tool, some organizations such as the Financial Services Information Sharing and Analysis Center working with the Financial

Services Sector Coordinating Council developed an automated version. The tool development is a good example of how sharing organizations can support government agencies to improve the cybersecurity effectiveness. FFIEC also committed to change the CAT to be in alignment with the FFIEC IT Handbook as changes are made. The tool was updated on May 31, 2017, reflecting the new mapping to the FFIEC IT Handbook, which changed in September 2016 through the issuance of a new Information Security Booklet to realign the tool and the handbook and reflect the current threat environment.

The FFIEC tool may be "voluntary" to use; however, the astute CISO will want to ensure that the requirements are met within the tool, or if the costs are prohibitive, that documented compensating controls are specified. While they may not be required today, this can change in the future or the information from the tool could be leveraged by regulators and auditors requesting results of the tool. Many of the controls specified in the tool are security controls that would be expected within an organization to mitigate risk. The CISO must determine how the tool will be used and likely, there is already measurement against another control framework using similar requirements (or declarative statements as in the case of FFIEC).

ISO/IEC 27001:2013 Information Security Management Systems Requirements

The ISO/IEC 27001:2013 Information Security Management Systems Requirements provides a model for establishing, implementing, operating, monitoring, reviewing, maintaining, and improving an Information Security Management System (ISMS). This was an evolution from British Standard (BS) 7799-2 and the subsequent issuance of ISO17799.

The U.K. Department of Trade and Industry Code of Practice for information security, which was developed from the support of industry in 1993, became BS 7799 in 1995. The BS 7799 standard was subsequently revised in 1999 to add certification and accreditation components, which became Part 2 of the BS 7799 standard. Part 1 of the BS 7799 standard became ISO17799 and was published as ISO17799:2000 as the first international information security management standard by the International Organization for Standardization (ISO) and International Electrotechnical Commission (IEC). The ISO 17799 standard was modified in June 2005 as ISO/IEC 17799:2005 containing 134 detailed information security controls based upon 11 areas. The ISO standards are now grouped together by topic areas, and the ISO/IEC 27000 series has been designated as the information security management series. The ISO17799 standard was renamed the ISO/IEC 27001:2005 standard in 2005. The next revision was released in 2013 by releasing ISO/IEC 27001:2013, which reduced the number of controls to 114 and categorized the controls in 14 groups and listed them in Appendix A of the standard. The control groups are as follows:

A.5 Information security policies
A.6 Organization of information security
A.7 Human resources security
A.8 Asset management
A.9 Access control
A.10 Cryptography
A.11 Physical and environmental security
A.12 Operations security
A.13 Communications security
A.14 System acquisition, development, and maintenance
A.15 Supplier relationships
A.16 Information security incident management
A.17 Information security aspects of business continuity management
A.18 Compliance

The changes to the standard in 2013 placed more emphasis on leadership involvement and risk management and updated controls to reflect the threats such as those related to mobile devices, online vulnerabilities, secure development and testing, project management, analysis of security events, ensuring security policies for supplier relationships, and ensuring the availability of information.

The ISO27001 process involves a scoping process, such as a business unit or major system within an organization. Since embarking on an ISO27001 certification process can involve many person-hours to achieve certification, this is one way that organizations can focus the certification efforts on the information assets most critical to the organization. Certification involves two stages: (1) a preliminary review by a company certified to conduct audits consisting of a documentation review to determine if the requirements of the ISO27001 standard have been met, and (2) the auditor verified the activities are compliant with the standard and with the internal company documentation proposed to certify to the standard. The first stage is sometimes done offsite, as it is a matter of an auditor verifying the requirements of the standard are met from a documentation-only perspective. If the organization is not compliant with the documentation, e.g., there is no risk management process or management review, then there is no need to proceed to Stage 2 until the issues are mitigated. Typically, the external audit firm will provide time to correct the issues, say 30–60 days, before coming onsite to perform the Stage 2 review. If major nonconformities (required clause within the standard, such as risk management) are experienced during the Stage 2 audit, the company cannot be certified. Major nonconformities can also result if there was a critical process that clearly was not being executed on a regular schedule. Minor nonconformities, such as some individuals having no record of security awareness training, can still become certified. Before embarking on an ISO27001 project, the CISO should have a clear understanding with the certifier of what types of process failures represent a major nonconformity and which ones represent a minor one. Once the certification is granted, a periodic (typically annually) ongoing review must be performed to ensure the ISMS is still operating as intended.

The ISO27001 standard is an excellent standard for global organizations, as this is the oldest information security standard and recognized internationally. Most of the other standards are mapped to this standard due to the popularity of the standard. When rolling out this standard in a global firm, I found that there was an eagerness by the different countries to "become ISO27001 certified" first. Once one country achieves certification, celebrate it globally and encourage other countries to venture down this path. To speed the process for these global organizations, it makes sense to draft "ISO27001 templates" for the process working with an external firm and license the product to be able to be used in multiple countries. Even though the individual country processes and controls may be different, the clauses needed for compliance will be the same. Walking through the process of attaining the standard and providing training on such as documents as the Statement of Applicability (whereby the controls necessary to satisfy the scope statement are designated), will accelerate the certification efforts. The standard has been used for several years to provide assurance to external parties of the security practices. Granted, the scope could be specified as very small and the risk tolerance high for an organization, and then, the certification would not mean much; however, many organizations going down the ISO27001 path do so to provide assurance and improve the existing security practices. As a CISO, there is a tangible benefit of having an external, independent party certify the ISMS, as some third parties will accept the certification in lieu of filling out a 500 security controls questionnaire, or will ask only a limited number of questions. Many major software vendors have embraced the ISO27001 Framework as a method to demonstrate assurance and may supply a copy of the ISO certification and an overview document indicating how the standard is implemented when signing contracts vs. providing internal policy documents.

The NIST Framework for Improving Critical Infrastructure Cybersecurity (NIST Cybersecurity Framework)

The NIST Framework for Improving Critical Infrastructure Cybersecurity, more commonly referred to as the NIST Cybersecurity Framework, or NIST CSF for short, was developed by NIST 1 year after the U.S. President issued Executive Order 13636, citing "repeated cyber intrusions into the critical infrastructure demonstrated the need for improved cybersecurity." The order directed NIST to lead the development of a framework to reduce the risks to the critical infrastructure and include a set of standards, methodologies, procedures, and processes to align policy, business, and technological approaches to address the cyber-risks. The order also suggested that the framework should be consistent with voluntary international standards. The framework was created by a collaboration between government and the private sector. The version 1.0 was released February 12, 2014, and after collaborating and holding workshops with the government and private sector, released final version 1.1 April 18, 2018. The voluntary framework gained much popularity due to the ease of communication represented by organizing the security controls into five functions: identify, protect, detect, respond, and recover. The five functions and the categories that make up the functions are shown in Figure 8.3. The framework has been used by organizations to describe the current security posture, define a target state for cybersecurity, identify opportunities for improvement using a repeatable process, assess the progress, and use as a communication tool internally and with external stakeholders about cybersecurity risk.

The framework consists of three elements: (1) Framework Core, (2) Framework Implementation Tier, and (3) Framework Profile. The first element, the Framework Core, contains four subelements: functions, categories, subcategories, and informative references. Functions are the high level (identify, protect, detect, respond, and recover) to enable conversation with management as well as to align the basic activities of the organization. These functions can be used at the board level, showing metrics and the "direction of travel" within these areas, as well as used to capture metrics at the operational level, which ultimately feed this high level. The functions are broken down into *categories* and *subcategories* to express cybersecurity outcomes desired from the activities supporting a function. For example, as shown in Figure 8.4, the communications category indicates "response activities are coordinated with internal and external stakeholders," and to further define this, the subcategories include the following: (1) personnel know their roles and order of operations when a response is needed, (2) incidents are reported consistent with established criteria, (3) information is shared consistent with response plans, (4) coordination with stakeholders occurs consistent with response plans, and (5) voluntary sharing occurs with external stakeholders to achieve broader cybersecurity situational awareness. The informative references provide references to other standards, such as CIS CSC, COBIT 5, NIST Special Publication 800–53, and ISO/IEC 27001:2013, and ANSI/ISA 62443-2 (Security for Industrial Automation and Control Systems). The second element is the Framework Implementation Tier, which characterizes how the organization views the cybersecurity risk and an assessment of the processes managing that risk. There are four tiers as follows:

Tier 1 Partial—ad hoc, sometimes reactive cybersecurity processes
Tier 2 Risk informed—approved by management, may not be established as organization-wide policy

Function	Cat ID	Category
Identify (ID)	ID.AM	Asset Management
	ID.BE	Business Environment
	ID.GV	Governance
	ID.RA	Risk Assessment
	ID.RM	Risk Management Strategy
	ID.SC	Supply Chain Risk Management
Protect (PR)	PR.AC	Identity Management and Access Control
	PR.AT	Awareness and Training
	PR.DS	Data Security
	PR.IP	Information Protection Processes and Procedures
	PR.MA	Maintenance
	PR.PT	Protective Technology
Detect (DE)	DE.AE	Anomalies and Events
	DE.CM	Security Continuous Monitoring
	DE.DP	Detection Processes
Respond (RS)	RS.RP	Response Planning
	RS.CO	Communications
	RS.AN	Analysis
	RS.MI	Mitigation
	RS.IM	Improvements
Recover (RC)	RC.RP	Recovery Planning
	RC.IM	Improvements
	RC.CO	Communications

Figure 8.3 NIST Cybersecurity Framework functions and categories. (Adapted from National Institute of Standards and Technology, *Framework for Improving Critical Infrastructure Cybersecurity, Version 1.1,* **2018.)**

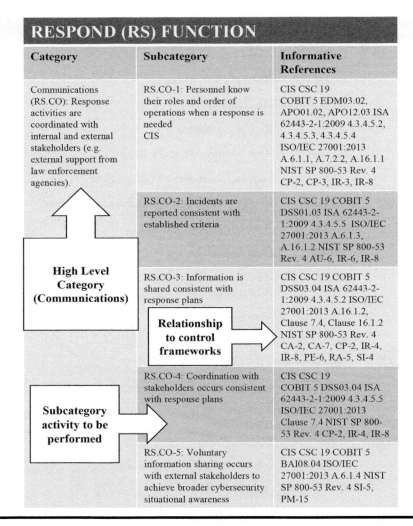

Figure 8.4 NIST Cybersecurity Framework core example. (Adapted from National Institute of Standards and Technology, *Framework for Improving Critical Infrastructure Cybersecurity, Version 1.1*, 2018.)

Tier 3 Repeatable—risk management practices formally approved and expressed as policy

Tier 4 Adaptive—organization adapts cybersecurity practices using lessons learned and predictive behaviors

The third and final element of the framework is the Framework Profile, which provides a road map for the organization by aligning the functions, categories, and subcategories with the business requirements, risk tolerance, and resources of the organization. Current and target profiles can be created to show where the organization is now with respect to maturity within each of the five functions and develop a target profile to drive investment.

As should be apparent by now, the framework does not replace the other standards and is intended to facilitate risk and cybersecurity management communications with various stakeholders. The standards noted in the informative references can be leveraged to provide further detailed requirements for the organization, as well as to map the efforts already in place, as well as the existing compliance with these other standards to the NIST CSF. This is a useful tool that the CISO should not look at as a replacement for other standards, but rather as an overarching way to organize the cybersecurity practices into an understandable communication tool, whether up, down, or sideways in the organization. The simplicity of the framework provides the ability to communicate in simple terms contrasted to trying to explain the cybersecurity status across 20 CIS CSC, 20 800–53 control families, 37 COBIT processes, or 14 groups of ISO27001! Each of these control specifications provides valuable content for their focus and can be integrated with the NIST Cybersecurity Framework for higher-level communication and cybersecurity risk discussions.

MATTHEW SMITH: USING THE NIST CYBERSECURITY FRAMEWORK IN AN INTERNATIONAL SETTING

Senior Security Engineer, G2, Inc.

In 2013, the U.S. administration initiated an exciting project—tasking the NIST with leading development of an agile framework for reducing cybersecurity risk. Through a series of workshops and outreach efforts, NIST and the cybersecurity community developed a "prioritized, flexible, repeatable, performance-based, and cost-effective approach to … identify, assess, and manage cyber-risk" (Executive Order 13636). Many standards bodies participated in this process [e.g., British Standards Institution (BSI), Information Systems Audit and Control Association (ISACA), ISA99, PCI, Information Security Forum (ISF), Center for Internet Security (CIS), The Open Group, X9). Notably, one of the earliest findings that CISOs and other leaders told NIST was that we did not need yet another set of controls, but rather we needed a better way to organize and communicate about the controls and processes that were already well established.

In the years since that first release, NIST has heard from CISOs that leaders find it challenging to communicate about cybersecurity and measure progress across varied subdivisions with diverse types of risk. The lesson learned from organizations such as hospitals, universities, and even entire national governments is that the Cybersecurity Framework's functions and categories provide a model with which leaders can set priorities, direct resources, and observe results across varying business units. Using the Cybersecurity Framework's five functions, an organization can *Identify* what matters, including critical resources and the known threats to those resources, then understand what is needed to *Protect* them appropriately, *Detect* events that need a response, *Respond* effectively when that happens, and *Recover* from disruptions rapidly and efficiently. The Cybersecurity Framework describes a set of desirable outcomes that CISOs have recommended as helpful for building an actionable plan.

As mentioned above, the Framework complements, rather than replaces, effective application of existing standards. For example, organizations that use ISO standards can immediately leverage ISO Technical Report 27103, which includes a mapping of many different ISO standards to the Framework. Organizations can check if they are achieving their unique set of desired outcomes against their ISO certifications and can identify gaps in current practices.

As organizations apply the Framework, CISOs are finding that it provides a common language for aligning senior executives' strategic cybersecurity goals with detailed business drivers. The Framework provides a key to unlocking the complex world of international regulations, laws, and directives. Because multiple countries (e.g., Japan, Israel, Italy, Uruguay, Philippines) are using the five functions to organize their national cybersecurity frameworks, business leaders can leverage common components to improve efficiency in cybersecurity risk management worldwide.

The NIST Recommended Security Controls for Federal Information Systems (800–53)

The standards and guidelines reference the minimum set of controls that must be implemented to protect the Federal System based upon the risk level determined. Implementation of the 20 families of security controls establishes a level of "security due diligence" for the Federal agencies and the contractors that perform work for the government. While the controls' document by the title infers this is only for Federal systems, the documentation is very comprehensive, freely available, and an excellent resource to supplement the other control frameworks. There is also a companion document, 800–53A entitled "Assessing Security and Privacy Controls in Federal Information Systems and Organizations: Building Effective Assessment Plans" to provide guidance for auditing the controls specified in the 800–53 document. In August 2017, NIST released version 5 in draft in response to a cybersecurity assessment by the Defense Science Board in 2017 iterating that due to the increasing security landscape outpacing the U.S. efforts to reduce vulnerabilities, "a more proactive and systematic approach to U.S. cyber deterrence is urgently needed." Version 5 of the security controls therefore was created to provide a comprehensive set of security and privacy safeguards for all types of computing platforms including general purpose computing systems, cyber-physical systems, cloud and mobile systems, industrial control/process systems, and Internet of Things devices. NIST indicated the major changes in this 800–53 version 5 over the prior releases included the following:

- Making the security and privacy controls more outcome-based by changing the structure of the controls
- Fully integrating the privacy controls into the security control catalog creating a consolidated and unified set of controls for information systems and organizations, while providing a summary and mapping tables for privacy-related controls
- Separating the control selection process from the actual controls, thus allowing the controls to be used by different communities of interest including systems engineers, software developers, enterprise architects, and mission/business owners
- Promoting integration with different risk management and cybersecurity approaches and lexicons, including the Cybersecurity Framework
- Clarifying the relationship between security and privacy to improve the selection of controls necessary to address the full scope of security and privacy risks
- Incorporating new, state-of-the-practice controls based on threat intelligence and empirical attack data, including controls to strengthen cybersecurity and privacy governance and accountability.

To support the privacy control aspects, two new families of controls were added in version 5 (prior version had 18 families of controls): individual participation (IP) and privacy authorization (PA). The control families are as follows:

1. (AC) Access Control
2. (AT) Awareness and Training
3. (AU) Audit and Accountability
4. (CA) Assessment, Authorization and Monitoring
5. (CM) Configuration Management
6. (CP) Contingency Planning
7. (IA) Identification and Authentication
8. (IP) Individual Participation
9. (IR) Incident Response
10. (MA) Maintenance
11. (MP) Media Protection
12. (PA) Privacy Authorization
13. (PE) Physical and Environmental Protection
14. (PL) Planning
15. (PM) Program Management

16. PS (Personnel Security)
17. RA (Risk Assessment)
18. SA (System and Services Acquisition)
19. SC (System and Communications Protection)
20. (SI) System and Information Integrity.

NIST has also included in the Special Publication 800–53r5 document mapping to ISO/IEC 27001:2013 and ISO/IEC 15408 (common criteria for developers of IT products). This is extremely useful for developing detailed control specifications to supplement the ISO27001 controls.

The NIST 800–53 controls are arguably the most detailed security controls available through the various control frameworks. These controls may have been created under the direction of the U.S. Government; however, the generic nature and richness of the controls enable their use in any environment. Government agencies and their contractors audited to these controls may complain at the detailed nature of the controls; however, for the most part, it is hard to argue that implementing many of the controls would not add to a security program. One of the challenges with government agencies required to implement NIST (i.e., all agencies in the Federal Government and their contractors) is that the "risk assessment process" is sometimes minimized and the acceptable risk level is many times at a very low level. In other words, there is a conservative stance and reluctance to accept the risk of not implementing all the controls. Contractors to the government typically do not have much flexibility, as it is ultimately the government agency that determines if the risk will be accepted or not. This results in much expense implementing and reviewing most of the controls in 800–53 without deciding on a risk-based basis which ones are truly important. In order words, if a control is specified in the 800–53 control set, it is most likely expected to be adhered to. NIST also provides an extensive set of cybersecurity publications in the Special Publication 800 series covering a broad range of topics.

Cloud Security Alliance Cloud Controls Matrix

The CSA was formed in December 2008 in response to concerns about cloud computing and the security capabilities of those environments. In 2009, the newly formed CSA issued the first comprehensive best practices paper for cloud computing, "Security Guidance for Critical Areas of Focus for Cloud Computing." The document and subsequent revisions provided extensive information in one place regarding cloud computing and had the benefit of many security leaders to work on the effort. I recall around that time being asked to participate on a cloud computing panel at a major conference with the founder, Jim Reavis and I declined. Why? Not because of the topic, but because I was uncomfortable as I had not been responsible for implementing in the public cloud at that time, as I was working for a large health insurer and the last place we would be putting our PHI was the cloud. Well, here is the kicker—hardly anyone else in the audience had either! These were the beginning days of the cloud conversation. Only the large, well-funded organizations were implementing in the cloud at that time. What a difference a decade can make, where cloud applications and platforms are commonplace and progressive organizations employ a "cloud first strategy."

The CSA created the CCM, which has gone through multiple revisions since inception. The latest major version (CCM 3.0) was released in September 2017 to provide fundamental security principles to guide cloud vendors and assist potential customers in assessing the overall security risk of the cloud vendor. The framework attempts to normalize the expectations between the vendors and customers, provide a consistent cloud taxonomy and terminology, and provide security measures for implementing in the cloud. The CCM is mapped to many other standards and contains 136 controls in 16 domains as follows:

1. Application and Interface Security
2. Audit Assurance and Compliance
3. Business Continuity Management and Operational Resilience
4. Change Control and Configuration Management
5. Data Security and Information Life Cycle Management.
6. Datacenter Security
7. Encryption and Key Management
8. Governance and Risk Management
9. HR Security
10. Identity and Access Management
11. Infrastructure and Virtualization
12. Interoperability and Portability
13. Mobile Security
14. Security Incident Management, E-Disc, and Cloud Forensics
15. Supply Chain Management, Transparency, and Accountability
16. Threat and Vulnerability Management

JIM REAVIS: BUILDING A BRIDGE TO THE FUTURE WITH CLOUD CONTROLS MATRIX

CEO, Cloud Security Alliance (CSA)

When CSA was in its formative stage in 2008, we recognized cloud computing as nothing less than a revolution. Not just a new model for orchestrating usage of compute, but in fact a major economic and societal trend. Compute is power, and cloud heralded a shift from large-scale compute being a constrained resource in the hands of a relatively few number of people and companies to a ubiquitous commodity in the hands of anyone. This revolution is ongoing, it has had many surprising winners and losers, and in its "teenager" phase, its disruption of the status quo is accelerating. Information security as an industry has always sought to help us from avoiding the pitfalls of new technologies. Often, this has been manifested as a form of conservatism that has caused organizations to miss out on the benefits of tech trends by assessing the actual risks incorrectly. This is quite understandable, managing risks in a tech whirlwind is nothing less than predicting the future. We all seek to be problem solvers in our lives; the trick to being really good at this is when you can solve future problems. In the early days of CSA, we recognized that having best practices for cloud security was not as important in the present as it would be in the future when organizations had massive adoption of cloud fueled by broadbased innovation. Our strategy for building research tools for the information security industry was to create "bridges" between where the industry was and where it needed to go. Arguably, our most popular "bridge" has been the Cloud Controls Matrix (CCM), which was first released in 2010. The CCM is a metaframework of security control objectives appropriate for cloud computing. It is organized into 16 comprehensive domains. We focused on making it high level ("strong authentication is important" vs. "use X type of multifactor authentication") in order to keep it relevant in consideration of the rapid changes in the cloud that we could anticipate occurring. This focus on principles resonated with practitioners, who made it our most popular download. We also mapped our control objectives to several other standards and regulations, from ISO/IEC 27001 to COBIT to PCI, and many others. This provided the bridge for the industry that allowed organizations to relate cloud security and risk issues to their existing frameworks, compliance requirements, and ISMSs. We have further enhanced it by characterizing controls as provider vs. customer vs. shared responsibility. We also try to categorize controls as relevant to all parts of the stack, from physical infrastructure to application to organizational governance. CCM has become the heart of many industry programs, inside and out of CSA. It is the foundation of many security programs and IT audits and is the heart of CSA's organizational certification, the CSA Security, Trust, and Assurance Registry initiative. CCM provides a tremendous amount of value as a freely available research artifact and has been translated into many languages. For all its benefits, CCM is not perfect. Mapping between other standards is often a laborious process, as human languages lack the precision of a computer language. Some standards articulate highly prescriptive controls, which can become quickly outdated and need constant revisions. The continuous updating of cloud software and configurations can run counter to the concept of periodic audits that was one of the design principles of CCM. For us at CSA, the CCM represents the journey, which is never ending, to improve the security of the cloud across all countries, industries, and organizations.

Center for Internet Security Controls (Formerly Sans 20 Critical Security Controls)

The Center for Internet Security (CIS) maintains the CIS Controls that include a set of recommended actions for cyberdefense providing specific and actionable methods to reduce the likelihood or damage resulting from the most common attacks. Formerly known as the SANS 20CSC, these controls provide actions organizations should perform first to minimize their risk. The attraction is the sequential and logical nature of the controls. The 20 CIS Controls are as follows:

Control 1: Inventory and control of hardware assets
Control 2: Inventory and control of software assets
Control 3: Continuous vulnerability management
Control 4: Controlled use of administrative privileges
Control 5: Secure configuration for hardware and software on mobile devices, laptops, workstations, and servers
Control 6: Maintenance, monitoring, and analysis of audit logs
Control 7: Email and web browser protections
Control 8: Malware defenses
Control 9: Limitation and control of network ports, protocols, and services
Control 10: Data recovery capabilities
Control 11: Secure configuration for network devices, such as firewalls, routers, and switches
Control 12: Boundary defense
Control 13: Data protection
Control 14: Controlled access based on the need to know
Control 15: Wireless access control
Control 16: Account monitoring and control
Control 17: Implement a security awareness and training program
Control 18: Application software security
Control 19: Incident response and management
Control 20: Penetration tests and Red Team exercises

Each of the controls is subdivided into sub-controls with actionable, mostly technical advice to comply with the control. For example, to achieve CIS Control 1, Inventory and Control of Hardware Assets, an organization can form several actions:

1.1 Use an active discovery tool
1.2 Use a passive asset discovery tool
1.3 Use Dynamic Host Configuration Protocol (DHCP) logging to Update Asset Inventory
1.4 Maintain detailed asset inventory
1.5 Maintain asset inventory information

1.6 Address unauthorized assets

1.7 Deploy port-level access control

1.8 Utilize client certificates to authenticate hardware assets.

The CIS Controls also provide descriptions for executing each of the sub-controls, indicate the asset type (applications, devices, network, data) related to the control, and map the control to the NIST Cybersecurity Framework Function.

TONY SAGER: JUMP-STARTING CONTROLS PRIORITIZATION WITHIN A CONTROL FRAMEWORK

SVP, and Chief Evangelist, CIS (Center for Internet Security)

"What do I do first?" When I started taking the National Security Agency (NSA) cyberdefense mission "public" in the early 2000s, this was the most frequent question from audiences. That caught me surprise, so you can tell I was never a CISO with the responsibility to solve problems. As a career-long software vulnerability analyst and executive manager at NSA, I got to point out problems. I was also struck by the irony—never in history have cyberdefenders had such great access to tools, training, guidance, threat information, control catalogs, and security frameworks. But all of this technology, information, and oversight had become a veritable "Fog of More"—more options, priorities, and opinions than an enterprise could manage. While security wizards can dream up countless ways that systems might be attacked, a useful priority scheme starts with how systems are being attacked. And while every enterprise is different, we all have more in common in cyberspace (e.g., technology, connectivity, attack types) than we do that is different. So, a community-level strategy of shared labor for threat analysis, translation into action, content development, and support is the only sensible path. If our social goal is to get all enterprises to a foundational level of security, and we will never get there if every enterprise has to go it alone. This is the motivation that led to what we now call the CIS Controls and the CIS Benchmarks, and is central to the work of the CIS. Starting from the community-developed content of the CIS Benchmarks and Controls provides an independent, vetted, and no/low-cost starting point for prioritization. They inherently address the most important needs for visibility, control, and ability to take defensive action. There is also a rapidly growing marketplace of complementary tools for implementation, adaptation, and measurement, as well as a way to map to any security framework. By starting from what we have in common and building to that, we gain great leverage for rapid action, consistency, and leverage to create a strong foundation for cyberdefense, and spend more of our scarce resources on things that really are unique about us.

An interesting new development in 2018 was the publication of Version 1.0 of the CIS Risk Assessment Methodology (CIS RAM), which recognizes the need to balance information security controls implementation with the organization's purpose and objectives. The risk assessment method supplements the implementation of controls to provide a common language between not only security professionals, but also the regulators, business management, and legal authorities. Today, the language of "due care" and "reasonable safeguards" used in the legal system after a breach does not connect well with the traditional establishment of maturity levels provided by the frameworks. What does a "3" mean in terms of due care? Is it enough? When management accepted the risk of the system, did they consider the potential harm to the public? The legal system is operating on a "duty of care," which require organizations to demonstrate they used controls to ensure the risk was reasonable to the organization and appropriate to other interested parties at the time of the breach. In an effort to bridge the gap in this communication, CIS and Halock Security Labs worked together to produce the CIS RAM. In short, the standard would allow an organization to demonstrate they implemented adequate controls, considering the "burden" to the organization of implementing the controls, thus finding balance between what you *should* do to protect others and what you *can* do as a business. CIS RAM is the first control standard to be applied to the new Duty of Care Risk Analysis Standard (DoCRA). It will be interesting to see how the acceptance of DoCRA progresses and the achieved level of adoption between the legal and security communities, as it directly marries the risk assessment techniques noted in the *Risk Management* chapter, the legal practices noted in the security incident and it's the law chapters, and this chapter on security control frameworks. There are clearly benefits of morphing to a more seamless conversation between the cybersecurity, legal, and business communities.

Information Technology Infrastructure Library (ITIL)

Information Technology Infrastructure Library (ITIL) is a set of books published by the British government's Stationary Office between 1989 and 1992 to improve IT service management. The framework contains a set of best practices for IT core operational processes such as change, release and configuration management, incident and problem management, capacity and availability management, and IT financial management.

ITIL's primary contribution is showing how the controls can be implemented for the service management IT processes.

Security Technical Implementation Guides (STIGS) and National Security Agency (NSA) Guides

Configuration standards for Department of Defense Information Assurance are freely available and used as the basis for technical standards for many private organizations.

These standards, if implemented, support many of the high-level requirements specified within the requirements of the other control frameworks in this section.

Payment Card Industry Data Security Standard (PCI DSS)

A set of comprehensive requirements for enhancing payment account security, formed by several major credit card issuers, to facilitate the broad adoption of a comprehensive security standard were designed to protect cardholder data. The standard, founded in 2006 by American Express, Discover, JCB International, MasterCard, and Visa, applies to all parties that are involved in credit card processing, such as merchants, processors, acquirers, issuers, and service providers as well as other entities that store, process, or transmit cardholder data. The standard contains 12 requirements to address each of the following areas:

- Build and maintain a secure network (proper network device configuration).
- Protect cardholder data (storage and encrypted transmission across open networks).
- Maintain a vulnerability management program (i.e., secure systems, antivirus software).
- Implement strong AC measures (logical and physical access, need to know).
- Regularly monitor and test networks (regularly test, track, and monitor access).
- Maintain an Information Security Policy (maintain a policy that addresses information security for all personnel).

The reviews are to be performed annually to ensure that cardholder data is protected. Depending upon the size of the entity participating in the program, the review may need to be conducted by an external assessor.

Control Objectives for Information and Related Technology (COBIT)

COBIT is a framework and supporting tool set initiated in 1996, issuing multiple versions with the latest version released in 2012 (COBIT 5) that allow managers to bridge the gap with respect to control requirements, technical issues, and business risks, and to communicate that level of control to stakeholders. COBIT can be used to integrate other standards as an umbrella framework.

COBIT 5 processes describe an organized set of practices and activities to achieve certain objectives and produce a set of outputs in support of achieving cybersecurity objectives aligned with enterprise objectives. The processes shown in Figure 8.5 were adapted from two professional guides designed to assist in the understanding and implementation of the COBIT 5 Framework, specifically the ISACA COBIT 5 Implementation (COBIT 5, 2012) and COBIT 5 for Information Security (COBIT, 2012) Professional Guides.

The risks related to IT implementations are noted as "risk sources" in the matrix, and a sampling of the COBIT 5 processes that could be used to mitigate the risk is shown in the far-right column as "COBIT 5 process capabilities." The COBIT 5 Framework contains processes for the enablement of IT, much of which can apply to cybersecurity practices. The COBIT 5 for Information Security Professional Guide extends the definition of these processes by adding processes specific to cybersecurity.

Risk Sources and COBIT 5 Process Capabilities		
	Risk Sources	*COBIT 5 Process Capabilities*
If the scenario is relevant and inherently likely…	…given these threats	…then consider whether these COBIT 5 processes need improvement. Note: In this column, next to each process number is an example from the process to consider. These are not the process names.
Benefit/Value Enablement Risk		
IT program selection	• Incorrect program selected for implementation and misaligned with corporate strategy and priorities • Duplication among different initiatives • New and important program creates long-term incompatibility with the enterprise architecture	• Alignment of cybersecurity with IT and business frameworks (APO02) • Cybersecurity is integrated with architecture (APO03) • Innovation promoted in cybersecurity (APO04) • Establish cybersecurity target investments (APO05) • Cybersecurity requirements in feasibility study (BAI01)

Figure 8.5 Cyber-risk and process capabilities using COBIT 5 for information security. (From Fitzgerald, T., Chapter Treating Cyber Risks Using Process Capabilities in Cyber Risk Handbook by Antonucci, D., 2017, John Wiley & Sons.)

(Continued)

New technologies	• Failure to adopt and exploit new technologies (i.e., functionality, optimization) in a timely manner • New and important technology trends not identified • Inability to use technology to realize desired outcomes (e.g., failure to make required business model or organizational changes)	• Measure effectiveness, efficiency, and capacity of cybersecurity resources against business need (EDM04) • Define target state for cybersecurity (APO02) • IT and cybersecurity architecture aligned with current technology trends (APO03) • Scan external environment, and identify emerging cybersecurity trends (APO04) • Create feasible new technology solutions while minimizing risk (BAI02) • Integrate cybersecurity in new technology design (BAI03)
Technology selection	• Incorrect technologies (i.e., cost, performance, features, compatibility) selected for implementation	• Develop clear information security criteria (APO02) • Cybersecurity architecture is aligned and evolves with changes (APO03) • Cybersecurity specifications in line with design (BAI03) • Security impacts of technology selection (APO13)
IT investment decision making	• Business managers or representatives not involved in important IT investment decision making regarding new applications, prioritization, or new technology opportunities	• Value management direction and/or oversight for cybersecurity (EDM02) • Business and cybersecurity involvement in IT strategic planning (APO02) • Cybersecurity investment fit with target enterprise architecture (APO03)

Figure 8.5 (*Continued*) Cyber-risk and process capabilities using COBIT 5 for information security. (From Fitzgerald, T., Chapter Treating Cyber Risks Using Process Capabilities in Cyber Risk Handbook by Antonucci, D., 2017, John Wiley & Sons.)

(Continued)

		• Cybersecurity investments allocated by risk appetite (APO05) • Develop cybersecurity budget (APO06) • Understanding of business how cybersecurity enables/affects it (APO08) • Program management stage-gating (BAI01)
Accountability over IT	• Business not assuming accountability over those IT areas it should such as functional requirements, development priorities, and assessing opportunities through new technologies	• Executive management accountability for cybersecurity-related decisions (EDM01-05) • Business, IT-related, and cybersecurity roles and responsibilities (APO01) • Clear and approved service agreements including cybersecurity (APO09) • Supplier relationship and requirements based on risk profile (APO10) • Visible leadership through executive commitment to cybersecurity (BAI05)
IT project termination	• Projects that are failing due to cost, delays, scope creep, or changed business priorities not terminated in a timely manner	• Cybersecurity roles, reporting and monitoring established (EDM05) • Value governance monitoring (EDM02) • Resource governance monitoring (EDM04) • Program/project management stage-gating (BAI01) • Effective portfolio management decision making (APO05)

Figure 8.5 (*Continued*)   Cyber-risk and process capabilities using COBIT 5 for information security. (From Fitzgerald, T., Chapter Treating Cyber Risks Using Process Capabilities in Cyber Risk Handbook by Antonucci, D., 2017, John Wiley & Sons.)

(*Continued*)

		• Investment monitoring (APO06) • Cybersecurity monitoring process and procedure (MEA01)
IT project economics	• Isolated IT project budget overrun • Consistent and important IT projects budget overruns • Absence of view on portfolio and project economics	• GEIT policies, organization structures, and roles (EDM01) • Value governance monitoring (EDM02) • Resource governance monitoring (EDM04) • Cybersecurity investment monitoring (APO06) • Independent project assessment to ensure cybersecurity requirements included (BAI01)
Program/Project Delivery Risk		
Architectural agility and flexibility	• Complex and inflexible IT architecture obstructing further evolution and expansion	• Define information security expectations (APO01) • Governance over resource optimization (EDM04) • Responsive cybersecurity planning (APO02) • Maintenance of enterprise architecture aligned with cybersecurity (APO03) • Cybersecurity innovation is promoted (APO04) • Portfolio management decision taking (APO05) • Agile development life cycle methods include cybersecurity (BAI02,03) • Maintaining security in an agile and flexible environment (APO13)

Figure 8.5 (*Continued*) Cyber-risk and process capabilities using COBIT 5 for information security. (From Fitzgerald, T., Chapter Treating Cyber Risks Using Process Capabilities in Cyber Risk Handbook by Antonucci, D., 2017, John Wiley & Sons.)

(*Continued*)

Integration of IT within business processes	• Extensive dependency and use of end-user computing and ad hoc solutions for important information needs • Separate and non-integrated IT solutions to support business processes	• GEIT policies, organization structures, and roles (EDM01) • Business and IT-related roles and responsibilities (APO01) • Define cybersecurity strategy, and align with IT and business strategies (APO02) • Align cybersecurity and enterprise architecture (APO03) • Stakeholders recognize cybersecurity as enabler (APO08) • Definition and understanding of business requirements and cybersecurity aspects (BAI02) • Define cybersecurity specifications with high-level design (BAI03) • Managing organizational changes with regard to cybersecurity (BAI05)
Software implementation	• Operational glitches when new software is made operational • Users not prepared to use and exploit new application software	• Monitor security quality metrics (APO11) • Project management (BAI01) • Requirements definitions (BAI02) • Solution development (BAI03) • Managing organizational changes with regard to software implementation (BAI05) • Cybersecurity requirements incorporated into infrastructure, process, and application changes (BAI06)

Figure 8.5 (*Continued*) Cyber-risk and process capabilities using COBIT 5 for information security. (From Fitzgerald, T., Chapter Treating Cyber Risks Using Process Capabilities in Cyber Risk Handbook by Antonucci, D., 2017, John Wiley & Sons.)

(*Continued*)

		• Ensure cybersecurity acceptance in test plan (BAI07) • Cybersecurity knowledge support through awareness training (BAI08)
Project delivery	• Occasional late IT project delivery by internal development department • Routinely important delays in IT project delivery • Excessive delays in outsourced IT development project	• GEIT policies, organization structures, and roles (EDM01) • Value governance monitoring (EDM02) • Investment monitoring (APO06) • Program/project management planning and monitoring (BAI01)
Project quality	• Insufficient quality of project deliverables due to software, documentation, or compliance with functional requirements	• Architecture standards and reuse of cybersecurity components (APO03) • Consistent and effective quality management activities (APO11) • Program/project quality management planning and monitoring (BAI01)
Service Delivery/IT Operations Risk		
State of infrastructure technology	• Obsolete IT technology cannot satisfy new business requirements such as networking, security, and storage	• Resource management direction and/or oversight (EDM04) • Identify potential cybersecurity gaps (APO02) • Align cybersecurity and enterprise architecture (APO03) • Identifying important cybersecurity trends (APO04) • Maintaining security infrastructure (BAI03)

Figure 8.5 (*Continued*) Cyber-risk and process capabilities using COBIT 5 for information security. (From Fitzgerald, T., Chapter Treating Cyber Risks Using Process Capabilities in Cyber Risk Handbook by Antonucci, D., 2017, John Wiley & Sons.)

(*Continued*)

		• Planning for and addressing capacity and performance issues (BAI04) • Identify cybersecurity requirements for assets (BAI09)
Aging of application software	• Application software that is old, poorly documented, expensive to maintain, difficult to extend, or not integrated in current architecture	• Resource management direction and/or oversight (EDM04) • Defining target state for cybersecurity (APO02) • Maintaining enterprise architecture (APO03) • Identifying new and important cybersecurity trends (APO04) • Maintaining applications with cybersecurity (BAI03) • Identifying cybersecurity requirements for assets (BAI09) • Business process controls (DSS06)
Regulatory compliance	• Non-compliance with regulations of accounting or manufacturing	• GEIT compliance policies and roles (EDM01) • Policies and guidance on regulatory compliance (APO01) • Planning for regulatory requirements (APO02) • Identifying and defining regulatory requirements (BAI02) • Monitoring compliance requirements and current status (MEA03)
Selection/ performance of third-party suppliers	• Inadequate support and services delivered by vendors, not in line with SLAs	• Effective supplier selection, management, and relationships based on cybersecurity risk (APO10)

Figure 8.5 (*Continued*)   Cyber-risk and process capabilities using COBIT 5 for information security. (From Fitzgerald, T., Chapter Treating Cyber Risks Using Process Capabilities in Cyber Risk Handbook by Antonucci, D., 2017, John Wiley & Sons.)

(*Continued*)

	• Inadequate performance of outsourcer in large-scale, long-term outsourcing arrangement	• Ensure cybersecurity part of procurement planning (BAI03)
Infrastructure theft	• Theft of laptop with sensitive data • Theft of a substantial number of development servers	• Policies and guidance on protection of assets (APO01) • References and background checks on new hires and contractors (APO07) • Protection of critical assets during maintenance activities (BAI03) • Physical security measures (DSS05)
Destruction of infrastructure	• Destruction of data center due to sabotage or other causes • Accidental destruction of individual laptops	• Environmental protection and facilities management (DSS01) • Physical security measures (DSS05)
IT staff	• Departure or extended unavailability of key IT staff • Key development team leaving the enterprise • Inability to recruit IT staff	• Use certification to develop cybersecurity skill set and enable retention (APO07) • Managing tacit knowledge (BAI08)
IT expertise and skills	• Lack or mismatch of IT-related skills within IT due to new technologies or other causes • Lack of business understanding by IT staff	• Definition and development of business and cybersecurity staff competency requirements (APO07) • Cybersecurity knowledge support through awareness training (BAI08)

Figure 8.5 (*Continued*)   Cyber-risk and process capabilities using COBIT 5 for information security. (From Fitzgerald, T., Chapter Treating Cyber Risks Using Process Capabilities in Cyber Risk Handbook by Antonucci, D., 2017, John Wiley & Sons.)

(*Continued*)

Software integrity	• Intentional modification of software leading to wrong data or fraudulent actions • Unintentional modification of software leading to unexpected results • Unintentional configuration and change management errors	• Definition of cybersecurity control requirements (BAI02) • Cybersecurity requirements incorporated into infrastructure, process, and application changes (BAI06) • Ensure cybersecurity part of acceptance testing (BAI07) • Establish cybersecurity configuration baselines (BAI10) • Access controls (DSS05) • Business process controls (DSS06)
Infrastructure (hardware)	• Misconfiguration of hardware components • Damage of critical servers in the computer room due to accident or other causes • Intentional tampering with hardware such as security devices	• Protection of critical assets during maintenance activities (BAI03) • Physical security measures (DSS05) • Establish cybersecurity configuration baselines (BAI10)
Software performance	• Regular software malfunctioning of critical application software • Intermittent performance problems with important system software	• Software development quality assurance (BAI03) • Planning for and addressing capacity and performance issues (BAI04) • Root cause analysis and problem resolution (DSS03)
System capacity	• Inability of systems to handle transaction volumes when user volumes increase	• Architecture principles for scalability and agility (APO03) • Maintaining infrastructure (BAI03)

Figure 8.5 (*Continued*) Cyber-risk and process capabilities using COBIT 5 for information security. (From Fitzgerald, T., Chapter Treating Cyber Risks Using Process Capabilities in Cyber Risk Handbook by Antonucci, D., 2017, John Wiley & Sons.)

(*Continued*)

	• Inability of systems to handle system load when new applications or initiatives are deployed	• Planning for and addressing capacity and performance issues (BAI04)
Aging of infra-structural software	• Use of unsupported versions of operating system software • Use of old database system	• Resource management direction and/or oversight (EDM04) • Recognizing and strategically addressing current IT capability issues (APO02) • Maintaining enterprise architecture (APO03) • Identifying new and important technology trends (APO04) • Maintaining infrastructure (BAI03) • Problems relating to business process controls (DSS03)
Malware	• Intrusion of malware on critical operational servers • Regular infection of laptops with malware	• Policies and guidance on use of software (APO01) • Malicious software detection (DSS05)
Logical attacks	• Virus attack • Unauthorized users trying to break into systems • Denial-of-service attack • Web site defacing • Industrial espionage	• Policies and guidance on protection and use of IT assets (APO01) • Security requirements in solutions (BAI03) • Access controls and security monitoring (DSS05)
Information media	• Loss/disclosure of portable media [e.g., CD, universal serial bus (USB) drives, portable disks] containing sensitive data	• Policies and guidance on protection and use of IT assets (APO01) • Protection of mobile and/or removable storage and media devices (DSS05-06)

Figure 8.5 (*Continued*) Cyber-risk and process capabilities using COBIT 5 for information security. (From Fitzgerald, T., Chapter Treating Cyber Risks Using Process Capabilities in Cyber Risk Handbook by Antonucci, D., 2017, John Wiley & Sons.)

(Continued)

	• Loss of backup media • Accidental disclosure of sensitive information due to failure to follow information handling guidelines	
Utilities performance	• Intermittent utilities (e.g., telecom, electricity) failure • Regular, extended utilities failures	• Relationships/management of key utility suppliers (APO08) • Environmental protection and facilities management (DSS01)
Industrial action	• Inaccessible facilities and building due to labor union strike • Unavailable key staff due to industrial action	• Staff relationships and key individuals (APO07) • Managing staff knowledge (BAI08)
Data(base) integrity	• Intentional modification of data (e.g., accounting, security-related data, sales figures) • Database (e.g., client or transactions database) corruption	• Information architecture and data classification (APO03) • Development standards (BAI03) • Change management (BAI06) • Managing data storage (DSS01) • Access controls (DSS05)
Logical trespassing	• Users circumventing logical access rights • Users obtaining access to unauthorized information • Users stealing sensitive data	• Policies and guidance on protection and use of IT assets (APO01) • Access controls and security monitoring (DSS05) • Contract staff policies (APO07)
Operational IT errors	• Operator errors during backup, upgrades of systems, or maintenance of systems	• Staff training (APO07) • Operations procedures (DSS01)

Figure 8.5 (*Continued*) Cyber-risk and process capabilities using COBIT 5 for information security. (From Fitzgerald, T., Chapter Treating Cyber Risks Using Process Capabilities in Cyber Risk Handbook by Antonucci, D., 2017, John Wiley & Sons.)

(*Continued*)

	• Incorrect information input	• Business process controls (DSS06)
Contractual compliance	• Non-compliance with software license agreements (e.g., use and/or distribution of unlicensed software) • Contractual obligations as service provider with customers/clients not met	• Monitoring service agreements (APO09) • Supplier agreements and relationship monitoring (APO10) • Software license management (DSS02) • Contractual compliance requirements and current status monitoring (MEA03)
Environmental	• Use of equipment that is not environmentally friendly (e.g., high level of power consumption, packaging)	• Incorporation of environmentally friendly principles in enterprise architecture (APO03) • Selection of solutions and procurement policies (BAI03) • Environmental and facilities management (DSS01)
Acts of nature	• Earthquake • Tsunami • Major storm/hurricane • Major wildfire	• Environmental and facilities management (DSS01) • Physical security (DSS05) • Manage continuity (DSS04)

Figure 8.5 (*Continued*) Cyber-risk and process capabilities using COBIT 5 for information security. (From Fitzgerald, T., Chapter Treating Cyber Risks Using Process Capabilities in Cyber Risk Handbook by Antonucci, D., 2017, John Wiley & Sons.)

Components of the Cybersecurity Processes

Each of the cybersecurity processes has a life cycle by which the process is defined, created, monitored, updated, and subsequently retired. New technologies are introduced which may negate the need for a process or significantly alter the process. For example, a cybersecurity policy in the past may have required that sensitive files be placed on a network server and not on the laptop or desktop. A change to the process by moving to a cloud storage provider with contractual backups or implementing laptops with encryption and backup software may remove the need to store information on a central network server to ensure the contents are appropriately backed up on a regular schedule.

The cybersecurity process components would include the process description, identification of stakeholders (internal and external), goals, life cycle, good practices (i.e., process practices, activities, work product inputs, and outputs), as well as including metrics for achieving and monitoring the goals and ensuring the stakeholder needs are met.

Cybersecurity Practices and Activities

Enabling processes are developed from practices, activities, and creating detailed activities through increasing levels of detail. Practices are statements of action that develop benefits, provide the appropriate level of risk, and manage the appropriate level of resources to meet the business objectives. An example of a security-specific practice to support the *Manage Security Services* process would be *Manage Endpoint Security*. This practice would ensure that endpoints (laptop, desktop, server, and other mobile and network devices or software) are secured at a level that is equal to or greater than the defined security requirements of the information processed, stored, or transmitted. Inputs to the process could include the information security architecture, service-level agreements, physical inventory audits, or reports of violations of security of these devices. These practices are somewhat generic and may be adapted for the needs of each enterprise. The organization also decides, through the governing bodies, which practices would apply, the frequency of the practice execution, how the practice is applied (manual or through automated means), and the acceptance of the risk if the practice is not implemented.

Cybersecurity-specific activities provide guidance to achieve the practices. Activities are, in short, the primary actions taken to operate the process. Each of the practices will have a set of either COBIT 5 activities or cybersecurity-specific activities to achieve the operation of the practice. Continuing the *Manage Endpoint Security* practice example, some of the cybersecurity activities may be to configure the endpoints in a secure manner, categorize the types of endpoints and the controls needs, identify potential entry point targets of the endpoints, analyze the target attractiveness for each endpoint, implement network monitoring on devices, dispose of endpoints securely, and examine the history of attacks and compare against the current endpoint population.

These activities would be based upon generally accepted and good practices, provide a sufficient level of detail to achieve the cybersecurity-specific practice, support definition of clear organizational responsibilities [i.e., responsible, accountable, informed, and consulted (RACI) charts, governance structures], and support the development of more detailed procedures. Some processes may need to be more detailed than others depending upon the criticality of the activity and the experience level of the group performing the task.

Different Types of Cybersecurity Processes Work Together

The processes need the input from other enablers to be effective. For example, processes need information as input and provide information as output to other processes and enablers. The five domains of processes are (1) evaluate, direct, and monitor (EDM);

(2) align, plan, and organize (APO); (3) build, acquire, and implement (BAI); (4) deliver, service, and support (DSS); and (5) monitor, evaluate, and assess (MEA).

EDM Domain

The EDM domain of processes is geared at providing governance for cybersecurity and is focused on ensuring the appropriate direction is provided and monitoring mechanisms are in place. Processes to ensure a governance framework and maintenance, benefits delivery, risk optimization, resource optimization, and stakeholder transparency are specified. For example, as shown in Figure 8.5, the risk "Obsolete IT cannot satisfy new business requirements such as networking, security, and storage" would be addressed through process capability EDM04—resource management direction and/or oversight. Judgment would be made on whether the current cybersecurity resources (people, process, or technology) are sufficient to satisfy the needs of the business. A laptop may have had sufficient processing power, memory, and storage in the past when encryption was not required; however, now that encryption is loaded on the device along with other security controls, the device may no longer be adequate.

APO Domain

The APO domain of processes contains cybersecurity management processes that are helpful to embed cybersecurity within the IT management framework, align the cybersecurity strategy, define the architectural components necessary to support the enterprise architecture, manage the cybersecurity portfolio, set a budget and provision expenses for breaches, manage the training process for cybersecurity professionals, obtain vendor Service Level Agreements for outsourced services, identify risk and treatment plans, and manage cybersecurity innovation with new technologies and other management practices. Essentially, the APO cybersecurity process capabilities ensure that cybersecurity is appropriately inserted into the processes to support the development of existing and new technology to meet the business objectives.

BAI Domain

The BAI domain defines process capabilities to assist in the execution of the cybersecurity program. Such capabilities include processes for defining cybersecurity requirements, selecting cybersecurity solutions, embedding cybersecurity in change management processes, managing normal and emergency changes, managing the collective knowledge of cybersecurity practices across the organization, and managing requirements risk. Project management practices are crucial to ensuring that the solutions selected meet the business requirements in a timely and budget-sensitive manner.

DSS Domain

The DSS domain defines those process capabilities that provide operational support and "keep the cybersecurity lights on." These apply to outsourced services as well as internally run services. The cybersecurity operations management is developed with input from the security architecture, information security policies, and facilities information. A process capability exists for identifying, classifying, escalating, and managing security incidents, managing the ticketing system for cybersecurity items, managing problems through root cause analysis, and reducing the likelihood of reoccurrence, managing crises, and ensuring that an appropriate business continuity plan and disaster recovery of IT-related equipment and data is in place. IR and recovery operations should be integrated with the overall business continuity management program. A key control today for recovering from ransomware attacks is the restoration of the data files using the backups obtained through the documented disaster recovery process. If these controls are not in place and integrated with business continuity, data may be unrecoverable, and if effective processes are not defined, the delay in processing may be unacceptable.

MEA Domain

This set of management process capabilities in the MEA domain provides the cybersecurity monitoring, self-assessments, and ensuring that reporting requirements satisfying compliance with various laws and regulations are being executed properly. Periodic reviews of cybersecurity through a formal approach are defined. Corrective cybersecurity actions are also tracked, and performance is reported. These processes ensure that the appropriate internal control mechanisms for cybersecurity are developed and operating effectively.

Each of the COBIT 5 domains contributes to the maturing of the cybersecurity program processes by contributing either governance or management practices and related activities to address the planning, building, or ongoing operation of the cybersecurity environment. The processes are the enablers which provide the who, what, when, and where actions need to be taken. Holistically, this reduces the risk that actions necessary to protect the confidentiality, integrity, and availability of the information critical to the business are missed.

Using the COBIT 5 process, enablers provides a very holistic set of cybersecurity processes to manage the cybersecurity program. Once the organization has implemented these processes, it will be clear as to who in the organization is accountable and responsible for each of the governance and management practices supporting cybersecurity, and who else needs to be involved to change or implement the process by being informed or consulted. A clear definition of the cybersecurity governance and management practices necessary to achieve each cybersecurity process that makes up the cybersecurity program will be established. Assurance can be provided that the detailed activities are defined and based upon good practices, leveraging those technical definitions defined by other standards built on good practices at that level. The organization has a mechanism to have the comfort that processes are in place to ensure that the risks inherent in implementing technology have associated processes to mitigate the risk.

COBIT 5 cybersecurity process capabilities provide the governance and management practices necessary to effectively and efficiently align the cybersecurity program with the business enterprise objectives. Detailed activities are developed to support the cybersecurity practices to provide governance (EDM), manage the work (APO), create solutions (BAO), sustain (DSS), and improve (MEA). These processes taken together form a cybersecurity life cycle with defined inputs and outputs based upon generally accepted good practices, taken together holistically, can serve to reduce the organizational cybersecurity risk.

Information Security Forum—The Standard of Good Practice for Information Security

The Standard of Good Practice for Information Security maintained by the Information Security Forum (ISF) addresses and is aligned to many of the security controls previously mentioned in the other frameworks and provides coverage for topics covered in ISO/IEC 27001:2013, COBIT 5 for Information Security, NIST Cybersecurity Framework, CSA CCM, CIS CSC, and PCI DSS. The ISF is a paid membership-based organization providing free access to the tool for use by its members.

The standard consists of areas similar to the other standards including security governance, information risk assessment, security management, people management, information management, system development management, system development life cycle, business application management, system access, system management, networks and communications, electronic communications, external supplier management, supply chain management, technical security management, threat and incident management, local environment management, business continuity, and security monitoring and improvement. Each of the areas is broken down into principles and objectives, as well as guidance or requirements related to the principles and objectives. The framework also provides links to other related content and resources to assist in achieving compliance results.

Federal Information System Controls Audit Manual

Issued by the General Accounting Office, this provides guidance for information systems auditors to evaluate the IT controls used in support of financial statement audits. This is not an audit standard but is included here because auditors are typically testing the control environment in government audits using this standard.

There has been increased emphasis on the use of NIST 800–53 controls and the NIST 800–53 A assessments; however, Federal Information System Controls Audit Manual is still used by government auditors, and therefore, it is worthwhile to understand the contents.

Open Web Application Security Project

The Open Web Application Security Project (OWASP) represents good development practices and worth including in the cybersecurity team's inclusion in frameworks and standards due to the risk that could be minimized by implementing appropriate application controls. Each year, OWASP generates a listing of the top ten application security risks for the prior year. These risks should be factored into the security program and checked as part of the system development life cycle for their consideration at each stage. The 2017 year risks included, in order of priority, (1) injection (Structured Query Language (SQL), NoSQL, operating system commands, Lightweight Directory Access Protocol (LDAP), etc.), (2) broken authentication, (3) sensitive data exposure, (4) XML external entities, (5) broken access control, (6) security misconfiguration, (7) cross-site scripting, (8) insecure deserialization, (9) using components with known vulnerabilities, and (10) insufficient logging and monitoring. OWASP has also created an OWASP Top Ten Proactive Controls Project to provide guidance for developing secure code, including the following controls in order of importance, (1) define software requirements, (2) leverage security frameworks and libraries, (3) secure database access, (4) encode and escape data, (5) validate all inputs, (6) implement digital identity, (7) enforce access controls, (8) protect data everywhere, (9) implement security logging and monitoring, and (10) handle all errors and exceptions.

CMMI Institute Cybermaturity Platform

In 2016, ISACA acquired the CMMI Institute (CMMI represents Capability Maturity Model Integration), well known for their CMMs for assessing IT departments. In 2018, the CMMI Institute announced the availability of a cybersecurity maturity platform to feature risk profiles, assessments, and gap analysis to provide a road map from the current maturity state to a desired maturity state. The platform focuses on the cybersecurity capabilities required within an organization to deliver secure systems. The capabilities are associated with a level of risk, with the notion that the CISO can place the focus on the areas where building the capabilities will have the most impact vs. focusing on the specific security controls. The platform is comprised of over 3,100 "best practice statements" across 80 practice areas, each associated with a 1–5 maturity level. These statements are oriented at what the organization does well (capability) vs. a specific individual control. Unlike the other control standards that are available for free or for a nominal cost to receive the framework, this is a cloud-based subscription with reporting capabilities and is fee-based.

North American Electric Reliability Corporation

The North American Electric Reliability Corporation (NERC) is a nonprofit organization whose beginnings trace back to 1968 to create standards in response to a major blackout in 1965. Voluntary standards were initially issued, and in 2007, these standards became mandatory with penalties for noncompliance. In July 2016, version 5 of the CIP standards was required, representing a shift from a risk-based assessment methodology to an impact-rating criterion that would be consistently applied across the utilities. The standards continue to be enhanced to address increasing concerns around network connectivity between utilities (supply chain and remote access), intermediate devices, encryption latency, and sufficiency of overall security controls. The CIP standards cover many of the same infrastructure areas as the other overall frameworks (i.e., ISO27001:2013, NIST Cybersecurity Framework, CIS Controls).

The 11-Factor Cybersecurity Risk Assurance Manifesto

The regulations, control frameworks, standards, technical implementation guides, and penalties for noncompliance provide insight into "what" needs to be achieved to provide the organizational compliance assurance to the various security-related regulations. Now, this begs the next question, "What actions need to be taken to achieve and maintain compliance with the regulations?"

To answer that question, the 11-Factor Cybersecurity Risk Assurance Manifesto, was originally published as the "Security Compliance Manifesto" in 2008 to provide guidance for sustaining information security as organizations were wrapping heads around how to comply with the plethora of various regulations and emerging changing control frameworks, as shown in Figure 8.6, sets out the principles by which cybersecurity risk assurance may be achieved.

1. *Designate the individual responsible for cybersecurity risk assurance oversight.* Whereas many of the policy-type regulations may not appear to change on a frequent basis, the supporting documents, technical specifications, and current areas of concern do change over time. New laws are also created, such as the New York Cybersecurity regulations and the GDPR previously mentioned. Staying on top of these changes and ensuring that someone is directing the cybersecurity risk assurance efforts are essential. In medium-sized organizations, this is likely to be the manager or director of security, whereas in larger organizations the CISO, Chief Security Officer, or Security Officer

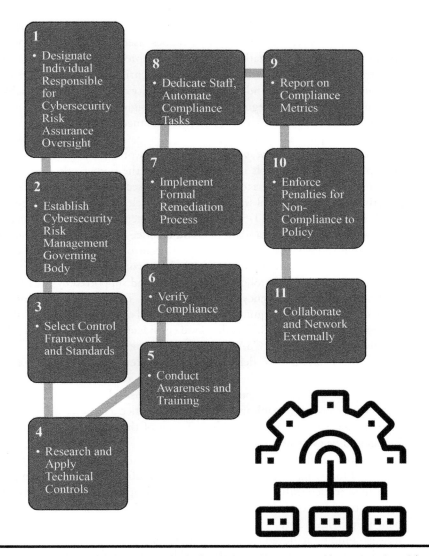

Figure 8.6 Eleven-Factor Cybersecurity Risk Assurance Manifesto. (Updated from Fitzgerald, T. *Information Security Governance Simplified: From the Boardroom to the Keyboard,* **p. 179, 2012, Boca Raton: Auerbach/Taylor & Francis.)**

is likely to be responsible for ensuring that the cybersecurity risk assurance activities are performed. The CISO's organization and the other business units carry out the mitigation work as appropriate.

  2. *Establish a cybersecurity risk management governing body.* To achieve support for the implementation of security policies throughout the organization and to ensure that the security policies do not disrupt the business, it is advisable

to establish a cybersecurity risk management council or committee. Councils or committees (name consistent with names used for other collaborative groups within the organization) made up of representatives from IT, business units, HR, legal departments, physical security, internal audit, ethics, and compliance, privacy, and information security can be effective in achieving compliance with the regulations. Their oversight and interaction provide feedback as to whether the security activities planned are feasible and whether there is a high probability of success.

3. *Select control framework and standards.* The frameworks offer an excellent place to map the security controls that are in place to the framework, uncover the gaps, and create action plans to increase the cybersecurity assurance with these objectives. Multiple control frameworks can be selected for different levels of detail. For example, COBIT 5 for Information Security, NIST Cybersecurity Framework, and the ISF Standard of Good Practice may be selected to provide a governing framework, whereas ISO27001 controls may be mapped to the framework (already available from multiple framework sources) and then linked to the NIST 800–53 control objective families and supported by the Defense Information Systems Agency (DISA) Security Technical Implementation Guides (STIGs) or vendor guidance. The technical controls used in the 20 CIS Controls can also be linked. Specific cloud considerations from the CSA CCM may also be leveraged (the CSA CCM contains linkages to many other frameworks). The mapping provides a mechanism to review how a set of technical controls supports the higher-level statements in the other frameworks. The same controls serve multiple purposes. Comprehensive frameworks are created through this process, enabling the other compliance assurance activities. An organization may not use the totality of each of these frameworks; however, they should be evaluated and leveraged.

4. *Research and apply technical controls.* There are many approaches at the technical level for being compliant with the control objectives. Analysis must be performed to determine the best control based upon the risk profile of the organization. For example, achieving security risk assurance with a requirement to provide adequate offsite backups of information in the event of a disaster could be achieved in a small regional office by placing a daily backup in a fireproof safe and rotating the weekly backup off-site. Alternatively, a small office may decide to store the backups remotely with a storage facility, transmit the backup information securely over the Internet to a cloud storage provider for backups, mirror the environment, or assign an individual to take home the backup nightly. Each of the scenarios has their own costs and risks inherent in the control selection.

5. *Conduct awareness and training.* The documented security policies and procedures are necessary; however, if individuals do not truly understand their responsibilities to comply with the security controls, the likelihood that the appropriate processes will be followed is greatly diminished.

6. *Verify compliance.* Vulnerability assessments, external penetration tests, Red Team exercises, and internal audit reviews of the security controls ensure that the policies and procedures that were created are being followed. Implemented security on the computing platform can be tested and compared with the documented baselines, configurations, and change control records to provide assurance that the security controls are being maintained per the requirements implemented through the control frameworks.

7. *Implement a formal remediation process.* When weaknesses in the security controls are discovered, through internal audits, external audits, vulnerability assessments, risk assessments, or other internal reviews, the issue must be logged and tracked to completion. Accountability should be placed at a middle management or senior management level to ensure the appropriate attention and priority are placed on remedying the issue. Completion dates must be assigned (preferably no later than 60–90 days after creation of the action plan, shorter for higher risk issues). Documentation of the remediation (evidence) must be provided when the issue has been resolved. The existence of a formal tracking of the security issues provides the assurance that security is an ongoing, management-supported process.

8. *Dedicate staff, automate compliance tasks.* Compliance initiatives are very time-consuming and drain the organization of resources to collect evidence, provide explanations, participate in interviews, and locate the policies and procedures that support the regulations. Without an organized automated process, this activity becomes even more challenging and time is wasted on inefficiencies. The same information may be requested multiple times to answer similar questions, where one report may have provided a reasonable answer. Initially, more staff should be allocated to the compliance efforts to provide a focus to the activity. When the compliance tasks are added to the regular jobs of predominantly IT staff, they may be given lower priority and resources. As automation increases, the staff required to support the compliance efforts should either remain constant or decrease. A constant staff may be needed to ensure that the new regulations and changes are adequately addressed and enable the team to increase coverage (i.e., more testing on different platforms, increased focus on business partners, analyzing trends).

9. *Report on compliance metrics.* Dashboards of red, yellow, and green or heat maps are useful tools to demonstrate where security is weak within the organization and where more focus should be placed. These metrics should be reported in a manner that is meaningful to the business, such as unavailability issues, which could impact major, mission critical applications, confidentiality concerns that may affect the consumer trust in the brand and integrity issues causing mistrust in the decisions based on the information.

10. *Enforce penalties for noncompliance to policy.* Does one grin and bear it when the security control objectives are not followed or grit one's teeth? This is one area that needs...teeth! There must be sanctions in place for those that do

not follow the security policies. Associates must also be trained that compliance with the security controls is part of their job responsibilities. The individual responsible for cybersecurity risk assurance must ensure that the guidelines are established for sanctions and that the appropriate parties follow through with the sanction (which may be the manager, legal, and HR representatives).

11. *Collaborate and network externally.* Many organizations must comply with the same regulations, why not leverage that experience? Working with peers, within the industry vertical for dealing with industry-specific regulations, and across industries for understanding various methods to implement the control frameworks, standards, and technical controls, can be invaluable. For example, nonprofit organizations such as the HIPAA Collaborative of Wisconsin were formed to bring together health-care providers, payers, and clearinghouses to discuss approaches to implementing HIPAA. The presentations, network contacts, and information sharing that happen are phenomenal. Attending conferences such as RSA, EVANTA, Gartner Security and Risk Summit, and industry associations such as the Information Systems Security Association, ISACA, Management Information System Training Institute, SANS Institute, International Association of Privacy Professions (IAPP), and others helps to gain a common understanding of the regulation and implementation approaches. This also provides input as to what the "herd" is doing to be compliant with the regulation.

RON HALE PH.D. CISM: THE POSITIVE POWER OF COMMUNITY ENGAGEMENT

Vice President Cyber Training, Development, and Policy, DarkMatter LLC

A group of 15 CISOs from various companies and industries had already gathered in the meeting room as I entered. As the last few came and got their coffee, the moderator began to explain how the CISO Forum was going to operate. While there was an agenda of short presentations and topics for discussion, the event was more of an open forum where the CISOs could explore topics of the greatest importance to the group. Over the years, I have participated in several CISO Forums. Each has provided participants an opportunity to connect with colleagues, to talk about pressing issues, and to share ideas. The Forums have provided an opportunity to come together as a community to share experiences and to explore common areas of interest. For me, the ability to build trust and form lasting friendships has been the most significant outcome of these events. As ISACA's Chief Knowledge Officer, I have had the tremendous pleasure of working with information security professionals from around the world. In addition to CISO Forums, I have worked on projects with ISACA colleagues and members of other associations. The associations we are members of, the certifications we earn, and the professional resources we use have come to us mainly through the efforts of individuals who saw a problem or had a good idea. Coming together to solve problems has been a tremendous force. It provides an opportunity to contribute and allows everyone to build new skills as well as their personal brand. At ISACA, I have had to bring together groups of practitioners from around the world. These practitioners have worked through hours of conference calls at inconvenient times, to contribute to a project deliverable, or to review draft documents. Those working on certification examinations spend hours writing and reviewing examination items. While it is hard work, those who get involved come away with a great sense of achievement and the personal satisfaction knowing that they are creating something of value. So, what is in it for you? I have found that the price of participation is small compared to the personal and professional rewards you receive including the following:

- Gaining executive-level experience by taking on project management activities.
- Working with luminaries and recognized leaders in the profession.
- Building your resume and personal brand.
- Expanding your world of professional connections.
- Increasing your knowledge and capabilities.
- Gaining personal satisfaction by being involved in a significant global project. Opportunities to engage with the community are everywhere. The local or international association you belong to is always looking for volunteers. There are multiple projects available through groups such as ISACA, the CSA, The Open Group, and OWASP. Take advantage of the many opportunities and experience the positive power of community involvement.

The Standards/Framework Value Proposition

Control frameworks and standards provide the road map to build a successful information security program. Once in place, continuous review of the policies, standard operating procedures, and implementation of the controls will enhance the effectiveness of the program. Monitoring through audits accompanied by corrective actions and tracking enables refinement of the control framework and standards to reduce the risk of a security event impacting the business in a significant way. Each of the frameworks provides their own unique contribution to the overall management of cybersecurity to reduce the risk, and we can leverage all of them. For example, for us to get from point A to point B on a map, we can walk, drive, schedule a pickup from a ride-sharing service such as Uber or Lyft from our smartphone; call for a taxicab;

take a train, a plane, a boat; or someday soon, board a self-driving or flying car. The point is that we have multiple methods, and depending upon the situation, the risk we are willing to take in getting there safely and on time determines the method we will use. Control frameworks, standards, and the controls contained within these are the same way, and one size does not fit everyone. Thankfully, the hard work of mapping these controls has already been done for us and is connected. Imagine if we needed to get to the train station but had no idea what vehicles could be available to get us there. With control frameworks, we have a map.

Suggested Reading

1. Federal Information Security Management Act of 2002 (FISMA). 2002. November 27. http://csrc.nist.gov/groups/SMA/fisma/index.html.
2. National Institute of Standards and Technology, Special Publications. http://csrc.nist.gov/publications/PubsSPs.html.
3. Recommended Security Controls for Federal Information Systems, Special Publication 800–53. http://csrc.nist.gov/publications/PubsSPs.html.
4. Defense Information Systems Agency (DISA). Security Technical Implementation Guides (STIGS). https://iase.disa.mil/stigs/Pages/index.aspx.
5. National Security Agency, Security Configuration Guides. www.nsa.gov/.
6. ISO/IEC 27001:2013 Information Security Management Systems Requirements www.iso.org/standard/54534.html.
7. ISO/IEC 27002:2013 Information Technology Security Techniques—Code of Practice for Information Security Management, International Organization for Standardization (ISO). www.iso.org/standard/54533.html.
8. Federal Information System Controls Audit Manual (FISCAM). GAO/AIMD-12.19.6. January 1999. www.gao.gov/special.pubs/12_19_6.pdf.
9. Federal Information System Controls Audit Manual (FISCAM). GAO-09-232G. February 2009. www.gao.gov/new.items/d09232g.pdf.
10. Information Technology Infrastructure Library. www.itil-officialsite.com/home/home.asp.
11. Tolle, E. 2005. *A New Earth: Awakening to Your Life's Purpose*. Penguin, London.
12. PCI Data Security Standards Council. www.pcisecuritystandards.org/security_standards/documents.php.
13. Fitzgerald, T. 2008. Compliance Assurance: Taming the Beast. In *Information Security Handbook*, eds. Harold Tipton and Micki Krause, Auerbach Publications, Boca Raton, FL.
14. IT Governance Institute. CobiT® Framework. Governance, Control and Audit for Information and Related Technology. www.isaca.org/About-ISACA/IT-Governance-Institute/Pages/default.aspx.
15. CobiT® 5.0, IT Governance Institute. www.isaca.org/COBIT/Pages/default.aspx.
16. National Institute of Standards and Technology (NIST). 2018. NIST Releases Version 1.1 of its Popular Cybersecurity Framework. (April 16). www.nist.gov/news-events/news/2018/04/nist-releases-version-11-its-popular-cybersecurity-framework.
17. Information Security Forum. The ISF Standard of Good Practice for Information Security. www.securityforum.org/tool/the-isf-standardrmation-security/.

18. National Institute of Standards and Technology (NIST). 2017. Security and Privacy Controls for Information Systems and Organizations. Draft NIST Special Publication 800–53 Revision 5. (August 2017). https://csrc.nist.gov/csrc/media/publications/sp/800-53/rev-5/draft/documents/sp800-53r5-draft.pdf.
19. Cloud Security Alliance. 2017. Cloud Controls Matrix v3.0.1 (9-1-17 Update). https://cloudsecurityalliance.org/download/cloud-controls-matrix-v3-0-1/.
20. North American Electric Reliability Corporation (NERC). www.nerc.com/pa/Stand/Pages/CIPStandards.aspx.
21. Health and Human Services. Health Information Privacy. www.hhs.gov/hipaa/for-professionals/security/laws-regulations/index.html.
22. Sanches, L. 2017. Update on Audits of Entity Compliance with the HIPAA Rules. U.S. Department of Health & Human Services Office for Civil Rights. (September 2017). www.nist.gov/sites/default/files/documents/sanches_0.pdf.
23. Federal Financial Institutions Examination Council. 2015. FFIEC Releases Cybersecurity Assessment Tool. (June 30). www.ffiec.gov/press/pr063015.htm.
24. Federal Financial Institutions Examination Council. Cybersecurity Assessment Tool. www.ffiec.gov/cyberassessmenttool.htm.
25. Federal Financial Institutions Examination Council. 2016. FFIEC Cybersecurity Assessment Tool Frequently Asked Questions. (October 17). www.ffiec.gov/pdf/cybersecurity/FFIEC_CAT%20FAQs.pdf.
26. Financial Services Information Sharing and Analysis Center. 2015. FSSCC Automated Cybersecurity Assessment Tool. (December 28). www.fsisac.com/article/fsscc-automated-cybersecurity-assessment-tool.
27. Cloud Security Alliance. Security Guidance for Critical Areas of Focus in Cloud Computing V3.0. https://downloads.cloudsecurityalliance.org/initiatives/guidance/csa-guide.v3.0.pdf.
28. Center for Internet Security. CIS Controls. www.cisecurity.org/controls/.
29. Open Web Application Security Project (OWASP). www.owasp.org.
30. OWASP Proactive Controls for Developers v3.0. 2018. www.owasp.org/images/b/bc/OWASP_Top_10_Proactive_Controls_V3.pdf.
31. DoCRA. Duty of Care Risk Analysis Standard. docra.org/wp-content/uploads/2018/04/Duty-of-Care-Risk-Analysis-Standard-v05.pdf
32. Center for Internet Security. CIS RAM for CIS Controls V7. learn.cisecurity.org/cis-ram

Chapter 9

Risk Management Practices

> Great blunders are often made, like large ropes, of a multitude of fibers.
>
> **Victor Hugo, 1802–1885**

If one was to answer the question, "What does a Chief Information Security Officer really do?", a simple response would be risk management. These two words really sum up the essence of the Chief Information Security Officer (CISO). So, what is risk management? The Merriam-Webster definition of risk is "the possibility that something bad or unpleasant (such as an injury or loss) will happen; someone or something that may cause something bad or unpleasant to happen; a person or thing that someone judges to be a good choice for insurance, a loan, etc." A business dictionary provides a more targeted definition of "the identification, analysis, assessment, control and avoidance, minimization or elimination of unacceptable risks. An organization may use risk assumption, risk avoidance, risk retention, risk transfer, or any other strategy (or combination of strategies) in proper management of future events."

These definitions pack a mouthful of activity into a few short words, which this chapter will address each of these areas. With respect to cybersecurity, the term "unpleasant" seems to be a bit light on explaining the issue—the events that occur because of a cybersecurity breach are much more than unpleasant and clearly fall into the *very bad* category!!! Applying appropriate risk management practices will reduce the probability of bad things happening and reduce the impact of these events should they occur. Risk management practices are ongoing processes, as organizations are continually changing their environments, people, technology, products, and services offered with the ability to change the risk model. Several models have emerged for risk management providing that the appearance risk management is the result of a scientific model; however, in practice, assessing risk properly more often seems to be more art than science. The models can increase the level of objectivity when reviewing an organization's risk while at the same time providing the ability to evaluate the companies' specific risks. The caution is that these models provide "an answer" and not "the answer," as there is always an element of subjectivity introduced into the models by the individual reviewing the risks based upon their past experiences. Nevertheless, an organization proceeding with developing an information security strategy and leading the program to increasing levels of maturity will not be effective without some form of risk management practice to ensure deliberate decisions are being made with respect to protecting the organization's assets. Risk management provides the point-in-time information necessary to understand the strategies in place to mitigate the risk for the various assets.

Risk Management Is a Key Issue to Get Right

Risk management does not have to be hard, and yet, it was one of the most frequent failings of organizations in the past when reviewing compliance with the Health Insurance Portability and Accountability Act of 1996 (HIPAA), and for the 2016–2017 Desk Audits conducted by the Office for Civil Rights (OCR), risk analysis and risk management practices were two of the key controls audited for compliance, as shown in Figure 9.1. If the risk analysis is not done properly, an organization cannot provide adequate assurance their security program understands all the risks having a large impact to the organization. Security controls may be in place and not addressing the larger risks. Risk management permits the organization to take a step back, review the current risk posture, and formulate a plan over time to address the risks. Once the initial risk management process is done, updating this on a regular basis can be done with fewer resources as many of the primary processes in place will not have changed substantially. The Department of Health and Human Services found organizations had some controls in place and had not reviewed the entirety of their organization's risk to determine if the right controls were in place to sufficiently mitigate the impact of a disclosure, loss, or destruction of information. Figure 9.2 shows the concern with risk management, continuing after several years of HIPAA Audits. The diagram clearly shows the 2016–2017 Desk Audits of Covered Entities indicating much improvement is needed in the risk analysis and management areas, with no covered entities audited being fully compliant in performing risk analysis and less than 2% fully compliant on risk management. Figure 9.2 further illustrates only 43% of covered entities audited were substantially or minimally compliant with risk analysis practices and 25% compliant with risk management practices, indicating much room for improvement.

This is somewhat disturbing given that the HIPAA Security Rule was communicated and in existence for almost 15 years prior to the health-care covered entity desk audits and given that the risk analysis and risk management processes are key to implementing reasonable security practices.

2016-17 HIPAA Phase II Desk Audit (Security Focus)

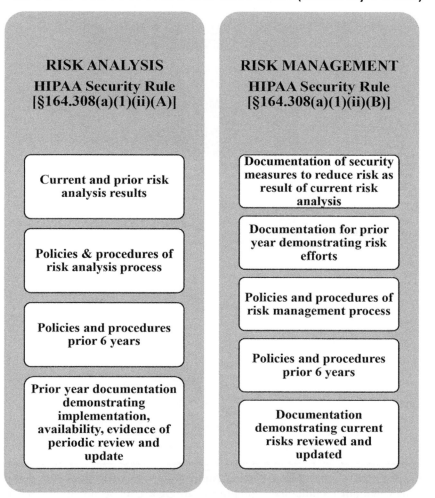

Figure 9.1 HIPAA 2016–2017 Phase 2 Desk Audit security risk focus areas. (Adapted from OCR Update on Audits of Entity Compliance with the HIPAA Rules, September 2017.)

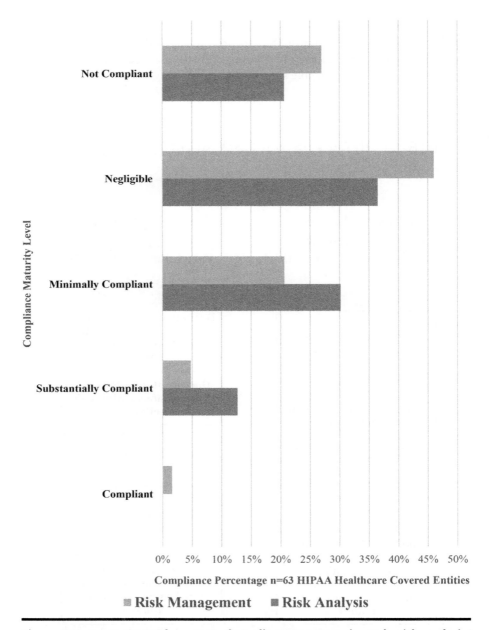

Figure 9.2 2016–2017 Phase 2 Desk Audit HIPAA Security Rule risk analysis/ risk management compliance. (Adapted from OCR Update on Audits of Entity Compliance with the HIPAA Rules, September 2017.)

Daily Risk Analysis

In our daily lives, we conduct risk management activities daily without even think-ing. Have you ever noticed how much time on the evening news is dedicated to the weather? On a normal basis, the weather is a lead-in to get us to watch the show, followed by a teaser in the first 5 minutes of the news program, with the remain-ing weather maps occupying another 5 minutes later in the show for the rest of the story. This raises the question, "Why are we so concerned about the weather, 365 days a year that we spend up to 33% of the local evening newscast talking about it?" Risk. We are managing risk. We want to know what the weather will be like so we can measure the probability of a sunny, rainy, cold, snowy, hurricane-filled, tornado-driven day so we can make appropriate plans. We would not plan an out-door barbecue if the weather channel told us there was a 90% chance of rain on that day. Or, maybe we would and mitigate the risk by moving the barbecue under cover. If there was a 30% chance of rain, we may decide to accept the risk and go forward with plans anyway. The interesting part of this is that two people may make different choices with the same "facts." Some of you, as you read this, were thinking, "go ahead with the barbecue anyway with a 90% chance of rain—is he nuts?" I would wait for a sunny day! Others (those very risk averse) might think a 30% chance of rain was too much to do anything and would postpone the event. Some of you would buy umbrellas as insurance, and we all know what happens when you have an umbrella with you—it never rains (only rains when the umbrella is left in the car).

The weather analogy provides a couple of key insights into risk management. First, different people will want to make different choices based on the facts pre-sented. The same is true within our organizations—some executives will see these as acceptable risks, while the others will think the risk needs to be mitigated. This is the job of the CISO to accurately communicate the risks and arrive at a consen-sus of the path forward. In this sense, the CISO is a facilitator of the risk manage-ment process and is not the decision maker. The other executives may rely heavily on the opinion of the CISO, and they should be able to as this is the CISO's area of expertise, all the while understanding their role to help make an educated, thoughtful, risk-based decision. Since other executives will make different deci-sions based on the same facts, it becomes important to ensure the terminology being discussed regarding threats, vulnerabilities, exposure, impact, probability of occurrence, and risk has a common set of definitions. The measurement and maturity metrics used also need to be standardized and understood by the team. People have different risk tolerances in their personal lives, as demonstrated by the different approaches to the weather, and will carry these into their professional lives. The risk appetite of the individual should be understood—is this person very conservative and risk-averse? Is this person a large risk-taker as demonstrated by a willingness to take on large projects with unknown payoffs in new markets? How does this person invest in the stock market, have they invested most of their money in Certificates of Deposits and bonds, or are they investing in emerging market stocks, gold and Bitcoin? These can provide clues to their personal risk appetite. The CISO needs to then communicate the risk appetite of the organization, potentially different from their individual risk appetite. Second, the facts are not really facts; rather, they are assertions. The meteorologist is more than just a pretty or handsome face and studies computer models of different weather patterns to predict the future weather that we may expect. These models are predicated on a science of atmospheric conditions and contain many variables. While the models may represent the atmospheric conditions as "facts," they are an interpretation of what is happening at a point in time. The "answer" after evaluating all the underlying variables is the predicted weather and may seem like it is predicted as a fact; however we all know, this is not a fact and is more of a "best guesstimate" of the future weather state. Someone once said that being a meteorologist was the best job, as what other job can you be wrong 50% of the time and keep it? The predicted state, even after the extensive risk analysis, plugging all the variables into the model, does not compute a fact of the risk value. The predicted risk value is after all an opinion and needs to be regarded as such. Third, just as three meteorologists will come to different conclusions, three different security risk assessors may have different opinions, creating a variance in the results. This does not mean that wide variability should be expected in the opinions of the current state (current weather patterns)—the variability is most likely to surface in the mitigating solutions presented to mitigate the risk. Assessors also come from different backgrounds and have different risk tolerances and experiences shaping their review of the systems. For example, an assessor working in a government contracting organization may take a harder line with respect to risk, pointing to the letter and verse of the detailed documented security requirements of the government, whereas the security officer in a nonprofit organization, not bound to the same rigorous regulations, may opt for a less formal risk assessment. The key is to match an assessor familiar with the environment or type of organization being assessed as well as the regulatory environment the organization must comply with. Finally, even after considering all the variables, such as inputting the weather patterns to come up with the best forecast possible, the calculated risk may be... wait for it... wrong! Yes, after the extensive analysis after many months, there may be a variable that was not considered, or a calculation missed, and the risk was either underrated or overvalued. In the case of the 2017 Florida and Atlantic Basin Hurricane Season, the experts predicted 14 named storms, six of those hurricanes, and two would be a category 3 or higher storm. The final tally was 17 named storms, ten were hurricanes and six were category 3 or stronger, including devastating Florida Hurricanes Irma and Maria, which destroyed the power grid and key infrastructure of Puerto Rico (category 4). In addition, Hurricane Irma was projected to make landfall in Miami; however, it shifted and made landfall on the other side of Florida, in the Tampa area. Were the meteorologists incompetent? No. The predictions were changed as more information was learned, highlighting the need to accept that (1) the original assessment may have been right based on the best-known available information at the time and (2) the variables now presented may have shifted the direction of the risk and the risk needs to be re-evaluated.

The weather scenario also highlights that even with the most comprehensive models available, supported by the best computing resources and best-known variables, the projections are estimates with an element of subjectivity, requiring monitoring over time. The hope is the more risk assessments are made, the more accurate the risk methodology and prediction will be. Risk management is about thoughtfully evaluating the risks and making the best decision, based upon the best facts available, at the time. Just as the meteorologist cannot accurately predict the weather 100% of the time, the security assessments also need to be viewed as an aide and input into the business decision-making process.

Cybersecurity Risk in Context

Cybersecurity is a risk, and potentially a large risk to an organization; however, it is important to keep the perspective of "this is one more risk the organization must evaluate and reduce to an acceptable level." Organizations face many risks including financial, operational, risks of an upcoming merger, the introduction of a new product or service, and performance risks. Risks are managed daily, and decisions are made on a big picture level by the Chief Executive Officer and daily within each of our jobs. We make decisions on how long it will take to develop a product and recognize we may not introduce the product to market before our competitors as part of the organizational and *7-S Framework Applied to Cybersecurity Leadership* strategy factor. We take risks with the staff we have, deciding they are the right staff with the right skills (two other *7-S Framework Applied to Cybersecurity Leadership* factors), or we supplement the staff with external expertise. We make long-term capital decisions not knowing whether the technology will continue to be supported near the end of life for the equipment. We buy businesses and sell others, all assuming we have formulated the right vision for our organization. Each of these events contributes to ensuring the organization can sustain itself with a stream of income and manageable expenses. These decisions are "opinions" based on past results and attempt to predict a better future for the company, employees, shareholders, and the public. Cybersecurity risk is one of the risks managed similarly. It is important to recognize this, as the executives will view this as one of the risks, and if they are presented with "the sky is falling" scenarios, even though it may be, the attention may turn to other risks communicated by other departments containing deeper analysis on the probability and impact of a "very bad thing" happening and the steps to mitigate it.

The context of the organization is important. For example, if the organization is a health insurance company and comfortable calculating the probability of occurrence of an event happening based upon the likelihood of someone needing surgery based on a certain diagnosis vs. the likelihood of someone avoiding surgery based upon that individual using a chosen drug, they are going to want to see a similar analysis for cybersecurity. Their analysis may follow the rigor of actuaries using statistical analysis and may expect the same. Alternatively, an organization may be used to a red/green/yellow or high/medium/low method of communicating and will more readily understand risks communicated in this way.

Management Risk Acceptance

Since management owns the risk decision, does not it seem appropriate they should sign off to accept the risk? After all, ensuring things get done within an organization requires someone be ultimately accountable, or the result is that no one is accountable. It should be easy to find the management person responsible for the risk, right? Unfortunately, in practice, this is more difficult for several reasons.

Cross-functional Boundaries

Business functions and projects typically cross organizational boundaries and as such, by definition, would have multiple people with a role in the risk acceptance. One person may be uncomfortable accepting the risk when the business function is not completely within his or her control. Second, when the risk item involves a business function and technology, which it most always will, who is responsible? The Chief Information Officer (CIO) responsible for the computing hardware and software platform? Or the business executive sponsoring the development? Or is it both? Take for example the case where a key application used by a business, say a transaction to conduct wire transfers from one bank to another, is compromised because one of the underlying systems is using unsupported vendor software past its end of life. Who is responsible for managing this risk? One could argue that the issue lies with the CIO for lack of upgrading the infrastructure to support the current version of the software. Or, one could argue the responsibility lies with the business executive that failed to influence the management team to provide additional funding to the CIO to upgrade the infrastructure over the other project priorities being considered. From this example, it is easy to see how both individuals could feel they were "right" in the decisions made; however, neither may desire to wholly own the risk for the software being exploited.

Lack of Funding

Accepting the responsibility for the risk without being provided the necessary funding to fix it can occur even when the function is contained within one department. The question of "Why should I accept responsibility for an unsecure product, when I have asked for funding during each of the past 3 budgeting sessions and was always turned down?" appears to be a valid concern. There will be a reluctance to accept the risk. In this scenario, it would be important to document these requests as evidence other higher probability risks were mitigated before this risk would be allocated any funds.

Control Ability

The executive may also have the sense they cannot control the risk, even if provided the funding and does not want to be held accountable. To these executives, this would be analogous to signing off that there should be on two major storms this year vs. six. While their assessment of the cybersecurity risk may be their best estimate, they may not be comfortable with accepting the risk.

CISO's Job

"Why am I accepting the risk for security—isn't that the CISO's job?" Yes and No. The CISO's job is to ensure that the best information is made available about the security risks so that management can make an informed decision. Since the CISO is part of the management team, they also have a responsibility to evaluate and provide recommendations on how the risk could be mitigated. In the end, the decisions for information security risk must be owned by the business managers responsible for the products and services. Building in proper security is part of the process of building and offering the product or service. The executive is going to know the viability of the product and what the market will bear in terms of price, timing of delivery, and whether the security recommendations are feasible, and the product or service will remain competitive. For example, two-factor authentication may be recommended by the security officer to provide an additional level of security to a mobile-recruiting application; however, the executive may determine this would be cost-prohibitive for what is being charged for the product and opts for stronger controls in the authentication process without two-factor authentication. The CISO can support the analysis by recommending different options and levels of security.

Wet Signatures

To ensure the organization's management takes the risk management function seriously, the organization may require a "wet signature" or handwritten signature accepting the risk. There is something about providing a handwritten signature that expresses our self-identity and is more meaningful than sending an email or verbally agreeing in a meeting to acceptance. Handwritten signatures still play an important role in our lives, as we use them to sign our name on documents to authorize, initiate, or complete transactions (many credit cards, even with the embedded chip, are still chip and signature vs. chip and PIN). The signature is used on important documents to commit to years of marriage, finalize a divorce, buy a house, or sign up for the military. The signature reflects our self-identity, bringing the totality of ourselves, identities, and schemas that form one's sense of self together when signing the document. In other words, we see something needing our signature as important. Because it is important, we provide it more attention than the casual glancing at the document and we pause to consider the implications of the document we are signing.

You may be thinking at this point—wet signature? That is impractical, as we move more to electronic transactions and building the digital economy. Initially, when risk assessments are first introduced, wet signature should be required, and this document can be scanned in and distributed electronically, as many documents are today. Executives and team management are used to this process, as they scan in receipts for reimbursement for travel and expense records, or the signing of contracts. Once the wet signatures have been put into practice and the workflow is understood, the organization can migrate to a document management solution whereby a scanned image of their signature can be affixed to the document and maintained electronically. Many real estate transactions today are conducted using this type of software to distribute the series of offers, acceptances, and closing transactions among the buyers, sellers, realtors, banks, and title companies to complete the transaction. Likewise, the cybersecurity risk acceptance could follow a workflow between the CISO, executive management approvers, management requesters, and related risk management departments to facilitate the transaction and maintain a historical record of the risk acceptances.

If a management team member has indicated they are willing to take accountability for the risk, the process must include more than a statement "I accept the risk." These risk acceptances need to be time-bound, such that there is an expiration date on accepting the risk before it needs to be reviewed again. Circumstances may change, and a risk deemed acceptable in the beginning may no longer be acceptable. For example, having an informal data retention policy may have been acceptable for many years as other priorities required more urgent resources; however, with the introduction of new security and privacy regulations, requiring information to be retained only as long as necessary, increased consumer rights with respect to accessing their information, and provisions for the "right to be forgotten," it may no longer be cost-effective for an organization to maintain a lengthy archive of records. Furthermore, without an adequate data retention strategy defined, it would be unclear how much information was stored, and present a greater risk and cost if this information was required to be produced or was accessed by unauthorized individuals or intruders. Thus, the risk acceptance needs to be time-bound and reviewed periodically. Figure 9.3 shows some of the items to include in a risk acceptance template.

Figure 9.3   Risk acceptance template items.

Qualitative vs. Quantitative Risk Assessments

"There is an 80% probability that today I will exceed the speed limit by more than 15 miles per hour on my way home today, and a 90% chance the impact will be zero dollars. There is a 20% probability I will exceed the limit by 15–25 miles per hour and a 50% chance the cost will be $250 (ticket)." Some individuals like the precision of quantitative methods to establish the net dollar value of a decision. These methods tend to be more time-consuming and complicated as much time is spent understanding the specific impact costs related to a risk exposure and the probability of past occurrences, requiring data on historical events. These calculations have the aura of precision, even though there will always be subjectivity in their application. Quantitative risk analysis attempts to allocate a dollar on the cost of accepting risk vs. implementing controls to reduce the risk level. The analysis can be very voluminous as each risk is evaluated using historical information and statistical analysis.

Qualitative methods have given way over the past decade to more user-friendly, qualitative methods that express risk more in terms of high, medium, and low (HML) as a result of assessing the probability of occurrence and impact on a similar scale. The HML methods tend to be easier for management to digest and facilitate better communication among executives. If the objective is to communicate, discuss, and evaluate the risks vs. attempt to get a precision dollar figure of the loss, this makes this approach very beneficial.

Jack Jones has created a risk management methodology known as factor analysis of information risk (FAIR), which provides a framework for quantitative analysis, incorporating Monte Carlo simulations, program evaluation and review technique distributions, and other graphs, charts, etc. Tom Peltier created the facilitated risk analysis process in the early 2000s as a method to qualitatively analyze risk in a matter of days. A more recent exploration of risk was created in the "How to Measure Anything in Cybersecurity Risk" (2016), also promoting quantitative methods used to measure in other disciplines to apply more rigor to the cybersecurity space. The Cyber Risk Handbook (2017) also discusses how to create and measure effective cybersecurity capabilities, leveraging the expertise of the risk management community and thought leaders experienced in measuring risk. While these approaches may vary with the depth of the quantitative analysis, formulas, and presentation of the risks, the goal is the same—to provide a methodology to determine if the underlying risk is acceptable or if additional controls need to be applied, and if so, how much this will cost and what will the resulting risk be. Each organization needs to determine the best fit and methodology for their organization. If parts of the organization are already performing extensive quantitative risk analysis, such as in the case of a bank evaluating investments, wealth management, and credit risk, it may behoove the CISO to adopt a more rigorous approach, as these parts of the organization will ultimately be competing for funds from the same "pot of gold." Alternatively, a small organization may be more comfortable with performing a workshop and discussing the relative risks on a high, medium, and low scale, while having discussions of potential controls to reduce the higher value risks.

JACK JONES: MEETING THE COST-EFFECTIVE IMPERATIVE

Chairman, The FAIR Institute

The cyber and information risk landscape is complex and highly dynamic, and we have limited resources with which to manage it. Consequently, two of the most important responsibilities for any CISO are to (1) prioritize effectively and (2) choose cost-effective risk management solutions for the things we focus on. These both inherently require an ability to measure risk accurately and defensibly, and in terms that business leaders will understand and support.

As a CISO for one company, I was faced with a Payment Card Industry (PCI) Audit that had identified the absence of data-at-rest encryption on my company's primary business databases. These systems contained massive volumes of credit card and other sensitive information. Unfortunately, when brought in to pitch their solutions the encryption vendors all admitted that (1) their products had not been applied to databases of that size/

architecture before and they could not guarantee there would not be problems and (2) any implementation would take at least 18 months, require significant changes to the business applications, and cost millions of dollars. It was also anticipated that this effort would cause potentially significant business disruption.

Before taking that message to my executive leadership, I needed to be able to articulate the value proposition of encryption (beyond simple compliance) from a risk reduction perspective. I also needed to know whether there were alternatives to encryption that would be more cost-effective in our environment. In order to achieve this, I used Factor Analysis of Information Risk (FAIR to evaluate and compare the current state of loss exposure, the loss exposure reduction expected to result from data-at-rest encryption, and the loss exposure reduction expected from an alternative set of controls. These alternative controls included, but were not limited to the following:

- Stronger internal network segmentation
- Hard token authentication controls for system, application, database, and network personnel
- Improved logging, detection, and response controls,
- Improved processes for ensuring that hard drives would be wiped before leaving controlled areas.

In order to be meaningful to business executives, these analyses had to express risk, risk reduction, and cost-benefit in economic terms. High, medium, and low were not going to cut it.

At the end of the analyses, I was able to show that the alternative controls provided greater risk reduction than encrypting data-at-rest. Better yet, these alternative controls required no changes to applications, no business disruption, a much faster time to implementation, and cost under $500,000. However, another important consideration conveyed to executives was the potential for accusations of negligence from taking a course other than encryption if a loss event ever occurred. After examining the analysis, their direction was clear—do the cost-effective thing.

The question, of course, was whether the PCI Qualified Security Assessor would sign off on anything other than encryption. Fortunately, when presented with these analyses, the PCI QSA had no problem signing off on the solution. After all, they recognized the need to be as cost-effective as possible in managing risk, and they appreciated the quality of our analyses and the fact that budget not spent on encryption could be applied to strengthen other, more important dimensions of our program.

Terminology

Before getting into the nitty-gritty of the risk analysis and management process, we need to clarify some terms to ensure we are discussing the same thing. Sometimes security and risk professionals use these terms interchangeably, leading to confusion when discussing risk. For this reason, when working with executives and subject matter experts when performing the risk analysis, it is a good idea to document the definitions on a slide or two, so everyone is talking about the same thing.

Threat Events

Threat events are those circumstances with the potential to cause harm to an information resource by exploiting vulnerabilities in the system. We can have natural threats such as floods, fires, hurricanes, earthquakes, and spreading diseases. The threats may be environmental or physical in nature including unintentional physical threats such as cable cuts, loss of power, equipment failure, or broken water pipes. They may be intentional human threats including items such as espionage, phishing/website access, terrorism, fraud, hacking, identity theft, or social engineering attacks. Human threats can also be unintentional, including such items as data input errors, carelessness, or leaving sensitive information exposed. Threats may also be technical such as a lack of logging, installed malware/spyware, or session takeover. A longer list of these threats is shown in Figure 9.4.

Threat Actors

Threats by themselves are benign unless there is a stimulus willing and able to act upon the threat. These are known as threat actors—the perpetrator or the event that serves to execute the threat. For example, the threat may be issuing a phishing email to trick the user into clicking on a link, thus installing malware on their system, and the threat actor could be sourced from a nation-state, organized crime, a hacker with a financial motive, a hacker testing their skills, an activist or "hacktivist," or a malicious disgruntled employee. The days of the "script-kiddies" whereby people with limited skills were using tools crafted by more experienced hackers to deface websites is less of a concern today, as the dangerous intrusions today are those that extract information to monetize it on the black market, or to extract money from vulnerable financial institutions and individuals.

Vulnerabilities

A vulnerability is a condition that leads to exposure and that may be exploited by a threat to cause harm. If there was no vulnerability, either through the application of additional controls or through an inherent protection built into

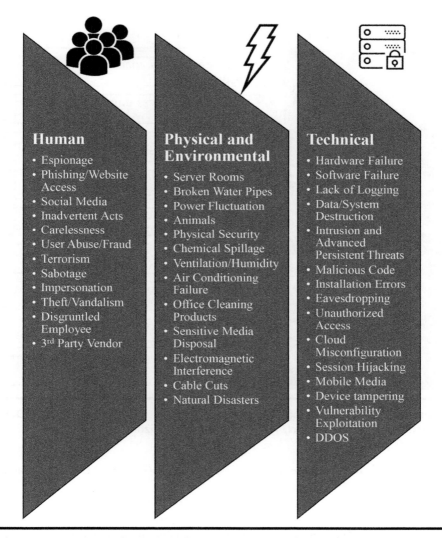

Figure 9.4 Human, physical, environmental, and technical threats.

the system, then the threat would not be able to be executed by the threat actor to cause harm. In the case of the phishing email example, possible vulnerabilities could include the lack of a filtering email gateway to detect phishing emails, lack of security awareness training for the end user to not open these emails, or the lack of controls to detect the execution of the payload or malware (code written to cause harm) once the email was clicked. The vulnerability could also be the result of a system not being patched, thus permitting the malware to exploit the system. When reviewing vulnerabilities, it is important to consider the totality

ATTACK PATTERN	• HOW TO REDUCE RISK
Crimeware	• Software updates, macro-enabled document risk
Cyber-Espionage	• Security Awareness training, phishing exercises
Denial of Service	• Test DDOS mitigation services
Insider and Privilege Misuse	• Limit, log, monitor use, large data transfer and usb awareness
Miscellaneous Errors	• Disposal processes, 4-eye policy for publishing information
Payment Card Skimmers	• Train employees, monitor terminals with video, review tapes regularly
Physical Theft & Loss	• Encrypt where possible, corporate policy limiting printing sensitive data
Web Application Attacks	• Promote varying Passwords, 2FA, limit data in web-facing applications
Point of Sale Intrusions	• Review 3rd party POS vendors and remote access

Figure 9.5 Nine breach patterns and what to do. (Adapted from 2017 Data Breach Investigations Report, 10th Edition. 2017, Verizon.)

of the controls to determine if a condition really exists where the information or system could be exploited.

The Verizon Data Breach Report identified nine patterns where systems were exploited, with 75% of these threat actors coming from hackers on the outside of the organization. The nine patterns where vulnerabilities were exploited are shown in Figure 9.5.

Risk

Risk is simply the chance a consequence will occur. Risk analysis evaluates the threats and vulnerabilities, examines their positive and negative consequences, assesses the likelihood that these consequences may occur and their impact, and assesses whether any existing controls minimize the risks. While the concept is a simple one, in practice, as previously mentioned, this is more of an art form; however, there is a process to perform a risk management as shown in the upcoming sections.

Asset

An asset is anything of value to the organization which should be protected. Assets are typically thought of as electronic in nature; however, this also includes paper document, oral communications and may include intellectual property, computer storage, networks, voice communications, email, applications, mobile devices, credit card numbers, strategic documents, etc. In order words, what is considered an asset to the organization can range from an electronic medium to a physical nonelectronic asset needing protection from a vulnerability exploited by a threat actor.

Risk Management Process

To bring these elements together, the diagram in Figure 9.6 from the National Institute of Standards and Technology (NIST) shows the relationship between these elements. As shown in the diagram, the threat source or actor initiates a threat event that exploits a vulnerability causing an adverse impact, therefore resulting in risk to the organization. To the extent the organization has applied proper security controls to minimize the likelihood that the vulnerability will be

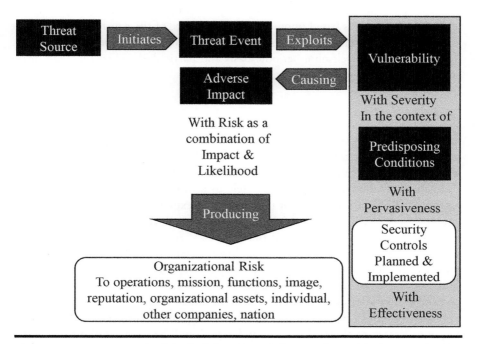

Figure 9.6   NIST generic risk model. (Adapted from NIST Guide for Conducting Risk Assessments, Special Publication 800-30 Revision 1. September 2012.)

exploited, the organizational risk can be reduced. It is through this thoughtful analysis and understanding of each of these elements that are essential to ensure an adequate level of control is provisioned to protect the information assets. Failure to execute this process or understand any one of these components properly may result in overspending on some security controls and underspending on others.

Failure to understand each of the components also paints an incomplete picture of the risk. In practice, this is a very tedious and difficult process, in part due to the lack of historical information and the lack of sharing of real intelligence of attacks across companies. Companies tend to want to keep this knowledge of compromises private, although the past few years have seen an increased level of sharing between organizations such as the Financial Services Information Sharing and Analysis Center, the Retail Cyber Intelligence Sharing Center formed after several retail-focused credit card breaches, the National Health Information Sharing and Analysis Center. In these forums, the vulnerabilities are shared, and nonpublic details of the threats, vulnerabilities, and defenses are shared among the membership, typically composed of companies operating within that selected vertical market.

Risk analysis generally follows steps of understanding the information systems that combine to provide the organization's business capability, select an initial set of security controls, implement the security controls, assess the security controls, authorize the systems based upon the risk acceptance of the controls, and monitor the controls on a continuing basis to ensure the controls are operating correctly. This cycle repeats itself on a periodic basis and particularly when there are infrastructure or system changes to the environment.

Risk Analysis

The following steps are those steps, as shown in Figure 9.7, for conducting the risk analysis. To conduct a proper risk analysis, it is important that the appropriate stakeholders are included so important details are not left out of the assessment. Individuals may be interviewed separately or as a group; however, if reviewed as a group, utilize the "soft skills of interaction" as explained in the *CISO Soft Skills* chapter, especially if there is a mix of management and employees. Some employees may be uneasy speaking up about the true risks within the organization if interviewed alongside their management, as they may feel this reflects upon the performance of the job they are doing, which may or may not be the case. The objective of the risk analysis is to obtain a clear picture of the current state, so the appropriate controls can be selected to enhance the environment to keep up with the threats (or alternatively reduce redundant controls not adding significant value and representing unnecessary cost). The following individuals will be useful in the risk analysis process:

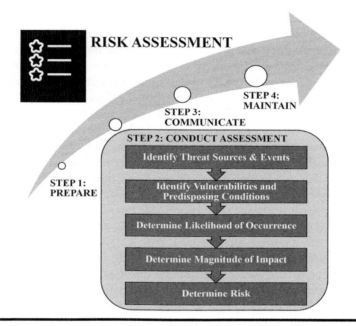

Figure 9.7 Risk assessment process. (Adapted from NIST Guide for Conducting Risk Assessments, Special Publication 800-30 Revision 1. September 2012.)

- CIO
- Chief Security Officer/CISO
- Senior management
- Middle management
- Internal audit
- System and information owners
- Business and functional support owners
- Information technology (IT) security practitioners
- Infrastructure personnel
- Physical security
- Chief risk officer/legal/C-suite.

Step 1: Prepare for the Risk Assessment

The scope of the risk assessment is formulated in this step to help the organization know what information needs to be provided to conduct the assessment, as well as to know the organizational level the risk assessment is targeting. The risk assessment may be focused upon the governance, security strategy, and operational or strategic issues at the top level of the organization. Another way to characterize this risk assessment is one focused on the management and governance of the security program and engagement of the other internal and external stakeholders. The risks assessment could be focused on an internal business process at the functional business management level, or middle management layer. The most common risk assessments conducted by audit firms appear to operate at the system level to determine technical vulnerabilities and what controls need to be implemented to mitigate the threat.

The purpose of the risk assessment should also be established—is this an initial risk assessment to obtain a big picture view of where the risks may be? Or is the purpose to update an existing risk assessment on a predetermined cycle (i.e., every 3 years)? Were there changes in hardware, software or changes to the organizational mission due to a change in strategy or acquisition/merger? These should be articulated so the focus is placed on the appropriate parts of the organization. For example, one would not want to initiate a risk assessment intended to be a risk assessment on the governance of the security program and whether employees were responding to the training, only to spend 25% of the time reviewing the vulnerability management program execution for an Oracle database server.

During the preparation step, the artifacts for threat sources, potential threat events, vulnerabilities, determining likelihood and impact, the approach, and the risk appetite are determined before the analysis is conducted. As a matter of practicality, the first time an organization performs a risk assessment, they rarely have all these artifacts defined, as external organizations are typically brought in to perform an independent assessment. They also have not had the experience to build up this documentation. Some artifacts such as security logs, monitoring reports, system diagrams, technical and process flows, and an understanding of the shared systems can be provided during this step to enhance the analysis. Any assumptions and constraints should be articulated. These usually are covered off by the purpose and scope statements.

Step 2: Conduct the Risk Assessment

This step produces a listing of information security risks to be subsequently prioritized by risk level and actions taken to mitigate the risk as much as possible. Threats and vulnerabilities are evaluated, and those relevant to the organization are analyzed to determine if the vulnerabilities could be exploited by a threat actor. The likelihood the threat actor would initiate a threat event and the likelihood a threat event would be successful are evaluated. Likewise, the impact of these events is evaluated to determine the severity of the event. Controls are evaluated, and recommendations for reducing risk are also evaluated. The tasks of the risk assessment are as follows:

Tasks 1 and 2: Identify Potential Threat Sources and Events

Threats serve to inflict harm on the information assets, or targets of the organization. Each organization needs to discover the potential threat sources for their organization, the threats (harm) these sources may cause, and the targets of the threats. It is also useful to examine the motivations of the attackers, their capabilities, intentions, and the effects of the actions by the threat sources. For example, a nation-state seeking to obtain information on individuals for future extortion attempts, possibly to extract intellectual property involving a design for a new product, may be interested in targeting human resource systems, employee medical information, and servers containing technical design documentation. Understanding the motivation of the attacker and the type of information they may be interested in facilitates modeling of the threat scenario. Without this understanding, the company would need to apply the same security controls to all information, increasing the costs. Some information may need to be segmented or layered with additional controls for protection, and without understanding where the specific information is, applying controls may be problematic. As noted earlier in the definitions, the threats or threat sources are defined in Figure 9.4. These may be used in the analysis to determine the threat events causing the organization concern.

These will vary by industry as well and has typically represented a challenge for CISOs to obtain information specific to industry verticals. The Verizon Data Breach Report over the past few years has done an excellent job articulating the major threats for each industry. Figure 9.8 shows the breakdown by industry vertical and the top three or more incident patterns resulting in a data breach. A data breach is the confirmed disclosure of information to an unauthorized party, whereas a security incident is the occurrence of a security event that compromises the integrity, availability, or confidentiality of an information asset. In some cases, the top security incidents do not result in actual breaches. The version data on incident patterns and those causing the most breaches was used to create this combined table. For example, in the financial and insurance industry, the top three patterns of compromise were denial of service, web application attacks, and payment card skimming representing 88% of all security incidents. With this knowledge in hand, the CISO could focus the analysis more on these threat vectors within their organization related to the specific industry the firm is operating within.

Task 3: Identify Vulnerabilities

A threat remains just a threat without having a vulnerability to exploit. Consider having a castle with stone walls, turrets with cannons, and a moat containing alligators surrounding the castle. Add in some barbed wire and some minefields outside and a person walking up to the main entrance carrying a knife may not be much of a match! In another circumstance, meeting someone on the street who is unarmed, the threat source may have the ability to cause harm and rob the individual, using intimidation and a knife. For a threat to be successful, there needs to be a vulnerability that can be exploited and the conditions protecting the vulnerability are insufficient. This is a key point for CISOs to consider.

Incidents by Industry (security events compromising integrity, confidentiality or availability of an information asset)									
Patterns	Accommodation	Education	Financial	Healthcare	Information	Manufacturing	Professional	Public	Retail
Crimeware	21	19	49	154	57	294	248	5988	26
Cyber-Espionage	1	12	9	24	4	82	41	120	
Denial of Service	13	151	336	1	580	74	104	703	85
Everything Else	13	48	59	63	81	39	41	68	12
Lost /Stolen Assets	4	10	16	96	3	15	17	3728	7
Miscellaneous Errors	2	16	22	181	34	3	30	1774	11
Pay Card Skimmers	6		49	5		1		1	81
Privilege Misuses	7	7	21	138	5	22	28	10311	11
Point of Sale	306		2	1	2		1		11
Web Applications	11	29	36	88	277	17	34	97	73

Shaded box = Top patterns accounting for <u>breaches by industry</u> (confirmed disclosure to an unauthorized party)

Figure 9.8 Key compromise concerns by industry. (Adapted from 2018 Data Breach Investigations Report, 11th Edition. 2018, Verizon.)

A vulnerability must be considered with respect to the control environment within which the vulnerability exists. Vulnerabilities may exist within our environments if we have not maintained the current releases of software or applied the critical security patch levels or configured and monitored our systems according to a standard baseline configuration. Our computing environments are also never monolithic or comprised of just one piece of software. Consider the desktop computing environment, whereby the latest version of Windows 10 may be running with the latest security updates; however, there may be instances of older software such as Adobe, Java, user-installed applications, movie-maker software, and business applications containing security vulnerabilities. Each of these also represents vulnerabilities for exploit within the system. The same could be said for the mobile devices, particularly those devices procured by the individual through a bring your own device (BYOD) program without device management software. Do we know the vulnerabilities existing on these devices for each of the applications used? An analysis of a flashlight application revealed that application was granted all the administrative privileges, including location tracking through the default installation.

Systems are also interconnected and a primary system housing the confidential design documentation for a new automobile may be locked down within the servers where the designs are stored, multifactor authentication may be implemented, and access granted to very few users. What happens when the user of the system exports the information from the design database into a spreadsheet and emails the information to others working on the project? Or downloads the latest design to a server to make updates? Or what about the encrypted communication to a part's inventory system to determine if new parts would need to be manufactured, and the downstream parts system does not have the same controls as the automobile design system? Due to these interconnections and the possibility for export, vulnerabilities need to be analyzed in the context of the threat actor/source, the target they are after, and what vulnerability could be exploited to gain access to this information. In the case of the castle, while the fortress may appear to have too many defenses to obtain information, one must ask, are there other ways to gain entry? Could a tunnel be dug under the castle, could the alligators be sedated, or could a drone at night unlock a door from the inside? While these ideas may sound farfetched, the lesson is the threat actor will be thinking this way, so it is prudent to think about methods around the vulnerabilities. Joaquin "El Chapo" Guzmán, a Mexican Drug Lord with an estimated net worth of $1 billion escaped prison twice, most recently through a one-mile-long tunnel terminating in his shower stall floor. More than 40 people colluding with Guzmán were arrested in connection with the 2015 escape, including 15 federal agents and 8 prison staffers. We need to evaluate vulnerabilities in terms of those with the right motivation, money, and ability, could they be exploited?

Where it was once unimaginable, "flash mobs" have brazenly entered stores and stolen merchandise, as in the case of seven teens who stormed an Apple store to steal $13,000 worth of Iphones. The Iphones were tethered by security cables, and the perpetrators cut the cords to the phones. In this case, the security videos of the store and around the mall were the secondary controls used by police to try and apprehend the youths. Systems will always have some level of inherent risk associated with vulnerabilities that cannot be fixed. The department store selling iPhones needs to be able to display the phones for consumers, or their ability to sell would be greatly minimized. They could sell the phones from behind bulletproof enclosures; however, their sales would not be very high as the consumers would not be able to shop and interact with the device freely. The same is true for our systems—there will always be some measure of vulnerability within our systems. They will never be patched to a 100% level, as once the patches are released, more patches are released for 0-day vulnerabilities. There will always be a lag time between when a vulnerability can be mitigated and when it can be fixed. We may identify the need to remove local administrative privilege as a local administrator for all the end users; however, there may be exceptional cases whereby certain groups of users need the ability to add new applications. This will require the purchase and installation of software to provide the ability to whitelist, blacklist, or graylist applications that may be installed by the user. The implementation of this software will require a project and time to implement before local administrative rights are removed. This clearly will take time to implement, and during this time, the vulnerability of having local administrative rights on each user machine may provide the attacker with the ability to escalate access rights. The vulnerability needs to be identified as a potential vulnerability while it is being mitigated. Figure 9.9 shows the threats of most concern, highlighting the vulnerabilities, exploits, and threat actors.

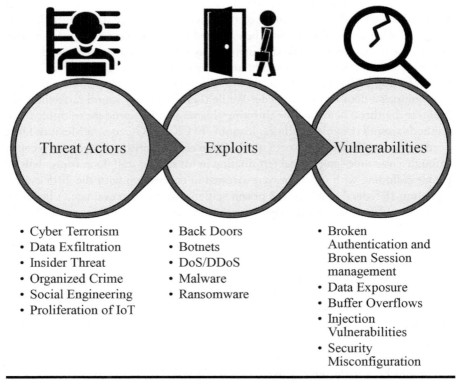

Threat Actors

Exploits

Vulnerabilities

- Cyber Terrorism
- Data Exfiltration
- Insider Threat
- Organized Crime
- Social Engineering
- Proliferation of IoT

- Back Doors
- Botnets
- DoS/DDoS
- Malware
- Ransomware

- Broken Authentication and Broken Session management
- Data Exposure
- Buffer Overflows
- Injection Vulnerabilities
- Security Misconfiguration

Figure 9.9 Threats of most concern. (Adapted from *2017 Global Information Security Workforce Study*, Frost & Sullivan, ISC2.)

The identification of vulnerabilities requires an honest assessment of the people, processes, and technology in place. Too often, individuals will inappropriately debate the existence of a vulnerability, as they perceive this is an indictment on their job performance (i.e., why have these vulnerabilities existed under your leadership?). If an organization under review is not able to take an objective view regarding the vulnerabilities, it may be prudent to enlist the internal audit department or external independent review of the vulnerabilities. The attacker does not care whether the owner of the control perceives it to be a vulnerability or not: if it is, it will be exploited; if it is not, an alternative path will be pursued until a vulnerability can be exploited. Not to minimize the task of the cybersecurity program, as this is more difficult in practice to mitigate the vulnerabilities within a reasonable time frame and with the budget constraints many CISOs are under—the underlying position an organization should adopt is, simply stated—until the vulnerability can be closed, it should be regarded as open and exploitable.

Task 4. Determine Likelihood of Exploitation Given Existing Controls

Once the vulnerabilities are discovered, the likelihood an attack will be successful is estimated. Qualitative analysis does not compute the likelihood from a rigorous statistical model, as in many cases, information is just not available or may be difficult with current staffing to obtain in a reasonable time frame. Estimates of likelihood of an event occurring may come from experience, information contained in systems (i.e., incident records, help desk calls, system fixes), market research, internal experiments such as conducting an internal awareness campaign (and testing 6 months after wards to see if the message is retained), or expert advice from the industry. As shown in Figure 9.10, a table may be constructed from a negligible, or unlikely to occur frequency, to an extreme level where the event is expected to occur multiple times per day, with varying frequencies in between.

It is important to create some concrete measurements when determining the likelihood, as better clarity is provided for the individuals discussing the likelihood. If the terms "high likelihood," "medium likelihood," and "low likelihood" were used without any description, different users would interpret the meanings of likelihood based upon their own normative perception of what is likely. In other words, I may feel it is highly unlikely would steal a desktop from inside one of the 100 branch offices due to the proximity readers and cameras protecting the office during off hours; however, another employee may view this as a high risk at last one of the offices would be compromised, with one being too many in their eyes. However, from Figure 9.10, a concrete discussion using frequencies can be discussed to arrive at a more accurate view of the likelihood. In this case, they may agree the likelihood of this type of theft may come from an insider threat or from the contractors having 24-hour access to the facility, and expect this to occur once every 6 months, resulting in a moderate likelihood, given the current control environment.

Likelihood of Occurrence	Adversarial	Non-Adversarial
Very Low	Adversary is highly unlikely to initiate the threat event.	Error, accident or act of nature is highly unlikely to occur, or occurs less than once a year, or occurs less than once every 10 years.
Low	Adversary is unlikely to initiate the threat event.	Error, accident or act of nature is unlikely to occur, or occurs less than once a year, but more than once every 10 years.
Moderate	Adversary is somewhat likely to initiate the threat event.	Error, accident or act of nature is somewhat likely to occur, or occurs between 1-10 times per year.
High	Adversary is highly likely to initiate the threat event.	Error, accident or act of nature is almost highly likely to occur, or occurs between 10-100 times per year.
Very High	Adversary is almost certain to initiate the threat event.	Error, accident or act of nature is almost certain to occur, or occurs more than 100 times per year.

Figure 9.10 Likelihood of occurrence.

Ownership of the likelihood determination is the domain of the business users, facilitated by the CISO. For future changes in the environment to be supported, the business users are the ones closest to the processes and have the best view of the likelihood of an event occurring in the absence of reporting metrics demonstrating otherwise. They can establish the starting point for measurement.

The likelihood considers the probability of the adversarial event being initiated such as a targeted nation-state attack or whether a non-adversarial event, such as a careless loss of laptop, is likely to occur. A small donut shop, e.g., may not perceive they would be the target of a persistent attack by a nation-state, as they would not have the type of information that a foreign government would be interested in. However, if this location was a suspected hangout for terrorist activity or meet-ups, the network may be of interest. Furthermore, while the donut shop may not view themselves as a target for a nation-state attack, if they are processing credit card information they could be an easy target. Small businesses are also increasingly becoming targets for ransomware, due to the perception they may not have rigorous controls in place, spend less time educating employees on phishing attacks, and have limited funds to allocate to cybersecurity practices. When discussing the likelihood, organizations should look at their specific threats for their industry; however, they also need to be aware the likelihood of being a target will never be zero, as they have assets available for theft, as in the credit cards, or assets available for monetization through ransomware. Organizations also must consider the likelihood their security controls will be breached to use to attack other systems or store hide information on their servers (i.e., pornographic material).

Likelihood also involves analyzing whether once these actions are initiated by the attacker, if they will be successful and result in disclosure, loss, destruction, or other adverse events. If there is little likelihood the event will succeed due to the existing administrative, technical, and operational control environment, then the likelihood is apt to be a very low likelihood. The capabilities of the attacker are taken into consideration here. For example, a nation-state attack will have the resources necessary to bypass simple controls and more extensive threat modeling will need to occur. Consider the case in 2014 where JPMorgan Chase and other banks were targeted by nation-states, acquiring intelligence in a targeted attack. The sophistication required to penetrate an institution that spends $250 million per year on cybersecurity and announced plans to spend more than $500 million per year, is clearly extensive, and could only be afforded by those nation-states with resources to allocate with sufficient interest and motive, whether financial or political. Thus, firms such as large banks may have a higher likelihood that would be a target of this type of attack vs. the mom and pop donut shop.

For those threat events whereby there are no vulnerabilities available for exploitation, the likelihood would most likely be assessed at a very low level of occurrence, as the threat is deemed to not have the capability to penetrate the system. The likelihood of these threats may change over time based upon new developments and must be monitored. When the National Security Agency (NSA) hacking tools were leaked by the Shadow Brokers in 2017, offering "monthly dump services" of their stolen tools, this changed the likelihood for organizations their systems could be compromised. These tools were being used for 14 years by the NSA to exploit that vulnerabilities were now available to hackers and nation-states, increasing the likelihood of compromise. The message here is clear—likelihood changes based upon the new vulnerabilities that exist and the control environment protecting the information assets and thus needs periodic review, particularly when events such as the availability of previously unknown exploits become available.

Task 5. Determine Impact Severity

The organization next determines the impact of the event in terms of criticality such that the impact may be very low where the impact would have a negligible impact on operations, assets, individuals within the organization, supply chain, or external parties. Alternatively, the impact may be large enough to cause extensive disruption, such as an attack on the power grid impacting thousands of lives, or making an entire commuting environment inoperable for health care, as in the case of the 2017 WannaCry incident infecting thousands of U.K. computers and paralyzing the National Health Service. The impact assessment evaluates the damage which is caused if such an event were to occur, evaluating the capability of the threat and the ability to spread to a larger problem, or if it would be localized to a small group of users or inconsequential transactions. Finance departments can be a big help in estimating the impact, as they typically will understand the cost of users being down for 1 hour. There may be contractual impacts whereby organizations are fined if information is not processed in a timely manner. For e-commerce-type organizations, the cost can be tremendous. For example, Google went offline, and it caused a 40% drop in Internet traffic, impacting those depending upon ad revenue. Amazon costs were estimated to be $66,240 per minute for downtime in 2013, and with the increased reliance on the AWS platform and retail sales by Amazon, this number is sure to increase over time. Consider that 13% of all Black Friday sales are generated on the Cyber Monday following Black Friday and the impact of a 1-day outage.

A severity of impact assessment scale, as shown in Figure 9.11, communicates varying degrees of impact based upon whether the attack resulted in catastrophic, severe, limited, or negligible effects to the company or entity. Some organizations use an assigned scale to represent a semi-qualitative value (similar values could be used for the likelihood determination as well).

The impacts consider the organizational impacts to people, operations, assets, buildings, technology, as well as the impacts to the IT resources. Harm to the operations may include items such as the inability to carry out the mission in a timely manner, inability to manage the environment with the current resources (i.e., support personnel now focused on restoring systems after a ransomware attack vs. support the end users or completing system updates they were working on), or damage to reputation and trust relationships (controls were assumed by the business to be in place). Intellectual property may be lost; damage to physical facilities and information systems may occur. Personally identifiable information (PII) may be lost, regulations may be violated, and other fines or sanctions may be

Impact	Threat Event Description
Very High	The threat event could be expected to have multiple severe or catastrophic adverse effects on organizational operations, organizational assets, individuals, other organizations, or the Nation.
High	The threat event could be expected to have a severe or catastrophic adverse effect on organizational operations, organizational assets, individuals, other organizations, or the Nation. A severe or catastrophic adverse effect means that, for example, the threat event might: (i) cause a severe degradation in or loss of mission capability to an extent and duration that the organization is not able to perform one or more of its primary functions; (ii) result in major damage to organizational assets; (iii) result in major financial loss; or (iv) result in severe or catastrophic harm to individuals involving loss of life or serious life-threatening injuries.
Moderate	The threat event could be expected to have a serious adverse effect on organizational operations, organizational assets, individuals, other organizations, or the Nation. A serious adverse effect means that, for example, the threat event might: (i) cause a significant degradation in mission capability to an extent and duration that the organization is able to perform its primary functions, but the effectiveness of the functions is significantly reduced; (ii) result in significant damage to organizational assets; (iii) result in significant financial loss; or (iv) result in significant harm to individuals that does not involve loss of life or serious life-threatening injuries.
Low	The threat event could be expected to have a limited adverse effect on organizational operations, organizational assets, individuals, other organizations, or the Nation. A limited adverse effect means that, for example, the threat event might: (i) cause a degradation in mission capability to an extent and duration that the organization is able to perform its primary functions, but the effectiveness of the functions is noticeably reduced; (ii) result in minor damage to organizational assets; (iii) result in minor financial loss; or (iv) result in minor harm to individuals.
Very Low	The threat event could be expected to have a negligible adverse effect on organizational operations, organizational assets, individuals other organizations, or the Nation.

Figure 9.11 Severity of impact.

imposed due to noncompliance. By thoughtfully engaging the business users in a discussion with scenarios such as, "what would happen if system X was unavailable for 48 hours, what would the impact be?" these items can be uncovered. All of these add up to impact the brand or reputation of the firm, another impact that should be noted.

Task 6. Determine Risk

Once the likelihood and impact have been determined in tasks 4 and 5, respectively, the risk value can be computed using the table shown in Figure 9.12. The likelihood occurrence is in the first column, the impact is in the row across the top, and the intersection of the two is the starting risk value. Each threat and vulnerability pair identified through tasks 1–3 is evaluated with respect to the impact and likelihood and subsequently looked up in Figure 9.12 for the risk value. For example, consider an organization assessing the risk of an insider threat to their payroll system. The likelihood of a threat of accessing the payroll system, given the current controls in place, may be rated as moderate, as the system is a few versions behind the current version and some exploits are available for the software, and there are some disgruntled insiders that may want to access this system due to the current layoffs that were rumored. Normally, the likelihood may be assessed as low; however, the organization is concerned with the recent actions they are taking. As far as impact, if an employee was to reveal the salaries of individuals, this could be detrimental to the organization by making confidential executive information public, as well as revealing individuals on the layoff list prior to the announcement. The system records could also be destroyed; however, the organization has mitigated this risk by frequent backups and sees the impact minimal in this aspect. The overall impact may be assessed as high to the organization, as there would be reputation damage at a time when the organization is considering a merger with another company and this would reflect very negatively on the ability to keep information confidential. In this scenario, since the likelihood was rated as moderate and the impact was determined to be high, by following the impact rows and likelihood column in the table, the resulting risk is determined to be moderate.

This process can be very effective with executives and staff discussing the risks because the conversation is focused on the likelihood and impact with descriptions of each item, and not on debating the risk value. This makes the assessment much more objective, as each person may have wildly different views on what constitutes "risk." Albeit a similar argument could be made when creating values for likelihood and impact, except the descriptions of likelihood frequency and the impact descriptions (sometimes expressed as $$$ ranges instead of a description), are more likely to produce thoughtful results based on these two parameters. The process can be further simplified into a high/medium/low scale if this works better for the organization. In practice, the HML scale is used more often, as it may be difficult for the organization to clearly delineate between low/very low or high/very high.

Step 3: Communicate the Results

After the risks have been determined, these are typically ordered by the severity level of the risk so that highest risk items can receive the proper management attention. There will usually be some debate as to how the risk values were generated,

Likelihood (Threat Event Occurs and Results in Adverse Impact)	LEVEL OF IMPACT				
	Very Low	Low	Moderate	High	Very High
Very Low	Very Low	Very Low	Very Low	Low	Low
Low	Very Low	Low	Low	Low	**Moderate**
Moderate	Very Low	Low	**Moderate**	**Moderate**	**High**
High	Very Low	Low	**Moderate**	**High**	**Very High**
Very High	Very Low	Low	**Moderate**	**High**	**Very High**

Figure 9.12   Risk determination.

thus another reason for approaching the risk assessment from a likelihood/impact discussion based upon the perceived threats and vulnerabilities existing in the environment. The reporting should be available with multiple reporting levels, a high-level aggregation of the results for the executive discussions backed up with the detailed findings through a report commonly known as a Risk Register. The Risk Register commonly provides for the specification of a management response for mitigating controls to be applied to lower the risk. In practice, high risk levels are rarely accepted for long without the specification of a plan to lower the risk level. Controls may be implemented for moderate/medium risk levels to lower these to a low risk level. Low risk levels are many times accepted by the organization, depending upon their risk tolerance or appetite, as there are typically very high/moderate risk items which must be addressed first. If the organization uncovers many low risk items, these may rise to the level in the aggregate of a moderate risk level and should not be dismissed or ignored because they were rated as a "low" risk level.

The resulting level of risk after the additional controls are implemented is known as the residual risk. The controls suggested for implementation because of the risk analysis should be sufficient to lower the residual risk to a level acceptable to the organization as defined by the executives. For example, if the company decides they cannot accept any high-level risks for more than 90 days, and all very high risks must be mitigated within 30 days, this provides clarity for what should be acceptable. There will always be exceptions; however, these exceptions will need formal risk acceptances as described earlier, until the risk can be mitigated.

Step 4: Maintain Assessment

Risk assessments are not a once-and-done activity since organizations are not static. New threat events, vulnerabilities, and changes in infrastructure or processes can necessitate change. Without taking on this activity on a regular periodic basis, at least annually, and making updates as necessary, the organization may implicitly be taking on greater risk than necessary.

Risk Mitigation

The preceding framework for evaluating organizational risk may be tweaked to be more qualitative or quantitative depending upon the organizational culture. When additional controls are evaluated as part of the risk mitigation, they can take several flavors according to the financial investment desired, strategic direction of the organization, or leveraging the impact of the existing or planned projects. Here are some of the options available to organizations.

Select and Implement Additional Controls

The most common approach to mitigating a risk is to identify and select a control to reduce the likelihood or impact and thus the resulting risk level of the threat. The controls can be administrative—such as implementing and enforcing a new policy, creating a procedure, or increasing training; technical—such as patching a vulnerability in a file server, implementing a mobile device management solution, or enhancing the firewall environment; or operational—such as creating server baseline configurations and monitoring these for compliance, or implementing disaster recovery solutions.

The controls can be preventive, detective, corrective, compensating, or deterrent controls. Preventive controls attempt to stop security violations from occurring in the first place and include such controls as authentication to applications, encryption of information, and enforcement of policies such as logical and physical access control mechanisms. These controls have typically received the most attention in the past as CISOs invest to try and prevent the attack from occurring. The goal with this type of control is to have the mechanism robust enough that the effort to attack exceeds the value of the information or financial gain obtained because of the attack. Prevention is also key to protect confidentiality, since once the information is known, knowledge of the information is hard to "forget." Contrasted to financial information, when this information is stolen, the information could be replaced, and the customer made whole without the same level of damage as a disclosure of an individual's personal health diagnosis (granted there may be repercussions from disclosing financial information of certain individuals; however, the issue is typically more of loss vs. confidentiality). Detective controls warn of situations where an attempted violation of security policy may be occurring, such as intrusion detection systems, security analytics, alarms, audit logs, and threat intelligence indicators of compromise. Corrective controls remediate vulnerabilities such as the disaster recovery and business continuity solutions to bring systems back up after a natural disaster, data center outage, or corruption of data. Compensating controls are additional controls that are in place to mitigate the risk to make up for other weaker controls. An endpoint workstation may have additional malware software based on behavioral analytics in the event the antivirus product does not have the latest signature for a zero-day threat. Deterrent controls attempt to persuade attackers not to violate policy, such as warning banners on systems of the consequences, or signs indicating the area is under surveillance by video cameras. These controls combine to make up a defense in-depth, layered strategy where no one control is depended upon for the security of the information assets. Different control methods will be used based on the ability to implement the control, the effectiveness of the control, and the efficiency.

Risk Assumption/Risk Planning

The organization may decide the risk is acceptable and will formally accept the risk. This happens with many low risks where the organization perceives the likelihood and impact do not rise to the level of concern. Given unlimited funds, all risks would be mitigated; however, organizations must make the choices between which risks should be accepted and which should not, as funds are not unlimited. This is a perfectly acceptable approach provided that there is a thoughtful analysis of the financial, operational, and reputation concerns. Risks may also be accepted for the time being, knowing a different solution will eliminate the risk. For example, servers running an old version of the database server may be allowed to operate, knowing the system was due for replacement soon with a new architecture running current servers hosted by a third party in the cloud.

Risk Avoidance

Risks are avoided by removing the system or situation creating the risk. Vulnerabilities may have existed on an early release such as an early release involving Android phones, and the organization may decide to change the strategy to replace the phones with iPhones. Risks are usually avoided as the cost analysis determines the cost is easier to replace the device vs. manage the vulnerabilities.

Risk Limitation

Risks may not be able to be easily mitigated, perhaps as the result of key software running on a non-supported operating system and old hardware. Administrators may be leery to patch or upgrade the system, as other individuals have left the company and the support team is unsure they could rebuild the environment if they were to make changes. In this case, the risk may be limited by placing monitoring software or access software on top of the application, such as a firewall to limit access to the application or segment the application in its own environment.

Risk Research

The solution for the vulnerability may not be immediately known requiring further analysis. This is acceptable; however, the activity should be treated as a project and time-bound such that a determination can be made on a new control to mitigate the risk, or one of the other risk mitigation options is decided upon.

Perfection and Risk Management Do Not Mix

It is easy to have the eyes glaze over when thinking about the seemingly daunting task of assessing risk for an organization. The process seems complicated as there are many inputs into the process, and unlike typing the name of a destination into a smartphone mapping application and it tells you exactly on the map where the destination is, risk management involves a high degree of "guesstimation" or "best guesstimation" and ambiguity to arrive at the answer. More importantly, we need to recognize this is our best guess at best. Sometimes, we will be right; sometimes, we will miss threats and risks to the environment. The best we can do is learn from our experience and continually enhance the knowledge of our organization information assets, systems, and practices, the vulnerabilities that could be exploited, the impact of the damage, and the risk mitigation strategies we are employing to be consistent with our risk appetite. The risk management process is one of the CISO's key "systems" or tools to be used in applying the 7-S Framework Applied to Cybersecurity Leadership.

Suggested Reading

1. Department Health and Human Services. 2016. HIPAA Privacy, Security & Breach Notification Compliance Audits phase 2, Informational Webinar. (July 13). www.hhs. gov/sites/default/files/OCRDeskAuditOpeningMeetingWebinar.pdf.
2. Sanches, L. 2017. Update on Audits of Entity Compliance with the HIPAA Rules. U.S. Department of Health & Human Services Office for Civil Rights. (September 2017). www.nist.gov/sites/default/files/documents////sanches_0.pdf.

3. HIPAA Collaborative of Wisconsin. www.hipaacow.org.
4. Waynar, J. 2017. 2017 Hurricane Season Devastates Florida, Caribbean islands. Florida Today (November 30). www.floridatoday.com/story/news/2017/11/30/2017-hurricane-season-devastates-florida-caribbean-islands/906545001/.
5. Kettle, K. and Haubl, G. 2011. The Signature Effect: Signing Influences Consumption-Related Behavior by Priming Self-Identity. *Journal of Consumer Research* Vol 38, No. 3 (October):474–489. www.jstor.org/stable/10.1086/659753.
6. Peltier, T. 2001. *Information Risk Analysis*. Boca Raton. CRC Press/Taylor & Francis.
7. Jones, J. 2015. *Measuring and Managing Information Risk: A fair Approach*. Waltham, MA. Elsevier.
8. Hubbard, D. and Seiersen, R. 2016. *How To Measure Anything in Cybersecurity Risk*. Hoboken, NJ. Wiley.
9. Antonucci, D. 2017. *The Cyber Risk Handbook*. Hoboken, NJ. Wiley.
10. Jervis, R. 2016. Mexico's Challenge: Stop Another 'El Chapo' Escape. USA Today (January 31). https://eu.usatoday.com/story/news/world/2016/01/30/el-chapo-mexico-arrest-corruption-extradition/79454512/.

SHARED VALUES

5

5 SHARED VALUES

Chapter 10

It's the Law

The law must be stable, but it must not stand still.

Roscoe Pond, 1870–1964

Some automobiles are built to travel at a very high rate of speed, with the 2019 Chevrolet Corvette ZR1 with 755 horsepower able to reach a top speed of 212 miles per hour. The Tesla Model S is also capable of going very fast and has the speed limited by the manufacturer, just as some European sports cars such as BMW, Audi, and Porsche are limited as well, to a speed of 155 miles per hour to avoid serious accidents on the Autobahn, where cars are permitted to go extremely fast. Each year since 2004, I have attended just one annual car race, the "greatest spectacle on Earth" with 250,000 of my closest friends—the Indy 500 in Indianapolis, Indiana, where cars routinely reach almost 225 miles per hour on the 2.5-mile-long race track. Going back 50 years to 1969, the legendary race car driver Mario Andretti won the race with an average speed of 157 miles per hour compared to an average speed of 74.6 miles per hour in the inaugural 1911 Indy 500. Amazing how far the technology has come that individuals are able to drive these cars at a high rate of speeds, experience few accidents, and incur relatively few serious life-threatening accidents given the number of racing events held. And now, street cars such as the Corvette and Tesla and others can not only achieve high rates of speed but can also accelerate quickly to 60 miles per hour in a matter of 3–4 seconds.

But wait, if the cars can go this fast, why do we still have laws on the books that we can only travel at 55–70 miles per hour (except for State Highway 130 between Austin and San Antonio, Texas, where it is legal to go 85 miles per hour)? Are these laws outdated and need to be changed to accommodate the new car speed capabilities? Are the laws out of touch with reality? Many would argue, slow down cowboy, not so fast! If the speed limit was raised to 212 miles per hour, then the serious accident rate would dramatically increase as the drivers are not skilled enough to handle the rate of speed and the roads were not built for it. While some car enthusiasts may disagree, one could argue this would not be in the public's best interest. Instead, we enforce the laws on the books, regardless of the capability of the vehicle.

What does this have to do with cybersecurity? Plenty. Laws and regulations are created to stand the test of time due to the lengthy process to pass a regulation or law. Laws are created for the public best interest. Laws are formed by committees in response to a need given enough visibility for a legislator to see it in their best interest to act upon it. Then, these law proposals are debated, voted on, and then pass the protocol for review and acceptance defined by the legal structure. For example, in the United States, for federal regulations, Congress (legislative branch) first proposes a bill that if approved, will become law. If Congress approves the bill, it goes to the President who can approve the bill or veto it. The new law if approved is then called an act or a statute. The House of Representatives standardizes the text and publishes it in the U.S. Code (U.S.C.) once every 6 years, with supplements issued in the interim.

Cybersecurity Flexibility in the Law

The codified laws do not explain the details as to how to apply the law, as typically regulatory agencies are given the detailed task of indicating how to comply with the law such as providing specific requirements about what is legal and what is not. The Health Insurance Portability and Accountability Act (HIPAA) of 1996 sets forth the law to protect health-care information (along with insurance portability, the primary focus of the law); however, the designation of specific requirements and enforcement has been delegated to the Office of Civil Rights (OCR). For example, the HIPAA law would require a risk analysis be performed to determine the existence of Protected Health Information (PHI), while the OCR would determine the specifics as to what constitutes an acceptable risk assessment to comply with the law. They would also determine the penalties for noncompliance within the scope of the limits determined by the law and subsequent legal revisions. Laws are thus written generally and discuss the policy, or the "what" to be achieved and do not address the "how" compliance is satisfied. This provides much leeway for the regulators to determine the rules within their mandated area. While some Chief Information Security Officers (CISOs) may desire more specificity in the law—as in "just tell me what to do!"—this is also where "be careful what you ask for" could not be more appropriate. If the specific requirements were codified into the laws, this would thwart innovation by not providing adequate flexibility. Specification of an eight-character password, one uppercase letter, one lowercase letter, one digit, and one special character may provide clarity, but it would not allow for innovations such as fingerprint biometric devices, addition of PINs, multifactor authentication, location- or device-based identity authentication, and digital certificates to authenticate the individual. Imagine if hardware-based authentication tokens (generating six-digit random numbers) were codified at a time when they were popular 10–15 years ago, and now an organization wanted to change over to a soft token using an application on the person's smartphone to provide the authentication—this implementation would be viewed as "noncompliant" with the letter of the law, as a hard token would be required. Laws need to be written to be flexible enough to ensure adequate protections available today are adhered to, while at the same time providing the flexibility for technical innovation.

Laws also must support organizations of various sizes and industries, whereby there is an implicit expectation that the larger organizations have more resources to spend on cybersecurity and failure to do so would be viewed as not exercising due care. The reasoning follows the organization is more concerned about profits than the protection of the employees, customers, and other stakeholders. Failure to pay any attention at all to information security can be seem as willful neglect. Under the law, these regulators have the capability to determine if cybersecurity neglect is occurring and levy fines that should not be ignored.

Laws and Regulations vs. Control Standards and Frameworks

Some regulations that must be complied with are not laws per se but are rather regulations formulated by an industry body. The Payment Card Industry Data Security Standard (PCI DSS) is a good example of this, whereby the standard was formed by the major credit card issuers to ensure security between the merchants and card processors. Even though the standard is not a law, it is a requirement established by the issuers that must be complied with to participate within the industry. Sometimes these are referred to as regulations, giving deference to the requirements that our organizations are held to, just as formal laws passed by legislative bodies, and sometimes referred to as control frameworks or standards, in deference to their ability to be used to guide the security programs to a more secure state. Hence, some of these "regulations" will often appear interchangeable when discussing the overarching law or regulation and when discussing the security controls used to achieve compliance with the regulation, control framework, or standard.

Civil Law vs. Criminal Law

Criminal laws exist to punish the perpetrator of the crime, protect society from future actions, and hoping to also serve as a deterrent to others considering committing the same crime. Since computer crime prosecution is not very prevalent and very few criminals go to jail, some of the criminal penalties associated with the various laws do not seem to serve as a large deterrent. As more criminals are prosecuted and sent to jail, maybe the criminal penalties will provide the deterrent that the law prescribes. It seems that the conduct would need to be egregious and willful to move to a standard of criminal prosecution. In large cases, such as when Albert Gonzalez received 20 years for hacking into Heartland Payment Systems, TJX, BJ's Wholesale Club, OfficeMax, Boston Market, Barnes & Noble, and Sports Authority, it is obvious that an example was made of the fraud to deter others from engaging in similar activity. Another reason for the lack of criminal prosecution may be that for criminal law the plaintiff must demonstrate beyond a reasonable doubt to a jury of their peers that an offense occurred, which, given the complexities of hacking, may be difficult to explain in understandable terms to the jury. Prosecutors must weigh the odds of a successful outcome before investing valuable time and resources into the case.

The more likely scenario is the leveling of civil monetary damages in the form of statutory damages that may be assessed as a matter of law. If the law has been violated, then there is an entitlement to the award. This may also present itself by way of fines, such as the Federal Trade Commission's (FTC) 2002 landmark assessment of $15 million in fines for Eli Lilly's accidental email/website disclosure of customers that were using an antidepressant drug. Since then, large fines have been levied by the FTC, such as the 2015 $100 million fine of LifeLock for not complying with a 2010 Federal Court Order, where they were fined $12 million, to secure consumer's personal information and refrain from deceptive advertising with claims that alerts would be issued as soon as they received information indicating a consumer may be a victim of identity theft. Civil cases are much more likely to be pursued to make the victim whole, as the standard of proof is much different. Whereas criminal cases must determine "beyond a reasonable doubt," civil cases only require that a "preponderance of the evidence" is sufficient to find the person guilty of the infraction. Regulators follow their internal prescribed processes for determining the fines; however, the fines may be appealed to the Federal Court. To date, these appeals have been largely unsuccessful and expensive for the companies challenging the decisions.

The CISO and the Lawyer

The CISO and the security department are often in a position where they are interpreting the law's requirements for senior management. The legal staff will know the ins and outs of the legal system which can be very helpful, particularly with their understanding of contract laws. Customers entrust their data to a business with the expectation that the information is adequately protected and used for business purposes. This expectation does not change if the business decides to subcontract and share the information with another entity. From the perspective of the consumer, they still have that expectation and do not care who is at fault if there is an incident. The legal staff must be involved in contracts of services or products of other organizations to ensure that the appropriate information security language is included. The language includes clauses that require the subcontractor to protect the confidentiality, integrity, and availability of the information, ensure there is the right to audit the controls of the sub-entity, and establish communication protocols and expectations between the subcontractor and the contracting business in the event there is a breach. Privacy laws have been very clear on the responsibility of both the responsibility of the data controller and the processor to maintain appropriate security and ensure the appropriate downstream contracts were in place. Organizations must manage these vendor relationships to reduce risk. The security department can provide the technical expertise to the legal department, or the assurance as to how the laws or regulations are being met. Regulations such as this generated a renewed interest by the legal department to be involved in cybersecurity practices due to the potential liability of failing to be compliant with the regulations.

MARK RASCH: HOW TO TALK TO YOUR LAWYER

Principal, Law Office of Mark Rasch

In William Shakespeare's Henry VI, Part 2, Act IV, Scene 2, the knave "Dick the Butcher" extolls the virtues of lawlessness, and exclaims that the way to achieve it is, "The first thing we do, let's kill all the lawyers." There probably is not a CISO who has not at least at one time or another, felt the same way about the legal profession. Lawyers are often perceived as either "Dr. No," or worse, autocrats and automatons who do not understand the "real world" and do not understand technology and demand the impossible from the CISO (in an impossible amount of time). They also refuse to give a direct answer to a direct question like, "Am I allowed to do this?" preferring an answer like "it depends," or "I'll look it up and get back to you." While many, if not most, CISOs have an excellent working relationship with inside and outside counsel, dealing with lawyers can be a challenge, mostly because lawyers and engineers, and lawyers and CISOs do not, in many cases, speak the same language.

But lawyers can, and in most cases should be, a CISO's best friend within an organization. When properly educated and trained (a rolled-up newspaper can help), counsel can be the most effective advocate for a CISO's projects and goals and help obtain the necessary funding and management support for a host of essential security, privacy, compliance, and other projects. This is because many of a CISO's objectives are—or more accurately can be framed as—requirements necessary to comply with legal requirements. Legal requirements are just that—requirements. As such, a company must comply or face significant consequences. So, a lawyer as an advocate for specific security objectives or goals can help make the case that the specific project, training, testing, implementation, etc. are required (or at least suggested) by law, by contractual requirement, by good risk management and negligence policies, by insurance company requirements, or just as a fiduciary of shareholder's assets. A good lawyer can help draft agreements with vendors, suppliers, and third parties (including software vendors, Software as a Service, and other vendors, cloud vendors) mandating not only good security practices, but testing, validation, verification, and assigning rights and responsibilities for things like data breaches and breach notification. Every CISO knows that their network and data are only as secure as the weakest link within the network—a good lawyer can help shore up that link, at least with an agreement.

Some lawyers are very conservative, while some are very permissive. A conservative lawyer might tell you that you are not permitted to do something that the CISO thinks is necessary, or that you are required to do something that the CISO thinks is either unnecessary or in some cases, dangerous. Take this as an opportunity for a dialogue—and not necessarily a mandate (well, at least not yet). Find out WHY the lawyer thinks the action is necessary, what law they rely on, and develop a work-around. Often, when a lawyer says that you MUST do something, it is based on an objective, not a procedure. So, while you MUST have access controls, you are not REQUIRED to have specific password lengths. Learn how lawyers think—usually in terms of "rights" and "obligations," and couch your pleas in those terms. Be familiar with the actual requirements of information security and privacy laws and see what your colleagues are doing. If your lawyer is telling you to do something that nobody else in your industry is doing, your lawyer is either very smart, or very wrong (or both?).

Above all, use your lawyer as an ally and a resource. Use them for training—let them educate your staff, while you educate theirs. Use them as leverage for funding and resources. Use them to justify new initiatives. Get them to validate your goals and objectives. Take them out to dinner— lawyers like to eat dinner. And buy them a beer. And remember, when Dirk the Butcher said "let's kill all the lawyers," he was suggesting that this was the best way to achieve anarchy.

Emergence of Cybersecurity Regulations Early 2000s

As indicated in the evolution of the CISO discussion earlier, the early 2000s saw much activity focused on safeguarding the information assets in large part to support the emerging concern over privacy of information with the computerization of more and more information, as well as a concern over the security of our critical infrastructures after the events of 9/11/01. The 1995 EU Data Directive included safeguard provisions, as did the Federal Government 1974 Privacy Act; however, more laws were introduced and noteworthy during this time, each playing large roles in their respective verticals. These are noted here, as the CISO should understand the genesis of these laws and regulations still in force and expanded upon today.

The subsequent sections present a brief synopsis of some of the key laws that have driven cybersecurity in recent years, as well as some of the high-level controls that are required. These sections should be regarded as an Executive Guide to the Information Security Laws impacting information security decisions. Many times, individuals are working within their own vertical industry and are unaware of the laws, regulations, control frameworks, and standards that are being discussed in other industries. Each of the laws has a specific purpose, genealogy, and differences with the other standards, but after working with these different laws, it is also clear that by following a consistent framework, whether it be COBIT 5 for Security, the National Institute of Standards and Technology (NIST) 800-53, ISO27001/27002, CIS Controls, PCI DSS, The ISF Forum Standard of Good Security Practice, NIST Cybersecurity Framework, Cloud Security Alliance Cloud Controls Matrix, or some other framework, there are requirements in these frameworks, which, if followed, would more than likely satisfy the law or regulation in most cases. This is since many of these laws and regulations are grounded in security principles to begin with and it should be no surprise that these requirements are presented within the regulation. The difference will typically be that the control framework will be more prescriptive and granular than the higher-level law to permit changes in technology, as articulated earlier.

Electronic Communications Privacy Act of 1986

The Electronic Communications Privacy Act of 1986 (Public Law 99-508), also known as the "Wiretap Act," was passed by Congress to extend the protections of the wiretap law to electronic communication forms, such as email, text, video, audio, and data. Under the law, messages may not be intercepted in transmission or in stored form while in transit. Law enforcement would need to obtain a court order to obtain information such as account activity logs showing the IP addresses that were visited by a subscriber of Internet services or the email addresses from who the subscriber exchanged emails. Law enforcement can also obtain a court order to compel cellular phone companies to provide records showing the cell phone location information for calls made from a person's cell phone. To increase the foreign intelligence gathering activities after the events of 9/11, the U.S. Patriot Act was made law by President George W. Bush on 10/26/2001. The U.S. Patriot Act weakened the restrictions and increased law enforcements ability to obtain telephone, email communications, and records such as medical and financial. For example, a search warrant could be issued for voicemail communications, bypassing the more stringent Wiretap Act. In subsequent years, this ability came under fire in privacy circles for being able to obtain this information.

The Computer Security Act of 1987

Congress enacted a law that reaffirmed the NIST as being responsible for the protection of unclassified, nonmilitary government systems and information. The National Security Agency (NSA), which provided for the protection of classified information for the U.S. Military, provided technical assistance to the nonmilitary parts of government, as Congress felt that it was more appropriate to have a nonmilitary agency responsible for the creation of guidance for protecting civilian information. The Computer Security Act of 1987 became Public Law 100-235. The key implications of the act were that it required that minimum acceptable security practices would be established for federal computer systems, systems security plans would be constructed for these systems defining the security controls in use, and that appropriate training would be provided. Computer systems were defined to include the computers, ancillary equipment, software, firmware, services, and the computer systems operated by any federal agency or a contractor of a federal agency that processes information on behalf of the Federal Government to support their processing.

Several attempts have been made to amend the Computer Security Act (1997, 1999, and 2001) to address technical changes that had occurred since 1987 and to designate a single agency to lead the computer security activities; however, these measures passed the House of Representatives and made their way through the Senate subcommittees, but were not presented to the Senate for a vote. No attempts have been made to change the law since 2001. This may be due in part to having more focus on the Federal Information Security Management Act of 2002 (FISMA).

Sarbanes–Oxley Act of 2002

Public Law 107-204 was enacted on July 30, 2002 and is referred to as the Public Company Accounting Reform and Investor Protection Act by the Senate and the Corporate Auditing Accountability and Responsibility Act in the House of Representatives, but is most widely known as Sarbanes–Oxley Act of 2002 (SOX). The bill came about as there were several accounting scandals which cost investors and employees of companies such as Enron, Tyco International, and WorldCom dearly. The SOX established the Public Company Accounting Oversight Board (PCAOB) to provide an independent oversight of public accounting firms providing auditing services. Arthur Anderson, a well-known and respected audit firm and auditor for Enron, ceased doing business as an accounting firm after the Enron scandal. The act also established standards to ensure auditor independence and avoid conflicts of interest, with a key provision restricting companies that provide consulting from providing audit services. Executives were also required to take individual responsibility for the accuracy and completeness of the financial reports, which was represented by their signing off and attesting to the documents. Within organizations, this resulted in a series of management signoffs to ensure that appropriate governance was achieved. For the CFO and CEO to sign off on the documents, it was not unusual for them to also require attestations of the management staff as well.

The most significant section of the law is Section 404, which requires an assessment of the internal controls. This part of the law has received criticism in recent years for the costs associated with compliance. Initially, many auditing firms took a very conservative view of what was required to comply, resulting in some cases extensive auditing, documentation, and testing of the automated controls. However, the increased attention to the internal controls has had a positive effect on the controls which in the past were overridden by management. The laws did represent more risk to the audit firms, as more work needed to be done to ensure that there was no undetected fraud being committed.

The PCAOB approved auditing standard No.5 on July 25, 2007, replacing the guidance provided in standard No.2 issued in 2004. The guidance refers to the report of the Committee of Sponsoring Organizations of the Treadway Commission (also known as the COSO report) as a framework for demonstrating the internal controls.

The law is important for cybersecurity, as organizations need to be able to ensure integrity in the financial statements, and to do so, they must have the assurance that minimally, the financial systems have the appropriate security controls. Organizations will want to identify and prioritize those financial systems, users, and access rights within the Identity and Access Management (IAM) systems to ensure access is controlled. An organization may have thousands of applications requiring access reviews, and the scope for SOX can be manageable if the subset is identified.

Gramm–Leach–Bliley Act

Public Law 106-102, also known as the Financial Services Act, was enacted on November 12, 1999, repealed part of the Glass–Steagall Act of 1933 and provided the ability for banks to function as an investment bank, commercial bank, and insurance company. The act also provided the Financial Privacy Rule, which permitted individuals to opt out of having their information shared with unaffiliated parties. The policy needed to be published to the individuals, as well as republished each time the policy changed. As such, the Financial Privacy Rule established a privacy policy between the individual and the company. Section 501(b) of the Gramm–Leach–Bliley Act (GLBA) required the Federal Deposit Insurance Corporation, Federal Reserve System, Office of the Comptroller of the Currency, and Office of Thrift Supervision (OTS) to develop standards for the examination to ensure that adequate safeguards are being implemented. The examination procedures were developed to determine the involvement of the board of directors, evaluate the risk management process, evaluate the adequacy of the program to manage and control risk, assess measures taken to oversee service providers, and determine where an effective process exists to adjust the program.

The Safeguards Rule of the GLBA requires the development of a written information security plan and must protect the current and past client's financial information. Title 15, Chapter 94, Subchapter I, Section 6801(b) requires that the financial institution, "establish appropriate standards for the financial institutions subject to their jurisdiction relating to administrative, technical, and physical safeguards (1) to insure the security and confidentiality of customer records and information; (2) to protect against any anticipated threats or hazards to the security or integrity of such records; and (3) to protect against unauthorized access to or use of such records or information which could result in substantial harm or inconvenience to any customer." The Federal Financial Institutions Examination Council IT Examination Handbook, substantially revised in September 2016 (and specifics expanded on in the *Control Frameworks* chapter), can be used as a basis to meet the GLBA requirements.

Health Insurance Portability and Accountability Act of 1996

The HIPAA of 1996 was enacted by Congress (Public Law 104-191) with two purposes in mind, (1) to reform health insurance to protect insurance coverage for their workers and families when they changed or lost their jobs and (2) to simplify the administrative processes by adopting standards to improve the efficiency and effectiveness of the nation's health-care system. Title I of HIPAA contains provisions to address health insurance reform, while Title II addresses national standards for electronic transactions, unique health identifiers, privacy, and security. Title II is known as Administrative Simplification and is intended to reduce the costs of health care through the widespread use of electronic data interchange. Administrative Simplification was added to the Title XI of the Social Security Act through Subtitle F of Title II of the enacted HIPAA law.

While the initial intent of the Administrative Simplification portion of the law was to reduce the administrative costs associated with processing health-care transactions, Congress recognized that standardizing and electronically aggregating health-care information would increase the risk of disclosure of confidential information, and the patient's privacy rights needed to be protected. Security provisions were needed not only to protect the confidentiality of information, but also to ensure that information retained the appropriate integrity. Consider the situation where the diagnosis or vital sign information is changed on a medical record, and subsequent treatment decisions are based upon this information. The impact of not being able to rely on the information stored within the health-care environment could have life-threatening consequences. Thus, privacy issues are primarily centered on the confidentiality of information to ensure that only the appropriate individuals have access to the information, whereas the security standards take on a larger scope to ensure also addressing issues of integrity and availability of information. While this focus has been primarily on confidentiality, the WannaCry breaches of U.K. National Health Service in 2017 raised the awareness within health-care environments regarding the disruption that could occur because of a massive breach, with patients moved to other facilities and treatments postponed. Until this time, much of the conversation within health-care environments was oriented towards keeping confidential information from being disclosed vs. concentrating on the availability concerns. As Internet of Things (IoT) and medical devices receive more focus, the conversation then involves the integrity aspect of security, highlighting the importance of being able to rely on the information created by the medical device.

The proposed security and electronic signature standards were originally published in the Federal Register on August 12, 1998. The HIPAA Security Rule was delayed on several occasions, as resources were committed to and focused on the proposed HIPAA Transaction and Code Set and Privacy Rules, both of which generated many public comments. These public comments must be reviewed, and the numbers can be large. Several thousand comments were received on the Privacy Rule and on the proposed Security Rule. The Security Rule was initiated during the Clinton administration and was carried over into the Bush administration, which created political challenges for expedient passage of the rule. As a result, the language was rewritten during 2002 to coincide with the Privacy Rule (issued on December 28, 2000, and was subsequently modified on August 14, 2002, with a compliance date for most covered entities, April 14, 2003), which needed to go through the U.S. Department of Health & Human Services (HHS) clearance process prior to final rule publication. The Final Security Rule was submitted by the Centers for Medicare and Medicaid Services to the Office of Management and Budget (OMB) in early 2003 and was published in the Federal Register as 45 Code of Federal Regulations (CFR) Parts 160, 162, and 164 on February 20, 2003. The regulations became effective on April 21, 2003, and covered entities were required to comply with the requirements by April 21, 2005, and small health plans had until April 21, 2006.

The Administrative Simplification (Part C of Title XI of the Social Security Act) provisions state that covered entities that maintain or transmit health information are required to "maintain reasonable and appropriate administrative, physical, and technical safeguards to ensure the integrity and confidentiality of the information and to protect against any reasonable anticipated threats or hazards to the security or integrity of the information and unauthorized use or disclosure of the information." The administrative, technical, and physical safeguards were divided into addressable and required implementation specifications. The addressable standards were more flexible; however, the required safeguards had to be implemented according to the rule. The contractors supporting Medicare claims processing, today known as Medicare Administrative Contractors, were given the directive that all the required and addressable security controls were to be regarded as required, setting a higher and more stringent standard for the protection of Medicare information maintained by the contractors.

Since the Final Security Rule was written to be consistent with the Privacy Rule, the focus of security standards applied to "health information" in support of the Administrative Simplification requirements was shifted to PHI and specifically to electronic PHI. The applicability statement of the Final Security Rule states, "A covered entity must comply with the applicable standards, implementation specifications, and requirements of this subpart with respect to electronic protected health information." Covered entities are defined as (1) a health plan, (2) a health-care clearinghouse, and (3) a health-care provider who transmits any health information in electronic form in connection with a transaction covered by Part 162 of Title 45 of the CFR.

The Security Rule was meant to be scalable such that small providers would not be burdened with excessive costs of implementation, and the large providers, health plans, and clearinghouses could take steps appropriate to their business environments. For example, a small office may be able to control access and enforce segregation of duties between the staff with a manually documented process with the supervisory review, while a larger organization would most likely need automated support through the IAM system, management approval processes, and automated reporting tools to achieve the same level of assurance. Decisions must be made to reasonably protect the information, and document how the decisions were made. While earlier it was recognized that security is always a risk-based decision, it is sometimes difficult to determine what will be "reasonable" under the circumstances.

One of the criticisms of the Final HIPAA Security Rule since its mandated implementation has been the lack of enforcement. When the HIPAA Law first was issued, many organizations were very focused on achieving HIPAA compliance and formed steering committees, hired consultants, and tracked compliance. Investigations were handled on a complaint-basis only, which resulted in a small number of complaints given the number of health-care providers. In February 2006, HHS issued the Final Security Rule for HIPAA enforcement, setting the civil monetary penalties and procedures for investigations. Since the OCR, who oversees the enforcement (since July 27, 2009), has tried to work out arrangements between the offender and the victim vs. pursue prosecution, there were few prosecutions under the law in the early days of HIPAA. In 2007, Piedmont Hospital was the first to undergo a HIPAA-type audit, with enforcement and fines not garnering much attention until after the 2009 Health Information Technology for Economic and Clinical Health (HITECH) Act that required government audit requirements and increased the fine capability. As shown in the timeline in Figure 10.1, HIPAA underwent several changes since inception.

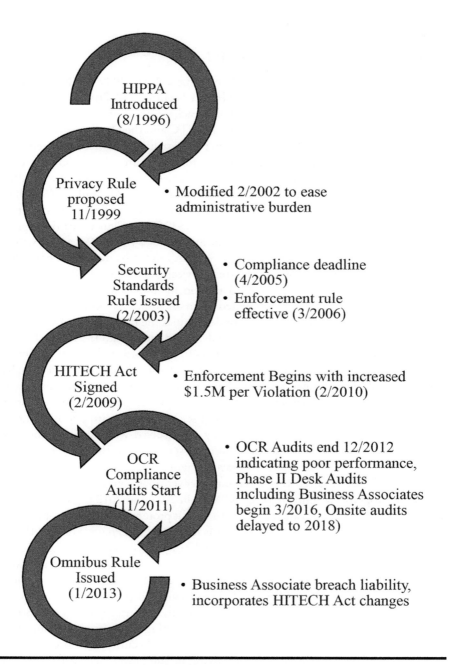

Figure 10.1 HIPAA progression time line.

Health Information Technology for Economic and Clinical Health Act

As part of the American Recovery and Reinvestment Act of 2009 (ARRA), Subtitle D of the HITECH Act extended the HIPAA Security and Privacy rules to the business associates of the covered entities. Breach notification requirements were also added to the HITECH Act, requiring the FTC and the Department of Health & Human Services to issue guidance on the breach notification requirements. Additionally, the organization must account for disclosures when using an electronic health record. The HITECH Act strengthened the civil monetary penalties by raising the maximum fine from $25,000 under HIPAA to $1.5 million ($50,000/day per violation, capped at $1.5 m/year) under HITECH. The first Civil Monetary Penalty of this magnitude was issued by the HHS OCR to Cignet Health (Cignet) for violating the HIPAA Privacy Rule in the amount of $4.3 million, citing willful neglect, indicating that Cignet violated 41 patient's rights by denying them access to their medical records that were requested between September 2008 and October 2009. These violations resulted in $1.3 million in fines, and Cignet's failure to fully cooperate in the investigation netted them an additional $3 million in fines. This is an example whereby the regulator determines the fine to be paid within the parameters of the law based upon their analysis and judgment. The rationale cited was for failure to cooperate due to "willful neglect not corrected within 30 days of when the covered entity (i.e., the provider) knew or with the exercise of reasonable diligence would have known of the violations." The OCR receives approximately 20,000 complaints a year, with nearly 90% of those investigated. The top five issues in 2016 were access, impermissible uses and disclosures, safeguards, administrative safeguards, and technical safeguards. Many are resolved without fines; however, in recent years, the fine amounts have been substantial with the greater amounts permitted via the HITECH Act, as shown in Figure 10.2.

HITECH also required the initiation of government audits, beginning with pilot audit programs (administered by KPMG) in 2011 and 2012 to assess the controls of 115 covered entities and developed an audit protocol to evaluate compliance with HIPAA. In 2013, the initial process was reviewed, and Phase II of the HIPAA Audits was launched in mid-2016 randomly selecting 167 covered entity candidates representing a broad spectrum of entities, varying in size, type (i.e., payer, provider, clearinghouse, business associate), and operations. The audit process in the past has spanned years and an additional 1–2 years can also pass after the audits are completed before the information is shared generally. A phishing email purporting to be an official OCR Audit communication prompting the users to click on a link regarding "possible inclusion in the HIPAA Privacy, Security, and Breach Rules Audit Program" was issued after Thanksgiving in late November 2016. With the increased fines in recent years and wanting to comply, the timing of this email was clearly playing on fear!

Advocate Health System $5.55M	3 breaches, 4 million individuals, unencrypted computers stolen during burglary
Memorial Healthcare System $5.5M	Former employee credentials not deactivated, 105,646 individuals accessed
NY-Presbyterian/ Columbia University $4.8M	Patient info accessible on Internet search engines
Cignet Health $4.3M	Denied 41 patients access to PHI
Triple-S $3.5M	Multiple breach notifications
Univ Mississippi Medical Center $2.75M	Missing laptop containing 10,000 patients without notification
Oregon Health & Science University $2.7M	7K patients, unencrypted stolen laptop; storage in cloud
CVS Pharmacy $2.25M	Disposing pill bottles with PHI in dumpsters
NY-Presbyterian $2.2M	Allowed film crews for 'NY Med' unfettered access
Concentra Health Services $1.7M	Unencrypted laptop stolen
Alaska DHSS $1.7M	Stolen USB Drive
WellPoint (Now Anthem) $1.7M	Data Breach exposed 612,000 individuals in database

Figure 10.2 Largest hospital fines.

Source: Updated data from 10 Largest HIPAA Settlement Fines, 2016, Becker's *Health IT and CIO Report, www.beckershospitalreview.com/healthcare-information-technology/10-largest-hipaa-settlement-fines.html.*

After serving on the board of directors for a leading a nationally recognized nonprofit volunteer-run HIPAA organization named the HIPAA Collaborative of Wisconsin (www.hipaacow.org) almost since the inception in 2001 whereby 200–300 health-care security, privacy, and electronic data interchange professionals from providers, payers, and clearinghouses meet twice a year, I can tell you from the OCR presentations that their intentions are to further the security and privacy of the systems and not to penalize the companies for noncompliance. The Department of Health and Human Services, Centers for Medicare and Medicaid Services, and the OCR have attended and presented regularly with the purpose of sharing their findings and enhancing protection of patient information. Used to illustrate the focus on risk management in the *Risk Management* chapter, it was noted that making a proper risk assessment, the fundamental requirement to protect information assets, is still either not being done or being done poorly by many organizations. Since few organizations performed the risk assessment well in the 2012–2013 Audits, the 2016–2017 Desk Audits focused on the risk analysis and risk management aspects of the HIPAA Final Security Rule (along with the Breach Notification Rule controls and Privacy Rule controls). The latest round of audits found that none of the covered entities audited had fully met all the HIPAA security risk analysis and management requirements.

The Centers for Medicare and Medicaid Services has also done an outstanding job of bringing together Medicare Administrative Contractor (administrators and processors of Medicare and Medicaid information) security officers twice a year in a conference called "CSCOUT" to discuss security, predicated on rigorous NIST 800-53 requirements since 2001, prior to the HIPAA rule passage. All the security controls are based on the risk assessment and systems security plan and audited multiple times per year. This due diligence of focusing on the detailed security controls by the contractors, auditing the controls, making security part of the contract award criteria, and reducing the number of data centers storing the information has limited the breaches within Medicare systems. Many times, the issue comes down to the funding capability of the health-care provider, which includes many organizations that in the past have not had the resources to allocate significant dollars to information technology (IT) or security. Those implementing HIPAA controls would be well served to examine the security practices of Medicare systems and network with those working in that community. Since the Centers for Medicare and Medicaid Services as an agency of the Department of Health and Human Services, these practices eventually become guidance for HIPAA systems in private sector through the issuance of Acceptable Risk Safeguards and HHS-driven guidance.

Federal Information Security Management Act of 2002

The primary purpose of the FISMA, enacted as Title III of the E-Government Act of 2002, is to provide a comprehensive framework for ensuring the effectiveness of security controls over information resources supporting federal operations and assets. These requirements extend to information systems and data managed by another agency, contractor, or source, such as cloud services. The law also provided funding for NIST to develop the minimum necessary controls required to provide adequate security. The government publishes an annual report card based upon their assessment of compliance with the framework. FISMA applies not only to the Federal Government, but also to those contracted to perform actions on behalf of the government. The metrics for compliance are organized around the five functions (identify, protect, detect, respond, and recover) of the NIST Framework for Improving Critical Infrastructure Cybersecurity, also known as the NIST Cybersecurity Framework.

The law was updated in December 2014 through Public Law 113–283, after multiple U.S. Office of Personnel Management incurred several breaches and the U.S. Office of Management and Budget recognized the need for a performance assessment to provide agency Deputy Secretaries with an understanding of the security hygiene. The shift was intended to shift from measuring compliance of the security controls to the effectiveness of the controls. Effectiveness measures the extent to which the controls are implemented correctly, operating as intended, and producing the desired outcome vs. checking a box that the control is in place (compliance). As a result, the OMB developed the President's Management Council Cybersecurity Assessment in late 2014, leveraging the FISMA Metrics data and assessment criteria from the NIST Cybersecurity Framework. The new process used a maturity scale (vs. a yes/no "program in place" under the 2002 law). The latest FISMA report to Congress indicates several areas of weakness and strengths for each agency, as shown in Figure 10.3. The new system permits richer information for evaluation year over year for each government agency.

Post-2015 Cybersecurity Laws

Cybersecurity Information Sharing Act of 2015

The Cybersecurity Information Sharing Act of 2015 (CISA) was signed into law December 18, 2015, requiring the heads of several agencies including National Intelligence, Department of Homeland Security, Department of Defense, and the Department of Justice to develop procedures to promote the sharing of classified and declassified threat indicators in possession of the Federal Government, private entities, and state, local, and tribal governments, as well as cybersecurity best practices—particularly support for small businesses without the resources to adequately manage the threat intelligence. Passing of the bill was met with controversy and opposition by some privacy advocates, who see this as a method for companies to freely share information with government agencies, such as the NSA and Federal Bureau of Investigations without having to follow the legal processes,

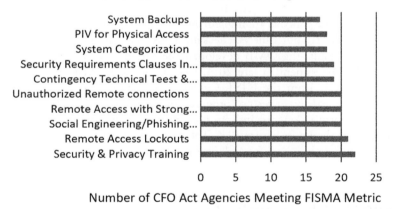

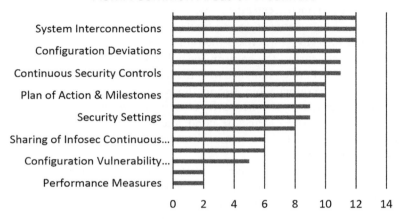

Figure 10.3   FY2016 FISMA common areas of weakness and common areas of strength.

Source: Data from Sheridan, P. and Hasan, K., Information Security and Privacy Advisory Board October Meeting Presentation: Evolution of OIG FISMA Metrics, October 27, 2017, https://csrc.nist.gov/CSRC/media/Presentations/Evolution-of-OIG-FISMA-Metrics/images-media/BriefingofIGMetricsSheridanandHasan.pdf.

such as obtaining a warrant for the information. The purpose of the law is to provide a mechanism to share information between companies and the government to thwart major cyber threats, without fear of breaching privacy laws. Companies are required to strip out personally identifiable information before sharing the information. The companies are not required to share information under the bill, and the information that is shared with the government is to be used for cybersecurity purposes. If the provisions of the act are followed, the entity sharing the information is protected from liability (i.e., sharing a cyber threat indicator of compromise or defensive measure). Examples of what could be shared are items such as a software vulnerability discovered by a software publisher; a phishing email contents, subject line, name and address of the sender, but not the email address or name of the targets; discovery of a technique that allows unauthorized access to a system; or the types of files exfiltrated after an intrusion.

Sharing information between organizations predated this executive order, as many organizations are currently involved in sharing information through the Information Sharing and Analysis Centers (ISACs), which started formation after Presidential Decision Directive-63 (PDD-63) signed May 22, 1998. Several of these are relatively new, such as the Legal Services Information Sharing and Analysis Organization for law firms formed in mid-2015 with support from the existing Financial Services ISAC (FS-ISAC) formed in 1999. The breaches in the retail sector in 2013 prompted the establishment of the retail ISAC in 2014, followed by a portal announced in March 2015, also with the support of the FS-ISAC. These are clear examples of collaboration and leveraging the capabilities and experience from other sectors.

2017 Executive Order 13,800—Strengthening the Cybersecurity of Federal Networks and Critical Infrastructure

Executive Order 13,800 placed the responsibility for cybersecurity risk on the individuals in charge of each federal agency by indicating, "The President will hold heads of executive departments and agencies (agency heads) accountable for managing cybersecurity risk to their enterprises." The law also posited that since decisions made by the agency heads can affect risk to the executive branch and to national security, the policy of the United States is to manage cybersecurity risk as an executive branch enterprise. Agency heads were directed to use *The Framework for Improving Critical Infrastructure Cybersecurity (NIST Cybersecurity Framework)* developed by the NIST and provide a report to the Secretary of Homeland Security and the Director of the OMB within 90 days, or by September 2017, documenting the risk mitigation and acceptance choices; the strategic, operational, and budgetary considerations informing these choices; any accepted risk and unmitigated vulnerabilities; and a plan to implement the framework and any budget impacts. There was also a clear push within the executive order to implement shared IT services as a preference, including such items as email, cloud, and cybersecurity services.

The order also promoted transparency of the cybersecurity practices and assigned the Secretary of Commerce and the Secretary of Homeland Security to lead an open and transparent process to improve the resilience of the Internet to reduce the threat by automated and distributed attacks (botnets). The Mirai Botnet attack in September 2016 and subsequent attacks in October 2016 causing a distributed denial of service of sites including Amazon, Twitter, PayPal, and Spotify surely provided an impetus to include botnet mitigation in the executive order.

Multiple agencies were required by the executive order to provide reports to the President on their findings and actions for periods ranging from 90 days to 1 year after the order was signed. These reports may be classified, and the results of the findings and investment changes may not be realized until well into the 2020s; however, the message was clear that cybersecurity needs to be treated with increased focus in the government agencies. The challenge for the agency heads is they are dealing with antiquated technologies, limited budgets, and ever-increasing hacker sophistication. Several themes surfaced in the Federal IT Modernization Report required by the executive order, including (1) network modernization and consolidation, prioritizing high-risk, high-value assets, modernizing the connections between systems and the Internet, and consolidating network acquisitions and management; (2) providing shared services enabling the use of commercial cloud products, accelerating adoption of cloud email, and collaboration tools, and improving existing and additional shared services; and (3) realigning the current IT resources to support the efforts. The government has been engaged in modernization efforts in the past as well, such as the Federal Risk and Authorization Management Program in 2011 to standardize security assessment, authorization, and continuous monitoring of cloud products and services. These efforts have improved the security; however, the federal attack surface is still too large, and the gaps will need to be reviewed to reduce the attack surface in the future.

2017 New York State Cybersecurity Requirements for Financial Services Companies

The rising number of security threats and concern over nation-states, terrorist organizations, and other criminal actors targeting the financial services industry prompted the New York State Department of Financial Services to issue a state cybersecurity regulation effective on March 1, 2017, with an annual report and certification of compliance to be submitted to the department beginning February 15, 2018. The law, Part 500 of Title 23 of the Official Compilation of Code, Rules, and Regulations of the State of New York, is entitled "Cybersecurity Requirements for Financial Services Companies" and includes in the concept of a "covered entity," curiously like the HIPAA definition of a covered entity but applied to the financial services industry. A covered entity, or one subject to the requirements of the legislation intended to protect customer information and the IT of regulated entities, means "any person operating under or required to operate under a license, registration, charter, certificate, permit, accreditation, or similar authorization under the Banking Law, the Insurance Law, or the Financial Services Law." There are several exemptions to the law carved out primarily for small financial services companies such as those with fewer than 10 employees located in New York, less than $5,000,000 in gross annual revenue for the prior 3 years, or less than $10,000,000 in year-end assets.

The regulation requires each company assess their risk profile and design a program that addresses their risks in a "robust fashion." The law requires many of the foundational elements necessary for a good cybersecurity program, highlighting many of the topics discussed throughout this book, including the items shown in Figure 10.4.

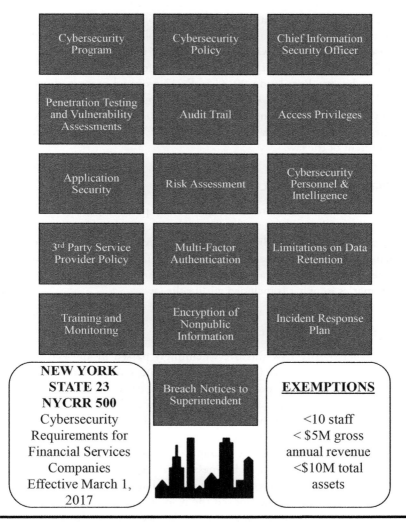

Figure 10.4   New York state cybersecurity requirements.

Source: Data From New York State Department of Financial Services 23 NYCRR 500 Cybersecurity Requirements for Financial Services Companies. *2017. New York State Department of Financial Services. March 1. https://www.dfs.ny.gov/ legal/regulations/adoptions/dfsrf500txt.pdf.*

As Figure 10.4 indicates, each covered entity must have a CISO designated and must develop a security program to review the internal security program, plus any third-party risks to the system. Some would argue this bill is not necessary, as many financial institutions fall under the GLBA of 1999 and are already regulated. However, some smaller banks not subject to GLBA would now be subject to compliance under this regulation. California initiated the first Data Breach Notification Law in 2003, and now 50 states plus the District of Columbia have enacted legislation. Similarly, some fear that other states will follow New York's lead and enact state-based cybersecurity laws, duplicating other regulations in place. While the Breach Notification Laws target one aspect of information security, another state law, Massachusetts Regulation 201 C.M.R. 17 required organizations to encrypt personal information stored on devices and transmitted wirelessly through networks by March 2010. In other words, there has been a precedent for states enacting their own cybersecurity laws prior to the New York Law and expanding on the original intent of the law.

International Cybersecurity Laws

The U.S. laws and regulations mentioned in the preceding section relate primarily to regulate cybersecurity and privacy practices within their applied industry vertical or focus area. In addition, international cybersecurity laws also have been advancing to protect information globally. Articulating all the international laws would be a book all by itself, and thankfully, some of the law firms prepare research and summaries for what is included within the laws.

China's Cybersecurity Law

China's Cybersecurity Law was overwhelmingly passed by the National People's Congress in November 2016 (154 for, 0 against, and 1 abstention) with an effective date of June 1, 2017, after several iterations dating back to early 2014. The law has provisions for (1) personal information protection and individual privacy protection; (2) clear definitions of network operators and security requirements; (3) protection of the critical infrastructure; (4) restrictions on the transfer of data outside of China, indicating that sensitive data must be stored domestically; and (5) penalties including the suspension of business activities. With so many organizations operating business activities within China, these laws can have significant impacts. For example, Apple Computer moved the iCloud accounts for Chinese customers to a state-owned Big Data storage company housed within China, along with the encryption keys. These types of changes change the privacy model for consumers, whereby in the past, for the government to gain access to the information, the U.S. legal system would be used; in this case, since the keys are now in China and managed by a state-owned company, the practices for obtaining personal information would follow the Chinese legal procedures. Portions of the law have been delayed from the initial implementation dates to provide more clarity and determine appropriate processes.

Russian Federation Critical Data Infrastructure Law

In mid-2016, Russia similarly enacted Federal Law 187-FZ entitled "On the Security of the Russian Federation's Critical Data Infrastructure" or the CDI Law; Federal Law 276-FZ "On Amendments to the Federal Law" and "On Data, Information Technologies and Data Security" regulating technologies that can be used to access restricted websites in Russia, known as the VPN Law; and Federal Law 241-FZ "On Amendments to Articles 10.1 and 15.4 of the Federal Law" and "On Data, Information Technologies and Data Security," introducing specific regulations for instant messaging service providers. Social media companies were informed by these laws they needed to store Russian citizen data on servers within Russia, or they would be added to a blacklist and the access would be restricted. LinkedIn website access was blocked following a Russia Court ruling that LinkedIn had not complied in November 2016. This demonstrates the impact of these laws, whether created for means of protecting the personal information of the country's citizens or for increasing surveillance as some would assert, has significant implications, particularly for technology companies with large numbers of customers currently accessing information stored in another country. Russia already had laws regulating the export and use of encryption technologies, requiring a state license for the encryption. This does not mean that encryption in Russia is not impossible; it just means that there may be restrictions on the encryption software used and the version to obtain the license and thus a high likelihood the Russian Government can obtain access to the information through their processes if necessary.

Approaching Laws and Regulations

While the preceding discussion of some of the information security laws is not a comprehensive list, the laws represented provide most of the driving U.S. legislation in force today, highlight some key foreign laws, and should give the perception that cybersecurity and privacy concerns are being addressed by laws and regulations in multiple industries and governments. The laws have come about in large part because cybersecurity is not something that businesses will normally invest in initially just because "it is the right thing to do." Without this legislation, it is unlikely that the security posture of the impacted industries would not be where they are today, albeit there is much work that needs to be done. Smaller organizations often find it difficult to obtain the appropriate resources to comply with the regulations, and larger organizations may become complacent after the initial implementation following a new law's introduction if the appropriate security oversight and governance mechanisms noted in the other chapters are not put in place.

Between the privacy laws requiring safeguards and the sector-based cybersecurity regulations contained within HIPAA, GLBA, North American Electric Reliability Corporation, FISMA, state laws, Presidential Directives/executive orders, etc., most CISOs in practice would want to say "stop" to the creation of more cybersecurity laws. The issue is not the lack of cybersecurity regulations, but rather cybersecurity activities are often underfunded by many organizations to match the risk of an ever-increasing threat environment. Many of the regulations repeat the requirements of other regulations and frameworks without adding much new. The laws keep getting created because breaches continue to happen, and the level of security is not at an acceptable maturity level.

So how should the CISO approach the laws? If we accept the premise that many of these regulations are very similar, and only add a couple of "new security requirements," then we should look to the frameworks that organizations have spent millions of dollars to develop and for our benefit, for the most part, are either available free or at a nominal cost. The control frameworks can all be leveraged to demonstrate compliance across the various regulations. These regulations can be simply mapped by using a spreadsheet and identifying the common elements and choosing one framework as the starting point. For example, security awareness training will appear in several regulations and could be recorded once and referenced by an "x" in a column in a spreadsheet to indicate compliance with that regulation, with specific additional requirements to be added and assigned to the regulation to which they apply. This can be a one-time exercise with updates when significant changes in the law/regulation or the control itself occur.

While it may appear that some laws have been on the books for a substantial amount of time and we should all be complying by now, the reality is that technology has not stood still. The laws are typically in a catchup mode and a lagging indicator. Laws and regulations are normally established in response to an undesirable event, as the preference is for businesses to have the flexibility to operate with innovation, creativity, and without excessive costs of compliance to a regulation. The reality for the CISO is that new regulations will continue to be created and the CISO needs to be aware of the regulations forthcoming and involve legal counsel to assess their impact or ensure there is someone on the team with the appropriate expertise or in the organization performing this task. Failure to do so can result in costly consequences.

More Cybersecurity Laws and Regulations Are Coming

As a final note, each Presidential administration from here until the end of time will likely pass some type of "Cybersecurity Bill" either to fix an issue not previously explicitly articulated and covered by another regulation or to provide the appearance of acting to improve cybersecurity. Whatever the motivations, passing new regulations has the effect of focusing attention on cybersecurity and causing an initial heightened level of anxiety for CISOs! As the saying goes, this too shall pass, and the regulation becomes another addition to the security risk and compliance area to certify to. The question is often asked why these laws are not harmonized, and the short answer is that the establishment of comprehensive laws would cross jurisdictions and require the rewriting of many other codified laws, with existing processes for compliance. Today, while this has been suggested, over 50 different federal statutes alone exist highlighting some reference to a cybersecurity issue, not counting emerging state cybersecurity laws and the foreign privacy laws (containing requirements for cybersecurity). The role of the Federal Government is complex with respect to facilitating cybersecurity—different agencies must secure the federal systems, provide national security, protect the critical infrastructure, and provide guidance for the nonfederal systems. The CISOs can be ensured that laws will continue to be added and most likely with increasing frequency as privacy and security issues receive public attention and legislators are compelled to act by their constituents.

As long as technology continues to push the envelope and create cars capable of going 212 miles per hour, clearly against today's "lawful driving standards" for any road except a race track, the laws will lag what is required. As CISOs, we need to find was to ensure the technology brought into our organizations is running safely and securely, regardless of the specific requirement to do so.

MICHAEL J. DAUGHERTY: FINDING THE RIGHT LAWYER TO DEFEND YOUR COMPANY

CEO, LabMD

If I only knew back in 2008 what I know today. So many lessons learned and so much to share. But if I only had one thing I could share, it would be about the lawyers. It is so hard to find a lawyer that has the skill, expertise and will to defend you because so many live in the silent and complicit world of Washington, DC, where everyone goes along to get along. After 2 or 3 years of relentless LabMD investigation by the Federal Trade Commission (FTC), my lawyer felt over her head, unclear, and outside her area of expertise. She really wanted me to find someone else who understood how this bizarre group of government attorneys really operated. I did not want to because I trusted her but, finally, I relented. When I started to call around Washington, DC, for an attorney who had regulatory experience with the FTC, I was demoralized by my discovery. Every single lawyer listened for 3 minutes maximum and told me to settle. They said the content of the case was irrelevant. Their tone of voice was what one would expect when you are being informed you have a terminal illness. Hopeless, impossible and settle were the routine words. This was shocking, but as time has passed, I now understand why they had such strong opinions. The bottom line is this. Lawyers that have experience fighting the government usually come from the government. You want to stay as far away from these people as possible. They get their jobs precisely because of their DC relationships. Because they are still in the neighborhood but no longer in the house, they will not risk bad relationships with the government simply for you. They will never tell you this. When you hire a lawyer, who used to work for the agency that is investigating you send a signal to the agency that you want to settle. If you want to fight, or even just know how the game is really played, hire a lawyer that has never worked for the government but has litigated against the government. He will know all the government machinations and horror stories, so you will not have to. Sad to say, but some lawyers hired to defend you will not cross lines that harm their ties with the Feds. You will never find that information in an engagement letter, and you do not want to finally figure it out when you are bewildered and confused after your grind through the government crosshairs is over.

Suggested Reading

1. Snyder, B. 2015. LifeLock Fined $100 Million for False Claims. CIO Online (December 18). www.cio.com/article/3016785/privacy/lifelock-fined-100-million-for-false-claims.html.
2. Department Health & Human Services. Enforcement Data. www.hhs.gov/hipaa/for-professionals/compliance-enforcement/data/index.html.
3. Becker's Health & Hospital Report. 2016. 10 Largest HIPAA Settlement Fines. (August 10). www.beckershospitalreview.com/healthcare-information-technology/10-largest-hipaa-settlement-fines.html.
4. Federal Register. 2009. Vol 74, No.148. Office for Civil Rights; Delegation of Authority. (August 4). www.hhs.gov/sites/default/files/ocr/privacy/hipaa/administrative/security-rule/srdelegation.pdf?language=es.
5. Department of Health & Human Services. HIPAA Privacy, Security, and Breach Notification Audit Program. www.hhs.gov/hipaa/for-professionals/compliance-enforcement/audit/index.html.
6. Sanchez, L. H. H. S. 2017. Office for Civil Rights (OCR) and National Institute of Standards and Technology (NIST). Safeguarding Health Information Conference: Building Assurance through HIPAA Security Conference. Presentation Update on OCR's Phase 2 HIPAA Audits. (September 6).
7. Sheridan, P. and Hasan, K. 2017. Evolution of OIG FISMA Metrics Presentation. (October 27). https://csrc.nist.gov/CSRC/media/Presentations/Evolution-of-OIG-FISMA-Metrics/images-media/BriefingofIGMetricsSheridanandHasan.pdf.
8. Federal Register. 2017. Strengthening the Cybersecurity of Federal Networks and Critical Infrastructure. Executive Order 13800. (May 16). www.federalregister.gov/documents/2017/05/16/2017-10004/strengthening-the-cybersecurity-of-federal-networks-and-critical-infrastructure.

9. Report to the President on Federal IT Modernization. 2017. Final IT Modernization Report. (December 13). https://itmodernization.cio.gov/.
10. Congress.gov. 2015. S.754- To U.S. Congress. Improve Cybersecurity in the United States Through Enhanced Sharing of Information About Cybersecurity Threats, and for Other Purposes. (October 27). www.congress.gov/bill/114th-congress/senate-bill/754.
11. Karp, B. et al. 2016. Harvard Law School Forum on Corporate Governance and Financial Regulation. Federal Guidance on the Cybersecurity Information Sharing Act of 2015. (March 3). https://corpgov.law.harvard.edu/2016/03/03/federal-guidance-on-the-cybersecurity-information-sharing-act-of-2015/.
12. Business Wire. 2014. National Retail Federation Announces Information-Sharing Platform. (April 14). www.businesswire.com/news/home/20140414006079/en/National-Retail-Federation-Announces-Information-Sharing-Platform.
13. New York State Department of Financial Services. 2017. New York State Department of Financial Services 23 NYCRR 500 Cybersecurity Requirements for Financial Services Companies. (March 1). www.dfs.ny.gov/legal/regulations/adoptions/dfsrf500txt.pdf.
14. New York State Department of Financial Services. 2017. Cybersecurity Filings, Key Questions About the Recent Cyber Regulation Notice. https://dfs.ny.gov/about/cybersecurity.htm.
15. Federal Trade Commission. Financial Institutions and Customer Information: Complying with the Safeguards Rule. www.ftc.gov/tips-advice/business-center/guidance/financial-institutions-customer-information-complying.
16. National Conference of State Legislators. Security Breach Notification Laws. www.ncsl.org/research/telecommunications-and-information-technology/security-breach-notification-laws.aspx.
17. Triolo, P. 2017. China's Cybersecurity Law One Year on An Evolving and Interlocking Framework. New America (November 30). www.newamerica.org/cybersecurity-initiative/digichina/blog/chinas-cybersecurity-law-one-year/.
18. Nellis, S. et al. 2018. Apple Moves to Store iCloud Keys in China, Raising Human Rights Fears. Technology News (February 23). www.reuters.com/article/us-china-apple-icloud-insight/apple-moves-to-store-icloud-keys-in-china-raising-human-rights-fears-idUSKCN1G8060.
19. Taylor, A. 2016. Russia Moves to Block Professional Networking Site LinkedIn. Washington Post (November 17). www.washingtonpost.com/news/worldviews/wp/2016/11/17/russia-moves-to-block-professional-networking-site-linkedin/?noredirect=on&utm_term=.437ad569799a.
20. Fischer, E. 2014. Federal Laws Relating to Cybersecurity: Overview of Major Issues, Current Laws, and Proposed Legislation. Congressional Research Service (December 12). https://fas.org/sgp/crs/natsec/R42114.pdf.
21. Moscaritolo, A. 2010. Hacker Albert Gonzalez Receives 20 years in Prison. SC Magazine (March 25). www.scmagazineus.com/hacker-albert-gonzalez-receives-20-years-in-prison/article/166571/.
22. U.S. Department of Homeland Security. Federal Information Security Modernization Act of 2014 (FISMA 2014). www.dhs.gov/fisma.
23. U.S. Department of Justice. 1974. Privacy Act of 1974. www.justice.gov/opcl/privstat.htm.
24. Federal Trade Commission. 2002. Eli Lilly Settles FTC Charges Concerning Security Breach. (January 18). www.ftc.gov/news-events/press-releases/2002/01/eli-lilly-settles-ftc-charges-concerning-security-breach.

25. National Institute of Standards and Technology (NIST). 1987. Computer Security Act of 1987. (June 11). http://csrc.nist.gov/groups/SMA/ispab/documents/csa_87.txt.

26. Securities Exchange Commission. 2002. Public Law 107–204 (Sarbanes-Oxley Act). (July 30). www.sec.gov/about/laws/soa2002.pdf.

27. HITRUST Central. http://hitrustalliance.net/.

28. Vijayan, J. 2011. HIPAA Privacy Actions Seen as Warning: HHS hit Cignet with $4.3 M Penalty; Mass General Settles for $ 1M. Computerworld. (February 25). www.computer-world.com/s/article/9211359/HIPAA_privacy_actions_seen_as_warning.

29. Standard of Good Practice for Information Security. Information Security Forum. www.securityforum.org/tool/the-isf-standardrmation-security/.

30. National Institute of Standards and Technology (NIST). 2002. H.R.2458-48. Federal Information Security Management Act of 2002. http://csrc.nist.gov/drivers/documents/FISMA-final.pdf.

31. Krok, A. 2018. Watch the 2019 Chevy Corvette ZR1 hit its 212-mph top speed on track. Road Showby Cnet (April 23). www.cnet.com/roadshow/news/chevrolet-corvette-zr1-top-speed-video/.

32. Sorokanich, B. 2017. The Tesla Roadster Is Not the "Fastest Car in the World." Road and Track (November 17). www.roadandtrack.com/new-cars/news/a30536/tesla-model-s-p100d-quickest-not-fastest/.

33. Acocelle, N. 2003. Andretti's Only Indy 500 Win Came in 1969. Espn Classic (November 19). www.espn.com/classic/s/add_andretti_mario.html.

34. Department of Health & Human Services. 2011. Final Determination. February 4. www.hhs.gov/sites/default/files/ocr/privacy/hipaa/enforcement/examples/cignetpenaltyletter.pdf.

35. Daugherty, M. 2013. The Devil Inside the Beltway. Atlanta. Broadland Press.

36. Cohen, D. et al. 2018. What Litigating the LabMD Case Showed us About US Cybersecurity Regulation. International Association Privacy Professionals (June 27). https://iapp.org/news/a/what-litigating-the-labmd-case-showed-us-about-u-s-cybersecurity-regulation/.

Chapter 11

Data Protection and Privacy Every CISO Must Know

> The poorest man may in his cottage bid defiance to all the forces of the Crown. It may be frail – the storm may enter – the rain may enter – but the King of England cannot enter – all the force dares not cross the threshold of the ruined tenement!

William Pitt, Earl of Chatham, 1708–1778

Organizations, large and small, have been sensitized to the need for information security due to the widespread media coverage of the breaches over the past several years. Companies do not want to be in the headlines for these breaches. There was a time when this concern was limited to those organizations maintaining financial information (where information assets were money and could be monetized and stolen directly), those organizations maintaining intellectual property (IP), such as manufacturing organizations with proprietary designs, or those organizations creating highly technical products. Today however, with the high visibility of the breaches in the health-care and retail space, these breaches are viewed by organizations of all types as "yes, this could happen to our company."

So, this is a good thing, right? Companies now understand that breaches are possible, and not only possible, but *likely* given that any organization can be subject to ransomware to monetize the damage. Furthermore, there is a real penalty for not complying with the various laws today. Failure for organizations to take these threats and regulatory requirements seriously has ramifications for an organization most executives would prefer to avoid. No one wants the spotlight of extra scrutiny on their systems by regulators or to suffer the downtime and costs associated with a breach, thereby detracting valuable resources from the mission of the business. The real question here is not whether this is a good thing or not, but is the threat from an attacker or the threat of paying regulatory fines enough to motivate an organization to do the right thing?

Before this question can be answered, it is necessary to pause for a moment and consider what is the right thing to do? What is the real objective organizations should be working towards? Is it to add in enough security controls so that the organization passes the next audit by the regulators and has no high-risk findings? Is it to ensure that sufficient backups are taken so that when there is a breach, the organization can recover quickly? Is it to download a checklist of security controls and check the box that each of these controls has had some level of compliance with the framework selected? While all the items are important for delivering a comprehensive security program, each one of them misses the point of why we are performing information security.

Impact for Chief Information Security Officers

Just as we make security decisions every day about security risk, we make decisions every day regarding privacy. We decide what information we want to share with the world and what information we want to keep private. We "assume" various levels of privacy protection through our online activities, as well as a level of privacy that we come to expect in our homes. When we vote, we cast our ballots in a private voting booth with the expectation that our votes are kept private and counted in the final tally. It is our right to decide whether we want to divulge our political party or the candidate we voted for. We expect that the activity within our homes is private and not subject to surveillance. In short, we traditionally have assumed we have a right to privacy.

A common expression in the industry is that "you can have security without privacy, but you can't have privacy without security." Until the recent past, most Information Security Officers appeared to have been focusing on the former part of this statement—focusing more on the information security controls within an organization vs. directing efforts towards understanding the nuances of privacy regulations. I would attribute part of this to the increased use of the cloud for processing and the concern of global organizations over the level of protection of the information. Beginning in 2015, I started providing a "One-hour Privacy Primer for Security Officers" session at the USA RSA Security Conference held annually in San Francisco, CA, representing the largest security conference with 42,000 attendees in 2018. Fully expecting a small group to show up, especially when the President of the International Association of Privacy Professionals (IAPP) was speaking in another room at the same time on current trends, was I ever surprised when a packed room of 400 people showed up. Really? To not hear about gory details of the latest advanced persistent threat or how threat intelligence was being used, but to learn about information privacy? It was at that moment that the light-bulb went on—there was a shift occurring within security professionals to embrace this "new privacy language" within the Chief Information Security Officer (CISO) and security professional community. I was humbled to repeat the session the next several years, and not only repeat, but was asked to present the session twice multiple times during the conference due to the demand. This is a very positive development, as security officers really do need to embrace the privacy concepts.

Here are a few reasons why the change of focus to "you can't have privacy without security" may be the result of the following events:

1. *Increased Regulation.* Several laws raised attention over the past several years to the need for privacy controls. Within the USA, the Health Insurance Portability and Accountability Act of 1996 (HIPAA) was gaining more attention as large fines were levied. The Office of Civil Rights was providing more visibility to privacy issues through increased audits of providers. The EU-U.S. and Swiss-U.S. Privacy Shield Frameworks were issued by the U.S. Department of Commerce and European Commission and Swiss Administrations to provide companies with a mechanism to conduct cross-border business and comply with the data protection requirements, thus facilitating transatlantic commerce. The replacement of the European Union Data Directive with the General Data Protection Regulation (GDPR) had widespread global implications.
2. *Increased Breaches.* The rise in security breaches involving organizations containing personal information has increased the conversation as to what information is retained on individuals and how is it protected.
3. *Contract Language.* Legal departments are engaging privacy and security personnel to review the contracts at an increasing rate, particularly with the information being captured within the systems.
4. *Cloud Processing in Other Countries.* As global organizations access and share information beyond their borders, more attention is being paid to (1) what information is being stored and (2) where is this information being stored. This should not be confused with the requirement to adequately secure the information, but rather the focus is on the information and are the privacy rights of the individual being protected with respect to the information.
5. *A Phone in Every Pocket, a Video on Every Street Corner.* As more and more information is being captured on events, locations of photographs and videos are tracked, and the information is posted online, individuals are more sensitive to how the information is being used.

Whatever the reasons may be for the increased focus on privacy, CISOs must understand the language of privacy to be effective Information Security Officers.

"VERY IMPORTANT" FOR PRIVACY COLLABORATION

Figure 11.1 Privacy collaboration with other functions. (From *Benchmarking Privacy Management and Investments of the Fortune 1000*, 2014, IAPP 2014 Research, www.iapp.org.)

According to a survey by IAPP, 76% of Fortune 1,000 companies surveyed indicated that information security was "very important" for privacy collaboration. This also represented the largest percentage of mentions for collaboration with the privacy function as shown in Figure 11.1 Information technology (IT) and legal were also high percentages eclipsing the other business areas by a wide margin.

Forrester research noted in a report regarding the strengths needed for the 2018 CISO that one of the necessary critical success factors was to "widen vision to privacy, data management, and compliance," and failure to do so could lead towards extinction within the role.

Aside from the commentary that "privacy is dead" or "privacy is thriving online," organizations have a responsibility to the customers and shareholders to abide by the regulations, which are clearly not dead and are increasing in importance.

SAMANTHA THOMAS: PRIVACY HUNGER GAMES: CHANGE THE RULES

Former CSO, CISO, CPO, CIO

During your time as a CISO, you will find yourself challenged with balancing the risk of information security and privacy in the Need-To-Know paradigm. Amidst one of these Need-To-Know challenges, my team found our organization at risk related to privacy for approximately 90 health-care entities to whom we provided Protected Health Information (PHI). Upon examination, we found that many of our divisions were providing the PHI with little to no structure. And vice versa. Our entity was often the primary health-care provider. The other entities provided mostly after care and tertiary services, and often, a patient would return to our care. And our organization was beginning to deploy a new electronic health record system. The other entities were mostly small government agencies with little staff, even less funding, and most used outdated technology. Methods of PHI exchanges were a shambled and archaic method of postal mail, courier, fax, hand delivery, unencrypted email, etc.

With communication at the forefront, my team and I reached out to the Chief Information Officers (CIOs), CISOs, and Chief Privacy Officers (CPOs) at each entity to discuss the issue and introduce a possible solution. We made presentations at the CIO's annual meeting and the CISO's annual meeting. In tandem, we engaged their CPOs to keep them appraised and validate our understanding of concerns for legal compliance. We documented conversations and decisions, and communicated our findings back to all CXOs. We were astute in tailoring this information to ensure it be direct and valuable enough for leaders to make the right decisions for their organization while having enough information to be cognizant of the larger picture.

With the information security specifics vetted, all parties agreed to solution "X." Multiple meetings and hours of research and agreements ensued with continual updates to key leaders and status updates to effected parties.

One problem continued to exist: all entities involved were at various levels of city, county, and state government. Developing a new solution and implementing a change are two different endeavors in this arena. Although we could identify and implement a solution for how our entity would send PHI outside our infrastructure, we had no authority to require how the other parties shall send PHI to our organization or how they should exchange it with one another.

So, we wrote a requirement into law.

Working with our legal team and legislative representatives, we authored suggested content and requested input from key players (e.g., health records management). As the process can be lengthy and filled with constant change, we continually updated the CXOs and assisted them in moving forward with other PHI protective measures until legal language was approved. This was a critical part of building trust with all involved and would create a new level of confidence by which involved entities worked together in the future.

Upon language being promulgated into law, the CXOs had the leverage they required to implement the necessary changes in their organization.

Due to the complicated nature of information sharing in this endeavor, the structure our team used was documented. This structure for "communicate, not dictate" with our collegiate health-care providers is now the de facto illustration for our organization when there is a need to engage multitiered/cross interest entities for privacy and information security concerns.

The Real Information Security Objective

The focus all too often is on the establishment of security controls to reduce the likelihood of the next breach of keeping the organization out of hot water and save money if there is a breach. However, there is a more fundamental reason why we should be implementing security and privacy controls within our organizations—to protect the data from those who do not have a legitimate need to access the information and enable the use of the information for those that require access to it, when they need it. Period. In other words, the real objective of any information security program should be to protect the information to which it has been entrusted—or rather to focus on *Data Protection*. This primary objective seems to get lost in the translation of the latest breach and what companies are doing to "fix" the mess after the breach.

Let us imagine for a moment that we have an organization that takes a data protection approach to their information vs. worrying about the next breach. Instead of focusing on what security technologies need to be in place to protect everything at the same level, the focus on data protection will lead the organization to decide what information is important for running the business, who should have access to it, and how it is protected. Notice the shift in focus away from talking about security controls, generally applicable to the entire dataset of the organization, to having a meaningful discussion regarding the information being most valuable to the mission of the business and how it should be protected. This represents moving security away from securing the "computing infrastructure" to securing "the data" of an organization. Securing the infrastructure typically involves attempting to understand the computing assets the organization maintains (not an easy task as this is a constantly moving target), applying security controls against those assets, and then monitoring and ensuring the controls are being maintained. Most organizations operating in this context do not have a clear view of where the critical information is located to run the business let alone the data sensitivity or classification of the information to be protected, or the level of security protections required to adequately protect the information asset. As a result, all the information residing on a computing platform, such as a SharePoint server, Oracle database, an unstructured One Drive cloud storage, or a mobile device, will have the similar baseline levels of protection. Access is also typically not created a granular enough level to the information resulting on these platforms, thereby resulting in excessive privileges to access the information. Organizations ultimately end up with charts depicting security controls across technologies; however, they are unable to articulate how the information related to a specific business function is protected end-to-end.

Why have organizations focused on securing the infrastructure vs. the data? As noted in the discussion regarding the *Evolution of the CISO*, information security was viewed predominantly as an IT issue in the past, and in many organizations lower on the maturity curve, and they still are. When a firefighter is in the middle of fighting a fire, keeping back the flames, his priority is on extinguishing the fire in front of him in a safe manner to protect themselves and the surrounding area from further damage. The focus at that point is not on whether the facility had good preventive controls in place and whether the most valuable items were placed in a fireproof safe and saved. Of course, the firefighter will first prioritize human life with everything else being of secondary importance. The fireman's focus is on the entire environment in front of him and returning the property to a safe state (extinguished fire). The same is true with organizations today starting the process of paying attention to their information security programs. This is not to suggest organizations abandon the focus on applying good security controls to the infrastructure, but rather organizations should determine the "minimal security standards" necessary to secure the business for the protection of all information at a "minimum acceptable level" and also should be focusing on where the valuable information is and how should it be protected (the discussion on strategies in Chapter 3 outlined several approaches for approaching strategy and the importance of determining the crown jewels in the strategy). For example, years of security controls suggest that connecting a personal computer to the Internet without running an antivirus (AV) program with daily signature updates would be taking on an unacceptable risk. While there may be other emerging technologies replacing this technology using mathematical calculations and behavioral analytics, few organizations are willing to advocate removal of the AV programs as a component of their infrastructure security program. These programs may be installed across the entire business with no knowledge of where the information resides, and that is ok. Vulnerability management is a fundamental control needed to be in place for all systems. Implementation of the vulnerability management program will check a box with the regulators and control frameworks as well. What it does not do, however, is (a) recognize the value of the information being protected, (b) provide understanding of what data is lost when a breach does occur, (b) provide knowledge of where valuable data exists within the organization, (d) assist in prioritization of systems for recovery during a catastrophic event, and (e) provide the ability to demonstrate how sensitive information is protected. To protect the "data" vs. the "systems," a different focus is required.

Privacy Laws and Common Principles

To appreciate the data protection and privacy principles we are faced with today, it is useful to review the history of privacy laws put in place in the past to increase privacy. Each law at the time was enacted based upon the concerns and technologies at that point in history. Knowing the global prior history allows us to appreciate how we have arrived at the place we are today with privacy being a key topic of discussion.

Privacy vs. Data Protection

The protection of information concerning individuals is commonly referred to as privacy law in the United States and some other countries, and data protection law in the European Union (an economic union of 28 member states located in Europe to provide free movement of goods and services across the member states). The references to privacy and data protection are almost interchangeable and focus on the protection of privacy. Different regions of the world may view privacy concerns with more rigor, as in the European Union, whereby privacy is regarded as a fundamental human right. In December 1948, the United Nations passed the Universal Declaration of Human Rights, proclaiming that, "no one shall be subjected to arbitrary interference with his privacy, family, home or correspondence." When working across countries, it becomes important to shift the lens to understanding the history and social origins within that country as to why the level of passion surrounding the topic may evoke a greater level of emotional response. Privacy rights may be regarded as much more than the implementation of a regulation and lean more towards the protection of the private activities of their citizens and protections from government interference. There may also be a view held that the privacy protections of other countries are not as strong as the protections within their own country, creating hesitation to allow information outside of their country without some assurance of adequate controls. The key point here is that it is necessary for the CISO to listen and appreciate the level of concern for privacy issues, taking into consideration the other country requirements.

Early Privacy History

While most countries in recent years have implemented privacy laws, many of the principles contained in the current laws dated back to specifications created many years ago. Privacy was mentioned in the Bible, Qur'an, and Jewish law regarding the discussions of prayer. England enacted the Justices of the Peace Act in 1361 providing for the arrest of "peeping toms and eavesdroppers."

Entick vs. Carrington (1765)

In the 1765 English case of Entick vs. Carrington involved the principle that the prerogative powers of the monarch were subordinate to the law of the land.

This assured that government officials could not exercise power unless there was a law authorizing the activity. The government suspected that Entick was writing derogatory material against the majesty and about both houses of the parliament. A warrant was created, and Carrington and three others broke into Entick's house with force of arms and against his will, spending more than 4 hours looking at his personal papers and causing damage to his property. Documents were also removed, Entick latter sued, and Lord Camden found the defendants liable, stating, "if this is law it would be in our books, but no such law ever existed in this country; our law holds the property of every man so sacred, that no man can set foot upon his neighbors close without his leave." William Pitt echoed this response in his 1763 speech on the excise bill, very eloquently by stating, "the poorest man may in his cottage bid defiance to all the force of the Crown. It may be frail; its roof may shake; the wind may blow through it; the storms may enter, the rain may enter,—but the King of England cannot enter; all his forces dare not cross the threshold of the ruined tenement!" These early ideas of privacy within our homes having the protection from outsiders gave rise to privacy laws and the separation between the executive and legislative branches of government to ensure that there was an existing law of the land decided before an executive of the law could act.

Warren and Brandeis (1890)

Regarded as the publication in the U.S. positing privacy rights, Samuel Warren and Louis Brandeis wrote a paper called the "Right to Privacy" published in the 1890 Harvard Law Review. In the paper, "recent inventions and business methods" were called out as a threat to the "right to be left alone." What were these "recent inventions and business methods?" These were referred to in the paper as the "instantaneous photographs and newspaper enterprise have invaded the sacred precincts of private and domestic life; and numerous mechanical devices threaten to make good the prediction that 'what is whispered in the closet shall be proclaimed from the house-tops'." Warren and Brandeis were eluding to the invention of the camera and the use by the newspapers to publish photographs! In the past, there were the "gossip columns" whereby gossip could be printed; however, it was subject to someone's belief that it happened. With the camera, it would be difficult to refute the "evidence." We can see similarities in the discussions today with the widespread availability of cameras and video recording capabilities in smartphones. Brandeis and Warren felt that individuals had "the right to be left alone."

In the paper, the protections for privacy are best stated by, "…the design of the law must be to protect those persons with whose affairs the community has no legitimate concern, from being dragged into an undesirable and undesired publicity and to protect all persons, whatsoever; their position or station, from having matters which they may properly prefer to keep private, made public against their will. It is the unwarranted invasion of individual privacy which is reprehended, and to be, so far as possible, prevented." This provides for the protection of all individuals from libel and slander.

Louis Brandeis served as an associate justice on the Supreme Court of the United States from 1916 to 1939. Louis was born in Louisville Kentucky in 1856. It is interesting how the introduction of new technology (cameras) brought about concerns over privacy, and over the years, introduction of new technology continuously re-energizes the focus on privacy as more information is collected, aggregated, and reviewed for appropriate use—all protecting the fundamental human rights of the individual for protection.

1948 Article 12 of Universal Declaration of Rights

In December 1948, the General Assembly of the United Nations adopted the Universal Declaration of Human Rights to address, "…disregard and contempt for human rights have resulted in barbarous acts which have outraged the conscience of mankind, and the advent of a world in which human beings shall enjoy freedom of speech and belief and freedom from fear and want has been proclaimed as the highest aspiration of the common people." The declaration provides for a right to private life in Article 12 stating, "No one shall be subjected to arbitrary interference with his privacy, family, home or correspondence, nor to attacks upon his honour and reputation. Everyone has the right to protection of the law against such interference or attacks."

The right to freedom is expressed in Article 19 as follows, "Everyone has a right to freedom of opinion and expression; this right includes freedom to hold opinions without interference and to seek, receive and impart information and ideas through any media and regardless of frontiers." The individual rights articulated in Article 19 are not absolute, with constraints clarified in Article 29(2) stating, "In the exercise of his rights and freedoms, everyone shall be subject only to such limitations as are determined by law solely for the purpose of securing due recognition and respect for the rights and freedoms of others and of meeting the just requirements of morality, public order, and the general welfare in a democratic society." In other words, individuals have a right to their privacy and reputation, as well as the right to freely express their ideas, provided that existing laws and morality are followed in expressing these opinions.

1950 European Convention on Human Rights

The Council of Europe, in Rome, invited the individual European states to enter into an agreement known as the European Convention on Human Rights, which among other provisions, provides for "respect for private and family life" in Article 8, similar to Article 12 of the Universal Declaration of Rights, but with the added enforcement by the European Court of Human Rights. These provisions protect the right of citizens to maintain the privacy of their personal information.

First Modern Data Protection/Privacy Laws

1970 Fair Credit Reporting Act

The 1970 Fair Credit Reporting Act, addressing the collection and processing of information related to consumer credit, is the first national law passed regarding privacy in the United States in response to the growing technological capabilities provided by the growth of mainframe computers in the 1960s and concern over surveillance activities. During the same year, the German state of Hesse enacted the first modern data protection law, a regional law, in part to prevent personal abuse during Hitler's Third Reich, particularly with the increased collection of personal information. Several European countries started putting data protection laws in place during this period. Sweden subsequently created the first European national data protection law in 1973; however, much energy towards privacy did not occur until the 1980s.

1974 U.S. Privacy Act

The Privacy Act provides restrictions on the Federal Government in the collection, maintenance, and use of the information collected on individuals. The act provides protection from disclosure of information that is defined within a defined "record set." Information cannot be released unless it was specifically requested by a court and with an individual's express consent. While the HIPAA provided protections for the release of health-care information, for information contained within government systems such as Medicare and Medicaid, the release of information was already protected by the Privacy Act of 1974. The attempts to provide a balance between the Federal Government's need to collect information to go about their business and at the same time not collect so much information or release information that constitutes an invasion of privacy. From a historical perspective, the act was born out during the aftermath of Watergate, where information was collected on individuals related to the Watergate scandal. Also, with the interconnectivity between systems and networks in the 1970s and the subsequent introduction of the personal computer that followed the act in the early 1980s, there was concern over the potential aggregation of information using a single identifier, such as the social security number. The act established fair information practices by placing some structure on how agencies managed their records, provided individuals with increased access to the records held by federal agencies, provided the means to amend records that were not accurate, relevant, timely, or complete and restricted their disclosure to appropriate individuals.

Late 1970s European Data Protection Laws

By 1979, data protection laws were being established across Europe in seven member states (Austria, Denmark, France, Federal Republic of Germany, Luxembourg,

Norway, and Austria) and three others (Spain, Portugal, and Austria) specified privacy rights within their constitution.

1980 Organization for Economic Cooperation and Development (OECD)

The Organization for Economic Cooperation and Development (OECD), established in 1948, is an international organization that originally included the United States and European countries, but has expanded to include Australia, Austria, Belgium, Canada, Chile, the Czech Republic, Denmark, Estonia, Finland, France, Germany, Greece, Hungary, Iceland, Ireland, Israel, Italy, Japan, Korea, Luxembourg, Mexico, the Netherlands, New Zealand, Norway, Poland, Portugal, the Slovak Republic, Slovenia, Spain, Sweden, Switzerland, Turkey, the United Kingdom, and the United States, along with European Union participation. The OECD provides the opportunity for countries to discuss issues such as the economic, social, and environmental challenges of operating in a global environment, with representation of 39 countries accounting for 80% of the world trade and investment.

The OECD most notably created the most widely known framework for establishing fair means of transferring and handling information. In 1980, the OECD published a set of guidelines entitled "Guidelines Governing the Protection of Privacy and Transborder Data Flows of Personal Data." The guidelines contained eight principles standing the test of time to provide a privacy framework leveraged in the construction of many privacy laws (explained later in this chapter). While the definitions of what is personal data may vary by country and regulation, the definition offered by the OECD in 1980 specified personal data as "any information relating to an identified or identifiable individual (data subject)," which was left unrevised in the 2013 OECD modification, a testimony to the thoughtful privacy thinking at the time.

1990s–2000s Privacy Laws

Multiple laws were emerging in the United States in the late 1990s modeling some of the fair information practices evident in the European Data Directive. Laws were created on a "sectoral" basis, aligning to individual industry verticals vs. the "comprehensive" law within Europe, which was more broad-based by focusing on the flow of information between the member states. This approach resulted in many different laws regarding privacy. Laws were developed to apply to the private sector (not for profit and commercial business entities) and the public sector for U.S. Government agencies. Some key laws developed during this time were revisions to the Fair Credit Reporting Act including extending the powers of the Federal Trade Commission (FTC) to levy fines for violations of the act (1996): Children's Online Privacy Protection Rule (COPPA); Gramm–Leach–Bliley Financial Privacy

Rule went into effect (2000); First Data Security Case with FTC vs. Eli Lilly & Company for disclosing 669 names of Prozac patients in an email shutting down a website (2002); CAN-SPAM Rule goes into effect (2004).

Terminology

It is useful to understand the terminology before addressing the European Union directives and the supporting EU-US regulations to support transborder data flows. While earlier definitions of some of these terms appeared in the OECD principles, the following definitions are those in use today (i.e., taken from the 2016 GDPR) as the most current and relevant for exploring these laws. As shown in Figure 11.2, there are four primary definitions used to describe the responsibilities and transfer of information between the entities. The definitions are as follows:

Data subject is an identified or identifiable natural person who can be identified, directly or indirectly, reference to an identifier such as a name, an identification number, location data, an online identifier or to one or more factors specific to the physical, physiological, genetic, mental, economic, cultural, or social identity of that natural person.

Personal data means any information relating to the data subject. While the definitions of what constitutes personal data may vary by country regulation and definition, the personal data items listed in Figure 11.3 indicate items that have a high probability of relating to a data subject and thus being subject to the privacy law.

Controller means the natural or legal person, public authority, agency, or other body which, alone or jointly with others, determines the purposes and means of the processing of personal data; where the purposes and means of such processing are determined by Union or Member State law, the controller or the specific criteria for its nomination may be provided for by Union or Member State law. In other

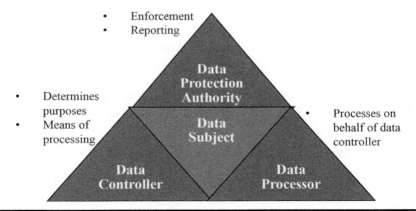

Figure 11.2   Personal data handling relationships.

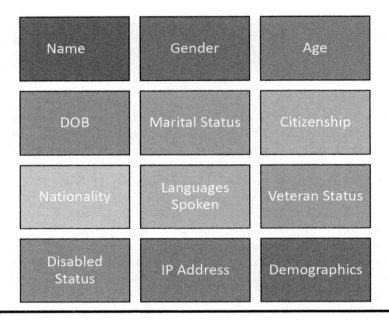

Figure 11.3 Personal data items.

words, most organizations using personal data in their business for the purposes of conducting their business would be considered data controllers, as they are directing the processing, either internally (own organization) or externally (third party) to process the information according to the organization's requirements.

Processor means a natural or legal person, public authority, agency, or other body which processes personal data on behalf of the controller.

Consent of the data subject means any freely given, specific, informed, and unambiguous indication of the data subject's wishes by which he or she, by a statement or by a clear affirmative action, signifies agreement to the processing of personal data relating to him or her.

Special categories of data (also known as "highly sensitive data in other regulations") have a different membership in the European Union than what would be "highly sensitive data" in the United States. There are special rules within the regulations such as requiring explicit consent (i.e., must opt-in) and limitations to the processing of the information. Figure 11.4 shows some of these differences.

1995 Directive 95/46/EC (EU Data Protection Directive)

1995 Directive 95/46/EC on the protection of individuals with regard to the processing of personal data and on the free movement of such data, also known as the EU Data Protection Directive, is a significant law in that has been viewed by many as the baseline for privacy laws created since. The directive incorporated the eight privacy

Figure 11.4   Differences in highly sensitive definitions.

principles specified by the OECD. The directive was drafted as there were emerging differences between the laws of the individual European member states, affording different levels of protection. The differences in the laws made it difficult to have a uniform flow of information across the borders without needing individual consent to pass the information between the borders. The European Union Data Protection Directive was passed to require each member state to develop laws that provided equivalent protection. Differences still existed within countries; however, the key issue of being able to export the information between countries was mitigated and information could move freely among European Union members. Since this was a directive (requiring each country to implement national laws to implement the principles stated in the directive) vs. a regulation (requirement of law by the European Union), it was up to each individual country to ensure they have created laws within their country.

The directive is consistent with earlier history whereby privacy is noted as a fundamental human right, as well as preserving the need to conduct business, stated as follows:

> Whereas data-processing systems are designed to serve man; whereas they must, whatever the nationality or residence of natural persons, respect the fundamental rights and freedoms, notably the right to privacy, and contribute to economic and social progress, trade expansion and the well-being of individuals.

The objective of the directive was clear, as noted in Article 1:

1. In accordance with this directive, Member States shall protect the fundamental rights and freedoms of natural persons, and in particular, their right to privacy with respect to the processing of personal data.

2. Member States shall neither restrict nor prohibit the free flow of personal data between Member States for the reasons connected with the protection afforded under Paragraph 1.

In other words, the intent of the directive was to maintain the privacy protections while enabling commerce. Other countries have adopted laws like the European Union, particularly to establish "adequate protection" for transborder flows with EU member states.

2000 EU Commission Decision 2000/520/EC (EU-US Safe Harbor)

The Data Protection Directive (95/46/EC) required the transfer of personal data to countries that lacked the adequate data protection to be forbidden. The United States was one of those countries determined by the EU to not have adequate privacy laws. To facilitate commerce between the United States and the European Union member states, the U.S. Department of Commerce worked with the European Commission to develop a "safe harbor" framework, whereby companies desiring to transfer personal data would agree to fair trade practices and certify to the U.S. Government their compliance on an annual basis. Two regulatory agencies, the FTC and the Department of Transportation agreed to facilitate this process. A set of principles were developed, modeling fair information practices such as those articulated within the Data Protection Directive including notice, choice, onward transfer, security, data integrity, access, and enforcement. The Department of Commerce maintained a listing of the companies certifying to safe harbor on their website.

2016 EU-US Privacy Shield Framework

The European Court of Justice declared the safe harbor principles as not being adequate for the protection of the information in October 2015. This decision resulted in declaring the US-EU Safe Harbor Framework as an invalid mechanism for satisfying the data protection requirements of the 95/46/EC Data Protection Directive. At the time, more than 4,400 US companies depended upon the Safe Harbor Framework to transfer information between the countries.

The case against Safe Harbor started when Max Schrems filed a complaint in 2013 with the Irish Data Protection Authority stating that his information in Facebook was being transferred to the United States and was not adequately protected. Information was also resident on Facebook's European servers; however, they were not the focus of the complaint. The complaint was lodged after knowledge about surveillance information captured by the U.S. National Security Agency was disclosed by Systems Administrator Edward Snowden. The reason for the ruling against Safe Harbor was that the agreement places "national security, public interest, or law enforcement requirements" over the privacy principles. This was deemed to conflict with the fundamental human rights of persons the European law was predicated on.

To resolve this logjam that could have been very detrimental to international trade, the U.S. Department of Commerce and the European Commission worked together in early 2016 to create a replacement for the EU-US Safe Harbor Framework. Since the United States was deemed to not have adequate privacy practices, primarily due to the government being able to access the information, controls beyond the principles stated in the original EU-US Safe Harbor Framework needed to be strengthened. On July 12, 2016, the new framework entitled the "EU-U.S. Privacy Shield Framework" was announced as the replacement for the EU-U.S. Safe Harbor Framework as an agreed upon, legal mechanism available for transferring personal data from the European Union to the United States. These new certifications started to be accepted on August 1, 2016, and the Safe Harbor certifications ceased being accepted as of October 31, 2016. On January 12, 2017, the Swiss Government announced a similar framework, the U.S.-Swiss Safe Harbor, for the transfer of information between Switzerland and the United States.

The key enhancements of the Privacy Shield over the Safe Harbor Framework were to address the concern over lack of oversight and transparency by implementing:

1. *EU Individual Rights and Legal Remedies.* Individuals may bring a complaint to the company, and the company has 45 days to respond. The individual may also submit a complaint to the Data Protection Authority in the EU. The FTC will also provide vigorous enforcement of the new framework.
2. *Program Oversight and Cooperation with EU Data Protection Authorities.* Verify completeness of company self-certifications and work together with the EU authorities, as well as make assessments of the program.
3. *New Requirements for Participating Companies.* Privacy policies must state a commitment to the Privacy Shield principles, along with links on the website to a complaint submission form. They must also disclose any information provided in response to a lawful request by public authorities. Onward transfers to third parties must also include contractual provisions; information will be processed consistent with the consent and specified purposes provided by the individual; and the information will be provided the same level of protection as in the principles.
4. *Limitations and Safeguards on National Security and Law Enforcement Access to Data.* Multiple layers of constitutional, statutory, and policy safeguards applying to U.S. Intelligence, along with active oversight by all three branches of the government, have been communicated in writing to the EU Commission. Limits to access were also provided by the US. Department of Justice. An ombudsperson was committed to being made available through this process for EU citizens to an inquiry regarding U.S. signals intelligence practices.

The Article 29 Working Party is a nonbinding group made up of representatives from each of the EU data protection authorities from each member state, the European Data Protection Supervisor, and the European Commission. This group reviewed the proposals to come to the final resolution, as they have done with other areas where there is uncertainty in the direction. In the earlier review of the Privacy Shield, they noted several areas with needed to be addressed before the final approval, specifically (a) massive collection of personal data by the United States was not fully excluded, (b) independence of the ombudsperson, (c) lack of a data retention principle, (d) inconsistency in the terminology, (e) protection for onward data transfers, and (f) need for a simple process for EU citizen redress. The party also suggested that the EU-U.S. Privacy Shield be reviewed after the EU GDPR became effective in May 2018 to ensure the new higher level of protection is also reflected in the Privacy Shield.

2016 General Data Protection Regulation

The GDPR was approved by the EU Parliament in April 2016, with a compliance date of May 25, 2018. This represents the largest change to the prior Data Protection Directive (titled as Directive 95/45/EC on the protection of individuals with respect to the processing of personal data and on the free movement of such data) guiding information privacy efforts for European Union citizens almost a quarter century. The new regulation, which superseded the directive, gained much attention and will have reverberations for years to come in the 2020s just as the EU Data Directive of 1995/1998 impacted the privacy regulations adopted around the world. The GDPR, first draft proposed in January 2012, was created to provide a comprehensive reform of the EU data protection rules to strengthen the online privacy rights and bolster Europe's digital economy. This resulted in an expanded territorial reach as organizations established outside the EU offering goods and services to or monitoring individuals in the EU are required to comply with the GDPR and designate a representative in the EU. The focus is on protecting the personal data of the data subjects residing in the EU, no matter where the controller or processor is located.

The prior privacy protection in the European Union was in the form of a directive vs. a regulation, meaning that each of the individual member states of the European Union was required to achieve a result by a specified date, but each of the 28 member states was free to decide the mechanism by which they would implement a solution. This created a variation between the member states interpretation and enforcement of the directive. An EU Regulation, on the other hand, as in the case of GDPR, is immediately applicable and enforceable by law. The member states can issue national laws to support the regulation and assign national authorities to administer the law; however, the law is in force without the passage of any additional laws in each member state.

Penalties of up to 4% of global annual turnover (revenue) or 20 million Euro, whichever is greater, can also be imposed on both controllers and data processors (previously not deemed directly liable under the prior directive, as the controller was primarily responsible per the directive).

Consent requirements were also modified, requiring clear consent for processing of personal data, in intelligible terms, and must have an affirmative response. Due to the GDPR regulation, many firms offering online services provided splash pages after the GDPR compliance date such as requesting "consent to set cookies on your device to use your search, location, and browsing data to understand your interests and personalize and measure ads on our products, and partner's products." If the affirmative "ok button" was not selected, the vendor denied access to the site or apps. It must also be easy to withdraw consent as well. Parental consent is also required for processing personal data for children under 16.

The law also includes the right to be forgotten and erased from records, as specified in Article 17 entitled "right to erasure." The data subject has the right to have their data deleted "without undue delay" where the data is no longer necessary for the purposes for which they were collected or processed, consent is withdrawn by the data subject or data subject objects to processing, the personal data was not lawfully processed, or the data was required to be erased for the controller to comply with a legal obligation. There are some exceptions to the right, such as excising the right of freedom of expression and information, handling of legal claims, reasons of public interest, and archiving for public interest, scientific or historical statistical and research purposes.

Google refused to remove from their search engine the past criminal conviction of an unnamed businessman conspiring to intercept communications over 10 years ago, whereby he spent 6 months in jail. His argument was that the information was no longer relevant. Google's argument was that the information was in the public interest; however, the U.K. High Court in 2018 overturned the lower court ruling and Google indicated that it would accept the ruling. The right to be forgotten was a legal precedent made by the European Union Court of Justice in May 2014 when Spaniard Mario Costeja Gonzalez requested Google remove information about his financial history. Mr. Gonzalez had run into some financial difficulties in 1998 and put his property up for auction, which was covered in the newspapers at the time. When people would search for his name, the stories about his financial difficulties would come up and he viewed them as damaging his reputation. The "right to be forgotten" has been codified into the GDPR. This does not mean that all information can be removed from newspapers upon request, as there are provisions and exclusions in the regulation which boil down to the information that can be removed if the impact on an individual's privacy is greater than the public's right to know it. The Google search engine cases are also good examples of the reach of GDPR, where the location of the servers (in Mr. Gonzalez's case, they were in the United States) is not viewed as an appropriate defense when protecting the privacy rights of EU citizens.

Where the controller has made the data public and is obliged to remove the data, the controller may remove the data, "taking account of available technology and the cost of implementation, shall take reasonable steps, including technical measures to inform data controllers which are processing the personal data that the data subject has requested the erasure by such controllers of any links to, or copy or replication of, those personal data." The assessment of what "reasonable steps" are in this context will most certainly be an area of debate. Is it reasonable that the organization know who and when they have provided the information to all other parties? The requirement as stated is to only "inform," but what is reasonable to ensure they received the message? Is it reasonable that all these parties be contacted? What is considered "undue delay?" Is it reasonable to expect confirmation and tracking of the "deletion" by the other parties which received the data, or will that be deemed unreasonable to expect this extra expense? Initial investigations will hopefully bring clarity. One thing is clear for the CISO and CPO, data retention becomes a larger issue than ever before, as the information is not to be retained longer than necessary "in relation to the purposes for which they are collected or otherwise processed," consistent with the purpose limitation principle ("data minimization"). The data subject may also request a copy of his information (Article 20) in a portable (common use and machine-readable) format.

Privacy by Design (PbD) principles have been built into GDPR, as specified by Article 25, "Data Protection by Design and by default." The article states, "The controller shall implement appropriate technical and organizational measures for ensuring that, *by default*, only personal data which are necessary for each specific purpose of the processing are processed." For the CISO, this provides another impetus for integrating security into the systems development life cycle for all applications processing personal data and extending these practices to critical applications at a minimum. Tracking by application of how the application implemented PbD principles should be retained and audited.

Controllers are required to report a data breach within 72 hours unless the data breach can be shown to have a low risk to an individual's rights. In supporting vendor risk management practices, the data controller must ensure they have contracts in place with the data processors. The data processors can be held directly liable for the security of personal data.

Data Protection Officers (DPOs) are required for companies that will be processing high volumes of personal data or "require regular and systematic monitoring of data subjects on a large scale" as articulated in Article 37. The DPO may be contracted and needs to be identified to the Data Protection Authority. International data transfers involve the concepts of Binding Corporate Rules, Model Contract Clauses, adherence to EU-US Privacy Shield, and ensuring an adequate level of protection.

The energy level of organizations implementing GDPR was very high, like implementing the HIPAA Privacy and Security Rules to protect sensitive personal data. And if the HIPAA compliance history of securing sensitive health information is any guide, with audits showing inadequate compliance 15 years after the implementation date (as detailed in the *Risk Management* chapter), along with the many privacy provisions in the EU Data Directive almost 25 years ago that are "not new" in GDPR, it is likely that there will be organizations not in compliance for several years. These organizations are risking the additional expense of large fines and reputation exposure in the event of a breach. What *is different* in today's world from when those earlier regulations were passed is the ability of the regulators to assess substantial fines, a lack of patience for those organizations not securing personal information, increased organizational and board visibility to cybersecurity risk, and a propensity for regulators to assess the fines.

GDPR prompted changes in business practices to ensure consent was obtained, data was retained for a reasonable amount of time, DPOs were recruited/retained as necessary, right to erasure could be supported, data could be reproduced in a machine-readable data format, and incidents could be responded to quickly. Those organizations not aware of where the personal data was being stored had much extra work to discover and map the flows of this information.

2018 California Consumer Privacy Act (CCPA)

California Governor Jerry Brown signed Assembly Bill No. 375 into law on June 28, 2018 to provide strong privacy protections that are being compared to the comprehensive European Union General Data Protection Regulation for its overarching provisions. As a result, legislators have since introduced amendments to the bill, such as 45 amendments passed by Senate Bill 1121 on August 31, 2018. The refinement of this law and challenges to the laws can be expected prior to the effective date of January 1, 2020. One area of concern is the possibility of ending up with 50 state privacy laws (vs 1 Federal law), similar to the data breach laws started by the introduction of the California data breach notification law (S.B. 1386) which became effective on July 1, 2003 and have now been enacted in all 50 states, along with the District of Columbia, Guam, Puerto Rico, and the Virgin Islands.

The law provides consumers several privacy rights, including the right to know the categories of information a business collects about a consumer, right to request deletion of information collected, and the right to instruct companies, or "opt out," to not sell their information to third parties. The consumer retains the right to receive equal service and pricing from a business, even if they exercise these privacy rights. To make these requests consumer-friendly, the business must provide a website link and a toll-free number to submit requests for disclosure and businesses have 45 days to satisfy the requests free of charge. There are extensions and exceptions for the requests; however, the message is clear that the privacy rights for the information collected are very consumer-oriented.

This represents another regulation focusing on the privacy rights of the individual, amplifying the need for businesses to understand what information is being collected, the purpose of the collection, and disposing the information when no longer necessary. The definition of "personal information" has also been broadened, with a listing in the law of personal information examples which may constitute personal information if "it identifies, relates to, describes, is capable of being associated with, or could be reasonably linked, directly or indirectly, with a particular consumer or household." As such, IP addresses, purchasing histories, and geolocation data may no longer be regarded as personal data if they cannot be directly linked to a specific consumer or household. Individuals also have a private right of action if a) there was a data security breach involving unredacted or unencrypted personal information and b) the breach was caused by a company's failure to maintain reasonable security measures. The company has a right to cure the alleged violation within 30 days and notifies the consumer in writing that the situation was corrected, and no further violations will occur.

Differences in Law Approach

Privacy laws developed by different countries have varied in their approach and focus on information privacy. While it has been noted in the discussions that the United States has not had "adequate privacy" with respect to the Data Protection Directive of the European Union with respect to the protection of personal data, this does not mean that there are not laws within the United States that are concerned with the privacy of information. I believe much of this thinking stemmed from the lack of a "comprehensive law" covering all personal data within the United States vs. the existence of a directive within the European Union. As seen above, even in the European Union, there were differences between the countries as to how the privacy laws were created and enforced from the directive as there was not a common unifying regulation (until GDPR) with enforcement capabilities. This is not to suggest that one countries laws are weaker than another's; rather, it is important to understand how the laws were created.

Comprehensive Privacy Law

The EU Directive and the GDPR are examples of comprehensive legislations whereby there is a unified set of policies that are governed by a single system of authority. Under the directive, each of the EU member states was required to create privacy laws and designate a Data Protection Authority to ensure the practices were carried out. Under the GDPR, there too is a set of regulations and enforcement mechanisms and a process for the countries to cooperate with each other to govern the privacy. The scope is all personal information and crosses all industries. This is an example of comprehensive legislation.

Sectoral-Based Privacy Law

The U.S. privacy laws were not created as one law but grew out of the need for different areas of government and private enterprise to protect information at different times. Different industries had different legal requirements and different economic sectors. The U.S. approach is referred to as a "sectoral"-based approach as the laws were created across health-care, government, financial, and other sectors specific to the needs of those areas. For example, the HIPAA introduced privacy for health-care records as the concern over the computerization and aggregation of this information was thought to be a threat to individual privacy. The Gramm–Leach–Bliley Act of 1999 focused on the collection of financial records and promoted the proper permissible use and safeguards to ensure the privacy of financial information was supported. The previously mentioned Privacy Act of 1974 was targeted at federal agencies to ensure the safeguarding of records within their care (note that this act applied to the protection of government held Medicare and Medicaid records, health information for the elderly and indigent, many years prior to the passage of specific health-care record legislation provided by HIPAA).

One key difference between the European legal briefs and the U.S. interpretation is that the U.S. Constitution does not explicitly provide a right to privacy. Recall that this differs from the privacy belief granting privacy as a "fundamental human right." It was not until 1890 with Brandeis and Warren that privacy was the right to be free from intrusion.

Co-regulatory Privacy Law

The co-regulatory approach relies on the industry within the different sectors to promulgate the specific standards and procedures to reflect the national privacy principles. Australia has created this type of environment by providing 13 principles addressing the following:

1. Open and transparent management of personal information
2. Anonymity and pseudonymity
3. Collection of solicited personal information
4. Dealing with unsolicited personal information
5. Notification of the collection of personal information
6. Use or disclosure of personal information
7. Direct marketing
8. Cross-border disclosure of personal information
9. Adoption, use, or disclosure of government-related identifiers
10. Quality of personal information
11. Security of personal information
12. Access to personal information
13. Correction of personal information.

There are also other nuances between how countries establish their laws. Canada, for example, is like the European model through the implementation of the Personal Information Protection and Electronic Documents Act of 2000. The law has goals of instilling confidence in electronic commerce and to establish a common playing field for all businesses. Canada also has variances of privacy laws according to the territory or province. In this regard, the laws may be viewed as sectoral as well.

Key Components for Data Protection

To adequately protect the data of an organization, several key components come into play as concepts to achieve this goal.

Data Discovery (Where Is the Data?)

The typical answer to this question when first asked is "I don't know" or "everywhere!" Even those organizations that have structured data stores and databases where the main customer information is held may think they know where all the information is stored and could point to a data store containing the "master record" for the information. However, without an explicit approach to data protection, the real location of this information is likely to be identified as only of a subset of where the real information is stored.

Documents (Word, Excel, PowerPoint)

How much information is extracted from the master databases or files and placed in Microsoft Excel files to be distributed across the organization? Information retained in databases is often difficult to access, as requests need to be processed by the access management team, resulting in minimally a one- to two-day delay in many organizations. Even if the access is promptly granted through a web interface, accessing the information in a database through the structured screens or via writing SQL queries is beyond the general skill level for most users. Most users within a company will have familiarity at a basic level with Excel, and for this reason, this has become a primary mechanism for exchanging information. Once information is extracted into this format, the security controls once in place are now removed unless the end user has taken steps to secure the individual files with passwords, encryption, and so forth. In the fast pace of organizations today, this step is often missed as end users are busy trying to complete their jobs and after all, they are exchanging the files with people with only a need to know, right? Unfortunately, these files typically end up on public internal company servers with limited protections implemented. Departments such as human resources (HR), finance, and legal may implement protections at a department level, or the proactive organizations at a more granular folder/file level; however, this is typically the extent of the departments that secure their information from others.

PCs, Laptops, Backups

The corporate security policy may state "No information may be stored on personal computers, all information must be stored on corporate servers." This would be a great policy—if only it was followed consistently by users. The policy usually gets adjusted or people are given a pass if they "temporarily need the information on the laptops." This is a valid request, considering the auditor working on some files on the train with limited or no Wi-Fi capability trying to finish his reports before the closing meeting or the business executive traveling by airplane for 8 hours overseas wanting to access their files with spotty, unreliable satellite Wi-Fi-access. If the organization does not provide a secure way to access the files, they will find a way that may be less secure. These policies allowing exceptions for PC or laptop storage, without thinking about the types of information that will be stored on the devices, add to the risk of not protecting critical data. When a laptop is lost, it becomes very difficult to know what was on the device other than by the user's recollection of what information may have been on the device. One method to ascertain this is through the examination of the PC backup logs, as they record the files and changes that were on the device—assuming the organization had a strategy to back up the PCs. Knowledge of the full contents is usually unknown by the user.

Few organizations teach the end users about where the best place to store information may be. Users may not recognize that document on their device was sitting in the temporary directory or that the file was not really deleted on the hard drive, but rather marked for deletion.

SharePoint/Intranet

Companies need to be able to share information across departments to accomplish their mission. Imagine the extreme where information within a department was not shared outside of the department—this would result in a siloed approach to business, where one department would not be able to know what was going on in another department. This would create large problems in communication across the company. For example, how effective would a security awareness program be if there was not the ability to share policies, procedures, standards, guidelines, news articles, and contact information for the rest of the organization? What if this content was limited only to the information security team? We can all agree that not sharing this information (except for the sensitive security detailed documents) would not be very effective.

SharePoint and sharing by a common intranet provide the company with the ability to broadly communicate information, and that is a great improvement from the prior generation of printed newsletters, institutional knowledge maintained by a few go-to people, and the occasional email or memo to communicate relevant information the organization needed to know. The SharePoint site or intranet becomes the "hub" for much corporate information and the reason why it is the home page for most people as they arrive to work. In the spirit of sharing, companies may have "gone too far" in what is shared. These intranet sites contain very capable search engines, like the Google search, whereby information is pulled from massive data stores and individuals may unintentionally have access to information they should not have. Since information to be useful needs to be found quickly, these powerful search engines default to returning as much information as possible, unless the information is specifically locked down. In the rush to make information immediately accessible outside of a department, these controls may not have been evaluated. For example, something as innocuous sounding as meeting minutes for a department may be posted to the department's intranet site for the department to share among themselves. However, the search engine will display the content of those minutes unless the files have been explicitly secured to only that department, as search engines are designed by default to return as much information as possible. Furthermore, unless there is clear guidance as to the level of detail that should be represented within the minutes with the note taker, embarrassing details of an employee discipline matter, salary discussion, or the divulging of an upcoming acquisition could be revealed.

Information that is shareable should be shared and encouraged. Unfortunately, the assessment for these sites usually comes after someone notices they have access to the information after it has been posted to the site, indicating a lack of policies and procedures regarding data protection.

Email Systems

Just as the information sprawls from the master files or databases to documents located on servers and intranet sites, information is passed from user to user across the internal and external email systems. Where did this file end up? How is the system/user receiving the information protecting it? As with the prior infrastructure discussion, how do we know that the platform the document is now stored has the appropriate infrastructure controls? This is what gives rise to the M&M candy analogy for how most organizations are protecting their information—hard on the outside and soft and chewy on the inside! Internally, we want information to flow quickly, and as such, we limit the number of controls on the individual files and want to "trust" our internal infrastructure. Externally, we do not have that luxury, as we do not have visibility into the security of external systems and must assume that they are insecure. This is the primary reason we encrypt files for external distribution—so we add Secure Socket Layer encryption and secure the files themselves by adding file-level encryption and distribute the keys through (preferably) another channel.

If the organization has not addressed data retention within the email system, imposed limits on the amount of storage available per user, or developed an archival strategy—excessive emails are likely stored within the email system. This can cause issues for e-discovery whereby large amounts of email would unnecessarily need to be presented to the court, potentially creating a disadvantage in the cost to acquire and analyze the information. As in the well-known case of a Sony Pictures breach (2014), embarrassing emails were revealed because of the breach causing reputational harm to the company.

Email systems used to be classified as a noncritical resource in business continuity/disaster recovery plans. Today, since email is still the primary means of communication within and externally by many organizations, the system and the contained information become critical information.

USB Drives

The inexpensive nature of USB drives makes retaining a backup of information easier than ever before. With capacities in recent years of 256 GB for thumb drives and multi-terabyte storage capacities for portable hard drives becoming the norm, company users are taking multiple backups (a good thing for disaster recovery) and storing copies of sensitive company confidential information (a bad thing for data proliferation). While some companies have resorted to blocking USB storage from their work computer systems, even those blocking these USB ports generally have an exception process for users needing to exchange information externally or create external presentations. In these cases, the focus tends to be more on "protecting the information" from external viewing vs. managing the location of the information. In other words, while an organization may put in protection mechanisms, there is a strong likelihood that data flow diagrams of where the information is resident do not exist. In other words, the USB drive becomes just another infrastructure component of the company with no visibility as to what type of information is stored on the device. This could be mitigated somewhat with data loss prevention to track the writing of sensitive information. Even at this level, this becomes a detective control vs. an organization proactively understanding why external storage needs to be used for a piece of information used in a business process.

Cloud Storage

Cloud storage could be viewed as the evolution of USB drives. USB drives were the evolution of CDs/DVDs, which were the evolution of floppy disks. The only real difference was the amount of storage—the effect was the same, passing information through "sneaker-net." This worked well when information was being exchanged in a local office or time expectations permitted mailing of the disks; however, in today's instant gratification world of same-day shipping and instant web transactions, the USB is rapidly becoming an outdated medium. The replacement technology that meets the need to communicate between disparate parties across the Internet is cloud storage. The enhanced capabilities of cloud storage provide better access control to the information, much like a "big database in the sky." The advantage of this platform with respect to data protection is that controls may be placed on the information to protect it while worrying less about losing or misplacing the actual (USB) device containing sensitive information.

The downside of this medium is that companies are typically surprised when a vendor offers to scan the environment to determine how many applications are being used outside of the "expected number of IT applications," only to find files are being stored in many external applications using cloud storage the organization is unaware of or has no visibility into.

Mobile Devices

More and more transactions are processed through mobile applications today as the platform of choice. Company user's login is through the mobile devices to portals, SharePoint sites, time and expense applications, cloud storage, Microsoft/Google office productivity applications, email, etc. With the Internet becoming ubiquitous, the model of "data access anywhere, anytime" can become a reality. Some of these applications provide access to other databases/files, while others retain access to information. What information is contained within the application? What information is contained on the device? How is this information being protected? Aside from the infrastructure of the mobile device—the pertinent question is, "What data flowing to the device and being retained on the device needs to be protected?" Is this information represented in a data inventory or data flow diagram? If the device is lost, is the information still protected (encrypted) or can it be wiped (eliminated)?

Storage Space Is Cheap

With all the places to store information and the ease by which we can drag/drop, cut/paste, and move information from one place to another, it should be no surprise that our information exists in more places than we initially think within our companies. Additionally, since storage has become very inexpensive, organizations have been less sensitive about the costs of the storage and in some cases have decided that buying more storage is cheaper than having employees spend extra time organizing and deleting their files. This may be true from an operational sense in the short term; however, as the information grows and backups increase in size, more information must be searched, a greater cost appears—*more information is at risk of disclosure*, it also becomes more difficult to comply with the industry regulations, as the premise of these regulations is that there is control over the information entrusted to the company.

WILLIAM MIAOULIS: DO YOU KNOW WHERE YOUR DATA IS?

CISO, *Auburn University*

Finding the crown jewels—Do you know where your data is? Data, data, everywhere. Data is everywhere, is it on home computers, in email, thumb drives, cloud storage, department drives, and paper. Do you know where your confidential data is located? How do we slow the spread of our confidential data? Below, we examine a couple of examples based on actual events, then offer some practical solutions.

- Jane worked at a Major Medical Center and wanted to work over the weekend, so she downloaded the file to a non-encrypted thumb drive. Her daughter took that thumb drive to school on Monday. It contained PHI which was seen by many at the school.
- John emailed confidential information to himself, then worked on the file on his home computer, and then emailed it back to his work email. Two weeks later, his home was broken into and his computer was stolen.
- James received a phishing email and gave up his credential to a bad actor. The bad actor, logged into the employee portal, changed James' bank deposit information, logged into James' email, and deleted the notice from HR. The bad actor would have access to all of James information in his email account, and in this case, an email contained numerous examples of SSN. In all three cases, the organization may have a reportable breach. The standard security controls that we have always used would have helped us in each of these situations.
- Jane and John could have been trained to use more secure methods of file storage.
- James could have been trained not to fall for phishing emails and not to store SSN in an email.
- The organization could have provided easily accessible secure locations to access the information.
- The organization could also have utilized data loss prevention software that looks for confidential information such as PHI, credit card numbers, social security numbers, and driver license numbers.
- The organization can install multifactor authentication to restrict access to data. We must remember the basics, know where your data is located, and then protect it.

Data Classification (What Is the Data?)

All data is not created equal; some have a higher-level risk attached to the information. The data is classified into normally three to four categories of information to specify how the information should be handled. The categories usually involve terminologies such as restricted, sensitive, or confidential data, private or company internal data, and public data. Some organizations will have two categories of restricted or sensitive data to denote the differences between say health or financial information requiring a higher level of protection and company confidential information. One approach is to regard all information processed or controlled as private data subject to baseline protection, unless it is specifically denoted as highly sensitive or sensitive information. In this manner, a thought process to deliberately identify the higher level of risk has been carried out, or the information was deliberately viewed as available for public consumption.

Information follows a life cycle and may have different classifications depending upon who the recipient of the information is. For example, information requested from a government entity through the Freedom of Information Act (FOIA), such as the high-level of an audit report, medical record for insurance purposes, or a criminal report, can be made available to the requesting entity by following a process. This information may be classified as sensitive information, even though it is subsequently available to the public by completing a request. A mistake would be to classify this information as "public" under the pretense that the public can "obtain the information anyway." Because there is a process of law that must be followed with records of the request and information delivered, this information is not public.

Why is it important to classify information? Simply stated, the costs are too high to protect all information to the same level. Protecting the spreadsheet containing the company's diversity program events would not rise to the same level as protecting an individual's health record. However, each organization needs to evaluate the risk of the information disclosure, destruction, or modification to the organization. For example, the log of the company upcoming diversity efforts could be classified as private/confidential in the event the company was targeted by activist groups perceiving them to have less than stellar records in promoting minorities or maintaining a low percentage of women in leadership positions. Knowledge of the timing of these events could be targeted with demonstrations representing a reputation risk to the company. The point here is that even those files that may seem on the surface to not contain confidential information should be reviewed on a periodic basis as the risks may have increased and changed the data classification. For most of the data within the organization, the challenge is not the changing classification of the information, but rather agreeing on the correct classification and implementing the appropriate security controls for the data classification.

Data stewards or data owners are charged with the responsibility to maintain the correct classification of the information, as well as ensure that the information is being handled across the business appropriately. This may include who has access to the information, how the information is protected, and a periodic recertification that access to the information is still required by each business area.

Data Protection (How Is the Data Secured?)

The answer will be different depending on the intersection of the two items above (what is the data and where is it stored). In other words, the data classification of the information and the application/technical platform containing the information will drive the level of protection afforded to the information requiring protection. A simple matrix can be created showing the classification on one axis and the technique to protect the information on the other axis and can guide the level of protection necessary. Additionally, the specific technical tools by platform could be noted to achieve the level of protection desired, forming a three-dimensional cube. (This could be a four-dimensional representation of data classification, method, application/platform, and tool alternatives; however, this level of complication is not necessary.)

If the security controls on one platform do not rise to the level the information is classified, then there is a risk at this point in the system. The system is only as good as the weakest point. Information encrypted while residing within the database system of record is not sufficiently encrypted if exported to a spreadsheet without encryption controls and password protection. By assigning different technologies to the methods of protection, these can subsequently be reused when other data types are added to the organization. In this manner, a well thought-out data classification strategy, combined with development of standards for data protection, can facilitate rapid deployment of secure solutions for new initiatives. This may require a substantial initial investment to identify all the information, where it is located, and how it is/is not being protected; however, the long-term ramp-up time should be considerably less.

MICHAEL BOUCHER: DATA PROTECTION: SECURITY INTELLECTUAL PROPERTY

Sr. Director, Information Risk Management, FTD

A project leader can typically expect to meet resistance due to a variety of reasons, including budget constraints, corporate culture, or lack of executive support.

When I was a manager at an international manufacturing company, I encountered many of these barriers when I was starting a data protection project. After being at the company for several months, I discovered that a large amount of company IP was not properly secured. This IP was hundreds of thousands of engineering drawings that were in .pdf and .dwg file formats. The hundreds of authorized users had full access to the files and could download them to their local machine without any record or log of the download. I began researching a better way to protect this information. I met with members of the engineering staff and management team to better understand who used the data and how it was used. They also confided that they had serious concerns about the security of the information and believed that former employees had taken sensitive information with them when they had left the company. I also met with the company's Chief IP Counsel to get his input about the issue. He agreed that the IP information was not adequately secured and confirmed that the company believed that its information was being used by one of our competitors. Armed with this information, we began to research security tools that would better improve the security controls for the company IP. After several months of research and review of technology tools, a tool was selected. When we proposed the purchase of the preferred tool to the CIO, he was hesitant to move forward, even though he had been informed of the project. He requestioned if the company really needed to bring in a "big brother" monitoring tool and how would it be funded. After several weeks, the Chief IP Counsel met with the CIO to convince him to move forward with the project. This tool became the foundation for a data protection program that included securing data for a joint venture with a company in China. Establishing a good relationship and building support with the engineering and legal teams were the key factors in getting the CIO to fund the project.

Data Flow (Relating Data to Other Information)

Understanding how the data flows throughout the system enables the opportunity not only to ensure that security is being maintained end-to-end, but also to enable the improvement of business processes. The process of documenting data flows can highlight inefficient processes, such as manual hand-offs to email systems and manual preparation of Word documents vs. leveraging the system to create the information. Gaps in access control may also be identified, whereby users are requesting access through decentralized means and the tracking of access is insecure (i.e., an application's logon and password information stored unprotected on a data owner's PC).

There may also be different understandings between how the user uses the technology and the capabilities of the application. For example, an application to support the recruiting function of an organization may restrict the ability to input social security numbers or driver's license numbers, resulting in the local recruiter setting up a local database to house this information outside of the application. The mapping of this business process to the application would identify this gap area and highlight the information stored outside of the protected application. The issue may be that the application delivered was too complex for the users, the training was deficient, or the appropriate functionality was missed in the design and development of the application.

Data Protection Regulatory Compliance

Data protection regulatory compliance could also be noted as the "why" for data protection; however, we need to be cautious that this is not the only reason we are protecting the information. As noted earlier, we have a fiduciary responsibility to protect the information entrusted to us. Not all companies unfortunately are as altruistic to invest money to do the right thing, so as a result, regulations are created to promote the compliance and move these organizations in the proper direction.

BEN ROTHKE: HOW TO ENSURE GDPR COMPLIANCE WITHOUT LOSING YOUR MIND

Principal Security Consultant, Nettitude Group

With the EU GDPR implementation date of May 25, 2018, behind us, firms are starting to catch their breath. Make no mistake, GDPR is the biggest data protection regulation ever enacted.

Many are now seeing that GDPR is not as prescriptive as they would have wanted. While there has been a lot of spending on data security hardware and software tools. Firms are waking up to the realization that the tools will not help much if they have not created the needed processes, policies, and enforcement mechanisms associated with the life cycle of their in-scope data from its collection and creation, up to its destruction. And if they do not have a mapping of their data, they do not have much in way of compliance.

There were fears that EU regulators would swoop down after the implementation date and that auditing and fining noncompliant data controllers. With fines for noncompliance maxing out at €20 million or up to 4% of a firm's worldwide annual turnover; fears of GDPR-based bankruptcy were overblown. Nonetheless, warnings and reprimands from EU auditors are still nothing to sneeze at.

As to the fears of hyper-enforcement, that has not been the case. The reality is that organizations that can show good faith effort and project plans towards meeting the regulation, and how they are implementing effective data-handling processes, are generally in good shape.

The D in the GDPR is data and its data that drives everything. If you do not know exactly where all your personal data is, then it is impossible to be compliant. Data discovery via data mapping is an integral part of GDPR. Here is how you do it:

1. *Create a data inventory*—the record of all personally identifiable information (PII) you have must be created.
2. *Data discovery*—some of the methods include.
3. *Data determination*—ascertain why the data is being collected. If you do not have a business or legal need to, then stop collecting it.
4. Once you have determined the data you do not need, go back and delete it from all data storage locations.

GDPR changes the nature of data from an asset to a liability. If you minimize your data collection and storage, you minimize liability and risk. And that is what GDPR is all about.

OECD Guidelines—Eight Principles

The following eight principles do not specify how the actions are to be carried out or the format of the information (oral, electronic, paper), contributing to standing the test of more than 30 years before there were changes made. The principles apply to personal data in both public and private sectors that may pose a risk to the privacy and personal liberties of those to whom the data is about. The exceptions to the principles, for cases involving national sovereignty, national security, and public policy should be (1) as few as possible and (2) made known to the public. The principles should be regarded as minimum standards, and additional measures of protection may be added.

Collection Limitation Principle

There should be limits to the collection of personal data, and any such data should be obtained by lawful and fair means and, where appropriate, with the knowledge or consent of the data subject.

In many cities, video cameras are used by businesses and law enforcement to record movement. An example of complying with this principle would be to ensure that the data subject has knowledge by posting a sign communicating the video surveillance. A company collecting driver's license information, or fingerprint biometrics when someone is paying cash at a grocery store would be an example of excessive collection of personal data.

Data Quality Principle

Personal data should be relevant to the purposes for which they are to be used and, to the extent necessary for those purposes, should be accurate, complete, and kept up-to-date. If an organization maintains personal data on an individual, they have an ongoing responsibility to ensure the data is correct. Consider the case of a credit reporting agency that fails to keep records up-to-date or stores misinformation on subjects applying for credit, and then using that information to determine their credit worthiness. This would not be viewed as a fair practice on behalf of the consumer.

Purpose Specification Principle

The purposes for which personal data is collected should be specified not later than at the time of data collection and the subsequent use limited to the fulfillment of those purposes or such others as are not incompatible with those purposes and as are specified on each occasion of change of purpose.

Ever sign up for a product and then start receiving emails from companies that no business relationship existed prior? Or junk mail starts piling up in the snail mailbox? Information collected by companies must state the purposes for which they will be using the information. Some companies try to broaden the definition to include future business areas they may want to venture into. On April 2, 2013, the Article 29 Working Party promulgated an opinion to help clarify the meaning of the purpose limitation principle, indicating that such statements in the privacy notices indicating broad and vague purpose statements such as "improving user experience" or "marketing purposes" are not sufficient to rise to the standards of a "specified, explicit, and legitimate" processing requirement. To determine the acceptability of an acceptable purpose, the following four factors need to be taken into consideration:

■ The relationship between the purposes for data collection and the purposes for further processing
■ The context in which data have been collected and the reasonable expectations of the data subjects regarding further use of the data
■ The nature of the data and the impact of the further processing on the data subjects
■ The safeguards put in place by the data controller to ensure fair processing and prevent undue harm to the data subjects.

The Working Party also reviewed the impact of Big Data with respect to the purpose limitation. In the scenario where Big Data was being used to analyze trends and detect correlations in the information, the Working Party indicated that the data controller needed to be able to ensure technical and organizational safeguards for the information to ensure confidentiality of the information, as well as to provide functionally separate processing environments. In the scenario where the use of Big Data directly affects individuals such as conducting profiling using behavioral advertising, location-based advertising, and tracking digital research, opt-in consent would almost always be necessary. Furthermore, organizations need to provide data subjects with easy access to their profiles and disclose the decision criteria.

The purpose needs to be stated when the information is collected, at the point when individuals are providing their consent through opt-in or opt-out mechanisms.

Use Limitation Principle

Personal data should not be disclosed, made available, or otherwise used for purposes other than those specified in accordance with Paragraph 9 (in the Purpose Specification Principle section) except (1) with the consent of the data subject or (2) by the authority of law.

This principle works in concert with the purpose specification principle to ensure that the ongoing usage of the personal data is used for the purposes specified at collection, unless there has been a positive affirmation of consent by the individual or the information is needed and requested through the appropriate procedures by law enforcement.

Security Safeguards Principle

Personal data should be protected by reasonable security safeguards against such risks as loss or unauthorized access, destruction, use, modification, or disclosure of data.

The term "reasonable safeguards" is always open for debate, as it depends upon the state of technology, the state of the industry, and most importantly, what are other companies in the same industries doing to reduce the risk of disclosure. The considerations for leading an effective security program are the genesis for this book. This clause is the one clause, in the absence of any other industry-specific regulation, that widens the requirement for information security to *every organization collecting, processing, using, or storing personal data. In other words, this is the clause applicable to almost every organization requiring the implementation of appropriate administrative, technical, and operational safeguards.*

Openness Principle

There should be a general policy of openness about developments, practices, and policies with respect to personal data. Means should be readily available of establishing the existence and nature of personal data, and the main purposes of their use, as well as the identity and usual residence of the data controller.

This clause promotes transparency of the operations and where the information is being processed. Individuals have a right to know how their information is being used. The organization can make information publicly available, such as the posting of their privacy notices on the websites along with contact information for questions. Information should be made available in different formats for different audiences, such as policies and procedures online along with downloadable PDF files for users.

Individual Participation Principle

Individuals should have the right (1) to obtain from a data controller, or otherwise, confirmation of whether the data controller has data relating to them; (2) to have communicated to them, data relating to them:

    i. within a reasonable time;
   ii. at a charge, if any, that is not excessive;
  iii. in a reasonable manner; and
   iv. in a form that is readily intelligible to them;

(3) to be given reasons if a request made under subparagraphs (1) and (2) is denied, and to be able to challenge such denial; and (4) to challenge data relating to them and, if the challenge is successful to have the data erased, rectified, completed, or amended.

This principle allows the individual to see what information has been captured on their behalf and who had access to the information. Hospital environments control access to information through the logging of access via electronic medical record systems. The benefit of capturing this information electronically is tremendous, as all the individuals interacting with the patient can see the full medical situation with the patient. The downside may be that sometimes hundreds of people may be involved with a person's care—from the physicians, to the person reading and interpreting the charts, nurses, to the billing office. While each of these individuals most likely has a legitimate need to view this information, the patient has the right to understand what records have been accessed and retrieve these for a reasonable cost. Consider the case of a divorce where the ex-spouse still works at the health-care provider and the patient wants to ensure their privacy is still being protected—they have the right to request this information at a reasonable cost. Sometimes it may be difficult to determine who the records were disclosed to, or the costs may be excessive, in which case the data controller has the responsibility to provide the information on all individuals to whom the information may have been disclosed to.

Also, consider the case of a credit reporting agency where information is kept on the consumer. The consumer has a right to understand what information has been collected and be afforded the opportunity to modify information if the information was deemed inaccurate. Credit reports may be obtained from each of the major credit reporting agencies (Equifax, TransUnion, and Experian) once a year free of charge to review the information maintained by them and could challenge the information stored by providing contrary evidence.

Accountability Principle

A data controller should be accountable for complying with measures that give effect to the principles stated above. The data controller cannot abdicate their responsibilities for maintaining accountability for personal data throughout the data life cycle. They are responsible for all stages, including the collection, usage, disclosure, and transfer to third parties for processing. Many organizations will appoint a CPO to assume this role to guide the program and demonstrate the organization is taking privacy seriously. Policies and procedures also provide the data organization with the mechanism to carry out their accountability.

2013 OECD Guideline Modifications

The OECD guidelines were not changed for several decades, until 2013 in response to a document released entitled "2008 Seoul Declaration for the Future of the Internet Economy" articulating the need for revision due to changing technologies, market and user behavior, and the growing importance of digital identities. The environment where privacy principles worked in the past had changed significantly (note the 1980 principles predated the general population use of the Internet and the existence of the World Wide Web as we know it today, along with other technical advances, and predated the CISO role). Attributes such as the volume of information processed, used, and stored had increased; wider range of analytics providing insights; value of the information increased; threats to privacy increased; the number and variety of actors capable of putting privacy at risk changed; substantial changes in the complexity and frequency of interaction of personal data that individuals were expected to comprehend were all factors contributing to the need to revisit the guidelines.

As part of the revision, the OECD Guideline 2013 revision focused on risk management and global interoperability when considering privacy issues. New concepts were also introduced including the strategic importance of national privacy strategies, implementation of privacy management programs, data security breach notification, strengthening privacy enforcement, and defining what it means to be regarded as an accountable organization. For example, the OECD revision included specific guidance in the 2013 version to articulate how to implement accountability as follows: "A data controller should: (a) have in place a privacy management program that (i) gives effect to these guidelines for all personal data under its control; (ii) is tailored to the structure, scale, volume, and sensitivity of its operations; (iii) provides for appropriate safeguards based on privacy risk assessment; (iv) is integrated into its governance structure and establishes internal oversight mechanisms; (v) includes plans for responding to inquiries and incidents; (vi) is updated in light of ongoing monitoring and periodic assessment; (b) be prepared to demonstrate its privacy management program as appropriate, in particular at the request of a competent privacy enforcement authority or another entity responsible for promoting adherence to a code of conduct or similar arrangement giving binding effect to these guidelines; and (c) provides notice, as appropriate, to privacy enforcement authorities or other relevant authorities where there has been a significant security breach affecting personal data. Where the breach is likely to adversely affect data subjects, a data controller should notify affected data subjects. "This change permits measurement of whether or not the organization has acted in an accountable manner with respect to privacy."

Privacy Impact Assessments

Privacy impact assessments (PIAs) are made to analyze how PII is collected, used, shared, and maintained across systems. The purpose is to demonstrate that an organization's program managers and system owners have consciously designed and incorporated privacy protections throughout the program, and where there are gaps, these gaps are being addressed. These are documents required in the United States by the E-Government Act of 2002, passed to improve the management of Federal Government services and processes. Checklists are leveraged to ensure

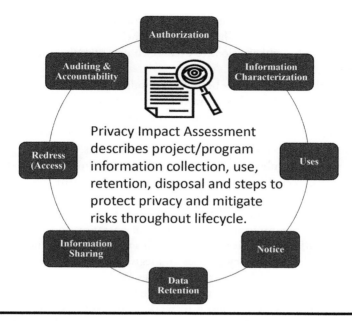

Privacy Impact Assessment describes project/program information collection, use, retention, disposal and steps to protect privacy and mitigate risks throughout lifecycle.

Figure 11.5   PIA coverage. (From U.S. Department of Homeland Security. *Privacy Impact Assessments.* **www.dhs.gov/privacy-impact-assessmentsAuthor.)**

systems are evaluated for privacy risks, and the relevant information is posted to government websites for full transparency (omitting sensitive information where appropriate). New systems require a PIA, as well as any systems incurring a major change, in addition to a periodic review. Legal and regulatory requirements are reviewed as well as the existing policies and practices. Figure 11.5 illustrates the coverage areas used in a privacy impact assessment.

Privacy by Design

PbD incorporates privacy into projects and data compliance activities keeping privacy in mind from the beginning of the effort. Too many times organizations are reactive and add on privacy in the back end, resulting in added unnecessary cost. The concept was developed in the 1990s by Ann Cavoukian, Ph.D., the Information and Privacy Commissioner in Ontario, Canada. The seven foundational principles were developed to address the impact of growing information systems and communication systems, recognizing that the privacy of information could not be adequately protected by implementing compliance activities focusing on regulatory frameworks alone. Instead, privacy needed to be a way of doing business if it was to succeed. Privacy by Design incorporates IT systems, accountable business practices, and physical design and network infrastructure. The principles may be applied to all types of information; however, particular care should be taken with sensitive information such as health-care and financial information. PbD principles provide a pathway for organizations to exercise control over the information under their control.

The PbD principles may have been first introduced several decades ago, so the focus was on IT systems and their infrastructures; however, the same principles can be applied today to Big Data, proliferation of mobile devices, Internet of Things (IoT), cloud storage across borders, etc., where there is a need to ensure privacy of the data contained within these applications and platforms.

The annual assembly of International Data Protection and Privacy Commissioners gathered in Jerusalem, Israel, in October 2010 and unanimously approved a resolution recognizing PbD as a fundamental component of privacy protection. What did this mean? The adoption of the principles should be encouraged as part of an organization's default mode of operation and invited the Data Protection Authorities and Privacy Commissions to promote the incorporation of the seven principles into privacy policies and legislation and encouraging research into furthering PbD. Based upon the references in the past few years of PbD in privacy guidance in different countries (including the EU GDPR), as well as being articulated by vendors seeking consulting work in the privacy space, it has become apparent that the principles are being woven into the privacy fabric. Subsequently, the U.S. FTC recognized PbD in 2012 as one of three practices for protecting online privacy, in addition to simplified choice for business and consumers (permitting users to make choices about their data at a relevant time and context), and greater transparency (pertaining to data collection and use). Additionally, the principles have been translated into over 31 languages.

The Seven Principles

These principles, when part of the general operation of a business, in other words, when thoughtfully evaluated when designing new products and services and conducting daily operations, should reduce the number of issues resulting from a lack of privacy and should also go a long way towards remaining compliant with the emerging regulations. The PbD foundational requirements are illustrated in Figure 11.6.

1. *Proactive not Reactive; Preventative not Remedial.* The PbD approach is characterized by proactive rather than reactive measures. It anticipates and prevents privacy invasive events before they happen. PbD does not wait for privacy risks to materialize, nor does it offer remedies for resolving privacy infractions once they have occurred—it aims to prevent them from occurring. In short, PbD comes before-the-fact, not after.
2. *Privacy as the Default Setting.* We can all be certain of one thing—the default rules! PbD seeks to deliver the maximum degree of privacy by ensuring that personal data are automatically protected in any given IT system or business

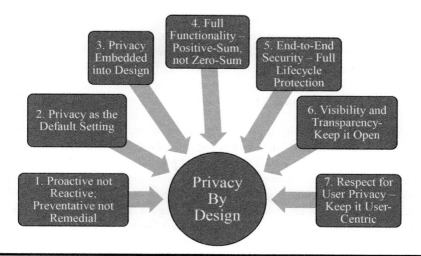

Figure 11.6 Privacy by design foundational requirements. (From Data from Cavoukian, A. *Privacy by Design: The 7 Foundational Principles.* www.ryerson.ca/content/dam/pbdce/seven-foundational-principles/The-7-Foundational-Principles.pdf.)

practice. If an individual does nothing, their privacy still remains intact. No action is required on the part of the individual to protect their privacy—it is built into the system, by default.

3. *Privacy Embedded into Design.* PbD is embedded into the design and architecture of IT systems and business practices. It is not bolted on as an add-on, after the fact. The result is that privacy becomes an essential component of the core functionality being delivered. Privacy is integral to the system, without diminishing functionality.

4. *Full Functionality—Positive-Sum, Not Zero-Sum.* PbD seeks to accommodate all legitimate interests and objectives in a positive-sum win-win manner, not through a dated, zero-sum approach, where unnecessary trade-offs are made. PbD avoids the pretense of false dichotomies, such as privacy vs. security—demonstrating that it is possible to have both.

5. *End-to-End Security—Full Life Cycle Protection.* PbD, having been embedded into the system prior to the first element of information being collected, extends securely throughout the entire life cycle of the data involved—strong security measures are essential to privacy, from start to finish. This ensures that all data is securely retained, and then securely destroyed at the end of the process, in a timely fashion. Thus, PbD ensures cradle to grave, secure life cycle management of information, end-to-end.

6. *Visibility and Transparency—Keep It Open.* PbD seeks to assure all stakeholders that whatever the business practice or technology involved, it is in fact, operating according to the stated promises and objectives, subject to

independent verification. Its component parts and operations remain visible and transparent, to users and providers alike. Remember, trust but verify.

7. *Respect for User Privacy—Keep It User-Centric.* Above all, PbD requires architects and operators to protect the interests of the individual by offering such measures as strong privacy defaults, appropriate notice, and empowering user-friendly options. Keep it user-centric.

By embracing these principles, as more and more personal information is collected from our mobile devices, IoT devices residing in our homes and workplaces, connected together and aggregated, there is the increased possibility information will be sufficiently collected, used, and stored in a manner as designed. This should give a competitive advantage to those organizations building in the trust for privacy practices, as well as gaining some efficiencies by not requiring the bolt-on to existing processes. Many organizations today are scrambling to meet regulatory privacy requirements, as privacy controls were not designed into the applications sufficiently to begin with.

ANN CAVOUKIAN, PH.D.: LEAD WITH PRIVACY BY DESIGN AND GAIN A COMPETITIVE ADVANTAGE

Distinguished Expert-in-Residence, Ryerson University— Privacy by Design Centre of Excellence

We are witnessing massive technological changes in all things connected. The creation of digital information is accelerating and attaining near immortality on the Internet. We know the value of personal information has increased— that it is being sold to others for profit and for purposes not always known to the individual. Its value also makes it a target for attack vectors. The explosion of social media has revived the "end of privacy" chants. What I submit without question is that there is little evidence to change our view that privacy remains a valued social norm. Privacy relates to freedom of choice and personal control in the sphere of one's personal information—choices regarding what information you wish to share and, perhaps more important, the information you may not wish shared with others. What has changed, however, is the means by which personal information is now readily exchanged. I admit that these trends carry profound implications for privacy, but we cannot give up. We need to change the paradigm—PbD is becoming essential to preserving our privacy now, and well into the future. From a privacy perspective, Information and Communication Technologies start off as being neutral. What matters are the choices made in their design and use— technologies may be designed to be privacy-invasive or privacy-enhancing. The framework of "Privacy by Design," which I developed in the late 1990s, emphasizes the need to embed privacy, proactively, at the design stages of information technologies, architectures, and systems. It highlights respect for user privacy and the need to embed privacy as the default setting. It also preserves a commitment to functionality in a doubly-enabling "win-win" manner or positive-sum strategy. This approach transforms consumer privacy issues from a pure policy or compliance issue into a business imperative. Organizations that proactively embed privacy into the design of their operations will benefit in a number of sustainable ways from the resulting "privacy payoff." Gain a competitive advantage by leading with PbD.

Privacy and Social Media

The focus on information privacy has gained much traction in recent years in large part due to the increased use of social media where information once regarded as private is now shared with many other people. In the early days of social media, when information was posted online and shared with "friends," there was this implicit expectation the information was only shared with those friends. Facebook has more than 2 billion active monthly users, Twitter over 330 million, and Instagram over 500 million and growing. For the past decade, the Smartphone has become a staple in everyone's pocket, and as such, social media has become the application commonly used, outside of the camera application—to take pictures to post to social media! These photographs that are being taken have geo-tags telling the social media sites when posted where you have been and when. Advertisers use this information to target ads directly to the consumer. This has bred mistrust and the thinking that the social media sites must be listening in on the conversations through the microphone (denied by the social media sites), as the appearance of targeted ads makes it seem that way. The items users search for on their mobile devices, PCs, desktops are tracked by cookies and can help advertisers target ads. Therefore, a user may be searching for a product and then later sees banner ads for the same or similar product on their email webpages or may receive an email alerting the user to a sale at that store.

Most of us click the end-user agreements without much thought to the 57 pages of license agreement we just signed up for, which included providing the information to the social media site to sell and use for marketing purposes. At the point where a friend tells us of a cool app to download, we are thinking less about our privacy and more about the functionality of the app. After all, for every life problem today, there must be an app for that. We need the immediate gratification of getting the application up and running and are not going to take the time to read a long license agreement. Even if we were, odds are we would have to click the ACCEPT button anyway, or we could not install the application! This is clearly a David vs. Goliath situation that cannot be easily resolved at the end-user level—it is more of a take-it-or-leave-it proposition.

Privacy regulations require companies make their privacy policies publicly available to indicate how the information will be used. Researchers at Carnegie Mellon University decided to explore how much time it would take for the average user to read every privacy policy a user should read. The median length for a typical privacy policy was 2,514 words; combined with a standard reading rate of 250 words per minute, this came out to about 10 minutes to read each privacy policy. This number was derived by looking at the top 75 websites that would be most frequently visited. The researchers then came up with how many websites does the typical user access, and they estimated between 1,354 and 1,518 websites, estimating 1,462 privacy policies encountered in a year. This is not surprising since the amount of time spent on social media per lifetime is estimated at more than we spend on eating and drinking (5 years 4 months vs. 3 years 5 months) and is increasing with teenagers spending as much as 9 hours a day on social media. So, what did the privacy policy researchers find? If every Internet user was to read each privacy policy for every site accessed during the day, they would spend 76 work days at 8 hours a day to just read the privacy policies! Assuming all the users in the United States alone read all these privacy policies, this would result in 53.8 billion hours with a hypothetical opportunity cost of $781 billion, or greater than the gross domestic product of the State of Florida.

This exercise highlights the unrealistic expectation that people know what is really happening with their data. The issue is not new, as prior to the Internet posting of privacy policies on the websites, the notices were mailed to individual homes as part of a bank or credit statement or acknowledgment signed as part of a healthcare provider's admissions process.

What Privacy Permissions We Are Granting

Beyond the privacy notice providing a high-level description of how the information may be used, let us take a deeper dive into the terms and conditions for the largest social media site Facebook. Recall the early days of Facebook when the stock price was around $20 a share and people wondered how they would make money? (2018 Facebook price exceeded $180/share). With a 60% penetration across Internet users for their products, which include WhatsApp and Instagram, Facebook is expanding into more international markets for revenue. The advertising revenue growth is almost $10 billion (2017)—in one quarter alone—and expected to increase 40% year over year. How are these numbers possible? Why are companies willing to pay to advertise on this platform? The answer becomes clear when we look under the covers and examine what privacy rights to our data have been willingly (or unknowingly) provided to Facebook. Facebook is used here as an example of how privacy of our information is given away; however, the information we let Facebook know about us is not unique from other companies that we are accepting the privacy notices and terms and conditions before we install the application.

Here are the key components agreed to by the Facebooks terms and conditions in early 2018, prior to revisions of policy after the Facebook/Cambridge Analytica situation, whereby Facebook changed the privacy policies on April 19, 2018. However, the language may have changed, but the concerns over the level of information rapidly granted to social media platforms by users have not changed much. Since these products are free to the user, users are giving up a level of privacy for the ability of the platforms to use the information to market to the users.

1. *We Agreed at Sign-Up.* That is right, when we clicked the sign-up button to when first signing up for the account, in addition to providing our name, mobile number, or email address, a password, our birth date (to ensure the right user experience for our age according to Facebook), and whether or not we are male or female—we agreed to "accept our (Facebook's) terms and that you have read our Data Policy, including our cookie use." We also agreed to receive Short Message Service text notifications and can opt out at any time (however, it is up to us to determine how to opt out of the messages and act). We have agreed to these policies before we understand what Facebook is and how it is used.

2. *Terms Are Lengthy.* The terms page agreed to at sign-up is 3,517 words and contains links to other documents. Beyond the terms page, there is also the Data Policy (over 4,500 words with April 2018 revision), which is a series of online links to review to understand the privacy policy, in addition to the cookies use policy. It is unlikely that the average user will take the time to review each of these documents before engaging with the product. It is also unlikely that users will review the privacy policies after the product. However, these policies are available in the event they are needed.

3. *Nothing Discussed on This Social Media Site Is Private.* The terms and conditions explicitly state they may use "all of the information we receive about you" to serve ads that are more interesting and relevant to you. Information supplied at registration time, during the use of the account, or timeline posting may be used. Items are shared on Facebook as to the likes and dislikes as well as any interactions with advertisements, partners, and apps. Keywords from stories that are posted may be used along with "things we infer from your use of Facebook." In other words, anything that is explicitly stated or can be deduced from the use of Facebook is fair game.

4. *Information Stays on the Network after a Person Leaves.* Videos, pictures, and content that may have been shared with other users may remain on the site and visible according to the other individual's privacy policies long after you have left the building.

5. *Profiles May Be Sold to Advertisers.* Permission is granted in the terms and conditions to "use your name, profile picture, content, and information in

connection with commercial, sponsored, or related content (such as a brand you like) served or enhanced by us." In fact, no compensation is due to the profile's owner either for this information. In other words, by the mere liking of a product or mentioning the product in a positive way during a post, we have granted the use of our endorsement to the creator of the product. This is an interesting granting of rights, considering that Hollywood actors charge for using their likeness in a commercial to promote a product. Here, we have given that right away for free. One could argue that the intent of this language is to limit any lawsuits whereby an accidental association with a product is being made through a Facebook picture; however, the granting of rights is clear here. Users that are viewed as key influencers are being targeted by marketing companies in the hopes that their liking of a product will induce others to like and purchase the product.

6. *Other Website Activity and Apps Are Being Monitored.* Beyond monitoring, the pages that are liked on Facebook, other websites, and applications accessed while using Facebook are tracked. This provides a wealth of information to them about the user's activity. Some make references to the spy state referred to in George Orwell's 1949 book "1984" about a future surveillance whereby much of what we did was under the watch by a government entity. The book was talking about telescreens that were dual-purpose devices playing a stream of propaganda while at the same time recording everything that is going on. Today, we have those devices in our pockets, call it a mobile or cell phone. Since many Facebook users are accessing Facebook from the mobile device, along with other websites, in some respects, this "1984" forecast made 35 years earlier may have manifested itself. While not eluding here to the possibility of turning on or off the microphone for average consumers as posited in conspiracy theories, the reality is that we are providing this information to Facebook—willingly through accepting the Statement of Rights and Responsibilities and the associated policies. After concern over the impact of Russian Fake News distributed on Facebook to influence the 2016 U.S. presidential election, Google and Facebook were taking steps to mitigate the distribution of Fake News, including prioritization of friends and family posts ahead of news stories. As many as 126 million people may have seen Fake News stories published by Russian Operatives during the election. Mark Zuckerberg's, Facebook CEO, goal was to minimize the spread of false information while resisting the urge to become the arbiters of the truth. To this end, Facebook was advocating for alignment with other fact-checking organizations such as PolitiFact and Snopes to perform this type of activity.

7. *Social Media Companies Partner with Data Brokers.* Data brokers collect information on the online and in-store purchases by consumers to determine the actual resulting behavior of the consumer. In other words, did the fact that someone liked a product in social media contribute to an actual

purchase? Demographic information is also collected, aggregated among multiple data brokers, and shared to make potentially sensitive inferences according to a study by the FTC, with some of the items collected shown in Figure 11.7. Information is collected whenever a consumer posts information online, shops online, registers on websites, shops at stores, fills out warranty cards, and buys houses and other purchase activity. Data brokers collect data from disparate sources and aggregate information to show consumer behavior.

8. *Access Granted to Use Information in Research.* As part of the research clause, "for internal operations, including troubleshooting, data analysis, testing, research, and service improvement," we have granted this access. Experiments

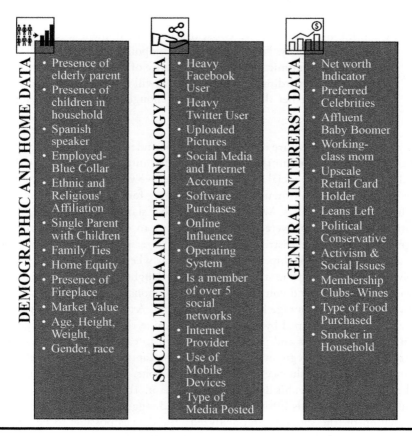

DEMOGRAPHIC AND HOME DATA
- Presence of elderly parent
- Presence of children in household
- Spanish speaker
- Employed-Blue Collar
- Ethnic and Religious' Affiliation
- Single Parent with Children
- Family Ties
- Home Equity
- Presence of Fireplace
- Market Value
- Age, Height, Weight,
- Gender, race

SOCIAL MEDIA AND TECHNOLOGY DATA
- Heavy Facebook User
- Heavy Twitter User
- Uploaded Pictures
- Social Media and Internet Accounts
- Software Purchases
- Online Influence
- Operating System
- Is a member of over 5 social networks
- Internet Provider
- Use of Mobile Devices
- Type of Media Posted

GENERAL INTERERST DATA
- Net worth Indicator
- Preferred Celebrities
- Affluent Baby Boomer
- Working-class mom
- Upscale Retail Card Holder
- Leans Left
- Political Conservative
- Activism & Social Issues
- Membership Clubs- Wines
- Type of Food Purchased
- Smoker in Household

Figure 11.7 Information collected and shared by data brokers. (From Federal Trade Commission. Data Brokers: A call for Transparency and Accountability, 2014, www.ftc.gov/system/files/documents/reports/data-brokers-call-transparency-accountability-report-federal-trade-commission-may-2014/140527databrokerreport.pdf.)

of whether good news or negative news impacted users' emotions positively or negatively for 700,000 people as research subjects and whether these emotions were spread across social networks were conducted, to which Facebook later apologized for the study. However, we have granted this right for research to be conducted, beginning in 2012.

9. *Government Access Is Granted.* The terms provide for turning over information to law enforcement relating to criminal cases, given that the legal request meets their standard of legal sufficiency and is not overly broad or vague. National security requests are another category where information will be provided.

10. *Amendments May Be Made at Any Time.* Changes to the policy are posted on a site governance page 7 days prior to the change-taking effect, whereby users may comment on the amendment. However, in the original terms accepted, by continuing the use of Facebook, this becomes implied acceptance of any changes to the policy. From a practical standpoint, this is more efficient for Facebook to communicate and get acceptance of the changes. As changes in the regulations regarding consent emerge, it will be interesting to see the test of time as to whether this implies strong enough consent for a change that may be instituted.

One could argue that we are in the beginning of understanding how privacy constructs should be applied in the digital age. Much information is captured about our daily lives through social media and the sites we visit. Credit card companies have been collecting information on user spending for years to target individuals through marketing efforts. Where is the line that should not be crossed? Target identified 25 items that were purchased together to determine if a woman was pregnant, so they could distribute coupons to the recipient, hopefully developing into a long-term relationship. A man was furious when his teenage daughter was receiving coupons from the store and said "My daughter got this in the mail, she is still in high school and you are sending her coupons for baby clothes and cribs? Are you trying to encourage her to get pregnant?" As it turns out, the predictive analytics model developed by the target to examine these products bought, such as vitamin supplements and purses large enough to carry diapers, led to the discovery that she was pregnant. Target wanted to capture individuals before they became pregnant to influence future shopping habits. As it turned out, unknown to the father at the time, his daughter was pregnant. This example underscores the complexity of using this information target had, aggregated with other external information on the shopper, and analyzed. The data is possible to be analyzed; the question is, "When are the privacy rights being violated, or have we entered an era where this is expected behavior where we shop?" Furthermore, our online behavior is being tracked and analyzed, as highlighted in the previous discussion, without us having to leave our homes. Much more is known about us today than ever before.

VALERIE LYONS: DOING PRIVACY RIGHT VS. DOING PRIVACY RIGHTS

COO, BH Consulting

Eric Schmidt (CEO Google 2001–2017) famously noted that his company's policy was "to get right up to the creepy line and not cross it." My first experience of this creepy line was in 2017; I typed the words "Dublin Airport" and Google search returned the landing time of the flight I was intending to search for. In just two words, Google searched my data and correctly guessed what I wanted to know. Although the experience left me feeling "robbed" of some level of control over my privacy, the benefit to me in that moment outweighed the invasion of my privacy. The creepy line can best be described as a boundary wall between consumer and organization that is built on values of ethics and trust. The closer an organization can get to this boundary wall, the more data they can leverage for profit maximization and personalization. Balancing the "creepy line" tensions is an increasingly delicate challenge— as one customer's great personalized experience may feel deeply creepy to another. Several factors mediate this creepy "context" within privacy such as the consumers' past experiences, their personal propensity towards privacy, their gender, age, and culture. In order to adapt to this "blurred creepy line," organizations such as Google have started allowing consumers to dynamically negotiate the collection and use of their personal data, in line with the consumers' own personal privacy requirements. However, how sustainable is a business if its information strategy is positioned right at the edge of the "creepy line"?

A SUSTAINABLE INFORMATION STRATEGY

Columbia Business School recently found that 75% of consumers are willing to share data if they trust the brand, and are willing to do so in exchange for offers or data-enabled benefits, such as reward points and personalized recommendations. In order to engender such privacy-related trust, privacy protection is undergoing a paradigm shift from compliance to data ethics, which increasingly places consumers at its center. This ethical approach to data privacy recognizes that feasible, useful, or profitable does not equal sustainable, and emphasizes accountability over compliance with the letter-of-the-law. Organizations, who ethically manage data and solve the consumer-privacy–trust equation, are more likely to win consumer loyalty with consumers more likely to pay a premium for products and services. Lego, for instance, has placed the protection of children's data at the heart of their information protection strategy. Activities include limits on integrating with social media, strong corporate responsibility regarding use of customer data by suppliers and partners, and no third-party cookies on websites aimed at children under age 13. Apple too mandates that any new use of Apple customer data requires sign-off from a committee of three "privacy czars" (top management) and a c-suite executive. The existence of, and compliance to, regulation will not be enough in the digital economy to engender consumer trust, and organizations need to find ways to let their consumers know that they are law-abiding, responsible, and fair. Organizations should understand the dynamics and profile of their consumer and the factors that lead their consumer to trust. In designing an information strategy, organizations should be combining four key risk dimensions: organization risks, consumer risks, ethics risks, and compliance risks together with a "no surprises" policy for data collection and use, with meaningful and unambiguous opt-in consent preferences.

Suggested Reading

1. Organization for Economic Co-operation and Development. 2013. OECD Guidelines on the Protection of Privacy and Transborder Flows of Personal Data. www.oecd.org/internet/ieconomy/privacy-guidelines.htm.
2. European Commission. 2013. Article 29 Working Party. Opinion on Purpose Limitation (March). http://ec.europa.eu/justice/data-protection/article-29/documentation/opinion-recommendation/files/2013/wp203_en.pdf.
3. Privacy Shield Framework. www.privacyshield.gov/welcome.
4. EU General Data Protection Regulation. www.eugdpr.org/.
5. EUR-Lex. 1995. Directive 95/46/EC of the European Parliament and of the Council 24 October 1995 on The Protection of Individuals with Regard to Processing of Personal Data and on the Free Movement of Such Data. http://eur-lex.europa.eu/legal-content/en/ALL/?uri=CELEX:31995L0046.
6. Moerel, L. and Prins, C. 2015. On the Death of Purpose Limitation. Iapp.org Privacy Perspectives (June 2). https://iapp.org/news/a/on-the-death-of-purpose-limitation/.
7. International Association Privacy Professionals. 2014. Full Report: Benchmarking Privacy Management and Investments of the Fortune 1000. Resource Center. https://iapp.org/resources/article/full-report-benchmarking-privacy-management-and-investments-of-the-fortune–1000/.
8. Whitworth, M. 2015. Evolve to Become the CISO of 2018 or Face Extinction. Forrester (August 17). www.forrester.com/.
9. Chang, L. 2015. Privacy is Dead, Says Mark Zuckerberg, Even for His Unborn Daughter. Digital Trends (October 8). www.digitaltrends.com/social-media/mark-zuckerberg-daughter-vr/.
10. Levin, A. 2015. Privacy Is Dead: What You Still Can Do to Protect Yourself. Huffington Post (August 27). www.huffingtonpost.com/adam-levin/privacy-is-dead-what-you_b_80 47530.html.
11. Klugman, C. 2016. A Generation Gap between Privacy and Confidentiality. Columbia University Bioethics Blog (February 17). www.bioethics.net/2016/02/a-generation-gap-between-privacy-confidentiality/.

12. Legistation.gov.uk. Justices of Peace Act 1361. www.legislation.gov.uk/aep/Edw3/34/1.
13. The Statutes Project. 1360: 34 Edcard 3 c.1: Justices of the Peace. http://statutes.org.uk/ site/the-statutes/fourteenth-century/1361-34-edward-3-1-justices-of-peace/.
14. LawTeacher. Entick V Carrington. www.lawteacher.net/free-law-essays/public-law/entick-v-carrington.php.
15. United Nations Human Rights Office of the High Commissioner. 1948. Universal Declaration of Human Rights. www.ohchr.org/EN/UDHR/Documents/UDHR_ Translations/eng.pdf.
16. German Hesse Data Protection Act. 1970. Hessisches Datenschutzgesetz (The Hesse Data Protection Act), Gesetz und Verordungsblatt I, 625.
17. Federal Trade Commission. Fair Credit Reporting Act. www.ftc.gov/enforcement/rules/ rulemaking-regulatory-reform-proceedings/fair-credit-reporting-act.
18. U.S. Department of Justice. 1974. Privacy Act of 1974. www.justice.gov/opcl/ privacy-act-1974.
19. EUR-Lex. 2000. Commission Decision of July 26, 2000. http://eur-lex.europa.eu/ legal-content/EN/TXT/PDF/?uri=CELEX:32000D0520&from=en.
20. Nakashima, E. 2015. Top E.U. Court Strikes Down Major Data-Sharing Pact between U.S. and Europe. Washington Post (October 6). www.washingtonpost.com/world/ national-security/eu-court-strikes-down-safe-harbor-data-transfer-deal-over-privacy-concerns/2015/10/06/2da2d9f6-6c2a-11e5-b31c-d80d62b53e28_story.html?utm_ term=.fd95dcb06db4.
21. European Commission. 2016. Adequacy of the Protection of Personal Data in Non-EU countries. ec.europa.eu/info/strategy/justice-and-fundamental-rights/data-protection/data-transfers-outside-eu/adequacy-protection-personal-data-non-eu-countries_en.
22. Privacy Shield Framework. Key New Requirements. www.privacyshield.gov/Key-New-Requirements.
23. U.S. Department of Commerce. 2016. Fact Sheet: Overview of the EU-U.S. Privacy Shield Framework. (February 29). www.commerce.gov/news/fact-sheets/2016/02/ fact-sheet-overview-eu-us-privacy-shield-framework.
24. U.S. Department Health and Human Services. Breach Notification Rule. www.hhs.gov/ hipaa/for-professionals/breach-notification/index.html.
25. Australian government Office of the Australian Information Commissioner. Australian Privacy Principles. www.oaic.gov.au/privacy-law/privacy-act/australian-privacy-principles.
26. Madrigal, A. 2012. Reading the Privacy Policies, You Encounter in a Year Would Take 76 Work Days. The Atlantic (March 1). www.theatlantic.com/technology/ archive/2012/03/reading-the-privacy-policies-you-encounter-in-a-year-would-take-76-work-days/253851/.
27. Asano, E. 2017. How Much Time Do People Spend on Social Media? {Infographic}. SocialMediaToday (January 4). www.socialmediatoday.com/marketing/how-much-time-do-people-spend-social-media-infographic.
28. Scherker, A. 2017. Didn't Read Facebook's Fine Print? Here Exactly What It Says. Huffington Post (July 21, 2014, updated December 06, 2017). www.huffingtonpost. com/2014/07/21/facebook-terms-condition_n_5551965.html.
29. Federal Trade Commission. 2014. Data Brokers: A Call for Transparency and Accountability. (May). www.ftc.gov/system/files/documents/reports/data-brokers-call-transparency-accountability-report-federal-trade-commission-may-2014/140527databroker-report.pdf.

30. Timberg, C. and Dwoskin, E. 2017. Russian Content on Facebook, Google and Twitter Reached Far More Users than Companies First Disclosed, Congressional Testimony Says. The Washington Post (October 30). www.washingtonpost.com/business/technology/2017/10/30/4509587e-bd84-11e7-97d9-bdab5a0ab381_story.html?hpid=hp_no-name_no-name%3Apage%2Fbreaking-news-bar&tid=a_breakingnews&utm_term=.e19140e4cc1c.

31. Lubin, G. 2012. The Incredible Story of How Target Exposed a Teen Girl's Pregnancy. Business Insider (February 16). www.businessinsider.com/the-incredible-story-of-how-target-exposed-a-teen-girls-pregnancy-2012-2.

32. Duhigg, C. 2012. How Companies Learn Your Secrets. The New York Times (February 16). www.nytimes.com/2012/02/19/magazine/shopping-habits.html?_r=1&hp=&page wanted=all.

33. U.S. Department of Homeland Security. Privacy Impact Assessments. www.dhs.gov/privacy-impact-assessments.

34. Cavoukian, A. Privacy by Design: The 7 Foundational Principles. www.ryerson.ca/content/dam/pbdce/seven-foundational-principles/The-7-Foundational-Principles.pdf.

35. Federal Trade Commission. 2012. Protecting Consumer Privacy in an Era of Rapid Change: Recommendations for Businesses and Policymakers. (March). www.ftc.gov/sites/default/files/documents/reports/federal-trade-commission-report-protecting-consumer-privacy-era-rapid-change-recommendations/120326privacyreport.pdf.

36. Trefis Team. 2017. Facebook's Strong Ad Revenue Growth to Continue. Forbes (October 30). www.forbes.com/sites/greatspeculations/2017/10/30/facebooks-strong-ad-revenue-growth-to-continue/#14054cb16fe7.

37. Burke, C. 2018. Zuckerberg Considers Prioritizing News Sources. Newsmax (January 11). www.newsmax.com/newsfront/mark-zuckerberg-facebook-fake-news-social-media/2018/01/11/id/836698/.

38. BBC News. 2018. Google Loses 'Right to Be Forgotten' Case. BBC News Technology (April 13). www.bbc.com/news/technology-43752344.

39. State of California Department of Justice. California Consumer Privacy Act (CCPA). https://www.oag.ca.gov/privacy/ccpa.

Chapter 12

Meaningful Policies and Procedures

It Don't Mean a Thing If it Ain't Got That Swing.

Duke [Edward Kennedy] Ellington, 1899–1974

When organizations first recognize they need to ensure the information assets of the organization are adequately protected, this usually results in asking the question, "What applicable policies are in place?" There may be some human resource (HR) policies that might apply, or corporate policies noted in the Ethics and Compliance Code of Conduct; however, these are normally insufficient to address the breadth of the information security needs. The next step is for the organization to embark upon the time-consuming task of developing cybersecurity policies.

To the seasoned cybersecurity practitioner, this may seem like a question with an obvious answer. The question is not so obvious to the end users of the organization, as many of them may feel that if everyone applies "common sense," there is no need for them to read and sign off on voluminous sets of policies. The reality is that each person has a different interpretation of what is "common sense." For example, leaving a scruffy old backpack containing books in a car may seem like a reasonable act to one employee who thinks, why would anyone want to steal a bag full of books? Another employee may think that because of the condition of the backpack, no one would want to steal it. Another may feel that their car is parked in broad daylight in a heavily traveled area, which would make the risk of stealing it quite low. Another employee may think that the car alarm would be a sufficient deterrent from anyone wanting to go through the trouble of stealing the backpack. Then along comes the Chief Information Security Officer (CISO), whose job is to evaluate the course of action that will provide reasonable security. The CISO knows the stories of break-ins all too well and knows that criminals do not know for sure what is in the backpack, and may assume that there is a laptop, money, credit cards, etc., that may be sold for a nominal amount to buy drugs, alcohol, or support rudimentary living expenses. Thus, the opportunity and motivation present an unacceptable risk that must be mitigated. The organization cannot afford to leave these individual decisions up to the "common-sense" internal barometer of thousands of employees. The organization must set forth advice or a baseline of what behavior is expected for each employee and not leave this up to individual discretion. This advice, and expected behavior, is manifested through a set of cybersecurity policies. The policies form the cornerstone to the information security program and are representations of management's intention that are needed to control the information security assets.

Beware of Policy Digital Dust

While information security policies are very important, they can easily become digital dust (or shelfware for paper documents) if their development, management, and distribution are not handled appropriately. Countless security departments have filled binders full of policies over the years that remain unread and require frequent dusting. As the Intranet-based environments started to take hold in the mid-1990s, these environments moved from paper-based shelfware to electronic-based shelfware. The security department may have had a large project to develop the cybersecurity policies, place them on the intranet, and then they were "done." Lengthy, technical documents with all the technical jargon may have sounded impressive to the security department but fail when end users are required to read them because they are not understandable. Who would read these lengthy documents? The same individuals who would read the complete car owner's manual after purchasing a new car before they put the key into the ignition—in other words, a very small segment of the population. The security policies should be written in a language from the user and be brief enough to get the point across, without overwhelming the end user. More detailed descriptions can be placed in standards documents that the user can read if they need additional information. An organization security policy beyond 30–60 pages is normally much more than would be required by any medium- to large-sized organization. Beyond that level, the policies are likely to go unread.

Security Policy Digital Transformation

It is also worth noting that intranets have evolved significantly from the publication of top-down, static content available to employees with the organization. The intranet evolved to where the starting page is taken for granted to be the company page, and integrations via hyperlinks to other tools were added, making this platform more of a collaboration tool than a tool dedicated to one-way content. Employees could access their HR information, 401Ks, access Twitter feeds, facilitate web conferencing, interact with and manage their supply chain, request travel, access productivity tools such as MS Office or Google Docs, utilize instant messaging, interact with external social networks, access collaboration tools such as SharePoint to interact with internal teams, or access their customer relationship management (CRM) systems. As the CISO, does not it make sense to view this platform as a method to *interact with the security policies* vs. see this as a static platform? In the age of digital transformation, where collaboration tools are creating efficiencies for business, the cybersecurity area could also leverage these tools to promote the security policies. For example, clickable buttons relating to a security policy could be used to play a short video to explain the policy, and comments about the policy could be solicited through instant messaging (assuming active monitoring by the security department), or provide a mechanism to send feedback through an online form. Internal social networks, such as Yammer, could be leveraged to post news stories about a topic or post external security-related stories and point to the policy and how the situation would be handled internally. The short story for the CISO is—while publishing the policies in a place where individuals can easily find them is important, periodic communication of these policies in a place where the users' hangout is an effective way to keep the message in front of them. These actions go beyond the regularly scheduled security awareness training and are focused on keeping the policies front and center, or they will become digital dust.

Maintaining Relevancy

To avoid shelfware in electronic policies, they need to be kept (1) brief, (2) updated, and (3) relevant. Web-based policies should each be no more than two online pages each to get the point across as to what is expected. Resumes are kept to two pages for a reason—people stop reading them if they have not received what is needed within the first two pages, and the second page is only read if enough interest has been maintained on the first. Posts placed on websites, such as Cable News Network (CNN), Forbes, USA Today, or social media sites such as LinkedIn are generally no more than two to three pages, as the reader may lose interest after that.

The policies need to be updated at least annually to ensure that the management direction is still desired. As an employee comes across a policy that was last updated 4 years ago, they may make the conclusion on their own that the policy no longer applies. The organization may have gone through a merger, and the conflicting policies may exist for the two organizations or worse yet; if the policies have never been integrated, the employees of the acquired company may make the erroneous assumption that they should still follow their old company policies and may not be aware of the new acquiring company policies.

Policies need to maintain their relevancy to remain effective. For example, if an organization has not addressed reporting requirements stemming from the ransomware attacks initiated by phishing in the past few years in their policies, the management and end users will have to rely on the existing policies to determine where this type of event should be reported. Or, suppose an employee just purchased a new iPad Pro tablet, but the policy indicates that no personal desktop or laptop computers may be used within the company—should the iPad be allowed? Technically, according to the policy, the iPad "tablet" has not been addressed, and the associate may leave it to an interpretation more favorable to the employee as to whether to use the device. If the iPad is allowed, what are the applications permitted for use and what are the requirements to implement mobile device management solutions on the device?

Policies posted should always ensure that the revision history is provided as well, so that users can see what changes were made to the documents and determine if they are looking at the correct version. Even with many companies becoming more socially responsible and implementing environmental-friendly initiatives to reduce wasteful printing and disposal costs, there are still times when an end user will prefer a paper document that can be referenced when needed. The revision update date and history help ensure that the correct document is being utilized.

Template Security Policies

Consulting organizations have sets of policy templates that are used to jump-start a client's need for information security policies. These are then tailored to the needs of the organization. This process may be more effective than writing the information security policies from scratch, if the policies meet the compliance, laws, regulations, and desires of the organization. It is not unusual to see where an organization has implemented a copied policy verbatim, sometimes even forgetting to change the company name on the template. During the British Petroleum Oil Spill, it was revealed that the business continuity/disaster recovery documents from several major oil companies appeared to have used the same templates for their disaster recovery plans.

While developing the complete cybersecurity policy is beyond the scope of this book, there are several information security books available with sample polices that can be used to jump-start the development. Three very good sources are Tom Peltier's *Information Security Policies and Procedures—A Practitioner's Reference*, *Information Security Policies Made Easy* by Information Shield (Author Charles Cresson Wood), and *Security Program and Policies: Principles and Practices* by Sari Stern Greene. These sources contain valuable information at a fraction of the cost of a security consultant for 1 day! The policy set has gone through numerous revisions, reflecting the changing environment that is constantly adding new requirements for policies adding policies such as cloud computing, email security including phishing, flash drive storage, third-party management and software development, social networking, mobile device security, and so forth. Vertical organizations have also made sample policies available for free, such as Health Insurance Portability and Accountability Act of 1996 (HIPAA) policies created by volunteers of the HIPAA Collaborative of Wisconsin (www.hipaacow.org) and mapped to the HIPAA regulations. Some online security publications such as CSOonline.com have provided templates free to use. These free policies are generally put together by volunteers contributing their knowledge for the benefit of others. Caution should be used to ensure the policies satisfy the laws the company may be subject to and can be modified as necessary. Every organization has budget constraints, and leveraging these free policies is a good place to start for those organizations with very limited resources unable to retain expertise. The various standards and control frameworks themselves can also be leveraged to create policies specific to the organization.

Distinguishing between Policies, Standards, Procedures, and Guidelines

Organizations typically do not have a consistent understanding as to what a "policy" is. This seems like such a simple concept, so why the difficulty? The reason is not the lack of understanding that a policy is meant to govern the behavior within the organization. The reason for the confusion has more to do with the fact that in the interest of saving time, organizations will combine policies, procedures, guidelines, and standards into one document and call it the "policy." This is not really a time saver because it makes it more difficult by introducing inflexibility into the policy each time the policy needs to change. This is like denormalizing a database structure to make the performance more efficient, when in fact it becomes harder to add new data elements to a table without redesigning the table. The policies and procedures end up getting fused together, and so when the procedure changes, the policy document by default is changing as well, when the policy does not need to change. Or, the employees begin to think that the procedure is the only way the policy can be implemented, when there may be multiple procedures across the organization that can be implemented to comply with the policy. For example, an organization may have a policy that users are to only have access to the information necessary to perform their jobs. To facilitate this, procedures may be developed to assign business or data owners to the information, highlighting the approval and periodic certification requirements to perform their jobs. Procedures also exist within the Identity and Access Management department to receive requests from end users and obtain approvals from their manager. Another procedure may exist to grant emergency access that temporarily bypasses this process with the appropriate management-level approval. System administrators may have a more rigorous approval process or may check IDs in and out of a digital vault. Remote users may have to follow a different process before the access can be granted. In the end, the policy is still to ensure the users only have access to the information necessary, but with different procedures. Fusion techniques are best left for food and not to combine policies, standards, procedures, and guidelines into one document.

Policy Development

Policies should be written at the highest level possible to still be able to communicate the intentions of the company. The higher the level of the policy, the more likely the policy can stand the test of time. The company does not want to be reissuing policies on a frequent basis unless they need to. This involves resources for development and, more importantly, the time and expense of each person to reread the complete policy. While changes in technology, company structure, laws and regulations, emerging trends, etc., warrant changes to the security policy, frequent changes due to minor technology changes are not desired. The reaction of most users will be, did not we just do this? For example, if authentication standards are written into the access policy for a primarily internal Windows-based environment, what happens when a cloud-based Oracle server supporting the new pilot digital transformation project is introduced? Will the authentication policy need to be redistributed and attested to by thousands of users, when the change impacted only a small number of users? Will there be changes in the method used to authenticate in this environment?

CISOs and their teams are charged with the responsibility of creating the security policies. The policies must be written and communicated at a level that is understood by the end users of the organization, if there is to be any chance of compliance. If their policies are poorly written or written at too high of an education level (common industry practice is to focus the content for general users at the sixth- to eighth-grade reading level), the policies will not be understood. CISOs may be charged with the development of the policies; however, the effort is normally a collaborative effort to ensure that the business issues are addressed. Utilization of a Cybersecurity Risk Committee, executive oversight committee, or a subgroup of that committee, depending upon the policy being drafted, is an approach that considers the business impacts of security policy decisions. Developing the policies solely within the information technology (IT) department and then distributing the policies without business input are likely to miss important business considerations. As always, deciding on the appropriate security controls is a decision of risk by the organization and ultimately should be decided by the business leaders. The organization is also more likely to accept security policies approved and endorsed by the business leaders vs. the Security Officer or the IT department.

Once these different documents have been created, the basis for ensuring compliance is established. These deliverables form the basis for organizational compliance with the cybersecurity policies. The most current version of the documents needs to be readily accessible by those that are expected to follow them. Many organizations have placed these documents electronically on their intranets or shared file folders to facilitate communication of the most current documents. Placement of these documents plus checklists, forms, and sample documents can save time for the individual and be an added value provided by the security department.

Policy Reasoning

Policies define *what* at high-level objectives the organization needs to accomplish and serves as management's intentions to control the operation of the organization to meet business objectives. The *why* should be stated in the form of a policy summary statement or purpose. If end users understand the why, they are more apt to follow the policy. As children, we were told what to do by our parents and we just did it—when the rules made sense to us. Today's organizations are no different; people need to understand the *why* before they can really commit. We want the employees and contractors to be successful and follow the policies vs. having to resort to punitive actions.

Security Policy Best Practices

Someone once said, "writing security policies is like making sausage, you don't know want to know what goes into it, but what comes out is pretty good!" Writing policies does not have to be a mystery, and there are several guidelines for creating good security policies practiced in the industry as follows:

- *Clearly Define Policy Creation Practice.* A clearly defined process for initiating, creating, reviewing, recommending, approving, and distributing the policies communicates the responsibilities of all parties necessary and the time expectations of their participation. This can be accomplished by process flows, swim lanes, flowcharts, or written documentation.
- *Write Policies to Survive 2–3 Years.* Policies are high-level statements of the objectives of the organization. The underlying methods and technologies to implement the controls to support the policies may change. By including these in the other related documents (procedures, standards, guidelines, and baselines), the policy statements will need less frequent change. This avoids frequent updates and subsequent distribution to the organization.
- *Use Directive Wording.* Policies represent expectations to be complied with. As such, statements such as "must," "will," and "shall" communicate this requirement vs. using weaker directives such as "should," "may," or "can." This latter type of language is better reserved for guidelines or areas where there are options.

- *Avoid Technical Implementation Details.* Policies should be written to be technology independent, as the implemented technology may change over time.
- *Keep Length to a Minimum.* Policies published online should be limited in length to two to three pages maximum per policy. The intent for the policies is for the end user to understand and not to create long documents for the sake of documentation.
- *Provide Navigation from the Policy to the Supporting Documents.* If the implementation of the policy is placed online, then hyperlinking the procedures, standards, guidelines, and baselines can be an effective method to ensure that the appropriate procedures are being followed. Some of the internal security procedures would not be appropriate for general knowledge, such as the procedure for monitoring intrusions or reviewing log files, and these need to be accessible by the security department and properly secured from general distribution.
- *Thoroughly Review before Publishing.* Proofreading policies by multiple individuals can catch errors that may not be readily seen by the author.
- *Conduct Management Review and Sign-Off.* Senior management must endorse the policies if they are to be effectively accepted by all management levels and subsequently the end users of the organization.
- *Avoid Techno-speak.* Policies are oriented to communicate to nontechnical users. Technical jargon is acceptable in technical documentation, but not in high-level security policies. This will also help the objective of having the policies last 2–3 years before revision and focus the policies to more business-friendly terminology.
- *Review Incidents and Adjust Policies.* Review of the security incidents that have occurred may indicate the need for a new policy, a revision to an existing policy, or the need to redistribute the current policy to reinforce compliance.
- *Periodically Review Policies.* A formalized review process provides a mechanism to ensure that the security policies are still in alignment with the business objectives.
- *Develop Sanctions for Noncompliance.* Effective policies have consistent sanction policies to enable action when the policies are not followed. These sanctions may include "disciplinary action up to and including termination." Stronger language can also be added for prosecution for serious offenses.

Policies provide the foundation for a comprehensive and effective security program. The company is protected from surprises, which may occur and gives the necessary authority to the security activities of the organization. By communicating the company policies as directives, accountability and personal responsibility for adhering to the security practices is established. The policies are utilized in determining and/or interpreting any conflicts that may arise. The policies also define the elements, scope, and functions of the security management.

Multiple Security Policy Types

Security policies may consist of different types, depending upon the specific need for the policy. The different security policies work together to meet the objectives of the comprehensive security program. Different policy types are as follows:

- *Organizational or Program Policy.* This policy is issued by a senior management individual who creates the authority and scope for the security program. The purpose of the program is described, and the assigned responsibility is defined for carrying out the information security mission. The goals of confidentiality, integrity, and availability would be addressed in the policy. Specific areas of security focus may be stressed, such as the protection of confidential information for a credit card company or heath insurance company, or the availability focus for a company maintaining mission-critical, high-availability systems. The policy should be clear as to the facilities, hardware, software, information, and personnel that are in scope for the security program. In most cases, the scope will be the entire organization; however, in larger organizations, the security program may be limited in scope to a division or geographic location. The organization policy sets out the high-level authority to define the appropriate sanctions for failure to comply with the policy.

- *Functional, Issue-Specific Policies.* While the organizational security policies are broad in scope, the functional or issue-specific policies address areas of security concerns requiring clarification. The issue-specific policies may be focused on the different domains of security and address areas such as access control, contingency planning, and segregation of duties principles. They may also address specific technical areas of existing and emerging technologies; for example, an Acceptable Use Policy may define the responsibilities of the end user for using the corporate computer systems for business purposes only or may allow the person some incidental personal use provided the restrictions of ensuring usage is free from viruses, spyware, downloading inappropriate pictures or software, or sending chain letters through email. These policies will depend upon the business needs and the tolerance for risk. Some financial institutions, e.g., have moved towards a more restrictive stance on the use of a business computer due to the ransomware and wire fraud/money transfer risks the organization faces, while other organizations view the openness of their systems (i.e., permitting Facebook, LinkedIn, and other external social media sites) as an important recruiting and employment engagement tool. The level of "lockdown" policies will depend upon the risk assessment and determined risk appetite of the organization. The policies contain the statement of the issue, the statement of the organization's position on the issue, the applicability of the issue, compliance requirements, and sanctions for not following the policy.

- *System-Specific Policies.* Areas where it is desired to have clearer direction or greater control for a specific technical or operational area may have more detailed policies. These policies may be targeted for a specific application or platform. For example, a system-specific policy may address which departments are permitted to input or modify information in the check writing application for the disbursement of accounts payable payments.

The more detailed and issue-specific that the policy is written, the higher likelihood will be that the policy will require more frequent changes. Typically, high-level organizational security policies will survive for several years, while those focused on the use of technology will change much more frequently as the technology matures and new technology is added to the environment. Even if an organization is not currently utilizing a technology, policies can explicitly strengthen the message that the technology is not to be used and is prohibited. For example, a policy regarding removable media such as USB drives, cloud storage, or one regarding the use of wireless devices or camera phones in the workplace would reinforce the management intentions of permissible storage mechanisms.

Standards

Whereas policies define that "what" an organization needs, the standards take this a step further and define the "how." Standards provide the agreements providing interoperability within the organization using common protocols. Standards specify the hardware and software security mechanisms selected as the organization's method of controlling security risks. Standards are prevalent in many facets of our daily lives, such as the electrical receptacle in our homes, specifications of the height, color, and format of our street signs, and the size of the headphone jack on our smartphones. Standards provide consistency in the implementation as well as permit interoperability with reduced confusion. There are many security standards we could choose to implement a solution. For example, the same secure baseline configuration for standing up a cloud-based virtual server could be specified for all new instances so there is consistency in the security controls.

Standards simplify the operation of the security controls within the company and increase the efficiency. It is costlier to support multiple software packages, which do essentially the same activity. Imagine if each user was told to go to the local computer store and purchase a personal firewall solution they liked the best. Some users would ask the salesperson for an opinion, some would buy the least expensive to meet their budget needs, and others might get the most expensive assuming this would provide the greatest protection. Without a consistent product standard for personal firewall products, the organization would be unsure as to the level of protection provided. Additionally, each of these different products would have different installation, update, and licensing considerations contributing to complex management. It makes much sense to have consistent products chosen for the organization vs. leaving the product choice to every individual. The user may also be unaware of the company-provided solution.

Determination of which standards meet the organization's needs must be driven by the security policies agreed by management. The standards provide the specification of the technology to effectively enable the organization to become successful in meeting the requirements of the policy. An organization may require all sensitive communications are encrypted when distributed to business partners; however, the large files may make this process impractical to send documents through email. In this case, the technology may not support the policy, and an alternative solution such as utilizing a cloud storage provider, encrypting the information, and distributing a link with access to the information may be a better solution. The technology to support the policy could be documented as a standard. The policy defines the boundaries within which the standards must be supportive.

Standards may also refer to those guidelines established by a standard organization from one of the many control frameworks and accepted by management.

Procedures and Processes

Procedures are step-by-step instructions in support of the policies, standards, guidelines, and baselines. The procedure indicates *how* the policy will be implemented and *who* does what to accomplish the tasks. The procedure provides clarity and a common understanding of the operation required to effectively support the policy on a consistent basis. Procedures are best developed when the input of each of the interfacing areas is included in the development of the procedure. This reduces the risk that important steps, communication, or required deliverables are not left out of the procedure. While a procedure provides step-by-step instructions to complete a task, a process is generally a function (also containing multiple steps or procedures) resulting in a desired business outcome, also containing a series of tasks. The terms "procedures" and "processes" are often used interchangeably. For the purposes or cybersecurity, the important aspect is ensuring the process or procedure accurately provides direction as to how the deliverable can be accomplished.

Companies must be able to provide assurance indicating they have exercised due diligence in the support and enforcement of company policies. This means that the company has tried to follow the policies and has communicated the expectations to the workforce. Having documented procedures communicated to the users, business partners, and anyone utilizing the systems as appropriate minimizes the legal liability of the corporation.

Creating documented procedures is more than a documentation exercise for the sake of documentation. The process itself creates a common understanding between the developers of the procedure of the methods used to accomplish the task. Individuals from different organizational units may be very familiar with their work area, but not as familiar with the impact of a procedure on a department. This is what I would call the "Chicago Bean Cybersecurity Effect." The Chicago Bean, also called "Cloudgate," created by Anish Kapoor, is a large 110-ton stainless steel structure measuring 33 by 66 by 42 feet, made up of 168 stainless steel plates welded together and polished to hide the seams. Standing in front of this structure in downtown Chicago, Illinois, at Millennium Park, you can see a distorted reflection of yourself. The stainless-steel "Bean" is massive, and it is impossible to know who is on the other side, or what they are doing. Our organizations sometimes feel like this, where individuals working in different departments can only see "their side" and may not understand the other parts of the organization. The constant reflection by their own peer group makes it appear as if everything is normal and working fine. The exercise of writing down a single, consistent procedure has the added effect of establishing agreement between the parties. Many times, at the beginning of the process, individuals will think they all understand the process, only to come to understand that people were really executing different, individual processes to accomplish the task.

Undocumented cybersecurity processes also create an efficiency and effectiveness issue as (1) it is assumed that everyone is doing the same thing each time, (2) the processes cannot be universally improved upon, (3) time is wasted communicating processes, (4) junior team members do not have the ability to learn from more senior knowledge of "best practices," and (5) the wheel is reinvented again and again. The lack of documented cybersecurity processes and charts depicting who is responsible, accountable, consulted, and informed lead to processes being missed, assumptions that processes are being executed when they are not, and uncertainty as to who owns the process and is accountable when the process fails.

Undocumented processes also result in tribal knowledge dependency. Processes are developed within an organization to include practices and activities to meet objectives set out by the organization through the creation of multiple outputs. Some organizations operate with processes that are either ill-defined or undocumented, resulting in inconsistent activities performed and different outputs of differing quality, depending upon the individual performing the process. For example, if cyber vulnerabilities are scanned monthly using tool A by employee A and the highly critical vulnerabilities are patched, or fixed, within 7 days, this will provide different results than the employee B using tool B and fixing all vulnerabilities found within 60 days. It would be difficult to be able to articulate the risk posture of the organization if multiple approaches are implemented, as it would be dependent upon the individual performing the work.

Having well-defined procedures/processes is important for any business process, so why the attention on processes with respect to cybersecurity? The answer is simple—even the slightest failure in one of these processes can cause issues with confidential disclosure, availability, or data integrity of the systems in place to support the mission. From the aforementioned example, it is found that not having a consistent vulnerability and patch management process could result in critical security vulnerabilities existing on the system that could be exploited by external hackers, insiders, or through carelessness. Executive leadership may assume that the processes are in place and they are being executed on a consistent basis, only to find out that the process was never implemented, the tool was removed, or the individual performing that task was pulled onto another project, and no one was informed that the process was no longer being executed. Unnecessary duplication of software application tool and training costs also result.

IT professionals generally dislike creating documentation of processes since this takes time away from exploring the new technology, creating new applications and databases, or resolving a system or end-user issue. Without clear direction and governance in place to ensure that process development is an organizational priority to support effective and efficient execution to meet the organizational mission, these processes are unlikely to be created and should not be assumed that they are. One way to ensure that processes are developed is to create a catalog of cybersecurity services with a periodic review of the processes to ensure they are still accurate and relevant, as well as ensuring that each process has a process owner responsible for maintaining and continuously improving the process.

Once the processes are documented, understood, and being followed, the end goal should be to automate these processes and move the routine actions into operations. Much discussion these days is around machine learning to minimize the amount of human interaction for items that can be automatically processed. Before this can be attainable, the current environment needs to be well understood. Information security personnel are more expensive resources relative to the computer operations areas that have been optimized for efficiency. Thus, these resources should be leveraged to design the most appropriate processes, with the view of moving these processes to a production operation as soon as possible, executed by automation or less-expensive resources. In the preceding vulnerability management example, most of the running of the vulnerability reports could be run by an external Security Operations Center, or a Managed Security Services Provider that operates the process and patches the vulnerabilities according to the risk acceptance level and the priority established by the cybersecurity team designing the process. This frees up the cybersecurity professional to focus on other high-value efforts vs. spending time managing the "routine" operational work. The cybersecurity team could be focused on the exception reports or those cybersecurity items that need further analysis and other potential technology tools to mitigate effectively.

Baselines

Baselines provide descriptions of how to implement security packages to ensure that implementations are consistent throughout the organization. Different software packages, hardware platforms, and networks have different methods of ensuring security. There are many different options and settings that must be determined to provide the desired protection. An analysis of the available configuration settings and subsequent settings desired forms the basis for future, consistent implementation of the standard. For example, turning off the telnet service may be specified in the hardening baseline document for the network servers. A procedure for exceptions to the baseline would need to be followed if the baseline could not be followed for a device, along with the business justification. The baselines are the specific rules necessary to implement the security controls in support of the policy and standards, which have been developed.

Testing of the implemented security controls on a periodic basis assures that the baselines are implemented according to the documented baselines. The baselines themselves should be reviewed periodically to ensure that they are sufficient to address emerging threats and vulnerabilities. In large environments with multiple individuals performing systems administration and responding to urgent requests, there is an increased risk that one of the baseline configurations may not be implemented properly. Internal testing identifies these vulnerabilities and provides a mechanism to review why the control was or was not properly implemented. Failures in training, adherence to baselines and associated procedures, change control, documentation, or skills of the individual performing the changes may be identified through the testing.

Guidelines

Guidelines are discretionary or optional controls used to enable individuals to make judgments with respect to security actions. A good exercise is to replace the word "guideline" with the word "optional." If by doing so, the statements contained in the "optional" are what is desired to happen at the user's discretion, then it is an appropriate guideline. If, on the other hand, the statements are considered as required to adequately protect the security of the organization, then this should be defined as part of a policy, standard, or baseline.

Combination of Policies, Standards, Baselines, Procedures, and Guidelines

Each of these documents is closely related to each other and may be developed as the result of new regulations, external industry standards, new threats and vulnerabilities, emerging technologies, upgraded hardware and software platforms, or risk assessment changes. The relationships between the policies, standards, baselines, procedures, and guidelines and the laws and regulations providing the requirement to implement these governing activities are shown in Figure 12.1.

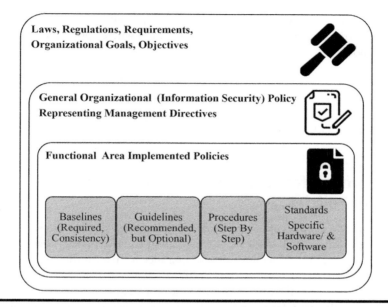

Figure 12.1   Laws, policy, procedure, standard, baseline, and guideline relationship.

Policy Analogy

A useful analogy to remember the differences between policies, standards, guidelines, and procedures is to think of a company that builds cabinets, which has a "hammer" policy. The different components may be as follows:

- *Policy.* "All boards must be nailed together using company-issued hammers to ensure end product consistency and worker safety." Notice the flexibility provided to permit the company to define the hammer type with changes in technology or safety issues. The purpose is also communicated to the employees.
- *Standard.* "11-inch fiberglass hammers will be used; only hardened-steel nails will be used with the hammers; Automatic hammers are to be used for repetitive jobs > 1 hour." Technical specifics are provided to clarify the expectations that make sense for the current environment and represent management's decision.
- *Guideline.* "To avoid splitting the wood, a pilot hole should be drilled first." The guideline is a suggestion and may not apply in all cases, or all types of wood. This does not represent a requirement, but rather a suggested practice.
- *Procedure.* "1. Position nail in upright position on board, 2. Strike nail with full swing of hammer, 3. Repeat until nail is flush with board, 4. If thumb is caught between nail and board, see Nail First-Aid Procedure." The procedure indicates the process of using the hammer and the nail to clarify what

is expected to be successful. Following this procedure, with the appropriate standard hammers, and practicing guidelines where appropriate, will fulfill the policy.

Analogies such as this can be effective when leading the team to develop security policies to ensure that they are on the same wavelength and not mixing policies, procedures, standards, and guidelines. These can also be useful in security awareness training to indicate when a user should refer to which.

An Approach for Developing Information Security Policies

Let us assume for a moment that the guidance in the preceding sections was followed, and the organization now has a set of information security policies that are easy to read, kept current, and generally available in a nice format on the internal website. However, no one seems to be reading them or following them, what could be the problem? Many times, the root cause is a lack of management support. How could this be? After all, the CISO has been designated with the role of developing and distributing information security policies, why would there be a low acceptance rate?

The answer usually lies in the fact that while the CISO may have done an excellent job at researching and developing security policies, the same diligence was not applied in ensuring that the rest of management was onboard with the policies prior to rollout. The CISO may decide to push out the policies once his department has developed them. As such, the policies become those "owned" by the CISO and not the rest of the management. These are then treated as departmental policies that have not greater enforcement requirements than the policies and procedures that are created by their organizational area. Then, when there is a conflict between the departmental desires and the security policy, the departmental desires win. For example, if an organization must get information quickly to a customer, they may fax (yes, those dinosaur devices still exist primarily due to security concerns over insecure networks) or email the information as part of their normal procedure. However, the information security policy may require that all transmissions over an open network, as in the case of email, that the transmission of all confidential information, be encrypted with the most stringent government standard encryption, such as FIPS 140-2 encryption requirements. The department sending the information may have a disagreement with the security department on the information classification of "confidential" in the information security policy or may feel that the requirement is a bit over the top, and does not agree with the policy at all, as it would hamper the speed of doing business and cause inferior relationships with the customers. Who is right? In this case, neither is—the CISO failed to obtain agreement with the policy before the procedures were executed and the executive from the other department is incorrect in not adhering to the policy. Unfortunately, this situation is all too common. The good news is that this can be avoided by following a different approach to developing and distributing the security policies.

Utilizing the Cybersecurity Risk Committee for Policies

Management support is essential in the development of cybersecurity policies. So, how is that attained? One method that is very effective is to form a security committee, also known as a Cybersecurity Council or Cybersecurity Risk Committee. The Cybersecurity Council can review the policies proposed by the information security department. The benefit of this approach is that (1) consensus of the policies is first built at the frontline supervisor/middle management/technical staff level, (2) senior management has greater comfort that the policies will be accepted by the organization as their management team has reviewed them before their approval, and (3) it builds grassroots ownership of the information security policies. While the committee can also serve as oversight for other security initiatives, serve as a sounding board, and prioritize information security efforts, they can be especially effective in vetting and discussing the information policies that are needed by the organization.

The Policy Review Process

Now that the organization has identified an individual responsible for the development and implementation of security policies the committee has been created, and an understanding of what makes a good policy has been communicated, there needs to be a process for reviewing the policies. This process may be developed during the creation of the committee, what is important is that the policy development process is thought out ahead of time to determine who will (1) create the policy, (2) review and recommend, (3) approve the final policy, (4) publish, and (5) read and accept the policies. The time spent in this process, up-front, will provide many dividends down the road. Many organizations "jump right in," and someone in the security department or IT department draft a policy and email the policy, without taking these steps. Proceeding along that path ends up with a policy that is not accepted by the organization's management and thus will not be accepted by the organization's end users. Why? Because the necessary discussion, debate, and acceptance of the policies by the leaders of the organization never took place. In the end, the question of management commitment again surfaces, when there was never a process in place to obtain the commitment.

The process could be depicted in a swim-lane-type chart showing the parties responsible, activities, records created through each activity, and decision boxes, or a flowchart format. Senior management will want this presented at a high level, typically no more than one to two pages of the process diagram. The process will vary by organizational structure, geographic location, size, and culture of decision making; however, a successful process for review should contain the following steps, as depicted in Figure 12.2.

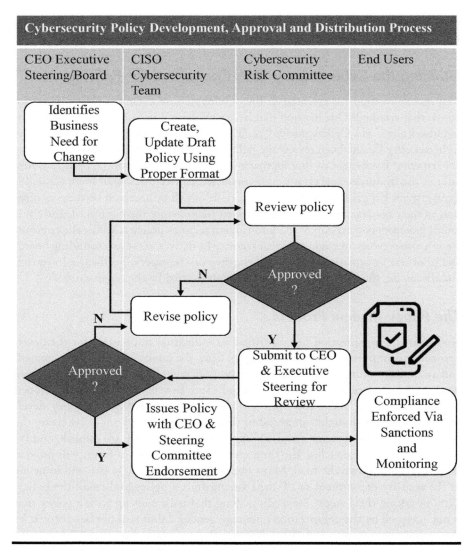

Figure 12.2 Policy development process.

1. *Policy Needs to Be Determined.* Anyone can request the need for a policy to the cybersecurity department. Business units may have new situations that are not covered by an existing security policy. If no security policies exist in the organization, the cybersecurity department needs to take the lead and establish a prioritization of policies that are necessary. The need for a policy is shown as driven from the CEO, the Executive Steering Committee (i.e., the senior leadership of the organization typically formed to review and provide

governance for business and IT initiatives), or emanating from the board of director concerns. The first swim line in Figure 12.2 represents these areas.

2. *Create, Update Existing Policy.* The CISO and cybersecurity team creates an initial draft for a new policy that can be reacted to. Caution must be taken not to copy and distribute these policies taken from books or Internet sources "as-is" as they may not be completely appropriate, enforceable, or supported by procedures within the organization.

3. *Internal Review by CISO and Cybersecurity Team.* People within the cybersecurity team will have varying levels of technical expertise, business acumen, and understanding of the organizational culture. By reviewing within the team first, many obvious errors or misunderstandings of the policy can be avoided before engaging management's limited review time. This also increases the credibility of the Information Systems Security department by bringing a quality product for review. It also saves time on minor grammatical reviews and focuses the management review on substantive policy issues.

4. *Cybersecurity Risk Committee Reviews and Recommends Policy.* This is arguably the most critical step in the process. This is where the policy begins the acceptance step within the organization. The policies are read, line by line, during these meetings and discussed to ensure that everyone understands the intent and rationale for the policy. The management commitment begins here. Why? Because they feel part of the process and have a chance to provide input, as well as thinking about how the policy would impact their own department. Contrast this method, with just sending out the policy and saying, "this is it," and the difference becomes clear. These are the same management people that are being counted on to continue to support the policy once it is distributed to the rest of the workforce. Failing in this step will guarantee failure in having a real policy.

   If we buy into the notion that a Cybersecurity Risk Committee is a good practice, logical, practical and appears to get the job done, what is the downside? Some may argue that it is a slow process, especially when senior management may be pushing to "get something out there to address security" to reduce the risks. It is a slower process while the policies are being debated; however, the benefits of (1) having a real policy that the organization can support, (2) buy-in from the management on a continuing basis, (3) reduced need to "rework the policies" later, and (4) increased understanding by management of their meaning and why they are important to outweigh the benefits of blasting out an email containing policies that were copied from another source, the name of the company changed, and distributed without prior collaboration. Policies created in the later context rarely become "real" and followed within the organization as they were not developed with a thorough analysis of how they would be supported by the business in their creation.

5. *CEO and Executive Steering Committee Approve Policy.* A committee made up of the senior leadership of the organization is typically formed to oversee the strategic investments in IT. Many times, these committees struggle with

balancing decisions on tactical "firefighting" 1–3-month concerns vs. dealing with strategic issues, and this perspective needs to be understood when addressing this type of committee. The important element in the membership of this committee is that it involves the decision leaders of the organization. These are the individuals the employees will be watching to see if they support the policies that were initially generated by the security department. Their review and endorsement of the policies are critical to obtain support in implementing the policies. Also, they may be aware of strategic plans or further operational issues not identified by middle management (through the Cybersecurity Risk Committee) that may make a policy untenable. Preferably, the committee would be an executive risk-oriented committee vs. an IT-oriented Executive Steering Committee; however, many organizations still have the CISO reporting to the Chief Information Officer (CIO), and if this is the case, the committee is likely to be the Executive IT-oriented Steering Committee.

Since time availability of the senior leadership is typically limited, these committees meet at most monthly and more typically, on a quarterly basis. Therefore, sufficient time for planning policy approval is necessary. This may seem to be run counter to the speed at which electronic policies are distributed; however, as in the case with the Cybersecurity Risk Committee review, the time delay is essential in obtaining long-term commitment.

6. *Publish Policy.* Organizations that go directly from Step 2 to this step end up with "shelfware," or if emailed, "digital dust." By the time the policy gets to this step, the security department should feel very confident that the policy will be understood by the users and supported by management. They may agree or disagree with the policy but will understand the need to follow it because it will be clear how the policy was created and reviewed. Care must be taken when publishing policies electronically, as it is not desirable to publish the same policy over and over with minor changes to grammar and terminology. Quality reviews need to be performed early in the development process so that the Cybersecurity Risk Committee and Executive Steering Committee can devote their time to substantive issues of the policy vs. pointing out the typos and correcting spelling. End users should be given the same respect and should expect to be reviewing a document free from error. The medium may be electronic, but that does not change the way people want to manage their work lives—with the amount of email already in our lives, we should try to limit the amount of "extra work" that is placed upon the readers of the policies.

Maintaining Security Policies

Security policy development is a repetitive process, where existing policies are updated and new ones are created as needed. Most of the work is in creating the initial security policies, and hopefully, if these policies were written to the appropriate level, modification of the policies should be minimal. Policy development evaluates the policies against the introduction of new technologies, law, and regulation changes, and changes to the business. Most often, the existing polices will suffice and not require major change. This rate of small change can cause organizations to not pay the appropriate attention to the policy review and update.

As a final note, it should be clear through the activities presented in this chapter that the CISO is the facilitator of the cybersecurity policy development but should not be the sole owner of them. The security policies should be owned by the organization, which, in most cases, is represented by the CEO and other members of executive management, including the CISO. Obviously, the CISO will be the one regarded as owning the policies in the organization in the absence of making it clear the security policies are owned and approved by the organization and the review committees and executive sponsorship of the direction. There will be much less challenging of the security policy if it is owned and issued at this level. All other security procedures, standards, guidelines, and implementations are dependent upon the construction of a consistent, easy-to-understand, coherent, and comprehensive cybersecurity policy. The time investment in this step is very valuable, and the impact to the organization should not be underestimated. Following the steps in this chapter will lead to more efficient and effective information security policy development and subsequent acceptance.

CHARLES CRESSON WOOD, JD: FIVE PITFALLS TO AVOID WHEN ISSUING INFORMATION SECURITY AND PRIVACY POLICIES

Independent Information Security and Privacy Consultant, InfoSecurity Infrastructure, Inc.

After working in the information security and privacy field for just under 40 years, I have had far too many occasions to notice the following five serious problems that just keep happening again and again. I hate for people to suffer needlessly, especially when the solutions are relatively straightforward and inexpensive, and so I offer five points here as warnings. For purposes of this note, I refer to these five warnings as "pitfalls," but what I mean are problems that CISOs need to avoid—if they are going to have a set of information security and privacy policies at their organization that is widely supported by the staff, consistently considered to be authoritative, and something that managers predictably point to as the way to make decisions (how to retain outsourcing firm services, how to structure new automated business solutions, how to handle nondisclosure agreements, etc.).

1. The first of these five pitfalls involves tailoring and customizing policies to fit the organization in question. Far too many organizations just copy polices that they found elsewhere, and then issue them internally without considering downstream impacts. Such an approach is a surefire way to communicate to internal staff that management is simply seeking to get an auditor's check mark in the policies box and that management does not consider policies to be an important and integral part of the internal information systems infrastructure. Every firm needs to do annual risk assessments, and those risk assessments need to expressly consider the existing policies and whether those policies are meeting the organization's unique needs. Based on such risk assessments, the internal policies should be annually updated, tailored, and customized to better fit the organization.

2. The second pitfall involves a blindness to incentive systems that already exist within the organization issuing the policies. It is unrealistic to expect people to support information security and privacy policies when internal incentive systems pull them to disregard, or even contravene, those same policies. For example, if confidential information about upcoming product releases is shared with salespersons, but they are told in policies to keep that information strictly confidential, it is predictable that salespeople will disregard the policies to make additional sales. This is because their commission structure, their quota system, and other incentive systems (perhaps that vacation in Hawaii going to the star salesperson of the year) are often in opposition to existing policies. I strongly recommend that every firm issuing policies consider how and why people would ignore, disregard, or even actively seek to defeat, the policies it has, and also the policies that it seeks to issue.

3. A third pitfall involves issuance of policies by the CIO, Chief Technology Officer (CTO), CISO, Chief Privacy Officer (CPO), or some other mid-level manager, rather than the CEO. Policies need to be observed consistently across the organization, and everyone should be expected to comply (including consultants, contractors, and temporaries). Of course, there should be a process for obtaining permission for out-of-compliance situations, but all that should be formally documented, so as to move those in an out-of-compliance state steadily towards a compliant state. Accordingly, everyone, even those who cannot currently comply, should be covered by policies and expected to abide by those same policies. If policies are issued by a mid-level manager, typically certain staff members will not recognize that mid-level manager as an authority to them, and so they will feel justified in disregarding or deliberately working against those policies. Be sure to take the time to make sure that the policies are signed off by, and clearly and visibly endorsed by, the CEO at the time of issuance.

4. A fourth pitfall involves issuing policies without accompanying training and awareness efforts. It is not realistic to assume that staff will take time out of their busy workdays, to then go on to read what many consider to be boring information security and privacy policies. It is also not realistic to assume that staff, without relevant training and awareness programs, will both understand policies and make the right choices in accordance with policies, as they go about their regular working routines. Policies need to be explained, and they need to be justified in the mind of staff members. Policy examples need to be provided, and staff needs to understand how those policies directly apply to their own working activities. The best way to do this is to deliver customized training for different types of staff members. Thus, the systems administrators should get a different training and awareness program than the end users in the marketing department. Make sure your budget for policies includes practical training and awareness programs. Requiring regular attendance at training and awareness programs and sign-off on forms acknowledging that they understood the material covered are both strongly recommended.

5. The fifth pitfall involves issuing policies as stand-alone components of an information systems infrastructure, perhaps simply posting them on an intranet server, without any tie-in with other business activities. To be effective, there must be multiple direct tie-ins with other activities at the organization. For example, if new software cannot be moved into any production web server, unless security and privacy tests have first been successfully performed, and the person in charge of change control diligently supports the policy requiring this testing step, now there is an action-forcing mechanism ensuring compliance. With such an enforcement system, developers will regularly read the relevant policy and design to the policy. There are many more opportunities to integrate policies into regular business processes and to provide policies in convenient places where people are making decisions, and it is this tight integration with existing business processes that make policies influential and consistently observed.

Suggested Reading

1. National Institute of Standards and Technology (NIST). 2014. Special Publication 800-16 Rev1 (Draft 3): A Role-Based Model for Federal Information Technology/Cybersecurity Training. https://csrc.nist.gov/CSRC/media/Publications/sp/800-16/rev-1/draft/documents/sp800_16_rev1_3rd-draft.pdf.
2. Peltier, T. R. 2007. *Information Security Policies and Procedures, A Practitioner's Reference.* 2nd edn. Boca Raton, FL. Taylor & Francis.

3. Wood, Charles Cresson and Information Shield. Information Security Policies Made Easy, Version13.https://informationshield.com/products/information-security-policies-made-easy/ispmenewinversion13/.
4. Greene, S. 2014. *Security Program and Policies: Principles and Practices*. 2nd edn. Upper Saddle River, NJ. Pearson.
5. National Institute of Standards and Technology (NIST). 2003. Special Publication 800–50: Building an Information Technology Security Awareness and Training Program. https://nvlpubs.nist.gov/nistpubs/Legacy/SP/nistspecialpublication800-50.pdf.
6. Chief Security Officer. 2016. Security Policy Samples, Templates and Tools. CSOonline (January 25). https://www.csoonline.com/article/3019126/security/security-policy-samples-templates-and-tools.html.
7. HIPAA Collaborative of Wisconsin. Security and Privacy Resources. http://hipaacow.org/resources/hipaa-cow-documents/.

STAFF

6

Chapter 13

Multigenerational Workforce Team Dynamics

We must not confuse dissent with disloyalty.

Edward R Murrow, 1908–1965

Just look around the workplace and we can see times are changing, morphing into a new work environment. In the words from one of the songs from the hit musical Hamilton, "Look Around, Look Around at how lucky we are to be alive right now." The musical itself is a prime example of how our tastes as a society have changed, as the musical reworks the story of Alexander Hamilton's efforts during the summer of 1776 to achieve American independence. The Founding Fathers and major character actors cast represented diversity, as well as utilizing nonstop hip-hop, rhythm and blues, pop music, soul music, and traditional show tunes to tell the story. The musical was critically acclaimed by receiving record 16 Tony nominations, winning the best musical award and ten others in 2016, and still experiences tremendous box office success today.

Our Workforce Is Changing

By now, the question must be surfacing—so, what does the Hamilton musical have to do with our workforce today? Everything. Everything that was taken for granted as "the way things were done" has shifted. Hamilton took an "old story" and modernized it, made a musical appeal to today's generation by speeding it up, changing the music to something catchy. The story also highlighted a "young, scrappy, and hungry" Alexander Hamilton who was determined to "not throw away my shot (at success)." Does this resonate with a new generation in the workforce that is predominant today? That is right, the millennial generation. Just as the boomer generation in their early years echoed the same sentiment—the desire to shift away from the way processes were performed to a new way of doing things. The success of Hamilton is not due to one generation watching the musical, or only those that liked hip-hop before they saw the musical. Nope. Just look at the crowd on any given sold-out performance, and Hamilton so brilliantly was able to bring all generations together through music, story, and history. Our workforces can become "Hamilton-like" and bring multiple, diverse generations together, even with ways of doing things much like the different music and style of musical delivery showcased in Hamilton, to create an experience valuable to each generation at the same time.

The *7-S Framework Applied to Cybersecurity Leadership* factors of *structure* (defining the functions of the staff) and *skills* (defining the skills to carry out the program) are complimented by discussing the a) workforce changes, b) generational differences, and c) individual-type preferences (using the Myers-Briggs Type Indicator® (MBTI) Personality Type Indicator). These forces presented in the rest of this chapter provide insight for the Chief Information Security Officer (CISO) into understanding the team beyond the specific job they are asked to perform. As a leader, this is essential to know where the "team is coming from" before addressing the individual skill requirement areas.

Types of Changes Impacting Work

Changes in the demographics of the global workforce, paired with other changes made by organizations to increase profitability, have clearly changed the way work gets done. While this is not an exhaustive list, the following indicate the types of workforce changes that must be navigated within our organizations.

1. *Technology.* Work is being changed by advances in technology whereby workers are being displaced at increasing rates. Consider McDonald's, the large chain feeds over 68 million people per day (1% of world's population) and is the largest beef purchaser in the United States at 1 billion pounds annually, who has rolled out self-service ordering kiosks in their stores. Customers would order their food on touch screen kiosks, and then, employees would serve them at their tables. Enhancements include ordering and paying through a mobile app. Think about this shift in product and the implications for not only the employees working in the store, but also for the types of individuals the company would need to recruit to develop this technology. What happens when the self-service menus malfunction? This requires a different skill set. Companies are experiencing transformations in the technology used and require employees willing to learn how to use the new technology.

2. *Talent Shortages.* Nowhere is this more evident than in the information security space—recruiting experienced staff is difficult to find. An estimated shortfall of 1.8 million security personnel is expected by 2022. This means organizations must not only be competitive with pay and benefit packages but must also know what attracts and retains their workers beyond these perks. According to Gallup, over 51% of the workforces are watching the job market or actively looking for a new job. This churn of employees can create considerable recruiting, training, and onboarding costs for companies. Given the talent shortages combined with the churn, this can result in months without a position filled, leading to other individuals having to pick up the work until a new employee can be found and trained, a transition that may take 6–9 months assuming a replacement can be found quickly. These talent shortages are illustrated in Figure 13.1.

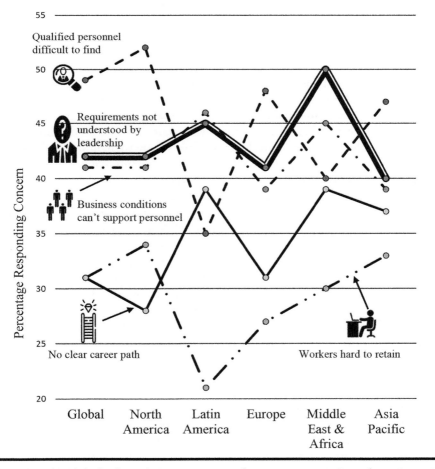

Figure 13.1   Global talent shortage reasons (by percentage). (Data from Frost & Sullivan, *2017 Global Information Security Workforce Study,* **2017.)**

GREG WITTE: USING NICE FRAMEWORK TO ATTRACT TALENT

Senior Security Engineer, G2

A critical element of the CISO's portfolio is a capable and engaged cybersecurity workforce. Support for an organizational cybersecurity program spans a broad range of work roles from oversight and governance, to operations, to monitoring and incident response. Cybersecurity is still an emerging technical area, and only recently have CISOs begun to understand the knowledge, skills, and abilities that are needed from workers in each type of role. Because such workers have been few, finding and keeping qualified candidates (without breaking the bank) has been a real challenge.

Some organizations have relied upon industry-recognized certifications as a measure of a candidate's qualification for a particular role. Many certifications help illustrate the person's understanding of a general body of knowledge about cybersecurity, but sometimes those certifications reflect a candidate's short-term memorization rather than their long-term understanding and ability.

Today, CISOs can turn to the National Initiative for Cybersecurity Education (NICE) to help better understand how to document, measure, and improve what is expected from their cybersecurity workers. An important element is the NICE Framework that describes more than 50 work roles that help support a CISO's needs. NICE maintains a dynamic database including typical tasks that are performed by staff in those roles, and the unique skills and abilities for successful achievement of organizational goals.

NICE helps CISOs to define what they are looking for in a candidate. The program is used by many schools to ensure that students are ready to fit the bill successfully. Because the job to be done is well described, the CISO can measure the worker's performance progress along a career path—the employee knows what is expected and can demonstrate capability and improvement, and that helps with job satisfaction. The process helps fulfill the CISO's need to recruit, hire, retain, and promote an effective and motivated workforce.

NICE is managed by the National Institute of Standards and Technology. More information is available by visiting www.nist.gov/nice.

3. *Workforce Consolidation.* Companies spread out across multiple inefficient offices are consolidating into campuses with greater interaction. Businesses go through cycles of change, with some relocating to urban areas to attract new, younger talent. McDonald's decided to relocate the corporate headquarters from the Chicago suburbs to Chicago for the first time in almost four decades, with the mayor of Chicago stating the reasons as, "McDonald's has identified the keys to success to today's global market, talent, technology, and

access to transportation networks." McDonald's stated that they wanted to "encourage innovation and ensuring great talent is excited about where they work." Amazon also searched for a second global headquarters in the eastern United States, building jobs for 50,000 employees, and initially narrowed the list to 20 different cities interested in attracting the second headquarters.

Companies are also collapsing the data centers through outsourcing activities, particularly in the cybersecurity discipline through the establishment of Managed Security Service Providers. Cloud technology, improved bandwidth speeds, and interconnectivity have made these changes possible and an affordable option. Skills sets are colocated physically in data centers, or individuals work remotely from home environments. I once visited a service desk center with many skilled employees speaking very good English in Romania, where employees were sourced from technical graduates from a nearby university. All the help desk calls from around the world were routed to Romania for resolution using advanced databases to quickly resolve issues from multiple clients. The information processing was performed at a data center in India. Prior to this change, help desk individuals were needed at many offices in the United States to field the technical calls. After the migration, only a small percentage of local onsite staff were necessary and then only for service requiring physical interaction. In fact, the local data center in Romania has only two people (one for redundancy and shift coverage) operating it, the management of the servers was administered remotely from India. They were only needed in the event a physical action was required—the rest was all controlled remotely from India.

JOHN IATONNA: DEVELOP FROM WITHIN OR HIRE A CONSULTANT?

CISO, Spencer Stuart

The right mix of talent and chemistry is key to the success of any security program, and the decisions made at the outset will have a lasting impact. But before making any staffing decisions, it is imperative to understand the challenges and risks the business faces. That risk assessment will guide the decisions you make when resourcing your program. One of the first judgments is whether to hire from outside or promote from within. Both have their merits and their drawbacks. That decision may already be made if there is an urgent need to resolve a significant exposure or a very specialized skill set that is lacking. But in the absence of a pressing risk, the hire vs. train question is a tough one. Early in my CISO career, when building out an information security program, I needed to address several near-term exposures as well as plan for the long-term development of information security talent on my team. It was a good learning experience for someone new to a leadership role. I had a requirement for an application security specialist for an urgent website launch; that person would also need to lay down the foundational elements to a formal Secure Systems Development Life Cycle (SSDLC) program. I brought in an external consultant for the engagement. The website security assessment was easily done, and the foundational SSDLC work was completed; but at the end of the contract, there was not an internal resource to transition the knowledge to. So much of the learning and SSDLC process understanding left with the contractor. In another situation when I sought to promote an internal candidate working in an information technology (IT) support role, I miscalculated the length of time it would take to train that resource up to a specialized security engineer. Additionally, I underestimated the difficulty in extricating that person from their legacy duties as an IT support analyst. It can be tough to reroute well-worn paths. Clearly, team chemistry will be of critical importance as well. A good mix of veteran team members willing to teach and mentor less experienced staff is a great model to develop talent at both ends of the experience continuum. As with any team dynamic, understanding the strengths and weakness of each team member and balancing those evaluations across the team will be critical.

4. *Aging Workforce.* The global workforce is getting older, and our companies are a microcosm of this aging process. In fact, the workforce is shrinking globally in developed regions, such as Europe, where in 2010 more people retired than joined the workforce. The group of 45- to 64-year-old individuals globally has been the main driver of the 1990–2010 workforce, growing 67% during this period. The group of 45- to 64-year-old individuals is expected to grow 41.2% globally between 2010 and 2030, mostly in the developing world. More retired men (35% of men aged 65–74) are expected to be in the workforce in 2020 vs. only 25% of this age group in 2000, in part due to the increase in the retirement age and in part due to economic events and lack of accumulated savings.

5. *Gender Diversity.* Slightly more than half of the global workforce are women (50.5%), and 76.8% of men are in the workforce. Within the cybersecurity space, women make up a statistically significant low number of positions. According to the 2017 Global Information Security Workforce Study, women comprised only 11% of the information security workforce, far less than the makeup of the global workforce. The percentages differ by region between North America (14%), Europe (7%), Middle East (5%), Latin America (8%), Africa (9%), and Asia-Pacific (10%). In terms of education, women command

a slight advantage with 51% having earned a master's degree or higher, compared to 45% of men. More men hold computer science degrees (48%) than women (42%), with a wider gap between those holding engineering degrees, where men (22%) hold an advantage over the women (14%). All of this adds up to that the industry must do more to attract women into the information/cybersecurity careers if these numbers are to increase. The 11% has held about the same over the last decade of the survey. There have been efforts by different conferences to appeal to women at an earlier age to engage them in the field of cybersecurity.

STACY MILL: WOMEN IN LEADERSHIP—PRACTICAL ADVICE

CISO and Vice President, Global Compliance, Spirit AeroSystems

This stigma attached to women leaders makes us sound special. In so many ways, that is true. We own the car pool lane at school, we give birth, and we are the core of our family support systems. I offer the same is true in business. It does not matter if you have ever been married or had children. Women are a grounding force in the industry today. What makes us stand apart is the fact that we must climb higher, prove ourselves countless times, all while being strategic thinkers who see the big picture to secure our business to achieve business goals. Heaven forbid we be seen as "Emotional!" And Man, have I worked for some emotional men. My point is that we are human! Our only difference as women is the pressure we put on ourselves to be perfect or the social stigma of "doing it all" (backward and in heals). As a tenured CISO, I have learned staying calm is very important. More importantly, listening is a key trait to understand what is important to people. Forget winning an argument for cybersecurity but understand that the argument should not happen in the first place. We must learn what is important for our business, our partners, and our counterparts in industry to achieve and build the conversation towards the achievement of those goals. I have used a couple of analogies: (1) Boy Scouts do not ask you "Would you like to buy a $5 box of popcorn for $20." They ask, "Would you like to help the homeless?"—How can you say no to a little kid? Some do but many do not. (2) The fastest race cars in the world have the best braking systems as well. It is not to keep them from winning the race. It is so they finish alive and intact. The same goes for the CISO role. We must have the conversation about what matters and work towards those goals—whether it is supply chain, manufacturing, banking, etc. All businesses run off some sort of technology. We need to win the race, the business race, and come out alive!

These changes will take some time to implement, as these demographics cannot change overnight without truly figuring out why women are not being attracted in large numbers to this field. The issue is not unique to the information security field, as women make up only 26% of the computer scientists and 12% of the engineers with the numbers decreasing over the past 30 years. Possible avenues to attract more women may include (1) engaging women early in school, (2) reframing the conversation to appeal to a passion for making a difference and using technology to achieve these goals, (3) reducing unconscious biases such as differences in how collaboration should be viewed as a strength, and being directive is not abrasive, (4) reimagining the tribe—we need to redefine the stereotype images that girls may have on Science, Technology, Engineering, and Mathematics (STEM) careers so they can see themselves as having these role models they can relate to and aspire to. The gap in women in the cybersecurity space and the distributions of the positions

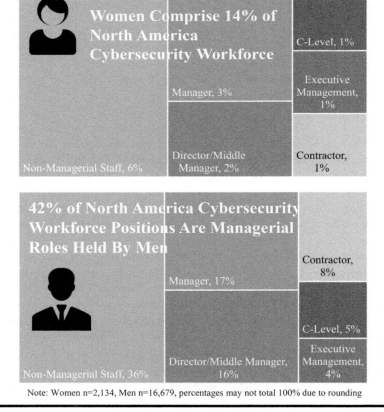

Note: Women n=2,134, Men n=16,679, percentages may not total 100% due to rounding

Figure 13.2 Cybersecurity workforce gender distribution by Organizational position—North America. (Data from Frost & Sullivan, *2017 Global Information Security Workforce Study: Women in Cybersecurity*, 2017.)

held can be seen in Figure 13.2, illustrating 14% women in the North America cybersecurity workforce as women. The number of women in the cybersecurity workforce is even greater than Europe (7%) and Asia (8%), with women in executive management positions being correspondingly less at 0% in Europe and 1% in Asia-Pacific, and 0% at the C-level positions. In other words, the gap is a global issue with similar distributions in the workforce as North America in terms of a) wide disparity in men vs. women population and b) disparity in women holding managerial positions.

EMILY HEATH: BUILDING A TALENTED AND DIVERSE TEAM

VP and CISO, United Airlines

At the time of writing, statistics say there are 20% more cybersecurity jobs than there are people to fill them. Add to this that the national average of women in cyber roles is 10%, and people of color is at 12%; clearly, we have a problem that we cannot sustain. Talent is in high demand and there is a shortage of people with the right skills in the cyber field and not enough focus on a diverse and creative workforce. These statistics cannot stay this way if we are to equip our organizations to tackle the ever-increasing threats of cyberattacks and plan for our futures. As leaders, it is our obligation to change this; it is a critical part of our job. So how do you build a talented and diverse team, and more importantly, keep them! In the last year at United Airlines, we have doubled the size of our cyber team, and we currently have 48% females and 42% people of color, statistics we are very proud of. Here are a few things we did that helped along the way.

1. Firstly, we made it a conscious goal to plan for talent pipelines, missing skills, and gaps in diversity. Every leader was involved, and we reported out on it every quarter to the entire team.
2. We made it mandatory that every open position had a diverse slate. I refuse to believe that diverse candidates do not exist, it is up to us to go and find them.
3. We dedicated resources to work with our human resources (HR) partners and build out talent pipelines in multiple ways. These not only included the corporate intern and graduate programs with some of the larger universities, but also included partnerships with local community colleges where the kids who may not have the financial ability to go to a bigger college still have oodles of talent and so much to offer. We also partnered with a number of nonprofit organizations who promote opportunities for minority groups.
4. How to keep people? Well, that is all about the secret sauce of leadership!

Adapting to Change

"I don't have an attitude problem, you have a perception problem!" may be the expression communicated in the hallways these days. There may be some truth in the statement if we have not taken the time to understand the changes taking place from the perspective of those making the changes.

Change impacts each of us in different ways, some readily embrace change, and others fight change until it is forced upon them. There are reasons for the resistance to chance that are not necessarily bad. For example, those resisting change may be of the mindset that more work needs to be done to develop the idea, as they can foresee the risks of rapidly implementing the change. These individuals are often thought to be more risk-averse, and this observation may be fair. These individuals may need more information or facts before coming fully onboard with a new idea. Conversely, others may jump head-first into the idea as they find making changes to be an exhilarating journey and believe whatever issues are raised along the way will ultimately be mitigated by a, sometimes creative, solution or workaround. These individuals are viewed as the risk-takers and believe in starting new ideas before the competition does, or the market or service opportunity will be missed if bogged down by the "why this can't work statements." The classic change curve published by Elisabeth Kubler-Ross describes the five stages of grief and was subsequently adapted towards organizational change by Schneider and Goldwasser in 1998 to the class change curve we are familiar with today. The curve shown in Figure 13.3 is the curve referred to most often today.

As seen in the change curve diagram, when changes are introduced, there is a shock, "Why would they do this?"—followed by denial, "surely, this isn't really happening," to anger, "don't they care about us who have been here and know this place?"—depression, "not sure we will get through this," acceptance, "I will have

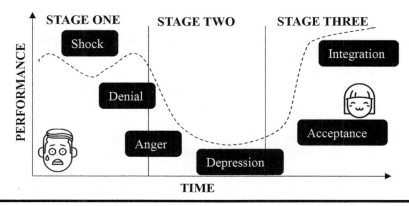

Figure 13.3 Adapting to change curve.

to figure out how to work in the new ecosystem," to integration, "this is really cool, I am learning so much and the new way is so much better." Organizational changes take a while to absorb and everyone does not accept the change at the same rate, again due to the risk aversion, experience, and personal impact the changes may have on the individual.

People change projects, jobs, skills, and experiences as part of a normal part of a career; however, these changes may not have as much impact as the changes created due to the emergence of a new generation in the workforce, bringing with them a new set of values, ideas, thought processes, and expectations for the work environment. Failure to understand these changes and how the company needs to adapt puts the company at a disadvantage with their peers. Individuals talk to colleagues outside of the organization to which they are employed, and their comments get around, positive or negative. In fact, a dissatisfied customer will tell between 9 and 15 people of a bad purchase experience, and around 13% of dissatisfied customers will tell more than 20 people! Think about relating these similar statistics to the workplace.

We are at a point in history where four generations are working side-by-side in the workforce, and with the emergence of the latest generation ("Generation Z" 1995-present) now in the postcollege workforce, it is imperative the differences between the generations be understood so that our organizations can appropriately structure and adapt for success. The oft (liberally)-summarized advice of Gandhi "Be the change you want to see in the world" clearly applies here—it is up to each of us to adapt and understand the environment to which we work in to become more effective. As the CISO, understanding the different generations and why they view the work differently and approach it differently is critical.

Six Different Generations Defined

Throughout history, generations have typically defined themselves in 15- to 20-year periods. These periods are not set in concrete, as it is only until after the generation grows up and moves into adulthood that time periods really established. Generations therefore are defined by the values of people in a period—a period that includes the teenage years these individuals were learning about the world they live in. It has been noted that the teenage years are very impressionable years, comprising the period where people are developing their own informed view of the world based upon their environment, education, world events, and upbringing. Consider, e.g., how different the views of a society may be that grew up during a time when the teenager saw parents struggling to keep the house and pay the bills, impacting what the teenager could do and buy vs. the teenager that grew up in a time where parent's jobs were plentiful, salaries were rising, and money flowed easily. These two teenagers would develop different perceptions of the world.

We must always use caution then attempting to put a generation's norms into a bucket and stereotype the generation. After all, we are all different and are free to make our own judgments and opinions. People may hold beliefs predominant in other generations or may choose to identify more with a different generation. However, history has shown that each generation can be defined by some high-level values, technologies, and norms that were seen through shared experiences. There are six generations in society today, primarily four that are in the workforce. The generations are as follows:

1. *The Greatest Generation.* Born before 1928, this generation (93 years old and over in 2020) became young men and women during the difficult times of World War II (WWII). As Tom Brokaw noted in his book "The Greatest Generation," this generation's perseverance through difficult times was a testament to their extraordinary character. These individuals were born and raised through an era containing economic depression and war and as a result, these individuals developed values of "personal responsibility, duty, honor and faith." Their resilience helped build the American economy, defeat the oppression of Adolph Hitler, and make advances in science. According to Brokaw, it was the efforts of this generation that the successive generations are experiencing the affluence and freedom to make choices in their futures. They are also as a group, not a boastful generation for what they have done; rather, they have been remarkably humble.

2. *The Silent Generation (aka Traditionalist Generation).* Born 1928–1945 (Ages 75–92 in 2020) holding several theories as to where the term "silent generation" came from. Children of this generation were very quiet and worked very hard and were to "be seen and not heard." Senator Joseph McCarthy's attempts to promote anti-communist sentiments in America may have resulted in people being afraid to speak their opinions and people were cautious about where they went and who they were seen with. They wanted to work within the system so that negative remarks would not be put in their permanent records. In other words, they kept their heads down. Time magazine also published an article in 1951 labeling the generation as such, noting they were unimaginative, unadventurous, cautious, and withdrawn. These children grew up during the period known as the Great Depression (1929–1939), affecting all social classes where people were losing their homes and starving. Over 24% of Americans were unemployed and many unemployed in Europe, such as 9.8% in the United Kingdom (reliable estimates are difficult to obtain as some individuals working in public works jobs were counted in the unemployment figures). While this generation grew up during the depression, they were born too late to be the war heroes of the prior "Greatest Generation" and born too early to be part of the changing boomer generation. This generation

initiated the "divorce resolution" as they were entering midlife, and Gail Sheehy popularized the term "midlife crisis" during this generation. This generation faced a booming economy when they came out of school; some would consider fortunate for their timing of not having to endure the wars and struggles (parents made the sacrifices for them). Pensions were the focus of job interviews, as they did not want to take chances and as they saw the devastation of the impacts of the depression on their parents and preceding generation.

3. *Baby Boom Generation.* Born 1946–1964 (Ages 56–74 in 2020), this generation was appropriately named due to the 76+ million births occurring during the postwar period. This generation became 40% of the population, resulting from the 10 million people coming home from the war. The WWII veterans benefited from the Government Issue (G.I.) Bill, paving the way for the parents to get an education and buy a home, leading to years of boomers to live in prosperity. Due to the G.I. Bill, 49% of those going to college in 1947 were veterans. Because of the size of this generation, they were very influential in creating change. The oldest of this generation reached the retirement age of 65 (when it started increasing to save the social security programs) in 2011, and the youngest will reach this age in 2029, with over 10,000 boomers retiring from the workforce daily. After the war, the average age of marriage had dropped and people in their early twenties were getting married and having babies creating this large generation. This resulted in overcrowding of schools, competition for colleges, and increased competition for starting jobs. This led to boomers ("Baby" has been dropped from the "baby boomer" term used to describe this generation in many news articles), competing for resources and success.

4. *Generation X.* Born 1965–1980 (Ages 40–55 in 2020), this generation was the named after the name of a chapter in a 1983 book by historian Paul Fissell entitled "Class: A Guide Though the American Status System," as well as the name of a 1991 book by Douglas Copeland entitled "Generation X: Tales for an Accelerated Culture." This generation was slightly less than the boomer generation with 61.2 million people, as the birth rates declined. This generation experienced the recession in 1991 and the dot-com bust in 2002. The name "Gen X" has remained in North America, along with other names highlighting the disenchantment including Generation Bof ("whatever") in France, the Latin America "Crisis Generation" representing the financial troubles in the region during the time. The generation marked times of uncertainty and social change. Some of the late-year boomers born from 1961–1964 sometimes identify more with the values of the Generation Xers. According to Pew Research, the number of Gen Xers is expected to surpass the number of boomers in 2028, while being a smaller population than the Millennials as shown in Figure 13.4.

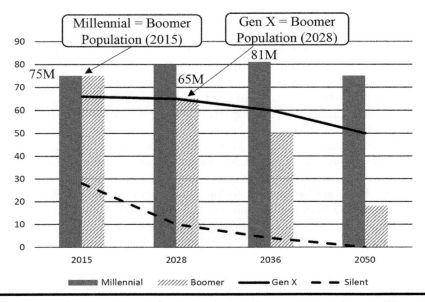

Figure 13.4 Projected population by generation. (Data from Fry, R., *Millennials overtake Baby Boomers as America's largest Generation*, April 25, 2016, Pew Research Center, Washington, DC.)

5. *Millennial Generation.* Born 1981–1995 (Ages 25–39 in 2020), this generation, also known as Generation Y, surpassed the number of baby boomers in the United States in 2016 with 75.4 million millennials, contrasted with 74.9 million boomers, representing 25% of the population. This generation is also more diverse than other preceding generations, with 44.2% part of a minority race or ethnic group. Demographics changed significantly with young men in 2014 being much more likely to live at home with their parents (35%) than living with a spouse or partner (23%) vs. the boomer generation whereby in 1960 only 23% lived in their parent's homes and 56% lived with spouse or partner. The employment and wages, and the 2008 recession, may have contributed to fewer individuals romantically settling down with a partner before age 35. Much has been written about the millennial generation in recent years, as large groups are heavily marketed to and there is a desire to understand the changes they bring to the workplace, culture, and society. Many of the millennials are predominantly children of the boomers and older-generation Xers. As young immigrants join the United States, this population is expected to grow and peak in 2036 with 81.1 million, also shown in Figure 13.4 (before net mortality begins decreasing the numbers), with the oldest millennial being 56 years old.

6. *Generation Z or the iGeneration.* Born 1996–? (Ages 24 and under in 2020), this generation is the "next" or the "current" generation reaching adulthood. While much focus has been on understanding the millennial population due

to their significant size, the first college graduates started emerging in 2017. This generation is coming out of college with an average school debt of $37,172 (2016); however, they are also willing to be flexible in terms of job location (41% willing to relocate and 38% willing to accept the first offer they receive). More than 58% considered it acceptable to work on evenings and weekends.

And so here we are, with a workforce as shown in Figure 13.5. As the figure illustrates, the number of "boomers" in the workforce has been steadily declining as the boomers age, and the number of millennials has now surpassed the number of

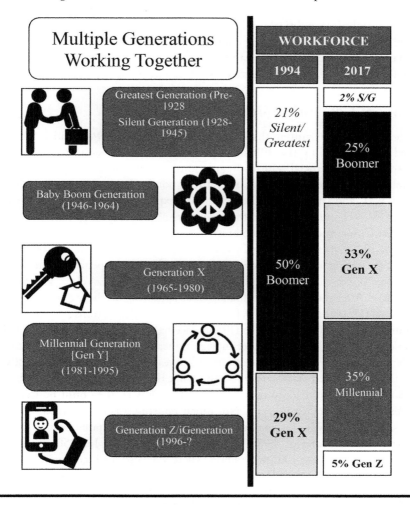

Figure 13.5 *Demographics and U.S. Labor Force participation by generation.* (Data from *Millennials are the largest generation in U.S. labor force*, April 10, 2018, Pew Research Center, Washington, DC.)

boomers and the number of Generation X individuals in the workforce and will serve as a large voice to influence the changes in how work is done.

How Was Each Generation Shaped?

While the above may be instructive in understanding the time frames of the generations that went before us, there is much more to the story. Each generation has been shaped through the events occurring in the environment at the time. Our values are shaped by growing up when we grew up. Let us examine some of these economic, technical, political, and social forces impacting the generations to further our understanding by putting context around the "teenage years" and how we may have been shaped. Then, we can review the events shaping each of the last five generations and how these values may have implications for the workplace.

The Silent Generation (Traditionalists)

This generation of 56 million shared the experiences of the 1940s and 1950s in the United States including the difficulties of the Great Depression, Roosevelt's New Deal (programs, financial reforms, regulations, and public works projects to provide relief for the unemployed and bring the nation back to prosperity), the Korean War, WWII, and the GI Bill. The generation experienced success with the allied forces in WWII and experienced the early days of the Cold War (tension between the Soviet Union and the United States).

In the 1940s, there were many inventions such as duct tape, the jeep built for the military, the Turing machine (to encrypt/decrypt information), penicillin, nuclear reaction/atomic bomb silly putty, the Bikini, instant photography, Velcro, and Legos to name a few! After the war, new technology was appearing on the scene including the credit cards (1950), television (1951), first video recorder (1951), transistor radio (1953), computer hard disk (1956), satellite (1957), pacemaker (1959), copy machine (1959), and microchip (1959). As with all technologies, there were versions of these technologies demonstrated as proof of concepts in earlier years; however, it was the 1940s and 1950s that experienced massive technology change that we take for granted today.

As people started to raise their families after WWII, they built houses in the suburbs at an ever-increasing rate. Not much housing was built during the Great Depression and the War, fueling demand for housing. The population was growing, and with low-cost loans for the G.I.s, houses were affordable. In 1950, more people lived in the suburbs than anywhere else. There was also an increase in consumer goods, as factories oriented the production towards consumer items such as appliances, cars, household goods instead of supporting the war efforts.

This generation could be best characterized as a hard-working generation that respected authority, hard work, honor, and delayed gratification. This was the generation that spent 30 plus years working for one company to retire with a company pension and a gold watch. There was a loyalty and identity between the company and the employee. One could regard this as the "company family," whereby when a job was no longer needed, the employee was retained and moved to another job vs. laid off, unless economic times were extremely dire for the organization. Work was considered a privilege by this generation, and promotions were something that was earned through tenure and productivity in the job. This generation has been referred to as the wealthiest generation.

While this generation has, for the most part, retired from the workforce (age 75–92 in 2020), they often had great interpersonal skills as they dealt with individuals in one-on-one situations. Technology adoption by this group may be slow to maintain a preference for the way things are done, as they value morals, security, safety, and consistency and may be more resistant to change as a result. The top-down chain of command and the hierarchy in communications and approval are viewed as something that should be respected. The bottom line is this generation were hard workers without a lot of fanfare and could be relied upon to take responsibility. Many of our organizations and the organizational structures in place today were designed by the Silent Generation and the Greatest Generation that preceded it.

The Baby Boom Generation (aka "Boomers")

Much has been studied, analyzed, analyzed some more, and dissected a third time for this generation over their history. Being the postwar children, this generation grew up in a time where there were many teenagers, many kids to play with. Their shared experiences of the 1960s and 1970s included Kennedy's "Camelot" Presidency that glorified the White House, ultimately experiencing assassinations of significant leaders—President John F Kennedy killed November 22, 1963, followed by Martin Luther King Jr., April 4, 1968, the most recognized spokesperson for the civil rights movement and still famous today for his speech determined to end racism entitled "I Have a Dream" 5 years earlier. A few months later, the assassination news continued with U.S. Senator Robert F. Kennedy, a younger brother of President Kennedy on June 6, 1968. In just a few short years, these assassinations robbed youth of their innocence—that the world was not as kind as the era of television, rock 'n' roll and fun times could have led them to believe.

With television reaching the widespread penetration where there were less than 10,000 TV sets in the country in 1945, by 1950 there were 6 million and 1960 almost 60 million or 9/10 households. As a child growing up in the 1960s, I never recall a time where we did not have a TV, and I recall clearly what a big deal it was to be one of the first houses on the block with a Color TV in 1965. TV was an essential part of this culture as a form of entertainment. There was also the steady stream of news about the Vietnam War on TV, and the protests of the war.

There are social issues such as the civil rights movement and Women's Liberation Groups fighting for equality. The generation witnessed the distrust of government, Watergate and Nixon's resignation as President. Credit cards were discovered and used by the generation in large ways, many times in "keeping up with the Jones" as more and more goods such as new houses, cars, and technology were coming to the market.

Boomers had a distrust for authority, unlike prior generations, and lashed out against "the establishment." Their goal was to change the world—and in fact, many changes were made, including putting a man on the moon. The motto of "sex, drugs (wanting them to be free) and Rock 'n' Roll" was the motto. Many boomers received identity through the work life—the job title, status, employee recognition, a parking space, and achieving a good salary leading to material wealth. This drove competitive boomers to increase the number of hours worked during their careers.

The boomers were known to build larger houses than prior generations, resulting in the "McMansions" averaging house size approaching 2,600 square feet as shown in Figure 13.6. The generation started to experience downsizing as employers were "reengineering" and moving jobs overseas. The social contract between the company and the employee was starting to see cracks. Employees also took advantage of company growth beyond their organizations and sought jobs where they could attain the promotion and the new shiny car as a perk. This generation also started to see the shifting of responsibility from employer to employee for their future, implementing 401K plans to shift more responsibility for retirement to the employee, and eliminating pensions. According to Towers Watson, less than 25% of Fortune 500 companies still offer pensions, and of those, less than 7% are of the traditional variety based on the worker's pay and number of years with the company as experienced by the prior generations. This change should not be a surprise, where boomers wanted to change the world and manage their own destiny, reflecting this in retirement as well. Due to the dot com bust and recession in 2008, many boomers saw their retirement savings drop. An American Association of Retired Persons (AARP) survey of boomers indicated that seven of ten boomers expected to work beyond the retirement age (generally 65, but higher for younger boomers). Where the prior generations have defined retirement as a time for leisure, travel, enjoyment, time with the grandkids and relaxation, the boomers, having placed a priority of work over their personal lives most of their working career, view retirement as a time to incorporate work into their work lives. With the average boomer today reaching 65 years old having a life expectancy into the 80s (50% chance), and boomers hearing the call from financial advisors that one or more of a couple has a greater chance than ever before with advances in medicine and more focus on healthier lifestyles of living into the nineties. In the 2010 census, the number of people over 90 tripled since 1980, reaching 1.9 million in 2010, and is expected to increase more than 7.6 million by 2050 according to the U.S. Census Bureau. The significance of this is that boomers with increased longevity expectations and less savings combine to their cohort remaining longer in the workforce. As a result, the last boomers that could have been expected to retire at full retirement age of 67 were born as late as 1964, meaning that boomers may be in the workforce until 2031 or later should they desire to work beyond this age.

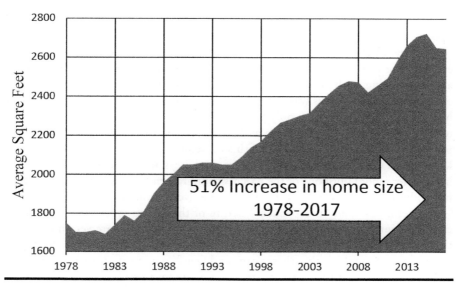

Figure 13.6   Average square feet in new single-family houses sold 1978–2017. (From Census Bureau. 2018. www.census.gov/construction/chars/pdf/soldsquarefeet.pdf.)

Generation X

The name given to this generation could not have been more appropriate, as this generation felt as if they were in some ways, the generation left in the middle. Just as the middle child grapples for identity and role within the family, whereby the older child defines the role of what it means to be a child, the middle one is "second" by definition and then the praise and expanded responsibility is showered upon the cuteness and freedoms the last child has (forged by the children that preceded them), so goes the generations. Generation X has the dubious place in the history of being sandwiched in between the baby boomers getting much attention and experiencing many new changes in society, and that of the generation to follow, another large generation, the millennials.

Since attitudes are shaped during the teenage years, this generation witnessed increases in unemployment among adults getting reengineered out of their jobs and having to "start over" with other employers. The large-scale layoffs ended the loyalty between organizations, with members of the Silent/boomer Generations (their parents or older siblings), being laid off in their later years as they were approaching retirement age. This bred mistrust in the eyes of Gen Xers for corporate environments. Who would believe that a company would be there for them as they got older? Those with older siblings, possibly late-stage boomers, also witnessed them in the workforce with shifting employment as companies downsized, moved factories, automated, and so forth. The impact of this was to develop a generation of "free agents," whereby building of skills and being resourceful as an individual (vs. the team orientation of the prior boomer generation), as there was a reliance to depend upon oneself to survive.

The layoffs were not the only reason for this reliance on self—more women were entering the workforce during these years, in part due to the rising divorce rates and in part due to the increase in women attending college and pursuing careers outside of the home. This was the first generation on a wide scale to see parents at home during the early years, only to leave the home when they reached school age to join or rejoin their employers. In many cases, it took two working spouses to support the household. The net effect of this movement was the creation of "latchkey kids"—kids were named this as they were given keys and came home to an empty house after school until one of the parents could return home from work. The kids had to become resourceful and fend for themselves during this time, building the "resourcefulness" and "independent" nature of this group today. The term "helicopter parents" has also surfaced today as well, where parents are very involved in the lives of their children. Some physiologists posit this was due to the feeling of being alone as a child during these years, and Gen X parents wanting their children to feel loved and that their parents are always there for them.

A few years ago, I had a Gen X employee who asked if he could attend a 9:30 AM event on a Monday at his school called "Donuts with Dad." The "workaholic boomer" would have never considered such a request and may have viewed it as career-limiting, as Monday morning would be a key part of the week, most likely filled with prescheduled meetings. Of course, I obliged, and it occurred to me that deep inside, as a boomer, this is *exactly* what I would have loved to have requested in my early work days, but with the constraints of the career, would not have asked. This would have been the type of activity that most likely would not have even been scheduled, as schools would fear no dads would be available to show up, especially on a Monday, and instead would have made a grandparent's day where they knew they would be available. The exceptions were holiday programs; however, these would have likely been scheduled in the evening (with dads standing in the aisles with their video cameras). But Donuts with Dad on a Monday morning? Blasphemy! Now here is the interesting part—later I found out that not only would the member of my team attending Donuts with Dad, but the President of our company was also there with his child! It could have been a career-limiting move to not permit the employee to attend the event!

This generation also experienced the Challenger Disaster, children in school witnessed live on January 28, 1986, as Challenger exploded 73 seconds into the flight, killing a teacher, Christa McAuliffe. In the months and weeks leading up to the tragedy, students were provided with stories about space and the honor of the first teacher to be in space. The horror experienced by these children watching a TV to be turned off by the teacher and experiencing this demonstration between life and death and how fragile life can be. It also demonstrated a mistrust in the ability of the United States to provide protection, adding to the mistrust in government. The Tylenol packaging scare, whereby cyanide was placed in some bottles, resulting in a massive recall of all Tylenol from store shelves (and ultimately responsible for the sealed packaging in place today), added to the mistrust of our companies and government regulation to protect us.

This generation also witnessed nonstop television news through the likes of CNN, as well as the introduction of online videos via MTV (1981). Microsoft was started during this era (1975), as well as the introduction of the Apple Personal Computer (1977). Video games were emerging and became a staple of Generation X growing up. The 1980s had a philosophy of "greed is good" with the use of credit cards and typified by such movies as "Wall Street." School shootings such as Columbine in 1999 contributed to an unease and mistrust of safety, leading to a "live life now, it may not be here tomorrow" attitude. The job market for many members of generation X was abysmal when they graduated from college, with the first graduates experiencing the stock market crash of 1987. Generation X came in behind the boomers gobbling up the jobs. These early years of adulthood continued with employment challenges that also contributed to the mistrust.

In some ways, Generation X was given a raw deal that continued with stagnant wage growth through the 1900s and 2000s and hit with recessionary times as they invested in houses at peak prices (driven up by the boomer demand) and stock markets to build wealth, without having the early year job opportunities and investment success many boomers experienced at the same stage of their lives. However, there are benefits that have accrued to this generation as well. Due to the distrust in institutions and a life-long belief from children that they had to figure out how to fend for themselves—this generation has emerged as a very resourceful generation, with highly credentialed education. Unlike the boomers, who many immersed themselves into the world of work, Gen X has viewed work more as a means to an end—to provide the financial independence and personal goals beyond work. Finding work that is interesting and fulfilling while at the same time providing the independence experienced by Gen X throughout their lives is the ultimate life balance. As the boomers leave the workforce, this generation is "next in line" for the leadership jobs—if they want them. However, they are facing the pressure from the emerging millennial generation, who are also looking to accelerate their movement into these same roles.

Generation X values money, as it helps maintain self-reliance; being good parents for those with kids; having strong bonds with friends, sometimes stronger than family (note the TV shows airing during the young adult years highlighting friends getting together and nonmarried relationships, such as the show Friends from 1994 to 2004 and Seinfeld from 1989 to 1998); freedom to choose how time is spent between work and nonwork.

The Millennial Generation or Generation Y

Just as the boomer generation due to their size was intensely studied by marketers, this generation has been discussed greatly in recent years for their differing values and approach to life. One must not forget that the fascination with youth and their values is not new, as evidenced by Time Magazine naming the "Twenty-five and Younger" as the 1967 Man of the Year (which reflects the values at that time in history as well, having since been renamed from Man or Woman of the Year to Person of the Year in 1999). Millennials grew up as teenagers predominantly in the mid-1990s through the late 2000s in the United States. The Millennial generation is called different names around the world, usually relating to some aspect of the millennial's life, whether it be the increasing amount of student debt they have incurred as states shifted costs to the individual for tuition, lack of housing (living with parents), unemployment (coming into the job market during recessionary times) or related to technology or indecision of future direction. In Sweden, they are called generation curling, in reference to the sport, indicating that the parents of millennials have "cleared any obstacles from their children's paths, refusing to set boundaries, and defending them to teachers that try to discipline them, including going to job interviews." They are called Generation Serious in Norway, and in Japan, they use a term "nagara-zoku," which scolds them for not giving undivided attention to anything, "the people are always doing two things at once." In the United States, United Kingdom, and Australia, they typically are called Generation Y. In Germany, they are called Generation Maybe, defined by a group that is highly educated, multilingual, globally minded, with plenty of opportunities, but who have so many possibilities that they "commit" to nothing.

So, is all this fair? It seems to be a favorite pastime of the press to write articles indicating the millennials are the entitled and difficult group to manage, expecting promotions very quickly, having low attention spans, limited social skills, and so forth. What some people forget—is some of the same things were said about the boomers when they were entering the workforce. The millennials expect much of themselves and their employers, and as a result, they are likely to disagree openly with missions, decisions, and existing reward systems.

We must examine history to understand this generation, the largest generation in the workforce. This generation was the first generation raised in families with both parents working as the norm (Generation X saw mothers going back to work during their childhood, vs. always being in the workforce). The culture was a very pro-child culture with parents heavily supervising, coordinating, coaching, and rewarding them for their efforts. Organized sports and activities were the norm. Sports teams rewarded everyone on the team with a participation trophy as opposed to prior generations where only the "winner" received a trophy. Parents were cautious to criticize their children, in part because they wanted a relationship with their children. The boomer generation was typically sent out to play and return at the end of the day, and the relationships with parents were not as close (40% enjoyed being around their parents) as that of the millennials who were with their boomer parents (90%). In other words, they actually liked their parents and spending time with them.

It should not be a surprise that this generation raised to be the center of the boomer's lives, possibly making up for the lack of relationship the parents had with their own parents, helped to create a culture where this generation sees the world as transactional in nature and expects a return for their efforts. With parents striving to treat the millennials as equals, this transcends into the workplace causing the same expectations to be placed on their supervisors and employers. Millennials thus freely state their opinion and expect shorter-term results. Is this not just an extension of the lack of loyalty in the workplace that started in their parents' generation years ago? The millennials trust "the system" less than the Generation X that preceded them—articulating a career path of 5, 10, 20 years in the future will not mean much—the expectation is what skills can be attained today.

This generation grew up on technology with access to the Internet. As such, they are referred to as a very technology savvy generation—willing to try new technical approaches to solve problems. This has also made them more interconnected and heavy users of social media, keeping in touch with many friends. The Internet is expected to be everywhere—including the office, with the answer to a question being only a "Google Away" or "just ask Siri" when hands-free is needed. Much information is shared through online social media platforms.

They are also the highest educated generation to date based on 22.3% of 18- to 34-year olds earning a bachelor's degree by 2013, compared to 15.7% in 1980. However, salaries were less as they followed the recession, with $33,883 average annual salary in 2013 compared to $35, 845 in 1980 (stated in 2013 dollars). This generation is concerned with paying student loans and funding the longer-term programs such as Social Security and Medicare, particularly with people living longer in the large boomer generation and straining the program. This generation has fears the fund will run out of money, the length they will have to work will be increased, or taxes will be raised to cover the shortfall.

This generation grew up with innocence removed as well through the 9/11/2001 terrorist attack on the world trade center. The event raised the level of patriotism and defending of America within this group, with waving of flags and chants of "USA" periodically at sporting events. This has also translated in volunteerism, with as many as 83% of freshman in 2005 volunteering in school. In the recent elections, there were significant increases in voters. Most of the millennial life has lived with increased security measures and warnings, such as the Transportation Security Authority taking over the airport security after 9/11. The fear is always there according to a Brookings Survey indicating 85% of Millennials believed that terrorism would always be a threat in their lives.

This generation has grown up as a very diverse generation, more accepting of diversity, different religions, civil liberties, and respecting differences between people. Millennials are eager to engage with other cultures, and many have traveled internationally or attended school in another country prior to college graduation. As the boomer generation declines, and this generation exercises its voting rights, they could conceivably drive the agenda going forward and election of public officials. The generation has been described as more liberal. In the 2016 Presidential election, more than 80% of the voters under 30 in Iowa, New Hampshire, and Nevada voted for Bernie Sanders, a candidate that poked holes at the Washington "system" for years. Whichever way this generation leans, they will be influencing the election for a very long time and their views and expectations need to be understood.

Generation Z/iGeneration

By 2020, this generation will have made up almost one-third of the U.S. population. This generation, born in 1996 and later, is still being analyzed; however, there are some observations taking shape surrounding this generation. This generation is now primarily the children of Gen Xers and late-stage boomers. As a reference point, the Huffington Post (2016) compared Generation Z with the prior millennial Generation and made some comparisons.

1. *Less Focused*—with information fired at this generation through continuous social media updates and apps such as Snapchat, Vine, and Instagram to briefly share instant real-time images, the attention level may be lower than with millennials.
2. *Better Multitaskers*—due to the multi-platform capabilities to perform work anywhere, creating documents on a school computer, researching on a phone or tablet, and finishing in front of a TV with a laptop. Oh, and do not forget taking notes and using Apple's Facetime to communicate with a friend at the same time. Prior generations, such as my mother (Greatest Generation), would do something similar with a different technology—watching TV, a radio earpiece in one ear, a police scanner in the other, and completing a crossword puzzle all at the same time! The difference was this was at home on the couch, with wires plugged into everything—this generation is working on the go. Internet is expected everywhere, one does not "get on the Internet" today; they are just always connected virtually to their work, home, and each other. Generation Z may be able to shift quickly between work and play, with multiple distractions in the background.
3. *Less Interested in Bargains*—millennials are more likely to go to a website to get a coupon (67%), whereas only 46% of Gen Z would go there. This may be due to the recessionary period the millennials experienced upon college graduation. Millennials also click on more ads online (71%) vs. Gen Z (59%).
4. *Gen Z Are Early Starters.* Employers are predicting that many Gen Zers will go straight into the workforce at ages 16–18, bypassing the route of higher education and debt and possibly completing school online and finding other ways to obtain an education.
5. *Gen Z Will Be More Entrepreneurial.* 72% of teens indicated they wanted to start a business someday. Their experiences may be traced back to seeing the impact of the 2008 recession within their families and wanting a greater sense of control.
6. *Gen Z Has Higher Expectations than Millennials.* Millennials recall the dial-up Internet and early days of "You've Got mail" (AOL), while for Generation Z, the technology is just there, and they expect it to work.

7. *Gen Z Is Big on Individuality.* This generation was born into the social environment, with 92% of them having a social digital footprint. Gen Z seeks uniqueness through the brands they buy and the celebrities and media they follow. This is much like their Gen X parents as they sought individuality.
8. *Gen Z Are More Global.* Millennials started the movement towards global connectivity with the Internet and travel abroad; however, Gen Z becomes more global in their thinking, interactions, and relate-ability with their peers in other countries.

One hallmark of this generation that is clear through casual observation is that this generation appears to always be on their digital devices, be it a phone, tablet, or laptop computer. The Huffington Post asked Gen Zers, "Would you call yourself addicted to your digital devices?" to which they were 25% more likely than millennials to admit they were, and 40% identified themselves as self-identified digital device addicts. The boomer generation became addicted to TV, with common words spoken "Why do not you go out and play with your friends," giving rise to the term "couch potato." Today, this phenomenon still exists thanks to the binge TV watching, of all generations; however, the time on device by Gen Zers may shift where the marketing $$$ will need to be focused to reach this group.

Gen Zers are entering employment at a time when technology is replacing jobs, more women will be in executive roles, work may be virtual and have less social interaction, the careers may be in multiple disciplines, and multiple careers over a lifetime may be the norm.

Unlike the millennials that grew up during a relatively peaceful and prosperous period of the 1990s, and subsequently had the shock of 9/11, and financial crashes of 2000 and 2008, the Gen Zers have had to live their lives from a more guarded lens from the start according to Neil Howe, a generational expert. He has also coined the term for them as the "Homeland Generation" vs. Gen Z or the iGeneration (coined for the launch of the iPhone in 2007 and widespread adoption).

CAITLIN MCGAW: OPTIMIZING FOUR GENERATIONS IN THE WORKFORCE

President, Candor McGaw, Inc.

Loneliness is a crisis that impacts all three working generations equally. There is little to suggest that Gen Z will be immune. Loneliness is a disrupter driving poor performance, conflict, lower productivity, and turnover. Root cause: when coworkers do not really know each other, they have a harder time being productive on their own or as a team. Harmonizing the generations requires connection and understanding.

Recently, I got a call from a senior information security analyst (Gen X) who had changed jobs 8 months ago, leaving a major hospitality company and joining a global bank. Previously, he had both team interaction and meetings with key stakeholders. Now, he runs his projects alone, and his meetings are virtual. In his open plan office, his colleagues (millennials, Gen X) all sit with headphones on. His manager (boomer) has little time for 1:1 meetings. He was depressed because of the lack of interaction with people at work; he was desperate to leave.

In contrast, an information security team at a prominent fin-tech firm recently hired a consultant (millennial) from a cybersecurity consulting firm; this was her first job in the industry. She was paired up with a seasoned director who had been with the company for 15 years and in the profession for 30 (boomer). When asked how her new job was going, she could not say enough about how amazing it was to work with someone with such deep experience who was willing to transfer knowledge and help her navigate a complex organization. She noted her manager's sense of humor, and the time they spent talking together. No generational conflict there!

Actionable steps are as follows:

- Pair team members of different generations who can learn from each other.
- Listen for shared interests among coworkers and find ways to bring that up informally so they can connect on a more personal level.
- Make time for team-building exercises as part of in-house training.
- Check in with each of your staff, listening for their level of satisfaction with the relationships they are developing with coworkers. Are they getting enough social interaction or are they feeling isolated and lonely?

Generation Differences and Leadership Implications

With the shifting of generations in the workplace, and the 2020 workforce looking similar to the workforce proportions shown in Figure 13.5 (slightly modified following a trajectory of the respective declining generational declines and increases following the trajectories illustrated in Figure 13.4), as well as the late-stage boomers still 10 years away from the virtual "gold watch," assuming they work until full retirement age, the organizations must lead and manage this mix of talent to obtain the best outcome for the business. Some millennials have now reached an age and experience level where they are occupying more of the senior and executive-level positions in some organizations and are no longer the new kid on the block. Millennials, according to a Brookings report "How Millennials Could Upend Wall Street and Corporate America," are expected to comprise 75% of the work-force by 2025. The authors note the millennials may end the confrontational and bottom-line financial world generated by boomers and Gen Xers. The millennials are viewed as team players that will discuss projects with others before jumping into projects that involve them. Consider the changes to the office space occurring today, such as cubicles replaced with open floor plans, management offices with glass walls, and rooms for private calls if necessary. Lunch rooms and break areas are set up with long tables to spend time together. Did social media influence this level of collaboration? Possibly, the existing interconnectedness desire of this generation needs to be supported.

Teachers also promoted group dynamics in school, which carried into college group projects—a concept somewhat foreign to prior generations (albeit the boom-ers were known as great team players, except when individual promotions and sta-tus conflicted with the celebration of the team). This may create a workforce where team members are better able to work together to accomplish a goal.

Corporate social responsibility will also be a big factor, with 9/10 millenni-als surveyed by Cone Communications (2015 Study) indicated they would switch brands to one associated with a cause. The rise in philanthropic efforts can be attributed in large part to the Millennials, wanting to work for and support orga-nizations that are kind to the environment and making real positive changes in people's lives outside of the corporation and generating money.

While the millennials and Generation Z have grown up with technology most or all their younger years and this skill will aide them in the workplace, there may be a deficiency in navigating the social verbal and facial cues, along with reading body language, as the focus has been looking into their devices. This may be a place where the boomers and Gen Xers can mentor the younger employees on face-to-face communication and building longer-term relationships. The reverse is also true—the younger generations can "reverse mentor" the older employees in the use of technology.

The use of technology and team focus may cause an eventual elimination of job titles for future generations. Job titles were important and sought after by the boomer generation as it portrayed status, recognition and provided a sense of (false) job security. The capabilities and team projects completed may bear weight on the future generations. With the work environment being the main motivation for work, and individuals looking for a lifestyle that includes home and work, along with the "contracting out" of work to freelancers, the job title becomes less important. Figure 13.7 shows the motivations, rewards, and sum-marizes how best to communicate with four of the predominant generations in the workforce.

- Connect actions to overall organization good
- Appreciate decisiveness
- Be organized, don't use profanity, slang
- Set long term goals, clear direction
- Clear job expectations
- Appreciate their experience
- Reward with symbols of loyalty (service awards, plaques)

Silent Generation

- Get them involved and show how to make a difference
- Be open to input, show interest, don't 'one-up'
- Treat as equals, consensual
- Show warmth and caring
- Appreciate phone calls, personal interaction
- Value their opinion
- Reward with personal appreciation, promotion and recognition

Boomers

- Allow them to complete job on their own schedule and in their own way.
- Be genuine, informal, results-oriented
- Support growth and training
- Communicate via voicemail and email
- Walk the talk, don't micro-manage
- Free time rewards, resource upgrades, and certifications and skills to add to resume

Gen X

- Connect their actions to personal and career goals
- Be positive, collaborative, coaching, and motivational
- Appreciate their technical savvy, treat them as valuable
- Communicate via instant/text messages, blogs, emails.
- Don't be cynical/sarcastic
- Reward with awards, certificates, tangible evidence of their credibility

Millennial

Figure 13.7 Motivating different generations in the workforce. (Adapted from Murphy, PhD, S. *Leading a Multigenerational Workforce*, AARP, 2017, Washington, DC.)

Understanding Individual Motivations

The differences between the generations provide a macro view of the external factors that may have impacted our beliefs and behavior, but what about our individual personalities? When building our cybersecurity teams and interacting with others up, down, and across the organization, would not it also be useful to understand more how the personalities are different? Could we not communicate better and provide them with what they need? Or at least understand why they may approach a problem differently?

Ideas emanating from the early work of Carl Jung, a Swiss psychologist, were extended through the development of an instrument to indicate personality-type differences by Isabel Myers and her mother Katharine Cook Briggs in 1943. This later became known as the MBTI which has been taken by millions of people since. The MBTI is a very powerful tool, which in its simplest form, breaks down all the personalities into 16 "types." Understanding each of these 16 types can help the CISO communicate more effectively with different individuals based upon their type. In other words, it helps to know how they may be wired to understand how they take in information, make decisions, where they get their energy from, and how they organize their lives. Paul and Barbara Barron-Tieger observed in their book *Nurture by Nature: Understand Your Child's Personality Type—And Become a Better Parent* that a child starts to show these preferences starting at age 4.

Four Dimensions of Personality Type

The complete psychology explanation of the 16 different types is well beyond the scope of this book, and there are many useful books written on the MBTI type noted at the end of this chapter: however, it is useful to provide a brief primer on the 16 types and more importantly, what the implications are for the CISO. There are four different scales, with each person having a natural preference for one of the two opposites on each scale. While we all use each of the opposites at different times, one feels more natural to us most of the time. This "natural" tendency becomes our preference, or the place where we are the most comfortable. The combination of the four different scales, each with two opposite values, yields 16 different combinations of letters. Each set of letters yields a describable personality, not in a stereotypical manner, but rather a mechanism to explain the personality and what may be expected behavior, career interests, reactions to certain events, etc. from that personality type. It is important to note that no "preference" is better than another, it is just different. Each of us uses all the dimensions of preference at some point, and we flex our behaviors depending upon the situation. For example, an introverted parent may flex their extraversion when providing discipline to a child.

Extraversion vs. Introversion Scale

The first preference is about where you prefer to get your energy from the external world (extraversion) or from the inside world (introversion). Extraverts tend to get energy from the people, interactions, and events, whereas introverts tend to derive their energy from their internal thought, feelings, and reflections. It is sometimes said that extraverts are processing information as they are talking, while introverts

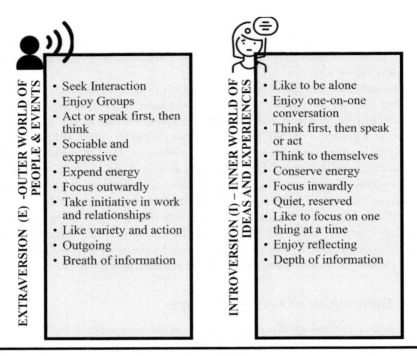

Figure 13.8 Obtaining and expending energy (extraversion vs. introversion).

tend to crystallize the idea internally first before speaking. Introverts draw their energy from being alone, while the extravert may feel drained by spending long periods without interaction. Figure 13.8 shows where extraverts and introverts obtain and expend their energy.

Sensing vs. Intuition Scale

This preference indicates how information is gathered. Sensing individuals prefer to take in information through their senses, such as seeing, hearing, and smelling to see what is happening. They are observant of what is going on around them and very good at determining the practicality of the situation. Information presented is preferred to be delivered in a very specific manner. Sensors tend to prefer to be presented with the facts and details of what they are reviewing. About 70% of the world prefers to gather information this way.

Individuals that prefer to see the big picture to take in information most likely prefer intuition to gather information. They focus on the relationship between various facts, facts that may not appear to have any relationship to the sensor. They are good at seeing new possibilities and new ways of doing things. Figure 13.9 shows some of the characteristics of sensing and intuition preferences.

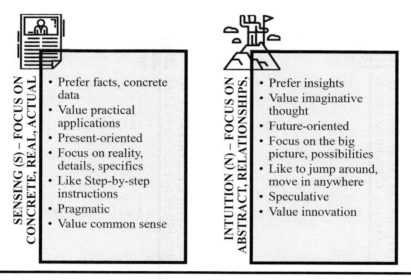

Figure 13.9   Sensing vs. intuition.

Thinking vs. Feeling Scale

How decisions are made is attributed to the decision-making preference, which has two ends of the scale, thinking (T) and feeling (F). Thinkers tend to look at the logical ramifications of a course of action. The goal of the thinker is to make a decision from an objective viewpoint and tend not to get personally involved in the decision. They are often called firm-minded and seek clarity in the decision. They are good at figuring out what is wrong with something so that problem-solving abilities can then be applied.

The feelers (F) tend to approach decision making based upon what is important to them and to the other people. While the decision-making of the thinker may gravitate towards what is right, lawful or concludes with justice, the feeler may base the decision on person-centered values to achieve harmony and recognition of other individuals through understanding, appreciating, and supporting others. In short, feelers tend to prefer empathy over intellect. Figure 13.10 shows some of the characteristics of thinkers and feelers.

Judging vs. Perceiving Scale

The last preference indicates the preference as to how you orient your world. Judgers (J) want to regulate and control life by living in a scheduled, organized, and structured way. They do not like things unsettled and want order in their lives. They enjoy their ability to stick to a schedule and get things done. For the judgers, there is usually a right way and a wrong way to do things.

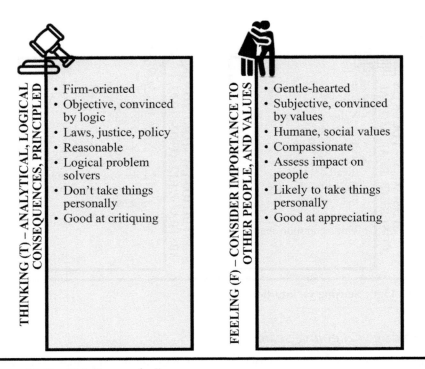

Figure 13.10   Thinking vs. feeling.

Perceivers (P) prefer to be flexible and adaptable in different situations. They want to be able to be spontaneous and flexible to rise to the opportunity as it presents itself. They are called "perceivers" due to their ability to keep collecting new information, rather than draw premature conclusions on a subject. In other words, they prefer the open-endedness and ability to change their decision based upon new information. Figure 13.11 shows some of the characteristics of judgers and perceivers.

Determining Individual MBTI Personality

Using the descriptions and characteristics above, by now it should be possible to determine your approximate MBTI or set of four letters describing your personality. This can be used as a guide for the next section in determining the individual temperament. The actual determination of the letters is more accurately determined by taking an assessment of the MBTI® by Consulting Psychologists Press, Inc containing over 200 preference questions and determining the letters with more accuracy. In real life, we must learn to approximate the MBTI of our peers, unless we ask them if they know what theirs are, as they are not going to take a 200+ question assessment for us! Over time, speed-reading the types for individuals becomes easier and a very valuable tool for interacting with others. The 16 types are shown

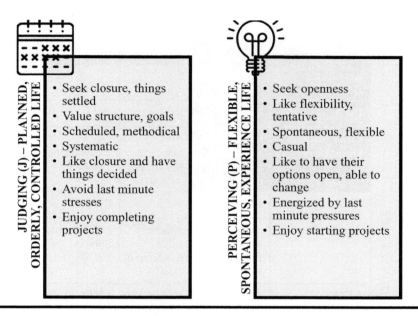

Figure 13.11 Judging vs. perceiving.

in Figure 13.12, reflecting an archetype to understand the individual preferences. The table also shows the grouping of the four different temperaments as explained in the next section.

The Four Temperaments

To distill the 16 different types into commonalities for ease of discussion, David Keirsey portioned the 16 types into four temperaments by grouping the "SPs," "SJs," "NTs," and "NFs" together. While there are individual differences due to the other two letters that make up each set of four letters (for an individual's personality), there was a strong commonality within these groups, which simplifies the discussion of their temperament.

Following is a brief description of some of the characteristics of personality types which fall into each of the four temperaments, along with the implications as to how security should be communicated with each temperament. For example, the SJ temperament consists of those individuals that have the ESTJ, ISTJ, ESFJ, or ISFJ personality preferences. The ESTJ natural preferences are to obtain their energy from extraversion, gather information through sensing (concrete, detail-oriented), make decisions based upon thinking (logical, analytical values), and orient their world through judging (schedule-oriented, organized). The ESTJs share some common characteristics with the other SJs (ISTJ, ESFJ, ISFJ), even though they may vary on one of the other dimensions.

(SJ) DUTY SEEKERS		(NF) IDEAL SEEKERS	(NT) KNOWLEDGE SEEKERS
ISTJ	ISFJ	INFJ	INTJ
Life's Natural Organizers	Committed to getting the job done	An Inspiring Leader and Follower	Life's Independent Thinkers
ISTP	ISFP	INFP	INTP
Just Do It	Action Speaks Louder Than Words	Making Life Kinder and Gentler	Life's Problem Solvers
ESTP	ESFP	ENFP	ENTP
Making The Most of The Moment	Let's Make Work Fun	People Are The Product	Progress Is The Product
ESTJ	ESFJ	ENFJ	ENTJ
Life's Natural Administrators	Everyone's Trusted Friend	Smooth-Talking Persuaders	Life's Natural Leaders
(SJ) DUTY SEEKERS			

(SP) ACTION SEEKERS

Figure 13.12 Sixteen MBTI types and four temperaments—bringing it all together.

SJ "Guardian" Temperament

Those personality preferences sharing the SJ temperament (ESTJ Supervisor, ISTJ Inspector, ESFJ Provider, ISFJ Protector) share characteristics of being reliable, organized, task-focused, and hard-working at their best. At their worst, they may be perceived as being judgmental, controlling, inflexible, or close-minded. They typically respect the laws and traditions of society, like to be in charge, have a standard way of doing things, expect others to be realistic, strive to belong and to contribute, have high expectations of themselves and others, are critical of mistakes and may fail to reward expected duties, have difficulty refusing to take on other assignments, and do not like surprises. They are also good at anticipating problems.

While people of any temperament can be successful at any job, there are some careers that attract this temperament more than others. The SJ temperament may choose careers as a project manager, regulatory compliance officer, budget analyst, Chief Information Officer, bank manager/loan officer, government employee, administrative assistant, nurse, auditor, pharmacist, engineer, or an accountant as examples. These are jobs typically involving adhering to a set of rules and standards without a large amount of ambiguity, which is attractive to the SJ temperament. SJs are also attracted towards positions which can create financial security.

When communicating information security issues with the SJ temperament, it is important that if something was done wrong, that regret is expressed and a simple "I'm sorry" is used. This can set things straight and allow the SJ to move forward. SJs should be appreciated for their responsibility and willingness to handle the details of the situation in the form of compliments. For example, individuals in the security group managing the very detailed logging and monitoring may be of the SJ temperament as evidenced by their willingness to handle and organize the vast amount of detail.

Commitments must be kept with SJs to win their trust. If the CEO is an SJ and there were promises made to implement a security initiative by the end of March so that a new product could be launched in May, the CEO that shares this personality-type preference will most likely be less forgiving than the SP type, e.g., when the deadline is not met.

Communications with SJs should be specific and practical, as the old Dragnet Shows' Joe Friday would iterate, "Just the Facts Ma'am, Just the Facts." They are also resistant to change and need to be brought into change more slowly with logical reasons for the change. However, once the change has been embraced, they can be one of the strongest supporters of the change.

SP "Artisan" Temperament

The SP temperament (ESTP Promoter, ISTP Crafter, ESFP Performer, ISFP Composer) personality types may be viewed as the "action seekers." They may be viewed as optimistic, generous, fun-loving, adventurous, realistic, and adaptable at their best or hyperactive, impatient, impulsive, or scattered at their worst. They enjoy life in the here and now, highly value freedom and action, like risk and challenge, are spontaneous, may be perceived as indecisive, observe and ask the right questions to get what they need, respond well to crisis, like short-term projects, and dislike laws, standard ways of doing things routine. This is a sharp contrast to the SJ temperament previously discussed, which thrives on standards and ensuring that the rules are being followed.

For career selections, the SPs tend to gravitate towards careers that permit them to experience life. Potential career choices for the SJ may include emergency room nurse, medical assistant, photographer, police officer, public relations specialist, fire/insurance fraud investigator, news anchor, airline mechanic, marine biologist, or paramedic/firefighter. In the security field, individuals wanting the excitement of responding to a disaster recovery situation, ransomware event, or an intrusion may gravitate towards this area.

When communicating with the SP temperament, appreciation should be shown for their enthusiasm, common sense, and ability to deal with crisis. Joining in some of their activities may be appropriate, such as an invitation to meeting them and a group of security vendors after work. Business executives of this type may be part of the golf club or bowling league, and this would be a good opportunity to network with these individuals and build rapport to create a non-adversarial environment. Given choices and alternatives, those sharing the SP temperament will want to do things their own way in their own time frame. Issues should be pinpointed and overwhelming them with information avoided. They also do not like being told how to change or what to do.

NF "Idealist" Temperament

Those sharing the NF temperament (ENFJ Teacher, INFJ Counselor, ENFP Champion, INFP Healer) known as the "Ideal Seekers" share the characteristics of being compassionate, loyal helpful, genuine, warm-hearted, and nurturing at their best, or may be perceived as moody, depressed, or over sensitive at their worst. They are warm-hearted, loyal, stimulated by new ideas, take an anti-authoritarian attitude, often sides with the underdog, sees possibilities in institutions and people, searches for meaning and authenticity, self-actualization, maintains close contact with others, gives freely and needs positive appreciation, and are good listeners.

NF temperaments may gravitate towards jobs such as psychologist, sociologist, facilitator, career counselor, travel agent, HR recruiter, teacher (health, art, drama, foreign language), social worker, or hotel and restaurant manager.

When communicating with the NF temperament, cards, gifts, compliments, and adoration go a long way. They are sensitive to criticism, so extra tact is necessary. Patience is needed to understand their need to express their feelings. Their support can be gained by appealing to their creativity and vision of their ideals.

NT "Rational" Temperament

Individuals sharing the NT temperament group (ENTJ Field Marshal, INTJ Mastermind, ENTP Inventor, INTP Architect), known as the "Knowledge Seekers," have strengths of being innovative, inquisitive, analytical, bright, independent, witty, and competent at their best, or they may be perceived as arrogant, cynical, critical, distant, or self-righteous at their worst. They work well with ideas and concepts, value knowledge and competency, understand and synthesize complex information, anticipate future trends, focus on long-term goals, like to start projects (although not as good on follow-though), not always aware of other's feelings, aim for mastery, and deal with the day-to-day details, but have little interest in them.

Knowledge seekers may be found as an executive, senior manager, personnel manager, sales/marketing manager, technical trainer, network integration specialist, technical writer, investment banker, attorney, psychiatrist, database administrator, credit analyst, technical project manager, architect, or web developer/computer programmer.

When communicating a security concern or initiative with the NT temperament, the security professional should attempt to appreciate their objectivity, quick minds, and knowledge. Since they value mastery in what they do, conversations that are intellectually stimulating should be pursued, feelings should be avoided in conversation, and debate with them, letting them you value their insights frequently. Many of the technical staff involved in connecting patterns together, such as the network engineers or database administrators, can become supportive of the security program by simply asking them for their input and genuinely incorporating their insights into the security strategy and subsequent implementations.

What Does All This Mean for the CISO?

Communication is so important and goes well beyond providing a written report or an oral presentation—it is how we interact with others daily. As the security program must remain credible to be effective, we must ensure that we are communicating the security messages with our teams and the organization clearly, and in a way, they will be heard. We tend to communicate by default by the manner that we are comfortable receiving. Unfortunately, and fortunately, we are not all the same, and we take in and process information differently. To be successful within the organization, the security officer and his or her team need to be able to communicate at an appropriate level.

The CISO that takes the time to understand and appreciate the personal preferences and understanding the generational differences will be able to build better teams beyond the normal skill and management development of the team.

SUZAN NASCIMENTO: BUILDING A DIVERSE SECURITY LEADERSHIP TEAM (MBTI)

SVP, Application Security, MUFG

Most leaders hire primarily for technical competence or knowledge. Most leaders never consider how that person's personality preference will impact the group, such as how they manage their energy, process information, make decisions, or manage their time. Generally, leadership teams are formed mainly on skills or knowledge than by intentional design. Rarely are leaders courted to the team because their strengths will balance the rest of the team. Or worse, leaders will pick people who are a lot like themselves. Not everyone solves a problem or develops new ideas the same. Thus, how will your team grow, adapt, or innovate if everyone is the same?

Individuals do not need to be balanced, but teams need to be. Great leaders surround themselves with diverse members, thus balancing the group. To create diverse teams, use the 60/40 rule when designing a team. Sixty percent weighting towards skill/competency and 40% towards team personality. How do I evaluate a team personality fit? One method I use is the Myers-Briggs Type Indicator® (MBTI®). I have all existing members take the MBTI® assessment. I then learn four styles of energy, cognitive, values, and self-management. Each preference is reported in terms of two varieties positioned on opposite ends of a range. For example, your energy style may be either extraverted or introverted. From there, I plot my team's MBTI combined. Consequently, I have been able to determine if I need new hires to have different styles. For example, on one leadership team, I had mostly people who processed info in a sequential, step-by-step manner. They are known as sensors because they focus on fact and raw data through their five senses. Therefore, I focused on recruiting people who processed info in a big-picture way. They are known as intuitives because they take a broader view, seeing patterns, connections, and potential in the world around them. As a result, I balanced my team with concrete vs. abstract thinkers. Subsequently, we had better initiatives because of higher innovation, a more engaged team, and less turnover.

Suggested Reading

1. Wilkinson, D. Is the Change Curve a Myth? The Oxford Review. www.oxford-review.com/is-the-change-curve-real/.
2. Shaw, C. 2013. 15 Statistics That Should Change the Business World—But Haven't. June 4. www.linkedin.com/pulse/20130604134550-284615-15-statistics-that-should-change-the-business-world-but-haven-t.
3. Ranseth, J. 2015. Gandhi Didn't Actually Ever Say "Be the change you want to aww in the real world." Here's the Real Quote… August 27. https://josephranseth.com/gandhi-didnt-say-be-the-change-you-want-to-see-in-the-world/.
4. Kowitt, B. 2016. Why Eating at McDonald's Is about to Undergo A Massive Makeover. Fortune (November 18). http://fortune.com/2016/11/18/mcdonalds-kiosks-table-service/.
5. Nash, K. 2017. Companies Face Growing Shortage of Security Personnel. Fortune (March 15). https://blogs.wsj.com/cio/2017/03/15/companies-face-growing-shortage-of-security-personnel/.
6. Glassdoor for Employers. Top HR Statistics. www.glassdoor.com/employers/popular-topics/hr-stats.htm.
7. Gallup. 2015. What Job-hopping Employees Are Looking For. Gallup Business Journal (November 13). http://news.gallup.com/businessjournal/186602/job-hopping-employees-looking.aspx.
8. Economist Intelligence Unit Limited. 2015. Future Global Trends Affecting Your Organization. http://futurehrtrends.eiu.com/report-2015/profile-of-the-global-workforce-present-and-future/.

9. Cilluffo, A. and Cohn, D. 2017. 10 demographic trends shaping the U.S. and the world in 2017. Pew Research (April 27). www.pewresearch.org/fact-tank/2017/04/27/10-demographic-trends-shaping-the-u-s-and-the-world-in-2017/.
10. Korn Ferry. The Six Global Megatrends You Must Be Prepared For. www.haygroup.com/en/campaigns/the-six-global-megatrends-you-must-be-prepared-for/.
11. He, W. and Goodkind, D. 2016. U.S. Census Bureau, International Population Reports, P95/16-1, An Aging World: 2015. U.S. Government Publishing Office, Washington, DC.
12. Peters, S. 2017. Women still only 11% of Global Infosec Workforce. Dark Reading (March 15). www.darkreading.com/careers-and-people/women-still-only-11--of-global-infosec-workforce/d/d-id/1328409.
13. Datta, M. 2016. I Belong Here: 3 Ways to Attract More Women to STEM. Entrepreneur (May 6). www.entrepreneur.com/article/272966.
14. Pew Research Center. 2018. Millennials became the largest generation in the labor force in 2016. April 10. www.pewresearch.org/fact-tank/2018/04/11/millennials-largest-generation-us-labor-force/ft_18-04-02_genworkforcerevised_lines1/.
15. Brokaw, T. 2001. *The Greatest Generation.* New York. Random House.
16. Black, W. 2013. Comparing Unemployment During the Great Depression and the Great Recession. New Economic Perspectives (April 5). http://neweconomicperspectives.org/2013/04/comparing-unemployment-during-the-great-depression-and-the-great-recession.html.
17. Howe, N. 2014. The Silent Generation, "The Lucky Few." Forbes (August 13). www.forbes.com/sites/neilhowe/2014/08/13/the-silent-generation-the-lucky-few-part-3-of-7/#.
18. Paulin, G. and Riordon, B. 1998. Making It on Their Own: The Baby Boom Meets Generation X. Monthly Labor Review (February). www.bls.gov/mlr/1998/02/art2full.pdf.
19. Kane, S. 2018. Baby Boomers in the Workplace, How Their Generational Traits and Characteristics Affect the Workplace. The Balance (April 19). www.thebalance.com/baby-boomers-2164681.
20. CNN. 2013. American Generation Fast Facts (November 6). www.cnn.com/2013/11/06/us/baby-boomer-generation-fast-facts/index.html.
21. Fry, R. 2016. For First Time in Modern Era, Living with Parents Edges Out Other Living Arrangements for 18–34-Year-Olds. Pew Research Center (May 24). www.pewsocialtrends.org/2016/05/24/for-first-time-in-modern-era-living-with-parents-edges-out-other-living-arrangements-for-18-to-34-year-olds/.
22. Dishman, L. 2017. Gen Z Is Starting to Graduate College This Year, With Lots of Debt and Optimism. Fast Company (May 10). www.fastcompany.com/40419195/gen-z-is-starting-to-graduate-college-this-year-with-lots-of-debt-and-optimism.
23. CBS. Meet Generation Z. www.cbsnews.com/pictures/meet-generation-z/8/.
24. Timetoast. Technology in the 1950's. www.timetoast.com/timelines/technology-in-the-1950s.
25. Weebly. 1940's: The Greatest Generation. https://rf1940s.weebly.com/inventionstechnology.html.
26. Mims, C. 2012. The McMansion Trend Has Peaked. Grist (February 13). http://grist.org/cities/the-mcmansion-trend-has-peaked/.
27. Marte, J. 2014. Nearly a Quarter of Fortune 500 Companies Still Offer Pensions to New Hires. The Washington Post (September 5). www.washingtonpost.com/news/get-there/wp/2014/09/05/nearly-a-quarter-of-fortune-500-companies-still-offer-pensions-to-new-hires/?utm_term=.76f9c49ac463.
28. Longley, R. 2017. Living Past 90 in America is No Decade at the Beach. ThoughtCo. (May 4). www.thoughtco.com/living-past-90-in-america-3321510.

29. Wallace, K. 2016. From 80's Latchkey Kid to Helicopter Parent Today. CNN (March 30). www.cnn.com/2016/03/30/health/the-80s-latchkey-kid-helicopter-parent/index.html.

30. Lyons, K. 2016. Generation Y, Curling or Maybe: What the World Calls Millennials. The Guardian (March 8). www.theguardian.com/world/2016/mar/08/generation-y-curling-or-maybe-what-the-world-calls-millennials.

31. Feeney, N. 2015. Millennials Now Largest Generation in U.S. Workforce. Time (May 11). http://time.com/3854518/millennials-labor-force/.

32. Rattner, S. 2015. We're Making Life Too Hard for Millennials. The New York Times (July 31). www.nytimes.com/2015/08/02/opinion/sunday/were-making-life-too-hard-for-millennials.html.

33. Towns, E. 2011. The 9/11 Generation. Center for American Progress (September 8). www.americanprogress.org/issues/religion/news/2011/09/08/10363/the-911-generation/.

34. USA Today College. 2016. How We Voted—By Age, Education, Race, and Sexual Orientation. http://college.usatoday.com/2016/11/09/how-we-voted-by-age-education-race-and-sexual-orientation/.

35. Beall, G. 2017. 8 Key Differences Between Gen Z and Millennials. Huffington Post (November 6). www.huffingtonpost.com/george-beall/8-key-differences-between_b_12814200.html.

36. Schawbel, D. 2014. Millennial Branding and Internships.com Release First Ever Study on High School Careers. February 3. http://millennialbranding.com/2014/high-school-careers-study/.

37. Scott, R. 2016. Get Ready for Generation Z. Forbes (November 28). www.forbes.com/sites/causeintegration/2016/11/28/get-ready-for-generation-z/#6b1f45cc2204.

38. Benedit, G. 2018. Why Embracing the Uncomfortable Is the Key to Driving Business Success? Forbes (January 9). www.forbes.com/sites/workday/2018/01/09/why-embracing-the-uncomfortable-is-the-key-to-driving-business-success/#642b052b5e38.

39. O'Rourke, P.J. 2014. *The Baby Boom.* New York. Grove Press.

40. Erickson, T. 2008. *Plugged In: The Generation Y Guide to Thriving at Work.* Boston, MA. Harvard Business Press.

41. Espinoza, C., Ukleja, M. and Rusch, C. 2010. *Managing the Millennials: Discover the Core Competencies for Managing Today's Workforce.* Hoboken, NJ. John Wiley & Sons.

42. Tulgan, B. 2009. *Not Everyone Gets A Trophy: How to Manage Generation Y.* San Francisco, CA. Jossey-Bass.

43. Erickson, T. 2010. *What's Next Gen X?* Boston, MA. Harvard Business Press.

44. Marston, C. 2007. *Motivating the "What's in It for Me?" Workforce: Manage Across Generational Divide and Increase Profits.* Hoboken, NJ. John Wiley & Sons.

45. Tieger, P, and Barron-Tieger, B. 1998. *The Art of Speedreading People: Harness the Power of Personality Type and Create What You Want in Business and in Life.* Boston, MA. Little, Brown and Company.

46. Tieger, P. and Barron-Tieger, B. 1998. *Do What You Are: Discover the Perfect Career for You Through the Secrets of Personality Type.* Boston, MA. Little, Brown and Company.

47. Tieger, P. and Barron-Tieger, B. 1997. *Nurture by Nature: Understand Your Child's Personality Type—And Become a Better Parent.* Boston, MA. Little, Brown and Company.

48. Myers, I. and Myers. P. 1995. *Gifts Differing: Understanding Personality Type.* 2nd edn. Palo-Alto, CA. Davies-Black Publishing.

49. Kroeger, O. and Thuesen. J. 1992. *Type Talk at Work.* New York. A Tilden Press Book.

50. Bolton, R. and Bolton, D. 1996. *People Styles at Work: Making Bad Relationships Good and Good Relationships Better.* Ridge Associates. New York. American Management Association.

51. Keirsey, D. 1998. *Please Understand Me II: Temperament, Character, Intelligence.* Del Mar, CA. Pometheus Nemesis Book Company.
52. Myers, I. 1993. *Introduction to Type.* 5th edn. Palo Alto, CA: Consulting Psychologists Press, Inc.
53. Laney, M. 2002. *The Introvert Advantage: How to Thrive in an Extrovert World.* New York: Workman Publishing.
54. Cain, S. 2013. *Quiet: The Power of Introverts in a World That Can't Stop Talking.* New York. Broadway Books.

SKILLS 7

Chapter 14

CISO Soft Skills

We may give advice, but we do not inspire conduct.

Francois, Duc de La Rochefoucauld, 1613–1680

The Chief Information Security Officer (CISO) must be able to interact with multiple levels of management. Often when employees respond to the first survey an organization issues on employee satisfaction, a frequent issue surfacing is "lack of communication." What does this really mean? Did the associate not feel listened to? Were their ideas not acted upon? Was there an avenue to provide input? Was the manager/supervisor sharing relevant news in a timely manner? It could be any one or more of those items or something else.

The CISO must be able to communicate with individuals in different levels of the organizational hierarchy, from the board of directors to the end users and everywhere in between. There are different personalities that must be communicated with, different styles of working, and different ways that people deliver, receive, and process information, as highlighted in the previous chapter regarding generational differences and individual personality preferences. The subsequent techniques can improve the ability of the security officer, or for that many, any security professional, to communicate with others.

The *skills* factor of the *7-S Framework Applied to Cybersecurity Leadership* focuses on the leadership "soft" skills of the CISO to navigate the organization.

Executive Presence

If I asked you to picture a "colorful bird," an image would come to mind. You may pick a bright red Cardinal, a beautiful Blue Jay or a multicolored Peacock. The picked birds would vary between us, but they would most likely all fit the definition and we would be able to know one when we see one. Have you ever worked with an executive and noticed—they really seem together and in command of what they are doing—but you are not sure why you feel that way? Welcome to the club of executive presence. Want to know the answer why they are that way? It is simple—just do an Internet search—there are four traits, no wait, there a ten, oh, another says seven… and on it goes.

The bottom line is that executive presence is an elusive trait as to "what" it is, just as leadership and colorful birds can take many flavors. What is clear—executive presence is how one appears to others, and appears to be able to handle difficult situations, even when the individual is having a bad day. Executive presence is a set of behaviors and emotional intelligence that provide the ability to promote your ideas and influence others. People want individuals they can trust in uncertain and difficult times. The CISO's world may be calm today, but the organization needs to know it can rely on the CISO tomorrow when there is a crisis. Those with executive presence come across as calm, approachable, and in control. The world may be in a hurry; however, the one with executive presence is not the flustered one in the room. The one with executive presence can take control of difficult situations, many times unpredictable. They can make the tough decisions and hold their own with other members of a typically smart, motivated executive team.

Here are the 4, 7, 10, 99 traits of executive presence distilled down to a short list to create this confidence. After all, an individual may have an extensive amount of technical security knowledge, knowledge of the business, knowledge of all the cybersecurity and privacy laws and regulations, and control frameworks, and these will all go to waste if a) the organization does not have confidence in their ability to move forward and b) the person does not seem to be in control of themselves.

1. *Appearance*—Do you dress like a senior executive? The dress should convey success, confidence, and respect. How do the executives in the company dress? Even on jeans Fridays, most likely, if the senior executives choose to participate, they are wearing sport coats with jeans and nice outfits and not wearing tennis shoes. To be on the championship sports team, you need to wear the uniform of the team—this is no different. And the uniform should be neat and pressed.
2. *Body Language*—Stand with good posture, shake hands firmly, and speak firmly and speak with authority. This means believing in yourself and not being tentative. If speaking as if you are unsure of yourself, others will not have confidence in you. This does not mean you know it all, it just means being deliberate.
3. *Elevator Pitch*—The 60-second elevator pitch is great training. I have used this at security conferences several times, randomly selecting people for a

60-second pitch, and it is amazing how hard some found it to speak for even 30 seconds in small talk. We should practice how we intend to add value the next time we see others and be able to articulate how we are adding value.

4. *Listening Skills, knowing when to engage*—Extraversion is not a requirement for success, and listening and knowing when to enter the conversion can be very powerful.

5. *Calmness*—Exercising calmness when others are emotional increases respect for the individual. When challenged, a point can still be made without being confrontational, gaining the respect of others.

6. *Presentation Skills*—Public speaking to a large audience demonstrates the ability to handle pressure with other executives. The Question and Answer section provides the ability to think on your feet.

7. *Be Genuine*—Use straight talk of the truth, give people a reason to trust you.

8. *Passion*—Those that exude passion inspire others to see that you love what you do and in turn will trust you want to do the right thing.

9. *Intelligence*—People respect intelligence, and it will come through in the interactions.

10. *Humility*—We all make mistakes and we need to be able to own up to and admit them. We also may be fearful and uncertain of some activities, and communicating the concerns shows we are real people also. Acknowledging these concerns can lead to solutions.

11. *Humor*—This is listed last; however, this is the secret sauce that can reduce tension and other people's defenses.

None of us will have all the strengths above, as we are all different individuals with different backgrounds, experiences, and strengths. Each of us needs to find what makes us authentic and unique to the point where we exude confidence. We may be nervous inside or wondering how we are going to do the task just assigned to us; however, we must be able to have enough confidence in our abilities, including our ability to reach out and partner with others in those areas we do not do so well, to project a "can do" attitude in having the back of our peers. Imagine being in an airplane that is having engine trouble and the pilot comes bursting into the passenger compartment screaming, "Help, we have an engine on fire!!!" How would we feel? Or would we rather receive an announcement, "Ladies and Gentlemen, we are experiencing some minor mechanical issues and expect the next couple minutes to experience some turbulent conditions, please remain seated with your seat belt fastened," even though they are trying everything possible up front in the cockpit to avoid disaster.

That is executive presence.

MARCI MCCARTHY: EMOTIONAL INTELLIGENCE

CEO and President, T.E.N.

While having a strong working knowledge of security best practices, technical insight, and a strong business acumen are all very important qualities for the modern CISO to possess, another often overlooked but extremely valuable aspect needed for truly impactful and effective information security leadership is emotional intelligence. At its core, information security is not simply an information technology (IT) issue, but a key business driver that affects the organization at large. Communication is key when it comes to being a CISO. It is vitally important that you possess the ability to properly articulate and translate business needs from analysts to board members and to the other departments that comprise your company. For example, the way in which a CISO must communicate business goals to their Security Operations Center might be more technical and methodical in nature, often involving specific solution or visibility needs as it relates to the security stack. However, using this same approach to inform the board of critical business needs would miss the mark. With proper emotional intelligence, the modern CISO can quickly deduce the most effective means to translate information security needs to all audiences. Strong emotional intelligence also means practicing proper self-care and introspection as well. With all of the threats and challenges the modern CISO faces day-in and day-out, it is not uncommon to see stress, anxiety, and frustration erode overall mental clarity. If left unchecked, this can also lead to serious burnout. Part of being an effective leader is being able to take a step back, temporarily remove oneself from a situation, and come back to it with a renewed sense of vigor and clarity. A CISO cannot be an effective leader or communicator if they do not also stop to take care of themselves. The ability to properly self-regulate and re-examine what you are doing is essential to maintaining positive motivation and continuing your ability to be an effective leader.

Talking vs. Listening

Many people appear to believe that they are best communicating while they are talking; however, when we are listening, and the other person feels they have been heard, our ability to communicate is much greater. Unfortunately, we block ourselves from effective listening by not paying full attention to the person speaking. Those that are good listeners tend to draw other people to them, people confide in you, and you become a trusted member of the team. By not listening, it sends the message of what they have to say is not very important. Critical information is then missed, and opportunities to demonstrate that the person is cared about are also missed. True listening involves providing our full attention.

Blocks to Effective Listening

There are 12 blocks that get in our way of effective listening, which make it hard for us to truly listen to what the other person is saying. Because listening is so crucial in communications, we should continuously be aware of our behavior when another person is speaking.

1. *Comparing*—While the other person is talking, you are trying to determine if you have had that situation before and was it worse or not. They may be talking about an issue that you have had before, and the thought is running through your mind, "hey, it isn't that tough to complete that, why are they having a problem." By comparing, it is difficult to listen to what their problem is, as the mind is busy analyzing our own past experiences.

2. *Mind Reading*—Instead of focusing on what the person is saying, the focus is on trying to understand the meaning behind what they are saying and interpret a different situation and driving the comments. For example, they may be saying "I have worked long hours to review these security violation reports, and I am tired of reworking them," while the listener is thinking, "oh, they just had a long day because they are going to school in the evenings and are probably just tired." This may not be the case at all, and in fact, the real issue is that the rework is preventing other work from being performed.

3. *Rehearsing*—The mind is too busy thinking of what the listener will say next, that they are not focusing on the message that is being delivered. In this case, the listener "appears" to be interested in what is being said.

4. *Filtering*—The listener listens just long enough to hear whether the person is angry, unhappy, or in danger. Once the emotion is determined, then the listening stops and focuses on other activities or plans that the person is thinking about. The listener only hears half of what is being said.

5. *Judging*—Judging occurs when someone is prejudged before they even start talking. A negative label is placed on the person who devalues what they may have to say. If the person is seen as unqualified, incompetent, or lacking the necessary skills by the listener, they may discount what they have to say. This causes insights to be missed that could provide valuable insight into the solution.

6. *Dreaming*—When the talker mentions a thought that causes you to think of something in your own life that is unrelated to what they are saying, this is dreaming. They may be talking about what happens if the contract that the company is bidding on is not won, what will happen to the security staffing levels, but before they get to ask the questions, your mind has drifted off to the last company that you worked for that lost a huge contract and how you hated going through the reduction in force motions with your staff.

7. *Identifying*—Similar to dreaming, in this case, everything the person is telling gets related back to by the listener to an experience in their own life. This is commonly shown when people are talking about a situation and then a similar situation is parroted back from the listener's life.

8. *Advising*—In this scenario, the listener is too busy thinking of the solution to the problem from the first few sound bites that they miss important information or fail to pick up on how the listener is feeling.

9. *Sparring*—Quickly disagreeing by the listener causes the listener to search for items to disagree with. This can take the form of a put-down where the talker does not feel listened to and possibly humiliated.

10. *Being Right*—This person will go to great lengths to demonstrate they are right, including standing by their convictions, not listening to criticism, making excuses, shouting, twisting the facts, and so forth.

11. *Derailing*—The conversation is ended by changing the subject and avoiding the conflict. This is sometimes done by joking to avoid the discomfort of having to discuss the subject.

12. *Placating*—The listener is very agreeable, as you want people to like you, see you as nice, pleasant, and supportive. Listening may be at the level just enough to get the idea of what is being said; however, you are not fully engaged.

By being conscious of these blocks, they can be avoided to become a better listener. Embedded in these actions above is our tendency to not really be listening, but rather trying to fix, control, confirm the point of view, hear whether I am liked, gain approval, avoid being dominated, avoid conflict, or be right. As a result, we are not present with the other person. While conducting "culture shaping workshops" at a major health insurer, we placed people into pairs for a coaching exercise and asked one person to speak and have the other person to listen without interruption, except to ask, "How could you make this situation even more effective?"—without providing advice. The experience of many people was a feeling of being heard, of being cared for. This act helped the other person work through the issue and process their problem.

There are also four steps to becoming a better listener: (a) be present—pay attention to the other person and give them your full attention, including putting distracting devices away, very challenging these days, but necessary to let the other person know you care, (b) listen for accuracy—practice paraphrasing back to the speaker and ask for confirmation so important details are not missed, (c) listen for empathy—try to understand the perspective and feelings from the other person's point of view, and (d) listen for mutual creativity—only after listening with accuracy and empathy can we stand in the other person's reality and work together for a mutual solution. These four steps can diffuse tension in a conversation and create more constructive conversations.

JOHN CERAOLO: LISTENING AND USING CREATIVITY IN YOUR SECURITY PROGRAM

CISO

Often, we do not get the opportunity to be creative when it comes to information security. Risk-driven, compliance control-based solutions rarely offer a chance to think out of the box. I was faced with a similar challenge in my past where we needed to institute picture identification badges for all employees. The CEO was not initially supportive and did not want his company referred to as "another corporate clone." While it was easy for me to detail why a picture of everyone that included their names also helped with identifying our coworkers, it just gave him too much of a "factory feel" and he dismissed the control (even though we had already been socially engineered the year before and suffered laptop theft). As I left his office, my departure brought me by his guitar collection that he proudly displayed on a long wall in our office area. Fifteen varieties, some handmade by our CEO, and others once owned by famous rock stars adorned the wall. While not in the music industry, it was a unique display that set our company apart and was something that always became a conversation piece for tours and interviews. It was then that idea occurred to me, how do I connect a security control with the company owner? Like many of us, he clearly had a passion for music, musicians, and the rock concert scene. Security is an integral part of a rock concert, and it is backstage passes that set apart fans from the stars and their crew. Then, it all comes together for me; create the normal mundane corporate card that provides auditable access but sheath it in the guise of a backstage pass! I enlisted our marketing department to come up with four different styles of music designs and gave employees the choice, including bright lanyards. The CEO was ecstatic, and to this day, he is never seen in the office without it. Using creativity to appeal to a stakeholder's style and company culture is not easy to come by but was made easier but expanding the mindset of "what will actually work to achieve the security goal but also be fun?". These opportunities are not always available, but with a little more creative thought, you can find these hidden gems.

Generating a Clear Message

Effective oral communication depends upon generating a series of clear, straightforward messages that express the thoughts, feelings, and observations that need to be conveyed. Since over 90% of what we "hear" is not from the words, but from the volume, pitch, and rhythm of the message and the body movements, including facial expression, it is important that our messages are congruent. We cannot be verbalizing the need for a new, exciting security initiative, with our posture slouched in the chair, and expect the recipient of the message to be as excited as we are (or potentially not!) Double messages should be avoided without hidden agendas. Over the long term, hidden agendas serve to undermine the security department's credibility.

DAVID NOLAN: ACHIEVING SECURITY BUY-IN: CHANGE THE APPROACH, NOT THE CULTURE

Director of Information Security, Aaron's

How do you achieve information security buy-in within your unique company culture? How can you avoid the perception of only dictating requirements, being the office of "Slow and NO," and sounding like the sky is falling?

To overcome these pitfalls and to achieve the most effective security buy-in, we have to change our approach and adapt to today's unique and fast-moving technology environment. Based on my experience, adapting your security program and matching the approach to your culture, rather than focusing on "changing the culture," result in greater success.

A CISO's first focus should be to understand the company/industry culture and the risk tolerance of the business. A surefire way to halt adoption is implementing a slow and highly restrictive cybersecurity program in a fast-paced, innovative company. By aligning with the overall culture of the company, security becomes part of the success, not a roadblock.

Rather than following my painful footsteps of focusing only on security requirements and leading conversations with "NO," a more successful way is to lead with "know" or the adage of "yes, but." This approach focuses on understanding the business objectives first and identifying security solutions that meet these objectives.

To avoid being perceived as a chicken little, [THE SKY IS FALLING!], focus on articulating risk in terms of company objectives. Connect realized risk to the impact on core business goals. This moves security concerns from a theoretical impact to something the business can internalize as helping successfully achieve company objectives.

Moving your company forward requires a willingness to challenge the security industry "status quo." A traditional methodology, industry magic quadrant, or white paper's way of security does not mean that it is the right way of achieving effective risk reduction in your environment. The best security successes I have seen are the result of not being happy with an existing approach in our industry.

Lessons learned are as follows:

- First, understand your business and company risk tolerance.
- Speak of risk in the context of company objectives.
- Challenge the security "status quo"—innovate security solutions and fail quickly.
- Understand the "what" (business objective) of a situation, and develop a secure solution to enable that objective.

Influencing/Negotiating Skills

Not everyone is going to automatically sign up for the cybersecurity initiatives, especially if this means spending money that could be allocated to other programs, involves an increase in the number of rules, or adds perceived overhead to their business operations. To successfully negotiate when discussing a position, the security leader must be able to separate the problem from the individual. Direct attacks based upon prior experience with a department will not help gain their support. The key is to look at the security initiative being proposed from the perspective of the person that you are trying to influence. It is also dangerous to try and read the other person's mind (as noted in the listening discussion) and come to prejudged conclusions of their support or nonsupport of the project. It is ok to postulate in advance what the stakeholders may think about the situation to assisting the preparations; however, it is not prudent to come to foregone conclusions about their reaction.

Consider various options to implementing a strategy that may be pliable to the stakeholder. There is always more than one way to perform something. A request by a business manager may be met with resistance by the CISO. However, by brainstorming various options, one of these solutions may be palatable, with some investigation, for both the business manager and advancing cybersecurity initiatives to provide adequate protection. Once options are determined, these can be generated into requirements that are not demands, but rather where the solution is mutually agreeable.

Forrester research has suggested that there are three ways the CISO needs to change the way to communicate, approach technology, and extend the network, as shown in Figure 14.1. A larger and diverse set of stakeholders are interested in the program, especially those in legal, privacy, marketing, finance, and other roles who do not spend much time thinking about information security. They need to understand why security matters, using stories, connections with business objectives, and engaging conversations with the executives and the board by asking questions regarding risk tolerance and priorities. The CISOs also need to be involved in product development, understanding how third parties interact with partners, and can anticipate the future road map by knowing how the company plans to use emerging technologies. The CISO should also work to build security champions to help influence the culture.

BEST PRACTICE	TACTICS
GOAL: EXPLAIN WHY SECURITY MATTERS	
Use stories before metrics	• Describe real-life and hypothetical scenarios. • Make your colleagues and their business the main characters. • Craft positive and negative scenarios, and describe the difference.
Tie every effort to business objectives	• Memorize your corporate objectives. • Document how each project, initiative, and budget item supports at least one. • Report your security metrics using this alignment.
Communicate with the board	• Build a profile of each board member. • Consider their backgrounds when developing your presentation. • Ask them questions about priorities, risk tolerance, and reputation.
GOAL: KNOW YOUR TECHNOLOGY TOUCHPOINTS	
Get involved in product development	• Work with marketing to understand customer security expectations. • Work with legal and compliance to meet privacy requirements. • Use DevOps development to streamline security reviews.
Map your digital ecosystem	• Create blueprints of data flow, payments, and other customer engagement. • Integrate inventory with IoT, smart agents, mobile apps, and other new technology.
Anticipate the technical road map	• Create formal planning sessions with the CTO, CDO, or other roles developing new systems. • Inquire about long-term product and technology wish lists. • Recommend training for team members based on likely future requirements.
GOAL: BUILD A LEGION OF FOLLOWERS	
Foster security champions	• Implant security experts in lines of business (LOB), or identify LOB partners. • Use contacts to gather business intelligence and communicate priorities. • Maintain your connections with ongoing training and communication.
Prioritize culture over process	• Establish a sense of joint responsibility rather than sets of rules. • Use existing culture and communication channels where possible. • Highlight success stories more than losses and violations.
Empower your team	• Give your staff face time in front of key meetings and audiences. • Provide cover for your staff so they're comfortable enforcing rules without retribution. • Place team members on customer-facing projects or other innovation linked to revenue.

Figure 14.1   The superstar CISO checklist. (From *"How to Become A Superstar Security Leader,"* Forrester Research, Inc., February 13, 2017.)

Building Relationships across Departments

To build effective relationships with other department stakeholders, it is critical to understand what is important to the management and technical staff in the organization. One approach when joining a new organization as the CISO is to schedule 1-hour meetings with each senior management member, middle management, frontline supervisor, and a cross-section of end users and key technical staff. In the first 20 minutes, the CISO discusses at a high level some of the information security concerns today facing companies with respect to the confidentiality, integrity, and availability of information. It may be helpful to provide some statistical information, new stories of events within similar industries, external threats impacting the industry, and some specifics of events that have occurred with the company. This is followed by a brief 10-minute discussion of the functions of the cybersecurity department and ways that the cybersecurity department can help. The next 30 minutes is devoted to listening (leveraging the active listening skills noted previously) to the challenges of the business area and identifying where the security area may be able to help. Through this process, a champion or two for the cybersecurity strategy may emerge in addition to learning what the issues are. For example, it may be learned that an executive is trying to reduce their costs per transaction and that the facility costs are a major expense. They may also indicate a desire to not want to incur the expense of maintaining another machine for everyone. As a possible solution, the executive was thinking about a work-at-home solution and did not know if this would increase the likelihood that information would become exposed. As the CISO, this should ring a bell that maybe a secure virtual private network solution coupled with virtualization of the desktop may be a feasible alternative. The CISO may also need to support a bring your own device program and consider authentication and device management issues. In short, the opportunities to solve current issues should be actively listened to.

Face-to-face interviews also serve to build rapport with key people within the business. By just taking the step of demonstrating that the cybersecurity department cares about their needs, concerns, and issues, begin to build the relationship. These are the same individuals that may be called upon later to support the implementation of the strategy by the departmental projects that are initiated.

MARK WEATHERFORD: RELATIONSHIPS MATTER

SVP and Chief Strategist, vArmour

When I was CISO for the State of Colorado back in the mid-2000s, one of the most challenging aspects of my job was working and coordinating with over 20 state agencies and departments, including elected officials' offices like Secretary of State, Attorney General, and Treasury. These agencies had extremely diverse mission requirements, policies, and regulations that governed how they operated, and security responsibilities varied widely across the organizations. When I was appointed by Governor Schwarzenegger in 2008 as the first CISO for the State of California, those Colorado challenges seemed trivial as I came to grips with how to work across more than 200 different agencies, departments, offices, boards, councils, and commissions. In a matrixed environment with over 150 information security officers [and an equal number of Chief Information Officers (CIOs)] responsible for securing the IT infrastructure in the sixth largest economy of the world, to say that the security community in California State Government was resource-challenged on a daily basis would be a vast understatement.

One of the most important things you need to learn early when working in state government is how funding works. It is not intuitive, and it is not written down anywhere, and while there is a lot of overlap, in general, there are three primary sources of funding for state organizations. The first is federal funding provided by various federal agencies for organizations such as health care, transportation, and support to military affairs. These agencies receive a mix of state and federal funding with most coming from the fed. Secondly, there are those agencies and departments who, through their own cost recovery mandates, are able to self-fund much of their operations and activities. Organizations such as the Department of Motor Vehicles, Treasury, Tax and Revenue, Higher Education, and Department of Regulatory Agencies who charge fees for services are able to budget better since they have more control over their overall budget process. Finally, as someone disparagingly told me early on, there were the legislature-dependent. There are those agencies and departments such as personnel and administration, public safety, corrections, and emergency services who depend almost solely upon the state legislature for all of their funds. No one would say that these organizations are unimportant; however, funding is always a threat because there are NEVER enough state government funds for everything the state needs. Sadly, budgeting often becomes a political battle for who can get the most attention or who has the best friends in the legislature.

Unfortunately, back in the early-mid 2000s, information security was just beginning to get acknowledgment as something both the executive branch and legislative branch should be paying attention to. Even though security incidents were becoming more commonplace, most agency and department heads had never experienced a security breach or incident and been responsible for answering to the public. When it came to budgeting crunch time, just like training is always one of the first things to be cut, security was definitely at the bottom of the priority list for most state executives. My challenge was how to elevate security in a state with a very real lack of urgency.

I will not say we completely solved the problem but I think we were able to make significant headway through a committed process to develop relationships. Not just between me and the agency and department security officers, but by being a vocal advocate and catalyst for interagency and inter-department conversations and relationships. I began by holding periodic meetings where we would bring all of the state information security officers together to bring them up to speed on my activities with the governor's office and the legislature, as well as any policy and programmatic activities my office was working on that would have agency- and department-level impacts. These meetings helped introduce people to others that they might never have had a relationship otherwise.

We were then able to begin identifying security programs the different organizations were embarking on or already involved with that might have a corollary in other agencies. This is where the magic came together. By security officers' understanding what others were working on, we were able to identify opportunities within agencies that did have money, to help agencies that were struggling with funding. We found a whole new universe of opportunities. Everything from adding a few extra pieces of hardware or extra software licenses to a large contract, to adding a few extra seats in a training class, these new personal relationships went a long way to expanding and promoting security across state government. We also began identifying and cataloging people with specific security talents such as programming and scripting, networking, firewall management, and even forensics, in each organization so if another agency had an issue, we knew where we could go for the right resources. People became much more willing to share when they knew it could be reciprocated if they ever needed it.

While we certainly did not solve all of the security problems in state government, I am convinced that by taking a focused and personal approach to developing and fostering relationships among very large and diverse agencies and departments, we identified a key that others can use to become better security organizations.

Written Communication Skills

Written communication takes on several forms in today's world from email, texting, twittering, social media posting, report writing, policy/procedure writing, and writing memos. Email is the predominant written form of communication and is much different than writing a memo or a policy and procedure. Care must be taken to know the audience and the purpose of the written communication. While email is a very quick method to communicate across the organization, it is amazing how many emails people send that have incorrect grammar, misspelled words, or use negative language. Since there is no "tone button" on the email that is sent, words must be chosen carefully to not alienate the recipient. A simple request may turn into hurt feelings if not written in a clear, nonconfrontational manner. Emails are also received almost as quickly as the send button is pressed, so extra care needs to be made when constructing the message. While it may be easy to become emotional over an issue, these are best handled by picking up the phone if they cannot be addressed using a fact-based, diplomatic written approach. Typing an all-caps subject line or highlighting in the red font may grab attention the first time, but to the recipient, this will portray an image of being frantic and not in control of the messaging. Long email messages are also ineffective—people do not read them, or they file them to "look at later," and "later" never comes. If a response is desired, a good technique is to have a question as the last line in the email, as this will be the last thought on their minds as they read the email.

Networking Skills

Networking is much more than sending out an email with your resume and asking if anyone knows of a CISO job available (bad idea anyway). Networking is not connecting to someone on LinkedIn or Facebook either. Networking is about building sustained relationships over time. While LinkedIn is a great professional tool to stay enable the CISO to stay connected, it is just that—a *tool* that enables that possibility. Networking is about helping others and sharing information and showing up at events well before you need a job. When someone is laid off at a company or decides to move on, it is interesting how the volume of connection requests suddenly increases. This is the wrong time to start building a network, as everyone knows you want something vs. trying to build a relationship.

Successful networking is built by attending events and being part of the community. The CISO who remains solely in the office will be limited by only the thinking of the staff in the office. While the teams in the office may be excellent, they cannot replace the hundreds of other CISOs that they may meet—at just one event. Networking forums take different shapes, from breakfasts, awards programs, to conferences. Over time, CISOs come to know other CISOs and security leaders who can help, or they can help to provide insights into an issue.

Networking also includes involvement with security standards bodies and professional organizations. Working with these groups can not only expand knowledge of the different frameworks, but also provide access to other individual experts in security, as well as be at the forefront of the guidance being produced by the organizations. Involvement with these groups provides a deeper understanding of the rationale behind the guidance issued.

BILL SIEGLEIN: NETWORKING WITH PEERS

Founder, CISO Executive Network

CISOs should participate in a peer network that meets regularly. Whether formal or informal, collaboration among CISOs is, "I believe, the #1 way to grow professionally." The CISOs I know who do this are quite successful and avoid the "speed bumps" that others have already hit.

In recent years, I have been fortunate enough to connect CISOs who have had very specific needs to learn from their peers. Not too long ago, a CISO in our network asked me to help find others that had deployed a specific Identity and Access Management product. Several other members in our network responded to his request, and they collaborated on a few phone calls. That member told me he likely saved hundreds of thousands of dollars in consulting and customization costs due to the input from his peers.

Similarly, another member of our network approached me about the challenges she was facing with her Managed Systems Security Provider. She wanted to speak with other members who were using the same provider. We were able to find a handful of members using that provider and connected her on a conference call with them. She learned that several were having similar challenges and heard recommendations on ways they had resolved their issues with that provider. She told me she was able to use some of those recommended methods to improve the service she was receiving.

In addition to sharing experiences about products and services, it is valuable for CISOs to compare their best practices and processes. For example, one of our network members shared how his team recently took over the management of all end-user infrastructures because they had become so frustrated with their IT department counterparts who were failing to effectively patch vulnerabilities on those end-user devices. This information was very informative to many of our members who are considering similar moves in their own firms.

These are just a few examples of the value CISO networking and collaboration. There are many more I could share. I think this quote from one of our members sums it up fairly well. "I get invited to many industry events and I am selective about which events and organizations in which I agree to participate. I specifically joined the CISO Executive Network and participate in their member events because I find them to be a valuable use of my time. It is important for me to periodically meet with my peers to share with them and learn from them. I recommend that other CISOs join this network."

Get Certified—For the Knowledge

In the early days, anyone wanting to work in the security field worked to attain the Certified Information Systems Security Professional (CISSP) certification from ISC2 to demonstrate an understanding of the security common body of knowledge. The CISSP credential, considered the "gold standard" for security certifications, is not the only certification available and relevant to CISOs, as ISACA provides certifications such as Certified Risk and Information Systems Control (CRISC), Certified Information Security Manager (CISM), Cybersecurity Nexus (CSX), Certified Information Systems Auditor (CISA) and others that are relevant. The International Association of Privacy Professionals provides privacy professional and management certifications focused on laws in different geographic regions such as the Certified Information Privacy Professional (CIPP) with specializations in the US via the CIPP/US certification, European Union (CIPP/EU), Canada (CIPP/C), Government (CIPP/G), and IT (CIPT). The IAPP also provides a Certified Information Privacy Manager (CIPM) certification. The E-C Council is best known for the Certified Ethical Hacker certification also offers a Certified CISO (C|CISO) certification. Sysadmin, Audit, Network, Security also provides technical certifications such as the SANS Global Information Assurance Certification (GIAC) Security Essentials, along with other vendors providing vendor-specific technical certifications. CISOs should also understand project management techniques, whereby the Project Management Institute offers the Project Management Professionalcredential.

The certifications do not replace experience, just as a college degree does not make someone an expert practitioner in the discipline. The real value of certifications is not in the credential itself, but rather the investment of time to learn the subject matter at a deeper level than normal, knowing there is a test at the end on the material. *The act of pursuing the credential drives knowledge enhancement for the CISO at a more rapid pace than would otherwise be learned.* A good practice to "the years do not start to pass the knowledge by" is to obtain one certification a year on something to ensure knowledge is continually increasing. This does not necessarily mean attending a seminar either (although that is ok if that is the best learning method), as there are many online and self-study methods to achieve the same result.

CANDY ALEXANDER, CISSP CISM: CISO APPROACH TO TRAINING

Cybersecurity Executive, Independent Consultant

You have finally made it, you are now a CISO and have reached the top of the cybersecurity career ladder. There is a misperception that many of us have when we reach this stage, and that is—we should know all there is to know about security. But, let us face it; that is an impossible task. No one can know everything. So, where do CISOs go to learn and just how do you fit it into your already-booked schedules?

It is important to recognize that formal training sessions and conferences that are designed for the general profession do not fit our needs. The exception to that, of course, is if it has been specifically designed for the CISO. The challenges we face are not so much how to configure a security application, but how to speak the language of the business, how to have a conversation with business leadership and executives as to what the cybersecurity risks are, how best to mitigate them, AND then, to learn it is the business leader's call as to except the risk, mitigate it, or transfer it.

Because CISO's need for knowledge is so individualistic, fluid, and sometimes urgent, the most effective means for CISO training is through peer interactions. This can be obtained through books, guides, CISO events, online communities, or one-on-one exchanges like through an informal mentorship. Simply put, put your pride aside and determine what it is that you need to increase your knowledge of; if it is a specific topic— search your personal network to see who an expert in the area is, or who has dealt with a similar situation—then connect with that person. If it is a more general area of knowledge you seek, check out the various CISO events offered throughout your area. The events range from the "free" to attend to those that are costly. Check with your peers to see which are of true value.

The key to it all is to never stop learning and seeking knowledge. As the saying goes, knowledge is power.

Presentation Skills

Presentations come with the territory, and every CISO will find themselves in the position of having to deliver a presentation to senior management. Since they have limited time and need to "get to the point," presentations need to be focused with, "What do I hope to obtain or convey with this presentation?" Sometimes presentations will be an impromptu-type, such as the 30-second elevator pitch, or it may be at the other extreme in the form of a memorized presentation. Most presentations are a combination of the two—whereby the presentation slides serve to guide the presentation, with much of the material being an impromptu delivery (albeit prepared) by the presenter. Presentation DOs and DON'Ts are shown in Figure 14.2.

CISOs should be engaged actively in public speaking internal and external to the company. The act of public speaking alone builds confidence in abilities and

DO	DON'T
❏ Know the audience- end users? Technically-oriented? Management?	❏ Assume audience has same level of understanding
❏ Engage by asking questions	❏ Speak non-stop for length of presentation
❏ Use mixture of audio, video, and visual artifacts to make a point	❏ PowerPoint® audience to death
❏ Translate technical issues using analogies, relating to daily language	❏ Use technical security jargon when unnecessary
❏ Make eye contact	❏ Read presentation slide by slide or from note cards
❏ "No Dumb Question" rule	❏ Act superior to the questioner by failing to recognize their comments as valid, as they may be coming from a different perspective
❏ Leave time for questions	
❏ End presentation 5 minutes early to respect their next meeting	❏ Speak about subjects you know little about or are not prepared
❏ Text at least 24-36 pt font	❏ Use graphics that are hard to see from the back of the room or are distracting (excessive animation)
❏ Always use microphone, back of the room can not hear, those with poor modulation may not speak up	
❏ Provide takeaways	❏ Fail to follow-up with responses to questions afterwards

Figure 14.2   Presentation dos and don'ts.

SHAUN CAVANAUGH: FROM TECHIE TO CISO—IDENTIFY WHERE YOU WANT TO BE AND HOW TO GET THERE

CISO, National Park Service

A little over 10 years ago, I was about 1 year into my first real job as an IT software developer for the U.S. Army. I was having my first annual review with our CIO when I was asked what my goals were for the future and I did not have an answer. I have thought about that moment a lot, and it really set the tone for my future.

Little did I know that I started my transition to CISO way back then by sitting down, thinking about where I saw myself in 10 years, and writing out a plan that would help get me there. Just the act of writing this plan gave me much needed confidence that I would be able to achieve this seemingly far-off goal if I took it one step at a time.

I identified what I really enjoyed doing and made a switch to work on the cybersecurity team. From there, I became aware of all the other nontechnical things that went into managing a successful program.

To help make myself more well rounded, I started taking classes on things outside of cybersecurity such as leadership, organization, project management, and public speaking.

I had to apply my newfound knowledge and get outside of my comfort zone, so I started volunteering for challenging projects and forcing myself to grow as a person by purposely putting myself in uncomfortable situations. One of the more uncomfortable times was when I voluntarily said I would run our security awareness program. That included doing a lot of public speaking. I had to give a presentation multiple times to an auditorium of around 350 people. It was a great experience, and I met around 5,000 of the people I worked with!

Beyond what I have mentioned, I would recommend to anyone looking to make a switch from techie to CISO (and quickly), must be willing to learn the "soft skills," be willing to move, embrace uncomfortable situations, and must learn how to write a resume and how to interview.

I truly wish you the best!

prepares for the critical presentations. Organizations are always looking for speakers on a topic. The preparation that goes into the making of an external presentation can be leveraged for internal presentations as well.

Budgeting

Budgeting is listed in this section as a "soft skill" because in practice, this is more of an art form than a science. While reports need to be made periodically with the board of directors indicating the cost of cybersecurity and what was done with the money provided, first the funds need to be procured within the management structure of the organization. Obtaining funding requires making the case of why funds spent for cybersecurity are more critical to allocate by the CEO and executive leadership team, than funds for a new marketing promotion or funds to upgrade a production facility—competition from the other business areas for the same pool

KEVIN RICHARDS: CREATING BUDGET WHERE THERE IS NO BUDGET

Global Head, Cyber Risk Consulting, Marsh Risk Consulting

Whether through merging of departments, company acquisition, or simply changing needs over time, many CISOs find themselves managing anywhere from 50 to 100 security tools at any given point in time. With that, many security teams find themselves with duplicative or redundant software tools (e.g., do you really need four antivirus products and three SIEMs?!?). In addition to the base annual software costs, these redundancies create system build complexities, extra training needs, increased help desk expectations, and additional hardware requirements—all taking away precious budget funds. Yes, clearly, the tools were selected for a specific need at a point in time, but as environments continue to change dramatically, the CISO security tool portfolio needs to adapt and evolve as well. The big benefits of this exercise are creating "space" in the annual budget—by not paying multiple times for the same capability, operational efficiencies—through reduced complexity, and improved security—by bringing unfunded needs back "on the table." The process starts with getting a current security tools inventory and service providers—which sounds simple, but it never is. With that inventory, capture annual costs (i.e., subscriptions, maintenance fees, etc.), integration costs (internal and consultants), internal and external full time equivalent support requirements, hardware/hosting costs, and training costs. As an additional overlay, map the tools to your security framework (e.g., NIST CSF, ISO 27002)—this becomes extremely helpful in understanding the "mix" of the annual security spend. With that full inventory, identify those areas that are duplicative or redundant. Those redundancies are the first items to be considered to be cut. Even small reductions can add up to make a big difference. Once the final list is in place, then build a governance process (or working group) to oversee the tool process. One example is "one-in, one-out"—meaning that if a tool is requested to be added to the portfolio, another tool must be decommissioned. While every security team is a bit different—and results may vary—many teams will be surprised by the amount of "space" that is created through effective security tool management.

of money. No matter what the company size is, there is a limit on the funding available (even though some banks have indicated that their expenditures on cybersecurity are "unlimited," there is a practical limit and individual project justification of this spending as well.)

Technical Excellence vs. Organizational Engagement

As discussed in the discussion on the evolution of the CISO, there has been a shift over time away from the technically oriented CISO to the risk-based business executive capable of partnering across the organization. So how is the impact of the CISO in the organization evaluated? By the technical practices in place or other "softer measures"? Some interesting research by the Institute for Applied Network Security (IANS) was conducted across 1,780 CISOs between October 2014 and May 2018 using 60-minute diagnostics to assess the CISO Impact in the organization. Two dimensions were evaluated: (1) eight domains of technical excellence and (2) seven factors of organizational engagement. Organizational engagement is important, as the CISO does not control all the assets within the business, and yet, the CISO is responsible for facilitating the continuous protection of information assets.

Technical excellence was evaluated on eight domains: (1) configuration and data protection, (2) software and vendor security, (3) access control, (4) security awareness and training, (5) analysis and detection, (6) defense, (7) incident response, and (8) recovery. Organizational engagement was evaluated using seven factors: (1) gain command of the facts, (2) get business leaders to own risk, (3) embed information security, (4) run information security like a business, (5) develop a technical and business capable team, (6) communicate the value of information security, and (7) organize for success. The results for each CISO were then plotted along five different zones, as shown in Figure 14.3. Each of the zones could be characterized as (1) foundational—new programs, programs that have stalled, firefighting, and basic responsibilities; (2) high foundational—focus on building processes vs. being ad hoc, engaging with business leaders and building teams, increased technical control; (3) transitional—using specific vertical industry threat data, building models, role clarity, business risk ownership conversations; (4) high transitional—the biggest leap in communicative value, critical asset understanding, pledges from business areas to become compliant; and (5) executive—reporting outside technology, risk stewardship signed off by board, rich risk profiles, configurations managed across full inventories, Red Team testing, internal and external providers verified for compliance.

As Figure 14.3 suggests, CISOs are on a journey with few running programs purely foundational in nature (151/1,780 or 8.5%) and even fewer at the executive end of the spectrum (54/1,780 or 3%). Most organizations indicated that the organizations were moving towards a transitional level with 33.8% (602) in the high foundational zone, or 38.6% (687) already operating in the transitional zone. The remaining 16% (286) were in the high transitional zone working towards the executive level. It becomes clear from the data that to have a successful program, both technical excellence and organizational engagement need to be focused on to rise to the next leadership level.

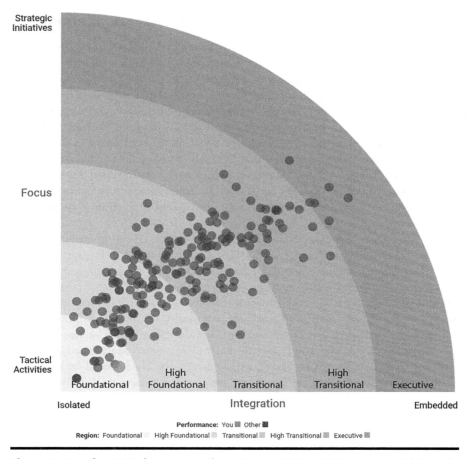

Figure 14.3   The CISO impact quotient. (From IANS, *CISO Impact: Lighting the Path to Leadership*, 2018. www.iansresearch.com/insights/reports/ciso-impact-lighting-the-path-to-leadership.)

DANE SANDERSEN: MOVING FROM A LARGE COMPANY TO SMALL- TO MEDIUM-SIZED COMPANY AS CISO

Global Security and Infrastructure Director, Trek Bicycle

So, you have decided to move on to a new, smaller company! Compared with a larger enterprise, you may notice a few differences—such as a less security savvy of the board of directors, lack of risk management allies, and you will probably be required to take a much more of a hands-on approach. Whether you seek greater autonomy, or a better title, moving from a large enterprise to a small- to medium-sized business can be exciting and rewarding, but also can come with challenges too. The board of directors at a smaller company (if one exists at all) will likely not have the same understanding of security issues of their counterparts at a larger enterprise. You must start educating them gently and deliberately, covering both the low-hanging fruit and the big rocks that present the largest risks. Do not use FUD as a shortcut—you will likely lose their trust in the long term. One tactic to make quick progress with a security program is to "circle the wagons" with other risk managers. If they do not exist or are not up-to-date with the latest security information, you must work diligently to educate those that are present and root out others who are sensitive to protecting the company's information. I would also recommend seeking out senior leaders in the product, and financial departments, as they can be fantastic security advocates. Budgets and resources at smaller companies can seem meager compared with those at their larger counterparts. In many cases, you have to be willing to roll up your sleeves, wear multiple hats, and be able to react to a swiftly changing business environment. You also might not be able to hire the people you need or buy a platform you want. However, you might be able to borrow an IT resource to tighten down that department's controls, or piggyback a security initiative on an existing project. For many, the lure of a smaller business can be strong—you will be closer to the business, able to make a more of a difference, and have less rules to deal with… But, you will likely have an equal amount of challenges and may be in for a bit of culture shock. My advice is to be flexible, engaged, and stay motivated!

Soft Skills Are Hard and Require Practice

Soft skills involve understanding and interacting with people from different experiences, backgrounds, and their own motivations and current life situations. People are unpredictable and have their own "vulnerabilities." Practicing the soft skills increases the CISO's effectiveness to deliver on the technical aspects of the role. When the CISO was buried deep in the data center, it was possible to get by primarily on technical knowledge. This model has clearly changed, with the CISO operating at all levels of the organization, to be trusted and viewed as a business partner; these skills must be viewed as just as important, if not more, than the technical cybersecurity skills that advanced the technical security practitioner into the CISO role.

BOB BRAGDON: WHAT IS IT THAT MAKES A GREAT CISO?

SVP and Founding Publisher, CSO—A Publication of IDG Communications, Inc.

Since launching CSO in 2002, I have spoken with, quite literally, thousands of CISOs and been able to observe what makes a few of them stand out among their peers. Despite what many would think, I believe it has less to do with their ability to specifically prevent security incidents and more to do with how they set their organizations up to manage the response when things go south (because things will always go south). It becomes more about resilience and less about prevention, more about collaboration and less about mandates, and more about leadership and less technical "chops."

I can list-off the key traits I see among the best CISOs: understanding their company's business, focus on strategic issues, collaboration with other parts of the business, a keen sense of what risk means to their business, the ability to think outside the box, and never being afraid to fail. But the best of them focus on two things in particular: the business and the future.

A couple CISOs I met with early on were leaders in very different businesses, but they each explained to me the importance of balancing security and business opportunity. "Without one, you can't have the other." While I believe that many security leaders inherently knew that was true, for most, it took the better part of a decade for them to get their organizations to the point where they would embrace that.

A great CISO also invests in the future of this profession by farming. I am not talking about raising wheat, and what I am talking about is helping their employees grow professionally. These unique individuals understand the importance of growing not only their staffs, but also the next generation of CISOs. In the short term, it pays them dividends in higher retention rates. In the long term, when their direct reports decide it is time to move on, they take what they have learned and become CISOs at other leading organizations where they, too, become farmers.

It sounds so simple, but there is a lot of work behind it. Be a great leader, and the benefits will flow.

Suggested Reading

1. McGrath, H. and Edwards, H. 2010. *Difficult Personalities: A Practical Guide to Managing the Hurtful Behavior of Others (and Maybe Your Own).* New York. The Experiment, LLC.
2. Keller, G. and Papasan, J. 2012. *The One Thing: The Surprisingly Simple Truth Behind Extraordinary Results.* Austin, TX. Bard Press.
3. Littauer, F. 2005 (39th Printing) Personality Plus: How to Understand Others By Understanding Yourself. Grant Rapids, MI. Fleming H. Revell.

4. Dweck, C. Dr. 2008. *Mindset: The New Psychology of Success: How We Can Learn to Fulfill Our Potential*. New York. Ballantine Books.
5. Little, B. 2014. *Me, Myself, and Us. The Science of Personality and the Art of Well-Being*. New York. Public Affairs.
6. Sinek, S. 2009. *Start with Why: How Great Leaders Inspire Everyone to Take Action*. New York. Penguin Group.
7. Goleman, D. 2015. *HBR's 10 Must Reads On Emotional Intelligence*. Boston. Harvard Business Review Press.
8. Lewis, R. 2015. *When Cultures Collide: Leading Across Cultures*. 3rd edn. Boston, MA. Nicholas Brealey International.
9. Meyer, E. 2014. *The Culture Map: Breaking Through the Invisible Boundaries of Global Business*. New York. Public Affairs.
10. Palmer, H. 1995. *The Enneagram in Love & Work: Understanding Your Intimate & Business Relationships*. New York. Harper Collins.
11. Zichy, S. 2013. *Personality Power: Discover Your Unique Profile—And Unlock Your Potential For Breakthrough Success*. New York. American Management Association.
12. McKay, M. Dr., Davis, D. and Fanning, P. 1995. How to Communicate: The Ultimate Guide to Improving Your Personal and Professional Relationships. New York. MJF Books, Fine Communications.
13. Loder, V. 2015. 4 Steps to Effective Listening. Forbes (July 1). www.forbes.com/sites/vanessaloder/2015/07/01/4-steps-to-effective-listening-how-to-be-a-better-leader-overnight/2/#7c3b8a6c7067.
14. Duan, M. 2017. Improve Your Executive Presence. Stanford Graduate School of Business (September 27). www.gsb.stanford.edu/insights/improve-your-executive-presence.
15. IANS. 2018. CISO Impact: Lighting the Path to Leadership. www.iansresearch.com/insights/reports/ciso-impact-lighting-the-path-to-leadership.
16. Forrester Research. 2017. How to Become a Superstar Security Leader. Vision: The S&R Practice Playbook. February 13.

STYLE 8

Chapter 15

The CISO and the Board of Directors

A graveyard of buried hopes is about as romantic as one could imagine.

Lucy Maud Montgomery, 1874–1908

For the largest corporations, reporting to the board of directors (aka "the board") by the C-level suite and executive management on strategic initiatives is not something new. The board has a fiduciary responsibility to protect the shareholders and other stakeholders such as regulatory agencies, customers, and the social and cultural environment from negative impacts resulting from the company's actions.

Increased Visibility with the Board

In recent years, the board of directors has become more interested in cybersecurity issues. One could argue that the Target Breach starting the day before Thanksgiving 2013, extending until at least December 15th during the busy holiday season, impacting 40 million customers, and costing upward of $300 million, was the impetus for much of the board of director's attention in today's cybersecurity programs for businesses of all sizes. The following January Target reported the theft of personal information on 70 million additional customers. This was the first very visible instance of a Chief Executive Officer (CEO), Gregg Steinhafel, a 35-year company employee and leader of Target Corporation for the 6 years preceding the breach, being forced to step down. While there may be other contributing factors such as the underperformance of the expansion of Target stores into Canada, the timing of the resignation was such that it was clear that breach clearly had an impact on the decision. In addition, the Target board of directors was under pressure as a proxy firm, Institutional Shareholder Services, was alleging that the board failed to protect the shareholders from the data breach and was recommending that seven of the board members be removed. The board was able to convince the shareholders to reelect them and they continued; however, it now became clear that cybersecurity and any future breaches would be their responsibility.

In many Chief Information Security Officer (CISO) minds, the Target Breach was a very significant event, a watershed moment that was discussed at most security conferences at the time. Heretofore, there was some discussion about senior management in information security; however, this was not generally a "board" topic for most organizations, other than to know that someone within the organization was designated with the responsibility and authority to appropriately manage the cybersecurity risk. Having discussions at the board level regarding cybersecurity for many organizations was not the modus operandi and far from commonplace. CEOs, executive management, and boards were now increasingly concerned with their responsibility to cybersecurity from a company and a personal liability level. For years, CISOs have been yearning for a "seat at the table," and to achieve the level of visibility that the Chief Information Officer (CIO) has been fighting for over the past several decades as well—and what seemed to be "all of a sudden," security leaders were being asked by the executive management what condition the information security program was in and wanting some measure of "are we secure." How could this not be of concern? The newspapers were bombarded with stories about cybersecurity and with the Target Breach, and this was now a household dinner-time conversation with other family members and relatives that may have been impacted by the various retail breaches.

The focus here should not be to determine whether Target properly managed their information security program, but rather what the impact on the rest of the industry was—initially the retail industry and subsequently other industries asking themselves hard questions such as, "Could this have happened to us?" There were some fundamental lessons learned from the breach, which has strengthened all our industries. Aside from the lessons learned that were more technical in nature and expanded upon in the earlier chapter on security incidents, there were two key learnings at the management level:

Executive Management Is Accountable

The CEO resigned after the breach, which caused significant attention; however, it should be noted that there was no official CISO responsible for information security. The function was disparate and owned by several different departments. The closest executive management individual to cybersecurity was the CIO, who resigned as part of an overhaul of the information security practice by the CEO, who later himself resigned.

The Board of Directors Must Be Involved in Cybersecurity

The risk of loss due to a cybersecurity attack can be substantial and needs to be given the appropriate attention by the board of directors. The attacks are becoming more sophisticated and thus require increased investments requiring the support of the board of directors. Information technology (IT) has increased the complexity and interconnectivity of the systems being relied upon to carry out the mission of the business. Board do differ in where the involvement lies, whether the discussion should be the responsibility of the full board, viewing cybersecurity as having a potential impact on the strategic direction and risk undertaking of the company, or by the audit committee, typically focused on the financial and compliance risk. In either case, the full board needs to have a line of sight of the incidents and the protection risk that is being accepted on a periodic basis (semiannual or quarterly). Whatever the involvement of the full board or the subgroups, invitations to the cybersecurity discussions should be extended and there should be a minimum cybersecurity discussion at a deeper level with the full board on an annual basis. Many organizations have determined that annual is too infrequent and have discussions on a quarterly or monthly basis. A good practice would be to include the cybersecurity topic on the agenda of the full board or committee agendas, as well as being included in merger/acquisition, due diligence discussions, major investment decisions, and the creation of new products and services.

JASON WITTY: PROJECTING CONFIDENCE WHEN PRESENTING TO THE BOARD OF DIRECTORS

EVP, CISO, U.S. Bank

You finally made it. You have gotten a seat at the board room table. Maybe you are the first true information security executive (other than a Chief Information Officer/Chief Technology Officer or similar) to address them, or maybe they have heard from your predecessor many times. In either extreme, getting a seat at the table and keeping it are completely different things. You will need to earn their trust. The good news is that they already recognize you have the skills and experience—or you would not be here. However, you will need to deliver a concise message that properly sets up the *context* of your story as well as the *implications* of what you are telling them. "IT people" and, in particular, "information security people" are not typically good at this. Here are a few survival tips. (1). *Content*: You obviously need good content for the board. But it needs to be written in common business terminology and vernacular. When describing a complex topic, I always imagine I am trying to explain it to my mother—an intelligent woman who has no knowledge of my subject area. It also needs to convey concerns in real business risk context and/or provide implications to the business. You should then address what you are doing and how quickly you are managing to reduce those risks. (2). *Practice*: Once I have my materials together, I often find it useful to put together a speaker's script—AKA, how am I going to "tee up" what is on the slides. Literally, what words will I use? I edit that, reread it and reedit several times to ensure I am properly conveying my message. Then, I start a stopwatch and read the script. Did it take too long? Not long enough? Was I able to make all the points I needed? Once I have been through that exercise 2–3 times per slide, I am then very confident in both the content and its delivery. I should no longer need the script. AKA—Do not read the script—delivery should seem natural. That brings me to (3). *Delivery tips—Now Read This*: ummmm... Just... you know...right...so...like...real quick... I was going to say... I mean... I want to say... "Does that make sense?"... All of these are "filler words" or "filler phrases." Reread them right now and count. It will waste about 8 seconds of your life. You just used 24 words and said absolutely nothing. Practice NOT using fillers—just say what you need to say. (4). *Beware* of *Confidence Killers*. Phrases like I believe... I think...I am told...My team tells me...I think I heard...I feel...I am pretty sure...absolutely kill your credibility. If the answer is "5," say it is 5. Have hip-pocket materials with the list of five. Do that ahead of time so you are prepared. If you get cornered and do not know, admit it and take an action. (5). *Power of Peers*: Lastly, I would offer that many of your peers have "been there, done that." I have had experience presenting to boards (both my own and those of my customers) over 40 times in the past 6 years. Most of my peers have as well. We are usually willing to spend the time to go through a dry run of a peer's materials or to share tips on delivery. Doing so makes us all better!

NACD Cyber-Risk Oversight Guidance

In supporting corporate board of directors to ensure that the right oversight is executed, in 2014 the National Association of Corporate Directors (NACD), in conjunction with American International Group and the Internet Security Alliance (ISA), prepared guidance entitled "Cyber-Risk Oversight." The document cited that most leading companies were evaluating cybersecurity through risk–reward trade-offs, just as other critical business decisions are evaluated. Since the costs of a data breach could have serious cost implications and are competing with cost pressures to implement cost-effective technical solutions to enable the business, there needs to be a level of oversight ensuring that thoughtful decisions are being made to both protect the business and sustain and grow the business. The report highlights five steps all boards should take to improve the oversight of cybersecurity risks as follows:

1. **Directors need to understand and approach cybersecurity as an enterprise-wide risk management issue, not just an IT Issue.** This is welcome guidance recognizing that cybersecurity involves the implementation of people, processes, and technology and depends upon the leadership of executive management to set the tone for the organization. The controls can be put in place to mitigate some of the technical threats; however, a careless user can bypass these controls through their actions, such as sending unsecure email, leaving a tablet in the backseat of an airplane, or carelessly leaving sensitive documents in an unlocked car. The statement also expands the responsibility beyond those individuals having an official role with regard to cybersecurity, such as the CISO and his or her team.

   The statement also emphasizes cybersecurity as being a risk issue spanning the enterprise. While in the past security issues were assigned to the security department within IT to manage, this precluded the proper analysis necessary to solve business issues. For example, a common issue organizations grapple with is the issue of users having more access than necessary to perform their jobs or having access after they have transferred departments or left the company. In the past, and in immature organizations, this would have been assigned to the security administration area to manage by requesting manager recertifications of all the end users within their department on a periodic basis. It would also have resulted in manager approval of access as well. Without involving the business in this process design upfront, which could have led to the definition of role-based access for groups of business users, adding to the efficiency of the access control, the process at an individual user level may remain at an inefficient and error-prone process. By involving the business, say to define user roles to provide access, the resulting goal has increased probability of coming closer to the access control needed by the business. The issues should be regarded as involving multiple departments across the business to derive the best solution. This may take more resources and time in the planning and analysis stages; however, this can avoid the implementation of processes not conducive to maintaining efficient business operations.

   Companies that do not recognize cybersecurity as an enterprise-wide issue and still regard it as an IT issue also fail to instill ownership by the business areas for cybersecurity. While cybersecurity is certainly not the "mission" of the business units, as they have their own goals and objectives to fulfill the overall organization's mission, if it is not made clear that cybersecurity is something they need to consider when building new products and service offerings, this can lead to increased costs either through product rework, unnecessary work (i.e., working with a vendor to deliver an unsecure product and then starting over), or delayed rollouts, while security controls can be investigated and applied after the product development has nearly completed. Costs could also be incurred through the rollout of products and services to the marketplace without the involvement of the IT groups, increasing the possibility of a cybersecurity breach through the introduction of an insecure product. Cybersecurity risks should be addressed from a strategic level to ensure the risks are considered properly by each department.

Business areas are also in the best position to understand where the most critical assets of companies are located. These assets referred to earlier as the "crown jewels," taking the name from the English term to refer to the jewelry often used for the coronation of a monarch to symbolize power through the monarchy, represent those items unique to an organization if landed in the arms of someone external to the organization could be leveraged to damage the organization. For example, the recipes of Kentucky Fried Chicken (allegedly uncovered in 2016 by a Chicago Tribune Reporter, whereby the original recipe was in a family scrapbook), or the formula for Coca Cola, are stored in vaults with levels of defense, as the copying of these recipes or formulas by a competitor could cause harm by replication of their product. Intellectual property such as research and designs, manufacturing processes, or even the materials used would be useful to competitors. Customer lists, pricing lists, sensitive information, and so forth all represent crown jewels needing protection. The issue for most companies is due to the complexity of the systems and the assumption of information "inside the walls" of the organization is protected; many companies struggle with knowing where the most critical data assets are, how are they accessed, who has permission to access them, and are the system protections adequately tested to protect the information. With more and more information moving into the "cloud," or external environments, this problem is even harder to manage. It is imperative that the board directs the organization to understand where the crown jewels are located using an approach such as the one outlined in the *Strategy* chapter, and if the level of protection of these assets meets the risk appetite or tolerance they have set for the organization.

2. **Directors should understand the legal implications of cyber-risks as they relate to their company's specific circumstances.** Beyond cybersecurity being the right thing to do for an organization to protect the information assets, there is the aspect that if there is a breach, the company could be liable for the damages to individuals or other companies. There could also be lawsuits filed by Attorney Generals at the State and Federal level, fines levied by Data Protection Authorities and fines or sanctions levied by government organizations. The company needs to be familiar with the contracts in place and any indemnification clauses or acceptance of higher risk levels. Cyber insurance can mitigate some of these costs; however, the legal liability still most likely rests with the organization and the contractual relationships. Board members may be protected if they take reasonable steps following a

cybersecurity incident and remain engaged in limiting the risk to the organization, shareholders, and customers. One way to understand the response capabilities of the organization is to have the directors become engaged in an incident response simulation, or a tabletop exercise. These tabletop exercises can provide the board with visibility into the response processes of the organization and provide a sense of how prepared, or unprepared, the organization is should a breach occur.

The laws are overlapping, sometimes conflicting, and can be confusing to those not involved with their interpretation daily. An organization would benefit from the homogenization of the laws applicable to the organization where possible and developing an institutional understanding of the laws mandating compliance. This is becoming increasingly important as companies venture into new global markets, where each country may have several laws pertaining to privacy, security, or conducting trade through digital means. Depending on the country and the sector of the breach (financial, health care, manufacturing, government, etc.), different reporting requirements may apply. Discussions of the risks and mitigation strategies, security program discussions, and outcomes should be documented in the board meetings for possible later review by external parties to ensure compliance.

3. **Boards should have adequate access to cybersecurity expertise, and discussions about cyber-risk management should be given regular and adequate time on the board meeting agenda.** This guidance points to the board being adequately informed on cybersecurity issues, and there are meaningful discussions vs. checking a box indicating that the subject was covered. The board should understand the risk level the organization is accepting with cybersecurity and the impact of threats to the environment. For example, 2017 ransomware attacks such as WannaCry and Petya garnered boardroom attention as organizations wanted to understand the damage and whether more investments were needed to combat the increasingly complex and damaging cyber threat. Adequate access to cybersecurity expertise could mean many possible avenues depending upon the company. They may choose to rely on their internal expertise or to obtain an external viewpoint by engaging a consultant to inform them on the efficacy of the security program and strategic cybersecurity program using the guidance of the CISO, internal or external staff functions. According to the NACD, cybersecurity is discussed regularly at board meetings 89% of the time in public companies and 72% at private companies. This clearly demonstrates the concern over cybersecurity as a key company risk requiring the proper support, investment, and attention by the board.

The current approach to protecting the company's most critical data assets was cited as the most frequent topic (77%) discussed by boards, followed closely by reviewing the company's technology infrastructure (74%) as the second most reviewed cybersecurity oversight practice. As shown in Figure 15.1, there are many opportunities for the board to be involved in cybersecurity. A certain level of cybersecurity knowledge should be obtained by the board members. While the board members are not expected to design an Identity Access Management solution, configure a firewall, or perform malware analysis, they do need to have a conversant level of understanding the cybersecurity risks in business terms and some of the mitigating approaches that are being applied. The board should be in a knowledge position where they can understand where the protections are not commensurate with the risks through reading the risk and protection reports provided by the CISO. It is also the CISO's job to ensure the correct level of detail in understandable terms and how the business is impacted.

Board Sets the Cybersecurity Tone

- Full Board or risk committee participation
- Include technology savvy directors on the board
- View cybersecurity as a competitive advantage priority

Build Collaborative Relationships with CISO

- Stronger alliances deliver increased trust
- Ensure time on the agenda for cybersecurity
- Provides CISO with board background level of security

Expect Consistent Reporting

- CISOs must provide consistent benchmark reporting
- Industry and peer company activities should be solicited
- Framework selection and measurable actions to maturity

Review Appropriate Investment Levels

- Question if security spending is on the right priorities
- Is cybersecurity function staffed, aligned, skilled properly?
- Ensure spending is matched to organizational risk appetite

Expect Incident Management

- Ensure the CISO has appropriate attention on response
- Support the organization 'self-hacking' with red teams
- Encourage exercises to prepare organization for breaches

Figure 15.1 Board involvement in cybersecurity opportunities.

RICHARD A. CLARKE: GETTING THE BOARD ON BOARD

CEO, Good Harbor Security Risk Management

Every major corporate board is now aware that it has a responsibility for oversight of the company's cybersecurity, but almost none of them are comfortable that they know how to do it properly. As both a board member and a cybersecurity consultant who has often briefed boards, I suggest:

1. The board must determine or approve the risk appetite for the company. Boards should annually be given a cyber threat briefing by an outside expert. The board must also be made aware of the Risk Register and told what risks are existential for the company or could be highly damaging if they happened. Then, the CEO and board can determine the remediation priorities. The CISO should not be the highest corporate official who decides on the risk appetite.
2. Boards should be given metrics. They need to know how they compare to other companies in their sector. They need to track progress towards a goal. Commercially available FICO-like scores help, as does the NIST Framework.
3. The board should review the cybersecurity budget. As a benchmark, companies at scale should be spending between 5% and 10% of the overall IT budget on cybersecurity.
4. Each board should have a cybersecurity committee. It is not the job of the Audit Committee. The cyber committee should meet quarterly with the CIO, CISO, and General Counsel to review threats, risks, and metrics of progress.
5. Boards should review cyber insurance, regulatory compliance, and vendor/supply chain requirements. These are issues boards can get comfortable discussing and are within their responsibility.
6. The board should require cybersecurity due diligence early in an merger and acquisition decision process. The cost of remediation in an acquired entity can be considerable. Reps and warranty insurance should specifically address cybersecurity.
7. Boards should insist on an outside cyber-risk assessment, an independent review of the Risk Register and the overall culture of cybersecurity in the company.

4. **Directors should set the expectation that management will establish an enterprise-wide cyber-risk management framework with adequate staffing and budget.** Clearly, the organization must evaluate the risk reward of

initiatives competing for revenue from other parts of the business and the allocation of funds must be adequate. These are subjective measures, and this is where external benchmarking may come into play to ensure that the spend is in line with other businesses within the same industry with a similar threat profile. Adequate spending for a financial or health-care institution may be different than the expenditures allocated for an educational institution or a nonprofit that does not process financial transactions or sensitive information.

The organization should leverage a "security framework," such as one of the frameworks mentioned in the *Cybersecurity Framework* chapter. The key point here for consideration by the board of directors is that at least one framework needs to be selected and used, and progress continually reported and measured against this framework. The maturity of the security program should be increasing until the controls are at an acceptable level for the risk appetite of the organization, at which point the board can decide if the additional investment is warranted as a strategic imperative. In any case, adoption of a framework is not a "once-and-done" initiative, and there needs to have continued reporting and measurement to ensure that proper security is being sustained.

The cost of obtaining the framework is not the difficult piece, as the challenge is to accurately assess the control environment against the framework and determine appropriate courses of action. Depending upon the depth of the internal security team, this could be performed internally, externally using an auditing or cybersecurity consulting firm, or a combination of both. It is usually advantageous to have some access to an external resource and their expertise gained from conducting reviews across multiple companies of various types. The ability to benchmark with peers is an advantage, as most organizations for confidentiality reasons are unwilling to disclose, and rightly so, critical details of where the information security is deficient. Doing so would create vulnerabilities for the organization. However, the external firms are typically collecting and aggregating this information from their clients under non-disclosure agreements and subsequently anonymizing the information, enabling presentation of the company data in comparison with the aggregated anonymous data. This can be helpful to understand how industry peers are performing and if further investment is needed to increase the level of information security to remain competitive.

The NACD suggests an integrated approach to managing cyber-risk, adapted from the ISA and American National Standards Institute, including seven principles for reducing cyber-risk, as shown in Figure 15.2.

The integrated approach establishes that cybersecurity is a risk to the entire organization and needs the involvement of each of the business units, whereby the involvement means ensuring that appropriate resources are allocated to ensuring the security of the company.

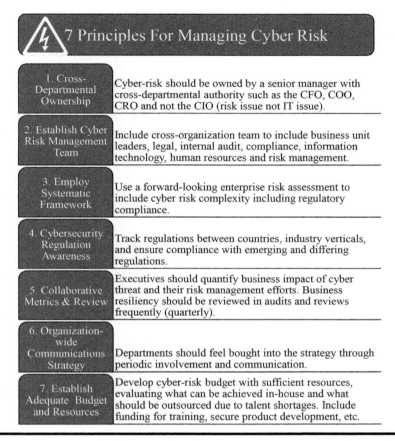

Figure 15.2 Seven board principles for managing cyber-risk. (Adapted from Clinton, L., *Cyber-Risk Oversight*, 2017, National Association Corporate Directors.)

DEVON BRYAN: THE COST OF CYBERSECURITY

Executive Vice President and CISO, Federal Reserve System

According to Internet security industry predictions, global spending on cybersecurity products and services will exceed $1 trillion by 2021. Researchers anticipate that there will be a 12%–15% growth year over year in the cybersecurity market. Despite these double-digit year-over-year growths in global cybersecurity spend, however, a growing degree of uncertainty by several corporate boards of directors still exists regarding the size of their organization's annual cybersecurity spend as they are seeking to have more quantifiable data on the size of the cybersecurity risk and the consequent reduction in risk exposures these projected investments should yield. And while growth in all other tech sectors is fueled by reducing inefficiencies and increasing productivity, the primary growth factor for cybersecurity is cybercrime. Internet security research firm Cybersecurity Ventures predicts that cybercrime will continue rising and cost businesses globally more than $6 trillion annually by 2021.

In light of the above harsh realities of the exploding cyber threat landscape and the known fact that to help keep our organizations ahead of these threats, annual investments in people and technology as very necessary operational and capital expenses are a must, many CISOs expect unlimited spend each year and really struggle when their boards or their Chief Financial Officers (CFOs) ask for more empirical data to support their investment strategies. Being able to apply a disciplined regimen to calculating the before and after risk score for an investment to derive the projected risk reduction efficacy, then being able to rack and stack all annual discretionary (non-legislative, regulatory etc.) investments by their projected risk reduction efficacy so you can quantitatively articulate the rationale for your investment portfolio based on the "buying down" of risks, is a coup d'état for our profession.

Further amplifying our message and cementing our position into the "good graces" of our Chief Risk and CFOs are also linking our individual investments to the various categories of an industry best practice risk management framework such as the 13 categories of the ISO27001 or the five domains of the NIST Cybersecurity Framework. This further allows the current-state maturity assessments against the chosen framework, the alignment with and prioritization within each framework's domain of the risk-quantified investments to demonstrate not only how the investments will reduce risks, but also how they will individually contribute to the maturity of the overall cybersecurity program.

JAMES CHRISTIANSEN: TOO MUCH SECURITY MONEY?

Vice President, CISO, Teradata

It is not often you have too much money, and in fact, it is typically the opposite. As a CISO, you are always justifying security projects and then hoping for funds. Often thinking deep down "Just a minor security breach—that would get their attention!" Of course, in the unlucky circumstance, you have a major breach, and with an immature security organization, it is a nightmare.

One year in my career, I decided to take a bold and unusual stance. At budget review time with the CEO, I started the meeting with a statement "This year we were responsible for $800 M in revenue." That caught both the CEO and CFO by surprise, and they then asked me how I brought in the revenue.

I quickly explained that during the past year, I had to meet with many of our existing customers that were up for contract review and all the new customers to articulate our security program. Having a security program that earned the confidence of our customers they choose us over the competition. The sum of those contracts was $800 M.

The budget meeting went well, and while other budgets were being cut, my budget was increased. But that is not the end of the story. A few weeks later, I was called by the CEO and he asked, "What would it cost to be best in class security?" I developed a laundry list of all the projects from my 3-year road map, added costs (people and technology), and went to review with him. Being an experienced executive, I had them risk-ranked, dollar amount, and summary justifications for each.

My expectation is that I would get some extra funding for the year— Yeah! Too my surprise, he approved all of them and wanted them completed by year-end. The beginning of the disaster...

For each project, we established an aggressive project plan, hired consultants, hired new employees, developed the new processes, and purchased the technology. Anyone from the outside witnessing, the activities would have thought we had experienced a security breach.

It is in this experience that I learned a lifelong lesson that I consider in each situation. An organization can only handle so much change, and each company has a different level of tolerance. Trying to change the company this rapidly leads to a total meltdown. The change control for the systems was a manageable task. But adding so many new people and new processes could not be absorbed by existing staff, and instead of having five successful projects, we had 15 failures. The change throughout the company was at such a rapid pace the employees did not have time to adjust to the heightened posture. While we did a lot of security awareness training to try to overcome their concerns, the disruption in the business was noticeable.

So, my lesson is there is such a thing as too much money. It takes 9 months to have a baby, and you cannot just add resources and make it go faster. An organization needs time to adjust and absorb new ideas and processes. Finding the right balance is key to your long-term success.

Tips
- Demonstrate the value of your security program in terms of revenue. Think about customers gained and customers retained because of the security program. Tie the security program to revenue as much as possible. It is a much stronger position than cost savings or cost avoidance.

■ Maintain a rolling 3-year road map of security projects that improve your security posture.

■ Always have a few of your unfunded projects ready to go with cost estimates and justifications just in case an opportunity arises.

■ If you find yourself in a situation where you are given too much funding, take the time to explain that while you appreciate the confidence but as a leader, you understand that the organization cannot absorb that much change at once. Submit a project funding list that is aggressive, but obtainable. It also helps build their faith in you as an executive in the company.

■ The situation does not happen often so relish the day and try to lock some of the additional funding into the next year!

5. **Board management discussion of cyber-risk should include identification of which risks to avoid, accept, mitigate, or transfer through insurance, as well as specific plans associated with each approach.** This guidance ensures that cybersecurity is not only discussed as informational, but also in the context of risks to be accepted or an alternative action is taken to mitigate or remove the risk. The ability to achieve absolute, complete cybersecurity protection is not possible, as the attacker has many entry points into the organization, and depending upon the sophistication and funding level of the attacker, the organization may not be able to afford defenses against a well-funded, determined adversary. Organizations need to apply appropriate security controls, such that if there is a breach, the damage caused will not be material to the company. Many companies apply the same security controls across the organization with no focus on the high-risk assets. Doing so wastes valuable resources to implement the controls. While it is true that some baseline controls need to be implemented throughout the enterprise, such as antivirus and malware controls or executing phishing campaigns to educate users, not all assets would require the level of monitoring equally. Therefore, administrative accounts, or those with elevated access, are reviewed on a periodic basis—these are the accounts whereby if credentials are compromised, the ability to delete files, establish accounts, and modify information is now in the hands of the attacker. This is more critical than compromising the credentials of someone able to view nonsensitive information.

Once the risk appetite is discussed and those risks are identified which are unacceptable, the organization has the choice of which risks to accept, mitigate, or transfer some of the risks. These need to be thoughtful discussions resulting in plans of action to handle the risk. The board needs to be involved in understanding the risks being accepted by the organization. Risk acceptance processes need to be in place to continually review the risk accepted by the organization.

ADEL MELEK: DETERMINING RISK APPETITE WITH THE BOARD

Global Vice Chairman\Risk Advisory, Deloitte

The challenge came about as a new CISO joined a large institutional fund organization, whereby the board was contemplating several things such as crafting appropriate risk appetite statements that would be relevant to managing cyber-risks and commensurate with the risk appetite statements that the organization has on various other risks such as financial, liquidity, geopolitical, concentration risks. The CISO was confronted with several challenges; such risk appetite statements in the cyber-risk space are less established, there are not too many known examples, and the level of maturity of the board's understanding of cyber-related risks was limited. In addition, several other matters also compounded the discussion including the board's appetite to allocate the necessary resources and funding to shore up cybersecurity defenses to a level that is aligned with the risk appetite, to explore outsourcing, and to purchase cyber-risk insurance. Deloitte was already engaged with the board on their broader risk framework and risk appetite. Through an iterative process, and multiple workshops with management and the board, several risk appetite statements were developed along the lines of (e.g., availability, recovery, confidentiality, data loss), and further refinement was also established (e.g., data leakage, loss of customer's data, loss of proprietary data, leakage of unpublished financial statements). A thorough assessment was conducted, identifying the size of the gap, along with the funds, resources, and timeline required to bring the organization in line with their new stated risk appetite. A prioritization exercise was conducted as well as tender to select cyber-risk services providers in select areas to assist the organization in mitigating their risks and over time achieving and maintaining the desired cyber controls and mitigants.

Show Continuous Improvement

The CISO needs to be aware that the board does not have the same depth of cybersecurity knowledge, nor do they need the depth of knowledge to accurately evaluate the security posture of the organization. The board wants to see continuous improvement of the security program, necessitating accurate, timely, and meaningful metrics on the operation of the cybersecurity program. These controls and metrics should be validated with the support of internal and external audits to gain support with the board as well. Not all controls need to be reported on; however, visual red, yellow, green traffic light-type reports with a sense of control prioritization will help communicate the message.

Advantage should also be taken of large initiatives supporting new business products and services or rollouts of new technology. This may include the transition to new operating systems such as Windows 10, new technologies such as blockchain, new mobile applications, or transition to cloud services. Other transitions may include mergers and acquisitions whereby cybersecurity due diligence can inform of the extra investment needed to bring on a new partner organization. New executive management added to the mix can also provide opportunities for furthering the cybersecurity agenda and support with the board, as they may have come from other organizations where cybersecurity was a higher priority and board interaction was higher. Audit results can also be leveraged to gain support with the board, indicating where there are issues and where the cybersecurity controls are helping to mitigate the risk.

Driving Effectiveness and Efficiency

The board and management should be concerned with driving effectiveness (doing the right things) and efficiency (doing things right) when implementing cybersecurity. All organizations have limited funds which must be allocated across multiple strategic

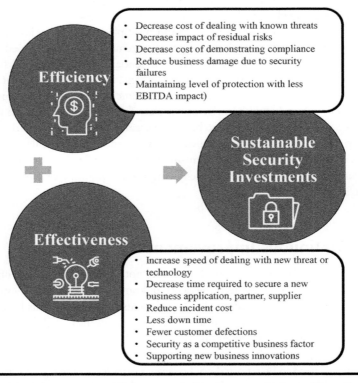

Figure 15.3   Cybersecurity efficiency and effectiveness. (Adapted from Pescatore, J. and Paller, A. *Briefing the Board: Lessons Learned from CISOs and Directors*. 2017. RSA Conference Presentation San Francisco, CA. (February).)

LANCE HAYDEN, PH.D.: MEASURING FOR EFFECT

Chief Privacy and Security Officer, Elligo Health Research

What to measure in security is a challenge. Perhaps even more fundamental is the challenge of why we measure security, because the why often drives the what, shaping it in ways CISOs and security owners may not even explicitly recognize. Over my career, I have seen one particularly important difference in why security gets measured, something I call measuring for effect vs. measuring for effectiveness.

Measuring for effect means developing metrics designed to convince someone to take action. A simple example is measuring the number of times an organization is "attacked" from the outside. Often, this metric includes everything from simple reconnaissance to concerted attempts to penetrate a perimeter and is deliberately dramatic. The effect is to convince the organization to devote more resources to security. Nothing gets the board's attention like stating "we're getting hit a million times each month...".

Of course, counting every time somebody probes the network perimeter does not really help an InfoSec team improve security posture (at least beyond keeping or growing the security budget, of course!) When measurement gives empirical insight into how well a security program functions operationally, providing insight for improvement, i.e., measuring for effectiveness. Such metrics might include the organization's information value at risk, vulnerability statistics for particular systems, or the mean time spent responding to actual security incidents.

The differences can be subtle, and it is not the case that one is a better measurement than the other. But a CISO should always know why they are spending the time and effort to produce a particular metric and understand whether their metrics portfolio is unbalanced. Spending all your time producing "wow!" metrics may be exciting, but counterproductive if they come at the expense of true operational insight. Conversely, understanding every nuance of your program may not add long-term value if the people that need to be impressed with your efforts do not care.

and operational initiatives and increasing the cybersecurity budget will likely result in the reduction of another budget to maintain the appropriate level of spending. Organizations are like balloons, where to increase the size of the "cybersecurity end of the balloon," another side of the balloon needs to be squeezed and becomes smaller in size. Therefore, we need to be prudent as to not waste the money allocated to cybersecurity efforts. As shown in Figure 15.3, there are multiple activities in the delivery of cybersecurity to be taken to reduce the cost of cybersecurity, and these activities may be demonstrated to the board. For example, by focusing the security investment on the crown jewels previously described, the organization can reduce the business impact due to security failures. Increasing focus on business resiliency can also reduce the business impact of an outage by quickly enabling the organization to get return to the normal state of operations. Likewise, having policies, procedures, and training in place and tested for incident response, thus increasing the preparedness, can increase the speed of response and minimize response time in dealing with a new threat. These practices can lead to increased effectiveness of the cybersecurity program.

No Shortage of Additional Board Reporting Guidance

The amount of guidance issued in the past few years for reporting to the board of directors has been enough to confuse the most experienced CISO. Each board is different and has a different makeup, background, cybersecurity experience level, risk appetite, etc. The common denominator is that the CISO must listen and determine what the board needs and not be afraid to say, "well, that didn't work," and move on to a new approach. The guidance from the NACD is solid, and each of these elements should be supported by the CISO.

Being curious as to what was in the guidance issued by all the companies, in preparation for a conference presentation, I reviewed as many reports as I could get my hands on focused on "how CISOs should report to the board." I came up with 39 discrete pieces of advice, as shown in Figure 15.4, in a couple of hours and decided to stop. No wonder this is a big area of concern and confusion for CISOs!

For simplicity sake, I believe this guidance can be greatly simplified into (1) understand the business priorities and how the CISO will add value to those, (2) have a mechanism to measure risk, (3) show progress towards a greater state of maturity and be able to explain why that is important, (4) communicate external threats and how these may impact the business, and (5) be action-oriented and demonstrate how you helped #1. These are the actions they hired you for. The rest are details that will vary board-by-board depending upon the makeup and challenges the board is facing.

Keeping the Seat at the Table

This book intentionally concludes with a discussion on interacting with the board of directors because without laying the foundation of the *7-S Framework Applied to Cybersecurity Leadership* factors of *strategy, structure, systems, staff, skills,* and *shared values* presented in this book, there is no need to discuss *style* factor for interacting with the board. The CISO needs to have the substance to bring to the board, just as we must diligently do our homework before we take an examination in school. This book was about strategically building the substance and leveraging the lessons learned from the 75+ prominent CISOs moving the needle in their organizations,

1. Use Analogies to explain complicated concepts

2. Understand the business goal-why is the CISO in the room?

3. Are we secure? Peers-Trends-Gaps-how to fill

4. Enterprise-wide risk management

5. How are you managing risk? Framework?

6. How is risk being mitigated, avoided, accepted, transferred?

7. Risk posture most important to the board, not so much to the CISO

8. Compliance maturity, incidents are important to CISO and Board

9. Must be 'business relevant', talk about 'who would target us and why', avoid security jargon

10. Credibility-share good news and bad and what you don't know

11. Share a story, don't drown them in metrics, talk in $$$ where possible (have available if asked)

12. Compare with peers, industry, maturity status, risks

13. Share incidents

14. Talk $$$ - budgets, cost of downtime

15.Efficiency – managing costs down

16. Effectiveness – oriented towards new business ops, new trends, threats, technology

17. Determine how security is viewed by the rest of the organization, be relentless in demonstrating business value

18. Engagement starts below the board level and works up one level at a time

19. Need to validate risks before taking to the board

20. Establish and communicate 3 lines of defenses (control oversight, assurance, audit)

21. Position board with their responsibility

22. Communicates clear organizational governance

Figure 15.4 39 Discrete industry advice suggestions for presenting to the board. (From Fitzgerald, T. *Are We Boring the Board?* 2017. COSAC Conference Presentation Naas, Ireland. (October).)

(Continued)

23. Communicate trends – invite regulators, government bodies, peers to present at add credibility

24. Communicate plan progress with a simple framework, deviation from industry standards

25. Explain the 'ideal' maturity level – risk appetite= difference from perfection and reality

26. What are the top 5 risks related to cybersecurity?

27. What are the actions in place to address these risks?

28. Are internal and external threats being examined?

29. Is the risk assessment holistic? Does it include vendors, suppliers– if not, could be 'willful neglect'

30. Carve program into security processes vs technology – such as threat management, incident response, vulnerability and patch management, security operations, security architecture, and risk management

31. Discuss how we would respond to an incident to educate the board that anyone could be vulnerable

32. 49% of CISOs reporting on vulnerabilities to board, followed by 25% on incident response

33. Many CISOs grasp for topics to connect with the boards!!!

34. Do we think the board really cares about lost laptops and website blocking?

35. Transparency on security risks new innovations carry

36. Prioritize assets, create common risk appetite with the board to fuel business growth and innovation

37. Implement security reporting discipline and engagement between CISO and board

38. Crowded board agenda, invisible payoff vs shareholder deliverables

39. "Not our problem" outside of military and financial services

Figure 15.4 (*Continued*)   39 Discrete industry advice suggestions for presenting to the board. (From Fitzgerald, T. *Are We Boring the Board?* 2017. COSAC Conference Presentation Naas, Ireland. (October).)

security leaders, professional association leaders, and cybersecurity standards setters. As presented in the introduction, failure in any one of these seven areas can reduce the effectiveness of the CISO, recruited for and relied upon to provide cybersecurity leadership for the organization.

I am convinced that paying attention to each of these areas will minimize the cybersecurity risk to the organization to meet today's threats and be resilient for tomorrow's emerging technologies and new threats presented.

Thank you for going on this CISO COMPASS journey with the other 75+ industry leaders sharing their insights for the benefit of us all.

It was my privilege.

Suggested Reading

1. Huston, W. 2017. Report: Cost of Target's Data Breach Nearing $300 Million. Breitbart (May 28). www.breitbart.com/tech/2017/05/28/cost-targets-data-breach-nearing-300-million/.
2. Basu, E. 2014. Target CEO Fired—Can You Be Fired If Your Company Is Hacked? Forbes (June 15). www.forbes.com/sites/ericbasu/2014/06/15/target-ceo-fired-can-you-be-fired-if-your-company-is-hacked/#4fb5972a7c9f.
3. Globe Newswire. 2017. National Association of Corporate Directors (January 12). https://globenewswire.com/news-release/2017/01/12/905421/0/en/NACD-and-ISA-Issue-New-Cyber-Risk-Oversight-Guidance-for-Corporate-Directors.html.
4. NACD Director's Handbook on Cyber-Risk Oversight. 2017. www.NACDonline.org/Cyber.
5. Gross, G. 2014. Target CIO Resigns Following Breach. CIO Magazine (March 5). www.cio.com/article/2378166/data-breach/target-cio-resigns-following-breach.html.
6. Rose, A. 2013. The CISO's Handbook—Presenting to The Board. Forrester (October 24). www.veracode.com/sites/default/files/Resources/AnalystReports/forrester-ciso-handbook-presenting-to-the-board-compliments-of-veracode-analyst-report.pdf.
7. Information Security Forum. Engaging with the Board: Balancing Cyber Risk and Reward. www.securityforum.org/research/engaging-with-the-board-balancing-cyber-risk-and-reward/.
8. Jones, J. 2017. Evolving cyberrisk practices to meet board-level reporting needs. *ISACA Journal* Vol 1. www.isaca.org/Journal/archives/2017/Volume-1/Pages/evolving-cyberrisk-practices-to-meet-board-level-reporting-needs.aspx.
9. Veltsos, C. 2017. Five Ways to Improve the CISO-Board Relationship. Security Intelligence (March 21). https://securityintelligence.com/five-ways-to-improve-the-ciso-board-relationship/?otm_medium=onespot&otm_source=onsite&otm_content=articles-units:right-rail-unit&otm_click_id=16546fdb-6705-4845-bc33-afe1cd23711a.
10. Pandya, D. 2009. CISO Reporting to Board of Directors: Myth or for Real? ComputerWeekly.com (November 23). www.computerweekly.com/news/1375176/CISO-reporting-to-board-of-directors-Myth-or-for-real.
11. Durbin, S. 2016. CISO and the Board—Triggers for Engagement, with Steve Durbin. Information Security Forum Youtube Podcast (November 24). www.youtube.com/watch?v=kaWhOMC9Cgo.
12. The White House Office of the Press Secretary. 2013. Executive Order—Improving Critical Infrastructure Cybersecurity (February 12). https://obamawhitehouse.archives.gov/the-press-office/2013/02/12/executive-order-improving-critical-infrastructure-cybersecurity.
13. Translating Security Leadership into Board Value: What Boards want to Know and CISOs Need to Say. 2017. Security for Business Innovation Council. (March). www.rsa.com/content/dam/en/report/sbic-translating-security-leadership-into-board-value.pdf.

Index